# HANDBOOK OF ENVIRONMENTAL SOCIOLOGY

# HANDBOOK OF ENVIRONMENTAL SOCIOLOGY

*Edited by* Riley E. Dunlap
*and* William Michelson

GREENWOOD PRESS
Westport, Connecticut • London

**Library of Congress Cataloging-in-Publication Data**

Handbook of environmental sociology / edited by Riley E. Dunlap and William Michelson.
    p. cm.
  Includes bibliographical references and index.
  ISBN 0–313–26808–8 (alk. paper)
    1. Environmentalism—Social aspects—North America.  2. Environmental policy—
North America.  3. Social ecology—North America.  4. Human ecology—North
America.  I. Dunlap, Riley E.  II. Michelson, William.
  GE195.H35   2002
  304.2'8'097—dc21      2001023880

British Library Cataloguing in Publication Data is available.

Library of Congress Catalog Card Number: 2001023880
ISBN: 0–313–26808–8

First published in 2002

Greenwood Press, 88 Post Road West, Westport, CT 06881
An imprint of Greenwood Publishing Group, Inc.
www.greenwood.com

Printed in the United States of America

The paper used in this book complies with the
Permanent Paper Standard issued by the National
Information Standards Organization (Z39.48–1984).

10 9 8 7 6 5 4 3 2 1

To Lonnie, Sara, and Chris, for their love, support, and encouragement over the years.

R.E.D.


In memory of Carin Boalt, Birgit Krantz, and Dagfinn Aas, for their influence in my understanding of the possibilities of built environment research.

W. M.

# Contents

# Preface

Several years ago we had a vision. It stemmed from the fact that we had both been fortunate to participate in the formative years of Environmental Sociology as it developed in North America in the 1970s. Over the years we have enjoyed an interchange of perspectives, ideas, and empirical results with a number of colleagues who shared our belief that our communities and societies, as well as the field of sociology, could benefit from sociological research focusing on environmental matters—ranging from the physical contexts in which we live to the resources on which we depend. Twenty-five years ago sociological interest in such environmental issues was formalized into what is now known as the Section on Environment and Technology within the American Sociological Society (ASA). Our subsequent vision was the creation of a book that captures the range, depth, and complexity of the innovative work being done by environmental sociologists. Although many important works exploring various perspectives and specific kinds of environmental contexts, issues, and problems have been published, we felt the need for a volume which would provide a relatively comprehensive overview of the field of environmental sociology. This volume is the result, and the realization of our vision.

We are grateful to Greenwood Press for its firm support for this vision, and for the numerous people there—from Mim Vasan to Suzanne Staszak-Silva—who have helped us bring it to fruition.

Our colleagues in the ASA Section encouraged us and cooperated actively in the creation of this volume, charging us with taking editorial responsibilities, but contributing ideas for the content and suggestions for contributors. In addition, numerous colleagues have kindly provided reviews of pre-publication versions of all of the chapters. We are therefore indebted to more environmental sociologists than we could possibly name here. Consequently, we will extend our thanks to the widest range of those who contributed to our vision, while directing specific attention to the many authors of the chapters that follow for their fine efforts in helping us make this volume a reality. In Chapter 1 we provide our view of the field and the place of various chapter contributions within it.

We have seen environmental sociology and kindred interdisciplinary subjects grow in size and maturity around the world in recent years, as social science research on environmental topics in general and environmental sociology in particular have clearly become institutionalized. By taking stock of the first quarter century of North American environmental sociology, we hope that this volume will not only help to codify the field, but will also provide guidance to those in the process of extending (and applying) it.

# HANDBOOK OF
# ENVIRONMENTAL
# SOCIOLOGY

*Chapter 1*

# Environmental Sociology:
# An Introduction

*Riley E. Dunlap, William Michelson,*
*and Glenn Stalker*

This book assembles for the reader a view of the breadth and depth of a recently developing field within sociology called environmental sociology. Twenty-five specialists in this field apply their knowledge and experience to fifteen subsequent chapters, each dealing with a specific topic or sub-area. In this chapter we provide our own appreciation of the substance, range, and progress of environmental sociology, both as a field and as represented by the chapters which follow.

Even the most casual glance at the content and references in these chapters indicates the diversity and richness of sociological work dealing with physical environments. This richness and diversity is also reflected in several book-length introductions to different perspectives on this subject (e.g., Bell, 1998; Harper, 1996; Humphrey and Buttel, 1982; Michelson, 1970/ 1976; Redclift and Woodgate, 1997), lengthy treatises on a point of view (e.g., Dickens, 1996; Hannigan, 1995; Klausner, 1971; Murphy, 1997; Schnaiberg, 1980; Schnaiberg and Gould, 1994), examinations of uniquely applicable research methods (Bechtel et al., 1990; Finsterbusch et al., 1983; Zeisel, 1981), and seminal articles providing conceptual guidance for the development of an academic field (Buttel, 1987, 1996; Catton and Dunlap, 1978; Dunlap and Catton, 1979, 1983, 1994). A good deal of progress toward integration and consolidation has surely been made; further, various topics have been researched in detail, and most of the major ones are covered in this volume.

We present in this volume our best efforts at a reasonably comprehensive overview of environmental sociology, albeit one with a strong North American focus. Indeed, the volume was stimulated by encouragement from colleagues in the American Sociological Association's (ASA) Section on

Environmental Sociology (now the Section on Environment and Technology), and our goal from the outset was to provide—to the extent possible—a state-of-the-art assessment of work in this new field. As a result, this volume is best viewed as an effort to take stock of the first quarter century of environmental sociology in North America. As will be obvious from a comparison of this volume with collections having a more international focus (e.g., Lash et al., 1996; Redclift and Woodgate, 1997; Spaargaren et al., 2000), North American environmental sociology has some distinctive characteristics. On the one hand, it tends to be highly empirical, as the richness of findings reported in the following chapters will demonstrate. On the other hand, it is more preoccupied with the development of mid-range, testable theories than the development of grand, macro-level theories that have been the focus on a good deal of European environmental sociology. In addition, we see a concern with a broader range of environments, from built to natural, in North American environmental sociology than is apparent in international environmental sociology.[1] Such characteristics, which will be touched on later, are neither better nor worse than their counterparts, but they provide environmental sociology in North America a unique orientation that this volume attempts to capture.

Even accomplishing the circumscribed task of presenting a good overview of North American environmental sociology has proven more difficult than imagined, because the field has grown rapidly and new areas of research have taken root and blossomed quickly. For example, when the present volume was originally conceived and chapters solicited, topics such as environmental justice and environmental racism were not nearly as prominent as they are at present, and thus in this volume they are dealt with in the context of chapters focusing on broader issues, such as environmentalism.

The rest of this chapter provides a guide to the field, one which served as the basis for the original selection of chapter topics comprising the book. We shall address environmental sociology's content, foci, boundaries, intellectual perspectives and trends, and current status (the latter internationally as well as in North America). Our original view of these issues helped shape our choice of topics for the chapters that follow; but it is equally true and certainly to be expected that the state of the art which these chapters reveal has come to influence our current assessment of the field.

## CONTENT OF THE FIELD

Many specialists in environmental sociology, particularly those who began work in the area when the field was being established, share an experience that shaped their subsequent careers. We discovered that an aspect of the environment which we thought had a real or potential significance for human life was simply not dealt with in any systematic way by then-current sociological knowledge and research. Not only was there a paucity of satisfactory sociological explanation regarding environmental phenomena, but there was a corresponding shortage of perspectives and conceptual schemes needed for investigating such phenomena. Without shared beliefs and intellectual perspectives, it is even more difficult to establish unique methodological tools for empirical investigation.

What aspects of environment demand the benefits of social inquiry? No fixed list is possible, as relevant topics become more numerous over time. For example, Michelson, who started with an interest in questions of housing and urban development, remembers questioning, not that long ago, how waste disposal could possibly be of interest to sociologists. The answer is now obvious. Similarly, Dunlap's interest in environmental issues was stimulated by a major instance of air pollution, and subsequently strengthened by a frustrating experience with the 1973–1974 "energy crisis," but for years he gave little thought to the linkages between either pollution or energy and the built environment. However, when thinking about aspects of the environment that sociologists may examine, we can start by distinguishing between "built" and "natural" environments (recognizing that in reality there is a continuum ranging from totally built to totally natural environments that is of potential interest to environmental sociologists).

### The Built Environment

The built environment consists of those tangible settings which people create for repeated use. These are settings with a shape and form which were not in place until someone decided to create them for a human purpose. Buildings are certainly a clear example of the built environment. Very few people now find shelter from wetness and cold (and from each other) in naturally existing edifices such as caves. Most people in industrialized nations work indoors as well, and they often travel to and from work in containers of some sort. If beings from other planets or galaxies observed Earth from afar, one of the puzzles they would face would come from the sighting of the huge agglomerations of built environments in which people live, work, and travel—namely, our cities. Earth is marked not only by its natural features (oceans, mountains, forests, deserts, etc.) but by huge numbers of built environments which also vary in size, shape, and function nearly as much as do natural environments and their flora and fauna.

Buildings, however, are but one example of built environments. People create environmental entities which fall within building units. Furniture is of potential human significance, whether as providing comfort and/or rest, indicating social status, giving opportunity for specific activities, or suggesting the relationship among people entering negotiations. Rooms, by their size, shape, color, materials, lighting, energy and resource supplies, and linkages to other rooms, impart their own degree of significance. By the same token, furniture and rooms are found in many settings other than in housing, including offices, factories, schools, hospitals, churches, and bars. Even at the level of the individual building, there are many variations and components with potential significance to people; and the social significance of built environments like furniture, rooms, and buildings goes much further than their potential impacts on people. Built environments are created by certain people for themselves or for other people. How and why this creative process takes the path it does is a social process. Understanding how environments get built; what objectives are chosen; how products and artifacts are distributed; and who benefits, who loses and in what way; are all matters of major importance that call for sociological analysis.

Nonsociological specialists in built environments have predominantly focused on the purviews of their own professions: on design, on distribution, on materials, or on the products created in occupational settings. Conversely, most sociologists have kept busy in pursuit of knowledge concerning social structure and interaction, generally ignoring how particular aspects of built environments intersect with more traditional concerns such as stratification, power, kinship, and the like. Environmental sociology has increasingly grown and taken shape as researchers have come to realize that both "sides" achieve insufficient understanding without explicit attention to the links between environment and sociology. The nonsociologists get into trouble in absence of knowledge about the impacts of their artifacts on people, as well as from an incomplete understanding of the social forces that come to bear on what gets built. The sociologists lack that part of their explanation which is based on the physical settings in which behaviors of interest occur. During periods when public policies came to focus on the provision of adequately functioning housing and institutions, it became clear to researchers that there was a vacuum of knowledge on the social aspects of built environments.

Built environments also deal with settings greater than the level of scale of buildings. Spaces immediately adjacent to buildings can facilitate or hinder a great number of human activities, some desired (e.g., social interaction, children's play, car parking, gardening) and others mostly to be avoided (e.g., crime, noise, disorder, pollution). As with other settings, the design, control, and distribution of such spaces is part of a social process (Gehl, 1987). Furthermore, spaces external to buildings but relevant to them extend outwards—sometimes quite far. The pattern of usage of the block (or other defined space on which a building is located) is typically the next greater scale of human relevance, but neighborhoods and communities are vital referents as well.

The environmental setting becomes more complex as it comes to include the combination and siting of different land uses, their absolute and relative scales (e.g., residential density, open space per inhabitant, sufficiency of necessary services), and their access to potential users. These levels of scale are traditionally dealt with by surveyors, developers, architects, landscape architects, and, more recently, urban planners. Such persons are adept at dealing with distribution and design, but less likely than social scientists to approach the issues which appear at this level from an empirical perspective. Hence, people in these professions are less likely to consider and especially to try to develop a well-grounded understanding of how such environments get formed and their subsequent impacts on individuals, families, and other relevant social groupings.

Environmental sociologists increasingly contribute to the realms of urban and regional planners. Settings at neighborhood, city, metropolitan, and regional levels are less tangible and less imageable than furniture, rooms, buildings, and blocks, but this does not mean that larger-scale environments are incapable of comprehension, understanding, and informed intervention by human beings. However, the conceptual schemes, theories, and research methods needed may not be the same as at the more tangible lower levels of scale (Hägerstrand, 1970; Lynch, 1960; Michelson, 1982, 1990).

Consequently, in this volume, chapters addressed specifically to built environments cover a range of settings from micro to macro. These chapters also deal with both the dynamics by which such settings impact people and how aspects of social structure bear on the nature of and changes in people's environments. In Chapter 4, Sherry Ahrentzen focuses on the lesser scale of environments, particularly on their socio-behavioral impacts on people; she deals specifically with the interrelationships between physical environment, social context, and activity. How the greater urban and metropolitan scales affect urban residents is the focus of David Popenoe and William Michelson in Chapter 5; they put particular emphasis on the contrast between central city and suburban environments. Leslie Kilmartin, in Chapter 6, addresses a range of scales, but changes the direction of explanation; his subject is the social explanation of environmental design, viewed broadly. Kilmartin examines such matters as how architects and planners are trained and rewarded, and how the social and economic systems intertwine to help explain how the public and private realms deal with various kinds of environments.

The various scales of built environments are not limited to urban artifacts and land-uses. The component parts are certainly found in rural areas, too, albeit at different concentrations. Although the problems addressed in rural areas are typically not the same as in urban areas, there is no a priori reason that the approaches largely developed in urban areas cannot be applied to them (Palm, 1981). Nonetheless, most research on built environments to this point has had a bias toward urban area applications.

Chapter 3, by Michelson and Willem van Vliet--, also deals with the built environment, but its focus on the role of theory in sociological studies of built environment extends across the many kinds and levels of applications and hence relates as well to the boundaries and perspectives of environmental sociology to be discussed below.

## The Natural Environment

If buildings represent obvious examples of built environments pertinent to people, then their counterparts in the natural environment might well be forests. Large stands of trees not planned or planted by people represent the epitome in history and literature of settings untouched by civilization. The deep, dark forest represented by the brothers Grimm was a fearsome, dangerous place, if only because it was outside the realm of human control; it often represented the realm of the supernatural (Ittelson et al., 1974). But now, whether still wilderness or else subject to incursions by human beings and enterprises, this "natural" setting poses questions in the realm of the environmental sociologist.

Sociologists assess what forests represent and potentially do to people in terms very different than did the brothers Grimm. One topic is the meaning of wilderness and wildlands to people (a refuge, untapped resource, or essential part of ecosystems?). Another is the recreational uses that people make of such areas, how this varies according to subgroupings of the population, and what impacts such use has for them. Still another is the conflict between recreational uses and other uses of forest land (e.g., timber or mining) or between different forms of recreation (e.g., snowmobiling versus cross-country skiing). (See Field and Burch, 1988:61–68, for a brief review of research on these and related topics.)

However, with major policy issues arising from human intervention into forests, considerably more sociological attention is being given to the dynamics of people's impact on forests as well as the social impacts of changes in the forest products industry (Lee et al., 1990). Concerns over logging by the timber industry have led to research on how decisions are made and implemented about forest use and management. Just as students of the built environment study the training and orientations of architects and planners, so do students of the natural environment study loggers, forest rangers, and bureaucrats. At the international level, worries about the clearing of rainforests may cause researchers in other disciplines to study soil erosion, oxygen generation, and species habitat, but they lead sociologists to study such topics as poverty and social stratification, land-tenure and distribution, and political power in nations whose rainforests are under siege (Rudel with Horowitz, 1993).

As members of the public at large become aware of environmental issues, they often form groups which take one or the other side on such issues. The result is that a large and active environmental movement has emerged in recent decades. How forest issues, for example, are dealt with is increasingly influenced by the actions of citizen groups and their interactions with industry and government. Sociologists actively study those involved in such citizen groups, the internal workings of these groups, and the strategies and tactics the groups employ in dealing with government and the private sector (Dunlap and Mertig, 1992).

The discussion above represents an attempt to explain the factors both influencing and reacting to environmental change. Such studies seek to illuminate the changes in social organization, societal priorities, and public policies that might be needed to develop alternatives to current practices and policies which are seen as having detrimental impacts on natural resources and the environment—impacts which in turn often lead to negative consequences for human communities.

Another subject having to do with the natural environment is natural hazards and disasters, such as earthquakes, floods, and tornadoes. These have major impacts on people, often involving direct impacts on life, limb, and economics, but they also have psychological and behavioral impacts. Some of the crucial questions pursued have to do with how people and their social structures relate to and deal with natural hazards and disasters. Consistent with other content areas dealing with built and natural environments, the study of natural hazards and disasters takes people as more than passive recipients of environmental outcomes; indeed, our collective and individual actions set many of the conditions under which such hazards are encountered, experienced, and potentially mitigated. Exactly what sociologists study in this realm (and the others) is what sets them off from other concerned persons like seismologists, engineers, and public officials (Mileti, 1999).

Energy and technology are now assessed in terms well beyond conventional factors of availability, cost, and potential for pollution. Sociologists study their impacts on human activities and well-being and, perhaps more importantly, the social processes underlying the adoption, use, change, and/ or continuation of differing forms of energy and technology. Further, the focus is expanding from specific geographical sites to dynamics involving all humankind.

It is arguable that energy and technology do not fit cleanly into the natural environment category. Certainly, Popenoe and Michelson show, in Chapter 5, how choices of technology in urban transportation both reflect and constrain the behaviors of segments of the population. Nonetheless, in modern industrial societies, technologies are inherent in the use of natural resources. Furthermore, subjects dealing with natural resources and technology are typically dealt with by different persons than those who deal with questions of housing and urban design. Consequently, within environmental sociology, energy and technology are more likely to be considered by researchers with an interest in natural environments than by those with an interest in built environments.

Many publics have become sensitized to the related processes of waste disposal and conservation. Schoolchildren are increasingly steeped in a new set of "3-Rs." Botanists, zoologists, and ecologists trace changes in the health and even existence of specific flora and fauna exposed to air and water with contaminants (e.g., acid rain). Epidemiologists document the impact of exposure to such substances as radioactive wastes, chemicals, and airborne pollution on humans, examining the effect of such contaminants on people's health, welfare, and life chances. Environmental sociologists have contributed to a rapidly growing literature on both the causes and effects of various waste disposal and conservation practices. Attention is paid to both social-psychological and behavioral dynamics, as well as social-structural factors, in assessing the causes and consequences of both contamination and conservation (Gardner and Stern, 1996).

With increasing public awareness of the above and similar issues has come—as noted above—the formation of organizations to represent interests other than those of economic and traditional governmental actors. Nonetheless, the environmental movement is dispersed among many groups, with different ideologies, degrees of commitment, and tactics. Differential participation in this movement across various sectors of society; differing meanings of environmental quality and conceptions of environmental threats held by diverse types of environmentalists; and the multiplicity of goals, ideologies, strategies, and tactics visible within the contemporary environmental movement are all topics addressed by environmental sociologists (Brulle, 2000; Szasz, 1994).

As in so many other areas of life these days, public opinion is an important consideration in environmental sociology. Once again, this is seen as both cause and effect vis-à-vis environments. Sociologists view public opinion toward the environment as a function of both environmental conditions and numerous social factors such as media attention, scientific evidence, and political leadership. Perceptions of environmental problems are clearly not simply (or even primarily in most instances) a function of the severity of particular events or conditions. Public opinion, in turn, influences the political salience and potential resolution of environmental problems (Dunlap, 1995; Szasz, 1994).

The chapters dealing with aspects of natural environments in this book were commissioned to reflect the range of topics being examined by environmental sociologists, as well as the necessity of considering both how environments influence society and social behavior and how social structures and people's behaviors impact environments and environmental practices. Chapter 2, by Frederick Buttel and Craig Humphrey, provides an overview of theorizing about natural environments, and will be discussed under both "boundaries" and "trends." In Chapter 7, Don Albrecht and Steve Murdock deal with rural environments and agriculture. Rural settings are not simply the obverse of urban built environments, but reflect the effects of agricultural resources, technology, and production on rural areas and peoples. Loren Lutzenhiser, Craig Harris, and Marvin Olsen, in Chapter 8, present a broad sociological work on energy that looks critically at the deficiencies of past energy policies and ends with an exhaustive review of research on energy and social behavior. The review indicates that sociological analysis of energy use has made a significant contribution in facilitating conservation by showing the limitations of individualistic, economistic, and purely technical perspectives.

The considerable literature on natural hazards and disasters serves as the basis for Joanne Nigg and Dennis Mileti's review of this topic in Chapter 9. Their chapter clearly indicates the many useful generalizations that have been developed by sociological research in this area; but hazards and disasters are no longer predominantly natural in origin. Hence, a separate analysis of technological hazards and disasters has been written by Steve Kroll-Smith, Stephen Couch, and Adeline Levine in Chapter 10. Their discussion highlights fundamental differences in the social impacts of technological versus natural hazards and disasters.

Both natural and technological hazards pose risks to modern societies, and lead to considerations of the broader topic of risk and society. In Chapter 11, Thomas Dietz, R. Scott Frey, and Eugene Rosa write about the social dimensions and dynamics of risk, and analyze the concept of risk assessment. The scale of risk increases in Chapter 12, on global environmental change, as Thomas Dietz and Eugene Rosa deal with human-induced changes to the global ecosystem that portend significant impacts on human societies worldwide. They provide an overview of recent sociological work on the causes and consequences of global warming and related phenomena.

Partly as a result of legislation, but partly also as a result of prior research activities, social and technological impact assessment became a major activity for environmental sociologists, and now offer opportunity for providing input into environmental/technological decision making. Kurt Finsterbusch and William Freudenburg discuss, in Chapter 13, both the strategies and methodologies associated with impact assessment. They show that impact assessment not only serves as a means of anticipating possible outcomes of environmental/technological developments and interventions, but that it can itself be a dynamic factor in environmental and technological policy making.

In Chapter 14, Angela Mertig, Riley Dunlap, and Denton Morrison trace the evolution of the American environmental movement from its conservationist beginnings to the present, and then proceed to analyze the organizational structure of the movement. They focus on both the institutionalization of the mainstream movement and the more recent emergence of various strands of environmentalism, such as the local grassroots and environmental justice movements. Chapter 15, by Riley Dunlap and Robert Emmet Jones, then deals with the question of public attitudes toward environmental issues. They examine public concern for environmental quality, paying special attention to the ways in which "environmental concern" is conceptualized and measured in empirical research—highlighting differences in studies based on attitude theory and those that take a more policy-relevant approach.

A final chapter (Chapter 16), by Barbara Payne and Christopher Cluett, examines environmental sociology in nonacademic settings, clarifying the roles played by environmental sociologists who work in government agencies, research firms, and private companies. They emphasize the different requirements and challenges involved in working in these settings compared to those inherent in academic settings.

## THE CHANGING FOCI OF ENVIRONMENTAL SOCIOLOGY

What then is the focus of environmental sociology? We have seen that it deals with both built and natural environments. Work on both types of environments (and the full continuum in between these two poles) can differ in scale from very microscopic to global; focus on a wide range of contexts; and require quite different methods, concepts, and explanations. In the face of such complexity, defining the field as the study of "societal-environmental interactions" or "relations between environment and society," as was done early on in an effort to codify the field and give it an identity (Catton and Dunlap, 1978; Dunlap and Catton, 1979), seems limiting. At the other extreme, one could define it very broadly and loosely as the work being conducted by everyone calling him/herself an environmental sociologist, as suggested by Buttel (1987). Perhaps a reasonable compromise is to recognize that environmental sociologists study not only the relations between humans and their environments (from built to natural, and from micro to macro), but also the multiplicity of ways in which these relations are often influenced by socio-cultural processes—including cultural representations, collective definitions, claims-making, political power, and public controversies, to name but a few.

This does not mean, however, that the diverse subjects studied by environmental sociologists are unrelated. It has been argued that the environment (or, more technically, ecosystems) can be seen as serving three distinct functions for human societies (Dunlap, 1994). The environment not only provides our home, or the space in which we conduct our activities, but it supplies us with the resources that are necessary for living and also acts as a "sink" for absorbing the waste products of modern industrial societies. These three functions, which can be termed the living space, supply depot, and waste repository functions, reveal the inherent interconnectedness of the subject matter of environmental sociology. Built environment specialists tend to focus on issues concerning living space, while natural environment specialists tend to focus either on issues involving the supply of natural resources or the use of the environment as a waste repository. Yet, any given environment is likely, or at least has the potential, to serve all three functions simultaneously to some degree.

Furthermore, the living space, supply depot, and waste repository functions of any given area may compete with one another. Using a given geographical area as a waste repository, for example, tends to make it less suitable as a living space or supply depot. Similarly, building a housing tract on former farmland obviously reduces the area's potential for production of agricultural resources. Figure 1.1 depicts the existence and growing competition among these functions. It suggests that in the past century human demand on ecosystems for each of these functions has grown substantially, with two consequences: First, as a result of increased human numbers and activities, nowadays there is substantially more conflict between these functions than in the past; second, the total human demand or "load" may be exceeding the long-term carrying capacity of both specific areas and even the global ecosystem (see, e.g., Vitousek et al., 1997).

The above-noted trends underlie the current emphasis being given to the notions of "sustainability" and "sustainable development," for these trends call into question the long-term sustainability of modern industrial societies. Efforts to understand and contribute to the resolution of the growing environmental problems that are seen as undermining sustainability will require environmental sociologists and other scholars to pay more attention to the inherent interrelatedness of the above-noted functions and the resulting complexity of environmental problems. Moving toward a more sustainable society, for example, will require using natural resources far more efficiently in order to minimize both resource withdrawals and pollution resulting from resource extraction, use, and disposal. This means making fundamental changes in our living and work environments and transportation systems as well as in production processes. Increasingly, therefore, built environment specialists will need to consider energy use and waste disposal issues, while energy specialists will need to consider the design of energy efficient buildings, transportation systems, and urban areas. Thus, we expect to see a trend toward greater consideration of both the built and natural components of environmental issues, and at larger scales, as environmental sociologists are forced to consider all of the functions that the environment performs for human societies.

Understanding these three functions performed by the environment (or ecosystems) provides insights into the evolution of environmental problems and issues of interest to environmental sociologists. In the late 1960s and early 1970s, when sociological interest in environmental matters was just beginning to emerge, primary attention was given to air and water pollution (problems stemming from the environment's inability to absorb human waste products), urban decay, and the importance of protecting areas of

Figure 1.1
Competing Functions of the Environment

**1a: Situation circa 1900**

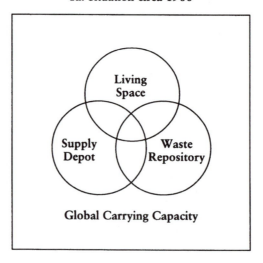

Living
Space

Supply
Depot

Waste
Repository

Global Carrying Capacity

**2a: Current Situation**

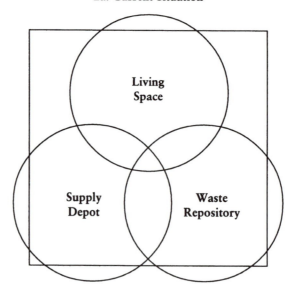

Living
Space

Supply
Depot

Waste
Repository

natural beauty. The "energy crisis" of 1973–1974 highlighted the dependence of the United States (and other industrialized nations) on fossil fuels and our nation's failure to develop energy efficient mass transportation systems; and it raised the specter of resource scarcity in general. A new problem came to the fore in the late 1970s when it was discovered that a neighborhood in Niagara Falls, New York, was built on an abandoned chemical waste site that had begun to leak toxic materials. "Love Canal" came to symbolize the growing problems of using an area as both waste repository and living space.

Throughout the 1980s, new and often more complex environmental problems emerged and garnered attention, including acid rain, rainforest destruction, ozone depletion, loss of biodiversity, catastrophic technological accidents such as Bhophal and Chernobyl, and the specter of global warming. Such problems are generally multifunctional in nature, as clearly illustrated by global warming. It is caused primarily by a rapid increase in carbon dioxide in the earth's atmosphere produced by human activities, particularly the burning of fossil fuels. The buildup of carbon dioxide traps more of the sun's heat, thus raising the temperature of the earth's atmosphere. While global warming thus results from overuse of the atmosphere as a waste site, the resulting warming may produce changes that make our planet less suitable as living space (not only for humans, but especially for other species) and affect the production of natural resources such as food supplies.

There are other features of this newer "wave" of environmental problems that distinguish them from their predecessors (which remain with us): The newer problems are often hard to detect by direct human sensory perception, making our awareness of them dependent upon scientific expertise; they often affect huge geographical areas, up to the global level; they have the potential of affecting future generations; and their potentially catastrophic consequences clearly exceed our ability to mitigate their impacts or adequately compensate their victims (see, e.g., Cohen, 1997). The emergence of this new set of "mega-hazards" and the risks they pose has major implications for environmental sociology: (1) The concept of risk has become more central to the field, and recognition that environmental/technological risks have become endemic to modern industrialized societies has led to the latter being described as "risk societies" (Beck, 1992); (2) the scale of contemporary problems has stimulated interest in the relationship between environmental conditions and globalization (Spaargaren et al., 2000); and (3) the inherent difficulties and ambiguities in identifying, documenting, and solving modern problems ranging from toxic contamination to global warming has led to an increased interest in the ways in which knowledge, claims, and policies are influenced by perceptions, cultural contexts, and political processes (Hannigan, 1995). In sum, the subject matter of environmental sociology—environmental conditions, contexts, and controversies—has become more complex since the emergence of the field.

Insofar as the supply of space in communities, regions, nations, and even the entire globe is becoming increasingly limited relative to the size and distribution of human populations and their socio-economic activities, interactions and potential conflicts among environmental uses will likely occur with increasing frequency and at larger geographical scales, creating shortages, contamination, crowding, conflicts, and other negative outcomes. The situation is further complicated by factors which crosscut the purely functional use of and competition among these three functions of given environments. People's subjective interpretations give meaning and direction to how they deal with environmental contexts and issues; risk, for example, has a highly subjective component. Similarly, how people organize to advance and/or handle the allocation and use of environmental context (including both environmental "goods" such as resources and "bads" such as pollution) represents a crucial force worthy of explicit consideration and understanding. Thus, it is not simply the "objective" environments, whether built or natural, that are of interest to environmental sociologists, but the ways in which those environments and the opportunities and conflicts surrounding them are perceived, defined, interpreted, and acted upon (Hannigan, 1995). In sum, there is every reason to believe that environmental sociologists will find ample subject matter to focus upon in the years to come. The challenge will be to cope with the growing interrelatedness, complexity, and scale of the topics noted above.

## BOUNDARIES OF THE FIELD

We noted earlier that many environmental sociologists initially focused on their subject area with the realization that it was simply not being "done" within existing disciplinary or professional divisions. The work by these people and subsequent cohorts has evolved into a specialty field because of the relative uniqueness of sociological research on physical environments. Nevertheless, despite much discussion, the question remains as to the intrinsic identity of environmental sociology, relative to both the larger field of sociology and to related disciplines.

This discussion begins with the question of whether environmental sociology is simply an extension of standard sociological thinking and research procedures to topics which happen to deal with the environment, or whether it truly represents a unique approach (Dunlap and Catton, 1979; Buttel, 1987). In their early effort to discern and legitimate a field of environmental sociology, Dunlap and Catton (1979) distinguished between a "sociology of environmental issues" and a true "environmental sociology." The former represented a "normal science" approach in which standard sociological perspectives were applied to environmental topics, such as analyses of public attitudes toward environmental issues and the environmental movement. The latter was reserved for the then-rare studies of "interactions" or "relations" between environmental and social phenomena, illustrated by analyses of the societal impacts of energy shortages or the relations between social strata and environmental degradation, which departed from the disciplinary norm of ignoring nonsocial variables. Such a distinction seemed useful in legitimating environmental sociology as a unique field on a par with areas like political sociology and social stratification, which were clearly demarcated by their emphases on political and stratification phenomena as independent and dependent variables. It is less essential now that analyses of the relationships between social and environmental variables, ranging from studies of the sources and impacts of tropical deforestation (Rudel with Horowitz, 1993) to similar studies of local toxic contamination (Szasz, 1994), have become more common. Consequently, while similar distinctions are still made (e.g., Kroll-Smith and Laska, 1994), we prefer a more inclusive view of the field as described in the prior section.

Nonetheless, the original distinction between approaching environmental topics from standard sociological perspectives (and thus concentrating solely on their social dimensions) and one that takes environmental phenomena seriously and tries to understand their relationships with social phenomena can still be discerned in contemporary work (see Kroll-Smith et al., 2000). A crucial reason stems from what Buttel and Humphrey, in Chapter 2 of this volume, term the "double determination" of environmental sociology. Building upon Buttel's (1986:338) earlier depiction of the "inherent duality in human existence," or the reality of "humans as strands in the web of life in the larger biosphere on the one hand, and humans as creators of unique and distinctly social 'environments' on the other," Buttel and Humphrey describe this double determination as follows: "theoretical postures in environmental sociology tend to be based on social theory at large on the one hand, and on empirical observations or theoretical/metatheoretical assumptions relating to humans as a species and to relationships between society and nature on the other." We would argue that some current work in environmental sociology emphasizes the development and application of sociological theory, but at the expense of paying careful attention to the environment and the ecological base of human societies. Conversely, other work takes quite seriously Buttel and Humphrey's observation that "This double determination, and especially the social significance of dependence on and interaction with the natural [and, we would add, built] environment, represents the uniqueness of the field."

In our view, at its best environmental sociology includes detailed analyses both of environments and social phenomena. Each aspect injects theoretical and practical considerations into the explanatory scheme and methods pursued (see Bechtel et al., 1990). Such work is unique among sociologists, for it requires special knowledge of the environments studied and sensitivity to the theoretical and methodological requirements needed for their conceptualization and empirical measurement. Insofar as this is still sociological analysis, environmental phenomena must be integrated with social factors and explanations (see Freudenburg and Gramling, 1993 for an excellent example). Even if this may not always constitute a form of double determination in the strictest sense, at the least it is a double consideration or double dynamic. Environmental sociology is *not* simply just one more extension of standard sociology. There *is* an environmental sociology, a field that departs from the larger discipline by its willingness to consider and investigate non-social variables such as aspects of built and natural environments (Catton and Dunlap, 1978, 1980; Dunlap, 1997).

Still, is environmental sociology narrowly sociological on the social explanation side of things? Certainly not. But then again, neither is much conventional research by sociologists. Reality seldom falls within the boundaries of only one discipline, exclusive of all others. A number of special fields within sociology traverse boundaries: Social psychology, political sociology, economic sociology, and sociology of health and medicine are examples.

The content of environmental sociology brings the field immediately into contact with other disciplines, occupations, and professions that deal with the various environmental contexts and subjects studied; but sociological insights influence the types of explanation, the factors considered, and the levels of scale employed by environmental sociologists. Michelson and van Vliet--'s review of theory in the sociological study of built environments, in Chapter 3, indicates a heavy use of psychological concepts, perspectives, and theories; many influences from economics and political science; extremely helpful guidance from geography; and, of course, engagement with architecture and urban planning. Psychology, for example, proves extremely useful again in the chapters on natural hazards and disasters and on risk, while aspects of economics and political science are an integral part of many of the chapters on natural environments. And, of course, the work of environmental scientists, ecologists, and other natural scientists provide essential input to sociological analyses of natural environment phenomena.

In short, environmental sociology is inevitably highly interdisciplinary in its outlook and composition. As such, albeit with its unique combination of factors, considerations, and questions to be addressed, it crosses boundaries not only with the conventional field of sociology, but with a range of relevant sibling disciplines in the social and behavioral sciences as well as natural science and various applied disciplines and professions.

## INTELLECTUAL PERSPECTIVES AND TRENDS

By now it is apparent that environmental sociology is a diverse field, as diverse as the demands of the many topics studied. There is no single perspective followed, but there are many characteristics of the varying approaches which allow for further examination of the field. In addition, although unanimity is lacking, some trends can be noted. What follows is a selection of criteria on which choices in the direction of research approaches are made, implicitly or explicitly. We shall discuss our views of the balance of, and when possible apparent trends in, work in environmental sociology with respect to each one.

### Built versus Natural Environments

This distinction has already been introduced as the most basic one for the content of environmental sociology. The question raised now has to do with the brunt of recent research in the field. Surely, pressing public policy questions remain regarding both kinds of environment, requiring extensive sociological research. However, public attention has shifted from the major concentration on urban built environments in the 1950s and 1960s to the identification of more and more problems having to do with natural environments that have occurred since then. While work continues apace on questions of appropriate housing and urban infrastructure in the absence of solutions to urban problems, there has been a relative shift of interest toward research on natural environments. The headlines given over to nuclear disasters, oil spills, hazardous waste disposal, environmental protests, international conferences, extreme weather events, and so forth have generated both supply and demand for work on natural environments. Even when governments fail to respond to the enormity of the challenge, this only generates more sociological research investigating why this is the case. Yet, as noted earlier, the growing emphasis on sustainability, and recognition of the interrelations among the living space, supply depot, and waste repository functions, creates potential opportunities for increased integration of work on both built and natural environments.

### Level of Scale

We noted previously that with regard to both built and natural environments there is a huge range in the levels of scale addressed, from furniture to the entire globe. Another trend within environmental sociology has been an escalation of the geographic scales studied. The lower, more imageable scales (e.g., housing and city blocks) are surely not abandoned, but the larger ones have become increasingly identified as relevant for pursuit. More attention (for example, on built environments) is given to metropolitan and regional settings and the opportunities and constraints which land-use and transportation patterns present for people. Attention to more universal phenomena such as the status of women in relationship to the objectives behind and functioning of built environments has grown rapidly. Regarding natural environments, there has been a definite trend toward issues of global scope as rainforest destruction, loss of biodiversity, ozone depletion, and global warming have become subjects of sociological attention (Yearley, 1996). Of course, the siting and impact of a local landfill or waste site remains as relevant as ever.

### Direction of Explanation

What is the relative emphasis that environmental sociologists put on understanding how environments impact people, compared to how people impact environments? At first, students of built environments were more likely to address the question of how environments affect human behavior. Although seldom taking a simple, deterministic form, as noted by Michelson and van Vliet-- in Chapter 3, such work has been important and useful. Architects demand checklists, for example, of what to build so as to produce the desired behavioral outcomes, while urban planners want to know if their designs will produce the expected results. Yet, considerable weight has swung around to understanding how environments get to be the way they are, representing a pendulum swing in the opposite direction.

The trend is not so clear in work on natural environments. Some early work looked at the effect of outdoor settings on social behavior, as well as the impact of energy and other resource scarcities on society; yet, examining the causes of environmental degradation has always been a central concern of environmental sociologists (e.g., Schnaiberg, 1980). The continuation of this bi-directional focus can be seen on topics ranging from global environmental change, where both the causes and consequences are given attention (as noted by Dietz and Rosa in Chapter 12), to local environmental hazards, where a similar dual focus is apparent (e.g., Szasz, 1994; and Chapter 10, this volume).

Both directions are appropriate subjects for sociological inquiry, and in numerous cases both will likely receive attention—as current conditions produce consequences that in turn help create new conditions. In a process akin to structuration, environmental conditions and social factors interact to create new situations that in turn alter environmental as well as social conditions.

### Environmental Degradation or Improvement?

Particularly in work on natural environments, environmental sociology has always placed emphasis on environmental degradation, whether investigating the causes or consequences of problematic environmental conditions. In recent years, however, environmental sociologists in some of the highly advanced European nations which appear to have made considerable progress in cleaning up their environments have begun to emphasize the need for sociological attention to the phenomena of environmental improvement. Typically termed *ecological modernization*, this school of thought has called for a fundamental reorientation of the field in order to account for processes by which environmental degradation is not only halted but reversed (e.g., Mol and Sonnenfeld, 2000). Although subject to many challenges, especially whether the presumed progress observed in wealthy northern European nations can be generalized to other regions of the world, ecological modernization has clearly added a new wrinkle to environmental sociology by expanding the field's traditional focus on environmental degradation (Buttel, 2000).

## Theoretical versus Empirical Approaches

At the outset we noted that American environmental sociology (akin to the larger discipline) has had a strong empirical orientation, as a majority of publications dealing with both built and natural environments report the results of empirical research. This empirical orientation will be obvious from reading the subsequent chapters in this book, as nearly all of them review numerous studies reporting data collected on the particular topics being reviewed. We believe this strong empirical bent contrasts with the overall situation in Europe, where (despite tremendous variation both across and within nations) there seems to be relatively more emphasis given to theorizing about environmental issues than to collecting data on them.

Furthermore, the more notable attempts to develop theoretical perspectives in American environmental sociology tend to be fairly middle-range in focus and amenable to empirical testing, as exemplified by Schnaiberg's well-known "treadmill of production" perspective (Schnaiberg, 1980; Schnaiberg and Gould, 1994). In contrast, European theorizing about environmental matters is often quite abstract, in the tradition of grand theory, and less amenable to empirical testing—as exemplified by Beck's (1992) provocative theory of the "risk society," Luhmann's (1989) abstract analysis of "ecological communication," and Giddens' (1990) portrayal of the role of ecological problems in an era of high modernity.

One of the results of the growing globalization of environmental sociology, to be discussed in the final section, is increasing cross-fertilization at the international level. One consequence of this is that American environmental sociologists are beginning to pay more attention to theoretical perspectives developed by their European (and other international) colleagues. Since the initial reaction has sometimes been critical (see, e.g., Buttel, 2000 on ecological modernization and Marshall, 1999 on the risk society), it is too soon to judge the outcome. Nonetheless, in the long run we expect to see an increased emphasis on theorizing within American environmental sociology—especially now that a good deal of empirical evidence yielding consistent generalizations has emerged in so many of the topical areas of interest to environmental sociologists, as reported in several of the subsequent chapters.

### Paradigmatic Stance

What stance do environmental sociologists take when they address environmental questions? As part of their effort to establish and legitimate environmental sociology as a distinct field, Catton and Dunlap (1978, 1980) not only defined its core as the study of societal-environmental interactions, but argued that seeing the physical environment as legitimate for sociological inquiry violated the disciplinary norm of explaining social phenomena only with other social phenomena. They further argued that reinforcing this norm was an implicit paradigm or worldview that blinded mainstream sociology to the relevance of the physical environments and ecosystem dependence of modern industrial societies. What they labeled the Human Exemptionalism Paradigm (HEP) captured the notion that humans, because of our exceptional characteristics relative to other species, were seen as being "exempt" from ecological constraints. In contrast, they argued that within at least some work in environmental sociology one could discern an alternative paradigm or set of background assumptions. By calling attention to the relevance of the physical environment, and the constraints that a finite planet poses for our species, the New Ecological Paradigm (NEP) offers a sharply contrasting image of human societies relative to that provided by the HEP. (See Chapter 2 of this volume for a full description of the HEP/NEP cleavage.)

The HEP leads to a view of the environment as something to be controlled by human beings for their own ends, and of humans as having the ability to exert such control. It is certainly a stance traditionally taken by engineers, whose role is to transform nature through the applications of science. Sociological work in this tradition focuses on environmental intervention for the express purpose of satisfying human objectives. Some call this social engineering. Work on built environments is often compatible with such a perspective, although growing recognition of the degree to which the living space function is inherently interrelated with the other functions may make this less common. In contrast, the NEP leads adherents to view natural environments as an essential context (or living space) for human social life, to see such environments as potentially fragile and limited in resources, and also as exercising constraints on the realization of human objectives. Much current interest in macro levels of analysis, especially that focused on global environmental change, is compatible with the NEP.

The more that environmental sociologists and the world at large learn about current environmental conditions, the greater the shift in stance toward the NEP (Dunlap and Catton, 1994). Yet, many policy makers and economic interests as well as portions of the public remain deeply wedded to the HEP, whereas most environmentalists, significant segments of the public, and some policy makers are endorsing the NEP. The resulting conflicts in perspectives provide a rich topic for sociological research (see, e.g., Olsen et al., 1992).

## Paradigms versus Theories

Because their original portrayal of the HEP/NEP distinction emphasized that mainstream theoretical perspectives—despite their diversity—all seemed premised on the HEP, Catton and Dunlap's (1978) call for environmental sociology to adopt the NEP was misconstrued as implying that the latter would replace existing theoretical perspectives. Buttel (1978) challenged this implication, appropriately arguing that existing theoretical perspectives (e.g., Marxian, Weberian, and Durkheimian) would remain relevant for analyses of environmental problems. Although Catton and Dunlap (1980) subsequently clarified their position, noting that they did *not* expect to see the NEP replace traditional theoretical perspectives *but* to lead to the development of more ecologically realistic versions of sociological theories, the original (mis)interpretation of their argument continues (see, e.g., Lidskog, 1998).[2]

Clearly, sociologists will continue to draw upon relevant theoretical perspectives in their research, and mainstream theoretical cleavages certainly find their way into environmental sociology. For example, the previously noted ecological modernization perspective is premised on a largely consensual image of society (with government, industry, and environmentalists all working toward the common goal of environmental improvement), one that rests solidly on a "social order" perspective. Conversely, the numerous political economy perspectives, ranging from Schnaiberg's (1980) treadmill of production argument to applications of World Systems Theory (e.g., Barbosa, 2000), are premised on a "social conflict" perspective.

However, a crucial development within the past decade has been the emergence of numerous efforts to develop "green" versions of classical and contemporary theories, resulting in perspectives that are quite compatible with the NEP. In the next chapter Buttel and Humphrey deal with some of these efforts (also see Dunlap et al., 2002) and note how they differ from their more traditional, exemptionalist-based predecessors. In the process they also demonstrate the point that Catton and Dunlap (1980) made in the clarification of their argument—namely, that the exemptionalistecological cleavage crosscuts rather than replaces traditional theoretical perspectives. We expect to see a continuing trend among environmental sociologists toward developing greener versions of existing theoretical perspectives, in order to be able to draw upon the insights that these perspectives offer for understanding the "societal" or "social" side of the societal-environmental equation.

### Simple versus Complex Explanation

Posing questions about how environments encourage certain behavior or how an interest group manages to inflict damage on the landscape is relatively simple and straightforward. Many questions are first posed in such simple terms. Unfortunately, reality is seldom so simple.

One of the clearest trends in environmental sociology is toward more complex, often interactive, forms of explanation. Certainly, the NEP stance implies recognition of complex ecological dynamics and the need for compatible explanations. The two chapters on hazards and disasters, both natural (Chapter 9) and technological (Chapter 10), clearly illustrate the merits of complex explanation, and the one on impact assessment (Chapter 13) indicates the increasing need for it in much applied research. More and more, the content of the field reflects how human–environment relationships are mediated by the nature and workings of social organization, often within the limitations set by environments and resources.

### Strong versus Weak Explanation

Chapter 3, by Michelson and van Vliet--, suggests that theoretical explanation on the impacts of environments on people is relatively weak because these impacts are seldom deterministic, but more likely reflect human motivation within broad limits set by environmental design. As scientific causality goes, this is weak. As reality goes, it is likely accurate. Strong and weak are not equivalent to good and bad for researchers, unless salaries are paid only as a function of the strength of predictability in results!

Some explanations in environmental sociology appear strong. For example, explanations of attempts to build similar upscale, central city commercial and recreational environments in city after city look strong, because of common interest group similarities across cities. Likewise, the operation of the treadmill of production can be expected to produce reasonably consistent results in differing communities.

Nonetheless, in a field with so many complex and interacting variables to consider, the impact of a single variable is not likely to be as strong as in fields in which research variables are abstracted away from real-world settings and their complex realities. Perhaps explanation is more appropriate to environmental sociology than is prediction. If explanation of past efforts can contribute wisdom to deal more adequately with future endeavors, this is not a minimal contribution. Indeed, Finsterbusch and Freudenburg (in Chapter 13) state that even work on impact assessment is not for the purpose of confident prediction. They observe that projection to the future from known conditions is possible and desirable, but that far too many factors can potentially intervene between present and future to enable prediction.

## Materialism versus Idealism

As Buttel (1996) has noted, early environmental sociology tended to emphasize the "materiality" of human existence, and the objective reality of environmental problems. Such NEP-oriented work more or less took pollution, resource scarcity, and the ecosystem dependence of modern societies for granted, and sought to analyze the causes, consequences, and implications of "ecological disruptions" (Schnaiberg, 1980) and resource constraints (Catton, 1980).[3] However, in recent years, influenced by the "cultural turn" of the larger discipline, environmental sociology has paid increasing attention to the less material and more "idealistic" aspects of environmental issues, focusing on their perceptual, cultural, and value-laden dimensions. In particular, borrowing from work on social problems, the sociology of science, and cultural sociology, many environmental sociologists have focused on the processes by which environmental conditions are "socially constructed" as problematic (see, e.g., Hannigan, 1995; Goldman and Schurman, 2000) while often remaining agnostic about their "reality" (Macnaghten and Urry, 1998; Yearley, 1996).

This trend, apparent by the early 1990s, provoked a lively debate over the merits of a "strong constructivist" approach. Such an approach sometimes appears to slip into ontological relativism and, by emphasizing the immateriality of environmental problems relative to their socio-cultural origins, impies human exemptionalism as well. Critiques of this approach (see, e.g., Dunlap and Catton, 1994; Murphy, 1997) have not only provoked a strong defense of the utility of constructivist analyses, but perhaps a more moderate version (involving epistemological but not ontological relativism) as well (see, in particular, Burningham and Cooper, 1999). Fortunately, fruitful new approaches that attempt to bridge the realist-idealist or objectivist-constructivist divide are being proposed (e.g., Bell, 1998; Rosa, 1998), and we hope to see the strengths of both approaches melded into richer perspectives for the field.

## Qualitative versus Quantitative Analysis

The realms of policy analysis have been partial to quantitative analysis for years. It parallels economic cost-benefit analysis and the medium of money. Quantitative analysis gives the appearance of precision, and the development of sophisticated statistical techniques enables very detailed examination and analysis of data and degrees of confidence accorded to results. Such analysis is taken as necessary and compelling by many decision makers. Quantitative analysis has become a regular part of sociological training and is utilized widely in sociological research. Use of quantitative analysis would appear straightforward when, for example, studying the impacts of activities on what are considered objective and delimited environments, or the social impacts of discrete events such as natural disasters.

Yet, at the same time, one of the contributions of sociology has been to show the relevance of people's subjective interpretation of phenomena like environments and contexts (Macnaghten and Urry, 1998). Another major contribution has been the understanding of how the interaction among different interests within the social structure underlies the creation, maintenance, and change of environments and environmental practices. These are subjects for which highly quantitative data are not always appropriate or forthcoming, but where qualitative data may be revealing.

There are pressures and advantages to the creation of quantitative data in as many research situations where such data can be gathered meaningfully. Environmental sociologists do gather such data. Indeed, in procedures like Risk Assessment and Impact Assessment, described in Chapters 11 and 13, quantitative data are nearly mandatory. Nonetheless, qualitative data have been extremely important for the assessment of meanings, impacts, and structural explanation in environmental sociology (as exemplified by Chapter 10 on technological hazards and disasters). A healthy balance can be found between these in the literature.

### Basic versus Applied Research

The distinguishing characteristic of environmental sociology, its perpetual focus on some aspect of the environment, tends to give it a relatively applied orientation. This does not mean that theoretical discourses linking environments to human behavior and social organization are lacking. Chapters 2 and 3 give many examples of such theoretical work, as do several of the subsequent chapters. Nonetheless, the purpose of conceptual and theoretical clarification is often to help achieve a better understanding of environmental problems, and thereby to be able to contribute to their resolution, or to improve situations involving human uses of environments. Thus, environmental sociology is relatively more applied than many other areas of the discipline.

## ACCOMPLISHMENTS AND CURRENT STATUS

While environmental sociology is still a young field, there are very positive signs suggesting its intellectual and professional maturation. We hope that the chapters in this book alone make evident the fact that a great deal of useful knowledge has been generated on a number of environmental contexts, issues, and problems, ranging from the local to the global level.

The final chapter, on environmental sociology in nonacademic settings, by Barbara Payne and Christopher Cluett, presents evidence of concrete applications being made on a day-to-day basis by environmental sociologists. These not only cover a number of important policy areas, but represent the introduction of sociological perspectives into institutions in which economic thinking has gone untempered for much of history. And, of course, academic environmental sociologists have also contributed substantially to policy and decision making. Several contributors to this book, for example, have been very active in working with government agencies and applied research projects.

Environmental sociology has become even more firmly rooted within academia than within agencies and research firms, first in North America and now increasingly in much of the rest of the world as well. Courses devoted to environmental sociology or dealing with environmental topics have become commonplace in undergraduate curricula, and a growing number of graduate departments not only offer courses but specializations in the field. The growth of student interest has helped stimulate these developments, as well as the spate of texts and related books in recent years (many of which were cited at the outset of this chapter). Similarly, sessions on environmental topics are commonplace and well-represented at sociology conferences.

An institutional base for environmental sociology within the discipline was secured long ago with formation of the Section on Environmental Sociology in the American Sociological Association (ASA) in 1976, following similar organizational developments in the Rural Sociological Society[4] and the Society for the Study of Social Problems (Dunlap, 1997). While these groups have had their ups and downs (the latter most noticeable during the 1980s), they have survived, and what is now the ASA Section on Environment and Technology appears to be thriving (Dunlap and Catton, 1994).

Perhaps the most significant trend in the past decade or so has been the enormous growth of interest in environmental sociology throughout much of the rest of the world. Environmental sociology groups and organizations have been formed, for example, within the national associations of the United Kingdom, Germany, Spain, and Italy, among other countries; Finland has an Environmental Social Science Association with a large contingent of sociologists; Japan has a separate Japanese Association of Environmental Sociology that publishes its own journal; and an environmental group has also been established within the European Sociological Association. More importantly, these organizational developments symbolize the vibrant intellectual communities being established in these nations that are yielding an increasing amount of scholarship (several chapters in Redclift and Woodgate [1997] illustrate these developments in various nations).

Earlier we noted some contrasts between the dominant thrusts of environmental sociology internationally and in North America, highlighting the strong emphasis on theorizing in at least some European environmental sociology relative to the strong empirical bent of American environmental sociology. Yet, even here it is important to note the existence of great heterogeneity within European scholarship. It is apparent that a wide variety of perspectives and emphases, including considerable empirical research, exist throughout Europe (see, e.g., journal symposia edited by Diekmann and Jaeger, 1996, and Fischer-Kowalski, 1993) as well as in most nations, as illustrated by the Netherlands (Leroy and Nelissen, 1999), Finland (Konttinen, 1996), and the United Kingdom (compare Macnaghten and Urry, 1998 with Dickens, 1996). The diversity of international environmental sociology is further illustrated by research on a wide range of topics in Asia (see, e.g., Iijima, 1993; Korean Sociological Association, 1994) and Latin American (see, e.g., Hogan and Vieira, 1995). While the amount and diversity of international contributions to environmental sociology make it difficult to offer detailed comparisons with North American work, the growing internationalization of the field ensures that increased cross-fertilization will occur and that environmental sociology is likely to be a richer and stronger area as a result.

In this regard, two organizational developments at the international level warrant mention. In the early 1990s, a Research Committee on Environment and Society (RC 24) was established within the International Sociological Association (ISA) and has quickly become one of ISA's most active research committees. RC 24 has provided a mechanism for increased interaction among environmental sociologists, particularly those interested in the natural environment, from several continents. Besides sponsoring sessions at ISA's quadrennial World Congresses, RC 24 has held several successful conferences of its own that are yielding valuable publications (Spaargaren et al., 2000; Dunlap et al., 2002). In the process RC 24 is proving to be an excellent vehicle for the globalization of environmental sociology, and we expect to see a rapid increase in international intellectual exchanges and collaboration among (natural) environmental sociologists as a result. A similar role is being played by the ISA Research Committee on Housing and Built Environment (RC 43), which recently grew out of working groups of sociologists in North America and Europe that have been meeting separately, and then together, since the early 1970s. Also one of ISA's most active research committees, RC 43 holds meetings between the World Congresses most years and is also producing a valuable and growing body of literature on built environments. It will be interesting to see if these two committees manage to collaborate in the future in an effort to reestablish the close connection between built and natural environment specialists that was the goal—albeit never fully achieved—of the original ASA Section on Environmental Sociology (see note 1).

In sum, there is good reason to be optimistic when contemplating the future of environmental sociology. Relatively few areas of specialization so thoroughly bridge the major theoretical and methodological debates that exist within sociology, or are assured that their subject matter will remain the subject of significant societal attention. Several years ago Buttel (1987) argued that (American) environmental sociology had taken on many of the characteristics of the larger discipline, including a propensity to specialize and fragment. While these trends are evident, the subject matter of environmental sociology also stimulates innovative efforts to transcend theoretical and methodological debates, divides, and dualisms (Bell, 1998). Environmental sociology demands that researchers employ a range of theoretical perspectives and methodological tools when investigating phenomena that can range from the micro to the global, the past to the future, the material to the ideal, and so forth. Doing so will involve transcending empiricism versus theorizing, realism versus constructivism, qualitative versus quantitative, agency versus structure, and other dualisms than plague sociology. The innovative treatment of these theoretical and methodological challenges will help to enlarge our audience and enhance the influence of environmental sociology on the larger discipline.

Thus, in our opinion, environmental sociology is well-established both in North America and, increasingly, in much of the rest of the world. Its active community of scholars, now an international community, produces a vast amount of important and interesting work that appears to be reaching a broader audience than in the field's early days—not just in the larger discipline of sociology and the other social sciences, but throughout the natural sciences and other professions as well as in policy-making circles. We hope that the chapters that follow will be useful both for understanding the substance and applications of the field and for fostering its further development.

## NOTES

Thanks are extended to Loren Lutzenhiser and Annamari Konttinen for helpful comments on an earlier draft of this chapter.

1. The concern with both built and natural environments was institutionalized in the bylaws of the ASA Section on Environmental Sociology (Dunlap and Catton, 1979:252). For an early effort designed explicitly to forge links between built and natural environment specialists, see Dunlap and Catton (1983). While this effort was reasonably successful in the first decade or so of the Section's existence, since then aspects of the natural environment seem to have become the primary focus of papers in Section-sponsored sessions, and one finds fewer built-environment specialists active within the Section.

2. Buttel's (1978) original interpretation that Catton and Dunlap (1978) were suggesting that the NEP would replace "existing" (i.e., contemporary) theoretical perspectives has evolved over time to the charge that they were suggesting that "classical" sociological theory was irrelevant (e.g., Buttel, 1987; Lidskog, 1998). Yet, except for criticizing "mainstream" sociology for having come to endorse Durkheim's dictum to avoid all but the social causes of social phenomena (something that had become highly ingrained by the 1970s), Catton and Dunlap totally ignored the issue of classical theory in their short article—not even citing Durkheim, much less Marx or Weber. Thus, subsequent efforts to show that the founding fathers, including Durkheim, paid some attention to ecological matters (e.g., Buttel, 1987, 2000; Foster, 1999; Järvikoski, 1996; Lidskog, 1998) are valuable and interesting, but irrelevant to Catton and Dunlap's critique of *contemporary* sociological approaches at the time they were writing.

3. Nonetheless, from the outset American environmental sociologists paid considerable attention to the processes by which environmental conditions came to be defined and recognized as problematic (see, e.g., Albrecht, 1975).

4. The relationship between natural resource sociology, which is based in the Natural Resources Research Group of the Rural Sociological Society, and environmental sociology has been the subject of considerable debate. Some see natural resource sociology as more or less a sub-area of environmental sociology (e.g., Dunlap and Catton, 1979), some see the two as essentially synonymous (Buttel, 1996), while others see natural resource sociology as a separate field with roots in early rural sociology (Field and Burch, 1988).

## REFERENCES

Albrecht, Stan L. 1975. "The Environment." Pp. 556–605 in *Social Problems as Social Movements*, edited by A. L. Mauss. Philadelphia: J. B. Lippincott.

Barbosa, Luiz C. 2000. *The Brazilian Amazon Rainforest: Global Ecopolitics, Development, and Democracy*. Lanham, MD: University Press of America.

Bechtel, Robert, Robert Marans, and William Michelson. 1990. *Methods in Environmental and Behavioral Research*. Malabar, FL: Robert E. Krieger Publishing.

Beck, Urich. 1992. *Risk Society: Towards a New Modernity*. London: Sage Publications.

Bell, Michael M. 1998. *An Invitation to Environmental Sociology*. Thousand Oaks, CA: Pine Forge Press.

Brulle, Robert J. 2000. *Agency, Democracy, and Nature*. Cambridge, MA: MIT Press.

Burningham, Kate, and Geoff Cooper. 1999. "Being Constructive: Social Constructionism and the Environment." *Sociology* 33:297–316.

Buttel, Frederick. 1978. "Environmental Sociology: A New Paradigm?" *The American Sociologist* 13:252–256.

———. 1986. "Sociology and the Environment: The Winding Road Toward Human Ecology." *International Social Science Journal* 109:337–356.

———. 1987. "New Directions in Environmental Sociology." *Annual Review of Sociology* 13:465–488.

———. 1996. "Environmental and Resource Sociology: Theoretical Issues and Opportunities for Synthesis." *Rural Sociology* 61(Spring):57–76.

———. 2000. "Ecological Modernization as Social Theory." *Geoforum* 31:57–65.

Catton, William R., Jr. 1980. *Overshoot: The Ecological Basis of Revolutionary Change.* Urbana: University of Illinois Press.

Catton, William R., Jr., and Riley E. Dunlap. 1978. "Environmental Sociology: A New Paradigm." *The American Sociologist* 13(February):41–49.

———. 1980. "A New Ecological Paradigm for Post-Exuberant Sociology." *American Behavioral Scientist* 24:15–47.

Cohen, Maurie J. 1997. "Risk Society and Ecological Modernisation: Alternative Visions for Post-Industrial Nations." *Futures* 29:105–119.

Dickens, Peter. 1996. *Reconstructing Nature: Alienation, Emancipation and the Division of Labor.* London: Routledge.

Diekmann, Andreas, and Carlo C. Jaeger (eds.). 1996. "Symposium on 'Umweltsoziologie'." *Kolner Zeitschrift fur Soziologie und Sozialpsychologie* 36:5–584.

Dunlap, Riley E. 1994. "The Nature and Causes of Environmental Problems: A Socio-Ecological Perspective." Pp. 45–84 in *Environment and Development: A Sociological Understanding for the Better Human Conditions*, edited by the Korean Sociological Association. Seoul: Seoul Press.

———. 1995. "Public Opinion and Environmental Policy." Pp. 63–114 in *Environmental Politics and Policy: Theories and Evidence*, 2nd ed., edited by J. P. Lester. Durham, NC: Duke University Press.

———. 1997. "The Evolution of Environmental Sociology: A Brief History and Assessment of the American Experience." In *The International Handbook of Environmental Sociology*, edited by M. Redclift and G. Woodgate. Cheltenham: Edward Elgar.

Dunlap, Riley E., Frederick H. Buttel, Peter Dickens, and August Gijswijt (eds.). 2002. *Sociological Theory and the Environment.* Boulder, CO: Rowman-Littlefield.

Dunlap, Riley E., and William R. Catton, Jr. 1979. "Environmental Sociology." *Annual Review of Sociology* 5:243–273.

———. 1983. "What Environmental Sociologists Have in Common (Whether Concerned with 'Built' or 'Natural' Environments)." *Sociological Inquiry* 53:113–135.

———. 1994. "Struggling with Human Exemptionalism: The Rise, Decline and Revitalization of Environmental Sociology." *The American Sociologist* 25(Spring):5–30.

Dunlap, Riley E., and Angela G. Mertig (eds.). 1992. *American Environmentalism: The U.S. Environmental Movement, 1970–1990.* Philadelphia: Taylor & Francis.

Field, Donald R., and William R. Burch, Jr. 1988. *Rural Sociology and the Environment.* Westport, CT: Greenwood Press.

Finsterbusch, Kurt, Lynn Llewellyn, and C. P. Wolf (eds.). 1983. *Social Impact Assessment Methods.* Beverly Hills, CA: Sage Publications.

Fischer-Kowalski, Marina (ed.). 1993. "Symposium on 'Environmental Sociology'." *Innovation in Social Sciences Research* 6:383–531.

Foster, John B. 1999. "Marx's Theory of Metabolic Rift: Classical Foundations for

Environmental Sociology." *American Journal of Sociology* 105(September): 366–405.

Freudenburg, William R., and Robert Gramling. 1993. "Socioenvironmental Factors and Development Policy: Understanding Opposition and Support for Offshore Oil." *Sociological Forum* 8:341–364.

Gardner, Gerald T., and Paul C. Stern. 1996. *Environmental Problems and Human Behavior.* Needham Heights, MA: Allyn and Bacon.

Gehl, Jan. 1987. *Life Between Buildings: Using Public Space.* New York: Van Nostrand Reinhold.

Giddens, Anthony. 1990. *The Consequences of Modernity.* Stanford, CA: Stanford University Press.

Goldman, Michael, and Rachel A. Schurman. 2000. "Closing the 'Great Divide': New Social Theory on Society and Nature." *Annual Review of Sociology* 26:563–584.

Hägerstrand, Torsten. 1970. "What About People in Regional Science?" *Papers of the Regional Science Association* 24:7–21.

Hannigan, John A. 1995. *Environmental Sociology: A Social Constructionist Perspective.* London: Routledge.

Harper, Charles L. 1996. *Environment and Society: Human Perspectives on Environmental Issues.* Upper Saddle River, NJ: Prentice-Hall.

Hogan, Daniel Joseph, and Paulo Freire Vieira (eds.). 1995. *Dilemas Socioambientais e Desenvolvimento Sustentavel.* Campinas, Brazil: Editor a da Unicamp.

Humphrey, Craig, and Frederick Buttel. 1982. *Environment, Energy, and Society.* Belmont, CA: Wadsworth.

Iijima, Nobuko. 1993. *Proceedings of the International Symposium on Environmental Problems in Asian Societies.* Tokyo: Tokyo Metropolitan University.

Ittelson, William, H. Proshansky, L. Rivlin, and G. Winkel. 1974. *An Introduction to Environmental Psychology.* New York: Holt, Rinehart and Winston.

Järvikoski, Timo. 1996. "The Relation of Nature and Society in Marx and Durkheim." *Acta Sociologica* 39:73–86.

Klausner, Samuel. 1971. *On Man in His Environment.* San Francisco: Jossey-Bass.

Konttinen, Annamari (ed.). 1996. *Green Moves, Political Stalemates: Sociological Perspectives on the Environment.* Turku, Finland: Department of Sociology, University of Turku.

Korean Sociological Association. 1994. *Environment and Development.* Seoul: Seoul Press.

Kroll-Smith, Steve, Valerie Gunter, and Shirley Laska. 2000. "Theoretical Stances and Environmental Debates: Reconciling the Physical and the Symbolic." *The American Sociologist* 31(Spring):44–61.

Kroll-Smith, Steve, and Shirley Laska. 1994. "The GEC Debate: Notes on Theorizing and Researching the Environment." *Environment, Technology, and Society* (Newsletter of the ASA Section on Environment and Technology) 74(Winter):1–3.

Lash, Scott, Bronislaw Szerszynski, and Brian Wynne (eds.). 1996. *Risk, Environment & Modernity: Towards a New Ecology.* London: Sage Publications.

Lee, Robert G., Donald R. Field, and William R. Burch, Jr. (eds.). 1990. *Com-*

*munity & Forestry: Continuities in the Sociology of Natural Resources.* Boulder, CO: Westview Press.

Leroy, Pieter, and Nico Nelissen. 1999. *Social and Political Sciences of the Environment: Three Decades of Research in the Netherlands.* Utrecht, The Netherlands: International Books.

Lidskog, Rolf. 1998. "Society, Space and Environment: Towards a Sociological Re-Conceptualisation of Nature." *Scandinavian Housing & Planning Research* 15:19–35.

Luhmann, Niklas. 1989. *Ecological Communication.* Chicago: University of Chicago Press.

Lynch, Kevin. 1960. *The Image of the City.* Cambridge, MA: MIT Press and Harvard University Press.

Macnaghten, Phil, and John Urry. 1998. *Contested Natures.* London: Sage Publications.

Marshall, Brent K. 1999. "Globalisation, Environmental Degradation and Ulrich Beck's Risk Society." *Environmental Values* 8:253–275.

Michelson, William. 1970 (rev. 1976). *Man and His Urban Environment: A Sociological Approach.* Reading, MA: Addison-Wesley.

———. 1982. "Basic Dimensions for the Analysis of Behavioral Potential in the Urban Environment." Pp. 17–27 in *Interaction Processes Between Human Behavior and Environment*, edited by G. Hagino and W. Ittelson. Tokyo: Bunsei.

———. 1990. "Measuring Macroenvironment and Behavior: The Time Budget and Time Geography." Pp. 216–243 in *Methods in Environmental and Behavioral Research*, edited by R. Bechtel, R. Marans, and W. Michelson. Malabar, FL: Robert E. Krieger Publishing.

Mileti, Dennis. 1999. *Disaster by Design: A Reassessment of Natural Hazards in the United States.* Washington, DC: National Academy Press.

Mol, Arthur P. J., and David A. Sonnenfeld (eds.). 2000. *Ecological Modernisation Around the World: Perspectives and Critical Debates.* Essex: Frank Cass & Co.

Murphy, Raymond. 1997. *Sociology, and Nature: Social Action in Context.* Boulder, CO: Westview Press.

Olsen, Marvin E., Dora G. Lodwick, and Riley E. Dunlap. 1992. *Viewing the World Ecologically.* Boulder, CO: Westview Press.

Palm, Risa. 1981. "Women in Non-metropolitan Areas: A Time-Budget Survey." *Environment and Planning A* 13:373–378.

Redclift, Michael, and Graham Woodgate (eds.). 1997. *The International Handbook of Environmental Sociology.* Cheltenham: Edward Elgar.

Rosa, Eugene A. 1998. "Metatheoretical Foundations for Post-Normal Risk." *Journal of Risk Research* 1:15–44.

Rudel, Thomas, with Bruce Horowitz. 1993. *Tropical Deforestation: Small Farmers and Land Clearing in the Ecuadorian Amazon.* New York: Columbia University Press.

Schnaiberg, Allan. 1980. *The Environment, from Surplus to Scarcity.* New York: Oxford University Press.

Schnaiberg, Allan, and Kenneth Alan Gould. 1994. *Environment and Society: The Enduring Conflict.* New York: St. Martin's Press.

Spaargaren, Gert, Arthur P. J. Mol, and Frederick H. Buttel (eds.). 2000. *Environ-ment and Global Modernity*. London: Sage Publications.

Szasz, Andrew. 1994. *EcoPopulism: Toxic Waste and the Movement for Environ-mental Justice*. Minneapolis: University of Minnesota Press.

Vitousek, Peter M., Harold A. Mooney, Jane Lubchenco, and Jerry M. Melillo. 1997. "Human Domination of Earth's Ecosystems." *Science* 277:494–499.

Yearley, Steven. 1996. *Sociology, Environmentalism, Globalization*. London: Sage Publications.

Zeisel, John. 1981. *Inquiry by Design: Tools for Environment-Behavior Research*. Monterey, CA: Brooks/Cole Publishing.

*Chapter 2*

# Sociological Theory and the Natural Environment

*Frederick H. Buttel and Craig R. Humphrey*

## INTRODUCTION

Environmental sociology, unlike many sociological fields, by and large has not been preoccupied with theoretical debate since its inception in the early 1970s. Taken positively, this means environmental sociology has been characterized by neither the overproduction of theory in a vacuum of empirical research, nor by the excessive internecine theoretical combat evident in some fields (Collins, 1987; Denzin, 1987). Taken less positively, it means that continuity in the assessment of relatively high-order theoretical propositions has been lacking. Although most research in environmental sociology addresses some theoretical proposition, the themes tend to be ad hoc and fragmented.

This chapter attempts to provide an overview of theoretical environmental sociology, particularly that dealing with the natural or biophysical (as opposed to the built) environment. Following work by Burch (1971), among others, we suggest that environmental sociological theory inherently must be characterized by a double determination; major theoretical postures in environmental sociology tend to be based on social theory at large, on one hand, and on empirical observations or theoretical/metatheoretical assumptions relating to humans as a species and to relationships between society and nature, on the other. This double determination, and especially the social significance of dependence on and interaction with the natural environment, represents the uniqueness of the field.

As we point out below, environmental sociology and theoretical debates in the field have their roots both in nineteenth-century social theory and later American sociology during its theoretical inception. The first section of this chapter is devoted to the classical tradition and its relevance to environmental sociological theory. We then examine human ecology, one of several precursors to environmental sociology. The remaining sections are devoted to other contemporary theoretical approaches and issues in the field.

## CLASSICAL THEORY AND ENVIRONMENTAL SOCIOLOGY

Recent years have witnessed increased attention to the work of classical theorists, particularly with regard to conflicting interpretations of their writings. Several of these controversies have a close relationship with environmental sociology. First and foremost, were environmental-biological considerations given sufficient attention in classical theory? Bock (1978), for example, has argued that biological analogies and evolutionary reasoning gave nineteenth-century social theory a distorted, deterministic view of social change and development, and Dickens (1992:xiii) has gone so far as to claim that classical sociology's reliance on biological concepts paradoxically inhibited the development of an adequate theory of society and nature. Lopreato (1984) has made a different argument—that nineteenth-century social theory was influenced by fundamental misreadings of Charles Darwin and others.

Different from these views, Catton and Dunlap (1978), two pioneers in environmental social theory, have argued that anthropocentrism is a key legacy of classical theory. Considerations relating to biology, the biophysical environment, and the relations of humans to other species in the ecosystem have been studiously omitted, they say, because of Durkheim's insistence that social facts must be explained by social facts, not heredity, race, geography, or personality. Religion, for example, must be explained by the functional role it plays for social solidarity. Lenski (1984) also has argued that social theory generally has accepted Durkheim's emphasis on social facts at the expense of ecological factors relevant to social structure and change.

A second controversy of relevance to environmental sociology relates to Social Darwinism. Most observers have credited Herbert Spencer, the nineteenth-century British social theorist, with providing the intellectual basis for Social Darwinism. The most prominent American Social Darwinist, W. G. Sumner, came under attack in American sociological circles for having founded this tradition of thought. The most articulate critic was Brown University's Lester Ward, who took strong exception to the Social Darwinists' interpretation of Darwinian fitness, particularly the notion that affluence or power is distributed according to merit (Lopreato, 1984). Ward's critique included a vigorous attack on Social Darwinists' tendency to legitimate poverty and class exploitation. Ward and other critics would soon find themselves vindicated by the Great Depression, during which the excesses of laissez-faire capitalism became dramatically apparent.

Social Darwinism soon dropped from favor in American sociology which, as Catton and Dunlap (1978) and others have noted, led henceforth to a strong aversion by sociologists to explanations using biological themes. Gouldner (1970:440), for example, argued that the assumption "society and culture shape men" served at one point to liberate people from biological or supernatural conceptions of their destiny. Others argued that this liberation has gone too far. Prevailing sociological theories are incomplete and inadequate because they fail to consider the role of ecological and biological factors in shaping and being affected by social structure and processes (Catton et al., 1986; Dickens, 1992; Lopreato, 1984).

While these scholars have valuable and important ideas about the neglect of ecological factors in classical and contemporary theory, it can be argued that environmental sociology is both old and new. Elements of environmental sociology have roots deep in nineteenth-century social thought. Marx and Engels frequently referred to the penetration of capitalism as a cause of massive air pollution and other threats to the health and welfare of workers, and to the need for political economy to treat relations between society and nature (Dickens, 1992; Parsons, 1977). Their schema positing the contradictory development of class societies and the revolutionary transformation from one mode of production to another contains an evolutionary component based on Darwin's work (Lopreato, 1984).

Durkheim also set forth a modified evolutionary schema and relied heavily on metaphors from Darwinian evolution and organismic biology. While Durkheim questioned Spencer's argument that evolutionary change led to continuous progress, his theory was based on an evolutionary view of social change (Turner, 1994). The master direction of change was from primitive societies with a low division of labor to modern societies with a complex division of labor. Durkheim, however, differed from Spencer in emphasizing the disruptive qualities of change. The transition from primitive to modern societies was accompanied by anomie and a breakdown of social solidarity and regulation. While Durkheim anticipated that modernizing societies ultimately would exhibit new, more effective organic solidarity, he regarded the establishment of adequate integration and solidarity to be problematic.

Durkheim freely used biological concepts in presenting his theories of social evolution and solidarity, as is evident above in the concept of organic solidarity. *The Rules of Sociological Method* (1895) referred to various types of societies along the continuum from traditional to modern as species or societal species. Moreover, as we will note below, his most famous work, *The Division of Labor in Society* (1893), set forth the major elements of a theoretical perspective that has come to be known as human ecology.

A final classical theorist widely considered to be among the most influential in Western sociology was Max Weber. While Marx and Durkheim largely assumed that there was an a priori direction of social change, Weber firmly rejected the theoretical viewpoint that there was a unilinear course of societal development. Social change was determined by shifting constellations of subjective, structural, and technological forces that ultimately were rooted in human motivations and history. Moreover, Weber (1922) was an outspoken opponent of Social Darwinism, and he frequently stressed how social science differed from biological sciences and that the methods and concepts of the former must be different from those of the latter. Weber's work thus has been taken to be the first decisive break from nineteenth-century evolutionism anchored in biological analogies (see Burns and Dietz, 1992; Dietz and Burns, 1992; and Sanderson, 1990 for comprehensive overviews of "social evolutionism").

It should be stressed, however, that Weber's break from nineteenth-century evolutionism should not be equated with his having rejected the notion that social structure and social action must be understood apart from biophysical factors such as natural resources. In fact, the works of Weber's in which his break with evolutionism and biological analogies was clearest (e.g., Weber, 1927/1981, 1976) were his comparative-historical, empirical studies in which he gave particularly extensive attention to natural resource factors. Weber treated environmental/resource factors as interacting with social factors (such as class, status, power relations, material and ideal interests, religious ethics, and so on) in complex causal models. Weber gave particular stress to how environmental factors "frequently affect complex societies through favoring the 'selective survival' of certain strata over others" (West, 1984:232). Thus, Weber's (probably unintended) use of Darwinian imagery was arguably truer to Darwin's notion of evolution than was the social evolutionism of Herber Spencer and others.

While West's (1984) account of Weber's embryonic sociology of natural resources was largely drawn from Weber's comparative macro-historical empirical studies, it should be noted that Murphy (1994a) has recently developed a neo-Weberian environmental sociology that differs considerably from that portrayed by West. Murphy's rendering of Weber is far less historical in approach and method than West's. Murphy draws primarily on Weber's ideal-types of rationality and orientations to action, and on his notion of Western rationalization. Murphy (1994a) agues that rationalization and the expansion of formal/instrumental rationality have involved tendencies to an ethic of mastery over nature, to a blind quest for new technologies with which to realize this mastery, and to a lack of attention to human threats to the environment. Similar to Weber's notion of charismatic authority, Murphy suggests that the ecological irrationalities caused by rationalization will stimulate social movements that aim at "derationalization" or "re-rationalization" of modern institutions.

## HUMAN ECOLOGY

Human ecology as a field can be defined as the study of structure and change in sustenance organizations or resource groups which support human populations within dynamic and constraining environments (Freese, 1988a, 1988b; Hawley, 1986; Kasarda and Bidwell, 1984). It focuses on patterns of activities for sustaining human populations, their functional relationships, and temporal change in their level of complexity. The transition from rural to urban organization of populations, its causes, and its consequences have been central phenomena in traditional human ecology (Hawley, 1950, 1971), although larger- and smaller-scale changes, including societal evolution (Hawley, 1986; Lenski and Nolan, 1984) and change in the population of organizations such as labor unions (Hannan and Freeman, 1988) and newspapers (Carroll and Hannan, 1989), fall within the domain of ecology.

The nature of organized sustenance activities, of course, involves more than productive organizations, supplies of natural resources, and other limits encountered by growing human populations. These activities reflect the cultural values and beliefs held by members of a society. Ways of earning a living, converting land from one use to another, constructing buildings, raising food, and other sustaining actions characteristic of a population emanate from a cultural milieu in which people are socialized and work (Firey and Sjoberg, 1982). Nonetheless, human ecologists, especially the neoclassical ones following Hawley (1950), traditionally analyzed the structure of human sustenance organization and how it is affected by technology, population, and environmental constraints irrespective of whatever attitudes and cultural values might be involved.

Human ecology has played an important role in sociology because of its ambitious conceptual scheme, including the notion of the environment as the phenomena surrounding and serving as a context for a human population (Turner, 1994). Scarce natural resources as well as other organizations, populations, and space are said to constitute the environment of any aggregate of people functionally related to each other in some enduring way. However, the ecological perspective contains ambiguous assumptions about the role of the environment in constraining the growth of human populations. In particular, despite frequent theoretical arguments within human ecology that the concept of environment includes nonhuman nature, for 70 years there has been a recurring tendency among ecologists to conceptualize the environment in one of two ways. Either it represents the friction of space limiting the daily range of human travel, or it consists of other human groups competing with other people for resources. While historically some of the leading human ecologists in the United States have acknowledged this problem (Hawley, 1984; Schnore, 1958), it has not been addressed in a systematic way. Indeed, the ambiguous, contradictory treatment of the relationship between population and the environment partly explains the emergence of environmental sociology as a separate field (Dunlap and Catton, 1979b).

Because of space limitations we must focus our discussion of human ecology on its main phases, highlighting those facets which at least address the relationships between population and the environment to some extent. First, we identify the roots of the field in innovative sociological work at the University of Chicago over one-half century ago. Then a strategic assumption in ecology—conceptualizing a human population as a territorially expanding sustenance organization—will be discussed. Finally, revisions to ecology centering on the idea of the ecological complex will be outlined. While one could cover even more recent phases in the development of the field (Freese, 1988a, 1988b; Hannan and Freeman, 1989), it is the concept of the human ecological complex which brought the field closest to the study of interrelations between society and the environment.

## AMERICAN SOCIOLOGY AND HUMAN ECOLOGY

Influenced by Darwin, Durkheim, and bioecologists, Park and Burgess postulated that competition and cooperation are basic forms of human interaction through which organized populations struggle to maintain an equilibrium within a constantly changing environment. Thus, the conceptualization of competitive struggles to gain resources among plants and animals in nature was adapted for human ecological analysis. Park and Burgess also recognized that the functional interdependencies within the human population required a certain amount of cooperation, so the basic process underlying much of human behavior amounted to competitive cooperation (Faught, 1986; Theodorson, 1982).

Park and Burgess made an analytical distinction between community and society in an effort to clarify exactly what they meant by ecological competitive cooperation within human populations. Ecological relationships were construed as biotic or functional interdependence binding people together, regardless of the values or motives for pursuing particular actions. In this way ecology presented a dual conceptualization of human society: (1) "biotic" or *community* relationships, based upon "non-thoughtful adjustments made in the struggle for existence," which became the major focus of human ecology; and (2) *societal* relations, based upon acquired values and motives to pursue goals prescribed by others, generally considered to be outside of the purview of human ecology (Theodorson, 1982: 3). While scholars now recognize that Park (1936a) viewed cultural aspects of human social interaction as the ways and means by which humans are related to the natural world (Lyman, 1990, Maines et al., in review), Park's distinction between community and society created endless debate and criticisms (Alihan, 1938; Michelson, 1976; Young, 1988). Ultimately, this imbroglio would lead to the demise of the classical school and to its replacement by neo-orthodox ecology developed by Hawley (1950) and others.

Park, Burgess, and their colleagues used Chicago as a natural laboratory for studying community growth and change. They viewed their industrial city as a territorially based ecological system—a Darwinian "web of life" (Park, 1936a). The in-migration and natural population increase resulting from the movement of people into an expanding industrial community were seen to cause a centrifugal movement of people from the congested central business district to sparse, outlying residential zones. A kind of Darwinian struggle over land use—competitive cooperation in an impersonal market— ensued. This process of urban population redistribution was seen to result, for example, in a segregated residential pattern, with the "fittest" (wealthiest) members of the community buying their way into the most sought-after residential locations. The poorest members of the community, those least able to compete in the housing market, resided in transient neighborhoods and slums, which later were often taken over by commercial activities from an expanding core or central business district. As Logan and Molotch (1986:5–6) have put the matter in their critique of human ecology,

In contrast to other species whose behaviors are genetically fixed, human beings have an equilibrating force in the property market and price system. . . . We thus end up in the ecological perspective with a "hidden hand" that secures the greatest good for the greatest number as an outcome of the market mechanism.

The process, referred to as ecological succession by analogy with bio-ecological succession, served as a major focus within Chicago human ecology, particularly in its application to changing urban land uses and residential population composition in a variety of neighborhoods (Cressey, 1938; Park 1936a, 1936b). In land-use succession, members of a population were seen to be competing for the control of territorial space, the net effect being outward growth of a community in wave-like, concentric zones. Any given stage of succession would be set in motion as pioneer migrants attempted to stake out new residential or commercial land uses in a location which was currently undeveloped or controlled by a competitor. Examples of residential succession have included the subdivision of farm land at the periphery of a metropolis for housing or commercial buildings (Patel, 1980; Rudel, 1989), the migration of working-class families into middle-class neighborhoods (Aldrich, 1973), and gentrification of inner-city neighborhoods (Hudson, 1987).

As with other branches in ecology, the Chicago human ecologists expressed an interest in the relationship between population and the environment, but they did so in a restricted fashion. The components of the environment germane to their work included natural barriers to the physical expansion of the community, travel time, access to sites within a community or region, population density, the size and function of other sub-areas, and the availability of natural resources. However, the optimistic influence of Durkheim, especially the idea that competition inevitably brought about more productive forms of social organizations, shifted attention away from the more problematic aspects of urbanization such as environmental pollution or natural resource depletion (Lenski, 1984). Instead, human ecologists focused on the location of neighborhoods and districts or land-use change in metropolitan communities.

While many other criticisms can be raised concerning classical human ecology (Gottdiener, 1985), research in the field ultimately paved the way for important revisions and innovations in other sociological fields as well, such as organizational theory (Aldrich and Pfeffer, 1976; Hannan and Freeman, 1989). Perhaps the chief contribution of the field from our vantage point is the implicit recognition that human populations, as other species, share functional interdependencies in a natural web of life. Neither Park and Burgess nor their students, however, fully examined the implications of this interdependence between human populations and their environments, especially the problems associated with biophysical constraints on growth or with the influence of natural resources on the structure of sustenance organization.

## HUMAN POPULATIONS: ADAPTIVE OR EXPANDING SYSTEMS?

Human ecology has the dual legacy of Malthusian and Durkheimian social thought. At least since Malthus published his famous *Essay on the Principle of Population* (1830), it has often been assumed that natural reproductive forces cause populations to grow exponentially until they encounter checks caused by finite natural resources, especially food supplies. In their efforts to acquire scarce resources, human populations can develop new technologies and an increasingly complex division of labor. Eventually, however, a population will stop growing as it reaches the limits of vital resources needed for further growth and development. In this sense ecological growth or expansion amounts to "a discontinuous and cumulative process in which change and equilibrium alternate until . . . a climax stage or steady-state equilibrium is reached" (Hawley, 1984:7). Human ecology is thus Malthusian in the sense that population processes constitute its major dynamic (Turner, 1994).

Human ecology has traditionally stressed the role of population growth in changing the organization of communities and societies, although some ecologists have been critical of Malthus for placing too much stress on population growth (Hawley, 1986:24–26). The emphasis of human ecology on population processes has ironically been due to Durkheim's (1893) *The*

*Division of Labor in Society* having played a formative role in human ecological theory, particularly in its emphasis on the ability of human population to transcend Malthusian limits and to grow by means of
technological innovation and a more complex and productive division of
labor. As human populations expand, the frequency and variety of social
contacts would increase in what Durkheim called a process of dynamic
density. The increased density of economic and social relationships and
exchanges, set in motion by population growth, become an engine for the
growth of ideas about innovative techniques and activities. Since these were
mutually beneficial to members of a population encountering intensified
resource scarcity, in Durkheim's view increased density thus tended to pro-
pel a population to new levels of complexity or structural differentiation
(Schnore, 1958).

The capacity for scientific and technological advance, spurred on by
transportation and communication processes, led ecological theory to emphasize cautionary optimism with respect to the continuing ability of human populations to expand their productive capabilities. In its more
straightforward form, the theory becomes one in which the limits to growth
are defined in terms of collective abilities of a population to organize productive activities and find new ways to sustain future generations. As a
prominent ecologist put it, "the power for technological and organizational
innovation implicit in the already accumulated fund of knowledge is ines-
timable and is constantly being enlarged" (Hawley, 1973:10). More recent
variants in the same paradigm envision the social and natural environment
as a set of limiting conditions for the development of human organization
(Hawley, 1986; Kasarda and Bidwell, 1984; McPherson et al., 1992).

Defined as a condition in which a community reaches the maximum
sustainable size and level of organizational complexity for its particular
environment (Micklin, 1984:55), the equilibrium-seeking tendency of a
population is an important property in ecological theory. Out-migration,
intensified resource exploration, technological innovation, declining rates
of natural population increase, and other adaptations can be explained in
terms of the equilibrium-seeking tendency of human ecological systems.
How equilibrium is maintained, of course, depends on a variety of influences. The changing ratio of population to resources, competition among
organizations, the availability of substitute resources, and the technological
innovativeness of a population influence the timing and nature of the equilibrium condition.

Perhaps the thorniest problem for human ecology in theorizing about the
relationship between population and the environment concerns adaptation
and the parallel concept of equilibrium. Curiously enough, only a few leading ecologists (Hawley, 1986) have scrutinized the concept of equilibrium.
Lacking unambiguous criteria for equilibrium, one is rarely certain, for
example, whether a phenomenon such as arrested population growth is an

equilibrating process, an indicator of disequilibrium, or a temporary phase in the longer-term process of expansion. This problem has become even more complex because recent work in population ecology suggests that human organizations have a characteristic known as structural inertia, so that individual organizations may or may not change significantly as their social and natural environment takes on new forms (Hannan and Freeman, 1984). Thus, while *populations* of organizations change over time, this occurs primarily through "births" and "deaths" of organizations (through a selection process), rather than through planning and strategic innovation among existing organizations.

Critics of human ecology in the past argued that notions about adaptation reflected a functionalist or conservative bias with a naively benign view of social change (Logan and Molotch, 1986:4–10).[1] If, on the other hand, entire populations of organizations grow and decline because environmental conditions change and organizations of like kind remain relatively inert or rigid in form, the problem is somewhat different. Then we have a kind of random change where organizations which happen to be suited to a particular set of conditions survive, while others, for a variety of reasons, die off (Burns and Dietz, 1992). Whether this haphazard sequence amounts to adaptation, however, remains problematic. It raises the question of adaptation for whom? Moreover, scholars have frequently observed that since one can always find some reason why a particular social practice is adaptive in terms of some group or population, the term is nearly meaningless (Freese, 1994; Turner, 1994).

Ecologically, adaptation refers to behavior that creates conditions, including biophysical ones, conducive to the successful reproduction of the next generation. Lopreato (1984) adds to this notion the idea that adaptation includes the enhancement of human satisfaction and avoidance of pain. Nonetheless, the human impact on the natural world and its consequences for the reproduction of the human population remain a very important part of the concept of adaptation. Yet, as we have already noted, sociologists historically have rarely examined interrelationships between social behavior and its biophysical consequences. Thus, we would have to concur with Burns and Dietz (1992) that after more than 70 years in the development of human ecology, we are a long way from a suitable understanding of the processes of societal evolution and human adaptation.

Although a few contemporary environmental sociologists were trained in human ecology or actively do ecological research, human ecology and environmental sociology have remained largely insulated from each other over the past two decades. This has probably been because many environmental sociologists were drawn to the field by strong feelings that the direction of social change in the advanced industrial countries was nonadaptive or maladaptive in terms of environmental and resource-scarcity threats to the sustainability of human societies—or even to the survival of the human species (Catton, 1976; Schnaiberg, 1980). Thus, many early environmental sociologists shared a conviction that the ecological expansion of modern society was undermining the very persistence of modern civilization. From this perspective, changes in the economy, government, and cultural values were needed to bring societal demands on the natural world in line with the resources and tolerance limits on the biosphere.

## THE ECOSYSTEM: HUMAN ECOLOGY REVISITED

Recognizing the limitations in a human ecology which focused almost exclusively on competitive cooperation in the spatial organization of metropolitan populations, a number of sociologists reworked the conceptual basis of the field during the 1950s and 1960s. Consequently, it came to be the study of interrelationships among four key properties of human ecosystems: population, organization, the environment, and technology, which are often designated as components of a "POET" model (Duncan, 1961, 1964; Sly, 1972). While this revised form still focuses on the ways by which populations are organized for sustenance or survival within dynamic and constraining environments, the model does isolate the concept of environment.

At times the use of the human ecological complex came close to an embryonic form of environmental sociology, although not always with a concern for the sustainability of organized social life. Duncan (1961), for example, observed the influence of atmospheric pollution on the redistribution of population in Los Angeles. During and after World War II, Los Angeles grew rapidly as a result of its location and function as a seaport and naval base (E→0). As the Los Angeles population grew and decentralized (P→0), the amount of particulate and gaseous substances emitted daily into the atmosphere increased, primarily as a result of increased travel in privately owned automobiles (T→E). With increasing levels of pollution or smog in the Los Angeles Basin after 1950, the residential population decentralized even further (E→P), thereby intensifying the causes of air pollution. Thus, Duncan's version of human ecological theory enables one to see the complex, reciprocal relationships among population, organization, environment, and technology.[2]

Other work, carried out at about the same time, examined the reciprocal effects of urbanization and the importation of raw materials and processed commodities (Gibbs and Martin, 1958, 1962). Using data from more than 40 countries, Gibbs and Martin demonstrated strong, positive statistical associations among levels of metropolitan population concentration, technological development, the division of labor, and the import of natural resources. Although the fossil fuels, nonfuel minerals, and food products imported to countries with high levels of metropolitan population concentration were not considered important in the classical version of human ecosystem theory, Gibbs and Martin (1958:267) stressed "the intensive and extensive organization of effort to convert natural resources into objects of consumption is a critically important part of human effort." Thus, the linkages among natural resources, an ever-increasing dependence upon technology, and a more complex division of labor have been recognized as important ecological processes for changing the sustenance organization of a human population.

These and other examples in the literature (Lenski and Nolan, 1984) suggest that human ecology can provide a useful perspective on the linkage between population and the environment. Nonetheless, the question of whether human populations and their organizations tend toward stability or growth remains unclear. Notions about the carrying capacity of particular environments, the functional as well as dysfunctional forms of adaptation (including technological innovations), and the nature of equilibrating processes remain to be adequately explored. These shortcomings, even after more than a half century of research, have led to the renewal of vigorous criticisms during the past decade (Catton, 1980, Catton et al., 1986; Catton and Dunlap, 1980; Logan and Molotch, 1986; Micklin and Choldin, 1984). Moreover, these criticisms and the neglect of social problems stemming from environmental pollution and natural resource scarcity by sociologists in human ecology and other fields have served as compelling reasons for the growth of environmental sociology during the past two decades.

## THE ORIGINS OF ENVIRONMENTAL SOCIOLOGY

Environmental sociology, of course, did not develop in a vacuum, and human ecology served as one entry point for sociologists with a growing interest in what would become a new field. There also was a literature on natural resources written by rural sociologists (Field and Burch, 1988). For decades rural sociologists have conducted research on agriculture, forestry, recreation, mining, and other primary industries.[3] Another important segment of the emergent literature, especially during the 1970s, consisted of sociological analysis of the environmental movement itself (Buttel and Morrison, 1977; Cotgrove, 1982; Humphrey and Buttel, 1982; Sandbach, 1980). Environmental sociologists (Burch, 1971) in the 1970s also drew extensively on the literature developed by ecological and cultural anthropologists (Vayda, 1969).

Other literature shaping environmental sociology came from several maverick scholars who periodically attempted to stake out a sociological human ecology. Their work remained dormant amid the disinterest of the 1940–1970 sociological mainstream in matters biological, ecological, and environmental. Sorokin and Ogburn made notable attempts earlier in the century (Catton, 1980), but the work of Cottrell (1955) and Firey (1960) would prove to be most influential, even though Cottrell's *Energy and Society* is now seen by many to reflect technological and environmental determinism (Rosa and Machlis, 1983), and Firey's *Man, Mind, and Land* had a highly abstract, functionalist overlay that made for difficult reading and for major problems in application to empirical research.

Two books played a particularly important role in synthesizing these transitional literatures and setting forth sociological postures relevant to modern ecological problems. Klausner's (1971) *On Man in His Environment* was strongly structural-fuctionalist in orientation and drew, in particular, on Firey's (1960) functionalist perspective. Klausner, for example, extensively focused on how diverse social science and ecological literatures could be synthesized within a functionalist framework; but structural-functionalism (Parsons et al., 1953) had been under sustained attack for nearly a decade, so it is probably fair to say that Klausner's work was far more influential in its synthesis of theoretical arguments and research findings from many disciplines, and in its setting forth a research agenda for environmental sociology, than it was in persuading its readers about the applicability of environmental structural-functionalism.

Burch's (1971) *Daydreams and Nightmares* shared certain theoretical and empirical common ground with Klausner's book. Burch, like Klausner, generally stressed the importance of values and norms in shaping societal resource use—a posture typically taken to be Durkheimian in nature. Burch also admirably synthesized a wide variety of social science and ecological literatures in a manner that, if anything, was more impressive than Klausner's and, in particular, was agnostic toward Parsonian functionalism. A principal argument of Klausner's *On Man in His Environment* was that well established sociological theory—particularly the Parsonian theory of action—was readily applicable to the sociology of environmental problems and policy, whereas Burch (1971:14–20) was critical of prevailing sociological theories for their inability to incorporate ecological insights.

## THEORETICAL ISSUES IN CONTEMPORARY ENVIRONMENTAL SOCIOLOGY

Following Burch's (1971, 1979) work and others (Catton and Dunlap, 1980), we have argued that the distinctive aspect of environmental social theory is its double determination in terms of general social theory on the one hand, and metatheoretical postures toward society and nature on the other.[4] Both dimensions are represented in Table 2.1. The first dimension is that of theoretical postures from the major classical sociological theorists: Marx, Weber, and Durkheim. The perspectives of the three major classical theorists are taken as the first axis of the typology, following the widely accepted premise that these classical sociologies continue to pervade mod-

1Table 2.1
A Typology of Environmental Sociological Theory

| Metatheoretical Paradigm* | Classic Sociological Roots | | |
|---|---|---|---|
| | Marx | Weber | Durkheim |
| Human Exemptionalism Paradigm (HEP) | 1. Baran and Sweezy (1966) | 1. Perrow (1984) 2. Resource mobilization theories of environmental movements | 1. Classical human ecology 2. Douglas and Wildavsky (1982) |
| | 1. Logan and Molotch (1986) | 1. Mitchell (1984) | |
| New Ecological Paradigm (NEP) | 1. Anderson (1976) 2. Enzenberger (1979) 3. Hardesty et al. (1971) 4. Benton (1989) 5. Bunker (1984) 6. Gorz (1982) 7. O'Connor (1994) 8. Dickens (1992) | 1. West (1984) 2. Morrison (1976) | 1. Firey (1960) 2. Burch (1971) 3. Klausner (1971) |
| | 1. Schnaiberg (1980) 2. Schnaiberg and Gould (1994) 3. Szasz (1994) | 1. Catton and Dunlap (1978) 2. Martell (1994) | |

*W. R. Catton, Jr. and R. E. Dunlap, "A New Ecological Paradigm for Post-exuberant Sociology," in *American Behavioral Scientist* 24:15–47, copyright © 1980 by Sage Publications, Inc. Reprinted by Permission of Sage Publications, Inc.

ern sociological theory (Alford and Friedland, 1985). We recognize, nonetheless, that this framework is most applicable to macro-sociology and is not adequate for representing micro-sociological theories such as phenomenology, symbolic interactionism, behaviorist social psychology, and so on.

The second dimension is a dichotomous representation of the arguments referred to by Burch (1971). One pole of the dichotomy involves the assumption that humans are a unique species due to their capacity for culture; human societies are accordingly seen as being shaped by socio-cultural forces. The second pole of the dichotomy reflects an assumption that humans are only one species among many in the biosphere; explanations of social structure and behavior must then be based, at least in part, on biological, ecological, or natural environmental forces. These poles of the continuum are referred to as, respectively, the Human Exemptionalism Paradigm (HEP) and the New Ecological Paradigm (NEP), following Catton and Dunlap (1980).

The typology in Table 2.1 yields six "ideal-types" of theoretical postures toward society and its natural environment. The table also recognizes the possibility of mixed types. For example, we categorize Dunlap and Catton as Weberian-Durkheimian/NEP, while Schnaiberg and Szasz are placed in the Marxist-Weberian/NEP category. Also note that Klausner, Burch, and Firey have been assigned to the Durkheimian/NEP category, despite differences in their work. Other examples include traditional human ecology and Douglas and Wildavsky's (1982) work on technological risk being classified as Durkheimian/HEP; Perrow's (1984) work on technological risk as Weberian/HEP; Baran and Sweezy (1966) as Marxist/HEP; Anderson (1976), Benton (1989), Dickens (1992), Enzenberger (1979), Gorz (1982), Hardesty et al. (1971), and O'Connor (1994) as Marxist/NEP; and Morrison (1976), Murphy (1994a), and West (1984) as Weberian/NEP.

## NEP AND THE SOCIETAL–ENVIRONMENTAL DIALECTIC

The schema set forth above, no matter how useful for understanding theoretical themes, is not appropriate for surveying the breadth of the field. Fortunately, this task has received treatment elsewhere (Buttel, 1987; Dunlap and Catton, 1979a, b). Instead we focus our remarks on a limited range of environmental sociology. We do so first in terms of attempts to conceptualize societal–environmental relations with regard to the biological duality of the human species—humans as one species among many, and humans as creators of unique and distinctly social environments. The works of Catton and Dunlap and Schnaiberg are chosen because the three are among the most influential American environmental sociologists and their work dovetails with the biology and society debates in the classical sociology tradition.

At the heart of Catton and Dunlap's (1978) environmental sociology is their observation at a broad paradigmatic level that "ostensibly diverse and competing theoretical perspectives in sociology are alike in their shared anthropocentrism" (p. 41). They have argued that theoretical perspectives as diverse as Marxism, ethnomethodology, and functionalism actually exaggerate their distinctive properties.[5] Instead of being "paradigms in their own right," they saw these theories as minor variants of a larger paradigm. "We maintain that their apparent diversity is not as important as the fundamental anthropocentrism underlying *all* of them" (p. 42; emphasis in original).

The anthropocentric worldview underlying contemporary theories based on otherwise divergent views among the classical theories was called the "human exceptionalism paradigm" by Catton and Dunlap (more recently, the "human exemptionalism paradigm"). In contrast to the HEP, they identified competing assumptions that comprise a "new environmental paradigm" or "new ecological paradigm" (NEP). A revised version of the two, along with a portrayal of the dominant Western worldview, is given in Table 2.2.

We have labeled Catton and Dunlap's work as an example of the Weberian-Durkheimian NEP. The Weberian component rests with an emphasis on changes in contemporary stratification which are deeply rooted in resource constraints and perception of these constraints. The Durkheimian aspect of their work is most clearly manifest in the primacy accorded to values (e.g., empirical work on the "dominant Western worldview"; see below). This worldview was bolstered by the boom of Western expansion underwritten by finite supplies of fossil fuels and other nonrenewable raw materials. Such growth led to notions that amount to assuming an environment's carrying capacity is always enlargeable as needed—thus denying the possibility of scarcity. The NEP assumptions represent an argument that the fundamental feature of the human species is its biological relationship with nature.

The HEP/NEP schema of Catton and Dunlap has had a curious influence on environmental sociology. On one hand, their work has been widely read and often cited, especially in theoretically oriented papers, and is the point of departure for most important recent works in environmental sociology (e.g., Dickens, 1992; Murphy, 1994a). In particular, the Catton and Dunlap argument of the anthropocentric/"unecological" legacy of the classical sociological tradition is widely acknowledged by observers from a variety of theoretical stripes (e.g., Benton, 1989; Martell, 1994; but see Mol and Spaargaren, 1993, for a dissenting view). On the other hand, there has yet been relatively little fleshing out of broad paradigmatic axioms of the NEP into more precise theoretical statements and testable hypotheses.[6] Perhaps the only major comparative macro-sociological study to work directly from the NEP is Catton's (1980) *Overshoot*, an elaboration of earlier work (Catton, 1976).

The other major application of the NEP in empirical sociological research has been in sample survey studies (Cotgrove, 1982; Dunlap and Van Liere, 1978, 1984). In these studies the NEP is construed not as a set of domain assumptions that guide sociological inquiry, but rather as a set of cognitive beliefs held by segments of the public at large. The object of this research has been to develop empirical attitudinal indexes of the NEP and HEP, and to examine the correlates of these beliefs and changes in beliefs. Dunlap's and Cotgrove's studies have indicated that these constructs can be measured in a reliable fashion and that their correlates are reasonably stable across sample survey populations in Western societies.[7]

Some environmental sociologists question the centrality or primacy of the HEP/NEP distinction (Buttel, 1978, 1986b; Humphrey and Buttel, 1982). The distinction is a valid one at the metatheoretical level, but there will be intense debate within the NEP and HEP reflecting the classical theoretical perspectives in Table 2.1. Catton and Dunlap initially argued that these differences lie only within the HEP.[8] The assumptions of the NEP also are at too high a level of abstraction to stimulate meaningful research. Stated so broadly, each of the classical theorists could be cited as exemplars of both the HEP and the NEP. It is not that the HEP/NEP distinction lacks utility. We consider it of such importance that it constitutes an axis in the table. However, the NEP cannot, in and of itself, be employed deductively to construct theory.

Schnaiberg's (1980) influential work, *The Environment* (see Schnaiberg and Gould, 1994, for an updated statement), serves as useful example of this argument. It draws on many of the sources—Marxist political economy, neo-Marxist and neo-Weberian political sociology—that are essentially dismissed as irrelevant anthropocentrisms by Catton and Dunlap. Moreover, the book begins with the point that ecological systems and human societies, especially those in an advanced capitalist-industrial form, have qualitatively different dynamics. Thus, natural ecosystems are transformed from relatively simple, rapidly growing organizations to complex systems which grow more and more slowly with time, while quite the opposite occurs in industrial society. Schnaiberg (1980:19) continues by saying, "But whereas the ecosystem reaches a steady-state by permitting the growth of just enough species and populations to offset the surplus [energy], societies tend to use the surplus to *accumulate* still more surplus in future periods" (emphasis in original).

Two concepts are particularly important in Schnaiberg's work: (1) the societal–environmental dialectic and (2) the treadmill of production. The dialectic was developed to explain the political-ecological dynamics of economic expansion in advanced industrial societies. Economic growth requires an increase in the extraction of resources, a process associated with the creation of environmental problems. These problems, in turn, can restrict future economic growth (Schnaiberg, 1975:5).

Table 2.2
A Comparison of Major Assumptions in the Dominant Western Worldview, Sociology's Human Exemptionalism Paradigm, and the Proposed New Ecological Paradigm

| | | Dominant Western Worldview (DWW) | | Human Exemptionalism Paradigm (HEP) | | New Ecological Paradigm (NEP) |
|---|---|---|---|---|---|---|
| Assumptions about the nature of human beings: | DWW[1] | People are fundamentally different from all other creatures on Earth, over which they have domination. | HEP[1] | Humans have cultural heritage in addition to (and distinct from) their genetic inheritance, and thus are unlike all other animal species. | NEP[1] | While humans have exceptional characteristics (culture, technology, etc.), they remain one among many species that are interdependently involved in the global ecosystem. |
| Assumptions about social causation: | DWW[2] | People are masters of their own destiny; they can choose their goals and learn to do whatever is necessary to achieve them. | HEP[2] | Social and cultural factors (including technology) are the major determinants of human affairs. | NEP[2] | Human affairs are influenced not only by social and cultural factors, but also by intricate linkages of cause, effect, and feedback in the web of nature; thus, purposive human actions have many unintended consequences. |

|  | DWW[3] | HEP[3] | NEP[3] |
|---|---|---|---|
| Assumptions about the context of human society: | The world is vast, and thus provides unlimited opportunities for humans. | Social and cultural environments are the crucial context for human affairs, and the biophysical environment is largely irrelevant. | Humans live in and are dependent upon a finite biophysical environment which imposes potent physical and biological restraints on human affairs. |

|  | DWW[4] | HEP[4] | NEP[4] |
|---|---|---|---|
| Assumptions about constraints on human society: | The history of humanity is one of progress; for every problem there is a solution, and this progress need never cease. | Culture is cumulative; thus, technological and social progress can continue indefinitely, making all social problems ultimately soluble. | Although the inventiveness of humans and the powers derived therefrom may seem for a while to extend carrying capacity limits, ecological laws cannot be repealed. |

*Source:* Catton and Dunlap (1980:34).

Resolutions to this dialectic have been presented in three separate syntheses. The most common historical resolution in industrial as well as industrializing countries, according to Schnaiberg (1975), is the economic synthesis (see also Schnaiberg, 1994). Here the antithetical relation between economic growth and ecological disruption simply is disregarded, maximizing growth without meliorating ecological problems. But as ecological problems mount, the economic synthesis gives way to a managed scarcity synthesis, as exemplified by American environmental policies during the 1970s. The underlying feature of this synthesis is its attention to only the most severe environmental problems which threaten to undermine production, public health, or both. Fundamental to the ecological synthesis would be a profoundly curtailed level of economic expansion such that production and consumption would be specifically constrained according to resource limitations.

Because Schnaiberg argues that the contradictory relations between economic expansion and environmental disruption have not yet resulted in the political and economic forces necessary for the ecological synthesis, the dialectic in practice consists of movement between just the economic and managed scarcity syntheses. In fact, Schnaiberg stresses that the historically nondistributive nature of the American political economy, where both capital and labor receive stable shares of benefits from additional production, creates a common interest among both corporations and labor in returning to a purely economic synthesis.

The treadmill of production serves as a second major concept in Schnaiberg's (1980) work on the forces underlying economic growth in capitalist-industrial society (see also Schnaiberg and Gould, 1994, for a particularly tightly argued version of this argument). The heart of the treadmill lies in the increasingly dominant role of monopoly sector firms both in terms of consequences from their investments and their relations with the state. The monopoly sector is the several hundred capital-intensive, multinational firms and their unionized workers. Their capital-intensive investments tend to displace labor, which later places pressure on the state to pay welfare and unemployment benefits and to solve related social problems. Also, the investments by monopoly sector firms require significant public expenditures for research, infrastructure, and education. Finally, these capital-intensive investments can create ecological problems requiring state expenditures for environmental restoration. The results are tendencies toward state spending, budget deficits, fiscal crises, and what O'Connor (1973) referred to early on as the taxpayers' revolt.

However, if investments in the monopoly sector lead to social and ecological problems, why would state managers not invoke policies to alter these investments? Schnaiberg's argument is that state managers will be constrained in implementing such policies due to the role of the state in capitalist society. The state faces two contradictory imperatives—to create

the conditions for capital accumulation and to foster legitimization or social order. Thus, the political response to problems caused by capital-
intensive economic growth will tend to be policies that encourage more
expansion, thus creating a treadmill of production. As the treadmill proceeds, environmental problems intensify, leading periodically to a planned
scarcity synthesis, but with compelling political and economic pressures to
return to the economic synthesis.

While Schnaiberg portrays the treadmill of production as a complex, self-
reinforcing mechanism, he does acknowledge that the treadmill has limitations or contradictions that may undermine it or make it subject to
reforms. For example, the trajectory of economic expansion after World
War II has resulted not only in ecological problems, but also, since the mid-
1970s, in seemingly insoluble crises of state fiscal stress and massive structural unemployment that threaten to erode social harmony. Schnaiberg
(1980:249) argues that the state really is the only social institution which
could redirect the course of economic growth in advanced capitalist countries (see also the essays in Schnaiberg, 1986). However, such an effort
would require both a collapse in faithful beliefs about the treadmill and
the mobilization of political support for growth in directions other than
capital-intensive technological change. This kind of widespread interest in
alternative forms of development has yet to surface in countries such as the
United States.

In the early 1980s, Schnaiberg identified the appropriate technology (AT)
movement as having the greatest potential to provide a politically viable
alternative to the treadmill of production, though his later comments became more pessimistic (Schnaiberg, 1983). He saw the early 1980s thrust
of the AT movement as being too utopian to appeal to more than a small
cross-section of the alienated middle classes. He argued that the movement
must appeal to much larger fractions of labor than it has heretofore con-
templated or attempted for it to have sufficient political resources to be a
realistic alternative to the treadmill of production. More recently, Schnaiberg and Gould (1994) have noted that "sustainable development" is essentially an updated variant of AT, and that, like AT, sustainable
development strategies in the Third World are not likely to challenge power
relations or the logic of the treadmill. Thus, in their view, sustainable development, if it enables marginalized people to provide for themselves and
in so doing patches over the problems of unequal, treadmill-based accumulation, will ironically tend to buttress capital-intensive industrialization
in the developing world.

A comparison of Catton and Dunlap with Schnaiberg raises a number
of controversies in the relations between sociology and biology discussed
earlier. Catton and Dunlap's objective has been no less than an effort to
reorient the larger sociological discipline along the lines of the new ecological paradigm, even though they (Catton and Dunlap, 1980) retreated

somewhat from their original notion that all theories derived from the classical traditions are outmoded for understanding contemporary reality. But, as yet, their paradigmatic work has not been codified in theoretical terms such that research involving the test of falsifiable hypotheses is possible.

Schnaiberg has been far less interested in reorienting sociology, and has largely directed his work toward the application of selected notions from mainstream sociology and political economy to the understanding of ecological issues. While the outcome is a refreshingly multicausal model, it is not without ambiguities, partly because of its abstractness. It is unclear, for example, whether the dynamic of the treadmill is induced primarily by the logic of capitalism, by the logic of the state, or by some combination of the two institutions. Also, his treatment of environmental issues is largely one of an undifferentiated mass of problems, a treatment that compares unfavorably with the ecological sophistication of Catton's *Overshoot* (1980).

There are important convergences between the approaches of Catton and Dunlap and Schnaiberg. Both argue, unlike many human ecologists, especially the classical ones, that human–environment relationships, at least at present, tend toward ecological disruption rather than societal–environmental equilibrium. Their work thus avoids the uncritical assumption of self-regulation of human–environment relations evident in some older forms of human ecology. They also agree that changes in public environmental consciousness will be required to address the ecological dilemmas of advanced industrial societies. Catton and Dunlap have emphasized the need for a general paradigm shift among the citizenry at large in the advanced industrial societies. Schnaiberg ties the values of economic growth more closely to dominant social classes and state managers. He suggests that new forms of consciousness must be rooted in the interests of labor as opposed to monopoly sector capital. Nevertheless, there are some convergences here which indicate that environmental sociology is beginning to come of age. Inquiry via substantially different assumptions and methodologies has begun to yield parallel conclusions.

## FURTHER EXPLORATION OF THE TYPOLOGY

So far, our discussion has emphasized differences between environmental sociologists whose work falls within the young tradition of the NEP. We would now like to explore the typology further by making two other comparisons. The work of Perrow (1984) and Douglas and Wildavsky (1982) is of particular interest to environmental sociology because of the recent explosion of interest in risk assessment and the sociology of risk (Beck, 1992; Mehta, 1995). Both Perrow and Douglas and Wildavsky can be categorized as falling within the HEP category in Table 2.1. Despite these commonalities, however, they have divergent perspectives on risk because of their different positions in social theory.

We have classified Perrow's work on technological and environmental risk as Weberian/HEP partly because of his *Normal Accidents* (1984). The book, however, can also be seen as an extension of a long career devoted to understanding complex organizations in relation to broader social structures and modalities of power, both of which are Weberian problematics. Perrow develops a structural perspective on technological risk, depicting "normal" or system accidents as inherent in complex, tightly coupled technical systems such as nuclear power plants, petrochemical plants, space missions, aviation, and so on. Perrow notes that risk adjudication and assessment have a strong tendency to ascribe the causes of accidents to operator error rather than to the inherent riskiness of technical systems. Using explanations based on operator error enables elite groups in society to legitimate risky systems and diffuse public scrutiny. It is also interesting to note that Perrow's work on normal accidents is one of the most frequently cited pieces of evidence in Murphy's (1994a) Weberian/NEP work.

Whereas Perrow argues that private and public sector power structures obfuscate the inherently risky nature of modern technical systems, Douglas and Wildavsky (1982) see obfuscation of a very different sort in their analysis of the environmental movement and its role in heightening public awareness of technological and environmental risks. More specifically, they suggest that public concern about risk has little or no basis in objective reality, but rather has its origins in sectarian groups, notably environmental organizations with their ritualistic and religious beliefs.

The emergence of environmental sectarianism is traced by Douglas and Wildavsky to the 1960s and 1970s when race riots, student demonstrations, the loss of the Vietnam War, capitulation to OPEC, and the Watergate scandal created a crisis in national self-confidence and collective identity. Concern over the future of the country became symbolized as concern over the future of the environment—in particular, in national celebratory rituals such as Earth Day, organized by environmental groups. The emergence of beliefs about pollution and the environment, however, is not seen by Douglas and Wildavsky as a cosmological concern of society as a whole. Rather, these concerns are rooted more narrowly in environmental groups, their ideologies, and their strategies for mobilizing the public. The consequences of widespread promulgation of sectarian environmental beliefs is a crisis of public confidence in technology that serves to exaggerate the risks involved and threatens to reduce public welfare if these technological systems are eliminated or overregulated.

Another exploration of the typology involves a comparison of HEP and NEP Marxism. It is useful to begin with Baran and Sweezy's (1966) *Monopoly Capitalism*, which has been one of the most enduring contributions. It should be noted that Baran and Sweezy's Marxism was a decisive break from more orthodox varieties in several respects. Perhaps the most important departure was their argument that because of the transition from competitive capitalism to highly profitable, monopolistic sectors in advanced capitalism, the fundamental problem of advanced capitalist political economies is no longer the falling rate of profit. They argued instead that monopoly had created a tendency for economic surplus to increase more rapidly than it could be productively absorbed. Accordingly, the advanced capitalist nations have become pervaded by excessive military expenditure, widespread advertising of products with planned obsolescence, the demise of public transport and its replacement by millions of private automobiles that travel on crowded, publicly funded highways, and so on. Writing prior to the surge of environmentalism in Western countries, Baran and Sweezy noted that this amounted to waste not only in the sense of foregone production and welfare, but also a waste of natural resources. However, they did not argue that there was a systematic relationship between monopoly capitalism and environmental degradation. Thus, we categorize their work as part of the Marxist/HEP tradition.

During the rise of environmental social science scholarship after 1970, however, there emerged at least three efforts to develop a Marxist tradition in which the dynamics of capitalist development could be linked to phenomena such as environmental degradation and the rise of the environmental movement. The first theoretical innovation, initiated by Enzenberger (1979), combines a critique of Marx's notion of unilinear progress with an argument that advanced capitalism is directly related to the degradation of nature and human social life. The second theoretical innovation, related to the first, elaborates the argument that capitalism is an inherently expansionist system and that there is a contradiction between advanced capitalist development and ecological integrity (Hardesty et al., 1971), what O'Connor (1994) has recently referred to as the "second contradiction of capital."

Gorz's (1982) work on French post-industrial capitalism, *Farewell to the Working Class*, serves as a third innovation in NEP Marxism, and it may prove to be one of the most important in the field. Gorz argued that because of changes in science and technology, especially automation and deskilling of manual industrial work, the traditional working class declined substantially as a proportion of the class structure, and work is no longer a central focus of the industrial workers who remain. The power of industrial workers has thus been broken, and this class is no longer the central force for change in capitalist societies.

At the same time, the imperative of private profitability continues to lead to wasteful, environmentally destructive growth. In the political vacuum created by the demise of the power of industrial workers new social movements have arisen—particularly the environmental, peace, and feminist movements—that Gorz (1982) contends are now the bearers of challenge to the social and ecological destructiveness of advanced capitalism. Their struggles are waged neither to increase movement members' share of the social product nor to advance the socialization of productive assets within the state. Instead, these new social movements have become mobilized to address the ecological destructiveness of capitalism and militarization, sexism, and so on—concerns that largely have their origins outside the sphere of work (see Buttel, 1992 Cotgrove, 1982; Faber and O'Connor, 1989; Frankel, 1987, for elaborations of this argument).

## ENVIRONMENTAL SOCIOLOGICAL THEORY IN THE 1990s

The theoretical arguments and debates that have been reviewed thus far can all be considered "modernist" in nature, in that they are, in one way or another, based on theorizing about the forces that have shaped societal-industrial expansion and ecological dynamics of the past two centuries. Environmental sociology has also been a largely materialist project, oriented as it has been to laying bare the fundamental, though often invisible, mechanisms by which social and natural forces are interrelated. But over the past decade or so, there has been under way a subtle but remarkable shift in social theory. Among the features of this new phase of social theory are the following. There has been a growing skepticism about whether comprehensive social theories can be largely structural in nature, and a growing momentum behind the notion that social theory must emphasize macro-micro linkages or subjectivity. There has been, in other words, a retreat from the project of anchoring social theory in a "grand narrative" that can provide an encompassing portrayal and explanation of the past two or three centuries of large-scale social change. Marxism—and, by implication, materialism—has rapidly fallen out of fashion, having been discredited by the disintegration of state socialism in Europe. There has been a turn away from the traditional unit of sociological analysis—the nation-state and national society—and toward increased emphasis on both more micro-situational and global levels of analysis. There has been a growing emphasis on subjectivity, and on cultural sociology in general. There has also been considerable flirtation with "postmodernist" ideas from literary and critical theory, semiotics, feminism, and so on (see Dietz et al., 1993; Seidman, 1991; and the essays in Ritzer, 1990, and Turner, 1990).

Recent environmental sociology has shown signs of being influenced significantly, albeit mostly indirectly, by these trends in late-twentieth-century social theory. There have been essentially no major pieces of theoretical scholarship in U.S. environmental sociology per se that have been at the cutting edge of the growing trend to postmodernist-culturalist social theory. But environmental sociology in the 1990s is tentatively taking on this new cast due to two factors: First, the empirical scope of environmental sociology has expanded into three areas—the sociology of science, the sociology of risk, and new social movements theory—in which interpretive or postmodernist theories have a strong foothold (e.g., Brulle, 1995; Buttel and Taylor, 1992; Freudenburg et al., 1995; Greider and Garkovich, 1994; Szasz, 1994). Second, scholars from the sociology of science, sociology of risk, and social movements (e.g., Beck, 1992; Martell, 1994; Scott, 1990; Wynne, 1994; Yearley, 1991) have become increasingly interested in environmental phenomena, and thus have "invaded" environmental sociology; in addition, some "general" theorists such as Giddens (1994) and Luhmann (1989) have begun to stress ecological beliefs and societal–environmental relations and important arenas for theoretical advance in sociology.

Most of the theoretical traditions reviewed earlier give considerable emphasis to science and technology as crucial intervening factors in social and environmental change. Yet until very recently, there was virtually no interchange between environmental sociology and the sociology of science. The sociology of science has historically been focused on the basic physical sciences, and has given relatively little attention to the sciences that relate closely to environmental issues. But given the crucial role of science and technological change in societal–environmental relations, environmental sociologists have increasingly found it necessary to expand the scope of their inquiries into the sociology of science literature, in which a "social constructionist," interpretive tradition has been well established, particularly in the United Kingdom, for about two decades. The sociology of science has likewise exhibited a rapidly growing interest in the biological and environmental sciences. Wynne's (1994) and Yearley's (1991) treatments of the interrelations between sociology of science and social movements perspectives on environmental mobilization have become influential works at the intersections of these subdisciplines.

It was stressed earlier that many modern environmental problems relate closely to technological risks posed to human health and environmental integrity, and that the sociology of risk has been of considerable importance to environmental sociology for nearly a decade. Since risk analysis intrinsically involves the need to treat perceptions and cultural factors, the sociology of risk has proven to be a particularly fertile area for application of the culturalist-postmodernist emphases of 1990s social theory (see Clarke's [1992] case study of the *Exxon Valdez* accident). Beck's *Risk Society* (1992) advances the concept of "risk society," in contrast to that of industrial-capitalist society, to depict the course of late-twentieth-century social change. Beck argues that the past two decades of global political-economic reorganization are leading to a fundamental reorientation of the social dynamics of modern societies. During the long era of Western development, the basic logic was that of industrial society and capital accumulation, with technological development and the orientation to technological risk being derivative of class structure and the class-related political party structure. In Beck's view, however, the rupture of the industrial-accumulation trajectory has led to a new dynamic. The dominant class has ceased to be merely an industrially based ownership class, but has become a class that controls technological knowledge. Antagonism and opposition have moved beyond the industrial working class and their struggles to achieve an increased "social wage," and now extend to the middle classes and intelligentsia, and are undertaken through "scientized" discourses of risk and ecology (see also Beck, 1995).

Environmental sociologists from the earliest years of the subdiscipline have stressed the social movement dimension of societal–environmental relations. Since that time there has been a major shift in the theoretical underpinning of work on social movements, one variant of which—new social movements theory—has experienced particularly significant cross-fertilization with the late-twentieth-century theoretical trends. Similar to the reasoning used by Beck, new social movements theory is based on the argument that the demise of post–World War II political-economic logic of industrial capitalism has led to new forms and functions of social movements. Ecology movements are normally portrayed as the prototype of new social movements whose social base is anchored in the noncorporate, white-collar "new class," whose major themes are orthogonal to the discourses of class-based political parties, and that serve as alternative modes of expression and political action to the traditional political parties (Buttel, 1992; Martell, 1994).

Although there has been a clear turn away from structural, "grand narrative" theorizing in sociology, there is by no means a consensus, inside or outside of environmental sociology, that the new late-twentieth-century theories will be enduring. Dickens (1992) and Benton (1989), for example, argue that theories of society and nature will need to keep one foot in the domain of nineteenth-century materialist reasoning, even as they take advantage of the insights made possible by postmodernist and cultural theories. Lipietz (1992) makes an even stronger argument: that treating nature and the environment more directly and integrally has been the missing element in twentieth-century materialism and that social theory will be ineffective unless it takes into account the material dimension of social life.

## CULTURAL SOCIOLOGY AND GLOBAL ENVIRONMENTAL CHANGE: CONTRADICTION OR CREATIVE TENSION IN THE RISE OF ENVIRONMENTAL SOCIOLOGY?

Environmental phenomena and environmental sociology are more prominent within sociology at large than many observers, including ourselves, might have thought possible a decade ago. It is useful to examine the reasons for the ascension of environmental sociology. In our view, there have been two principal factors: First, global environmental change (GEC)—particularly "global warming," but also related matters such as stratospheric ozone destruction, tropical rainforest destruction, and loss of biodiversity—has been particularly central to the revitalization of the environmental movement (Dunlap and Catton, 1994). This has not only bolstered commitment to the field among environmental sociologists, but has also generated attention to environmental matters on the part of sociology colleagues (e.g., Beck, 1992, 1995; Foster, 1994; Giddens, 1994:ch. 8; McNaughten and Urry, 1995). The rise of GEC has provided environmental sociologists with a provocative focal point for research and theory-building (e.g., Dietz and Rosa, 1994). There has been a very strong tendency for recent work in the field to embrace the notion that global environmental problems are the most serious and intellectually challenging ones (Martell, 1994; Murphy, 1994a; Redclift and Benton, 1994). Second, as alluded to earlier, the rise of cultural sociology has occurred in tandem with growing interest in and fascination with ecological movements, beliefs, movements, and knowledges.

Interestingly, these two forces leading to more attention to environmental sociology have some contradictory components. The notion that GEC should be privileged in environmental sociological theory and research, for example, has come under criticism from several quarters of environmental sociology that are influenced by cultural theories (e.g., Mol and Spaargaren, 1993; Taylor and Buttel, 1992). Further, some environmental sociologists (Mol and Spaargaren, 1993) feel that "ecological modernization" (environmental quality improvements made possible by the extension of formal rationality to resource use in the modern business enterprise and state organization) warrants more attention than "alarmist" or faddish notions such as GEC. Others (e.g., Wynne, 1994) have argued that GEC is a "social construction" which involves a somewhat arbitrary delineation of what are and are not important environmental problems that is rooted in ideology, values, or social movement strategy. Finally, it is argued that the conventional portrayal of environmental mobilization—which sees mobilization largely as a logical reaction to the realities and threats of global environmental problems—grossly oversimplifies the dynamics of environmentalism and ignores the situational-contextual nature of mobilization (Yearley, 1991). In turn, prominent environmental sociologists (Dunlap and Catton, 1994; Murphy, 1994a, 1994b) have strongly criticized the cultural-sociological relativization of GEC and global environmental knowledge. Not only has GEC as the basis of an innovative environmental sociology been defended, but some have taken the argument further—claiming that the fact that constructivist sociology of science's being unable to see the reality of GEC testifies to its fruitlessness in general (Murphy, 1994b).

More fundamentally, it may be noted that the essence of environmental sociology for many persons is its materialism, or its ability to reveal a substructure of "materiality"; at the same time, the essence of cultural sociology is a notion that culture and subjectivity, rather than social structure and material substructure, are the building blocks of social organization. Environmental-sociological materialism (both GEC- and non-GEC-anchored) and subjectivist/cultural frameworks are not necessarily incompatible, and some recent works have explicitly attempted to synthesize the two (Dickens, 1992; Freudenburg and Gramling, 1994; Freudenburg et al., 1995). The ability of environmental sociologists to reconcile structure/macro/materiality and agency/subjectivity/micro/cultural factors will be integral to its future. It should be stressed, however, that this is essentially the same challenge that faces sociological theory as a whole.

## CONCLUSION

This chapter has sought to place the emergence of environmental sociology in the historical context of Western sociological thought. Debate over the social and ecological duality of the human species has a long history, one whose roots extend well beyond the beginnings of the sociological discipline.[9] Contemporary North American environmental sociology is but the latest chapter in this history. The major argument of this chapter has been that environmental sociological theory continues to revolve around the double specification of traditional social theory, on one hand, and of postures on the nature of humans as a biological species in an ecosystem versus a conception of humans as creators of distinctly social environments, on the other. At the same time, environmental sociology, like the discipline as a whole, must continue to search for resolutions of structure/agency, macro/micro, and material/ideal dualisms.

The subdiscipline on environmental sociology can begin a new chapter in the dialogue between biology and society with some significant strengths other than its security and recent ascension within the sociological establishment. In addition to the work of Catton and Dunlap and Schnaiberg, it has the writings of Burch (1971), Dickens (1992), Morrison (1976), Murphy (1994a), Perrow (1984), a number of provocative NEP Marxists, practitioners of new cultural-environmental sociologies, and others to serve as diverse, enduring, innovative exemplars. Environmental sociology also has thriving applied research arms (Bunker, 1984; Catton, 1981; Finsterbusch, 1981; O'Riordan and Turner, 1983; Redclift, 1987) that are instrumental in grounding scholarship in real-world concerns and issues. Most importantly, the field has begun to stake out a set of theoretical positions in which ecologically informed analyses can be conducted without denying the validity of the sociological perspective.

## NOTES

We gratefully acknowledge the editorial work of William Michelson, and especially Riley E. Dunlap, who reviewed earlier versions of this chapter. Of course, the authors take full responsibility for any errors of omission or interpretation in this rapidly growing body of literature.

1. Orlove (1980) makes a comparable argument concerning much of the literature in ecological anthropology.

2. See also Duncan (1964), for an extended version of this human ecology.

3. C. C. Zimmerman, R. DuWors, P. H. Landis, H. F. Kaufman, C. E. Lively, and A. L. Bertrand did a series of studies on factors influencing natural resource use and conservation from the 1940s through the 1960s. Their work is analyzed in detail by Field and Burch (1988), Field and Johnson (1986), and Firey (1978).

4. Portions of this section draw heavily on Buttel (1986a).

5. At a more programmatic level, Dunlap and Catton (1979a, 1979b, 1983) have urged the use of Duncan's (1964) "ecological complex" or "POET" model comprised of population, organization, environment, and technology as an analytical framework for guiding the work of environmental sociologists (see also Martell, 1994).

6. At several junctures Catton and Dunlap have stated that the assumptions of both the HEP and NEP are not testable, but rather are broad "domain assumptions," to use Gouldner's (1970) expression. Put somewhat differently, the HEP and NEP are essentially metatheoretical postures.

7. The application of the HEP/NEP distinction in survey research raises certain noteworthy issues. If the NEP is so novel, how is it that one finds substantial variation in attitudes toward this idea? How stable and meaningful are these beliefs? To what degree is there an ongoing paradigm shift in the beliefs of the public? Will this shift be a significant future force for pro-environmental change?

8. Catton and Dunlap (1980) have moved toward the position we have advocated elsewhere (Buttel, 1978; Humphrey and Buttel, 1982). Here they state that the NEP and HEP are crosscut by theoretical perspectives such as Functionalism and Marxism.

9. See Magill (1986) for a parallel argument in human geography.

## REFERENCES

Aldrich, H. 1973. "Employment Opportunities for Blacks in the Black Ghetto." *American Journal of Sociology* 78:1403–1425.
Aldrich, H., and J. Pfeffer. 1976. "Environments and Organizations." *Annual Review of Sociology* 2:79–105.
Alford, R. R., and R. Friedland. 1985. *The Powers of Theory*. New York: Cambridge University Press.
Alihan, M. A. 1938. *Social Ecology*. New York: Columbia University Press.
Anderson, C. H. 1976. *The Sociology of Survival*. Homewood, IL: Dorsey Press.
Baran, P. A., and P. M. Sweezy. 1966. *Monopoly Capital*. New York: Monthly Press.
Beck, U. 1992. *Risk Society*. Beverly Hills, CA: Sage Publications.

————. 1995 *Ecological Enlightenment*. Atlantic Highlands, NJ: Humanities Press.

Benton, T. 1989. "Marxism and Natural Limits: An Ecological Critique and Reconstruction." *New Left Review* 178:51–86.

Bock, K. 1978. "Theories of Progress, Development, Evolution." Pp. 39–79 in *A History of Sociological Analysis*, edited by T. Bottomore and R. Nisbet. New York: Basic Books.

Bunker, S. G. 1984. *Underdeveloping the Amazon*. Urbana: University of Illinois Press.

Burch, W. R., Jr. 1971. *Daydreams and Nightmares: A Sociological Essay on the American Environment*. New York: Harper & Row.

————. 1979. "Human Ecology and Environmental Management." *The Environmental Professional* 1:285–292.

Burns, T. R., and T. Dietz. 1992. "Cultural Evolution: Social Rule Systems, Selection, and Human Agency." *International Sociology* 7:259–283.

Brulle, R. J. 1995. "Environmentalism and Human Emancipation." Pp. 309–328 in *Social Movements*, edited by S. M. Lyman. New York: Macmillan.

Buttel, F. H. 1978. "Environmental Sociology: A New Paradigm?" *The American Sociologist* 13:252–256.

————. 1986a. "Sociology and the Environment: The Winding Road Toward Human Ecology." *International Social Science Journal* 109:337–356.

————. 1986b. "Toward a Rural Sociology of Global Resources: Social Structure, Ecology, and Latin American Agricultural Development." Pp. 129–164 in *Resources and People: Disciplinary Attempts to Bridge the Natural and Social Sciences*, edited by K. A., Dahlberg and J. W. Bennett. Boulder, CO: Westview Press.

————. 1987. "New Directions in Environmental Sociology." *Annual Review of Sociology* 13:465–488.

————. 1992. "Environmentalization: Origins, Processes, and Implications for Rural Social Change." *Rural Sociology* 57:1–27.

Buttel, F. H., and D. E. Morrison. 1977. "The Environmental Movement: A Research Bibliography with Some State-of-the-Art Comments." Exchange Bibliography No. 1308. Monticello, IL: Council of Planning Librarians.

Buttel, F. H., and P. J. Taylor. 1992. "Environmental Sociology and Global Change: A Critical Assessment." *Society and Natural Resources* 5:211–230.

Carroll, G. R., and M. T. Hannan. 1989. "Density Dependence in the Evolution of Populations of Newspaper Organizations." *American Sociological Review* 54:524–541.

Catton, W. R., Jr. 1976. "Why the Future Isn't What It Used to Be (and How It Could Be Made Worse than It Has to Be)." *Social Science Quarterly* 57: 276–291.

————. 1980. *Overshoot: The Ecological Basis of Revolutionary Change*. Urbana: University of Illinois Press.

————. 1981. "Environmental Protection." Pp. 511–537 in *Handbook of Applied Sociology*, edited by M. E. Olsen and M. Micklin. New York: Praeger.

Catton, W. R., Jr., and R. E. Dunlap. 1978. "Environmental Sociology: A New Paradigm." *The American Sociologist* 13:41–49.

————. 1980. "A New Ecological Paradigm for Post-exuberant Sociology." *American Behavioral Scientist* 24:15–47.

Catton, W. R., Jr., G. Lenski, and F. H. Buttel. 1986. "To What Extent Is a Social System Dependent on Its Resource Base?" Pp. 165–186 in *The Social Fabric*, edited by J. F. Short, Jr. Beverly Hills, CA: Sage Publications.

Clarke, L. 1992. "The wreck of the *Exxon Valdez*." Pp. 80–96 in *Controversy*, edited by D. Nelkin. Beverly Hills, CA: Sage Publications.

Collins, R. 1987. "Looking Forward or Looking Back? Reply to Denzin." *American Journal of Sociology* 93:180–184.

Cotgrove, S. 1982. *Catastrophe or Cornucopia*. Chichester: Wiley.

Cottrell, F. 1955. *Energy and Society*. New York: McGraw-Hill.

Cressey, D. 1938. "Population Succession in Chicago: 1898–1930." *American Journal of Sociology* 44:59–69.

Denzin, N. K. 1987. "The Death of Sociology in the 1980s: Comment on Collins." *American Journal of Sociology* 93:175–180.

Dickens, P. 1992. *Society and Nature*. Philadelphia: Temple University Press.

Dietz, T., and T. R. Burns. 1992. "Human Agency and the Evolutionary Dynamic." *Acta Sociologica* 35:187–200.

Dietz, T., P. McLaughlin, and R. Brulle. 1993. "Reconstructing Human Ecology, Hermeneutics, and Habermas: Toward a New Human Ecology." Paper presented at the annual meeting of the American Sociological Association, Miami Beach, August.

Dietz, T., and E. A. Rosa. 1994. "Rethinking the Environmental Impacts of Population, Affluence, and Technology." *Human Ecology Review* 1:277–300.

Douglas, M., and A. Wildavsky. 1982. *Risk and Culture*. Berkeley: University of California Press.

Duncan, O. D. 1961. "From Social System to Ecosystem." *Sociological Inquiry* 31:140–149.

———. 1964. "Social Organization and the Ecosystem." Pp. 36–82 in *Handbook of Modern Sociology*, edited by R.E.L. Faris. Chicago: Rand McNally.

Dunlap, R. E., and W. R. Catton, Jr. 1979a. "Environmental Sociology." *Annual Review of Sociology* 5:243–273.

———. 1979b. "Environmental Sociology: A Framework for Analysis." Pp. 57–85 in *Progress in Resource Management and Environmental Planning*. Vol. 1, edited by T. O'Riordan and R. C. D'arge. Chichester: Wiley.

———. 1983. "What Environmental Sociologists Have in Common (Whether Concerned with 'Built' or 'Natural' Environments)." *Sociological Inquiry* 53:113–135.

———. 1994. "Struggling with Human Exemptionalism: The Rise, Decline, and Revitalization of Environmental Sociology." *The American Sociologist* 25:5–30.

Dunlap, R. E., and K. D. Van Liere. 1978. "The 'New Environmental Paradigm': A Proposed Measuring Instrument and Preliminary Results." *Journal of Environmental Education* 9:10–19.

———. 1984. "Commitment to the Dominant Social Paradigm and Concern for Environmental Quality." *Social Science Quarterly* 62:7–22.

Durkheim, E. 1893/1933. *The Division of Labor in Society*. Trans. G. Simpson. New York: Macmillan.

———. 1895/1964. *The Rules of Sociological Method*. Trans. S. A. Solovay and J. H. Mueller. New York: Free Press.

Enzenberger, H. M. 1979. "A Critique of Political Ecology." Pp. 371–393 in *Political Ecology*, edited by A. Cockburn and J. Ridgeway. New York: Quadrangle.

Faber, D., and J. O'Connor. 1989. "The Struggle for Nature: Environmental Crises and the Crisis of Environmentalism in the United States." *Capitalism Nature Socialism* 1:12–39.

Faught, J. 1986. "The Concept of Competition in Robert Park's Sociology." *The Sociological Quarterly* 27:358–371.

Field, D. R., and W. R. Burch, Jr. 1988. *Rural Sociology and the Environment*. Westport, CT: Greenwood Press.

Field, D. R., and D. R. Johnston. 1986. "Rural Communities and Natural Resources: A Classical Interest." *The Rural Sociologist* 6:187–96.

Finsterbusch, K. 1981. "Impact Assessment." Pp. 24–47 in *Handbook of Applied Sociology*, edited by M. E. Olsen and M. Micklin. New York: Praeger.

Firey, W. 1960. *Man, Mind, and Land*. New York: Free Press.

———. 1978. "Some Contributions of Sociology to the Study of Natural Resources." Pp. 162–174 in *Challenges of Societies in Transition*, edited by M. Barnabus et al. Dehli, India: Macmillan.

Firey, W., and G. Sjoberg. 1982. "Issues in Sociocultural Ecology." Pp. 150–164 in *Urban Spatial Patterns*, edited by G. A. Theodorson. University Park: Pennsylvania State University Press.

Foster, J. B. 1994. *The Vulnerable Planet*. New York: Monthly Review Press.

Frankel, B. 1987. *The New Utopians*. Madison: University of Wisconsin Press.

Freese, L. 1988a. "Evolution and Sociogenesis, Part 1: Ecological Origins." *Advances in Group Processes* 6:53–89.

———. 1988b. "Evolution and Sociogenesis, Part 2: Social Continuities." *Advances in Group Processes* 5:91–118.

———. 1994. "Evolutionary Tangles for Sociocultural Systems: Some Clues from Biology." Pp. 139–171 in *Advances in Human Ecology*, edited by L. Freese. Greenwich, CT: JAI Press.

Freudenburg, W. R., S. Frickel, and R. Gramling. 1995. "Beyond the Nature/Society Divide: Learning to Think about a Mountain." *Sociological Forum* 10: 361–392.

Freudenburg, W. R., and R. Gramling. 1994. *Oil in Troubled Waters*. Albany: State University of New York Press.

Gibbs, J. P., and W. T. Martin. 1958. "Urbanization and Natural Resources: A Study in Organizational Ecology." *American Sociological Review* 23:266–277.

———. 1962. "Urbanization, Technology, and the Division of Labor: International Patterns." *American Sociological Review* 27:667–677.

Giddens, A. 1994. *Beyond Left and Right*. Stanford, CA: Stanford University Press.

Gorz, A. 1982. *Farewell to the Working Class*. Boston: South End Press.

Gottdiener, M. 1985. *The Social Construction of Urban Space*. Austin: University of Texas Press.

Gouldner, A. W. 1970. *The Coming Crisis of Western Sociology*. New York: Avon.

Greider, T., and L. Garkovich. 1994. "Landscapes: The Social Construction of Nature and the Environment." *Rural Sociology* 59:1–24.

Hannan, M. T., and J. Freeman. 1984. "Structural Inertia and Organizational Change." *American Sociological Review* 49:149–163.

———. 1988. "The Ecology of Organizational Mortality: American Labor Unions, 1836–1985." *American Journal of Sociology* 94:25–52.

———. 1989. *Organizational Ecology.* Cambridge, MA: Harvard University Press.

Hardesty, J., N. C. Clement, and C. E. Jencks. 1971. "The Political Economy of Environmental Destruction." Pp. 85–106 in *Economic Growth vs. the Environment,* edited by W. A. Johnson and J. Hardesty. Belmont, CA: Wadsworth.

Hawley, A. H. 1950. *Human Ecology: A Theory of Community Structure.* New York: Ronald Press.

———. 1971. *Urban Society: An Ecological Approach.* New York: Ronald Press.

———. 1973. "Ecology and Population." *Science* 179(23 March):1196–1201.

———. 1984. "Sociological Human Ecology: Past, Present, and Future." Pp. 1–15 in *Sociological Human Ecology,* edited by M. Micklin and H. M. Choldin. Boulder, CO: Westview Press.

———. 1986. *Human Ecology.* Chicago: University of Chicago Press.

Hudson, J. 1987. *The Unanticipated City: Loft Conversion in Lower Manhattan.* Amherst: University of Massachusetts Press.

Humphrey, C. R., and F. H. Buttel. 1982. *Environment, Energy, and Society.* Belmont, CA: Wadsworth.

Kasarda, J. D., and C. E. Bidwell. 1984. "A Human Ecological Theory of Organizational Structuring." Pp. 179–236 in *Sociological Human Ecology,* edited by M. Micklin and H. M. Choldin. Boulder, CO: Westview Press.

Klausner, S. Z. 1971. *On Man in His Environment.* San Francisco: Jossey-Bass.

Lenski, G. 1984. "The Garden of Eden Revisited: Resource Depletion in Ecological and Evolutionary Perspective." Presentation at the meeting of the American Sociological Association, New York City, August.

Lenski, G., and P. D. Nolan. 1984. "Trajectories of Development: A Test of Ecological-Evolutionary Theory." *Social Forces* 63:1–24.

Lipietz, A. 1992. "A Regulationist Approach to the Future of Urban Ecology." *Capitalism Nature Socialism* 3:101–110.

Logan, J. R., and H. L. Molotch. 1986. *Urban Fortunes.* Berkeley: University of California Press.

Lopreato, J. 1984. *Human Nature and Biocultural Evolution.* Boston: Allen & Unwin.

Luhmann, N. 1989. *Ecological Communication.* Cambridge: Polity Press.

Lyman, S. 1990. "Robert Park Reconsidered: The Early Writings." *The American Sociologist* 21:342–357.

Magill, S. M. 1986. "Environmental Questions and Human Geography." *International Social Science Journal* 109:357–375.

Maines, D., J. Bridger, and J. T. Ulmer. In Review. "Mythic Fads and Park's Pragmatism: On Processor-Selection and Theorizing in Human Ecology."

Malthus, T. R. 1830. *An Essay on the Principles of Population.* London: J. M. Dent.

Martell, L. 1994. *Ecology and Society.* Amherst: University of Massachusetts Press.

McNaughten, P., and J. Urry. 1995. "Towards a Sociology of Nature." *Sociology* 29:203–220.

McPherson, J. M., P. A. Popielarz, and S. Drubnic. 1992. "Social Networks and Organizational Dynamics." *American Sociological Review* 57:153–170.

Mehta, M. D. 1995. "Environmental Risk: A Macrosociological Perspective." Pp. 185–202 in *Environmental Sociology*, edited by M. D. Mehta and E. Ouellet. North York, Ont.: Captus Press.

Michelson, W. 1976. *Man and His Urban Environment*, 2nd ed. Reading, MA: Addison-Wesley.

Micklin, M. 1984. "The Ecological Perspective in the Social Sciences: A Comparative Overview." Pp. 51–90 in *Sociological Human Ecology*, edited by M. Micklin and H. M. Choldin. Boulder, CO: Westview Press.

Micklin, M., and H. M. Choldin. 1984. "Research and Policy Issues in Sociological Human Ecology: An Agenda for the Future." Pp. 427–435 in *Sociological Human Ecology*, edited by M. Micklin and H. M. Choldin. Boulder, CO: Westview Press.

Mitchell, R. C. 1984. "Public Opinion and Environmental Politics in the 1970s and 1980s." Pp. 51–74 in *Environmental Policy in the 1980s*, edited by N. J. Vig and M. E. Kraft. Washington, DC: Congressional Quarterly Press.

Mol, A. P., and G. Spaargaren. 1993. "Environment, Modernity, and the Risk-Society: The Apocalyptic Horizon of Environmental Reform." *International Sociology* 8:431–459.

Morrison, D. E. 1976. "Growth, Environment, Equity and Scarcity." *Social Science Quarterly* 57:292–306.

Murphy, R. 1994a. *Rationality and Nature*. Boulder, CO: Westview Press.

———. 1994b. "The Sociological Construction of Science without Nature." *Sociology* 28:957–974.

O'Connor, J. 1973. *The Fiscal Crisis of the State*. New York: St. Martin's Press.

———. 1994. "Is Sustainable Capitalism Possible?" Pp. 152–175 in *Is Capitalism Sustainable?*, edited by M. O'Connor, New York: Guilford Press.

O'Riordan, T., and R. K. Turner (eds.). 1983. *An Annotated Reader in Environmental Planning and Management*. New York: Pergamon Press.

Orlove, B. S. 1980. "Ecological Anthropology." *Annual Review of Anthropology* 9:235–273.

Park, R. E. 1936a. "Human Ecology." *American Journal of Sociology* 42(July):1–15.

———. 1936b "Succession: An Ecological Concept." *American Sociological Review* 1:171–179.

Parsons, H. L. (ed). 1977. *Marx and Engels on Ecology*. Westport, CT: Greenwood Press.

Parsons, T., R. F. Bales, and E. A. Shils. 1953. *Working Papers in the Theory of Action*. New York: Free Press.

Patel, D. I. 1980. *Exurbs: Urban Residential Developments in the Countryside*. Washington, DC: University Press of America.

Perrow, C. 1984. *Normal Accidents*. New York: Basic Books.

Redclift, M. 1987. *Sustainable Development*. London: Methuen.

Redclift, M., and T. Benton (eds.). 1994. *Social Theory and the Global Environment*. London: Routledge.

Ritzer, G. (ed.). 1990. *Frontiers of Social Theory*. New York: Columbia University Press.

Rosa, E., and G. E. Machlis. 1983. "Energetic Theories of Society: An Evaluative Review." *Sociological Inquiry* 53 (Spring):152–178.

Rudel, T. 1989. *Situations and Strategies in American Land-Use Planning*. New York: Cambridge University Press.

Sandbach, F. 1980. *Environment, Ideology and Policy*. Montclair, NJ: Allanheld, Osmun & Co.

Sanderson, S. K. 1990. *Social Evolutionism*. Oxford: Basil Blackwell.

Schnaiberg, A. 1975. "Social Syntheses of the Societal-Environmental Dialectic: The Role of Distributional Impacts." *Social Science Quarterly* 56:5–20.

———. 1980. *The Environment*. New York: Oxford University Press.

———. 1983. "Redistributive Goals Versus Distributional Politics: Social Equity Limits in Environmental and Appropriate Technology Movements." *Sociological Inquiry* 53:200–219.

———. 1994. "The Political Economy of Environmental Problems and Policies: Consciousness, Conflict, and Control Capacity." *Advances in Human Ecology* 3:23–64.

Schnaiberg, A. (ed.). 1986. *Distributional Conflicts in Environmental-Resource Policy*. Aldershot, Hants, UK: Gower.

Schnaiberg, A., and K. A. Gould. 1994. *Environment and Society*. New York: St. Martin's Press.

Schnore, L. F. 1958. "Social Morphology and Human Ecology." *American Journal of Sociology* 63:620–634.

Scott, A. 1990. *Ideology and the New Social Movements*. London: Unwin Hyman.

Seidman, S. 1991. "The End of Sociological Theory: The Postmodern Hope." *Social Theory* 9:131–146.

Sly, D. F. 1972. "Migration and the Ecological Complex." *American Sociological Review* 37(October):615–628.

Szasz, A. 1994. *Ecopopulism*. Minneapolis: University of Minnesota Press.

Taylor, P. J., and F. H. Buttel. 1992. "How Do We Know We Have Global Environmental Problems? Science and the Globalisation of Environmental Discourse." *GeoForum* 23:405–416.

Theodorson, G. A. (ed.). 1982. *Urban Spatial Patterns*. University Park: Pennsylvania State University Press.

Turner, B. S. (ed.). 1990. *Theories of Modernity and Postmodernity*. Beverly Hills, CA: Sage Publications.

Turner, J. H. 1994. "The Ecology of Macrostructure." Pp. 113–138 in *Advances in Human Ecology*, Vol. 3, edited by L. Freese. Greenwich, CT: JAI Press.

Vayda, A. P. (ed.). 1969. *Environment and Cultural Behavior*. Garden City, NY: Natural History Press.

Weber, M. 1992/1968. *Economy and Society*, edited by G. Roth and C. Wittich. Berkeley: University of California Press.

———. 1927/1981. *General Economic History*. New Brunswick, NJ: Transaction Books.

———. 1976. *The Agrarian Sociology of Ancient Civilizations*. Atlantic Highlands, NJ: Humanities Press.

West, P. C. 1984. "Max Weber's Human Ecology of Historical Societies." Pp. 216–234 in *Theory of Liberty, Legitimacy and Power*, edited by V. Murvar. Boston: Routledge & Kegan Paul.

Wynne, B. 1994. "Scientific Knowledge and the Global Environment." Pp. 169–189 in *Social Theory and the Global Environment*, edited by M. Redclift and T. Benton. London: Routledge.

Yearley, S. 1991. *The Green Case: A Sociology of Environmental Issues, Arguments and Politics*. London: HarperCollins.

Young, R. C. 1988. "Is Population Ecology a Useful Paradigm for the Study of Organizations?" *American Journal of Sociology* 94:1–24.

*Chapter 3*

# Theory and the Sociological Study of the Built Environment

*William Michelson and Willem van Vliet--*

Theory is a primary concern within sociology. Sociologists are trained to regard theory as a justification for variable selection and data collection, a basis for expectations and interpretations, an integrator of phenomena and findings, and, often, the single most important component of an enterprise whose data only partially incorporate the complexities of the real world. Successful pursuit of theory is accorded approbation, while those neglecting it not only are criticized but internalize training-based guilt.

There is thus an irony in detailing the place of sociological theory in a field of specialization which is not avowedly theoretical. Students of built environment do not deal with theory for its own sake. Less and less is it an objective to build a comprehensive or general theory, and many of the theories used are not strong or decisive in the overall scope of human life. Competition among researchers to show the superiority of their own or their favorite theories in more and greater applications is less pronounced than in other sociological fields. In fact, the concrete artifacts or processes involved in built environment research are usually of more interest to such students than the particular theories they happen to use.

However, this indicates neither the absence nor disutility of theory in studies of the built environment; it means only that the theoretical issues are more subtle. In fact, though short of becoming a self-absorbing enterprise, theory permeates work in this field, just as prose constitutes even sociological literature. Therefore, we shall emphasize how different types, directions, and aspects of theory come to be used under specific substantive and situational demands. Furthermore, we draw in part from sibling disciplines because the theory used by environmental sociologists is highly interdisciplinary and eclectic, indeed wider in range than in many other specialties.

## THEORY FOR WHAT?

Chapters 4, 5, and 6 in this volume are guides to several directions of substance in the study of built environment. Our objective here is to consider what such substance requires of theory and hence what kind of theory responds appropriately.

Are the phenomena dealt with so singular and similarly patterned that a single theory, no matter how general, can apply meaningfully to their substance? Pursuit of theory within the larger field of sociology is replete with support for successive, overarching theories in pursuit of power of generalization. Auguste Comte, the founder of sociological theory, placed sociology at the top of the hierarchy of sciences, due to the degree that its theory was thought to interpenetrate all the others. Subsequent generations of students and practitioners have argued for and against, for example, structural-functionalism, reductionism, and historical/economic materialism as the one true path of theory. A relatively modest, but highly pragmatic question which has to be examined in this chapter is what implication the substance of sociological research on built environment has for the kind of theory which could be usefully employed.

The questions posed by sociologists in this area have a unique focus, yet, in other ways, represent considerable diversity. This reflects the defining substance: Some aspect of manipulable context is always involved, but people's contexts constitute a huge variety of types and scales.

Contextual diversity leads in an infinite number of theoretical directions, due to the number of possible combinations of an open-ended set of contextual factors. For example, explanatory dynamics will be of vastly different character and complexity according to the scale involved. The factors involved with ergonomic considerations in furniture vary greatly from the contextual issues of institutions like schools, hospitals, and retirement homes, from the local area considerations involved in residential, commercial, and industrial settings, which again vary from the dynamic components of metropolitan areas and regions, with their accompanying need for understanding land-use patterns and travel flows. Certainly, within any level of scale, considerations will vary by the types of environments (e.g., schools versus hospitals).

Further, considerations of any given context and scale will vary also by the attributes of the individuals and groups involved in any way with them, and the ways in which contexts are to be used: sleeping, eating, washing, associating, recuperating, teaching, creating, travelling, purchasing, exercising, praying, deciding, procreating, punishing, rehabilitating, manufacturing, storing, and countless more, not to speak of combinations.

Needless to say, perhaps, the complex matrix formed by these environmental and behavioral variables is complicated further by numerous variables that potentially interact with or intervene in any relationship found to occur. Social entities using built environments include individuals, families, neighborhood associations, building firms, banks, real estate firms, and government authorities. Each is characterized by a combination of social, cultural, economic, and political variables.

Thus, explanation must simultaneously address both the characteristics of the context itself and the demands placed on it. This need for specificity amid diversity will almost inevitably involve selection from among many complementary theoretical approaches, rather than one or a few general theories suitable for widespread application.

Additional theoretical variety, even given the choice of a specific situation, comes from what researchers choose to address. Theoretical approaches are not taken in a vacuum, but in response to particular questions. The questions asked of built environments are numerous, as in turn are the kinds of reasoning and empirical referents which are required to find answers. To illustrate, one very basic dichotomy in built environment research involves a focus which may vary between the impact of environment on people, on the one hand, and people's impact on environment, on the other. Pursuit of the former requires an explanatory perspective on what roles environments play in various forms of behaviors, subjective feelings, outcomes, and so on, of individuals, groups, and aggregates. Ahrentzen (Chapter 4) and Popenoe and Michelson (Chapter 5) deal with this side at different levels of scale. The latter half of the dichotomy characteristically involves analyses of structures and processes through which environments come to be formed and changed. What interests and interactions come to bear on the nature and design of environments built and interventions made not least in view of competing possibilities? Kilmartin (Chapter 6) deals with this side. Considerably different theories are employed not only between the sides of this dichotomy but, depending on contextual nature and scale, within each.

Nonetheless, the two sides of this dichotomy share an intrinsic dialectical dynamic. For example, low-density residential development in U.S. suburbs during the 1950s was a function of a combination of cultural, economic, and political factors. Once in place, it began to affect people, for example, through its relative inaccessibility to jobs for women (Andrew and Moore-Milroy, 1988).

Furthermore, even when the theoretical considerations already mentioned have been dealt with, the theories which prove relevant may vary in terms of the form of their causal reasoning. The kinds of relationships to be assessed are handled by different theoretical approaches.

In his many examinations of theory in environmental psychology, for example, Stokols (1977, 1981, 1986, 1995) distinguishes among theories which posit deterministic causal relationships and those which are inter-active and hence not subject to widespread generalizability, himself placing an emphasis on the latter. Stokols notes that the choice among such theories is in part a function of whether explanation is of enduring processes, caused at any one point in time, or rather of more situational dynamics reflecting transactional processes linking specific population groupings and particular aspects of environment for any length of time (1986). His own outlook on theory in built environment research disaggregates it into many specific theories, reflecting the variations of questions and causation which appear in a matrix of interpersonal considerations times environmental consider-ations (the latter including not only physical but social and cultural dimen-sions as well).

Sociologists typically distinguish among three types of causality in this context: deterministic, probabilistic, and possibilistic.

According to the deterministic view, environment directly causes behav-ior or certain other outcomes. The simplicity of this approach has made it appealing to many who are practice-oriented. Optimistic planners have ap-plied deterministic thinking to the design of new cities (Goodman and Goodman, 1960), neighborhoods (Perry, 1939), and blocks (Jacobs, 1960; Katz, 1994). Deterministic situations do occur. Unheated dwellings will induce hypothermia in elderly people during severe winter weather. An infant will not survive a fall from a 32nd-floor balcony. However, deter-ministic situations in studies of the effects of environment on people appear restricted to adverse effects (can design guarantee happiness?), only a small proportion of what's studied (Franck, 1984). Determinism is found some-what more frequently concerning how people affect environment, particu-larly in terms of economic determinism (e.g., money talks), but certainly not as an exclusively agreed-upon or universally applicable form of logic (Garavaglia, 1992).

While avoiding direct environmental causation of behavior, probabilism treats causation in terms of the likelihood of a certain outcome occurring in the absence of any confounding factors. Under this form of logic, and regardless of the direction of the person–environment relationship, a certain cause will likely produce a given effect; but the certainty of this is reduced by acceptance of the probability of competing and intervening forces found in all but the most simple situations. Hence, probabilistic theory is typically applied to many real-world situations in which knowledge of "the path of least resistance" is desirable. For example, the early literature on friendship formation (e.g., Festinger et al., 1950), showed a highly positive relation-ship between couples' door placement and friendship patterns in most cases. In a related vein, Newman (1972) proposed to induce greater poten-tial for mutual concern among residents and thus to increase their safety by designing housing environments according to principles of "defensible space," intended to increase the probability of responsible behaviors and to decrease the probability of criminal behaviors. Another example is the introduction of guidelines for the design of public open space into New York City's zoning ordinance, based on observations of what constitute effective environmental contingencies for user-preferred behaviors (Whyte 1978).

The least powerful of the three forms of causation is possibilism, which views a given variable as a necessary but not sufficient cause of an outcome. Built environment, for example, would make certain behavior possible but would not by itself explain whether or why it would actually occur. Built environment might be a requisite condition for this behavior, but such other factors as motivation, socio-economic and cultural characteristics, and perception might be needed to actualize expected or desired behavior. Although possibilism is undeniably weak in terms of the power given to or acting on environment, it is a strong theoretical tool in addressing certain kinds of questions. In many instances, the object of research is to determine why desired or expected behavior is absent. It is extremely important to determine whether some aspect of built environmental context precludes the possibility of occurrence. Along the same lines, studies during the program stage of architecture often need to ensure that opportunities for desired behavioral outcomes are created by specific design proposals, or that opportunities for undesired outcomes (e.g., vandalism) are eliminated (e.g., by "target hardening").

The point of complexity is really a simple one: There are countless empirical relationships between people and their built environment. These relationships are dynamic and reciprocal. To improve the quality of the built environment, we need to order and understand these relationships. For this, we need theory; but it is difficult to envisage any single theory that could inform all situations and kinds of questions about them.

With this in mind, we have to turn our examination to the kinds of theories that have been used to this point. This will be done in terms of both trends and characteristics of theories utilized in response to needs.

## WHAT KIND OF THEORY?

The crucial point of similarity among theories specific to studies of built environment, amidst the demands for diversity just sketched, was noted earlier as a concern for at least some aspect of manipulable context. Hence, theory in this area must to some extent represent a departure from general sociological theory by its inclusion of built environment as an explicit factor.

Much sociological thinking, not least among some of the well-known classical theorists who dealt with cities and their component contexts, has followed the form of the Human Exceptionalism Paradigm discussed so fully in Chapter 2 in connection with thinking about natural environments. For example, Comte started by examining the reconstruction of a collapsed feudal society on the basis of progress unhampered by environmental constraints (Turner and Beeghley, 1981); and Durkheim (1895) declared that the determining cause of a social fact should be sought among the social facts preceding it. Then when Weber (1921) carried out a detailed analysis of the city, he emphasized historical and institutional considerations exclusively, omitting any spatial connotations. In Tönnies' (1887) influential Gemeinschaft-Gesellschaft typology, one looks in vain for spatial referents, although the latter form of societal organization requires an entirely different spatial configuration, one where specialized land-uses reflect a greater division of labor.

The work of human ecologists such as McKenzie, Park, Burgess, and others associated with the so-called Chicago School, did incorporate the spatial environment, but merely as a medium or a stage for social phenomena. On this level, human ecology was less a theory and more a method of plotting the spatial distribution of (commonly pathological) behaviors. These behaviors might subsequently be correlated with social structural indices, but it was ultimately economic forces, governing processes of supply and demand in the built environment and assumed to be uncontrollable, which underlay all explanation of this genre. While not mainline human exceptionalism, this approach was even less one employing explicit contextual factors in explanation.

Subsequent work falling under the label of social area analysis (Shevky and Bell, 1955) utilized small residential areas in cities as units in explanation but took them as manifestations of processes associated with the division of labor, the structure of productive activity, and societal scale more generally, not in regard of their spatial structure.

## THEORIES OF PEOPLE AND ENVIRONMENT

Thus, when students of the built environment recognized the need to devise theory which incorporated physical context as an explicit factor, this was a major departure from precedent. There was no accepted model as to the place of built environmental context in sociological theories. Indeed, a major need was the conceptual clarification of the nature of relationship (or interchange) between people and their built environments.

Nowhere was this need more evident than in the ongoing work over many years on the effects of density and crowding on people. A major problem in the early work on this subject is that there was little or no theoretical basis for connecting the independent variable (density) with the dependent (human outcomes). While significant correlations between such variables were found more than occasionally, they were not credible without theoretical underpinnings. More recent work in this tradition has begun to posit more logical, causal relationships between environment and behavior, with mediating variables accounting for documented outcomes (Gillis, Richard, and Hagan, 1986; Gilmore, 1977; Michelson and Garland, 1974; Stokols, 1987).

However, conceptual clarification has come in many ways and with differing degrees of predictive strength. Some of the earlier attempts to grapple with the place of physical environment in social science explanation of human behavior delimited relevant classes of variables and put the various components thus implicated into meaningful relationships which made their mutual and integral consideration logical. This kind of patterned outline we call a paradigm. Its function is by and large descriptive and heuristic. When a paradigm is strengthened by an operational dynamic which potentially explains outcomes, we call this a model. Its function is primarily explanatory. Let us now examine some of the theoretical paradigms and models which have attempted to deal explicitly with people and their physical contexts.

### Paradigms

Kurt Lewin presented one of the first theoretical paradigms incorporating physical context in his field theory (1936). Coming from the field of social psychology, it turned psychological attention outward to extrapersonal contexts with probable influence on behavior, in the absence of countervailing factors. It did not, however, explicitly pinpoint any specific dynamic variables within the built environment having impact on people.

Bronfenbrenner's *The Ecology of Human Development* (1979) expands beyond Lewin's formulation by specifying hierarchically which social structural contexts serve to complement strictly developmental forms of explanation for child development (see also Moen et al., 1995). This work captures the essence of traditional sociology and anthropology, but still does not address dynamic aspects of physical environment.

Geographers like Smith (1988) and Dear and Wolch (1987) have demonstrated the utility of increased contextual analysis, even if largely excluding consideration of the form of built environments.

Somewhat more specification has come from the theoretical formulation of a field called "ekistics," a Greek word standing for a "Science of Human Settlement." Its founder, Constantine Doxiadis (1974), turned explicit attention to the relationships between people and environment, from the least to the greatest scale in each. The ekistics grid, classifying substance at the grid intersection of the two scales, has become a basis for retrieval of research information, as well as a taxonomic legitimation for research. However, its emphasis on structure rather than process renders it unsuitable for clarifying the etiology of built environments.

Another ecological approach originated in the work of Roger Barker (1968). One cannot do justice to this complicated scheme in a short section, but the essence of what Barker did was to break regularized behavior down into situation-specific episodes which are setting-dependent. The physical locus of behavior is the behavior setting. This is a place in which the physical design permits the behavior, while the accompanying culture, artifacts, and rules encourage and support its enactment. The interrelationships among the different aspects of a behavior setting are called "synomorphy," implying that mutual support provides expected behavior in high probability. Thus, you yell at a basketball game, pray in church, and chatter in the luncheonette. Research in this vein has specified a number of specific, prototypical behavior settings in small communities, portrayed life there in terms of the nature of such settings, and compared behavior in two or more communities as a function of differences in behavior settings there.

Barker's "ecological psychology" has had many adherents (Bechtel, 1990; Wicker, 1985) who have developed and used the paradigm extremely insightfully. Nevertheless, there are important person–environment interactions outside the specific scope of the behavior setting: microenvironments and artifacts; those which fail to have the synomorphic qualities of the behavior setting but which nonetheless guide behavior in some way (e.g., road signs and landmarks; see Lynch, 1960); larger complexes of behavior settings and nonbehavior settings; and the settings of movement from place to place, for example. Nor does ecological psychology concern itself with questions related to the life cycle of behavior settings; it remains unclear how they come into being, how they cease to exist or become dysfunctional, how they are transformed into new ones, and what the role of the built environment is in these processes. More to the point of its paradigmatic character, even the identification of synomorphy does not say what it is about built environments that makes them suitable for given behaviors, or what it is about people that has them seek out a particular environment. The behavioral ecological approach provides a taxonomic inventory that is useful in initial conceptual organization, but it has not linked behavioral processes to specific traits of built environments. Hence, it has contributed limited insights from which guidelines for design can be derived (Kaminski, 1989). Thus, although the behavior setting was specified by Zeisel (1975) as "Probably the most fundamental . . . concept" in studies of the built environment, Barker's formulation is still at the level of a nondynamic paradigm.

Other researchers have referred to what Barker called synomorphy by other names. Alexander (1964) adopted a fairly pragmatic approach to develop the concept of "fit" in describing the relationship between people and their environments. From an architectural viewpoint, he assembled what he called patterns, designs of space intended to fulfill stated behavioral objectives. From a collection of such patterns, the designer would select the necessary elements of a total environment that would, one by one, permit the assessed behavioral objectives of the given client or group, without any single pattern even indirectly violating the realization of an objective. The best pattern for a design would not only accomplish its own function but would be most accommodating to all the others—a lowest common denominator. The result of considering and selecting designs in terms of the range of behaviors desired was called fit. Once again, this had the effect of calling attention to the capacities of environment regarding behavior. A greater understanding of its underlying dynamics came from subsequent conceptual and operational advances utilizing space syntax, in which spatial arrangements have been documented for their impact on human contact and activity (Hillier and Hanson, 1984; Klarqvist and Min, 1994).

Working in a more deductive fashion, Michelson (1970) built a roughly similar theoretical framework around the concept called "congruence." The objective in this case was to present a conceptual understanding of how behaviors can be contingent on their environments. This framework suggests analysis of the ways in which environmental design facilitates or hinders access of people to each other and to logistically relevant land-uses. At the same time, individuals and groups can be examined in terms of their behavioral demands on variations of environment. The concept of congruence is central, signifying whether the people at hand can find it possible to realize their preferred or mandated behaviors in the specifically conceptualized setting, or not (incongruence). While possibilism remains its underlying logic, subsequent refinement and elaboration of this framework (Michelson, 1977) enhanced its conceptual accommodation of empirical dynamics; but in its basic form, ignoring accumulated content, Michelson's congruence remains a paradigm.

The paradigms selected for mention because they bring built environment into social science theory all deal with research questions focused on how environment has an impact on people. There have been parallel paradigms dealing with the reverse focus—how people come to bear on the generation of environments. Form (1954) and Long (1958), for example, have both contributed paradigms which specify aspects of social structure with potential to have impact on what gets done and in what way, without being either predictive or deterministic; but in studies on this direction of impact, the actual characteristics of the environmental product are seldom of concern in any detail. Policy alternatives concerning the creation of environment are paramount, and hence the focus is primarily on the structural processes contributing to support for one or another alternative rather than on any incorporation of environmental variables per se into theory. We shall thus postpone consideration of theoretical approaches for this direction, beyond the current section on theories of people and environment.

Paradigms such as these are heuristically valuable because they suggest considered inquiry into the interrelations of particular elements or phenomena. Furthermore, the act of specifying the general classes of such elements or phenomena involved and how they might be related leaves us with concepts that are potentially useful in later theoretical formulations, with additional operational specification. Thus, concepts like behavior setting, congruence, and fit may not rest on dynamic theory but can be incorporated into it. For example, although no specific process is conceptualized as affording congruence or fit, one can predict that its absence in relevant contexts will lead to dysfunctional outcomes.

## Models

Beyond paradigms, models add dynamic elements with the potential for explanation of observed and presumed relationships.

An early theoretical model rests heavily on cultural variables. Maslow's (1954) hierarchy of needs assesses the priority needs are accorded at a given level of life conditions, notably socio-economic class. This model hence provides a way of understanding what people expect from an environment and therefore which of the many kinds of person–environment relationships are likely to be pertinent. Hierarchy of needs has been applied successfully to a large number of social science research topics; within the scope of built environment, perhaps its best-known application is to user needs in housing (Rainwater, 1966).

Still at the cultural level, a very influential model called "proxemics" was advanced by anthropologist Edward T. Hall (1966). In this case, the critical dynamic linking people and built environments is culture-bound definitions of appropriate distances at which people separate themselves for specific activities, from intimacy to sociability, task performance, civility, and crowd behavior. Insofar as the culturally correct distances for given activities vary from society to society, spatial design will ideally take different shapes and scales according to client characteristics, in the absence of which considerations dysfunctional behavior will be more likely. Proxemic considerations therefore form at least a partial basis for the creation of environments, reactions to those encountered, and changes in existing ones. However, as indicated by its very name, proxemics is too limited in its coverage of scale and behavior to serve as an organizing theoretical focus for the field as a whole.

A related model comes from socio-biology. It is organized around the concept of personal space, which is seen as a mechanism to regulate social interactions with particular reference to the avoidance of conflict resulting from natural aggression. Intragroup relations are ordered by patterns of dominance, and intergroup relations by principles of territoriality (Aiello, 1987; Sommer, 1969). Incursions on the established socio-spatial order, whether intended or not, lead to predictable fight-or-flight reactions, and people attempt to manipulate environmental props individually and collectively to mark the order they seek. Empirical work along these lines ranges from the study of positions of active defense and optimal retreat in study areas to investigations of graffiti used by youth gangs to express their identity and stake out their turf. Like the models discussed previously, this one, too, adds a dynamic dimension to the paradigms outlined in the preceding section. Like the other models, it, too, does so by concentrating on one subset of the total realm of potentially relevant reality.

Psychological models have played a very important role in providing explanatory processes, although some of the major contributors (true to the interdisciplinary nature of the field) have not been psychologists by discipline.

One approach takes as its basis the processes of cognition. People commonly learn over time about their environments from their experiences. This learning forms internalized pictures of people's effective environments that serve as a basis for future experiences. Someone who regularly uses many different settings placed over a large urban area will thereby more likely have richer cognitive representations to guide future movements than someone whose activities remain confined to a single, suburban neighborhood (Orleans, 1967).

One prominent line of work in this tradition is mental mapping, in which people are asked to draw maps of a certain area, whether a neighborhood, city, or nation. Practical applications involve the development of public transit information systems and the routing of building egress in case of fire. Cognitive representations, dependent as they are on everyday routines and other sources of knowledge, are shown to provide a basis, for better and worse, for processes such as housing and job selection (Gould, 1974). They also help explain why residential relocation is such a major and potentially disruptive event to many elderly people who have lived in one place for some time (Danermark and Ekstroem, 1990; Rubinstein and Parmelee, 1992).

A second psychological model utilizes learning theory. Wicker (1972), for example, has suggested that congruence between people and their environments may be explained by operant or observational learning of behaviors appropriate in any given circumstance. Synomorphy in behavior settings could similarly be attributed to feedback in the form of discriminative stimuli that reinforce appropriate behaviors and discourage inappropriate behaviors. Likewise, a view of social exchange as a congruence-mediating mechanism involves a learning of costs and rewards associated with alternative situations.

A third psychological model involves perception. Quite apart from the mental images people carry around, people observe their environments selectively. It is an open question as to what people will pay attention. From the point of view of environmental design, the challenge is to understand enough of perception so as to build settings and artifacts that will be interpreted in a behaviorally functional way. Appleyard and Myer's work with highways (1964), for example, dealt with whether or not the characteristics of road design and signs captured the attention of motorists. Lynch's earlier classic (1960) dealt with how the structure and design of cities provide or withhold cues for guidance to get from place to place, as well as sensory enrichment in a given place. Such are all meant as the theoretical grounding for an empirically rooted basis for building better environments (Appleyard, 1976, 1981; Lynch, 1976, 1981). It is no wonder that many researchers stay within this model, given its detail and variation over a spectrum of scales (from the color of micro-environments to the layout of regions) and ways in which people experience their surroundings (e.g., smell, sight, touch, hearing, etc.; Rapoport, 1977:ch. 4).

Closely related is the mammoth *Experimental Sociology of Architecture* by Ankerl (1981), which attempts to anchor a unifying framework for research on built environments in communications theory. It relates design to the dynamics of various modes of human communication—sight, sound, smell, even gustation. Nonetheless, despite basic documentation of how these human processes relate to design considerations, application remains at the level of the room (and occasionally interrelations of a few rooms), where these kinds of considerations are most immediate.

Some sociologists explain person–environment relationships by treating aspects of environment as symbolic objects. Csikszentmihalyi and Rochberg-Halton (1981), for example, examine the meaning of homes in terms of behavior, status, culture, social integration, role models, and self-development. Thus, people use their environments in terms of the meanings these have for them (Arias, 1993). This focus is central to the phenomenological approach, which aims to reveal meaningful content and significance of built environments not captured by empiricist reductionism (Barbey, 1989). These kinds of transactions between people and symbolic aspects of the environment are incorporated in some of the previous models (e.g., behavioral ecology, learning theory), but are elevated to the chief focus in the symbolic interactionist model. This treatment of carefully defined physical environments is obviously a part of main currents in sociological phenomenology (Schutz, 1982). In recent years, this kind of model has been broadened beyond housing per se to choice of neighborhood (Stefanovic, 1992) and municipality (Weiher, 1991). Still others have argued that the scope of planning should be broadened to include considerations of environmental symbolism related to needs for identity, power, and status affirmation by individuals and groups (Appleyard, 1979; Johnson, 1995; Vale, 1992; van Vliet--, 1980.

A very different model, coming primarily from geography, is directed much more explicitly at how the (macro) environment affects human behavior. Hägerstrand (1970) built this perspective around the organization of time and space in cities and regions (most typically) to explain the extent of what people can accomplish within conventional time spans (usually a day), given the current structure of a person's physical surroundings. This time geography is not deterministic, but serves to show the constraining processes involved within time scheduling and land-use patterns in terms of how potential daily activities fit with each other according to availability in time and access in space (Carlstein, 1978; Michelson, 1990; Parkes and Thrift, 1980; Pred, 1977). Models of temporal and spatial structure can be created to assess the nature and degree of behavioral constraints in effect (Lenntorp, 1976). Although time geography rests on the very general theoretical principle that what you can do next is a function of current activity and location, in light of temporal and spatial contexts, applications have been made to a number of pragmatic situations: day care and political participation (Mårtensson, 1979), transportation (Matzner and Reusch, 1976), round-the-clock commerce (Melbin, 1987), and maternal employment (Friberg, 1993; Michelson, 1985).

The same kind of logic, as to how cities which have come to be structured over time on certain criteria then present their residents with definite constraints, is employed by Popenoe (1985). He analyzes how the emerging Western metropolis (especially in the United States) has become adverse to collective activities and supports as a function of structural trends on behalf of privatism.

These and other models provide a theoretical basis for formulating hypotheses directed to answering questions. While all are concerned with the person–environment problematic, they typically provide partial and distinctive explanations that reflect their disciplinary origin, which renders them appropriate to some questions and inappropriate to others. Understanding the impact of environments commonly requires combinations of these perspectives. How people use cities, for example, can benefit from combined knowledge of cognition, perception, and time geography, in varying degrees.

Research has begun to reflect this focus (Goss, 1988; Lawrence, 1987). In addition to multiple causation, where two or more variables act in concert (simultaneously or sequentially) to produce a given outcome, greater currency is also being accorded to plural causation (Pickvance, 1986; van Vliet--, 1990). The latter involves different causative dynamics producing parallel outcomes. An example would be the occurrence of inequalities in access to housing, explained in market economics as a reflection of differential ability to pay, and in centrally planned economies as a reflection of differentially privileged positioning in bureaucratic allocation processes. Theoretical models increasingly include a broad array of potentially relevant explanatory factors.

Furthermore, different models, by virtue of the essentially different spotlight they shed on reality, identify and seek different types of data and thus bring forward the need for new and different methodological tools. For example, an increasing interest in phenomenological approaches to design builds on qualitative research to gain better insights into "experienced space" (Barbey, 1989). This perspective supplements the more common quantitative orientation of empirical research on built environments, contributing a broader understanding of requisites for their successful planning and design.

While theories which interrelate people and environment are necessary to impart meaning and organization to research on the built environment, these are not the only theories which have been found useful for such research. Theories dealing more specifically with people or contexts, not just the interrelations of the two, are also useful to the practice of environmental planning and design.

### Theories about People Pertinent to Environment

It should come as no great surprise that theories from elsewhere in sociology and the other social sciences are useful also in this subfield for illuminating human behavior. Just as research on the impact of built environment on people demanded uniquely new theoretical initiatives to comprehend how built environment bears on people's lives, so, too, have students of the impact of people on environments been forced to contemplate their theoretical underpinnings. Ironically, some responses have been to the effect that studies of built environment have no unique theoretical considerations (Castells, 1977). More general structural theories account for built environment just as they do other objects of study. Whereas research in the one direction pointed to theories which build environment in, research in the other direction tended to take it out.

Studies in the Marxian tradition had a ready-made structural theory which accounted for built environment as all else. This was supported by the trend in physical design identified by Alexander (1964) from unselfconscious to self-conscious form-making. The former, typical of premedieval times (and still found in many Third World nations), is guided by tradition, produces little differentiation, and usually involves people building and altering the environment for their own use. Unself-conscious form-making is a process of direct, iterative responses to slowly evolving socio-physical requirements. In contrast, self-conscious form-making turns built environment into a commodity, produced by nonresidents, entrepreneurs, and bureaucrats, and for objectives which may diverge far from user needs in the direction of profitable investment and gain for nonusers (Mayo, 1988).

The advent of self-conscious form-making calls for theories pertinent to the production of objects for consumption. Housing and other aspects of built environment qualify as such objects. Historical-material explanation is of clear relevance, and hence writings by Marx have had a wide influence.

A number of researchers in this tradition share as a common element the view that the built environment is a commodity whose primary use, at least in capitalist political economies, is to generate profit by means of construction, trade, sale, rent, and so on. Private capital accumulation is seen as the driving force shaping the urban built environment (Dear and Scott, 1981; Harvey, 1973; Tabb and Sawers, 1984), ranging from suburbanization (Walker, 1978) to gentrification (Rose, 1984). Unquestionably, a number of these analyses rest on a compelling logic, corroborated by empirical evidence. Sufficient illustration is the juxtaposition of a proliferation of magnificent office buildings, shopping centers, and professional sports stadia with the rapidly increasing number of homeless, among whom women and children now make up the fastest growing segment (Bingham et al., 1987; Blau, 1992).

Increasing attention is now put on the interface of city development with worldwide economic links and trends—the so-called global economy (Gottdiener, 1994; Sassen, 1991).

However, not all researchers share the view that built environment does not have special characteristics which call for particular types of explanation besides undifferentiated historical-materialism.

A strong neo-Marxist approach continues to utilize concepts related to economic structure and profit, but focuses on uniquely urban structures dealing with allocation, power, influence, and decision making which have an impact on urban development and housing. The concept of "urban growth machine," for example, has been used to bring together analyses of the particular interest groups and processes currently exercising such strong influence in the sectors and styles of development, in many cities in the United States and other countries with so-called "free" market economies (Feagin and Parker, 1990; Logan and Molotch, 1987; Logan and Swanstrom, 1990). How this approach applies to land on the urban-rural fringe was assessed by Rudel (1989).

More recently, research has focused on commercial real estate development in large cities as an arena for investigation of the new localism (e.g., Fainstein, 1994). Conventional theory in this connection posits that the provenance of local outcomes lies in the hegemony of international forces (e.g., Peterson, 1981). Others have begun to advance less deterministic perspectives (corroborated by empirical evidence) that cities, in fact, *can* (and often do) play an important role in mitigating the effects of global restructuring, insofar as they express themselves in patterns of socio-spatial polarization and downtown revitalization at the cost of neighborhood decline (e.g., Davis, 1994; Goetz and Clarke, 1993; Wilson, 1995).

In many ways, the trend from Marxian to neo-Marxian theory was predated by a roughly similar trend from determination by supposedly uncontrollable forces arising from urban land values (according to the Chicago School) to the examination of the value of additional, alternative influences on urban land-use. Alihan (1938) first questioned the exclusivity of the explanatory power of land value, and then Firey (1947) presented examples in Boston in which shared historical sentiment and symbolism appeared to override economically determined land value. The previously mentioned eclectic paradigms of Form (1954) and Long (1958) followed in turn, inter alia, before the pendulum swung again to the strong theory of Marx.

Current structural alternatives, furthermore, are not all neo-Marxian. Caulfield (1994), for example, examines the process of gentrification of city neighborhoods as not only a potential function of structure and capital, but also of conscious will on the part of citizens. As such, he attributes this process primarily to a grassroots social movement (Castells, 1983), rather than to an inexorable structural imperative.

Others have turned again in time to cultural forces. For example, Zukin's deconstructionist analysis (1991) suggests that recent trends in urban development reflect consumption priorities over production (see also Abu-Lughod, 1991). As theoretical pendula swing, it is interesting to find critiques of Marxian and neo-Marxian approaches which are similar in important respects to those lodged against the Chicago School over 50 years ago.

Another major focus of theoretical work concerns professionals involved in the production of built environments. This focus includes the roles, employment structure, practice, values, and ideologies of planners (Howe and Kaufman, 1981; Michelson, 1977; Peattie, 1987; Schon, 1983), similar considerations about architects (Cuff, 1991; Gutman, 1975; Knox, 1987; Lang, 1988), modes of activity in real estate (Bassett and Short, 1980; Krohn et al., 1977; Salins, 1980), and, not at all as strange as the context might make it seem, the workings of local politics (Suttles, 1990). Complementary insights have been gained through structural studies of citizen participation (Medoff and Sklar, 1994; Simmie, 1974; Wireman, 1984).

A recent emphasis in environmental studies brings back an old one in sociology: inequality. Sociological analysis reminds the environmental researcher that there are important, structurally based subsectors within society that are faced with different conditions of life (van Vliet--, 1993). While there is a long history of assessing the nature and adequacy of housing for the poor, as well as implications of housing stock variations for such groups (e.g., Wilner et al., 1962), inquiry has expanded to include also other forms of differentiation.

Another spotlight is on environments for women (Altman and Churchman, 1994; Andrew and Moore-Milroy, 1988; Dandekar, 1993; Franck and Ahrentzen, 1989; Gilroy and Woods, 1994; Hayden, 1984; Michelson, 1985; Spain, 1992; Weisman, 1992) and for the handicapped, not to speak of youth and the elderly. All these and more are conceptualized as vulnerable groups—those at risk to varying degrees because many of their environmental needs have not been adequately considered by designers and planners or properly targeted by those making decisions about environment (Zimring et al., 1987). Here, too, multiple factors are being explored: for example, gender and socio-economic status; gender and sustainability (Eichler, 1995).

The usefulness of theories not unique to studies of built environment extends, of course, well beyond structural approaches. Developmental theories, for example, are very helpful. Studies of children and the elderly in particular benefit from knowledge of what capabilities persons in these and other stages of life bring to their environments. Work on children, for example, has emphasized the importance of play, local areas, and the problems of coping on the basis of incipient abilities and resources (Garbarino, 1982; Lynch, 1977; Michelson and Roberts, 1979; Pollowy, 1977; Wohlwill and van Vliet--, 1985). Similarly, the accumulating knowledge of aging has led to environmentally relevant theories on such subjects as competence and disengagement (Altman et al., 1984; Cohen and Weisman, 1991; Pynoos and Liebig, 1995).

How people address their environments has been informed by knowledge of human personality, its variations and contextual implications. In this connection, specific scales have been directed to dimensions of relevance to the use and evaluation of environments (e.g., Bunting and Semple, 1979; Craik, 1968, 1976; Stokols and Novaco, 1981).

The place of variables about people in theories and about people pertinent to environments varies by the topic and formulation. In many structural approaches, these variables are cast as independent variables, but in other instances, they are often antecedent (why specific people will or will not use a context which produces outcomes) or intervening (why a context may have a differential impact for one or another subgroup).

### Theories about Environment Pertinent to People

Finally, a whole corpus of specific theories about contexts has emerged in connection with empirical studies. They take various forms; but, while grounded in particular research questions and hence contexts, some of them are sufficiently general for use on related phenomena. For example, one of the classic theories in environmental psychology emerged from Glass and Singer's work (1972) on noise. In this theory, noise—defined so as to logically explain dysfunctional outcomes—was conceptualized as loud, from external, uncontrollable sources, and sporadic. Not only was this formulation fruitful for explanation in its immediate framework, but it has been seen as suitable for use in conjunction with other sources and types of interruptions—and the more general concept of control (Cohen et al., 1986).

Defensible space is a much disputed but potentially valuable scheme put forward by Newman (1972) and similar to work by Jeffery (1977) on "crime prevention through environmental design." The former is a scheme in which the vulnerability of a residential building or project to muggings and vandalism is seen as a function of design in terms of fostering surveillance and resident territoriality. Although its empirical basis is still in question, due to a plethora of intervening variables, its logic extends to many more aspects of social control.

A theory involving the concepts of overmanning and undermanning came up in studies of schools by Barker and Gump (1964). While in the tradition of ecological psychology, it is not dependent on the behavior-setting paradigm. It addresses the number of persons available in institutional settings to fill the number of valued roles open to them. When there are more people than needs for them, alienation is expected. Commitment, on the other hand, is felt to apply to those persons stretched to fill needs in the undermanned situations.

Thus, fruitful theories in studies of built environment have taken many forms: interrelating people and environment, illuminating people in ways pertinent to environment, and explaining the dynamics of environmental contexts with pertinence to human life.

## TRENDS AND CONCLUSIONS

Our overview of the use of theory in studies of the built environment has implicitly documented three trends:

1. Declining emphasis has been placed on any one (or general) theory and, indeed, on the desirability of such a theory, due to the specificity and diversity of subject matters treated and questions addressed.

2. Reference to a wide number of specific theoretical models with the potential for dynamic explanation of specific situations is increasing, as is the perceived applicability of multiple and plural causation.

3. Nonetheless, while understanding of the place of built environments in context-relevant explanation is absolutely essential—not only to accurate explanation but to the creation of more optimal environments as well—the degree of causal strength of environmental variables is often low. Environments are more typically necessary but not sufficient conditions for outcomes, and a paradigm or model must usually contain a wide variety of types of factors.

Our observations on these matters are not unique. Zeisel (1981), for example, stresses the use of models, concepts, and hypotheses which are pragmatically oriented to the demands and objectives of specific settings—a major disaggregation of theoretical direction. In a state-of-the-art review for the Environmental Design Research Association, Moore, Tuttle, and Howell (1985) concluded that "There is no single unifying perspective for the study of environment-behavior relationships" (p. 48).

Such a trend is fortunate because it is logical. If the content of research on built environments is so multifaceted as to denigrate the generalized applicability of individual theories, then the logical alternative is the cultivation of multiple formulations, reflecting specific considerations to be drawn upon in such combinations as befit the questions and settings at hand (Gärling and Valsiner, 1985; Goss, 1988). Indeed, in their "Introduction" to the *Handbook of Environmental Psychology* (1987), Stokols and Altman note that "recent research indicates an increasing emphasis on theoretical integration and coherence . . . [as] reflected in the linkages that have been drawn between the various research paradigms within the field" (p. 2). And a recent journal issue dedicated to "Priorities for Research on Human Aspects of the Built Environment" turned for such priorities in a number of different directions (*Architecture and Behaviour*, 1993).

Thus, we withhold the claim of need for the creation of increasingly general theory. The substantive justification is missing in this highly diverse field. Instead, the need we see is for still greater enrichment and guidance of empirical work with what we've called models of the interrelationship of people and environment, and with theories from the middle range of social sciences. Research on, for example, user needs and evaluation can vary enormously in the degree that it fishes for responses, on the one hand, or sifts out a significant catch by casting out appropriate theoretical nets, on the other. The aim, as we see it, is not to build magnificence in theory, but to use theory for the creation of fruitful research results that in turn lead to higher-quality environments.

## NOTE

Helpful comments on earlier drafts were given by David Popenoe and by many of Michelson's colleagues while on study leave at the Department of Building Functions Analysis, School of Architecture, University of Lund, Sweden.

## REFERENCES

Abu-Lughod, Janet. 1991. *Changing Cities*. New York: HarperCollins.
Aiello, John. 1987. "Human Spatial Behavior." Pp. 389–504 in *Handbook of Environmental Psychology*, edited by Daniel Stokols and Irwin Altman. New York: Wiley Interscience.
Alexander, Christopher. 1964. *Notes on the Synthesis of Form*. Cambridge, MA: Harvard University Press.
Alihan, Milla. 1938. *Social Ecology: A Critical Analysis*. New York: Columbia University Press.
Altman, Irwin, and Arza Churchman (eds.). 1994. *Women and the Environment*. New York: Plenum Press.
Altman, Irwin, M. P. Lawton, and J. Wohlwill. 1984. *Elderly People and the Environment*. New York: Plenum Press.

Andrew, Caroline, and Beth Moore-Milroy (eds.). 1988. *Life Space: Gender, Household, Employment*. Vancouver: University of British Columbia Press.

Ankerl, Guy. 1981. *Experimental Sociology of Architecture*. The Hague: Mouton Press.

Appleyard, Donald. 1976. *Planning a Pluralistic City*. Cambridge, MA: MIT Press.

———. 1979. "The Environment as a Social Symbol: Within a Theory of Environmental Action and Perception." *Journal of the American Planning Association* 45(2):143–154.

———. 1981. *Livable Streets*. Berkeley: University of California Press.

Appleyard, Donald, and John Myer. 1964. *The View from the Road*. Cambridge, MA: MIT Press.

*Architecture and Behaviour* 9(1) (1993).

Arias, Ernesto (ed.). 1993. *The Meaning and Use of Housing*. Aldershot, UK: Avebury.

Barbey, Gilles. 1989. "Towards a Phenomenology of Home." *Architecture & Behaviour* 5(2):99–101.

Barker, Roger. 1968. *Ecological Psychology*. Stanford, CA: Stanford University Press.

Barker, Roger, and Paul Gump. 1964. *Big School, Small School*. Stanford, CA: Stanford University Press.

Bassett, Keith, and John Short. 1980. *Housing and Residential Structure*. Boston: Routledge & Kegan Paul.

Bechtel, Robert. 1990. "Ecological Psychology." Pp. 191–215 in *Methods in Environmental and Behavioral Research*, edited by Robert Bechtel, Robert Marans, and William Michelson. Malibar, FL: Robert E. Krieger Publishing.

Bingham, Richard D., Roy E. Green, and Sammis B. White (eds.). 1987. *The Homeless in Contemporary Society*. Beverly Hills, CA: Sage Publications.

Blau, Joel. 1992. *The Visible Poor: Homelessness in the United States*. New York: Oxford University Press.

Bronfenbrenner, Uri. 1979. *The Ecology of Human Development*. Cambridge, MA: Harvard University Press.

Bunting, Trudi, and T. M. Semple. 1979. "The Development of an Environmental Response Inventory for Children." Pp. 273–283 in *Environmental Design: Research, Theory and Application*, edited by A. D. Seidel and S. Danford. Washington, DC: Environmental Design Research Association.

Carlstein, Tommy. 1978. "A Time-Geographic Approach to Time Allocation and Socio-Ecological Systems." Pp. 273–283 in *Public Policy in Temporal Perspective*, edited by William Michelson. The Hague: Mouton Press.

Castells, Manuel. 1977. *The Urban Question*. Cambridge, MA: MIT Press.

———. 1983. *The City and the Grassroots: A Cross-Cultural Theory of Urban Social Movements*. London: Edward Arnold.

Caulfield, Jon. 1994. *City Form and Everyday Life*. Toronto: University of Toronto Press.

Cohen, Sheldon, Gary Evans, Daniel Stokols, and David Krantz. 1986. *Behavior, Health, and Environmental Stress*. New York: Plenum Press.

Cohen, Uriel, and Gerald Weisman. 1991. *Holding on to Home: Designing Environments for People with Dementia*. Baltimore, MD: Johns Hopkins University Press.

Craik, Kenneth. 1968. "The Comprehension of the Everyday Physical Environment." *Journal of the American Institute of Planners* 34:27–37.

———. 1976. "The Personality Research Paradigm in Environmental Psychology." Pp. 55–80 in *Experiencing the Environment*, edited by S. Wapner, S. B. Cohen, and B. Kaplan. New York: Plenum Press.

Csikszentmihalyi, Mihaly, and Eugene Rochberg-Halton. 1981. *The Meaning of Things: Domestic Symbols and the Self*. Cambridge: Cambridge University Press.

Cuff, Dana. 1991. *Architecture: The Story of Practice*. Cambridge, MA: MIT Press.

Dandekar, Hemalata C. (ed.). 1993. *Shelter, Women and Development: First and Third World Perspectives*. Ann Arbor, MI: George Wahr Publishing.

Danermark, B., and M. Ekstroem. 1990. "Relocation and Health Effects on the Elderly." *Journal of Sociology and Social Welfare* 17:25–49.

Davis, John Emmeus (ed.). 1994. *The Affordable City: Toward a Third Sector Housing Policy*. Philadelphia: Temple University Press.

Dear, Michael, and Allen Scott. 1981. *Urbanization and Urban Planning in Capitalist Society*. New York: Methuen.

Dear, Michael, and Jennifer Wolch. 1987. *Landscapes of Despair*. Princeton, NJ: Princeton University Press.

Doxiadis, Constantine. 1974. *Anthropopolis: City for Human Development*. New York: Norton.

Durkheim, E. 1895. *The Rules of Sociological Method*. Glencoe, IL: Free Press (8th ed., 1958).

Eichler, Margrit (ed.). 1995. *Change of Plans: Towards a Non-Sexist Sustainable City*. Toronto: Garamond Press.

Fainstein, S. 1994. *The City Builders*. Cambridge: Blackwell.

Feagin, Joe R., and Robert Parker. 1990. *Building American Cities*. Englewood Cliffs, NJ: Prentice-Hall.

Festinger, Leon, Stanley Schachter, and Kurt Back. 1950. *Social Pressures in Informal Groups*. Stanford, CA: Stanford University Press.

Firey, Walter. 1947. *Land Use in Central Boston*. Cambridge, MA: Harvard University Press.

Form, W. H. 1954. "The Place of Social Structure in the Determination of Land Use: Some Implications for a Theory of Urban Ecology." *Social Forces* 32(4): 17–23.

Franck, K. 1984. "Exorcising the Ghost of Physical Determinism." *Environment and Behavior* 16(4):411–435.

Franck, K., and S. Ahrentzen (eds.). 1989. *New Households, New Housing*. New York: Van Nostrand Reinhold.

Friberg, Tora. 1993. *Everyday Life: Women's Adaptive Strategies in Time and Space*. Trans. Madi Gray. Stockholm: Swedish Council for Building Research.

Garavaglia, J. C. 1992. "Human Beings and the Environment in America—on 'Determinism' and 'Possibilism'." *International Social Science Journal* 44:569–577.

Garbarino, James. 1982. *Children and Families in the Social Environment*. Chicago: Aldine.

Gillis, A. R., M. Richard, and John Hagan. 1986. "Ethnic Susceptibility to Crowd-ing: An Empirical Analysis." *Environment & Behavior* 18:683–706.

Gilmore, Alan. 1977. "Density and Crowding: The Anatomy of a Spurious Rela-tionship." Doctoral dissertation, University of Toronto.

Gilroy, Rose, and Roberta Woods (eds.). 1994. *Housing Women*. London and New York: Routledge.

Glass, D. C., and J. E. Singer. 1972. *Urban Stress*. New York: Academic Press.

Goetz, Edward G., and Susan E. Clarke (eds.). 1993. *The New Localism: Com-parative Urban Politics in a Global Era*. Newbury Park, CA: Sage Publications.

Goodman, Paul, and Percival Goodman. 1960. *Communitas*, 2nd ed., rev. New York: Vintage Books.

Goss, Jon. 1988. "The Built Environment and Social Theory: Towards an Archi-tectural Geography." *Professional Geographer* 40(4):392–403.

Gottdiener, Mark. 1994. *The New Urban Sociology*. New York: McGraw-Hill.

Gould, Peter. 1974. *Mental Maps*. Hammondsworth: Penguin Books.

Gutman, Robert. 1975. "Architecture and Sociology." *American Sociologist* 10: 219–228.

Gärling, Tommy, and Jaan Valsiner. 1985. *Children within Environments: Toward a Psychology of Accident Prevention*. New York: Plenum Press.

Hall, Edward T. 1966. *The Hidden Dimension*. Garden City, NY: Doubleday.

Harvey, David. 1973. *Social Justice and the City*. London: Edward Arnold.

Hayden, D. 1984. *Redesigning the American Dream*. New York: Norton.

Hillier, B., and J. Hanson. 1984. *The Social Logic of Space*. Cambridge: Cambridge University Press.

Howe, E., and J. Kaufman. 1981. "The Values of Contemporary American Plan-ners." *Journal of the American Planning Association* (July):266–278.

Hägerstrand, Torsten. 1970. "What About People in Regional Science?" *Papers of the Regional Science Association* 24:7–21.

Jacobs, J. 1960. *The Death and Life of Great American Cities*. New York: Random House.

Jeffery, C. Ray. 1977, rev. ed. *Crime Prevention Through Environmental Design*. Beverly Hills, CA: Sage Publications.

Johnson, N. 1995. "Cast in Stone: Monuments, Geography, and Nationalism." *Environment and Planning D: Society and Space* 13:15–65.

Kaminski, Gerhard. 1989. "The Relevance of Ecologically Oriented Conceptuali-zations to Theory Building in Environment and Behavior Research." Pp. 3–36 in *Advances in Environment, Behavior, and Design*, vol. 2, edited by Ervin H. Zube and Gary T. Moore. New York: Plenum Press.

Katz, Peter. 1994. *The New Urbanism: Toward an Architecture of Community*. New York: McGraw-Hill.

Klarqvist, Bjoern, and Ye Min. 1994. *Design, Space and Use*. Stockholm: Swedish Council for Building Research.

Knox, Paul L. 1987. "The Social Production of the Built Environment." *Progress in Human Geography* 11(September):354–377.

Krohn, Roger, Roger Fleming, and Marilyn Manzer. 1977. *The Other Economy*. Toronto: Peter Martin Associates.

Lang, Jon. 1988. "Understanding Normative Theories of Architecture: The Potential Role of the Behavioral Sciences." *Environment & Behavior* 20(5): 601–632.

Lawrence, Roderick. 1987. *Housing, Dwellings, and Homes*. New York: John Wiley & Sons.

Lenntorp, Bo. 1976. *Paths in Space-Time Environments: A Time-Geographic Study of Movement Possibilities of Individuals*. Lund: CWK Gleerup.

Lewin, Kurt. 1936. *Principles of Topological Psychology*. New York: McGraw-Hill.

Logan, John, and Harvey Molotch. 1987. *Urban Fortunes: The Political-Economy of Place*. Berkeley: University of California Press.

Logan, John, and Todd Swanstrom (eds.). 1990. *Beyond the City Limits: Urban Policy and Economic Restructuring in Comparative Perspective*. Philadelphia: Temple University Press.

Long, N. E. 1958. "The Local Community as an Ecology of Games." *American Journal of Sociology* 64:251–261.

Lynch, Kevin. 1960. *The Image of the City*. Cambridge, MA: MIT Press.

———. 1976. *Managing the Sense of a Region*. Cambridge, MA: MIT Press.

———. 1977. *Growing Up in Cities*. Cambridge, MA: MIT Press; Paris: UNESCO.

———. 1981. *A Theory of Good City Form*. Cambridge, MA: MIT Press.

Maslow, Abraham. 1954. *Motivation and Personality*. New York: Harper & Row.

Matzner, E., and G. Reusch (eds.). 1976. *Transport as an Instrument for Allocating Space and Time*. Vienna: Technical University in Vienna, Institute of Public Finance, no. 11.

Mayo, James. 1988. "Urban Design as Uneven Development." *Environment & Behavior* 20(5): 633–663.

Medoff, Peter, and Holly Sklar. 1994. *Streets of Hope: The Fall and Rise of an Urban Neighborhood*. Boston: South End Press.

Melbin, M. 1987. *Night as Frontier*. New York: Free Press.

Michelson, William. 1970. *Man and his Urban Environment: A Sociological Approach*. New York: Random House (orig. Addison-Wesley).

———. 1977. *Environmental Choice, Human Behavior, and Residential Satisfaction*. New York: Oxford University Press.

———. 1985. *From Sun to Sun: Daily Obligations and Community Structure in the Lives of Employed Women and Their Families*. Totowa, NJ: Rowman & Allenheld.

———. 1990. "Measuring Macroenvironment and Behavior: The Time-Budget and Time Geography." Chapter 7 in *Methods in Environmental and Behavioral Research*, edited by Robert Bechtel, Robert Marans, and William Michelson. Malabar, FL: Robert E. Krieger Publishing.

Michelson, William, and Kevin Garland. 1974. "The Differential Role of Crowded Homes and Dense Residential Areas in the Incidence of Selected Symptoms of Human Pathology." Research Paper No. 67. Toronto: University of Toronto, Centre for Urban & Community Studies.

Michelson, William, and Ellis Roberts. 1979. "Children and the Urban Physical Environment." Pp. 410–478 in *The Child in the City: Changes and Challenges*, edited by William Michelson et al. Toronto: University of Toronto Press.

Moen, Phyllis, Glen H. Elder, Jr., and Kurt Leuscher (eds.). 1995. *Examining Lives in Context: Perspectives on the Ecology of Human Development*. Washington, DC: American Psychological Association.

Moore, Gary T., D. Paul Tuttle, and Sandra C. Howell. 1985. *Environmental Design Research Directions*. New York: Praeger.

Mårtensson, Solveig. 1979. *On the Formation of Biographies*. Lund: Gleerup.

Newman, Oscar. 1972. *Defensible Space*. New York: Macmillan.

Orleans, Peter. 1967. "Urban Experimentation and Urban Sociology." Paper presented to the annual meeting of the National Academy of Sciences, Washington, DC.

Parkes, Don, and Nigel Thrift. 1980. *Times, Spaces, and Places*. New York: John Wiley & Sons.

Peattie, Lisa. 1987. *Planning: Rethinking Ciudad Guayana*. Ann Arbor: University of Michigan Press.

Perry, C. H. 1939. "The Neighborhood Formula." Pp. 94–109 in *Urban Housing*, edited by W.L.C. Wheaton et al., 1966. New York: Free Press.

Peterson, Paul. 1981. *City Limits*. Chicago: University of Chicago Press.

Pickvance, C. G. 1986. "Comparative Urban Analysis and Assumptions about Causality." Pp. 162–184 in *International Journal of Urban and Regional Research*, edited by Michael Harloe. London: Edward Arnold.

Pollowy, Anne-Marie. 1977. *The Urban Nest*. Stroudsburg, PA: Dowden, Hutchinson & Ross.

Popenoe, David. 1985. *Private Pleasure, Public Plight*. New Brunswick, NJ: Transaction Books.

Pred, A. 1977. "The Choreography of Existence: Comments on Hagerstrand's Time-Geography and Its Usefulness." *Economic Geography* 53:207–221.

Pynoos, Jon and Phoebe S. Liebig (eds.). 1995. *Housing Frail Elders: International Policies, Perspectives, and Prospects*. Baltimore, MD: Johns Hopkins University Press.

Rainwater, Lee. 1966. "Fear and the House-as-Haven in the Lower Class." *Journal of the American Institute of Planners* 32(1):23–31.

Rapoport, Amos. 1977. *Human Aspects of Urban Form*. New York: Pergamon Press.

Rose, D. 1984. "Rethinking Gentrification: Beyond the Uneven Development of Marxist Urban Theory." *Environment and Planning D: Society and Space* 1:47–74.

Rubinstein, Robert L., and Patricia A. Parmelee. 1992. "Attachment to Place and the Representation of the Life Course by the Elderly." Pp. 139–163 in *Place Attachment: Human Behavior and Environment*, edited by Irwin Altman and Setha M. Low. New York: Plenum Press.

Rudel, Thomas. 1989. *Situations and Stragegies in American Land-use Planning*. Cambridge: Cambridge University Press.

Salins, Peter. 1980. *The Ecology of Housing Destruction*. New York: New York University Press.

Sassen, Saskia. 1991. *The Global City*. Princeton, NJ: Princeton University Press.

Schon, Donald. 1983. *The Reflective Practitioner: How Professionals Think in Action*. New York: Basic Books.

Schutz, Alfred. 1982. *Life Forms and Meaning Structure*. London: Routledge & Kegan Paul.

Shevky, E., and W. Bell. 1955. *Social Area Analysis*. Stanford, CA: Stanford University Press.

Simmie, J. M. 1974. *Citizens in Conflict: The Sociology of Town Planning*. London: Hutchinson.

Smith, Christopher. 1988. *Public Problems*. New York: Guilford Press.

Sommer, Robert. 1969. *Personal Space: The Behavioral Basis of Design*. Englewood Cliffs, NJ: Prentice-Hall.

Spain, Daphne. 1992. *Gendered Spaces*. Chapel Hill: University of North Carolina Press.

Stefanovic, Ingrid. 1992. "The Experience of Place: Housing Quality from a Phenomenological Perspective." *Canadian Journal of Urban Research* 1(2): 145–161.

Stokols, Daniel. 1977. "Origins and Directions of Environment-Behavioral Research." Chapter 1 in *Perspectives on Environment and Behavior*, edited by Daniel Stokols. New York: Plenum Press.

———. 1981. "Group x Place Transactions: Some Neglected Issues in Psychological Research on Settings." Pp. 393–415 in *Toward a Psychology of Situations*, edited by D. Magnusson. Hillsdale, NJ: Lawrence Erlbaum Associates.

———. 1986. "Transformational Perspectives on Environment and Behavior: An Agenda for Future Research." Pp. 243–260 in *Cross Cultural Research in Environment and Behavior*, edited by William H. Ittelson, Masaaki Asai, and Mary Ker. Tucson: University of Arizona Press.

———. 1987. "Conceptual Strategies of Environmental Psychology." Pp. 41–70 in *Handbook of Environmental Psychology*, edited by Daniel Stokols and Irwin Altman. New York: Wiley Interscience.

———. 1995. "The Paradox of Environmental Psychology." *American Psychologist* 50(10):1–17.

Stokols, Daniel, and Irwin Altman. 1987. "Introduction." Pp. 1–4 in *Handbook of Environmental Psychology*, edited by Daniel Stokols and Irwin Altman. New York: Wiley Interscience.

Stokols, Daniel, and R. W. Novaco. 1981. "Transportation and Well-being: An Ecological Perspective." Pp. 85–130 in *Human Behavior and Environment—Advances in Theory and Research, Transportation Environments*, vol. 5, edited by J. Wohlwill, P. Everett, and I. Altman. New York: Plenum Press.

Suttles, Gerald. 1990. *The Man-Made City*. Chicago: University of Chicago Press.

Tabb, W., and L. Sawers. 1984. *Marxism and the Metropolis*, 2nd ed. New York: Oxford University Press.

Tönnies, F. 1887. *Gemeinschaft and Gesellschaft: Community and Society*, edited by C. P. Loomis, 1957. New York: Harper Torch.

Turner, J. H., and L. Beeghley. 1981. *The Emergence of Sociological Theory*. Homewood, IL: Dorsey Press.

Vale, Lawrence J. 1992. *Architecture, Power and National Identity*. New Haven, CT: Yale University Press.

van Vliet--, Willem. 1980. "An Extended Comment on the Environment as Social Symbol." *Journal of the American Planning Association* (July):337–340.

———. 1990. "Cross-National Housing Research: Analytical and Substantive Issues." Pp. 1–82 in *The International Handbook of Housing Policies and Practices*, edited by Willem van Vliet--. Westport, CT: Greenwood Press.

————. 1993. "A City Is Not an Elephant." Pp. 555–564 in *The Meaning and Use of Housing*, edited by E. Arias. Aldershot, UK: Avebury.

Walker, R. A. 1978. "The Transformation of Urban Structure in the Nineteenth Century and the Beginnings of Suburbanization." Pp. 165–212 in *Urbanization and Conflict in Market Societies*, edited by K. R. Cox. Chicago: Maaroufa Press.

Weber, M. 1921. *The City*, edited by D. Martindale and G. Neuwirth, 1958. New York: Free Press.

Weiher, Gregory. 1991. *The Fractured Metropolis: Political Fragmentation and Metropolitan Segregation*. Albany: State University of New York Press.

Weisman, Leslie. 1992. *Discrimination by Design: A Feminist Critique of the Man-Made Environment*. Urbana and Chicago: University of Illinois Press.

Whyte, W. H. 1978. *The Social Life of Small Urban Spaces*. Washington, DC: Conservation Foundation.

Wicker, A. W. 1972. "Processes Which Mediate Behavior—Environment Interactions." *Behavioral Science* 17:265–277.

————. 1985. *An Introduction to Ecological Psychology*. New York: Irvington.

Wilner, D. M., R. P. Walkley, T. Pinkerton, and M. Tayback. 1962. *The Housing Environment and Family Life*. Baltimore, MD: Johns Hopkins University Press.

Wilson, P. A. 1995. "Embracing Locality in Local Economic Development." *Urban Studies* 32(4–5): 645–658.

Wireman, Peggy. 1984. *Urban Neighborhoods, Networks, and Families*. Lexington, MA: Lexington Books.

Wohlwill, J., and Willem van Vliet-- (eds.). 1985. *Habitats for Children: The Impacts of Density*. Hillsdale, NJ: Lawrence Erlbaum Associates.

Zeisel, John. 1975. *Sociology and Architectural Design*. New York: Russell Sage Foundation.

————. 1981. *Inquiry by Design*. Monterey, CA: Brooks/Cole Publishing.

Zimring, Craig, Janet Carpman, and William Michelson. 1987. "Design for Special Populations." Pp. 919–949 in *Handbook of Environmental Psychology*, edited by Daniel Stokols and Irwin Altman. New York: Wiley Interscience.

Zukin, Sharon. 1991. *Landscapes of Power: From Detroit to Disney World*. Berkeley: University of California Press.

*Chapter 4*

# Socio-Behavioral Qualities
# of the Built Environment

*Sherry Ahrentzen*

> The Palace Flophouse was no sudden development. Indeed when Mack
> and Hazel and Eddie and Hughie and Jones moved into it . . . [it] was
> only a long bare room . . . They had not loved it then. But Mack knew
> that some kind of organization was necessary particularly among the
> group of ravening individualists . . . Mack, with a piece of chalk, drew
> five oblongs on the floor, each seven feet long and four feet wide, and
> in each square he wrote a name. These were simulated beds. Each man
> had property rights inviolable in his space. He could legally fight a man
> who encroached on his square. The rest of the room was property
> common to all.
>
> —John Steinbeck, *Cannery Row* (1945)

Novelists and filmmakers recognized the connection between the built environment and social behavior long before it came under the purview of
sociologists and other social scientists. For example, we see in Charlie
Chaplin's film *The Great Dictator*, the two dictators Hynkel and Napaloni,
sitting next to each other in barber chairs being shaved, raising their chairs
higher and higher, spatially competing for social position. Filmmakers, television directors, novelists, playwrights, and performance artists are particularly adept at manipulating space to visually convey social relationships
and messages.

Indeed, social behavior does not operate in a vacuum: It operates on a
stage, complete with props (Goffman, 1959). As experimental theater
demonstrates, the play can go on without props and scenery, without
music or even lighting; but certain messages and nuances about the social

relations of the actors or of the narrative theme may be interpreted differently with different stage settings. Hamlet's soliloquy can occur on a deserted beach on a moonless night, on a site of a nuclear power plant, or in the confines of a mental hospital. The words may remain the same, but the message of those words may be interpreted differently in each place. Performance and meaning are influenced by the environment in which they are embedded.

In the last two decades there has been considerable research on the physical environmental conditions of our social lives and experiences. Reviews have expanded from articles in the *Annual Review of Psychology* and *Annual Review of Sociology* (recent reviews include: Buttel, 1987; Holohan, 1986; Saegert and Winkel, 1990), to books, texts, collected monographs, and series (recent ones include: Altman and Wohlwill, 1976 ad seriatim; Gifford, 1987; Lang, 1987; McAndrew, 1993; Veitch, 1995; Zube and Moore, 1987 ad seriatim), to extensive handbooks such as this volume and the *Handbook of Environmental Psychology* (Stokols and Altman, 1987). Reflecting an array of epistemological positions and methodological approaches (see Chapter 3, this volume), this empirical and theoretical work has not yet formed into an integrated and comprehensive discipline, but rather represents a federation of a number of active research areas in which researchers share a set of attitudes, perspectives, and metascience concerns (Darley and Gilbert, 1985). Since a single chapter cannot present a comprehensive review of all arenas of this prolific research, I have chosen to restrict my discussion here to that research examining the linkages between the built environment (i.e., those physical structures designed, constructed, and altered by people) and three aspects of social behavior: security, meaning, and socio-spatial control. I have chosen to focus on these social qualities because they are issues of particular relevance to the field of sociology; other socio-behavioral qualities such as sensory stimulation, legibility, and physical comfort have stronger psychological, physiological, and cognitive bases. In addition, the material covered in this chapter (1) is limited to the composition of single sites and buildings, the boundaries of which approximate a social group or organization; and (2) focuses on the built environment as it influences the social performance of people and the social meaning of places. (Built environments at a larger scale are examined in Chapter 5 in this volume. Similarly, how people's actions and attitudes shape the built environment is addressed in Chapter 6 in this volume.)

Yet even within this restricted subset of the field, much remains. To help organize the discussion of this material, I have developed a classification model, introduced in the first section of this chapter. Later sections use this model to describe the research addressing the role of the built environment in eliciting qualities of security, meaning, and social control.

## A CLASSIFICATION MODEL

In 1981, Weisman proposed a classification model of environment-behavior systems consisting of three constituent parts: social organization, individuals, and the physical setting. The product of these components produced what he called "attributes" of the environment (e.g., crowding, accessibility). In this chapter I use a modified version of this model. The central focus of my version is on what Weisman calls attributes, but which I refer to as experiential "qualities," in deference to those often unnamed qualities of which transactionalists speak (e.g., the "more enduring qualities of interdependence that can arise between people and places," Stokols, 1986:244) and to Alexander, Ishikawa, and Silverstein's (1979) timeless "quality that has no name." One enters a great cathedral and is immediately aware of the *tranquillity* of the setting before noting such details as the architectural style, the lighting source, or who else is there. An American enters a subway station in Tokyo and is immediately struck by the *crowdedness*, not the individual components per se that contribute to that feeling. It is these characteristics—in these examples, tranquillity, crowdedness—that reflect the experiential qualities of the setting, the connotative meanings behind the concepts of fit/misfit, congruence/incongruence, compatibility, and the like. They are the social constructions of the intermingling of built forms and people; they are the product of the transaction between the setting's physical environment, activities, and the social context (Figure 4.1). For heuristic and organizational purposes, I distinguish the various components of this model in the following manner.

### Physical Environment

When mentally imaging the "built environment," we often conjure up images of functional building types, such as a single-family house, a school, or a hospital. Yet this broad characterization of the built environment may hamper our ability to see similarities across or differences within pre-established functional types (Franck, 1994). Further, such a broad sweep diminishes our understanding of the impact that environmental details and smaller-scaled places and amenities make in our daily lives. Instead of thinking of the built environment solely in terms of broadly based "building types," we will consider a finer-grained classification in order to identify the elements of buildings which affect and reflect social behavior. In considering the physical environment as those tangible, physical features which are combined to create buildings, I propose five *conceptual* categories of the built environment (these are derived from a larger classification scheme by Geddes and Gutman, 1977):

1. *Spatial Organization,* or the structural layout in terms of the dispersion, concentration, clustering, proximity, juxtaposition, and/or alignment of facilities or

Figure 4.1
Model Illustrating Production of Experiential Qualities of the Environment

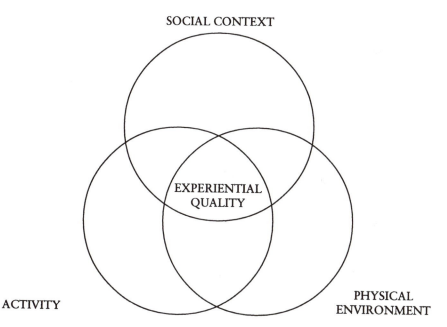

SOCIAL CONTEXT
Individual
Social
Organizational
Institutional

SOCIAL CONTEXT

EXPERIENTIAL
QUALITY

ACTIVITY

PHYSICAL
ENVIRONMENT

ACTIVITY
Type
Ritual or Routine
Temporal, Procedural
Symbolic Characteristics
Social Purpose

PHYSICAL
ENVIRONMENT
Spatial Organization
Communication Systems
Semi-Fixed Feature Amenities
Ambient Properties
Architectonic Details

spaces. It also includes massing, the type of enclosure, and circulation and movement systems, such as corridors, stairways, alleys, and aisles. Empirical measures would then include: square footage of floor area; distance between doorways; floor configuration; ceiling height and slope; changes in floor levels; and so on.

2. *Communication Systems* are those properties which give people information. They may include electric and electronic devices (e.g., telephone, computer) as well as other physical features which provide information, such as signs.

3. *Semi-Fixed Feature Amenities* are those nonstructural and moveable physical properties (not involving communication systems) of a setting, such as household appliances, furniture, play equipment, paintings, and plants.

4. *Ambient Properties* are those mechanical systems which serve to maintain or affect physiological and sensory functioning, such as illumination, heating, ventilation, and sound systems.

5. *Architectonic Details* include those fixed and stationary physical features which do not involve the organization of space but rather the embellishment of it: decorations, floor texture, and construction materials, for example.

### Activity

Although a building may be constructed primarily for one particular purpose, multiple activities occur in buildings and settings, and an activity type may cut across numerous settings. For example, nurses work in hospitals, baseball players work in stadiums, teachers work in schools, homemakers work in houses. Learning occurs in schools as well as in museums, galleries, residences, and on sidewalks. Thus, the activity context of this model needs to consider more than simply the manifest or instrumental function of the setting.

There have been various attempts to define and classify human activities. A classification system based on gross motor behaviors may be useful for ergonomic concerns, but is of limited help in understanding social behavior. On a larger scale, the Multinational Time Budget Study (Szalai et al., 1972) uses 97 activity categories clustered in nine groupings. There has been some international support for this typology, although it lacks activities not performed by individuals on a regular basis (e.g., to give birth, to celebrate, to commemorate, to wed).

However, we can also think of activities as reflecting either rituals or routines. *Routines* are patterns of actions done regularly, and are necessary for the maintenance of the setting or for the functioning of the individual. Taking out the trash, answering the phone, replacing a light bulb, all are typically routinized actions; but *rituals* are those patterns of action with much symbolism and emotion, whether done on a daily basis or not. Rituals are not necessarily spectacular, religious, or formal happenings: anthropologists maintain that secular, even "anti-ritual," cultures are full of ritual situations and events, very few of which take place in religious contexts (Douglas, 1966; Moore and Myerhoff, 1977).

*Daily rituals* involve the day-to-day essentials, such as eating, sleeping, and the like, but they are meaningful actions, often including symbols that express far more than do words. Because daily rituals happen frequently, it is likely that they will fall into set patterns over time without people becoming aware of how fixed they are. Making sure one's desk is clear of papers before starting to work in the morning; saying grace before a meal; or the television Walton family's "Good-night, John-boy" nightly farewell, are all daily rituals various people and families engage in.

There are also those rituals that occur regularly, on *special occasions*, or expectedly, as in *life-cycle rituals*. We often connect these to particular public or family celebrations and holidays (e.g., Bar Mitzvah, Macy's Thanksgiving Day parade); but they also occur in noncelebratory ways. In considering the art museum as a ritual, Duncan (1995) maintains that museum space is carefully delineated and culturally designated as reserved for a special quality of attention. One is expected to behave with a certain decorum, as this ritual site is a place programmed for the enactment of some kind of performance. In the art museum an individual may follow the ritual of talking quietly to her companions, or of following a prescribed route.

Hence, in considering the activity dimension of this model, we must go beyond identifying the activity proper to also recognizing routinized or ritualized intention embedded within the behaviors themselves. In particular, Rapoport (1977) calls our attention to temporal, procedural, and symbolic characteristics of activities.

Further, we must also recognize that activity follows a social purpose. One way to characterize this dimension of the activity context is to consider Franck's (1994) reformulation of building-use types. She advocates focusing on the social purposes and interests that use types promote. "Some of the purposes of use types may be quite obvious, particularly when only one use type is studied, i.e., a prison is for removing and controlling criminals. Other purposes are implicit, if not hidden, embedded in the images and ideology of the use types. These purposes are easier to identify if we examine an entire landscape of use types and uncover the common purposes that quite disparate types are designed to serve" (Franck, 1994:353). She discusses six such social purposes of various settings: (1) for removal and control; (2) for retreat or escape; (3) for protecting and honoring; (4) for producing and controlling capital; (5) for public service; and (6) for enabling and empowering. Any use type may serve more than one purpose, and exemplars of the same type may differ in the purposes they serve.

### Social Context

The social context component of the model includes four interdependent levels. The *individual* level includes the physiological, personality, cognitive, and motivational characteristics of individuals. The *social* level considers

102 *Handbook of Environmental Sociology*

the social characteristics of individuals and groups: ascribed and achieved status, social class, group identity or affiliation,[1] and lifestyle, for example. Race, ethnicity, and gender may likewise be considered social characteristics—not in the biological or physiological sense, but in how men and women, or members of a particular race or ethnic group, are socialized to act and communicate; and in how people of a particular sex or ethnicity are treated or perceived by others outside that group. For example, participants in a study by Jahoda, Markova, and Cattermole (1988), all of whom had a mild mental handicap, were aware of the social stigma attached to them by others; nonetheless, the majority of them conceived themselves as essentially the same as the general population. Another example, illustrated in this quote from Ralph Ellison's *Invisible Man* (1952:1), vividly demonstrates the social face and construction of race:

I am an invisible man. No, I am not a spook like those who haunted Edgar Allan Poe; nor am I one of your Hollywood-movie ectoplasms. I am a man of substance, of flesh and bone, fiber and liquids—and I might even be said to possess a mind. I am invisible, understand, simply because people refuse to see me. . . . When they approach me they see only my surroundings, themselves, or figments of their imagination—indeed, everything and anything except me.
Nor is my invisibility exactly a matter of a bio-chemical accident to my epidermis. That invisibility to which I refer occurs because of a peculiar disposition of the eyes of those with whom I come in contact. A matter of the construction of their *inner* eyes, those eyes with which they look through their physical eyes upon reality.

The *organizational* level of the model reflects the rules, procedures, and rituals of a collectivity. Harvard University, the Chicago School District, and the Disney Corporation, for example, are organizations, complete with policies for the enactment of daily life as well as special events. In much of the recent organizational literature, these organizations and other social groupings are often seen as cultures: the term "corporate culture," for example, has entered both the popular and business lexicon. One way to define culture is a group of people who have a set of values and beliefs which embody ideals and which are transmitted to members of that group, resulting in a characteristic way of looking at the world (i.e., a worldview). Culture can also include shared patterns of behavior and shared cultural meanings.

The final social level of the model, the *institutional* one, consists of ideologies, institutionalized norms, and regulations of institutions and societies. These often direct the operation and orientation of specific organizations and social groups. For example, there is a type of economy under which British Airways (an organization) operates; there is another type of economy under which China Airlines (again, an organization) operates.

We can see then that these four social levels—the individual, social, organizational, institutional—themselves are overlapping and relational. Many of the "individual" characteristics are likewise social constructs, even though we often may not consider them as such. For example, in a compelling argument, Higgins (1992) contends that disability is not a physiological or psychological attribute or limitation of the individual, but is rather socially constructed, in large part by the social and physical environment in which people who have disabilities function. In his book, Higgins demonstrates how disability is socially "manufactured," "experienced," and "serviced." While it may be difficult for many to completely accept his radical characterization of disability as entirely socially constructed, in large part Higgins' illustration and argument does reveal how social constructions as well as physical and mental conditions—and the important interaction between them—identify and characterize persons.

In addition, we must also acknowledge that none of the social factors are immutable for individuals. Cultural identity, gender, and other social constructs are "works in progress." They are fluid, and differ within and across cultures, times, environments, and other social and economic conditions. Further, there is a level of choice and agency in social affiliation that can occur several times across an individual's or a community's life course. In *Making Ethnic Choices*, ethnologist Karen Leonard (1992) describes the meaning of the lives of the rural Californians who changed inherited boundaries to actively create the Punjabi-Mexican community, formed out of immigrant communities of south Asians and Mexicans. Angela Davis (1992) appeals to the general public to acknowledge this tendency and desire for choice and agency when she asks that the "ropes" attached to the "anchors" locating individuals in primary communities be long enough to enable people "to move into other communities." Likewise, Alan Wolfe (1992:319) exhorts sociologists that they not "denigrate the capacity of people to change the definitions of the boundaries around them, for every boundary that is ascribed, others can be achieved."

Also, individuals are members of many different social groups or cultures; they have multiple identities, alliances, and affiliations. This fact challenged practices of the U.S. Census Bureau, since many people refused to identify themselves as belonging solely to one of the government's four racial categories. For 2000 the Bureau developed new categories and allowed people to identify themselves using multiple categories. Acknowledging the multiple affiliations, identities, and orientations of the individual poses many more questions than answers. As Hollinger (1995:106) claims:

[M]ost individuals live in many circles simultaneously and . . . the actual living of any individual life entails a shifting division of labor between the several "we's" of which the individual is a part. How much weight at what particular moments is assigned to the fact that one is Pennsylvania Dutch or Navajo relative to the weight assigned to the fact that one is also an American, a lawyer, a woman, a Republican, a Baptist, and a resident of Minneapolis?

M. Wolfe (1992) reminds us that the term *culture* is often used as a singular and static concept in the environment-behavior literature when describing the social milieu of a particular setting; such usage often obliterates and oppresses the other prevailing ways of living occurring there. Diversity within social groups and cultures exists as well: For example, the differences among Hispanic subgroups in the United States have been well documented (see Riche, 1991). But diversity is more than simply a mosaic of different people composing a setting. Williams' (1982) concept of residual, dominant, and emergent cultures helps us see diversity in relational, dynamic terms.[2] It is important to recognize that multiple and often conflicting cultural or social conditions permeate the production and reproduction of our built settings.

### Qualities

The combination of the three components of this model—activity, social context, and physical environment—produces the experiential qualities of the setting. Such intangible, perceived qualities include: meaning (e.g., self-identity); security; sensory stimulation (e.g., noisy); territorial control; crowding and spaciousness; privacy; power; imageability; legibility; physical comfort; psychological comfort; among others.

The three components of this model mingle like paint colors to produce a new hue. The combination of red and blue produces a qualitatively different color effect than simply placing red and blue side by side. Different amounts of each hue produce different variations of purple. Different saturations and intensities also contribute to the final effect. Researchers are concerned not only with identifying the correct types of "hues" to produce a desired quality, but also the process whereby such hues mingle to create that effect. A brief example below, on baseball stadiums, by sports journalist Bill James (Lenehan, 1983:60) illustrates how a change in one component of the model results in a changed experiential quality.

As the mountains make Wyoming folk rugged and the cities make city folk guarded or defensive, this environment, too, shapes the character of its inhabitants. It has always been my feeling that the cliquishness of the Boston Red Sox, their surliness and impatience with the press . . . was the Curse of Fenway, that it owed its origins to a long-dead architect. An absurd theory? So it sounds, but hear me out. Fenway makes ballplayers look like better hitters than they are. That inflates egos. Inflated egos cause resentment, in particular among those not favored by the park; the team divides into clusters of the favored and ill-favored.

The Astrodome is a negative image of Fenway, an exact opposite park in almost every way one can imagine. Beautiful, ugly. Quaint, modern. Vibrant, sterile. Cozy, spacious. Hitter's heaven, hitter's nightmare. And for what were the Astro players of the fine teams of 1978 to 1981 known? Their openness with the press, their closeness and almost family-like atmosphere. Odd, isn't it? As the park knocks twenty points off every player's average, it humbles hitters and it controls egos.

But even more than that, it is my feeling that the mere fact that in Fenway a hitter can create runs *by his own actions* tends to cause Fenway teams to pull apart over time. A key fact about the Astrodome is that it takes three players to make a run. In order to do your job in this park, you have got to see yourself as part of a plan, a cog in a machine.

Here the ritualized activity is a form of labor, playing baseball, and the physical and social accoutrements associated with it. In American culture, professional baseball is a system—some would say an industry—with institutionalized rules for the conduct of this activity (institutional level of social context). The social status of professional ballplayers (social level) as well as individual egos, physique, stamina, and expertise (individual level) are also aptly evident. The differences in social cohesion (experiential quality) that James notes is also due to the size of the stadium, in particular the dimensions of the field (physical environment). This physical size, in conjunction with the social context and activity, contributes to the level of camaraderie among ballplayers.

This is not to suggest that you simply add the various ingredients of this model, stir, and *viola!*, a particular quality—like a sense of community, safety, or tranquillity—appears. The manner in which the components manifest and interrelate (negate, synthesize, oppress, synergize, etc.) has an eventual effect on the manifestations of the experiential quality. *Theories* are developed to describe and explain the process by which these interrelations and manifestations occur.

While the model itself does not reflect the intricacies and diversity of dynamism inherent within, it is presented here simply as a schema for thinking about and conceptualizing socio-behavioral experiences, or qualities, as reflected in and affected by the built environment. I use this heuristic model in the following sections to review research of the social, behavioral, and physical environmental conditions, and the dynamic processes among them, in producing qualities of security, meaning, and social control (as manifested in privacy and power).

## SECURITY

Jane Jacobs (1961) was one of the first urban observers to consider the connection between the built environment and security.[3] Based on personal observations and anecdotes, she proposed three design principles which would help make residential streets "safer": (1) "eyes on the street," or a building's windows and doors oriented toward the street so that residents inside their homes have a natural opportunity to survey outdoor activity; (2) demarcation of public and private spaces; and (3) location of public outdoor spaces in close proximity to, or having visual access from, areas which are heavily used. She felt that such places close to buildings and walkways would feel "safe" and as a result would be used.

However, it was Oscar Newman's work, in 1972, which thrust into prominence the connection between security and the physical environment. His model of defensible space suggests that certain physical environmental characteristics can promote residents' feelings of territoriality and control over a space, feelings which in turn deter crimes of opportunity such as vandalism and certain forms of theft. His thesis was partly based on archival analysis of crime statistics and residential characteristics of various housing projects in New York City, although the weight of his argument lay with a comparison of two adjacent housing developments of similar densities but different designs.

Newman uses the term *defensible space* to refer to a range of mechanisms which bring the environment under the control of its residents. He identified four features which characterize defensible space: (1) territorial definition of space reflecting residents' areas of control and influence; (2) positioning of residential windows to allow residents to naturally survey the public areas of their environment; (3) building forms and idioms which avoid the stigma of peculiarity and the suggestion of vulnerability and isolation of residents; and (4) location of housing developments in areas adjacent to activities which do not provide continued threat.

After Newman's book was published, a number of researchers and scholars challenged his methodology and theoretical claims. Some criticized the assumed instinctual nature of territoriality; the environmental deterministic nature of the model; and the lack of social factors as mediating variables (Merry, 1981; Taylor, 1987). Replicated studies of other housing developments did not support Newman's defensible space contentions (Mawby, 1977). Others criticized Newman for providing no justification for the selection of the two case studies (Kaplan, 1973). A serious deficit in Newman's model is a fine-grain interpretation of the complexities of the social context. Brantingham and Brantingham (1993) demonstrate that strategies for reducing crime vary with the type of crime, offender, situation, and site. Those who live in a community with little social integration may not try to defend any territory, for example; and, arguably, the most serious conceptual limitation of Newman's thesis is that he does not provide any empirical evidence that the environmental characteristics he proposes actually produce the personal predispositions of territoriality and control, the intervening variables which subsequently act to deter crime and enhance security.

Nonetheless, Newman's work spurred interest in this area among academics as well as lawmakers and law enforcers, whose research and policy making continue to proliferate even today. For example, in 1995 the Secretary of the U.S. Department of Housing and Urban Development published a pamphlet advocating defensible space features as a method to deter crime and build community (Cisneros, 1995). Schools, shopping centers, transit stations, residential complexes and subdivisions, have been designed or redesigned according to defensible space principles. Police crime prevention planners are regularly given training in defensible space issues, and pass these ideas on to the community (Brantingham and Brantingham, 1988).

Researchers have begun to cast a wider methodological net, interviewing residents as well as convicted burglars, and undertaking behavioral and participant observation. Although Newman's work focused on urban residential settings, other researchers have examined suburban residential neighborhoods, banks and commercial buildings, parking lots, and schools. Most importantly, theoretical concepts were developed which included additional physical environmental variables and portrayed the social context as a much more vital player. The following reviews some of the salient findings of this recent research, highlighting aspects of the physical environment, the social context, and the activity context, and concluding with different theoretical proposals for explaining the enhancement of security by environmental design.

### Physical Environment

Most of the physical elements examined in the research involve spatial organization and communications systems. Perhaps the most consistently verified physical feature is that which encompasses Jacobs' (1961) notion of "eyes on the street": opportunities for visual surveillance. But surveillance is a complex activity with many actors. First, there are the victims and bystanders surveying the crime site or perpetrator; second, the victims and bystanders viewing appropriate intervention agents, such as a telephone or security guard: and third, the perpetrators surveying the crime site and surroundings both before and during the crime. Identifying appropriate surveillance features that enhance security necessitates understanding the surveillance processes from all three of these perspectives.

*Surveillance features allowing visibility onto the perpetrator or the site* of the crime have been studied most often. In interviewing incarcerated burglars, Macdonald and Gifford (1989) found they were deterred by those physical conditions that promoted surveillance onto the site, particularly the visibility of the intended robbery site from neighbors and people using the street. Simply providing windows is not sufficient. Window orientation may produce glare, making it virtually impossible for anyone outside to look into the building and see what is happening (Tiffany and Ketchel, 1979). Further, the balance between privacy and surveillance may be tenuous: Windows too close to other buildings or public areas from which outsiders can look in are often curtained or draped (Merry, 1981), hence deterring opportunities for surveillance.

The nature of the space is also important in allowing surveillance: Crowded settings and long, rectangular shapes minimize opportunities for staff to notice suspicious-looking patrons (Tiffany and Ketchel, 1979; Wise and Wise, 1985). Obstructions such as columns, bushes and trees, and stairwells may also prevent surveillance (Brown, 1984; Pablant and Baxter, 1975; Renegert and Wasilchick, 1985). Nasar and Fisher (1993) examined "hot spots" of fear—areas and situations having a concentration of fear— on a college campus, and found that fear increased in proximity to those buildings with features that allowed for concealment of a potential offender, and blocked prospect and escape for the victims (they also noted differences in these perceptions between men and women, and during the time of day). In the residential complex she studied, Merry (1981) noted that almost half of the robberies occurred in areas which reflected Newman's territorial definition of semi-private space; but, in such cases visibility onto these spaces was obstructed by physical elements such as landscaping or stairways.

Another aspect of surveillance involves *victims or bystanders being able to see appropriate interventions*: Once noticing a crime, one needs access to reporting it if so inclined. Banks more frequently robbed have high teller counters and wickets, resulting in a low degree of visibility between teller positions (Tiffany and Ketchel, 1979) or longer distances between teller positions (Wise and Wise, 1985). In both these spatial configurations, tellers needing to communicate crises have had difficulty doing so to other employees. Other appropriate interventions in public settings are emergency call boxes. Although these are increasingly found on American university campuses, I have informally observed that their design and location do not reflect concerns for heightened visibility or knowledge about environmental cognition (surveys I have conducted with my students bear this out). This aspect of surveillance is scarcely studied or acknowledged, and certainly deserves more attention.

A final aspect of surveillance is *from the perspective of the perpetrator "scoping out" a site and maintaining control* over it during the crime. Multiple entrances are difficult to watch and control while committing the robbery (Archea, 1984; Tiffany and Ketchel, 1979; Wise and Wise, 1985). Physical traces suggest people nearby may inhibit potential perpetrators. Brown (1984) found that compared to nonburglarized ones, burglarized homes had few physical traces, such as sprinklers or hoses running in the front yard, music emanating from inside the house, bicycles left on the front porch: traces that indicate that people may be in or around the house. Although Brown's observations of these traces occurred after the homes were burglarized, interviews with convicted burglars (Renegert and Was-ilchick, 1985) lend support to her hypothesis.

Besides environmental features which maximize visual surveillance for bystanders and minimize it for perpetrators, *physical features which deter physical accessibility* also act as crime deterrents (Newman and Franck, 1982). The most typical deterrents proposed by law enforcement agencies are target-hardening devices such as locks and other materials which deter physical movement and entry. But other physical elements may deter entry: fences or barriers which make the need for planning of entry and egress by a burglar greater than the rewards justify. Wallis and Ford (1980) mention several "movement-control tactics" which reduce the ease with which strangers move through a setting.

A final physical feature for consideration is one not associated with sur-veillance or accessibility, but with territorial markings, that of *personali-zation*. Among elderly residents, Patterson (1978) found a correlation between personalization of residences and fear of property loss, especially among men. Brown (1984) found that less burglarized homes had name plates on the residences, although there were no differences among other personalization features, such as flowers, lawn furniture, architectural uniqueness, or surface qualities of the home. In studies with line drawings (Brower et al., 1983), respondents felt that fences and, to a lesser extent, flowers would deter intrusions.

However, without additional empirical inquiry it is difficult to generalize these findings to actual criminal circumstances. Such features may have less to do with notions of territorial control than they do with affluence: People with residential name plates, flowerboxes, or lawn furniture are displaying more wealth than those without such displays; and affluent homes may be perceived as being more secure because crime rates are lower in more af-fluent areas; such homes may be in areas with stronger police protection and surveillance; burglars may stand out in such environments; or there may be increased efforts among residents to deter crime (e.g., installing burglar alarms).

Two studies suggest we need to further examine the connection between signs of affluence, personalization, and security. Shaffer and Anderson (1983) found that higher perceived safety was reported for those slide scenes depicting higher property values. In a multiple regression model, perceived safety was related first and foremost to maintenance and design factors reflecting affluence; second to building visibility; and finally to lot size and enclosure. In a study of the role of defensible space in a burglar's choice of single-family homes (Macdonald and Gifford, 1989), juvenile and adult offenders reported they would not be deterred from burglarizing homes showing territorial markers, measured by traces of occupancy, bar-riers, or personalization. In fact, in this study homes with signs of person-alization actually attracted the offenders, who associated them with greater house value. This and other studies suggest that surveillability—the possibility of surveillance by someone whom the offender believes might interfere—has a stronger effect on criminal decision making than do territorial markers (see Brantingham and Brantingham, 1993).

Notably, these latter two studies (by MacDonald and Gifford and Shaffer and Anderson) are some of the few studies examining the relative contribution of various physical factors to perceptions of security. Most of the research in this field examines physical variables in isolation and not in combination with each other, thus ignoring possible interactive or negating effects. Brantingham and Brantingham (1993) argue that perceptions of security as well as perpetration are based on complex interactions among individual cues, cue combinations, and cue sequences, rather than simply on individual cues. In support, Shaw and Gifford (1994) found that residents' perceptions of burglary risk had little to do with individual cues (and also were dependent upon the personal and social attributes of the perceiver). For example, a fence may decrease burglary risk if it does not affect visibility from the road; alternatively, it may increase such risk if it decreases visibility from the road.

### Social Context

Numerous surveys show that those who are most fearful of crime are not necessarily those people who are most likely to be victimized. *Those who are physically vulnerable or who are less able to resist attack are among those most fearful.* The elderly, for instance, express a greater fear of crime, yet they are among the least victimized. Numerous studies also show gender differences in perceptions of security, with women expressing more fear (e.g., Gordon et al., 1981). Compared to men, however, women are less likely to be victims of crime.

That women and men react differently to not only the fear of crime but also in their perceptions of a setting's safety is illustrated in a quasi-experimental study of two transit stations (Richards et al., 1978). At one station, extensive security surveillance equipment was installed. Surveys conducted both before and after installation revealed a reduction in women's expressed level of fear and an unexpected increase in men's after the installation. The researchers concluded that initially women are more fearful in such settings, but that added surveillance devices reduce the amount of fear. Women may feel they would be detected if a crime was committed, or that the surveillance devices might deter potential muggers from committing a crime. On the other hand, men did not initially perceive the station as unsafe. However, the addition of surveillance cameras may have indicated to them that dangerous events were occurring there, enough to warrant the installation of surveillance cameras. While being a good illustration of gender differences in perceived safety, this study also demonstrates that the type of research needed is that which examines the interactive effects between the social context and physical environment in enhancing security.

Recent studies focusing on women's perception of crime and assault have included a societal dimension to the equation as well (see Day, 1994 for a review). Urban institutions (particularly their attitudes toward sexual assault and its victims), government, laws, and popular myths regarding sexual assault all may play a role in projecting a picture (accurate or not) of where criminal behavior is likely to occur, and under what conditions. Such projections may reflect different mechanisms of social control. Fox (1977) identifies three types of *social control of women*: confinement, protection, and normative restriction—which is most inclusive over the life span and over the situations to which it is applicable. Day (1994) found all three forms of social control operative on the two college campuses she studied. Women were encouraged to stay indoors and to refrain from certain activities and from going to certain places because of the danger of sexual assault in those situations (confinement). When women would venture outdoors, especially at night, they were encouraged to go with someone else—for example, an escort service, a male friend (protection). Finally, women were encouraged to present themselves in such a way as to be perceived undeserving of sexual assault (normative restriction).

Further, Day found that the mechanisms by which women learn to associate fear with strangers in public space included childhood socialization, personal experiences and experiences of others, and media representations. In fact, a number of researchers have concluded that the news coverage of rape and crime influences women's fear of sexual assault; but while women feel at risk in certain places and at certain times, the geography of fear is not the same geography of violence. The latter—based on crime statistics and demographics—would suggest that women should be more fearful at home and of men they know (Hanmer and Saunders, 1983). Yet research reveals that women perceive themselves to be in greater danger from strange men and in public space (Valentine, 1992). Valentine's research also shows that the media create images about the spatial and temporal context of the violence they report. Women's perceptions of space appear to be partially constructed from the media's narrow and bias selection of assaults reported and their depiction of where violent assaults are committed.

Another aspect of the social environment pertinent to the enhancement of security is the *ability of residents to distinguish intruders from neighbors*. This lies at the heart of Newman's proposal for having a small number of households share hallways or public entries. With a small number, a resident is more likely to recognize who is an outsider and who is a resident. However, Merry's (1981) study of different ethnic groups residing in Dover Square, a public housing development, suggests expanding this notion beyond pure numbers to include the degree of shared cultural and physiological characteristics. She found that residents often failed to evict intruders or intervene in crimes, even when defensible space features allowed sufficient surveillance opportunities and territorial definition. She attributes this lack of intervention to two factors. First, the social fragmentation of the project made it difficult for residents to distinguish intruders from their neighbors' visitors. If their neighbor belonged to another ethnicity and was a stranger, residents did not know whether an outsider they saw was a dinner guest or a potential thief. She gives the example of one Chinese family who assumed that the man they saw going upstairs intended to visit the black family who lived in an upper apartment. Later they discovered that he had burglarized the other apartment. Although the design of the stairwell demarcated the space as semi-private, social heterogeneity thwarted effective intervention.

Another factor involves the choice of a viable strategy for intervention. Many residents observed incidents yet failed to act because they felt there was little they could do. Their inability to speak English left Chinese residents unable to call the police, or left them fearful that their phone call would implicate them in prolonged court proceedings resulting in days of lost wages. Merry concludes that while design can provide preconditions for effective control, it cannot create such control if the social fabric of the community is fragmented and ethnically divided, and territorial dominance is ambiguous. Willingness to defend public spaces around the home depends not only on physical features but also on cultural definitions of territorial dominance, the ability to identify intruders, and the availability of effective modes of intervention.

Such concerns are likely applicable to other social and physiological dimensions of residents, such as age. The fact that elderly tenants in age-segregated housing are more likely to intervene and survey public areas may reflect the greater ease within a homogeneous environment in which to interpret situations and users. As long as one's appearance is not out of keeping with the norms of the location, and diversity within that location is minimal, little attention will be called to a person. When a teenager, for example, steps into a housing environment for the elderly, that person immediately becomes tagged as an outsider. The interpretation is not so easy in family-occupied complexes.

When the settings are populated with a pluralistic group of strangers, *spatial order* may replace *appearential order* as the basis for assessing the security of a place (Lofland, 1973). Today many different types of people use the same services, facilities, and spaces, but the appearential distinction between valid users and unwarranted strangers is weak. Scarlet letters are not worn today, and both the rich and the poor wear stonewashed jeans. In such a pluralistic society, the meaning we assign to behavior is often more a function of the person's location in space than his/her appearance. The work of Zimbardo (1969) supports this idea: A person standing over a car with an opened hood in a residential driveway is a homeowner fixing his car, while the same person standing over the same car in a deserted parking structure is likely a thief.

In addition, the type of people in an area, whether homogeneous or not, influences the sense of security of the space. "Dangerous-looking" (as defined within the culture or social context) individuals hanging around spaces which are legible, territorial, and easily surveyed will make such places seem dangerous even if they are essentially crime-free. Social cognition influences one's sense of security in spite of the environmental situation. Day (1994) found that college women feared the unlike or incivil "other" because of what the person's appearance or behavior symbolized: This became manifested as a fear of sexual assault (and other violations). People desire to see others in public places supporting public, community, or subcultural norms (reported in Taylor, 1987). Social and physical signs of incivility may reflect social disorder. Such cues inspire fear, and this fear of social disorder may translate into a greater fear of crime.

### Activity Context

A theoretical model of the criminal and intervention activity process as a basis for this research has not yet been developed. Instead, assumptions of criminals' and victims' cognitions and decision-making behaviors are often made without sufficient empirical testing. Crime must be conceptualized not as an isolated event but as a dynamic, moving process (Merry, 1981; Renegert and Wasilchick, 1985). The decision-making process of the perpetrator, the surveillance process by all actors involved, and the process of intervention are, for example, three activity dimensions which need to be examined in conjunction with how they interact with the physical and social environments in enhancing security.

Brantingham and Brantingham (1993), throughout their extensive research in this area, acknowledge and treat crime as an event, as a behavior—but one that varies and is complex. Some crimes, for example, are highly opportunistic and highly dependent upon daily activities and the physical availability of suitable targets and crime situations, frequently including lack of surveillance or a feeling of anonymity. As they note, many juveniles walking to and from school steal goods from residences. If their normal travel path does not pass by empty houses or apartments, they are unlikely to steal. Conversely, juveniles spend hours in malls, where there are endless opportunities for theft. The desire for thrill among many teenagers is also great; and hence shoplifting is not an unexpected behavior. Those who commit crimes have their own behavior settings, influenced by social surroundings, but also by characteristics such as safe access.

The Brantinghams contend that the decision to commit an offense involves an appraisal of the situation and site, or a search for a target. In all cases, a crime template is used. Identifying the characteristics of the template has been at the center of much of their research to date, although its delineation is still embryonic. They have detailed template construction and use for understanding the decision to choose a place/situation for burglary (focusing on the role of nodes, paths, edges, and an environmental "backcloth"), but have little developed the strategy for shoplifting and robbery.

## Theoretical Frameworks

A comprehensive explanation of the relationship between environmental design and criminal behavior has not emerged since Newman's work. This may be explained partly by the lack of a detailed analysis of the victimization, surveillance, and intervention activities on which subsequent theoretical and empirical work can be built; and, unfortunately, there is very little work looking at additive, negating, or interactive effects between multiple environmental features, or physical and social factors.

There is continuing usage of *territoriality* (Brown, 1984; Taylor, 1987) to explain how burglars choose appropriate places to burglarize and how residents' control over such settings leads to crime deterrence. Unfortunately, the decision-making and control assumptions underlying these notions of territoriality have not been empirically tested.

Another theoretical orientation involves *environmental cognition*. Merry (1981) suggests that legible and clearly articulated residential layouts contribute to the development of clear cognitive maps which help residents avoid exposure to risk. She mentions the illegible site plan of the housing project she studied: Residents complained that the site plan was ambiguous and that "all the buildings look alike." They had difficulties finding their way around, which often resulted in a heightened sense of fear. Environmental cognition processes may also explain the intervention process—how people locate suitable intervention mechanisms. Latane and Darley (cited in Gold, 1980) suggest that people who are more familiar with the environment are also more aware of the way it works; consequently, they may have a greater sense of control in those situations and feel more responsibility for keeping those settings safe.

Brantingham and Brantingham (1993), as previously mentioned, also demonstrate that cognitive maps and knowledge of spatial relations influence crime location/selection. Cognitive representations of high activity nodes and the paths between them partially shape the location of crime, they contend.

The environmental cognition orientation is thus contingent upon point of view—the offender's or the victim's. Shaw and Gifford (1994) suggest that defensible space theory may be more closely linked to, or representative of, residents' rather than burglars' perceptions of burglary risk. The defensible space cues they examined in their research explain more of the variation in residents' than in burglars' vulnerability ratings. They suggest this orientation may be because Oscar Newman—the originator of the theory—is a resident, not a burglar; and that his own perception of the relations between the physical environment and burglary risk—being more similar to residents' than burglars' perceptions of burglary risk—may have resulted in a resident-centered defensible space concept.

Another model which focuses on the environmental aspects of the surveillance process is Archea's (1984) model of *visual access and visual exposure*. Here the surveillance process is examined from the standpoint of various actors (detailed explanation of this model is provided in the later section, "Socio-Spatial Control: Privacy and Power"):

According to this model, people's awareness of emerging social opportunities will vary as a function of their ability to see the spaces which surround them. This is defined as visual access. Similarly, an individual's accountability for his or her responses to these emerging opportunities will theoretically vary as a function of the likelihood of being seen from those same spaces. This is defined as visual exposure. (Archea, 1984:iii)

In conclusion, while there are many empirical studies identifying single environmental elements involved in security enhancement, it has only been in the last few years that researchers have begun to examine the complex interrelations and interactions among these factors. Such sociologists and other social scientists have begun to enrich our understanding of the various aspects of the social context which influence and reflect security of the built environment. In the past decade alone, a number of researchers have been attempting to develop a comprehensive model of environmental security/criminology through the processes of victimization, surveillance, informal social control, environmental cognition, and intervention—as viewed from and experienced by criminal offenders, their victims, and the general public (see Brantingham and Brantingham, 1993; Perkins et al., 1993; Shaw and Gifford, 1994). Future theoretical modeling needs to further incorporate and delineate not only the roles of these interconnected situations but also the interactive effects of the physical and social environments surrounding and producing them.

## MEANING

Physical environments "tell" us something about the places we are in, about the people who live or work there, about the social structure and the society to which those places belong. Messages we "read" might involve personal identity, social relationships, affect, instrumental use, or higher-level meanings. Studies involving the personal or social identity of occupants are particularly salient in the research on the meaning of home (e.g.,

Becker, 1977; Csikszentmihalyi and Rochberg-Halton, 1981; Duncan, 1982; Nasar, 1989; Rapoport, 1982a; Sadalla et al., 1987) as well as studies in office settings (see Sundstrom with Sundstrom, 1986). But the environmental symbolism of role, status, power, and hierarchy has been studied in various settings. For example, Goodsell (1988) demonstrates how architectural features of American city council chambers changed as the structure of city politics evolved from 1800 to the present. As the political distance between citizens and city governors was minimized, design of the chambers began to express this more intimate political relationship.

In this section I review only a part of the research on environmental meaning, that focusing on those physical cues, social contextual factors, and activities which reflect personal identity and social relations. At the end of this section I present some theoretical perspectives on how people "read" the environment and derive social meaning from it.

### Physical Environment

In considering a framework of environmental features which act as cues for meaning from the environment, Rapoport (1982b) uses Hall's (1966) concepts of fixed, semi-fixed, and nonfixed feature space. *Fixed feature spaces* are those physical features which are fixed and rarely changed, such as walls, square footage, and roofs. In many industrialized societies such features are under the control of codes and regulations. Because of the physical, economic, and political difficulty an individual faces in changing these, fixed feature cues are more likely to reflect social, organizational, cultural, and institutional meanings rather than those of the individual. *Semi-fixed feature spaces* are those features which can and do change quickly (e.g., furniture, wall color, posters, plants, light bulbs). Being changeable, inexpensive, and easily moveable, they are more likely to represent individual or social position. *Nonfixed features* are nonarchitectural elements such as clothes, kinesthesia, eye contact, and proxemics.

There has been considerable research on the former (i.e., fixed and semi-fixed) types of space in this field. Empirical studies of various fixed feature spaces demonstrate that interior spatial configuration is a physical cue embedded with significant social meaning. The amount of space allocated to employees, for example, may depend more upon status than work activities (Duffy, 1969; Sundstrom with Sundstrom, 1986).

Degree of enclosure is another fixed feature space which indicates status in Western societies: The more permanent the enclosure, the higher the status. A well-defined space differentiates a place and person from the background and establishes an identity different from it (Appleyard, 1979). However, in a provocative argument about how electronic media are changing our sense and meaning of place, Meyrowitz (1985) contends that the link between territorial space and status is changing. A well-defined territory is related to status and authority partially because it allows one to control information within one's territory and prevent others from seeing private, backstage behaviors. Today's forms of electronic media, however, circumvent territorial barriers. Having a well-defined space that is monitored by a television camera or having a space without a telephone is hardly an indicator of high status.

One's location in a building also acts as a sign. Signs of power are conveyed by visibility and imageability (Appleyard, 1979). Visibility depends upon access and location. An enduring image may be created by novelty and uniqueness. One's proximity to a power base or to limited amenities (e.g., corners, windows) are other signs of high status.

The facade and massing of particular building types are also significant cues in identifying the social characteristics of a place. Business owners, such as restaurateurs, are quite cognizant of this. Cherulnik (1991) demonstrates how easily college students can assess a variety of social conditions (price range, customer traits, for example) from the facades of different eating establishments; and Abrams (1986) documents the shift in design of the facades of McDonald's restaurants as the image of its customers changed over time.

Semi-fixed feature elements also are powerful cues of social position. In a national survey of office workers, Louis Harris and Associates (1978) found that the most prevalent status markers were style and material of desks, tables, and chairs; degree of physical enclosure; amount of personal space; paintings and posters; and materials used for the desk (see also BOSTI, 1984).

Illumination has been overlooked in the research literature for its symbolic qualities, although historically architects have paid attention to the symbolic quality of light. Lang (1987) reports a student survey in Philadelphia which found a correlation between restaurant quality and illumination type. The less expensive restaurants had high levels of light, typically fluorescent. The more exclusive restaurants had lower lighting levels, incandescent light fixtures on walls or tables, and rarely had overhead ceiling lighting.

## Social Context

According to those theoretical positions emphasizing a symbolic interactionist perspective or a cultural one (discussed later), a symbol in one culture or for one group may not be similarly shared by another group. As well, a symbol at one point in time may not be similarly recognized at a later date. Within a relatively homogeneous culture, there may be shared agreement on symbolism. Yet, in a society or group with different social groupings and affiliations, controversy ensues over different meanings, as witnessed in the fervor of the Vietnam Veterans' Memorial in Washington,

DC. The debate over the low-lying black "wall" reflected the serious divisions of feelings and opinions in the American population about the war itself, and how to publicly acknowledge it in a memorial (Capasso, 1985; Mayo, 1988).

Some researchers suggest that environmental meaning may be a more important quality for some individuals than for others. The poor may be more concerned about instrumental use and safety than the social meanings of the spaces they inhabit (Rainwater, 1966). In studies in the United States and India, Duncan and Duncan (1976) conclude that, compared to the nouveau riche, true elites have little need for display of social status in their homes because their identities are firmly established socially and interpersonally. Those more transient—the upwardly mobile, for example—depend more on environmental displays.

Another social difference is between lay individuals and architects. Groat (1982) investigated such differences using a multiple sorting task and found that the major concern among nonarchitects is that the building design be appropriate to the building type and use, and that it be related to one historical style. Architects, on the other hand, prefer more complex associations.

### Activity

Very few studies have examined the interactive effects of activity and environmental cues on meaning. As noted in the Groat study above, nonarchitects prefer a building's architecture to relate to the use and activities of the functional building type. However, in today's era of building rehabilitation, we see churches converted to bookstores and restaurants, monasteries to family housing, and gas stations become food stores and boutiques. Although no one has yet examined the meanings associated with such converted settings, Rapoport (1982b) suggests that physical environmental cues are less important when cues from other sources—clothing, activity—work well. Yet, this assumption needs further empirical substantiation. Ahrentzen (1989), for example, found families' and friends' perceptions of a home-based worker's status changed when the job was switched from an office setting to a domestic one—even though the nature of the activity or work, as well as the social and economic conditions surrounding it, remained the same. Here, the architectural cues of the domestic setting are not the traditional ones established for an occupational role and status. In some cases, such discrepancies led to conflicting interpretations of the homeworker's social status and work in the home: As one home-based sales operator claimed, "Working at home has made me a housewife."

### Theoretical Frameworks

Environmental meaning has been extensively analyzed by theoreticians attempting to develop comprehensive conceptual frameworks. This section presents a few prominent theories, offering a range of different perspectives in this arena.

Minimizing, although not negating, the role of the social world, Cooper Marcus (1974) uses the psychological theories of Carl Jung to suggest that the most basic of archetypes—the collective unconscious linking human beings to the primitive past—is the self. People use material objects as symbols of the manifestation of this self. For example, she suggests that the high-rise apartment building as a family home violates the archaic image of a house (and consequently the self) as a separate and unique personality. She stresses the unconscious and psychological nature of associating physical place, particularly the home, with expression of one's self-identity.

Another perspective—a behaviorist approach to meaning (see Lang, 1987)—maintains that particular physical elements historically associated with certain pleasurable experiences are subsequently constructed in order to perpetuate these positive associations. So, something that was once constructed purely for functional reasons is later retained primarily for the symbolic pleasure it conveys from past associations. However, empirical support for this perspective is minimal.

These two theoretical orientations either neglect or minimize the role of the social structure in producing and conveying meaning. The models discussed next not only acknowledge the internal feelings and behaviors of individuals in eliciting meaning from the physical environment, but they also incorporate the role of social structure and culture in this process. Many of these models derive their basic assumptions and foundations from the work of sociologists: Cooley, Durkheim, and Blumer, for example.

Rochberg-Halton (1984) contrasts the psychoanalytic view of object relations with that of symbolic interactionism of the early Chicago School. His "pragmatic" view of meaning dismisses Freudian and cognitive approaches which conceive the mind only as individual and internal to the person. Rather, he builds upon the work of Cooley (1964), maintaining that the essence of self lies in a communicative relationship with objects, a relationship which includes the real object as well as its representation in the mind. Objects and the built environment have an inherent character or quality that have an influence on people. We cultivate ourselves through transactions with our physical surroundings.

Rapoport (1982b:57) presents one of the most extensive models of environmental meaning, incorporating a nonverbal communication approach as well as a symbolic interactionist perspective (Blumer, 1969). As he states:

in many cases the environment acts on behavior by providing cues whereby people judge or interpret the social context or situation and act accordingly. In other words, it is the social situation that influences people's behavior, but it is the physical environment that provides the cues.

Physical environments are analogous to nonverbal behavior which communicates indirectly and also reinforces verbal communication. Cultural meanings are encoded in the physical environment, which people respond to if they know the cultural context. People in turn act toward these objects and events on the basis of the social meanings which these have for them.

Environmental meaning thus is derived from the interaction between human beings and the physical environment. The latter tells people how to act; social organizations and culture supply a set of cues which are used to interpret situations and help people act accordingly. However, meanings are not constructed *de novo* each interaction: Once learned they operate rather spontaneously. This enculturation process is a role the environment assumes in an individual's learning of cultural codes. As well, the environment assists in maintaining social order and in reinforcing culturally acceptable behavior. In short, the built environment, along with social agents, conveys and maintains the social relationships, expectations, and behaviors of a society.

Hillier and Hanson (1984) have developed an elaborate argument for the relationship between social structures and spatial structures, partially derived from Durkheim's (1964) two principles of social solidarity. They contend that spatial organization is embedded at the economic and political levels of society and reflected in the relationships between occupants and between occupants and outsiders.

Hillier and Hanson have also produced a morphologic method of analyzing the physical environment. The analysis focuses on the permeability of space—how "cells" and entrances are arranged to control access and movement. However, communication systems, such as the telephone, which may be viewed as a space-transcending device, and other elements such as mechanical systems and architectonic details, are not considered. This exclusive emphasis on the spatial organization differs from the majority of work in environmental meaning which generally focuses on building facades, details, furniture, decorations, and other subbuilding objects (i.e., architectonic details and semi-fixed feature space). In fact, they criticize architectural and urban semiologists who address the "systematics of appearances": those who assume social meaning is something added to the surface appearance of the object rather than something that structures its form.

In contrast to the research in environmental meaning which focuses on a psychological dimension, Hillier and Hanson (1984) posit a political dimension in the shaping of environmental meaning. They advocate that not only do spatial relationships convey social messages, but that spatial relationships objectify social norms—define them, sustain them, and reproduce them. Further, they maintain that meanings come about not simply through our perception of the world, but through our experience in everyday life. This argument, if verified, would possibly disconfirm much of the empirical research done in the field of environmental meaning which uses photographic simulations of unfamiliar settings. Their theory is one that goes simply beyond the notion of environment as communication device to consideration of the spatial environment as a means to maintain social order.

While all of these theoretical models present compelling arguments and perspectives, there has been little empirical, comparative testing between them. An exception is a series of studies by Sadalla and Sheets (1993), which examined the meaning of residential building materials from the standpoint of symbolic interactionist and self-presentation theories. Their careful, sequential series of experiments, while limited to college students, supported a symbolic interactionist analysis of material symbolism, particularly along three dimensions: creative expression, interpersonal style, and social class. Yet, in exploring the cognitive mechanisms of such symbolism, they found that each building material (e.g., brick, flagstone, wooden shingles) was associated with a unique character or personality, based on enduring, perceptual qualities of the material, that became attributed to the homeowner when the homeowner actively chose the material. Together the findings suggest that cultural as well as biological or archetypal models may be joint operative processes. Clearly, more extended, comparative analysis is needed if we are to further our understanding of the complex nature and development of environmental meaning.

## SOCIO-SPATIAL CONTROL: PRIVACY AND POWER

Much of our time is spent in the presence of others, or intentionally avoiding others. When one is able to *control* the desired level and type of social interaction with individuals who are similarly free to choose whether or not they want to be with others, *privacy* exists. When one has such social control not only for oneself but over others, a form of *power* exists. In the research literature, the spatialization of privacy has been examined much more extensively than the spatialization of power; yet we can see that both exist along a continuum of *social control*. Environmental psychologists typically define privacy as control over information and space for oneself, but not for others. Yet, we see in everyday situations in schools, factories, homes, military barracks, prisons, and other settings, that social control of information and space can extend from oneself to that of others. This is legally enforced in some settings (e.g., prisons) and for certain individuals (e.g., young children). I would like to extend here the more common definition of privacy—which limits social control to that over one's own space, interactants, and information—to a broader notion of socio-spatial control including power over space and information of other people (Figure 4.2).

In this section, I first review empirical findings of the activity, social context, and physical features enhancing the qualities of privacy, and then review some theoretical models focusing on the environmental context of social control.

### Physical Environment

Osmond's (1966) concepts of socio-fugal and socio-petal space emphasize the positioning of furniture. *Socio-petal spaces* are arranged so that eye contact is easy to maintain, and positions between people, or "stations," are at a socially proxemic distance (see the Theoretical Frameworks section for definition of "proxemic" terms). *Socio-fugal spaces* are arranged so that possibility of eye contact is minimized and/or spatial distances between stations are at a publicly proxemic distance. When desires for social interaction exist, socio-petal arrangements provide opportunities to elicit communication easily. When one needs to be in a space with others but does not want to interact with them, socio-fugal arrangements work well.

*Clearly demarcated boundaries*, notably walls and partitions, enhance privacy and social interaction in a number of different U.S. settings. In a quasi-experimental study of child care centers, Moore (1986) found more social interaction and cooperation in spatially well-defined settings (i.e., with walls) than in moderately or poorly defined settings. Additionally, cooperative interaction was related to well-defined settings staffed by teachers with open styles of educational teaching. In a similar vein, BOSTI (1984) found that privacy and task-related interaction were higher among office workers with self-contained, rather than open, offices—again a function of barriers; and in a psychiatric ward, Holohan and Saegert (1973) found that partitions surrounding a patient's bed were indicative of heightened social interaction between patients and staff, and between patients and visitors. Boundaries provide not only opportunities for social isolation, but also for control of desired interactions of small groups. These studies also suggest that the role of such barriers is in regulating both visual and auditory information.

In his study of office workplaces, Goodrich (1986) found that some design solutions had the unintended effect of reducing perceived privacy while creating more spatial privacy. When partitions were used for visual privacy for instance, noises and movements outside were sudden, unanticipated, and surprising. Standing out from surrounding sound levels, they tended to be more distracting. One company (Seiler, 1984) found that changing glass-enclosed cubicles to opaque panels actually reduced privacy as managers became afraid to talk to anyone in their offices for fear of who might

Figure 4.2
Two Models of Social Control in the Environment

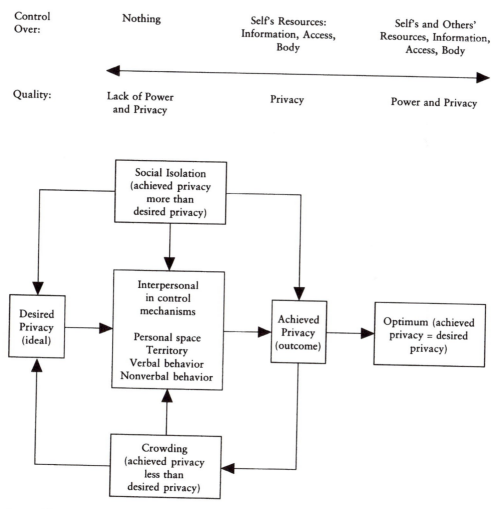

Control
Over:

Nothing

Self's Resources:
Information, Access,
Body

Self's and Others'
Resources, Information,
Access, Body

Quality:

Lack of Power
and Privacy

Privacy

Power and Privacy

Social Isolation
(achieved privacy
more than
desired privacy)

Interpersonal
in control
mechanisms

Personal space
Territory
Verbal behavior
Nonverbal behavior

Desired
Privacy
(ideal)

Achieved
Privacy
(outcome)

Optimum (achieved
privacy = desired
privacy)

Crowding
(achieved privacy
less than
desired privacy)

*Source*: Altman (1975).

overhear. In their glass offices, they had at least been able to determine who was within earshot before speaking confidentially. Thus, while enclosure may enhance privacy, it does not necessarily guarantee it. From his studies of privacy in the workplace, Sundstrom et al. (1980) concluded that architecture can enhance privacy when people in private quarters can *control their accessibility* to others more easily than in open and visible places. Hence the issue becomes not enclosure per se, but control over accessibility.

Another important physical characteristic is the *location of spaces* for socializing and gathering. In studies of congregate housing for the elderly, Lawton (1980) noted that places on the paths of everyday activity patterns were places where informal interaction frequently occurred. In offices, informal gatherings of co-workers generally occur in places that are centrally located, near pathways, used for daily activities, and comfortable for conversation (Sundstrom with Sundstrom, 1986). These places reflect Alexander et al.'s pattern (1977:621) of "common areas near the heart": "Create a single common area for every social group. Locate it at the center of gravity of all the spaces the group occupies, and in such a way that the paths which go in and out of the building lie tangent to it."

However, as Whyte (1980) has noted in his research on North American public plazas, informal meetings between strangers or casual acquaintances are facilitated not only by such spaces, but also by some type of *catalyst* (e.g., food, entertainment) which brings people to the space in the first place.

### Social Context

A number of researchers have explored the environmental context of privacy in Western and non-Western cultures. Rapoport (1982b) describes many examples, as do Altman and Chermers (1980). Front yards in American suburbs, tall shrubs in front of English homes, blank walls facing the roads in Middle East residential areas, fabric "walls" between Bedouin tents—all these are different manifestations of privacy regulation of the home occupants. Personal characteristics have also been identified and studied. Kinzel (1970), for example, found that violent people need further spatial distancing than nonviolent persons. Studies with children reveal that as maturity increases, so do privacy needs and corresponding spatial distances (see Parke and Swain, 1979).

Yet most of the research on the social context of privacy in the built environment remains atheoretical: Differences are noted but no general explanation is developed and tested. The work of Lawton and his colleagues (see Lawton, 1980), however, may provide a useful conceptual framework of the role of personal and social factors as they interact with physical environmental conditions. The underlying concept behind this model is *competence*. Internal competence is defined by biological health, sensorimotor functioning, cognitive skill, and ego strength; external processes of competence reflect social support, finances, and other social and economic resources. Environments make demands on users. The less competent the individual (e.g., poor health, low income), the greater the impact of environmental demands on that individual. As an illustration, Lawton contends that propinquity becomes a major factor in promoting social interaction among the elderly because as competence decreases, the need for mutual aid increases; and as competence decreases, the ability to traverse environmental barriers decreases, making opportunities for social exchange closer to one's home base more desirable and necessary.

## Activity

Hall's proxemics model provides a classification scheme of socio-spatial interaction, loosely based on the nature of the relationship between interactants (for a detailed description, see Theoretical Frameworks section below). However, other activity dimensions of social penetration include: (1) the size of the grouping (i.e., personal proxemics between a pair of friends may differ from that between a dozen friends); (2) the duration of interaction; (3) the direction of interaction (one-way or two-way); (4) the nature of the communication—task oriented, informational, social, directive, emotive, or perfunctory; (5) whether social interaction is the primary activity or a concomitant, secondary one; and (6) whether or not it is intentional and planned or simply accidental.

A study demonstrating the effect of activity on the environmental context of privacy had students rate the suitability of model rooms with different ceiling heights and under different activity conditions (Baird et al., 1978). Respondents preferred larger rooms (in terms of volume) for the public activities, smaller for the solitary condition (i.e., reading alone), and in-between these for the intimate (i.e., dancing), personal, and socially proxemic activities.

## Theoretical Frameworks

An early model illustrating the environmental context of social penetration was proxemic theory, or proxemics, a term coined by Hall (1966) to refer to the distances people space themselves from each other depending upon the formality of the social encounter. These distances are related to the amount and type of sensory information culturally appropriate to the social exchange. *Intimate distance*, one of heightened sensory input, occurs when touch is intended to overtake vocalization as the primary communication. This is the common proxemic distance between very close friends or relatives, lovers, and even bullies. *Personal distance* involves intense eye contact and some physical contact, but communication is more likely to be verbal than through touch. For *social distance*, common in casual gatherings and work situations, vision is less detailed, there is no touching, and people can easily engage or disengage. *Public distance* is formal and entails raised voice and exaggerated body movements.

For certain sentiments and messages to be adequately communicated, individuals have to be in appropriate proxemic positions. The consequences of the incongruency between social and spatial distance may be reduced attraction and empathy (Boucher, 1972), anxiety (Aiello and Thompson, 1980), and compensatory reactions such as body posturing and change in eye gaze (Argyle and Dean, 1965).

One of the most developed and cited theories of privacy in environmental psychology is that of Altman (1975). He defines privacy as an interpersonal, boundary-control process by which an individual or a group regulates social interaction with others. As a dialectical process, privacy involves both restricting and seeking social interaction. The mechanisms used to achieve one's desired level of privacy, that is, one's desired amount of interaction, include verbal and para-verbal behavior, personal space, and territoriality, the latter two involving spatial behavior. Underlying this framework of privacy is the ability to control and manage visual, auditory, and other sensory interactions with others.

Privacy is viewed along a continuum; too little of one's desired level of privacy results in social isolation, too much results in crowding. Although the search and desire for privacy is universal across cultures, the degree to which it is defined and the behavioral and spatial mechanisms used to achieve it are culture-specific.

The two preceding models minimally address the built environment in their schemes. Archea (1977), however, proposes a model with a strong emphasis on the architectural characteristics of the setting, independent of normative and symbolic associations. He focuses on the arrangement of the physical environment as it regulates the distribution of information on which social interaction depends. He develops a set of such arrangements—visual access, visual exposure, gradients, and terminals—which, by the amount, pace, and type of information accessed and exposed, structures social interaction and control.

In Archea's model, *visual access* is the ability to monitor one's immediate spatial surroundings by sight. It can be a function of doors, walls, mirrors, and opaque and reflective surfaces relative to one's position. *Visual exposure* is the degree to which one's behavior can be monitored by sight from the immediate surroundings. This also is a function of the placement of visual barriers, spaces, and illumination levels relative to people's positions. A *gradient*, the dynamic dimension of a setting, is the amount of change of visual access and/or visual exposure available as a function of proximity to edges or openings; shifts in position; the movement of doors and other semi-fixed barriers; and the size of the space. *Terminals* are formal communication or information networks (e.g., telephone systems, two-way television monitors).

In this model, privacy is not simply assessed architecturally. One's location and orientation in a setting affects the acquisition of information about surrounding activities and the abilities of others to notice one. This model emphasizes the role of visual information, as mediated and constructed by architecture and behavior, in privacy regulation.

Another perspective also emphasizes the role of visual information but in the context of the spatialization of power. If privacy is seen as a dialectic and a process of choice and control (e.g., Altman, 1975), then an extreme position would be the complete control over others, not just oneself, by means of the physical environment. In his analysis of "the birth of the prison," Foucault (1977) examines the materiality of the prison environment in English and French societies as an instrument of power. He first bases his commentary on Jeremy Bentham's development of the Panopticon of the 1830s, which became the architectural program of most subsequent prison buildings. It had a pinwheel configuration: a central tower pierced by windows directed toward the outer ring. The ring itself was subdivided into cells, each the full width of the ring, with windows on the side facing the tower and on the side furthest from the tower.

Like Archea's model, this one also emphasizes architecturally enhanced visibility. Here visibility becomes a trap when one has no control over it. It becomes a vector of power when one has visual and institutionalized control over others. Speaking of the prisoner, Foucault (1977:200) notes: "He is seen, but he does not see; he is the object of information, never subject in communication."

Foucault sees this phenomenon operating in any setting: hospitals, schools, factories, and so on. He contends that not only does the configuration allow for visibility, control, and power, but that this very configuration eventually induces in the inmate (i.e., the surveyed) a state of conscious and permanent visibility, resulting in perceptions which induce the automatic functioning of surveillance and, hence, power. Power is displaced from the individual person to the architecture itself.

Pader's research (1994a, 1994b) illustrates how the spatialization of power is embedded in law. She demonstrates how local, state, and federal housing policies define bedroom and acceptable sleeping arrangements. While often promoted as means to protect health, safety, and welfare of citizens, housing policies are also likely to protect dominant values and morals, disregarding the physical or emotional well-being of nondominant groups. In her study, Mexican and U.S. domestic spatial relations are compared within their larger conceptual frameworks to explain some sociocultural bases for housing regulations, hence leading one to question their social purpose as simply maintaining "health and safety."

Spain (1992) also considers the political perspective of socio-spatial control in her study of "gendered spaces"—that is, those spaces which separate women from knowledge used by men to produce and reproduce power and privileges. She describes settlement, work, and educational settings in various cultures in which women and men are spatially (both architecturally and geographically) segregated in ways that reduce women's access to knowledge, and hence diminish their power and status in the culture. Spatial barriers become established and then institutionalized for reasons that often have little to do manifestly with power, but which tend to maintain prevailing advantages. Using the theoretical position of Bourdieu, she further argues that together women and men create spatial segregation and stratification systems. Both subscribe to the spatial arrangements that reinforce differential access to knowledge, resources, and power: men because it serves their interests, and women because they may perceive no alternative.

To date there have been no attempts to integrate a richly developed architectural focus with a socio-behavioral one in explaining both privacy and power in settings.[4] Yet, the empirical research discussed previously on the activity, social context, and physical environment provides sufficient material to guide and develop such theoretical formulations.

## CONCLUDING REMARKS

This review covers only a fraction of the work in this field. Although I have organized the physical environment, activity, and social context into separate categories here, I have done so for heuristic and organizational purposes only. Certainly, in everyday life, the boundaries between behavior and social milieu, or social and physical environments, become blurred.

My intention to focus the chapter on "qualities" was a deliberate act to acknowledge space and architecture not only as tangible artifacts, but as social products and processes. In 1903, Durkheim and Mauss argued that space and time were forms of social categorization and that such categorizations expressed the societies they represented. My argument here is that the physical environment is an active, manipulable ingredient that, along with the social context in which that environment is embedded and represents, and with the human actions of the participants in that setting, produces and reproduces social life. Our experience of the built environment extends beyond bolts, bricks, and cement. As the atom is in chemistry and physics, space too is a social product. It is a function of our conceptual scheme of the physical world.

While assembling material for this chapter, I was struck by the disparity of the amount of work involving psychological and cognitive orientations compared to that involving sociological perspectives and theories. While I certainly maintain a multidisciplinary perspective on research, problem definition, and problem solving, I do think that a stronger sociological contribution and perspective to this field should be forthcoming. At the larger regional and urban scale, sociological perspectives certainly abound; at the interior and building scale, the contribution is far less. However, the work reviewed in this chapter demonstrates that sociological perspectives in the larger field of environment-behavior studies enrich our understanding of the role of social groups and situations in the built environment; expands our conceptual definitions and frameworks; and broadens our often myopic, or neglected, acknowledgment of the embeddedness of social ideology and social structure within the built environment.

Recent signs that sociological perspectives are increasingly permeating scholarly work of the built environment are encouraging. Contemporary social theorists such as Giddens (1984) have actively incorporated a spatial dimension. The work of Hillier and Hanson (1984) discussed in this chapter reflects a movement among scholars to address the intermingling of ideology and built form: Prior's (1988) study on the architecture of the hospital is a good example of this. Her work also represents a new wave of the socio-historical analysis of buildings and settings (e.g., Cromley and Hudgins, 1995; King, 1980). In particular, feminist scholars addressing gender issues of the built environment have also infused their analyses with sociological arguments and perspectives (e.g., Hayden, 1984; Spain, 1992; Weisman, 1992). With such orientation, the research activity itself can be transformed from an (assumedly) value-free method of discovery to a "communication process that can enhance the awareness, participation and cohesion of environmental users, and as a process for articulating and strengthening the values of the participants" (Stokols, 1990:643).

I am heartened by all of this recent activity which brings about an infusion of sociological perspective and imagination. This field, like the landscape it studies, is still quite large, multifaceted, and complex, rich with material for creative approaches.

## NOTES

I would like to thank Carole Després, Bill Michelson, and two anonymous reviewers for their helpful suggestions on an earlier, and much bulkier, version of this chapter.

1. The term *identity* is used extensively in multiculturalist discourse. But Hollinger (1995) argues that the use of this term can hide the extent to which the achievement of identity is a social process by which a person becomes affiliated with one or more acculturating cohorts. He contends that the word *identity* implies fixity and givenness; the word *affiliation* suggests a greater measure of flexibility consistent with a postethnic eagerness to promote communities of consent. Affiliation is more performative, while identity suggests something that simply is.

2. Williams describes these in terms of cultural production. The conditions of *dominance* are usually clear, in certain dominant institutions and forms. *Residual* is work made in earlier and often different societies and times, yet still available

and significant. *Emergent* is work of various new kinds, often equally available as practices. This new work may try to move, and at times succeed in moving, beyond the dominant forms and their socio-formal relations.

3. Used here, security refers to the absence of intended physical harm to one's self or one's property inflicted by other persons. Perceived security is one's perception of such a condition.

4. Much theoretical work exists on the spatialization of power in the urban realm (e.g., Castells, 1977; Harvey, 1973).

## REFERENCES

Abrams, J. Y. 1986. "Signs and Systems at McDonald's." Paper presented at Northeast Regional Annual Meeting, Association of Collegiate Schools of Architecture, New Jersey Institute of Technology, Newark, NJ.

Ahrentzen, S. 1989. "A Place of Peace, Prosect, and . . . a P.C.: The Home as Office." *Journal of Architectural and Planning Research* 6(4):271–288.

Aiello, J. R., and D. E. Thompson. 1980. "When Compensation Fails: Mediating Effects of Sex and Locus of Control at Extended Interaction Distances." *Basic and Applied Social Psychology* 1:65–82.

Alexander, C., S. Ishikawa, and M. Silverstein. 1979. *The Timeless Way of Building.* New York: Oxford University Press.

Alexander, C., S. Ishikawa, and M. Silverstein, with M. Jacobson, I. Fiksdahl-King, and S. Angel. 1977. *A Pattern Language.* New York: Oxford University Press.

Altman, I. 1975. *The Environment and Social Behavior.* Monterey, CA: Brooks/Cole Publishing.

Altman, I., and M. M. Chemers. 1980. *Culture and Environment.* Monterey, CA: Brook/Cole Publishing.

Altman, I., and J. F. Wohlwill (eds.). 1976 ad seriatim. *Human Behavior and Environment* (various volumes and subtitles). New York: Plenum Press.

Appleyard, D. 1979. "The Environment as a Social Symbol: Within a Theory of Environment Action and Perception." *APA Journal* 45(2):143–153.

Archea, J. 1977. "The Place of Architectural Factors in Behavioral Theories of Privacy." *Journal of Social Issues* 33(3):116–137.

Archea, J. C. 1984. "The Use of Architectural Props in the Conduct of Criminal Acts." *Journal of Architectural and Planning Research* 2(4):245–259.

Argyle, M. and J. Dean. 1965. "Eye-contact, Distance and Affiliation." *Sociometry* 28:289–304.

Baird, J. C., B. Cassidy, and J. Kurr. 1978. "Room Preference as a Function of Architectural Features and User Activities." *Journal of Applied Psychology* 63(6):719–727.

Becker, F. D. 1977. *Housing Messages.* Stroudsburg, PA: Dowden, Hutchinson & Ross.

Blumer, H. 1969. *Symbolic Interactionism: Perspective and Method.* Englewood Cliffs, NJ: Prentice-Hall.

BOSTI. 1984. *Using Office Design to Increase Productivity.* Grand Rapids, MI: Westinghouse Electric Corporation.

Boucher, M. L. 1972. "Effect of Seating Distance on Interpersonal Attraction in an Interview Situation." *Journal of Consulting and Clinical Psychology* 38:15–19.

Brantingham, P. L., and P. J. Brantingham. 1988. "Situational Crime Prevention in British Columbia." *Journal of Security Administration* 1:17–27.

Brantingham, P. L., and P. J. Brantingham. 1993. "Nodes, Paths and Edges: Considerations on the Complexity of Crime and the Physical Environment." *Journal of Environmental Psychology* 13:3–28.

Brower, S., K. Dockett, and R. B. Taylor. 1983. "Residents' Perceptions of Territorial Features and Perceived Local Threat." *Environment and Behavior* 15(4):419–437.

Brown, B. B. 1984. "Residental Territories: Cues to Burglary Vulnerability." *Journal of Architectural and Planning Research* 2(4):231–243.

Buttel, F. H. 1987. "New Directions in Environmental Sociology." *Annual Review of Sociology* 13:465–488.

Capasso, N. J. 1985. "Vietnam Veterans Memorial." Pp. 188–199 in *The Critical Edge*, edited by T. A. Marder. Cambridge, MA: MIT Press.

Castells, M. 1977. *The Urban Question.* Cambridge, MA: MIT Press.

Cherulnik, P. D. 1991. "Reading Restaurant Facades: Environmental Inference in Finding the Right Place to Eat." *Environment and Behavior* 23(2):150–170.

Cisneros, Henry G. 1995. *Defensible Space: Deterring Crime and Building Community.* Washington, DC: U.S. Department of Housing and Urban Development.

Cooley, C. H. 1964/1902. *Human Nature and the Social Order.* New York: Schocken Books.

Cooper Marcus C. 1974. "The House as Symbol of Self." Pp. 130–146 in *Designing for Human Behavior: Architecture and the Behavioral Sciences*, edited by J. Lang, C. Burnette, W. Moleski, and D. Vanchon. Stroudsburg, PA: Dowden, Hutchinson & Ross.

Cromley, E. C., and C. L. Hudgins. 1995. *Gender, Class, and Shelter: Perspectives in Vernacular Architecture, V.* Knoxville: University of Tennessee Press.

Csikszentmihalyi, M., and E. Rochberg-Halton. 1981. *The Meaning of Things: Domestic Symbols and the Self.* Cambridge: Cambridge University Press.

Darley, J. M., and D. T. Gilbert. 1985. "Social Psychological Aspects of Environmental Psychology." pp. 949–992 in *Handbook of Social Psychology, Volume II: Special Fields and Applications*, 3rd ed., edited by G. Lindzey and E. Aronson. New York: Random House.

Davis, A. 1992. "Rope." *New York Times*, May 24, section 4, p. 11.

Day, K. 1994. "Assault Prevention as Social Control: Women and Fear of Sexual Assault on Urban College Campuses." Unpublished doctoral dissertation, Department of Architecture, University of Wisconsin–Milwaukee.

Douglas, M. 1966. *Purity and Danger.* London: Routledge & Kegan Paul.

Duffy, F. C. 1969. "Role and Status in the Office." *Architectural Association Quarterly* 1:4–13.

Duncan, C. 1995. *Civilizing Rituals: Inside Public Art Museums.* London: Routledge.

Duncan, J. S. (ed.). 1982. *Housing and Identity: Cross-Cultural Perspectives.* New York: Holmes and Meier.

Duncan, J. S., and N. G. Duncan. 1976. "Housing as Presentation of Self and the Structure of Social Networks." Pp. 206–213 in *Environmental Knowing: Theories, Research and Methods*, edited by G. T. Moore and R. G. Golledge. Stroudsberg, PA: Dowden, Hutchinson & Ross.

Durkheim, E. 1964 (originally in French, 1893). *Division of Labor in Society*. New York: Free Press.

Ellison, Ralph. 1952. *Invisible Man*. New York: Random House.

Foucault, M. 1977 (translation). *Discipline and Punish: The Birth of the Prison*. London: Penguin Books.

Fox, G. L. 1977. " 'Nice Girl': Social Control of Women through a Value Construct." *Signs: Journal of Women in Culture and Society* 2(4):805–817.

Franck, K. A. 1994. "Types Are Us." Pp. 345–370 in *Ordering Space: Types in Architecture and Design*, edited by K. A. Franck and L. H. Schneekloth. New York: Van Nostrand Reinhold.

Geddes, R., and R. Gutman. 1977. "The Assessment of the Built Environment upon the Health and Behavior of People." Pp. 143–196 in *The Effect of the Man-Made Environment on Health and Behavior*, edited by L. E. Hinkle and W. C. Loring. Atlanta: Centers for Disease Control, U.S. Department of Health, Education, and Welfare.

Giddens, A. 1984. *The Constitution of Society*. Cambridge: Polity Press.

Gifford, R. 1987. *Environmental Psychology: Principles and Practice*. New York: Allyn and Bacon.

Goffman, E. 1959. *The Presentation of Self in Everyday Life*. New York: Doubleday Anchor.

Gold, J. R. 1980. *An Introduction to Behavioral Geography*. Oxford: Oxford University Press.

Goodrich, Ronald. 1986. "The Perceived Office: The Office Environment as Experienced by Its Users." Pp. 109–133 in *Behavioral Issues in Office Design*, edited by J. D. Wineman. New York: Van Nostrand Reinhold.

Goodsell, C. T. 1988. *The Social Meaning of Civic Spaces*. Lawrence: University Press of Kansas.

Gordon, M. T., S. Riger, R. K. LeBailly, and L. Heath. 1981. "Crime, Women, and the Quality of Urban Life." Pp. 141–157 in *Women and the American City*, edited by C. R. Stimpson, E. Dixler, M. J. Nelson, and K. B. Yatrakis. Chicago: University of Chicago Press.

Groat, L. 1982. "Meaning in Post-modern Architecture." *Journal of Environmental Psychology* 2:3–22.

Hall, E. T. 1966. *The Hidden Dimension*. New York: Doubleday.

Hanmer, J., and S. Saunders. 1983. *Well Founded Fear: A Community Study of Violence to Women*. London: Hutchinson.

Harvey, D. 1973. *Social Justice and the City*. Baltimore, MD: Johns Hopkins University Press.

Hayden, D. 1984. *Redesigning the American Dream*. New York: Norton.

Higgins, P. C. 1992. *Making Disability: Exploring the Social Transformation of Human Variation*. Springfield, IL: Charles C. Thomas.

Hillier, B., and J. Hanson. 1984. *The Social Logic of Space*. Cambridge: Cambridge University Press.

Hollinger, D. A. 1995. *Postethnic America: Beyond Multiculturalism*. New York: Basic Books.

Holohan, C., and S. Saegert. 1973. "Behavioral and Attitudinal Effects of Large-scale Variations in the Physical Environments of Psychiatric Wards." *Journal of Abnormal Psychology* 82:454–462.

Holohan, C. J. 1986. "Environmental Psychology." *Annual Review of Psychology* 37:381–408.

Jacobs, J. 1961. *The Death and Life of Great American Cities*. New York: Random House.

Jahoda, A., I. Markova, and M. Cattermole. 1988. "Stigma and the Self-concept of People with a Mild Mental Handicap." *Journal of Mental Deficiency Research* 32:103–115.

Jeffery, C. R. 1976. "Criminal Behavior and the Physical Environment: A Perspective." *American Behavioral Scientist* 20(2):149–174.

Kaplan, S. 1973. Review of *Defensible Space. New York Times Book Review*, April 29, 16.

King, A. D. 1980. *Buildings and Society*. London: Routledge & Kegan Paul.

Kinzel, A. F. 1970. "Body-buffer Zone in Violent Prisoners." *American Journal of Psychiatry* 127:59–64.

Lang, J. 1987. *Creating Architectural Theory: The Role of the Behavioral Sciences in Environmental Design*. New York: Van Nostrand Reinhold.

Laska, S. B. 1993. "Environmental Sociology and the State of the Discipline." *Social Forces* 72:1–17.

Lawton, M. P. 1980. *Environment and Aging*. Monterey, CA: Brooks/Cole Publishing.

Lee, Kyung Hoon. 1992. "Informal Social Control, the Physical Environment, and Residential Burglary." Unpublished doctoral dissertation, Department of Architecture, University of Wisconsin-Milwaukee.

Lenehan, M. 1983. "An Eye on the Records: The Bill James Theory of Winning Baseball." *Atlantic Monthly* (September):58–70.

Leonard, K. I. 1992. *Making Ethnic Choices: California's Punjabi Mexican Americans*. Philadelphia: University of Pennsylvania Press.

Lofland, L. 1973. *A World of Strangers*. New York: Basic Books.

Louis Harris and Associates. 1978. *The Steelcase National Study of Office Environments: Do They Work?* Grand Rapids, MI: Steelcase.

MacDonald, J. E., and R. Gifford. 1989. "Territorial Cues and Defensible Space Theory: The Burglar's Point of View." *Journal of Environmental Psychology* 9:193–205.

Mawby, R. I. 1977. "Defensible Space: A Theoretical and Empirical Appraisal." *Urban Studies* 14:169–179.

Mayo, J. M. 1988. *War Memorials as Political Landscape*. New York: Praeger.

McAndrew, F. T. 1993. *Environmental Psychology*. Pacific Grove, CA: Brooks/Cole Publishing.

Merry, S. E. 1981. "Defensible Space Undefended: Social Factors in Crime Control through Environmental Design." *Urban Affairs Quarterly* 16(4):397–422.

Meyrowitz, J. 1985. *No Sense of Place*. New York: Oxford University Press.

Moore, G. T. 1986. "Effects of the Spatial Definition of Behavior Settings on Children's Behavior." *Journal of Environmental Psychology* 6:205–231.

Moore, S. F., and B. Myerhoff. 1977. "Secular Rituals: Forms and Meanings." Pp. 3–24 in *Secular Ritual*, edited by S. F. Moore and B. Myerhoff. Assen/ Amsterdam: Van Gorcum.

Nasar, J. 1989. "Symbolic Meanings of House Styles." *Environment and Behavior* 21:235–257.

Nasar, J. L., and B. Fisher. 1993. " 'Hot Spots' of Fear and Crime: A Multi-method Investigation." *Journal of Environmental Psychology* 13:187–206.

Newman, O. 1972. *Defensible Space: Crime Prevention Through Urban Design.* New York: Macmillan.

Newman, O., and K. A. Franck. 1982. "The Effects of Building Size on Personal Crime and Fear of Crime." *Population and Environment* 5(4):203–220.

Osmond, H. 1966. "Some Psychiatric Aspects of Design." Pp. 281–318 in *Who Designs America?*, edited by L. B. Holland. New York: Doubleday.

Pablant, P., and J. C. Baxter. 1975. "Environmental Correlates of School Vandalism." *AIP Journal* 41(4):270–279.

Pader, E-J. 1994a. "An Ethnography of Occupancy Standards: Reconceptualizing Definitions of Discrimination on the Basis of National Origin and Familial Status." Pp. 1–7 in *National Fair Housing Summit Final Report*. Washington, DC: U.S. Department of Housing and Urban Development.

Pader, E.-J. 1994b. "Spatial Relations and Housing Policy: Regulations that Discriminate against Mexican-origin Households." *Journal of Planning Education and Research* 13:119–135.

Parke, R., and D. B. Swain. 1979. "Children's Privacy in the Home Development: Ecological and Child-raising Determinants." *Environment and Behavior* 11(1):87–104.

Patterson, A. H. 1978. "Territorial Behavior and the Fear of Crime in the Elderly." *Environmental Psychology and Nonverbal Behavior* 3:131–144.

Perkins, D. D., A. Wandersman, R. C. Rich, and R. B. Taylor. 1993. "The Physical Environment of Street Crime: Defensible Space, Territoriality and Incivilities." *Journal of Environmental Psychology* 13:29–49.

Prior, L. 1988. "The Architecture of the Hospital: A Study of Spatial Organization and Medical Knowledge." *British Journal of Sociology* 39(1):86–113.

Rainwater, L. 1966. "Fear and House-as-haven in the Lower Class." *Journal of the American Institute of Planners* 32(1):23–31.

Rapoport, A. 1977. *Human Aspects of Urban Form.* Oxford: Pergamon Press.

Rapoport, A. 1982a. "Identity and Environment: A Cross-cultural Perspective." Pp. 6–35 in *Housing and Identity: Cross-Cultural Perspectives*, edited by J. S. Duncan. New York: Holmes and Meier.

Rapoport, A. 1982b *The Meaning of the Built Environment: A Nonverbal Communication Approach.* Beverly Hills, CA: Sage Publications.

Renegert, G., and J. Wasilchick. 1985. *Surburban Burglary: A Time and Place for Everything.* Springfield, IL: Charles C. Thomas.

Richards, L., I. O. Jacobson, R. D. Pepler, and R. F. Bloom. 1978. "Perceived Safety and Security in Transportation Systems as Determined by the Gender of the Traveler." Pp. 441–478 in *Women's Travel Issues: Research Needs and Priorities*, edited by S. Rosenbloom. Washington, DC: U.S. Department of Transportation.

Riche, M. F. 1991. "We're All Minorities Now." *American Demographics* 13(1): 26–34.

Rochberg-Halton, E. 1984. "Objects Relations, Role Models, and Cultivation of the Self." *Environment and Behavior* 16(3):335–368.

Sadalla, E. K., and V. L. Sheets. 1993. "Symbolism in Building Material: Self-presentation and Cognitive Components." *Environment and Behavior* 25(2): 155–180.

Sadalla, E. K., B. Vershure, and W. J. Burroughs. 1987. "Identity Symbolism in Housing." *Environment and Behavior* 19:569–587.

Saegert, S., and G. H. Winkel. 1990. "Environmental Psychology." *Annual Review of Psychology* 41:44–77.

Seiler, John A. 1984. "Architecture at Work." *Harvard Business Review* (September–October):118.

Shaffer, G. S., and L. M. Anderson. 1983. "Perceptions of the Security and Attractiveness of Urban Parking Lots." *Journal of Environmental Psychology* 5: 311–323.

Shaw, K. T., and R. Gifford. 1994. "Residents' and Burglars' Assessment of Burglary Risk from Defensible Space Cues." *Journal of Environmental Psychology* 14:177–194.

Spain, D. 1992. *Gendered Spaces*. Chapel Hill: University of North Carolina Press.

Stokols, D. 1986. "Transformational Perspectives on Environment and Behavior." Pp. 243–260 in *Cross-cultural Research in Environment and Behavior*, edited by W. H. Ittelson, M. Asai, and M. Ker. Tucson: University of Arizona Press.

Stokols, D. 1990. "Instrumental and Spiritual Views of People–Environment Relations." *American Psychologist* 45(5):641–646.

Stokols, D., and I. Altman. 1987. *Handbook of Environmental Psychology*. New York: John Wiley & Sons.

Sundstrom, E., with M. G. Sundstrom. 1986. *Work Places: The Psychology of the Physical Environment in Offices and Factories*. Cambridge: Cambridge University Press.

Sundstrom, Eric et al. 1980. "Privacy at Work: Architectural Correlates of Job Satisfaction and Job Performance." *Academy of Management Journal* 23(1): 102.

Szalai, S., in collaboration with Philip E. Converse. 1973. *The Use of Time*. The Hague: Mouton Press.

Taylor, R. B. 1987. "Toward an Environmental Psychology of Disorder: Delinquency, Crime, and Fear of Crime." Pp. 951–986 in *Handbook of Environment Psychology*, edited by D. Stokols and I. Altman. New York: John Wiley & Sons.

Tiffany, W. D., and J. M. Ketchel. 1979. "Psychological Deterrence in Robberies of Banks and Its Application to Other Institutions." Pp. 81–87 in *The Role of Behavioral Science in Physical Security*, edited by J. J. Kramer. Washington, DC: U.S. Department of Commerce.

Valentine, G. 1992. "Images of Danger: Women's Source of Information about the Spatial Distribution of Male Violence." *Area* 24(1):22–29.

Veitch, R. 1995. *Environmental Psychology*. Englewood Cliffs, NJ: Prentice-Hall.

Wallis, A., and D. Ford. 1980. *Crime Prevention Through Environmental Design:*

*An Operational Handbook*. Washington, DC: U.S. Department of Justice, National Institute of Justice.

Weisman, G. 1981. "Modeling Environment-Behavior Systems." *Journal of Man-Environment Relations* 2:32–41.

Weisman, L. K. 1992. *Discrimination By Design*. Urbana: University of Illinois Press.

Whyte, W. H. 1980. *The Social Life of Urban Spaces*. New York: Conservation Foundation.

Williams, R. 1982. *The Sociology of Culture*. New York: Schocken Books.

Wise, J. A., and B. K. Wise. 1985. *Bank Interiors and Bank Robberies: A Design Approach to Environmental Security*. Rolling Meadows, IL: Bank Administration Institute.

Wolfe, A. 1992. "Democracy vs. Sociology: Boundaries and Their Political Consequences." Pp. 309–325 in *Cultivating Differences: Symbolic Boundaries and the Making of Inequality*, edited by M. Lamont and M. Fournier. Chicago: University of Chicago Press.

Wolfe, M. 1992. "Invisible Women in Invisible Places." *Architecture and Comportement/Architecture and Behaviour* 8(2):137–158.

Zimbardo, P. G. 1969. "The Human Choices: Individuation, Reason, and Order versus Deindividuation, Impulse, and Chaos." Pp. 239–308 in *Nebraska Symposium on Motivation*, edited by W. J. Arnold and D. Levine. Lincoln: University of Nebraska Press.

Zube, E. H., and G. T. Moore (eds.). 1987 ad seriatim. *Advances in Environment, Behavior, and Design*. New York: Plenum Press.

*Chapter 5*

# Macro-Environments and People: Cities, Suburbs, and Metropolitan Areas

*David Popenoe and William Michelson*

Metropolitan environments have in this century become the dominant residential environments in developed societies. Populations that formerly lived on farms and in rural villages and small towns now inhabit built environments that, in comparison, have been described as relatively large, dense, and demographically heterogeneous (Wirth, 1938). In the United States in 1990, 284 metropolitan areas were identified by the U.S. Census Bureau, ranging in size from 57,000 (Enid, Oklahoma) to 18 million (New York City and environs). These areas house 78 percent of the American population, an increase from 35 percent in 1910. The greatest population increase has been in the suburban parts of these metropolitan areas. In 1970, suburbs surpassed both central cities and nonmetropolitan areas in population, and today nearly half of all Americans live in suburban areas.

This momentous environmental shift has given rise to two broad questions of interest to environmental sociology. First, what has caused these environments to be the way they are? This is the concern of both urban ecologists (e.g., Berry and Kasarda, 1977; Hawley, 1981), who focus on spatial organization, and scholars with a structural perspective (e.g., Caulfield, 1994; Gottdiener, 1994; Logan and Molotch, 1987, who focus on how interest groups interact in the determination of urban land-use. (Leslie Kilmartin addresses some of these latter concerns in Chapter 6 in this book.)

Second, once formed, what difference does the physical character of such large-scale environments make in the lives of the residents who inhabit them? This question is the topic of the present chapter. We focus on the macroscopic aspects of metropolitan environments—the structure of metropolitan areas and their large constituent parts, that is, central cities, suburbs, municipalities, and other major sub-areas, but not blocks, buildings, or dwelling units per se (which fall more into the realm covered by Chapter 4 in this book). This chapter takes shape as follows. We first explore some of the issues and dilemmas basic to the study of metropolitan areas. Then we ask how such areas as a whole differ meaningfully from small towns and rural areas. After that, our focus turns to socially relevant differences between and then within metropolitan areas.

## METROPOLITAN BUILT ENVIRONMENTS: ISSUES AND DILEMMAS

Some issues frequently raised by the public are: Have metropolitan environments caused their residents to become more criminogenic, less familistic, more private? Each of these effects is abundantly supported by the testimonials of people who have actually moved from small towns or farms to cities or suburbs. They have some empirical support as well, at least in terms of statistical association: Crime rates are higher in metropolitan areas than elsewhere (Fischer, 1976:100–109); family decline is closely associated with urbanization (Fischer, 1976:160–166); and people in cities have been shown to lead more privatized life styles (Fischer, 1982).

A fundamental question for environmental sociology is, to what degree can effects such as these be attributed to the built environment per se, which interacts with other "environments": the natural environment (climate, natural resources), population (scale and density), and especially the sociocultural environment (politics, economics, values)? Unfortunately, this question is very difficult to answer because of the following issues:

1. These environments are so closely interconnected, and the number of interacting variables is so enormous, that it is very difficult to distinguish the separate impact of the built environment. Additional complexity stems from the fact that each environment is represented by all levels of scale, ranging from a room in a home to the entire world.

2. The behavioral impact of tangible elements of the built environment is typically mediated through the meanings that people assign to these elements; such meanings vary greatly, in keeping with the wide diversity of human cultures and personalities. "Although we live in physical environments, we create cultural environments within them" (Csikszentmihalyi and Rochberg-Halton, 1981:122).

3. Unlike animals in adapting to their environments, humans demonstrate much free choice. People are both highly adaptable to a wide range of built environments and able, if necessary, to change environments if a particular one does not suit them.

4. The physical characteristics of built environments are seldom a determinant of behavior, acting more to facilitate or foster what people already desire (Michelson, 1992).

5. Urban and suburban environments come in diverse shapes and sizes, and are not easy to define precisely.

6. With typical sociological cross-sectional research designs it is impossible to establish unequivocally whether social behavior has been caused by the effects of a given environment, or instead by particular characteristics of people who have chosen to live in that environment—the factor of social selection.

In the face of these issues, some sociologists who have studied built environments have thrown up their hands and proclaimed that the character of the built environment is of little consequence for human behavior, implying that the study of environment–behavior relations can be a waste of time (Berger, 1960; Gans, 1962a, 1962b). Most sociologists, dominated by an all-powerful cultural determinism, have simply refrained from dealing with the built environment as a social reality, as if it did not even exist (see discussions in Choldin, 1978b; Dunlap and Catton, 1994; Martell, 1994; Michelson, 1976).

However, does it really make little difference for human behavior whether a person, for example, lives in a built environment that is large and dense, with multifamily housing, a wide range of land uses, a public transportation system, and a centrally focused physical plan, rather than one with the opposite characteristics? On the face of it, an affirmative answer to this question seems highly dubious; certainly it violates everyone's commonsense view of the matter. More importantly, it has not been supported by the growing volume of research in this area over the last few decades.

The answer to such a question is of no small importance because the built environment, to a much larger degree than the socio-cultural environment, is something that can be manipulated by human agency (Arias, 1992; Cooper Marcus and Sarkissian, 1986; Franck and Ahrentzen, 1989). Residential environments can be molded to certain specifications; this, in fact, is continuously being done by builders, architects, and planners the world over (Eisner and Gallion, 1992; Hall, 1988). If there are *any* significant effects of these environments on human behavior, such information should be placed in the hands of these professionals, not to speak of the public at large.

In seeking seriously to examine environment–behavior effects, one must be careful how the research questions are phrased. There have been few findings to date which conclusively demonstrate a strong environmental causation for human behavior; it appears to be the case that only limited aspects of the built environment have a *determinative* (in the sense of necessary or inevitable) impact on human beings. In complex interrelations with personality, social structure, and culture, the effect of the built environment is best viewed as making certain choices more likely than others. "It supports rather than requires; it discourages rather than prohibits"

(Krupat, 1985:12). Thus, rather than viewing environment–behavior relationships as deterministic, they should be looked at in probabilistic or possibilistic terms (Chapter 3 this volume); people do, or do not do, things partly based on an assessment of environmental opportunities and constraints. And the phrase "environmental effect" is best thought of in terms of "relationships" (this notion is explored below with respect to "environmental congruence"). Through a constant round of interaction, we are continually shaping our environment and, in turn, being shaped to some extent by it (Michelson, 1992, 1995; Stokols, 1995). In this respect, the built environment is no different from any other aspect of what is sometimes referred to as our material culture (Gutman, 1972; Zukin, 1995); but what makes the urban phenomenon so complicated—and fascinating—is the number of other dimensions of built environment which simultaneously come to bear, not the least of which is the spatial dimension.

We now examine the metropolitan built environment as a holistic phenomenon, in comparison with nonmetropolitan contexts, with respect to human impacts and considerations. Then we shall turn to ways in which particular metropolitan areas and the sub-areas within them differ from one another and the social and behavioral significance of these differences.

## THE METROPOLITAN ENVIRONMENT AS A HOLISTIC CONTEXT

Urban and suburban environments (which can be incorporated within the category "metropolitan environments") are, of course, different from each other; but first it is useful to show how they jointly differ from the other main types of residential environments in which people live: small towns, villages, and farms. The primary difference, obviously, is scale. As the classical University of Chicago sociologist Louis Wirth (1938) long ago emphasized, metropolitan environments are larger, both in environmental and population terms, and this fact alone has important implications for the way people live (Sadalla, 1978). For example, it provides sufficient consumers or users, what Claude Fischer (1976) called critical masses, to support greater numbers and varieties of stores, institutions, and places of recreation.

Although metropolitan environments are typically denser as well as larger than their nonmetropolitan counterparts, density differences are less easily captured conceptually. Many a metropolitan single-family house suburb is less dense than a small town; the same holds true for entire cities that are built at low densities, such as Houston, Texas. Built environment densities are often best expressed through house type and lot size: Metropolitan areas tend to have a higher percentage of small dwelling units, such as those in multifamily dwellings, and they tend to use a larger percentage of available space for building.

Metropolitan areas are also typically more heterogeneous in an environmental sense, as expressed in the phrases "mixed land-uses" and "mixed housing types." Such environmental heterogeneity goes hand in hand with socio-cultural diversity. The scale of urban areas helps foster heterogeneity and diversity, insofar as it makes possible multiple subgroups in the population—the presence of critical masses of persons to support each of the units contributing to overall diversity (Fischer, 1976). For example, lifestyle diversity is much easier to maintain in a metropolis than in a hamlet because people with differing interests are more able to find others like themselves for stimulation and reinforcement.

## CLASSICAL VIEWS ON THE SOCIAL IMPACT OF METROPOLITAN ENVIRONMENTS

What is it like to live in these environments? We start with cities. The most influential classical approaches to the study of the effects of living in cities are those put forth by Georg Simmel (1905) and his successor, Louis Wirth (1938). Both focused on the city's outstanding characteristics as a type of environment. Wirth hypothesized that demographic scale and density (which he tended to combine into a single factor) generated socio-cultural diversity, and each of these factors, in turn, led to weakened kinship and neighboring; superficial social contacts, weak emotional ties, and personal isolation; the decline of informal social control mechanisms; and a generally weakened community consensus and "moral order" (Morris, 1968). Wirth's critics have long sought to refute his views through empirically demonstrating, for example, that such dimensions as kinship and neighboring still strongly exist in the city. Yet it has never been conclusively demonstrated that many aspects of social structure are not, as Wirth maintained, weaker in the city than in small towns and rural communities (the major empirical findings will be discussed below.)

Wirth has also been criticized for emphasizing "ecological" independent variables at the expense of such cultural variables as "capitalism" and "rationality," and for what is considered to be an overly negative evaluation of city life. Although a negative evaluation of contemporary city life has been generally subscribed to by a long string of American intellectuals (Mumford, 1961; White and White, 1962), to say nothing of most Americans, Wirth's stress on the role of cities in creating social disorganization and personality disorders did downplay the positive side of city life, such as enhanced excitement and stimulation, cultural creativity, personal freedom, and tolerance of diversity. These traits, too, presumably stem in part from scale, density, and heterogeneity, and they have been celebrated in such influential works as those of Jane Jacobs (1961) and Richard Sennett (1970) and applied more recently by Mats Lieberg (1995).

According to Claude Fischer's view of the subcultures made possible by critical masses of population, we can expect that at least some of these provide positive experiences for people with shared backgrounds, experiences, and/or interests (Fischer, 1976). Within some of these social worlds, in contrast to Wirth's conception, life may be just as warm and emotional as in the small town. This situation also helps to spawn unconventionality and deviance; the deviance can be both positive, leading to beneficial social change, and negative, as in crime and delinquency.

Georg Simmel (1905) had focused more on the "profusion of sensory stimuli" in the city. These abounded both in the physical environment, with the need for people to respond frequently and quickly to signals, noises, directions, and movements in the ambient context (with possible loss of life as a consequence for nonobservance), and in the social environment, with the need to deal appropriately with people known only according to delimited roles being played or with complete strangers. Simmel felt that urban dwellers in consequence became more rationally calculating and emotionally distant from one another, as well as more intellectual. He also saw them as, compared to rural and small-town dwellers, relatively blasé and reserved. Urbanites were said to relate to each other with their heads, not their hearts.

In the early 1970s, psychologist Stanley Milgram (1970) produced an influential refinement of this perspective. He too saw the city as stimulating, but sometimes overly stimulating, leading to the stress of "psychic overload." The profusion of sensory stimuli demands certain psychological adaptations on the part of urban dwellers that enable the screening out of certain inputs. These psychological adaptations include such maneuvers as disregarding low-priority inputs and shifting responsibility to others. Such maneuvers can be effective in preventing psychic overload, Milgram pointed out, but they can also deprive urban dwellers of a sense of direct contact and spontaneous integration with the life around them.

Another influential perspective on the impact of the urban environment is that of Lyn Lofland (1973), who sees the urban world not so much as one of psychic overload as of anonymity, brought about by the large size of cities, as well as by the separateness of heterogeneous subcultures. Urban anonymity has two faces: not knowing most of the people one encounters on a daily basis, and not being known by them. Unlike Wirth, Lofland does not see anonymity in a necessarily negative light. In order to deal with anonymity, urbanites create (mostly successfully in Lofland's view) a sense of social order through either judging the physical appearances of strangers or, more commonly in modern industrial cities, the ordering of urban space. Urban dwellers "privatize" urban public space in ways that enable them to cope with anonymity; one result is the reinforcement of the mosaic of social worlds. Also, the urbanite learns to get some satisfaction from even the most fleeting of social relationships, such as the segmented role relationship between shopkeeper and patron.

## AREAS OF METROPOLITAN ENVIRONMENTAL IMPACT: RESEARCH FINDINGS

These classic hypotheses about the social effects of city living are, of course, not meant to apply to all people under all urban conditions; they are generalizations, broadly contrasting urban and nonurban conditions. In recent years, many attempts have been made to empirically test one or another of these hypotheses, and the findings of this research, although not conclusive, are of considerable interest (Karp et al., 1991). Discussed here are the findings in three key areas of social impact—social relationships, sense of community, and social control—as well as the conclusions of a considerable body of research into the human effects of density and crowding. Much of this research has been undertaken in terms of an urban/rural continuum, that is, it involves a comparison of behavior in communities ranked on a continuum of size and density.

### Social Relationships

Although the variance is not exactly as hypothesized by the urban theorists, social relationships among people have been shown to vary along the urban/rural continuum, not only in terms of people's personal characteristics but also in terms of differing environmental settings. In urban/rural comparisons, several social differences stand out as simple effects of social scale: In more urban places, a higher percentage of the people one encounters are strangers; and (using the classic primary-secondary relationship distinction) a higher proportion of one's total social relationships are secondary (specialized, lacking in emotional warmth, and involving only a limited aspect of one's personality). The question of real interest is, however, do these fundamental urban/rural differences have any significance for the number and especially the quality of the city dweller's primary relationships (personal, emotional, not easily transferable, and involving a variety of roles and interests)? Does the relatively anonymous character of urban public life, for example, spill over into urban private life? Is it true that urbanites tend to be "physically close (in spatial terms) but emotionally distant?" Such questions are of special interest in view of the importance that primary relationships hold in people's lives.

The research that has been done on these questions is limited, but a number of studies have come forth with the following general findings. With urbanism, there is some decline in neighboring; relations among neighbors become less frequent and less positive, and fewer neighbors are personal friends (Keller, 1968). Greater neighborhood homogeneity created in part by the housing mix or lack thereof, on the other hand, promotes neighboring and neighborhood attachment (Silverman, 1986). Also, urban dwellers are substantially less helpful and considerate to strangers; this finding is based on a wide range of studies of such things as doing small favors, assisting a lost child, letting a stranger use the phone, and bystander interventions (Christy, 1994; Korte, 1980; Piliavin et al., 1981; Wolfinger, 1994). While many factors help to account for these findings, built environment factors are surely among them (although environmental factors have not always been the main focus of the research). Certain building site designs such as the use of cul-de-sac streets, for example, have been shown to promote neighboring in urban areas (Brown and Werner, 1985; Carey and Mapes, 1972; Michelson, 1992, 1994b), and group size, which is strongly affected by environmental conditions, is closely associated with the willingness of bystanders to intervene in emergency situations (Latane et al., 1981).

Relationships with family members, relatives, and friends, however, are apparently not so affected by type of residential environment. Both urban and small-town dwellers seem to have a similar number of friends and acquaintances (although there have been few studies of the quality of these relationships) but, in keeping with the neighboring finding noted above, urbanites tend to have to go further afield to find their friends (Fischer, 1982). There is also some indication that friendships take longer to make in cities (Franck, 1980). Although fewer urbanites live in nuclear family households, the differences in family relationships along the urban/rural continuum do not seem very pronounced. Toward the urban pole there is some dropoff in relationships with the extended family; this may be due largely to the fact that the relatives of urbanites live farther apart from one another. Among the nonenvironmental social factors of greatest importance in accounting for family relationships are social class and ethnicity; at lower social class levels and among certain ethnic groups, social relationships tend to be more within the kin group, and more localized geographically (Cochran et al., 1990).

### Sense of Community

The contribution of the built environment to the generation of "neighborly feelings" and a "sense of community" has long been a subject of speculation, especially by persons concerned about the presumed decline of "community" in modern societies (Newman, 1980; Thorns, 1976). Such decline has been a central theme in modern social thought (Lyon, 1987; Nisbet, 1969; Warren, 1972), and the theme has had a wide appeal among architects and planners. Many architects and planners have suggested that they could create community through their designs, and have made community a central planning goal (Buder, 1990; Chermayeff and Alexander, 1963; Duany and Plater-Zyberk, 1991; Lynch, 1981).

There is general agreement that the idea of the urban neighborhood which has identifiable boundaries, within which interaction among a relatively homogeneous segment of the population is intense, has become weakened with urbanization. This geographic community has been partially replaced by a "community without propinquity." The latter is a form of community that extends as a "social network" over broader distances with the help of advanced technologies of transportation and communication, and that to some extent includes friends and co-workers in place of kinship group members and neighbors (Webber, 1963; Wellman et al., 1988; Wellman and Wortley, 1990). The local neighborhood in the metropolitan area, in turn, has been said to become a "community of limited liability" (Greer, 1962; Janowitz, 1967), although strong, mostly working-class "urban villages" still exist in some parts of the contemporary metropolitan area (Gans, 1962b; Hannerz, 1969; Liebow, 1967; Suttles, 1968).

Over time, the social and physical characteristics of local areas have assumed a huge variety, including both traditional and nontraditional forms. Janet Abu-Lughod (1991:329–333) cites research identifying through empirical means 40 different types of local neighborhoods, according to life-style differences among residents.

To those who seek to rebuild the local community of propinquity in the metropolis through physical planning, the findings of social research provide only limited support. The most active attempts by planners to create a sense of community through design have been in the European nations, where the centralized planning of cities and suburbs has been much more common than in the United States. A review of Swedish attempts to create community concludes that variations of the physical environment have at best modest effects, and most of those are indirect, operating through the types of people that are attracted to differing environments and the capacity they have for local-level decision making (Hjärne, 1986).

However, a recent empirical study of four attempts in Sweden to foster social contact among neighbors through innovations in physical design and/ or social organization documented that even though there is a large amount of "self-selection" to particular housing areas, the relative degree of neighboring is to some extent influenced by opportunities within the residential contexts (Michelson, 1991, 1992). For example, neighboring is higher in collective housing areas. The concept of collective housing (often called co-housing in the English-speaking world) has spread from Scandinavia and been slowly adopted elsewhere as a way to foster social contact within residential settings (Fromm, 1991 McCamant and Durrett, 1988).

In the United States, it has been suggested that community identity is enhanced when residential environments are designed to promote "communities of interest," or "life style enclaves," collections of people in a limited geographic area who share the same life style (Newman, 1980). It has also been noted that community cohesion and a sense of community are promoted when local areas are identifiable and bounded, so that a certain residential exclusiveness is fostered (Suttles, 1972); when they are rich with community facilities that can be places of intimacy and companionship apart from home and work (Oldenburg, 1989); when they have appropriate public spaces (Altman and Zube, 1989; Whyte, 1988); and even when they have "livable streets" (Anderson, 1986; Appleyard, 1980). Because feelings of community have been found to be strongest among those who have lived the longest in a given environment (Kasarda and Janowitz, 1974; Sampson, 1988), another way in which the physical environment can potentially be effective in this regard is through reducing needless residential mobility. An example is the provision of a range of housing so that when people's needs for space change solely due to normal movement through the life cycle, they do not have to change communities (Cooper Marcus and Sarkissian, 1986).

### Social Control

Among the most widely researched areas of urban built environment impact is social control. The classic work of Jane Jacobs (1961) gave prominence to the idea that modern urban building and planning arrangements were helping to break down the mechanisms of informal social control, leading to an increase in crime. Some years later the work of Oscar Newman (1972) helped to focus attention on the ways in which informal social control could be enhanced through environmental design, especially through the provision of what he called "defensible space." The work of Newman and his associates pointed to the existence of anonymity, the lack of surveillance or "neighborhood watchfulness," and the presence of alternative escape routes as contributors to high crime rates in residential environments. To Newman, the kind of residential environment that would most effectively deter crime was one in which people outside their dwellings not only could see and be seen continuously, but also would be willing to intervene when a criminal act was observed.

The degree to which neighbors will engage in informal social control activities is clearly dependent on the level of neighborhood and community trust and solidarity, which in turn is partly based on environmental conditions, as well as a variety of nonphysical factors (Merry, 1981; Sampson and Groves, 1989: Skogan and Maxfield, 1981). In one empirical investigation of Newman's theory, higher crime rates (and greater fear of crime) were found to be related to large building size, in association with such environmentally related features as the number of people using a single entrance to a building and the degree to which the grounds and common parts of the buildings are not shared and "defended" by individual households (Newman and Franck, 1980). Other studies have shown that criminals tend to avoid, and residents have less fear of crime in, residential environments which have a number of the physical characteristics posited by Newman (Murray, 1983; Poyner, 1983; Taylor and Gottfredson, 1986).

One recent study found that "physical disorder" in the form of visual signs of negligence and unchecked decay, for example, abandoned buildings and broken streetlights, can seriously erode the impulse for neighborhood control over events and conditions (Skogan, 1990). Findings in the area of social control, then, provide a useful lesson in the ways in which environmental and social factors interact to affect human behavior. (Contextual aspects of social control are discussed in Chapter 4 of this volume from a more micro perspective).

### Density and Crowding

Perhaps the most obvious negative aspect of urban life, in the minds of many people, is the presumed stress and other personal problems associated with high density and overcrowding. Ever since Calhoun's (1962) studies showed that severe overcrowding produces stress and pathological behavior in rats, evidence for this relationship has been sought in human environments. Searching the cities for what Calhoun termed "behavioral sinks," urban density/crowding research has become a robust undertaking in the past few decades, albeit one with inconclusive results.

One pioneering study conducted in Chicago found that high population density was associated with tension in the home, less effective child care, and juvenile delinquency (Galle et al., 1972). Distinguishing crowding (often defined as persons per room) from density (as measured by persons per unit of land area), some sociologists have singled out crowding as having the more deleterious social consequences (Gove et al., 1979). A common explanation for the negative effects of crowding is that it generates a loss in people's ability to control the environment.

These studies and others that have found similar statistical associations, however, have been widely challenged on methodological grounds. Although crowding and density certainly have the capacity to be stressful, and may well be for many people both uncomfortable and unpopular, many scholars have found no conclusive evidence that either environmental variable on its own causes personal or social pathology (Booth, 1976; Choldin, 1978a; Freedman, 1975). Other sociologists have pointed to the positive side of density and crowding, stressing that the presence of others presents opportunities as well as constraints (Baldassare, 1979).

Environmental psychologists have tended to conceive of crowding as the personal experience of density, noting that there is an abundance of cultural and social factors affecting the conditions under which density feels like crowding (Baum and Epstein, 1978; Baum and Paulus, 1987). Studies of Pacific Rim nations such as Hong Kong and Japan have found few deleterious effects from housing conditions that in Western nations would clearly be regarded as severe overcrowding (Mitchell, 1971). It is suggested that people in Asian cultures, partly due to rigorously followed norms of interpersonal etiquette, are better adapted to high-density living, although a study of crowding among city dwellers in India found many negative effects there (Jain, 1987).

Scholars agree that the effects of density, especially the degree to which density leads to the experience of feeling crowded and to psychological stress, are widely variable among human populations and cultures.

Another mediating factor noted in the literature is the extent to which access to technology and resources in the local area is sufficient for the numbers of persons present. Do people have to wait unduly long for elevators or transportation, have to queue for food, or lack ready access to places of work or recreation? The degree of access to such resources can make dense situations either workable or frustrating (Michelson, 1984).

An outgrowth of scholarly interest in density and crowding is the assessment of the impact on people of urban areas that are growing or declining in population size. Municipal politicians typically assume growth to be necessary and desirable, as it suggests an expanded tax base and portrays vitality to the rest of the world. When Mark Baldassare (1981) examined this issue with systematic data from the United States, he found the politicians' hypothesis confirmed in slow-growth contexts. However, very rapid growth leaves new residents lacking expected facilities and services, with strains put on municipal budgets to provide them. His study of a particularly fast-growing area in California (Orange County) documented many sources of dissatisfaction which were unexpected from the upscale nature of development occurring there (Baldassare, 1986).

Now let us turn to another way of viewing metropolitan environments and people. What implications do differences of metropolitan context from one metropolitan area to another, and from one unit of a metropolitan area city to another, make in people's lives?

## THE SOCIAL IMPACTS OF DIFFERING METROPOLITAN CONTEXTS

Even in an age when people can create and experience their own virtual communities through various electronic devices, the literature suggests that the particular characteristics of the bounded areas where people live—well-defined neighborhoods, municipalities, and regionally governed areas, counties, or metropolitan areas—have an explicit place in people's minds and in their lives and life chances.

For example, research by Gregory Weiher (1991) makes a strong argument in favor of the continuing salience of the municipality in people's lives. Weiher argues that municipalities have the benefit of explicit boundaries as cues for people to identify and compare them. They also have governments, with the mandate to deliver a specific set of goods and services. Municipalities take on unique identities according to the decisions they make and the milieu which takes shape. To the extent, as in many suburbs, that municipalities have homogeneous populations, potential residents are drawn to a municipality by their image of who lives there, further reinforcing the special characteristics of the municipality both socially and in terms of policy directions. The criteria people use in selecting a municipality in which to live, according to Weiher, include a mixture of social and physical characteristics—quality of housing, provision of services, the kinds and levels of fees and taxes, the amenities, security, quality of life, social status, and the population characteristics of residents (particularly social class and race/ethnicity).

Weiher points out that most people feel they have more control over what happens at the municipal level than at other levels of government. However, local governance is increasingly carried out simultaneously at different levels. City government is no longer uniquely important, as larger functional service areas, regional or county governments, and states or provinces provide direction from above. In the other direction, neighborhood areas within cities not only remain as reference points for population subgroups but are dealt with formally by ward-level politicians and community-oriented city planning structures. Weiher does not argue that territorial units other than the municipality are unimportant, only that the formal borders of a municipality reinforce the distinct impacts this unit imparts.

Research on three regional governments in the greater Toronto area (covering areas sometimes thought to be larger than the size of territory which people can easily comprehend) shows that respondents clearly differentiate their special attributes (Michelson, 1997). Residents of the Municipality of Metropolitan Toronto—the center block of the whole metropolitan area but much more than the central city—felt that "Metro" was better than other nearby regions in terms of public transit and access to stores and services. In contrast, the more peripheral regions of York and Durham viewed their areas as superior on criteria of housing, open space, crime, raising children, and growing older.

Conceptually, the match between macro-environments and people has been viewed according to several roughly similar terms: fit, congruence, synomorphy (Michelson, 1976, 1988). A high-quality residential environment is one that does not "pinch"; it supports rather than discourages the desired behavior of its occupants. Such an environment presumably brings its occupants a high level of personal satisfaction and social efficiency. An environment which is incongruent, in contrast, causes dissatisfactions; if these dissatisfactions are great enough, the residents may flee (if possible) to a different environment, but only if they have reason to believe they won't be subject to a range of dissatisfactions there which are comparable or worse (Brown and Mikkelsen, 1990). If they have the freedom of choice, people will choose to live in those environments which they believe are most congruent with their needs and desires.

In considering the match between macro-environments and people, "people" must be considered according to concepts that are potentially relevant to interaction with the macro-environment. Fortunately, the social sciences provide concepts such as culture (and subculture), social class, age and stage in the life cycle, life style, and gender (Michelson, 1976, 1988). Conceptualizing macro-environment, however, is more difficult. Once one focuses on physical environments greater than, say, the block, it is more difficult to convey the image of how one setting differs from another in meaningful, systematic terms. It is one thing to describe the components of a living room or an office, but quite another to talk about the meaningful dimensions of metropolitan areas. Fortunately, some useful conceptual schemes have emerged.

## INTERMETROPOLITAN DIFFERENCES (METROPOLITAN FORM)

Far from arguing that cities and metropolitan areas are or should be even roughly similar in physical design, planners and architects have made special efforts to make differing macroscopic designs to serve diverse purposes. Many cities in the midwestern United States follow the gridiron pattern, with intersecting sets of north-south and east-west streets created at equal intervals. Not only does this enable rational wayfinding, but it makes the sale and development of (rectangular) plots of land extremely straightforward. In contrast, cities such as Washington, DC, have been designed as large circles, with radial roads serving and visually highlighting the city centers. In cities with radial form, land subdivision is more difficult, as may be getting to and from noncentral locations; but quick and secure access to the center is facilitated. This is one reason why the planner Haussmann imposed a radial design on the existing structure of Paris; it is particularly important for military purposes.

There is a tradition for architects to propose city plans with strong social goals in mind. Le Corbusier promoted urban form based on high-rise buildings with small functional apartments, in a park-like setting, and joined to city centers by public transportation lines, while Frank Lloyd Wright, to the contrary, proposed cities of extremely low densities, incorporating single-family housing, large private lots, and private means of transportation. Corbusier emphasized collective amenities, while Wright expressed individualistic objectives.

David Popenoe (1985) has explored the impact of such ideological perspectives, focusing on the collectivity versus the individual in metropolitan structure and functioning. He documents, through a comparative study of Swedish, English, and American cities, how the emphasis in American metropolitan development on placing amenities for the private consumption of households (i.e., single-family housing at low densities, with much recreation on private property and travel by private automobile) has the impact of (further) weakening intergroup contacts and the viability of public institutions, while widening the gap between rich and poor—what he calls "public plight." His comparison shows how the extent of public transportation networks is a vital element in the determination of how privatized metropolitan areas will become. Where cities are built around strong public transportation systems (as in Sweden), people have better access to city centers and public facilities; and where the emphasis is on collective rather than private amenities, public facilities are more likely to be available to all individuals, including those most in need of them.

Another illustration of the social impact of metropolitan form lies in Richard Sennett's analysis of how people regard the human body (1994). He traces, largely historically, how the shape and focus of cities has emphasized or repressed various functions of the body—talking, touching, and so on. Following upon Popenoe's privatization theme, Sennett notes that "this great geographic shift of people into fragmented spaces has had a larger effect in weakening the sense of tactile reality and pacifying the body" (p. 17). He argues that in modern, decentralized cities, "Space has . . . become a means to the end of pure motion" (p. 17), which removes the body from all kinds of contact with others.

Several conceptual schemes have been advanced to account for inter-metropolitan differences in physical structure which have human implications. The work of Kevin Lynch was dedicated to the clarification of urban form and its interactions with people (Lynch, 1960, 1961, 1977, 1981) Lynch and Rodwin, 1958. His early writings help explain the varying ease with which people can find their way around cities, as well as the richness of detail they feel in their urban surroundings. These are explained by virtue of such spatial attributes as the presence or absence of landmarks, edges (e.g., rivers, railway rights of way), nodes, and the like. His 1977 study for UNESCO suggests that adolescents are given opportunities for meaningful activities and contacts by some city structures but "experiential starvation" (p. 4) in others. His final book (1981) brings the physical and social parameters together for the guidance of planners and interested decision makers.

A very different approach deals with macro-environments in terms of their varying composition of spatial and temporal attributes (Carlstein, 1978; Hägerstrand, 1970; Michelson, 1990, 1994a; Parkes and Thrift, 1980). Torsten Hägerstrand, a Swedish geographer, addressed the question of "What about people in Regional Science?" (1970), by sketching out systematically how the commonly noted dimension of space assumes more meaning in people's lives when viewed in conjunction with time.

Hägerstrand took as assumptions that there is only so much time in the day and that all people share the same amount of it. He also took as an assumption that you can't be in two places at once. His underlying objective was to seek an understanding of what people can work into the limited time available in a day, given the structure of their macro-environments in terms of space and time. The spatial aspect covers what land-uses are available to a person within the parameters of a day in a given macro-environment, as well as where they are located vis-à-vis each other. For example, how clustered or dispersed are they? Are they proximate to those living centrally and distant for those living in the periphery? Ultimately, however, one needs to understand which land-uses a person or class of persons needs and/or desires to use during the day, together with how long it takes to get from one to another given the respective distances and available mode(s) of transportation. Given that some activities like employment and sleep are granted high priority, how many and which of the other activities can one realistically combine in the daily routine within the layout and travel parameters of a particular metropolitan area?

An additional constraint in this picture comes from the timetabling of the activities at the different land-uses. Time is viewed here not only in terms of duration, but as "timing." In view of given hours of employment, what opening and closing hours pertain to store, services, places of recreation, health facilities, and so on? Even if you can work a trip to a doctor or to a post office into your daily routine in terms of the total amount of time needed and available for travel and service, are they accessible in time beyond working hours?

Further understanding of the impact of metropolitan macro-environments comes from a comparison of different contexts within the same metropolitan area, an issue to which we now turn.

## INTRAMETROPOLITAN DIFFERENCES

### Central City–Suburban Differences

In earlier times, sociologists wrote about not only urban–rural differences but also about city–suburban differences. When they compared urban to rural, it was the central city they most had in mind. After World War II, much more notice was taken of suburbs, which, while not new at that time, were nonetheless expanding rapidly. Suburbs appeared to represent a newly important milieu whose social and physical characteristics required exploration and understanding. In the past 50 years, however, the dichotomous distinction between city and suburb has blurred, due to several developments. Especially in the American sunbelt, but also in other climates in which cities have grown from relatively small settlements in recent years, large areas within central cities often have the physical characteristics of the prototype suburbs. Also, as metropolitan areas have grown in size well beyond the borders of the original central cities, not only have the suburbs come to accommodate the majority of the metropolitan population in numbers, but they also have come to encompass more city-like land-uses, as well as a more diverse population (Fishman, 1987; Garreau, 1991; Muller, 1981; Sassen, 1990). These developments make urban–suburban comparisons increasingly difficult. Yet, before turning our attention to other intra-metropolitan differences, we should convey a summary of writings on suburban life as it differs from that of the central cities and small towns.

Like cities, suburbs come in all shapes and sizes—and are therefore difficult to define; some suburbs are really parts of the city, others are merely small towns that have become incorporated into metropolitan areas. The prototypical suburb is an environment that is specialized in terms of the residential function and therefore dependent on other environments (especially the city) to provide the functions of work, leisure, and even shopping. In addition, suburbs tend to be environmentally homogeneous, often containing, for example, just one or two housing types. In other respects, such as scale, the suburb (at least in Western, industrial nations) is intended to be a compromise between urban and nonurban environmental forms. But, as noted above, many suburbs around the world are gradually receding from the prototype and becoming less specialized and homogeneous.

The term *suburban environments* will be used here to refer to their prototypical form found in Anglo-American nations: the United States, the United Kingdom, and the British Commonwealth nations. This prototype consists of low-density, socially homogeneous, residential environments made up largely of single-family detached houses on relatively large lots and oriented to the automobile. Especially in the United States following the proliferation of such environments after World War II, there was widespread discussion in the popular press of the possible negative social effects of these new suburbs. The viewpoint most commonly expressed was of a suburban environment that fostered overconformity, hyperactivity, anti-individualism, conservatism, "momism," dullness and boredom, status seeking, and a host of problems including mental illness, sexual promiscuity, and alcoholism. In focusing exclusively on the negative side of an as yet unaccustomed form of living, the suburban debate resembled Wirth's earlier one-sided discussion of central-city life.

These popular critics were soon sharply challenged. One writer called the discussion "a critical onslaught of monumental, and largely nonsensical proportions" (Donaldson, 1969:1). Sociologist Herbert Gans concluded for the suburb that he intensively studied—Levittown, New Jersey—that "few changes can be traced to the suburban qualities of Levittown" (Gans, 1967: 288). A similar conclusion was reached by Bennett Berger, who followed the move of working-class families to a California suburb (Berger, 1960). In general, the work of these pioneering suburban sociologists stressed that the social characteristics found among residents of particular suburbs were ones they had "brought with them," not ones caused by their new environments. The early post–World War II suburban dwellers were largely young, white, middle class, and in the family stages of the life cycle; but as suburbs came to encompass a greater cross-section of the population, researchers discovered blue-collar suburbs, upper-middle-class suburbs, black suburbs, ethnic suburbs, and much more.

A later generation of sociological studies brought back important effects of the environment to some degree. Suburban living is home-centered, for example, with many leisure activities taking place within the home (Michelson, 1977), a phenomenon that is closely related to such physical characteristics of the suburban environment as the presence of detached and owned homes on large yards.

Compared to central-city dwellers, suburbanites also have increased contact with their neighbors (Fischer, 1982; Keller, 1968) and a slightly higher level of community participation (Fischer et al., 1977). These various social traits are often subsumed under the concept "suburban localism," a social life directed toward the immediate locality and its residents. An additional suburban social trait often discussed, and one also related to environmental characteristics, is the social homogeneity of suburban populations. At its worst, this trait is linked with racial and class segregation (Schwartz, 1976).

When compared to the typical small town, however, suburban localism is cast in a different light. Suburbs have less neighboring and community participation (and usually also less social heterogeneity) than do small towns. Thus, to someone moving to a suburb from a small town, suburbs can seem rather formal, privatized, and unfriendly. While this suburban social difference can be generated by such nonenvironmental factors as social class, elements of the built environment also play a role. Because suburbs are typically residentially specialized, with residents having to go elsewhere for work and to some extent for leisure and even shopping, the overlapping social networks and public life found in small towns are comparatively lacking (Fischer, 1982).

Due to the low-density character of suburban environments together with the geographic "scatteration" of employment, shopping, and leisure facili ties, a phenomenon popularly called "urban sprawl," it is useful to conceive of the suburb as the opposite of the city in terms of both geographic accessibility and social "stimulation." Especially for those without ownership of, or access to, an automobile, the suburban environment clearly involves a "deprivation of access" to needed facilities and services (National Research Council, 1974); and, the suburban environment might be thought to involve a stimulus deprivation, a deficit in those environmental elements that generate social activity and stimulation (Lynch, 1977; Popenoe, 1979). This is the reverse of the stimulus overload presumably found in urban settings.

Combining this stimulus deprivation with the social picture of the suburban environment drawn from a comparison with small towns, some scholars have even suggested that, far from being a place with "community," the suburb represents a kind of overprivatized anti-community (Popenoe, 1985; Schwartz, 1980). This lack of community, moreover, is commonly regarded in the highly suburbanized United States to be an increasingly serious social problem (Bellah et al., 1985). In combination with the dominance of individualism in American culture, for example, the privatized suburban environment may help to reinforce the weak feeling of collective responsibility and exaggerated sense of personal liberty that make this nation stand apart from the European welfare states (Popenoe, 1990). Such attitudes, in turn, seem to be exacerbating the American "urban crisis" (Kelly, 1989), and have led to movements within the fields of architecture and urban planning calling for the return of a "neotraditional," village-oriented urban form (Duany and Plater-Zyberk, 1991).

The contrast between the prototypes of central city and suburb has been shown to be related to some of the main sociological differences within metropolitan populations.

### Social Class

Some of the earliest studies to point up class differences in environmental congruence were those of the English sociologists Michael Young and Peter Willmott, focused on the London area (Willmott and Young, 1960; Young and Willmott, 1957); Herbert Gans for the Boston and New Jersey areas (Gans, 1962b; 1967); and Scott Greer for the Los Angeles area (1962). Although the word *congruence* was not used at this time, these studies concluded that urban working-class families had life styles which were consistent with dense, inner-city neighborhoods with abundant street life, neighborhoods that were often considered slums by middle-class observers. These families had life styles that emphasized local neighborhood interaction, and they relied heavily on nearby kinship networks for social contact and support. One of the interesting findings from this period was that such families, when forced to moved from their urban villages as the result of slum clearance programs, developed feelings akin to grief over the loss of their environments (Fried, 1973). Middle-class families, in contrast, were found to be well adapted to the single-family house areas of the suburbs; their privatized, home-oriented life styles, which relied less on local kinship networks, were congruent with the detached house and private yard. These conclusions have been supported by much research of a more recent vintage (see Fischer, 1982).

### Age, Stage of the Life Cycle, and Gender

Built environment research over the last few decades has convincingly demonstrated the fairly obvious fact that people's environmental needs change as they go through life. The environment best suited to the child is not the one desired by teenagers; and the environment best suited to the single adult is not the one preferred by the family with young children (Michelson, Levine, and Michelson, 1979; Michelson, Levine, and Spina, 1979; Weinstein and David, 1987; Wohlwill and van Vliet--, 1985). In general, lower-density, less stimulating environments are thought by many to be better suited to children, and higher-density environments are often favored by teenagers and by young, single adults. The geographic pattern of residence in cities and suburbs reflects such considerations, with families more often found in suburban locales and singles nearer the central city. In American cities, due in part to safety concerns accompanying high crime rates, this pattern is exaggerated over what it is in many other Western societies; families with children and also the elderly seek to live far from center cities and their high crime rates.

If density falls too low, however, the stimulus necessary for personal intellectual growth can become inadequate, and accessibility to necessary services and facilities in such areas as health, education, and welfare can become a serious problem. Much of environmental congruence, of course, rests on the availability of those facilities and services that a particular age group desires and needs; this is particularly true for the elderly (Altman et al., 1984; Cohen and Weisman, 1991; Huttman, 1977).

Determining congruence goes well beyond the assessment of individual preferences, however; there are multiple perspectives from which congruence may be viewed. For example, teenagers may desire a rich environment in which they have maximum freedom of movement, yet from society's point of view the best environment is one tempered by considerations of social control. It also is the case that because households often contain people of many different ages, some household members may be congruent with the environment in which they live, while others are not. The environment that is best to children may be stultifying to their teenage brothers and sisters, to say nothing of their mothers and fathers. Also, every environment represents a compromise; it maximizes some human opportunities while minimizing others.

The problems of designing congruent environments show up clearly when considering gender. Gender is a variable in which there is not much urban residential differentiation, with the exception of homosexual sub-communities; men and women tend strongly to live together in the same areas (smaller spaces within these areas can be highly "gendered," however; see Spain, 1992). Yet areas that are deemed suitable for men may not be so for women. There is some evidence, for example, that low-density suburbs are more supportive of the typical desires and social roles of men than of women (Michelson, 1977, 1985; Popenoe, 1977; Rothblatt and Garr, 1986; *Sociological Focus*, 1985; van Vliet--, 1989). To many men, the suburb is a desirable place of refuge from the tense work day. Their love of driving makes heavy reliance on the automobile less onerous, and they often enjoy the home maintenance and repair that come with an owned house. To the suburban housewife, in contrast, the large house can be a physical drain and the suburban community a bore; to the working wife, the suburb can generate real problems of accessibility to services and employment opportunities, not the least as men are more likely to claim first right to family transportation resources. For these reasons, low-density suburbs have been the frequent focus of feminist criticism (Altman and Churchman, 1994; Andrew and Moore-Milroy, 1988; Eichler, 1995; Friedan, 1963; Hayden, 1984; van Vliet--, 1989; Wekerle, 1984).

An irony of the wave of postwar suburbanization has been the impact of efforts of central-city interests to counter the exodus of development activity and capital with projects which focus heavily on upscale development, tourism and conventions, and recreational facilities (Logan and Molotch, 1987). Expensive hotels, restaurants, and boutiques, condominia, convention centers, and domed stadiums, for example, do little for the population of the poor, of minorities, and of the elderly, (who account for a disproportionate number of central-city residents) except to ratchet up the cost of housing and other aspects of living. It is no wonder that the number of homeless persons has mushroomed at the same time that strenuous efforts have been made to improve the tax base of central cities with impressive artifacts.

It is partly because the "most congruent" environment varies so much among different types of people that metropolitan areas in advanced societies have become so residentially differentiated in terms of life styles, with groups of Yuppies, families, the elderly, homosexuals, singles, and working-class ethnics each inhabiting their own special segments of the metropolis. This hyper-differentiation into homogeneous sub-areas is enhanced by general affluence and the advanced technologies of transportation and communication. What is congruent for each group, however, may not add up to a metropolitan environment that is in the best interests of the civic body as a whole.

## Other Kinds of Intrametropolitan Differences

The impact of differing macro-environments at a level more subtle than the central-city–suburban dichotomy has also been the focus of important research. The study by Gregory Weiher (1991) noted earlier, for example, which directs attention to the importance of the municipality in accounting for differential residential selection, is pertinent to ecological differentiation *within* the suburban areas of large cities. His study was of the band of suburbs surrounding St. Louis, Missouri. Weiher argues that the individual suburban municipalities are sufficiently different from one another that people consciously choose to live in one or another based on their unique patterns of physical and social attributes. Residential choice is not just between St. Louis and Kansas City (or some other metropolis) or between "the city" and "the suburbs."

Even a municipality largely lacking in many positive attributes can be actively chosen by some people if thought to enable living at a significantly lower cost. For example, in the Toronto area study also cited earlier (Michelson, 1997), the two suburban regions were largely viewed alike on positive attributes, but only one of them was thought by its residents to be "better" than other areas in terms of the price of available housing (by 72% in the Durham Region, compared to 30% in the Regional Municipality of York).

A much earlier study by Clark (1966) provided a qualitative appreciation of major differences among newly developing suburbs, also in the greater Toronto area. His descriptions, for example, of the differences between what he called packaged suburbs, pure suburbs, and cottage suburbs strongly reflect degrees of site planning, housing type, integration of land-uses, and institutional density, along with accompanying differences in the socio-demographic characteristics of persons choosing to live in them.

The 40 different types of local areas cited by Abu-Lughod (1991) clearly represent ecological differentiation *within* both central cities and suburbs. While some generalizations about city-suburban differences may be justified (e.g., gender-related implications), there are certainly different social worlds existing within both sides of the supposed dichotomy, each carrying with it a particular set of contextual contingencies relevant to everyday life.

Kilmartin (1996) applies the term *locational disadvantage* to the situation of some sub-areas of otherwise booming urban regions. All suburban areas don't suffer from locational disadvantage, and some central-city areas do. Newly built areas of housing, but with a paucity of institutions and local jobs, can be locationally disadvantaged; so can older areas whose jobs and hence tax bases have been eroded by technological change and globalization. Both cases represent a context in which access to the means of livelihood, transportation, sustenance, public recreation, and socialization is limited.

The consequences of locational disadvantage are very real. Individual residents are not necessarily more prone to difficulty than are people living elsewhere, but locational disadvantage presents common difficulties for all residents, which often cycle into further hardships at the aggregate level. Commerce, for example, moves away from disadvantaged areas. Also, individuals living in what get to be known as problem areas are subject to stereotypes, discrimination, and generally poorer treatment by authorities. A vicious cycle, once started, is difficult to change. Better knowledge and recognition of the role which macro-environments play in everyday life is essential to avoid the damaging consequences that stem from sub-areas with locational disadvantage.

## CONCLUSIONS

Long favoring a resolute cultural determinism, sociology has been relatively oblivious to the importance of the built environment in people's lives. Some sociologists have been interested in the way in which people distribute themselves in space, and the way in which cities are built, but few have gone on to analyze the effect of the physical environment on people that results. Those studies that have been done (including many by nonsociologists), however, present convincing evidence that the character of the environment in which people live should by no means be dismissed from social analysis. While any single physical element, such as density or house type, may not be very important on its own, the total gestalt of a built environment clearly has important social implications for those who come in contact with it; and while people's lives may not be governed by environmental exigencies, they certainly are made more or less satisfactory, agreeable, and efficient by environmental form and facilities.

Because people are so diverse in their needs and desires, there can be no single, ideal residential environment or city; but certain basic elements have been identified, by which the quality of any residential environment may be evaluated. The late Kevin Lynch (1981), architect and planner, who thought more about the "good environment" than almost anyone else, suggested that in addition to congruence or fit with human biological and social needs, the good environment should provide *access* (regarded by others as a dimension of fit), *control* (people's ability to modify the environment in desired directions), and *sense* (the degree to which, at the level of meaning, the environment can be perceived and understood). In common pursuit of environmental goals such as these, environmental sociologists, together with urban designers and policy makers, can make a signal contribution to the creation of more livable and humane metropolitan areas.

## REFERENCES

Abu-Lughod, Janet L. 1991. *Changing Cities*. New York: HarperCollins.
Altman, Irwin, and Arza Churchman (eds.). 1994. *Women and the Environment*. New York: Plenum Press.
Altman, Irwin, M. P. Lawton, and J. F. Wohlwill (eds.). 1984. *Elderly People and the Environment*. New York: Plenum Press.
Altman, Irwin, and Ervin H. Zube. 1989. *Public Places and Spaces*. New York: Plenum Press.
Anderson, Stanford (ed.). 1986. *On Streets*. Cambridge, MA: MIT Press.
Andrew, Caroline, and Beth Moore-Milroy. 1988. *Life Space: Gender, Household, Employment*. Vancouver: University of British Columbia Press.
Appleyard, Donald. 1980. *Livable Streets*. Berkeley: University of California Press.
Arias, Ernesto (ed.). 1992. *The Meaning and Use of Housing*. Brookfield, VT: Avebury.

Baldassare, Mark. 1979. *Residential Crowding in America*. Berkeley: University of California Press.

———. 1981. *The Growth Dilemma: Residents' Views and Local Population Change in the United States*. Berkeley: University of California Press.

———. 1986. *Trouble in Paradise: The Suburban Transformation in America*. New York: Columbia University Press Reviews.

Baum, Andrew, and Y. M. Epstein (eds.). 1978. *Human Responses in Crowding*. Hillsdale, NJ: Lawrence Erlbaum Associates.

Baum, Andrew, and P. B. Paulus. 1987. "Crowding." Pp. 533–570 in *Handbook of Environmental Psychology*, edited by in Daniel Stokols and I. Altman. New York: Wiley Interscience.

Bellah, Robert N., R. Madsen, W. M. Sullivan, A. Swidler, and S. M. Tipton. 1985. *Habits of the Heart: Individualism and Commitment in American Life*. Berkeley: University of California Press.

Berger, Bennett M. 1960. *Working Class Suburb*. Berkeley: University of California Press.

Berry, Brian, and John Kasarda. 1977. *Contemporary Urban Ecology*. New York: Macmillan.

Booth, Alan. 1976. *Urban Crowding and its Consequences*. New York: Holt, Rinehart and Winston.

Brown, Barbara B., and Carol M. Werner. 1985. "Social Cohesiveness, Territoriality, and Holiday Decoration: The Influence of Cul-de-sacs." *Environment and Behavior* 17(5):539–565.

Brown, Phil, and Edwin J. Mikkelsen. 1990. *No Safe Place: Toxic Waste, Leukemia, and Community Action*. Berkeley: University of California Press.

Buder, Stanley. 1990. *Visionaries and Planners: The Garden City Movement and the Modern Community*. New York: Oxford University Press.

Calhoun, J. 1962. "Population Density and Social Pathology." *Scientific American* (February):139–148.

Carey, Lynnette, and R. Mapes. 1972. *The Sociology of Planning*. London: B. T. Batsford.

Carlstein, Tommy. 1978. "A Time-Geographic Approach to Time Allocation and Socio-Ecological Systems." Pp. 69–82 in *Public Policy in Temporal Perspective*, edited by William Michelson. The Hague: Mouton Press.

Caulfield, Jon. 1994. *City Form and Everyday Life: Toronto's Gentrification and Critical Social Practice*. Toronto: University of Toronto Press.

Chermayeff, Serge, and C. Alexander. 1963. *Community and Privacy*. Garden City, NY: Doubleday.

Choldin, Harvey. 1978a. "Urban Density and Pathology." *Annual Review of Sociology* 4:91–111.

———. 1978b. "Social Life and the Physical Environment." Pp. 352–384 in *Handbook of Contemporary Urban Life*, edited by David Street and Associates. San Francisco: Jossey-Bass.

Christy, Cathryn. 1994. "Bystander Responses to Public Episodes of Child Abuse." *Journal of Applied Social Psychology* 24:824–847.

Clark, S. D. 1966. *The Suburban Society*. Toronto: University of Toronto Press.

Cochran, Moncrieff, Mary Larner, David Riley, Lars Gunnarsson, and Charles R.

Henderson, Jr. 1990. *Extending Families: The Social Networks of Parents and Their Children*. Cambridge: Cambridge University Press.

Cohen, Uriel, and Gerald D. Weisman. 1991. *Holding on to Home: Designing Environments for People with Dementia*. Baltimore, MD: Johns Hopkins University Press.

Cooper Marcus, Clare, and Wendy Sarkissian. 1986. *Housing as if People Mattered*. Berkeley: University of California Press.

Csikszentmihalyi, Mihaly, and Eugene Rochberg-Halton. 1981. *The Meaning of Things: Domestic Symbols and the Self*. New York: Cambridge University Press.

Donaldson, Scott. 1969. *The Suburban Myth*. New York: Columbia University Press.

Duany, Andres, and Elizabeth Plater-Zyberk. 1991. *Towns and Town-Making Principles*. New York: Rizzoli.

Dunlap, Riley E., and William R. Catton, Jr. 1994. "Struggling with Human Exemptionalism: The Rise, Decline and Revitalization of Environmental Sociology." *American Sociologist* 25:5–30.

Eichler, Margrit (ed.). 1995. *Change of Plans: Towards a Non-sexist City*. Toronto: Garamond Press.

Eisner, Simon, and Arthur B. Gallion. 1992. *The Urban Pattern*, 6th ed. New York: Van Nostrand Reinhold.

Fischer, Claude S. 1976. *The Urban Experience*. New York: Harcourt Brace Jovanovich.

———. 1982. *To Dwell Among Friends*. Chicago: University of Chicago Press.

Fischer, Claude S., R. M. Jackson, A. A. Stueve, K. Gerson, L. M. Jones, and M. Baldassare. 1977. *Networks and Places: Social Relations in the Urban Setting*. New York: Free Press.

Fishman, Robert. 1987. *Bourgeois Utopias: The Rise and Fall of Suburbia*. New York: Basic Books.

Franck, Karen A. 1980. "Friends and Strangers: The Social Experience of Living in Urban and Non-urban Settings." *Journal of Social Issues* 36(3):52–71.

Franck, Karen A., and Sherry Ahrentzen. 1989. *New Households New Housing*. New York: Van Nostrand Reinhold.

Freedman, Jonathan L. 1975. *Crowding and Behavior*. San Francisco: Freeman.

Fried, Marc. 1973. *The World of the Urban Working Class*. Cambridge, MA: Harvard University Press.

Friedan, Betty. 1963. *The Feminine Mystique*. New York: Norton.

Fromm, Dorit. 1991. *Collaborative Communities: Cohousing, Central Living, and Other New Forms of Housing with Shared Facilities*. New York: Van Nostrand Reinhold.

Galle, Omar R., W. R. Gove, and J. M. McPherson. 1972. "Population Density and Pathology: What Are the Relations for Man?" *Science* (April):23–30.

Gans, Herbert J. 1962a. "Urbanism and Suburbanism as Ways of Life: A Reevaluation of Definitions." In *Human Behavior and Social Processes*, edited by A. M. Rose. Boston: Houghton Mifflin. Reprinted in Robert Gutman and D. Popenoe (eds.), *Neighborhood, City and Metropolis*. New York: Random House, 1970, pp. 70–84.

———. 1962b. *The Urban Villagers*. New York: Free Press.

————. 1967. *The Levittowners.* New York: Pantheon.

Garreau, Joel. 1991. *Edge City: Life on the New Frontier.* New York: Doubleday.

Gottdiener, Mark. 1994. *The New Urban Sociology.* New York: McGraw-Hill.

Gove, Walter R., M. Hughes, and O. R. Galle. 1979. "Overcrowding in the Home: An Empirical Investigation of the Possible Pathological Consequences." *American Sociological Review* 44 (February):59–80.

Greer, Scott. 1962. *The Emerging City.* New York: Free Press.

Gutman, Robert. 1972. *People and Buildings.* New York: Basic Books.

Hall, Peter. 1988. *Cities of Tomorrow: An Intellectual History of Urban Planning and Design in the Twentieth Century.* New York: Basil Blackwell.

Hannerz, Ulf. 1969. *Soulside.* New York: Columbia University Press.

Hanson, Susan, and Perry Hanson. 1993. "The Geography of Everyday Life." Pp. 249–269 in *Behavior and Environment: Psychological and Geographical Approaches,* edited by T. Gaerling and R. G. Golledge. New York: North-Holland.

Hawley, Amos. 1981. *Urban Society,* 2nd ed. New York: John Wiley & Sons.

Hayden, Dolores. 1984. *Redesigning the American Dream.* New York: Norton.

Hjärne, Lars. 1986. "Planning for Community in Swedish Housing." *Scandinavian Housing and Planning Research* 3:193–215.

Huttman, Elizabeth D. 1977. *Housing and Social Services for the Elderly.* New York: Praeger.

Hägerstrand, Torsten. 1970. "What About People in Regional Science?" *Papers of the Regional Science Association* 24:7–21.

Jacobs, Jane. 1961. *The Death and Life of Great American Cities.* New York: Random House.

Jain, Uday. 1987. *The Psychological Consequences of Crowding.* Newbury Park, CA: Sage Publications.

Janowitz, Morris. 1967. *The Community Press in an Urban Setting,* 2nd ed. Chicago: University of Chicago Press.

Karp, David A., Gregory P. Stone, and William C. Yoels. 1991. *Being Urban: A Sociology of City Life,* 2nd ed. New York: Praeger.

Kasarda, John, and M. Janowitz. 1974. "Community Attachment in Mass Society." *American Sociological Review* 39:328–339.

Keller, Suzanne. 1968. *The Urban Neighborhood.* New York: Random House.

Kelly, Barbara M. (ed.). 1989. *Suburbia Re-examined.* Westport, CT: Greenwood Press.

Kilmartin, L. A. 1996. "Planning Urban Regions: Social Dimensions." Chapter 4 in *Urban Regions in a Global Context: Directions for the Greater Toronto Area.* Toronto: Centre for Urban and Community Studies, University of Toronto, Major Report 34.

Korte, Charles. 1980. "Urban-Nonurban Differences in Social Behavior and Social Psychological Models of Urban Impact." *Journal of Social Issues* 36(3):29–51.

Krupat, Edward. 1985. *People in Cities: The Urban Environment and Its Effects.* Cambridge: Cambridge University Press.

Latane, B., S. Nida, and D. Wilson. 1981. "The Effect of Group Size on Helping Behavior." Pp. 287–317 in *Altruism and Helping Behavior,* edited by J. P. Rushton and R. M. Sorrentino. Hillsdale, NJ: Lawrence Erlbaum Associates.

Lawrence, Denise L., and Setha M. Low. 1990. "The Built Environment and Spatial Form." Pp. 453–505 in *Annual Review of Anthropology* 19. Palo Alto, CA: Annual Reviews.

Lieberg, Mats. 1995. "Teenagers and Public Space." *Communication Research* 22(6):720–744.

Liebow, Elliot. 1967. *Tally's Corner*. Boston: Little, Brown.

Lofland, Lyn. 1973. *A World of Strangers*. New York: Basic Books.

Logan, John, and Harvey Molotch. 1987. *Urban Fortunes: The Political Economy of Place*. Berkeley: University of California Press.

Lynch, Kevin. 1960. *The Image of the City*. Cambridge, MA: MIT Press and Harvard University Press.

———. 1961. "The Pattern of the Metropolis." *Daedalus* (Winter):79–98.

Lynch, Kevin (ed.). 1977. *Growing Up in Cities*. Cambridge, MA: MIT Press.

———. 1981. *A Theory of Good City Form*. Cambridge, MA: MIT Press.

Lynch, Kevin, and Lloyd Rodwin. 1958. "A Theory of Urban Form." *Journal of the American Institute of Planners* 24:201–214.

Lyon, Larry. 1987. *The Community in Urban Society*. Chicago: Dorsey Press.

Martell, Luke. 1994. *Ecology and Society*. Amherst: University of Massachusetts Press.

Mårtensson, Solveig. 1979. *On the Formation of Biographies*. Lund: Gleerup.

McCamant, K., and C. Durrett. 1988. *Cohousing: A Contemporary Approach to Housing Ourselves*. Berkeley, CA: Habitat Press.

Merry, Sally Engle. 1981. *Urban Danger: Life in a Neighborhood of Strangers*. Philadelphia: Temple University Press.

Michelson, William. 1976 (1970). *Man and His Urban Environment*. Reading, MA: Addison-Wesley.

———. 1977. *Environmental Choice, Human Behavior and Residential Satisfaction*. New York: Oxford University Press.

———. 1984. "Density and Livability—People and Place." Occasional Paper No. 30, Human Settlement Issues. Vancouver: Centre for Human Settlements, University of British Columbia.

———. 1985. *From Sun to Sun: Daily Obligations and Community Structure in the Lives of Employed Women and Their Families*. Totowa, NJ: Rowman & Allenheld.

———. 1988. "Congruence: The Evolution of a Contextual Concept." Pp. 19–28 in *Housing and Neighborhoods: Theoretical and Empirical Contributions*, edited by Willem van Vliet--, Harvey Choldin, William Michelson, and David Popenoe. Westport, CT: Greenwood Press.

———. 1990. "Measuring Macroenvironment and Behavior." Pp. 216–243 in *Methods in Environmental and Behavioral Research*, edited by Robert Bechtel, Robert Marans, and William Michelson. Malabar, FL: Robert E. Krieger Publishing.

———. 1991. "Built Environment as a Mediator of Human Intentions." Pp. 98–107 in *Environment and Social Development*, edited by Toomas Niit, Maaris Raudsepp, and Kadi Liik. Tallinn: Tallinn Pedagogical Institute.

———. 1992. "The Behavioral Dynamics of Social Engineering: Lessons for Family Housing." Pp. 303–325 in *The Meaning and Use of Housing: International*

*Perspectives, Approaches, and Their Applications*, edited by Ernesto G. Arias. Brookfield, VT: Avebury.

———. 1994a. "Everyday Life in Contextual Perspective." Pp. 17–42 in *Women and the Environment*, edited by Irwin Altman and Arza Churchman. New York: Plenum Press.

———. 1994b. "Measuring New Objectives in Suburban Housing." Pp. 253–269 in *Research in Community Sociology*, edited by Dan A. Chekki. Greenwich, CT: JAI Press.

———. 1995. "Housing as Subject and Object: The Place of Surveys in Housing Research." Paper presented to International Symposium on Housing Surveys: Advances in Theory and Methods, Laval University, Quebec City, 5–8 July.

———. 1997. "The Place of the Municipality in Prospective LULU Impact." *Research in Community Sociology* 7:117–140.

Michelson, William, S. V. Levine, and E. Michelson (eds.). 1979. *The Child in the City: Today and Tomorrow*. Toronto: University of Toronto Press.

Michelson, William, S. V. Levine, Anna-Rose Spina, and Colleagues. 1979. *The Child in the City: Changes and Challenges*. Toronto: University of Toronto Press.

Milgram, Stanley. 1970. "The Experience of Living in Cities." *Science* 167:1461–1468.

Mitchell, R. E. 1971. "Some Social Implications of High-Density Housing." *American Sociological Review* 36:18–29.

Morris, R. N. 1968. *Urban Sociology*. New York: Praeger.

Muller, Peter. O. 1981. *Contemporary Suburban America*. Englewood Cliffs, NJ: Prentice-Hall.

Mumford, Lewis. 1961. *The City in History*. New York: Harcourt, Brace and World.

Murray, Charles A. 1983. "The Physical Environment and Community Control of Crime." Pp. 107–122 in *Crime and Public Policy*, edited by James Q. Wilson. San Francisco: ICS Press.

National Research Council. 1974. *Toward an Understanding of Metropolitan America*. San Francisco: Canfield Press.

Newman, Oscar. 1972. *Defensible Space*. New York: Macmillan.

———. 1980. *Community of Interest*. Garden City, NY: Anchor Press/Doubleday.

Newman, Oscar, and K. Franck. 1980. *Factors Influencing Crime and Instability in Urban Housing Developments*. New York: Institute for Community Design Analysis.

Nisbet, Robert A. 1969. *The Quest for Community*. New York: Oxford University Press.

Oldenburg, Ray. 1989. *The Great Good Place: Cafes, Coffee Shops, Community Centers, Beauty Parlors, General Stores, Bars, Hangouts, and How They Get You Through the Day*. New York: Paragon House.

Parkes, Don, and Nigel Thrift. 1980. *Times, Spaces, and Places*. New York: John Wiley & Sons.

Piliavin, J. A., J. F. Dovidio, S. L. Gaertner, and R. S. Clark III. 1981. *Emergency Intervention*. New York: Academic Press.

Popenoe, David. 1977. *The Suburban Environment: Sweden and the United States.* Chicago: University of Chicago Press.

———. 1979. "Urban Sprawl: Some Neglected Sociological Considerations." *Sociology and Social Research* 62(2):225–268.

———. 1985. *Private Pleasure, Public Plight: American Metropolitan Community Life in Comparative Perspective.* New Brunswick, NJ: Transaction Books.

———. 1990. "The Political Culture of Metropolitan Communities in the United States: A Cross-National Perspective." Chapter 2 in *Research in Community Sociology: Volume I—Contemporary Community Change and Challenge*, edited by Dan A. Chekki. Greenwich, CT: JAI Press.

Poyner, Barry. 1983. *Design Against Crime: Beyond Defensible Space.* London: Butterworths.

Rothblatt, Donald N., and Daniel J. Garr. 1986. *Suburbia: An International Assessment.* New York: St. Martin's Press.

Sadalla, Edward K. 1978. "Population Size, Structural Differentiation and Human Behavior." *Environment and Behavior* 10(2):271–91.

Sampson, Robert J. 1988. "Local Friendship Ties and Community Attachment in Mass Society: A Multilevel Systemic Model." *American Sociological Review* 53(5):766–779.

Sampson, Robert J., and W. Byron Groves. 1989. "Community Structures and Crime: Testing Social Disorganization Theory." *American Journal of Sociology* 94(4):774–802.

Sassen, Saskia. 1990. "Economic Restructuring and the American City." Pp. 465–90 in *Annual Review of Sociology* 16. Palo Alto, CA: Annual Reviews.

Schwartz, Barry (ed.). 1976. *The Changing Face of the Suburbs.* Chicago: University of Chicago Press.

———. 1980. "The Suburban Landscape: New Variations on an Old Theme." *Contemporary Sociology* 9(6):640–650.

Sennett, Richard. 1970. *The Uses of Disorder: Personal Identity and City Life.* New York: Alfred A. Knopf.

———. 1994. *Flesh and Stone: The Body and the City in Western Civilization.* New York: Norton.

Silverman, Carol J. 1986. "Neighboring and Urbanism: Commonality versus Friendship." *Urban Affairs Quarterly* 22:312–328.

Simmel, Georg. 1970 (1905). "The Metropolis and Mental Life." Pp. 777–787 in *Neighborhood, City and Metropolis*, edited by Robert Gutman and David Popenoe. New York: Random House.

Skogan, Wesley G. 1990. *Disorder and Decline: Crime and the Spiral of Decay in American Neighborhoods.* New York: Free Press.

Skogan, Wesley G., and M. G. Maxfield. 1981. *Coping with Crime: Individual and Neighborhood Reactions.* Beverly Hills, CA: Sage Publications.

*Sociological Focus.* 1985. "Structured Environments and Women's Changing Roles." 18(2) (special issue).

Spain, Daphne. 1992. *Gendered Spaces.* Chapel Hill: University of North Carolina Press.

Stokols, Daniel. 1995. "The Paradox of Environmental Psychology." *American Psychologist* 50:821–837.

Suttles, Gerald D. 1968. *The Social Order of the Slum*. Chicago: University of
    Chicago Press.
————. 1972. *The Social Construction of Communities*. Chicago: University of
    Chicago Press.
Taylor, Ralph. B., and S. Gottfredson. 1986. "Environmental Design, Crime, and
    Prevention." Pp. 387–416 in *Communities and Crime*, edited by Albert. J.
    Reiss, Jr., and M. Tonry. Chicago: University of Chicago Press.
Thorns, David. 1976. *The Quest for Community: Social Aspects of Residential
    Growth*. London: Allen & Unwin.
van Vliet--, Willem. 1989. *Women, Housing and Community*. Brookfield, VT:
    Gower.
Warren, Roland L. 1972. *The Community in America*. Chicago: Rand McNally.
Webber, Melvin M. 1963. "Order in Diversity: Community without Propinquity."
    Pp. 791–811 in Robert Gutman and D. Popenoe (eds.) (1970), *Neighbor-
    hood, City and Metropolis*. New York: Random House.
Weiher, Gregory. 1991. *The Fractured Metropolis: Political Fragmentation and
    Metropolitan Segregation*. Albany: State University of New York Press.
Weinstein, Carol S., and Thomas C. David (eds.). 1987. *Spaces for Children: The
    Built Environment and Child Development*. New York: Plenum Press.
Wekerle, Gerda R. 1984. "A Woman's Place Is in the City." *Antipode* 16(5):11–
    19.
Wellman, Barry, Peter Carrington, and Alan Hall. 1988. "Networks as Personal
    Communities." Pp. 130–184 in Barry Wellman and S. D. Berkowitz (eds.),
    *Social Structures*. Cambridge: Cambridge University Press.
Wellman, Barry, and Scot Wortley. 1990. "Different Strokes from Different Folks:
    Community Ties and Social Support." *American Journal of Sociology* 96:
    558–588.
White, Morton, and Lucia White. 1962. *The Intellectual versus the City*. New York:
    Mentor Books.
Whyte, William H. 1988. *City: Rediscovering the Center*. New York: Doubleday.
Willmott, Peter, and M. Young. 1960. *Family and Class in a London Suburb*.
    London: Routledge & Kegan Paul.
Wirth, Louis. 1938. "Urbanism as a Way of Life." *American Journal of Sociology*
    44:3–24. Reprinted in R. Gutman and D. Popenoe (eds.) (1970), *Neighbor-
    hood, City and Metropolis*. New York: Random House, pp. 54–68.
Wohlwill, Joachim F., and W. van Vliet-- (eds.). 1985. *Habitats for Children: The
    Impacts of Density*. Hillsdale, NJ: Lawrence Erlbaum Associates.
Wolfinger, Nicholas. 1994. "Reexamining Personal and Situational Factors in
    Drunk Driving Interventions." *Journal of Applied Social Psychology* 24:
    1627–1639.
Young, Michael, and P. Willmott. 1957. *Family and Kinship in East London*. Lon-
    don: Routledge & Kegan Paul.
Zukin, Sharon. 1995. *The Cultures of Cities*. Cambridge, MA: Blackwell.

*Chapter 6*

# Designing the Built Environment

*Leslie Kilmartin*

## INTRODUCTION

Some years ago, the development of a neutron bomb was proposed. This device would have the capacity to destroy life while preserving the built environment. Imagine instead a device which could achieve the opposite effect, that is, the preservation of life and the destruction of the built environment. A little reflection of this fanciful scenario reveals the utter dependence of humankind on the built environment. The built environment is indeed designed and created to meet human needs, and the more complex the society, the more complex the built environment. To draw upon the Wirthian model, the more people, the more densely settled they are, the more heterogeneous those people, then the more complex will the built environment need to be to support them.

What do we mean by the term *built environment*? For purposes of this review, it is that part of the environment constructed by human intention and effort. Two important features of built environments are the fixed location in space and their relative durability. There are five types of built environment which are central to environmental sociologists. First, there are small-scale behavior settings such as single buildings and behavior settings within buildings (such as offices, apartments, wards, cells, and so on). Within the design professions, these correspond with the focus of architects and interior designers. Second, there are designed spaces around and between single buildings, these constituting the domain of the landscape architect. Third, there are clusters of behavior settings such as neighborhoods, precincts, and special environments such as office, industrial, and technology parks, together with large-scale recreation centers. These may be the province of the architect, the planner, or the urban designer. Fourth, there are metropolitan areas and their major regions which together constitute the field of interest of the urban planner. Finally, there is the system of metropolitan and submetropolitan physical infrastructure such as household services (power, fuel), and the system for transportation of people and goods (roads, public transport networks)and information (telecommunications). These are the domains of the urban planner and the engineer.

Given that modern human life depends so fundamentally on the built environment, it is perhaps somewhat curious that more sociological attention has not been paid to the design, construction, ownership, and control of the built environment. After all, the built environment is intimately connected with and supportive of human affairs, and the processes of its design and construction are inherently social processes underpinned by human intentionality and action (see Logan and Molotch, 1987).

Notwithstanding these obstinate facts, and until very recently, sociology in general had comprehensively ignored the built environment. This curious state of affairs is in large measure attributable to a belief that humans are exempt from environmental constraints, and to an abiding fear among sociologists of being charged with reductionism and environmental determinism (Dunlap and Catton, 1983:115). For environmental sociologists, however, there is no alternative but to confront the question of the role of the built environment in social life.

It will be apparent that the term *built environment* incorporates an enormous variety of human artifacts, even though it is generally taken to include those environments which are settings for human activities. Equally diverse is the term *design* For the sake of simplicity, that term is used interchangeably with *planning*, though generally the two differ in the scale of activity referred to. Design is usually reserved for the small-scale such as work environments (offices, factories, and other interiors), residential units, houses, apartments and other single-building structures typified by the work of architects. Planning refers to large-scale activities such as neighborhood units, regional and metropolitan planning. Urban design is an activity which attempts to bridge the gap between architecture and planning, and is increasingly promoted as a new professional activity concerned with aesthetic and experiential aspects of the form of large-scale urban developments (Hack, 1984:127).

It is contended that sociology has two important roles in relation to the design and construction of the built environment. The basic content of such a focus is the understanding that the design and construction of the built environment are fundamentally social processes, for they involve human intention and social organization intended to design, construct, and allocate resources. It is assumed that these resources have the ability to promote or inhibit human well-being, to advance or impede life chances, and to promote or diminish the efficiency of social organization.

Second, sociology has the potential to inform the design and construction of the built environment by drawing upon sociological theory and methodology and the accumulation of empirical findings in the published literature.

Other chapters in this volume are devoted to the impacts of the built environment at both the small scale (Chapter 4) and the large scale (Chapter 5). The focus of this chapter, however, is upon the process of the design of the built environment, and I want to devote particular attention to the role of the environmental sociologist in that process. First, however, it is necessary to explore the sociology of design and to examine briefly some of the wider social forces which may exert significant effects on the design and construction of the built environment. As will be argued later, such factors may constitute central concerns for environmental sociologists engaged in the design of the built environment.

## THE CONTEXT OF DESIGN

Design of the built environment is a complex process of decision making whose dynamics are only superficially understood. One consideration which complicates analysis of the process is the fact that it occurs within a set of contexts which themselves exert degrees of influence on the process and its final outcome. In particular, one may consider the role of cultural, economic, political, and ideological factors, and even fashion. In this section, we shall examine these forces insofar as they bear upon the design of the built environment.

### Ideological Factors

It has been said that all dictators are patrons of architecture. It seems that dictators have an irresistible urge to create physical structures which will symbolize and reinforce their power and their ideology. In his autobiographical account of the Third Reich, Adolf Hitler's architect, Albert Speer, provides an excellent insight into this particular phenomenon. Such developments are possible when power is so concentrated in the hands of a single person or oligarchy that designers can be instructed to do the bidding of the powerful. Under such circumstances, whole cities can be designed or redesigned for ideological ends (Berlin of the Third Reich, and EUR, Mussolini's new town outside of Rome), or even whole societies can be so structured, together with the necessary changes to the built form. A notable and extreme example occurred in the racial segregation of South Africa's urban areas where the authorities employed a program of "organized urbanization." In 1986, 64,180 blacks, described as a "surplus people," were evicted from their homes—which were then bulldozed—and relocated to "homelands" (Bole-Richard, 1987).

Much of the process of urban development has a pervasive ideological content. Policies such as the construction of high-rise flats for public housing were adopted by many Western governments in the belief that society could be altered for the better through the medium of physical design (Dickens, 1990). Whether this is interpreted as a form of physical determinism or social control, it was nonetheless an ideologically and design-driven solution to a perceived problem. But a policy that was seen as progressive in the 1960s has often produced built environments "of a wholly malevolent and undesirable kind" (Dickens, 1990:158).

More benign examples of the physical representation of personal or group ideologies can be found. In a semiotic analysis of the production of Disneyland, Gottdiener (1982) argues that the Disneyland phenomenon ("the happiest place on earth") can be explained in part by Disney's attempt to create a spatial representation of "middle class virtues of small-town American life." Very few individuals, apart from the very wealthy, have the opportunity to create large-scale environments as manifestations of ideological positions. Even in Disney's case, the built environment he created is one without long-term residents. More compelling instances of built environments designed with ideological intent are to be found in the nineteenth-century industrial communities (such as Bournemouth in Britain and Pullman in the United States), and in a wide variety of total institutions. A modern parallel can be drawn with the "designer cities" being constructed in many waterfront redevelopments around the world. These cater almost exclusively to high-income earners, often at the cost of the gentrification of existing, low-income communities. The ideology being expressed in this new landscape of consumption (Cooper, 1993) is that of market capitalism.

Another type of example to fall into the category of ideological bases of design concerns the development of built forms meant to be urban landmarks or urban symbols. Sometimes these structures are purely symbolic with the apparent intention of providing a focus for the collective sentiments of the residents of a particularly urban area (Suttles, 1984). Other examples, such as the development of offices, sporting venues, and other special sites, are designed to serve both a symbolic role and an associated economic role. Bianchini et al. (1992) characterize this type of development as "flagship projects," and they are generally instigated by governments attempting to create an international economic and/or cultural focus for their city or region.

### Technological Factors

The development of new technologies has often affected the design and construction of the built environment. Advances in engineering, for example, water and sewerage provision, allowed the growth of large and dense settlements of human populations. The transition from craft-based to industrial building techniques (Ravetz, 1980) and the development of the elevator were key factors permitting high-rise buildings. More recent technological advances have seen the emergence of "smart buildings" and now offer the prospect of the "wired city" (Brotchie et al., 1985). Design education and design practice are increasingly affected by such developments.

Inevitably, then, the design of the built environment is influenced by the desire of professional designers to employ state-of-the-art technologies. Sometimes these developments are more driven by the desire to satisfy professional curiosity and to meet the needs of designers than by the satisfactoriness of the built environment for users, or by its suitability for local conditions. In this sense, the design of the built environment is subject to changes of fashion in professional practice, such as in the replacement of modernist architecture by postmodernist. Similar observations can be made about planning ideas generated not so much by technological change but by influential ideas which become fashionable in the design professions. Such a change is evident in the fall from favor of high-rise flats in many Western cities after the initial acceptance of this concept.

## Cultural Factors

The most compelling and enduring case for the role of cultural and symbolic factors in the built environment is Walter Firey's monograph *Land Use in Central Boston* (1947). It is, in the view of Suttles (1984:283), one of the most cited and least imitated books in sociology. In his view, this is due to a deficiency of current analyses of urban life which overlook cultural factors and opt, instead, "to treat urban life from the perspective of its end points, that is, from the standpoint of production and consumption" (p. 283). In a similar vein, Agnew et al. (1984:1) criticize "the enduring Western conceit" that "all contemporary cities can be explained by reference to a 'rational' economic calculus of profit and loss for the individual or group." These authors reject such a view and start with the assumption that "culture counts."

Certainly, when one takes a cross-national perspective, the role of culture in design of the built environment becomes clearer. Furthermore, such a role is by no means "residual" as various authors attempt to demonstrate. For example, Walton (1984) argues that it can be shown that culture can evolve in a form which is selectively independent of class interest. How can this occur? Culture for Walton is defined as "collective self portraits, the beliefs and ambitions that conflicting social (class and status) groups develop for themselves in joint action." Thus, genuine cultural interests transcend social-class interests. What is more, such cultural elements can manifest themselves (along with class interests, one assumes) in the physical and social organization of a city.

Walton shows, in the case of Guadalajara in Mexico, that there are four important cultures, all of which have manifestations in the built form. These were a civic culture, the modernity culture, the working-class culture, and the political culture of development.

In a comparative study of house design and use in Australia and England, Lawrence (1987) shows how these two similar but different cultures have evolved different housing forms. Whereas the terraced (row) house is the mode in England, it is the exception in Australia, where the detached bungalow was reported as early as 1825. Furthermore, the two cultures have evolved different arrangements of domestic space, especially around activities associated with the preparations and eating of food, with the separation of laundry activities from others (especially kitchen activities), classification of front and back of houses, classification of day/night, public/private. Lawrence notes that in the traditional English domestic system, dishwashing, laundering, and (sometimes) bathing were considered as one set of activities, all concerned with removal of dirt. In Australia, the kitchen has traditionally been reserved for those activities solely related to the preparation of food and dishwashing. A separate laundry was provided, and a separate bathroom was taken for granted.

In his discussion of local urban cultures, Suttles (1984) brings us back to the question of urban symbols, though not (as earlier) as ideological manifestations but here as manifestations of collective representations of urban residents. Such local cultures develop very slowly and the accumulation of local culture is a matter of age (p. 284). Essentially, there are three interrelated sets of collective representations which may be found in frequent repetition, and which form the basis for an accumulation of a local culture over time. There are collective representations concerning the community's "founders," the notable entrepreneurs and political leaders, and its "character" as represented by a host of catch phrases, songs, and physical artifacts, With the passage of time, there is a progressive "museumization" of these collective representations in the local areas, which aids the process of the maintenance of local culture and which, presumably, provides a foundation for its extension and augmentation. In the postmodern landscapes of consumption, such as the waterfront developments mentioned above, there is a tendency for culture and history to be reinvented and commodified. There is then the real possibility of a dilution and a blurring of "organic" culture with that which has been created as a marketing strategy.

The pro-culture propositions put by both Walton and Suttles are powerfully argued and intended to save the idea of culture from residual or epiphenomenal status. Undoubtedly, such factors are significant in the design and creation of the built environment. However, in the case of the

Western capitalist city, the culture which prevails is very pervasively the culture of market capitalism. It is inevitable, then, that we must consider political and economic factors which will manifest themselves in the design of the built environment.

### Political Factors

It is sometimes argued that the work of design professionals serves the interests of the dominant political grouping at the time (e.g., Lang, 1988: 627). It is by no means difficult, for example, to discern the impact of major political movements such as fascism and Nazism on architecture and urban design (Goodman, 1972:ch IV; Speer, 1970). The impact of industrial capitalism on design and the built environment has been extensively analyzed in recent time. As a consequence, more attention is now directed to the design, production, ownership, and control of the built environment in disciplines such as sociology, geography, and politics. Among these more political approaches, many diverse and competing strands can be identified, though most fall into a neo-Weberian or neo-Marxian perspective. Both of these perspectives attempt to understand urban development by reference to analyses of the society in which development occurs. The city is variously portrayed as a "gigantic resource system" (Harvey, 1973), "a machine to make money" (Feagin, 1982), or as a "growth machine" (Logan and Molotch, 1987; Molotch, 1976). The built environment is, then, part of the dynamic of the contemporary capitalist society.

If the city is a gigantic resource system, the built environment represents a significant resource whose ownership, management, and use will accurately reflect social structures and social processes. Proponents of neo-Weberian perspectives focus on the key urban actors whose role is the design, creation, and allocation of the city's resources, including the built environment. Such actors are called urban managers and urban gatekeepers (Kilmartin et al., 1985), and one relevant category of actors is the designers of the built environment.

Within the neo-Marxian perspective, there are quite marked variations in approach (see Ball, 1986) which cannot be developed here. However, the essentials of a political economy perspective can be taken to be the following:

In the first place, such a perspective proceeds from a class (Marxian) analysis of society. Thus, in examining the phenomenon of cities, the analyst attempts to explain the role of cities and the built environment in class terms. Central questions are: What is the role of the city in the process of capital accumulation and reproduction of labor power? What is the role of the state in urban development and the construction of the built environment? The skill of the capitalist is in creating more resources, making decisions to enhance profit-making activities, and to manipulate the system of externalities.

Fundamental to this view of the city and the built environment, then, is the notion that the city is a focus for the processes of production (of goods, services, etc.), of exchange of these commodities (through the free market), of consumption (of all manner of goods including the built environment), and circulation (of goods, information, people, etc.). What is the role of design in these complex processes? Here, we must proceed with our analysis in terms of the scale of the object being designed. In the first place, the design or planning of whole urban areas or regions is depicted as a process which falls to the urban planner.

Generally, the planner is employed, directly or indirectly, by the state. This gives rise to a view of the state as intervening in and controlling the processes of circulation in order to overcome the tendency of the free market to anarchy, and in order to promote orderliness and efficiency in urban processes. Now emerges the question of whether the state acts to assist capital accumulation or whether it acts autonomously and with evenhandedness with regard to all parties. In general, the neo-Marxian perception assumes that the state is the servant of the capitalist class and that the planner is an agent of the state.

Planning, therefore, is depicted as a thoroughly political process. Harvey (1985:175) summarizes the role of the planner as contributing "to the processes of social reproduction and in so doing the planner is equipped with powers vis-à-vis the production, maintenance, and management of the built environment which permit him or her to intervene in order to stabilize, then create the conditions for 'balanced growth,' to contain civil strife, and factional struggles by repression, co-optation, or integration."

Such a view may strike some, especially planning practitioners, as extreme. Such practitioners tend to possess an alternate, more benign and even progressive perception of their professional role. It would be difficult to refute the assertion, however, that political factors suffuse the practice of planning. Things could hardly be otherwise, given the fact that land and the built environment constitute such valuable urban resources, ownership and control of which cover significant advantage. Such realities inevitably influence the processes of urban planning and the work of planners (Beauregard, 1983). Thus, in his critique of urban-design professionals, Mayo (1988) rebukes those professionals for their lack of critical perspective on their work. He argues that, in practice, they have accepted capitalist assumptions about urban form and urban space, and that this has led to the political colonization of urban design thought (p. 654).

If we now move to the level of the designer of smaller-scale environments—houses, offices, neighborhoods—we can see some slightly different roles. For the capitalist, the built environment is a channel for capital investment and speculation. Unlike other forms of investment, the built en-

vironment is fixed and immovable in space. Thus, while there may be
locational advantages accruing from some investments, there will also be
certain disadvantages. Investment in the built environment is subject to the
same processes as investment in other areas:There will be booms and
slumps in the real estate market and investment will be switched in and
out of the built environment to optimize financial returns. One of the means
for enhancing investment in this sector of the market is its design. Design
often plays an important role in enhancing the values of the built environment, both for its users (use value) and as a medium for accumulation
(exchange value). In a competitive market environment, design professionals need to create "distinctive, novel buildings that will lease faster, for
higher rents and for a longer duration, yielding the eventual occupier a
headquarters rich in 'symbolic capital' accruing from possession of a building designed by a 'name' architect" (Crilley, 1993a:137).

As Crilley (1993b) states, the postmodern architecture of redevelopment
is fully incorporated into the ideological apparatus of place marketing. In
this respect, the design of commercial or symbolic structures, despite the
rhetoric of governments or architectural theory, ultimately serves an economic purpose.

These, then, are some of the more significant factors which impinge on
the processes of design and construction of the built environment, determining what gets built, where, and why. The design process operates within
a system of social, structural, and other constraints. In Western cities, there
is also a complex legal environment of design and the usual commercial
pressures to "get things done." Both clients and users—and governments—
may inject demands for expediency and pragmatism into the process. Any
particular development is more likely than not the result of the interplay
of several factors. Design rarely occurs, therefore, under circumstances
which the designer regards as "optimal." It is against this backdrop of
considerations that the role of the sociologist in design must be viewed.
Only infrequently do sociologists contribute to design. Only infrequently is
design informed by sound sociological theory, data, and methods of inquiry; and it is to these matters that we now turn in an attempt to assess
the contribution that sociology can make to the process of design of the
built environment.

## SOCIOLOGY AND DESIGN

While design and sociology are, on the face of it, both concerned with
behavior and social life, there is a great gulf between the two domains. This
is a matter to which we shall return toward the end of this section. For a
moment, we shall address the role of sociology in the process of design of
the built environment. In particular, I shall be concerned with the four

separate but intimately connected phases of programming, design, impact assessment, and post-occupancy evaluation.

Gutman (1975:219) defines programming as the process through which the requirements of the clients and users are investigated and set to right. It is during this stage that the architect is most likely to call in the sociologist, Gutman writes, for the architect is seeking to understand the objectives of the client or the user and to have an informed opinion on the reasonableness of the means of achieving the clients' and the users' goals (p. 222). Design is the process through which the form and characteristics of the building are developed in response to the information given in the program (Gutman, 1975:219). Impact assessment is the attempt to predict the satisfactoriness of the design from the point of view of the paying clients and the user clients, and to evaluate how well the design meets the programming needs.

The task confronting the sociologist is to evaluate proposed environments in terms of their consonance with sociologically derived standards or other related criteria of evaluation, to suggest spatial forms that might be responsive to user needs, and to suggest ways to obtain information about the adequacy of the plan in terms of the views of the probable user (Gutman, 1975:225). Post-occupancy evaluation is the process of evaluating the built environment from the point of view of the paying clients and the user clients once the built form is in use. Each of these phases informs the other and the processes outlined above are, ideally, cyclical.

What, then, is the role of sociology in these processes? At base, sociology is a discipline which seeks to apply rigorous techniques of inquiry to social phenomena. Sociology is a research-based activity which has as its ultimate goal the understanding of human behavior and social processes, and it therefore seeks to develop systematic methods of inquiry to generate cumulative knowledge in these domains. Thus sociology, like any other scientific form of inquiry, offers to designers theories which may be applied to the understanding of human behavior and social life insofar as these relate to the interests of designers. As well, it has a large body of empirical findings which shape its theories and which may also be applied usefully to the process of design. Finally, sociology has developed an impressive armamentarium of methodological techniques which facilitate its quest to accumulate empirical knowledge. These tools of theory, data, and techniques are what the sociologist brings when participating in design of the built environment.

Given the foregoing, the roles adopted by the sociologist who participates in design can include the following.

### Clarifying Assumptions

In general, design is intended to serve human needs, most obviously in the design of houses, work places, recreational areas, and so on. Even the

designs of monuments and other noninhabited structures eventually become the objects of human perception and evaluation. As a consequence
of this consideration, most designs incorporate theories about social processes and human behaviors, whether the designer makes these overt or
covert. The sociologist has the task of identifying these assumptions at the
programming and design phases. One of the greatest sources of debate,
then, between sociologists and designers centers upon the role of the built
environment in influencing human behavior and social processes. The view
of many designers that their work goes beyond simply providing pleasure
to those who view and use their work, and actually changes users, is one
that has drawn sharp criticism from social scientists. Those who adopted
such views were accused of committing the fallacy of physical determinism.
What is physical determinism and what does sociology have to say about
it?

In the 1950s and 1960s, social scientists identified a new orthodoxy,
namely, the view that the built environment could exert no influence on
human behavior or social life. The argument was based on the Durkheimian premise that social facts are explicable only in terms of other social
facts. Thus, the built environment, not being a social phenomenon, could
not be employed to explain social phenomena. Pioneering the identification
of the so-called "fallacy of physical determinism" were Herbert Gans
(1968) in the United States and Maurice Broady (1968) in the United Kingdom. So influential did this view become that little sociological study was
undertaken on environment/behavior relations for two decades. Even now,
environmental behavior research is only beginning to shrug off the varieties
of determinism it has been alleged to be guilty of—architectural, environmental, and physical. Increasingly, however, the case is being compellingly
made for a more sympathetic examination of environment–behavior relations, and environmental sociologists are increasingly prepared to agree
that it seems "as naive to believe that spatial organization through architectural form can have a determinative effect in social relations as to believe
that any such relation is entirely absent" (Hillier and Hanson, 1984:ix).

While acknowledging our inadequate understanding of the relation between space and social life, Hillier and Hanson assert that this deficiency
in our knowledge is the chief obstacle to better design (p. xi). Yet a continuing criticism of the design professions is their adoption of the view that
through design they can provide ideal environments, a view rejected by
most sociologists. However, one of the unfortunate implications of the sociologists' attempt to shake their faith in the beneficial effects of design is
to provide designers with a justification for a retreat from a concern for
social justice and for user-oriented design. Instead there has sometimes been
a return to a "design for designers," especially evident in contemporary
postmodernist architecture.

A resurgence of interest in the relations between environment and behavior has occurred over recent years through the fields of environmental

design and environment/behavior research. Progress has, however, been slow. One useful attempt to theorize environment–behavior relations has been that of Karen Franck (1984), in her article "Exorcizing the Ghost of Physical Determinism."

Franck recommends that the term *physical determinism* be avoided altogether, since it is too often employed in simplistic ways. In particular, she shows that there are four common weaknesses in the usual use of the term. In the first place, the term is used in a way which exaggerates the influence of the physical environment on behavior by ignoring or underestimating the influence of other factors. Examples of such a view would be the assumption that the built environment is the *only* factor affecting behavior, and that the built environment is more important than social and cultural factors. Franck argues that the term *physical determinism* should be reserved for such extreme positions, especially the former. The task then for social science is to theorize and undertake research on the more common and less certain cases where the built environment may be assumed to play some role in affecting social life and organization.

The second weakness of the determinist perspective identified by Franck is the assumption that the environment has only direct effects on behavior. Far more likely, she argues, is the proposition that the effects of the built environment are mediated through intervening variables or an effect which occurs as a result of an interaction between an environmental feature and some other factor. An example of the former indirect effects can be seen in the mediating role of the perceptual set of an observer of the built environment. Interaction effects can be illustrated by the combined effects of a physical feature and some social or cultural attribute such as gender or socio-economic status.

The third weakness of the determinist perspective is that it tends to depict human agents as passive, reacting to or submitting to environmental features that are thrust upon them. Yet a wide variety of empirical studies reveal that human beings are not passive in the face of environments, but that they make choices about environments and that they go to great lengths to modify their environments to meet personal, social, economic, and cultural needs. It could also be said that human beings also have a great capacity to adapt to their environments, particularly when change is enforced through natural disasters or other adversity.

The final weakness is the assumption that the features of the physical environment are given and immutable. Instead, it is obvious even to the casual observer that human beings, as mentioned above, invariably modify their environments to meet their life's needs. There is much agreement, Franck asserts, on the existence of a reciprocal relationship between people and the physical environment.

We see, therefore, that we are moving to a more sophisticated conceptual framework for understanding the subtle links between the built environment and human behavior. Environmental sociologists should abandon any defensiveness about the significance of the built environment for social life and work toward a clearer understanding of the undoubtedly subtle relationships that exist. Theorizing and empirical research should be directed toward clarifying those relationships with the ultimate aim of improving the information available to designers of the built environment. The role of the sociologist is to indicate to his/her designer the limit of the impact of environment on behavior. Moreover, we would do well to heed Gutman's (1975:226) advice that instead of asking how the built environment affects behavior, we ask what part the built environment can play in resolving problems at the social system level.

In examining the matter of physical determinism, we have seen how social theory can be developed to aid the process of design. The sociologist, of course, draws upon a vast literature in attempting to inform design. As Pahl (1977:145) notes, the sociologist is both a gatekeeper to the literature and a filterer of it for the benefit of the designer.

### Socio-Behavioral Data Relevant to Design

In addition to development of social theory, the sociologist is involved in collecting and/or analyzing data of relevance to programming and design. For example, in the case of urban design and planning, the analysis of official statistics can shed light on the processes of industrial and office location decision of firms, which have an important impact on the shape of metropolitan areas and on questions of regional planning and development. As well, the sociologist may collect data which is of similar significance. For example, data on journey to work or shopping behavior may have important consequences for planning urban form and services. The sociologist may then contribute to design and planning by identifying and dimensioning the demographic, social, economic, and life-style changes afoot in urban areas (Hack, 1984:128). While sociologists must avoid the temptation to equate their discipline with market research (Pahl, 1977), they should not eschew data when such data may lead to better design and planning outcomes.

Gary Moore (1984:108) argues that more research is needed on the topic of life style and architecture. He identifies several major contemporary social changes, such as the emerging new family types, and argues for more research aimed at identifying the special environmental needs of persons in such families. He poses two questions: First, what are the emerging or desired life-style patterns and what environmental characteristics are needed to support them? Second, how adaptable are our physical environments to the constant changes in the choices we are beginning to be faced with?

## Identifying Users and Their Needs

A third area of involvement for the sociologist lies in the identification of user needs and generally adopting a user orientation. Sociological critiques of design and planning have generally identified two deficiencies. First, it has been argued (as suggested earlier) that design has too often been guided by anticipated evaluations by professional peers. As a consequence, user needs have been downplayed or even overlooked altogether. The community architecture movement has been based, by contrast, on the assumption that "good design requires a dialogue with the users. It is an enabling form of empowerment intended to involve people in decisions about their environment" (Comerio, 1987:19). Second, where designers have attempted to plan for users, they have too often presumed an understanding of user needs and/or have failed to acknowledge the diversity of users' needs and preferences. A misfit or lack of congruence between the built environment and the users is therefore a common outcome. In considering the needs of special populations with respect to the built environment, Zimring et al. (1987:925) conclude:

When examining the accumulation of spaces, ways to get about between them and the rules and timetables associated with their use, it is hardly an exaggeration to observe the customary assumptions behind design reflect the situation primarily of mature, white, economically able, healthy males with wives at home to dedicate themselves to family health and welfare during standard business hours.

The tendencies to design for elite and advantaged users, on the one hand, or for presumed "normal" users, on the other, are unfortunate but widespread practices in the design professions, which sociologists can assist in overcoming.

At the stage of programming, the matter of the ultimate client frequently occurs. Zeisel (1981:35) makes a distinction between "user clients" and "paying clients," and at the programming stage it ought to be made clear whether the design is intended to meet the needs of the paying client or the users. The questions of advocacy occur again immediately. Traditionally, sociologists have taken a user perspective, but it is sometimes necessary to acknowledge that the paying client may so closely dictate the design that it primarily meets his or her needs. In such a situation, it would seem reasonable for the sociologist to point out that without user satisfaction with the built environment, there may be ultimate problems of tenancy turnover, damage, and vandalization, all of which are not desirable from the point of view of any paying client, whether in the public or the private domain. Perhaps a more complex situation arises where there are two or more sets of user clients. Marans and Spreckelmeyer (1981), for example, in their post-occupancy evaluation of a federal office building in Ann Arbor, Michigan, show that the building was used by both office staff and by members of the general public seeking the services offered.

At one extreme, this view raises certain moral issues, in particular that of the right of the sociologist to work as an advocate for users or for some relatively powerless group. Pahl (1977:145) identifies this as one of the roles he was expected to play in a planning team. In his work with planners, he tried to make value judgments which were progressive and not reactionary and which he could defend from the attacks of very clear minds. The question of whether sociologists have any superior knowledge or expertise when the issue of the rights of oppressed and powerless groups are involved is beyond the scope of the present discussion. It suffices for the moment to acknowledge that this is a role sometimes expected of sociologists in design and planning teams. It is not a question which is easily dealt with or which can easily be avoided.

Leaving aside such dilemmas, the sociologist is sometimes employed to facilitate the involvement of users in planning and design. It has long been a criticism of professional designers that they do not live in the buildings and neighborhoods that they design, that they do not work in the offices and factories they design. Increasingly, as Alison Ravetz (1980:270) notes, members of an urbanized society spend more and more of their waking lives in institutions and public places that they have no chance to influence. Moreover, it has often been the case that designers have not sought the views of users in preparing these designs. Leaving aside any professional values which assert the superior knowledge of designers, there are in fact great practical obstacles facing any designer seeking to incorporate user needs in design. Most obviously, the users may not be known or knowable, or the project may be of such a scale (for example, a whole new town) that tapping user and prospective user needs is nearly impossible and most certainly very costly, or the needs of users may be contradictory in quite fundamental ways.

It is almost certainly the case that the smaller the scale of the built environment being designed, the greater can be the participation of users and potential users. Thus, the innovative work of psychologists and architects at the Laboratory for Architectural Experimentation in Lausanne, Switzerland (Lawrence, 1987) allows users and architects to simulate built forms at full scale in the design phase. Such a technique is, of course, most applicable in the case of affluent persons designing a free-standing residence. However, its possibilities should also be explored for low-income tenants who are required to live in high-density housing.

As the scale of the proposed built environment increases, however, the problems of including large numbers of potential residents is usually too great to permit any meaningful participation. In such cases, small groups of surrogates may be used in determining potential user needs and preferences. Whatever the scale of the proposed development, the role of the sociologist is to devise means for accurately translating the needs of users—and including groups of users with special needs by virtue of social attribute—for incorporation by the designers.

The identification of users and their needs is, as Gans (1983:313) suggests, ultimately a political issue since built environments can rarely by designed to satisfy the needs of all users. At some stage decisions are made which, whether intended or not, will favor the interests of some users ahead of others, or the interests of the paying client ahead of some or all of the user clients. This is a conclusion also reached by Churchman and Ginsburg (1984). In addressing the question of varied and contradicting group preferences, they see a role for the socio-behavioral scientist in informing planners of potential conflicts between meeting the needs of disparate groups, for example, in mass housing projects. The designers should attempt to minimize these impacts while acknowledging the limitations of the effects of design. If design cannot be used to promote positive social contacts, it may still be useful in reducing those elements that cause conflicts between neighbors. In the final analysis, however, the designer may have no alternative but to choose one group's needs over those of others in a "conscious and informed manner" (p. 63).

### Impact Assessments

Once the designer has completed one or more designs intended to meet the goals identified in the programming phase, a process of design review or impact assessment occurs. This is the stage where an attempt is made to identify the likely impacts of the built environment, once constructed. It also allows an opportunity to assess the likely impacts during the construction phase. Here the work, whether it be of social scientists or other professionals, will be somewhat speculative. Nonetheless, techniques of impact analysis have been refined (see Chapter 13 in this volume) and provide a basis for some system rigor.

In Gutman's view (1975:225) predicting social consequences of built environments is potentially the most significant contribution of the sociologist. He also acknowledges that this is the contribution we are least able to do well.

### Evaluating Built Environments

As we have seen, designs for built environments are intended to achieve one or more goals which the programming phase identifies. Once the design has been implemented and the environment built and occupied, the process of evaluation can commence. By and large, systematic evaluation from the point of view of users of the built environment is the exception rather than the rule. This is regrettable, since good evaluation studies can inform the design process, and presumably, improve it.

Essentially, evaluation of the built environment is the examination of the effectiveness for human users of occupied design environments where effectiveness includes the many ways that physical and organizational factors enhance achievement of personal and institutional goals (Zimring and Reizenstein, 1980:429). The intention of the evaluation, according to these authors, is to improve design, usually in some future instance due to the inability to substantially alter built environments. The evaluation is intended to be used both to improve the local environment and to influence the vast, complex system of users, designer, planners, builders, managers, financiers, and regulators who plan, design, build, occupy, manage, alter, and raze designed environments (p. 430). Since the process involves the systematic analysis of user evaluations and perceptions, the skills of the sociologist are required for this phase.

While the collection and analysis of survey material are the stock in trade of the sociologist, it is important to remember the centrality of the designer from two points of view. First, the designer should collaborate in the preparation of the evaluation study in order to explicate design goals and intended socio-behavioral outcomes. Second, the sociologist's report must be intelligible to the designer if it is to have any effect on future designs.

As indicated earlier, evaluation is the exception rather than the rule. However, systematic, well-planned and well-executed evaluation is even rarer. Marans (1984:118) notes the absence of carefully planned approaches to evaluation, poor research designs, a lack of systematic execution of evaluation studies, failure to operationalize environmental indicators, poor presentation of findings, and lack of generalizability of findings.

Marans and Spreckelmeyer's (1981) evaluation of a federal office is a model of a well-planned and well-executed study which attempts to avoid the deficiencies referred to above. Their findings serve to highlight several important points. First, evaluations of built environments may vary according to the groups surveyed. Thus, Marans and Spreckelmeyer report that three out of four members of the general public thought the building was attractive and deserving of its architectural honors. This contrasted sharply with the views of the occupants of the building, who rated it low both in terms of architectural quality and as a work environment. Second, the findings demonstrated the difficulties faced by designers in achieving social goals through design of the built environment. One of the goals set for design was the creation of a sense of community among the workers in the building. The designers had pinned their hopes for achieving this goal on two design features: a lounge and open light-wells between the adjacent spaces of different federal agency employees. Neither feature was successful in achieving the desired goal, and the authors of this evaluation conclude that "in a building that serves different functions and contains diverse groups of individuals and organizations, fostering a sense of community is an unrealistic objective" (p. 197). Third, the study showed that the failure to implement design features can also be a source of dissatisfaction. The designers had planned for, and the workers had been promised, flexible furniture systems. Instead, old furnishings and improper moveable partitions were used in modern, open offices. This was undoubtedly a cause of user dissatisfaction, presumably because of incompatibility of fittings with the open office style and also because of the unfulfilled promise to workers. This latter cause was all the more unfortunate since, in the planning of the building, the architects had shown great sensitivity to the needs of the occupants in a pre-design user-needs survey.

In summary, the process of systematic evaluation of built environments is a useful but neglected phase of the design process. It provides an opportunity to assess the match between the goals of programming and design, on the one hand, and built environments, on the other. While it is most commonly employed in the case of single buildings, it is applicable to other types of built environments. However, with the increasing commodification of the built environment, particularly with speculative developments, there seems to be less likelihood that nonrentable use value will become an integral part of design.

### Analyzing the Design Process

A final role which the sociologist can usefully play is in assisting to understand the process of design and planning. In a review of types of research useful for design, Hack (1984) argues that it is important to obtain knowledge about effective processes of urban design, and he calls for basic research on how designers' minds work. Lang (1988) believes that one of the major contributions behavioral scientific research can make is in clarifying the normative positions taken by architects and explaining their reasons for doing so. In noting that the process of design is only poorly understood, Purcell and Heath (1982) propose that the methods of the human sciences be applied to the understanding of design processes themselves. The knowledge generated by such research could itself provide opportunities for bridging the applicability gap. In proposing research on process rather than product, Purcell and Heath argue that progress in collaboration is more likely to be furthered by better models of the designing process than by the expansion of knowledge or the translation of that knowledge into terms intelligible to the designer.

While it is undoubtedly the case that research into design and planning processes is likely to bear fruit, it seems unlikely that ignoring the other types of contributions the sociologist can make to the design/planning process constitutes a prudent approach. To concentrate our efforts exclusively on the process will certainly lead to a perception among many practitioners that social science is retreating to an extreme form of nonapplied, analytical activity unlikely to generate findings of much immediate use in design.

Moreover, the study of the design process will inevitably open a window on the many structural forces of a political and institutional kind that are at work on the process of design and planning, which were outlined in the beginning of this chapter. We come, then, full circle in our discussion to rediscover the importance of the contexts in which planning occurs. While it may be possible to draw conceptual distinctions between design and its contexts, in practice those distinctions evaporate. Attempts by some designers and environmental sociologists to deny the contexts of design—political, social, ideological, economic, and so on, are, then, doomed to failure.

## The Two Communities

As we have defined "design," it is clearly the province of the professional designer. It involves processes and skills alien to most social scientists. Where sociology is concerned with analysis, design depends upon synthesis; where sociology is literal, design is visual. Sociology depends upon theory-building and accumulation of knowledge; design depends upon intuition and novelty. Sociological research involves "the systematic analysis of phenomena under conditions allowing facts, laws and theories to emerge and be tested. Design is the application of knowledge to the solution of real work problems" (Moore, 1984:97). Snyder (1984:7) argues that the intellectual tradition of architectural education emphasizes precedent and adaptation rather than knowledge development. The designer mind is in fact almost diametrically opposed to the mind of the sociologist. As Seidel (1982:18) notes, architects harbor quite different ways of looking at problems and different methods of attempting to form solutions.

As far as designers and environment/behavior researchers are concerned, there are "two communities" (Seidel, 1979) that are increasingly operating in different spheres, giving rise to the so-called "applicability gap" (Purcell and Heath, 1982; Seidel, 1982). Why does this gap persist? Essentially, design and research are rather different cognitive processes. Brill and Villecco (quoted in Bender and Parman, 1984) argue that environmental/design research can usually be distinguished from design practice in a number of significant ways: First, design is unique; its products are singular and its methods less important than its results. Design is product-oriented; it is justified as the solution to a problem and the method needs not be replicated for evaluation. Design practice frequently welcomes intuitive leaps as it seeks to resolve the complexity of program and context into a single form. Its values are implicit in its product and its evaluation qualitative as well as quantitative.

Second, environment/design research, on the other hand, is concerned with the frameworks for all the activities that affect design, which allow evaluation and design to take place within a rational context. Research is both process- and product-oriented. The process must be replicable and its methods documented as a basis for evaluation of each research project's internal validity. It takes a specialized view of the world in order to push at limits and to new levels of understanding. It is exclusive, rather than inclusive, by nature. The purpose of research is to advance the state-of-the-art of design; and, while intuitive leaps used to create knowledge are an accepted or even preferred method in design, in research intuition must be tested for its utility against specific research objectives. Environmental/design research is not singular, but concerned with sets of cases and generic application; it must be generalizable to more than a unique situation.

Some authors argue that designers are becoming more sympathetic to research, especially environment/behavior research. King (1984:29), for example, asserts that there is relative unanimity that more and better research is needed by the architectural community. The facts appear, however, to contradict this view. Blau (1984:85), in discussion of the acceptance of widespread physical determinism among architects, claims that they are not very receptive to the findings of social research. King himself (1984:33) quotes a study conducted for the American Institute of Architects Research Corporation which acknowledges at the outset that:

1. Little relevant research exists on people in their environment.
2. The traditional design perspective has not easily integrated such research.
3. The field (environment/behavior research) is not recognized by most designers, clients, or researchers as a normal professional service.

With respect to point 2, we have already noted that designers and researchers have quite different agendas and modi vivendi. Design is often guided by the designer's attempt to provide a novel, unique solution to the paying client's problem. The quest for originality, in the view of the designer, obviates the need for social science theory, data, and methods. As Blau (1983:9) argues, architecture has potentialities beyond the banalities of existing form and these potentialities can be realized through visionary means, never by means of empirical social science research on existing forms and people's preferences. Likewise, according to Blau, social science is unable to deal with the uniqueness of place that characterizes every design problem. Perhaps points 1 and 3 are interrelated. If it is the case that there is little relevant research on people and their environments, of course the usefulness and legitimacy of environment/behavior research is in doubt. Is there a body of relevant research? An increasing number of design professionals are questioning the usefulness of social science in informing the design process (Pressman and Tennyson, 1983).

## Bridging the Applicability Gap

It is undoubtedly the case that sociologists and behavioral scientists have been tardy in developing their disciplines with the needs of designers and planners in mind. The socio-behavioral sciences have had their own internally generated research agendas, which have only infrequently been informed by interaction with design practitioners. That situation is now being improved with the emergence of professional associations representing both designers and researchers (for example, Environmental Design Research Associates and the International Association for the Study of People and Their Physical Surroundings). Gradually, a research literature is being developed that will meet the criticisms of the report cited above. These cross-professional contacts have also generated a great deal of thinking about possible bases of collaboration, and some new directions are emerging. In his review of methods of increasing environment-behavior research utilization, Seidel (1979:16) identifies three strategies (which he unhelpfully labels "theories").

The first is *communication strategies*. These are the strategies which acknowledge that few design practitioners have the expertise or the desire to grapple with technical research reports by social scientists. The technical jargon, the use of theory, the unfamiliar methodologies, and the use of quantitative data and statistical analysis all render most sociological reports unintelligible to design practitioners. The communication strategies address this problem by presenting reports in language and style familiar to the designer. Such a strategy inevitably places new responsibilities on the sociologist to prepare reports with practitioners in mind rather than sociological colleagues. Commonly, this means more everyday language and a more visual than verbal presentation of findings. Of course, there are difficulties in this strategy. In the first place, the bulk of sociologists—even environmental sociologists—will continue to publish in traditional ways and, as Purcell and Heath (1982:12) note, attempts to translate such reports into the language of designers will continue to be rare and unevenly successful. Nonetheless, as Purcell and Heath acknowledge, there have been some noteworthy contributions in the area of translation.

The second group of strategies is what Seidel calls *linkage strategies*. This is the use of professionals who can speak the languages of both the researcher and the designer. In this way, the results of research can be translated—not in general, as in communication strategies, but in particular situations where this is necessary. Seidel speaks of "middlemen" as well as the use of advisory committees, opinion leaders, and information transfer specialists. Gans (1983:314) also favors such a strategy, although his solution is to proceed in both directions. He advocates in the first place for the recruitment and training of architects who are "sufficiently sympathetic to, and familiar with, the social sciences, and with the use of social science data in architecture to initiate research." Second, he advocates the recruitment and training of social scientists who are interested in working with architects (p. 314).

Purcell and Heath also favor this double-pronged approach, observing that some of the most effective and fruitful collaboration has been produced by this kind of activity. Nonetheless, there are considerable difficulties facing such a new professional group, not the least of which will be the willingness of clients and practitioners to add to their costs by the inclusion of yet another professional group. This particular difficulty will probably mean that insofar as designers and environment/behavior researchers do work together, it will be as professional collaborators.

Thus, Seidel's third strategy is *collaboration*. This strategy eliminates the need for a specifically identified "middleman" as the linkage strategies require, and lays responsibility for communication directly upon the sociologist participating and collaborating on the project. This strategy can be most fruitful and stimulating for the participants, but it is necessary for collaboration to occur at each phase of the process: programming, design, user impact analysis, and evaluation.

## CONCLUSION

In a review of architectural research, James Snyder (1984) laments the absence of design research to inform the process of design. He argues that there is a growing awareness among building industry participants and the public at large that the built environment too often fails—in aesthetic, functional, social, and economic performance. While this chapter has not attempted to evaluate the performance of the built environment, if Snyder is correct in his assessment, then our discussion sheds some light on the reasons for its failure. In the first instance, there are society-wide forces at work on the design and construction phases which subvert those processes. These may be best understood through the political economy of the built environment or through an understanding of the intrusion of the interests of particular groups on the process. There are also problems more internal to the process of design. In particular, that process is too rarely informed by research, particularly behavioral and social research. An urgent task facing environmental sociology is the development of strategies which will facilitate the penetration of the process of the design of the built environment by socio-behavioral theories and methodologies and established empirical findings. Such strategies will need to acknowledge and address the growing skepticism among design professionals toward the social sciences.

# REFERENCES

Agnew, John A., John Merves, and David E. Sopher (eds.). 1984. *The City in Cultural Context*. Boston: Allen & Unwin.

Ball, M. 1986. "The Built Environment and the Urban Question." *Environment and Planning D: Society and Space* 4:447–464.

Beauregard, Robert A. 1983. "Planners as Workers: A Marxist Perspective." Pp. 183–207 in *Professionals and Urban Form*, edited by Judith R. Blau, Mark LaGory, and John S. Pipkin. Albany: State University of New York Press.

Bender, Richard, and John Parman. 1984. "The Question of Style in Research." Pp. 51–64 in *Architectural Research*, edited by James C. Snyder. New York: Van Nostrand Reinhold.

Bianchini, F., J. Dawson, and R. Evans, 1992. "Flagship Projects in Urban Regeneration." Pp. 245–255 in *Rebuilding the City*, edited by P. Healey, S. Davoudi, M. O'Toole, S. Tavasanoglu, and D. Usher. London: E & F. N. Spon.

Blau, Judith R. 1984. *Architects and Firms: A Sociological Perspective on Architectural Practice*. Cambridge, MA: MIT Press.

Bole-Richard, M. 1987. "South Africa's 'Organised Urbanisation' Disguises Sordid Reality." *The Guardian Weekly* 136(15):13.

Broady, Maurice. 1968. *Planning for People: Essays on the Social Context of Planning*. London: National Council of Social Service.

Brotchie, John, Peter Newton, Peter Hall, and Peter Nijkamp (eds.). 1985. *The Future of Urban Form: The Impact of New Technology*. London and Sydney: Croom Helm.

Churchman, Arza, and Yona Ginsberg. 1984. "The Use of Behavioral Science Research in Physical Planning: Some Inherent Limitations." *Journal of Architecture and Planning Research* 1:57–66.

Comerio, Mary C. 1987. "Design and Empowerment: 20 Years of Community Architecture." *Built Environment* 13(1):15–28.

Cooper, M. 1993. "Access to the Waterfront: Transformations of Meaning on the Toronto Lakeshore." Pp. 140–157 in *The Cultural Meaning of Urban Space*, edited by R. Rotenberg and G. McDonogh. Westport, CT: Bergin and Garvey.

Crilley, D. 1993a. "Megastructures and Urban Change: Aesthetics, Ideology and Design." Pp. 127–164 in *The Restless Urban Landscape*, edited by P. L. Knox. Englewood Cliffs, NJ: Prentice-Hall.

Crilley, D. 1993b. "Architecture as Advertising: Constructing the Image of Redevelopment." Pp. 231–252 in *Selling Places: The City as Cultural Capital, Past and Present*, edited by G. Kearns and G. Philo. Oxford: Pergamon Press.

Dickens, P. 1990. *Urban Sociology: Society, Locality and Human Nature*. Hemel Hempstead: Harvester Wheatsheaf.

Dunlap, Riley E., and William R. Catton, Jr. 1983. "What Environmental Sociologists Have in Common (Whether Concerned with 'Built' or 'Natural' Environments)." *Sociological Inquiry* 53:113–135.

Feagin, Joe R. 1982. "Urban Real Estate Speculation in the United States." *International Journal of Urban and Regional Research* 6(1):35–39.

Firey, Walter. 1947. *Land Use in Central Boston.* Cambridge, MA: Harvard University Press.

Franck, Karen A. 1984. "Exorcizing the Ghost of Physical Determinism." *Environment and Behavior* 16:411–435.

Gans, Herbert J. 1968. *People and Plans: Essays on Urban Problems and Solutions.* New York: Basic Books.

Gans, Herbert J. 1983. "Toward a Human Architecture: A Sociologist's View of the Profession." Pp. 303–319 in *Professionals and Urban Form*, edited by Judith R. Blau, Mark LaGory, and John S. Pipkin. Albany: State University of New York Press.

Goodman, Robert. 1972. *After the Planners.* Harmondsworth: Penguin Books.

Gottdiener, M. 1982. "Disneyland: A Utopian Urban Space." *Urban Life* 11:139–162.

Gutman, Robert. 1975. "Architecture and Sociology." *The American Sociologist* 10:219–228.

Hack, Gary. 1984. "Research for Urban Design." Pp. 125–145 in *Architectural Research*, edited by James C. Snyder. New York: Van Nostrand Reinhold.

Harvey, David. 1973. *Social Justice and the City.* London: Edward Arnold.

Harvey, David. 1985. *The Urbanisation of Capital.* Oxford: Blackwell.

Hillier, Bill, and Julienne Hanson. 1984. *The Social Logic of Space.* Cambridge: Cambridge University Press.

Kilmartin, Leslie, David C. Thorns, and Terry Burke. 1985. *Social Theory and the Australian City.* Sydney: Allen & Unwin.

King, J. 1984. "Research in Practice." Pp. 29–37 in *Architectural Research*, edited by James C. Snyder. New York: Van Nostrand Reinhold.

Lang, Jon. 1988. "Understanding Normative Theories of Architecture: The Potential Role of the Behavioral Sciences." *Environment and Behavior* 20(5): 601–632.

Lawrence, Roderick J. 1987. *Housing, Dwellings and Homes: Design Theory Research and Practice.* Chichester: John Wiley & Sons.

Logan, J. R., H. L. and Molotch. 1987. *Urban Fortunes. The Political Economy of Place.* Berkeley: University of California Press.

Marans, Robert W. 1984. "Evaluation Research in Architecture." Pp. 113–124 in *Architectural Research*, edited by James C. Snyder. New York: Van Nostrand Reinhold.

Marans, Robert, and K. Spreckelmeyer. 1981. *Evaluating Built Environments: A Behavioral Approach.* Ann Arbor: University of Michigan Press.

Mayo, James M. 1988. "Urban Design as Uneven Development." *Environment and Behavior* 20:633–663.

Molotch, Harvey. 1976. "The City as a Growth Machine: Toward a Political Economy of Place." *American Journal of Sociology* 82:309–332.

Moore, Gary T. 1984. "New Directions for Environment-Behavior Research in Architecture." Pp. 95–112 in *Architectural Research*, edited by James C. Snyder. New York: Van Nostrand Reinhold.

Pahl, R. E. 1977. "Playing the Rationality Game: The Hired Hand as Expert."

Pp. 130–148 in *Doing Sociological Research*, edited by Colin Bell and H. Newby. London: Allen & Unwin.

Pipkin, John S., Mark La Gory, and Judith R. Blau. 1983. "Introduction." Pp. 1–12 in *Professionals and Urban Form*, edited by Judith R. Blau, Mark La Gory, and John Pipkin. Albany: State University of New York Press.

Pressman, N., and J. Tennyson. 1983. "Dilemmas Facing Social Scientists and Designers." *Journal of Architectural Education* 36:16–21.

Purcell, Terry, and Tom Heath. 1982. "The Two Communities: Is There a Common Focus for Designer-Researcher Collaboration?" Pp. 3–15 in *Knowledge for Design*, edited by Polly Bart, Alexandra Chen, and Guido Francescato. Proceedings of the Thirteenth International Conference of the Environmental Design Research Association (EDRA), College Park, Maryland.

Ravetz, Alison. 1980. *Remaking Cities: Contradictions of the Recent Urban Environment*. London: Croom Helm.

Seidel, A. D. 1979. "Our Concern for Research Utilisation Continues." Pp. 219–223 in *Environmental Design: Research, Theory and Application*, edited by A. D. Seidel and S. Danford. Proceedings of the Tenth Annual Conference of the Environmental Design Research Association, Washington, DC.

Seidel, A. 1982. "Useable EBR: What Can We Learn from Other Fields." Pp. 16–25 in *Knowledge for Design*, edited by P. Bart, A. Chen, and G. Francescato. Washington, DC: Environmental Design Research Association.

Speer, A. 1970. *Inside the Third Reich: Memoirs*. London: Weidenfeld and Nicholson.

Suttles, Gerald D. 1984. "The Cumulative Texture of Local Urban Culture." *American Journal of Sociology* 90:283–305.

Snyder, James C. (ed.). 1984. *Architectural Research*. New York: Van Nostrand Reinhold.

Walton, John. 1984. "Culture and Economy in Shaping of Urban Life." Pp. 76–92 in *The City in Cultural Context*, edited by John A. Agnew, John Mercer, and David E. Sopher. Boston: Allen & Unwin.

Zeisel, John. 1981. *Inquiry by Design: Tools for Environment Behaviour Research*. Cambridge: Cambridge University Press.

Zimring, Craig M., and Janet E. Reizenstein. 1980. "Post-Occupancy Evaluation: An Overview." *Environment and Behavior* 12:429–450.

Zimring, Craig M., Janet E. Reizenstein-Carpman, and William Michelson. 1987. "Design for Special Populations; Mentally Retarded Persons, Children, Hospital Visitors." Pp. 919–949 in *Handbook of Environmental Psychology*, Vol. 2, edited by Daniel Stockols and Irwin Altman. New York: John Wiley & Sons.

*Chapter 7*

# Rural Environments and Agriculture

*Don E. Albrecht and Steve H. Murdock*

## INTRODUCTION

A vast majority of the land area in the United States, as well as the rest of the world, can be defined as rural. This means that it has relatively low population densities and lacks the residences, highways, industries, and commerce of urban areas. In fact, of the 3,618,770 square miles that comprise the United States, about 1 percent are urbanized. Obviously, the environmental conditions of the 99 percent of the land area that make up rural America, and changes that occur therein, are vitally important to all Americans.

Agricultural lands comprise a significant proportion of the rural land area of the United States as shown by the fact that in 1992, 1,477,391 square miles (41 percent) of the total land in the United States was in farmland. Within the conterminous 48 states, over 50 percent of the total land area was in farms in 1992. The environmental conditions of the nearly 1.5 million square miles of American farmland are critical because this land produces the majority of the sustenance on which we depend; the environmental problems originating on agricultural lands and from modern agricultural practices directly and/or indirectly affect all Americans, and are some of the most severe environmental and socio-economic problems that must be addressed in the coming decades (Bird et al., 1995; Buttel et al., 1981).

As with many other sociological subdisciplines, research in the sociology of agriculture has only recently begun to explore the effects of environmental factors on social phenomena. This is somewhat surprising because agriculture, more than virtually any other industry, is so closely tied to and directly dependent upon the natural environment (Albrecht and Murdock, 1990, Dunlap and Martin, 1983). However, like the rest of the discipline, researchers in the sociology of agriculture have tended historically to emphasize social and psychological explanations rather than structural or environmental ones (Buttel et al., 1990).

This chapter examines the agricultural environment in several ways. To begin with, we discuss some important component resources of the agricultural environment and how the quantity and quality of these environmental resources influence settlement patterns, carrying capacity and farm structure. This is followed by a discussion of both the macro- and micro-level consequences of changes in the availability of these critical natural resources, and the influence of resources on the adoption of agricultural technology. In the following section the impacts of modern agricultural practices on environmental quality are discussed. Finally, conclusions about the state of the sub-area are delineated, areas not adequately addressed in the existing literature base are noted, and some important questions for future research are suggested.

Obviously, there are numerous other environmental issues related to agriculture that cannot be discussed in this chapter. However, since all of these issues cannot be adequately covered, an effort has been made to select some of the more important ones that give an overview of the breadth of issues that could be covered.

## ENVIRONMENTAL RESOURCES AND AGRICULTURE

Agriculture, more than nearly any other endeavor in industrialized Western society, is very closely tied to the natural environment (Albrecht and Murdock, 1990, Dunlap and Martin, 1983). The quality and quantity of resources present in the environment play a major role in determining which commodities can be produced and the amount of production that occurs. While the number of environmental factors influencing agricultural production is innumerable, it is obvious that some factors are more critical than others. For example, successful agricultural production requires the appropriate combination of several environmental factors including soil, water, and temperature. If these factors are missing or vary too widely, production will either not occur or will be limited to some degree. Although the production of agricultural commodities requires all of these essential resources, the amounts required vary substantially from one commodity to another. For example, wheat can be produced in areas that experience harsh winters and have relatively short growing seasons, while citrus fruits cannot, and rice production requires substantially more water than cotton production. Thus, because of these basic environmental differences, farm production is severely limited in some areas, and certain commodities cannot be effectively produced in other areas.

To provide some indication of the importance of environmental resources in agriculture, two of the more important of such resources (soil and water) will be briefly discussed. The purpose of this discussion is to provide an indication of the importance that natural resources play in agriculture. In describing the relationship between agriculture and the environment, we are not attempting to argue that the environment alone determines agricultural development. Rather, the view taken in this chapter is that the natural environment is a major constraint to agricultural development, but numerous other factors are also important (Dunlap and Martin, 1983; Franck, 1984).

## Soil

Soil is an absolutely essential element in farm production, but one that is both limited and fragile. The thin layer of topsoil covering much of the earth (in most places about six inches thick) has always been, is now, and will likely remain the major source of human sustenance (Sampson, 1981).

The importance of adequate soil resources to a society can be appreciated by examining historical evidence. This evidence suggests that the rise of many of the great civilizations of the past has been founded on an extensive natural resource base and, in particular, an extensive base of fertile soil. A basis of fertile soil allows surplus farm production, which frees part of the population from agriculture and permits some persons to become artisans, engineers, scientists, writers, artists, and so on (Dale and Carter, 1955; Lowdermilk, 1953). However, with few exceptions, humans have not been able to continue a progressive civilization in one locality for more than a few hundred years. This is because the natural resource base (and in particular, the soil base) that permits the surplus production becomes depleted. As the resource is depleted, surplus production decreases and the civilization declines (Brown, 1981). In most cases, the more technologically advanced the civilization, the shorter its period of progressive existence and expansion (Dale and Carter, 1955).

The presence of adequate soil resources has also played a vital role in the historical development of agriculture in the United States. Because transportation capabilities were relatively limited, it was essential that each area of the country be able to produce its own food supply. Consequently, settlement was limited to areas where agricultural production was possible. Further, areas that had a rich soil base, if other important resources were adequate, generally attracted a larger farm population.

In the United States, the quality and quantity of soil resources varies extensively from one part of the country to another. About one-third of the land in the United States cannot be used for agricultural production because it is in federal ownership. What remains is about 1.5 billion acres of non-federal land, which varies extensively in the capability of the soil to support

Table 7.1
Percentages of Nonfederal Land in Various Soil Capability Classes by USDA
Farm Production Regions

| Farm Production Region | Land Capability Classes | | |
|---|---|---|---|
| | I–III Suitable | IV Marginal | V–VIII Unsuitable |
| Total | 45 | 13 | 42 |
| Pacific | 25 | 14 | 61 |
| Mountain | 18 | 12 | 70 |
| Northern Plains | 59 | 11 | 30 |
| Southern Plains | 44 | 13 | 43 |
| Lake States | 59 | 23 | 18 |
| Corn Belt | 76 | 10 | 14 |
| Delta States | 55 | 11 | 34 |
| Southeast | 45 | 23 | 32 |
| Appalachia | 43 | 13 | 44 |
| Northeast | 37 | 10 | 53 |

*Source*: Soil Conservation Service (1961, 1982).

intensive cropping. The U.S. Department of Agriculture (USDA) has developed a system, known as the Land Capability Classification System, that categorizes land into eight major classes based on its potential to support crop production without suffering permanent topsoil damage (Soil Conservation Service 1961, 1982). In this classification system, higher values indicate land which can support only limited crop production because of poor quality soils, steep slopes, or for some other reason. Soils that fall into Classes I through III are commonly referred to as land that is "suitable" for cropland; land in Class IV is "marginal"; and land in Class V through Class VIII is "unsuitable." Table 7.1 shows that about 45 percent of the nonfederal land in the United States is suitable for cropland. However, only 3 percent of this land is sufficient to be classified as Class I cropland. The distribution of land suitable for crop production is very unevenly dispersed throughout the country. As shown in Table 7.1, the proportion of nonfederal rural land suitable for crop production varies from a high of 76 percent in the Corn Belt to a low of 18 percent in the Mountain states. These differences are even more extensive than it may appear, because vast amounts of the land most incapable of crop production in the Mountain states are in federal ownership and not considered in this discussion.

In Table 7.2, data are presented which show the total land area (in-

Table 7.2
Farm Population and Gross Farm Sales by Region and State

| Region and State | Total Square Miles | 1990 Farm Population (1,000) | Farm Persons per Square Mile | 1992 Gross Farm Sales ($ million) | Farm Sales per Square Mile |
|---|---|---|---|---|---|
| **Pacific** | | | | | |
| Washington | 68,139 | 60.2 | 0.88 | 3,821 | $ 56,077 |
| Oregon | 97,073 | 68.7 | 0.71 | 2,293 | 23,621 |
| California | 158,706 | 151.5 | 0.95 | 17,052 | 107,444 |
| Total | 323,918 | 280.4 | 0.87 | 23,166 | $ 71,518 |
| **Mountain** | | | | | |
| Idaho | 83,564 | 44.9 | 0.54 | 2,964 | $ 35,470 |
| Montana | 147,046 | 45.7 | 0.31 | 1,730 | 11,765 |
| Wyoming | 97,809 | 15.9 | 0.16 | 824 | 8,425 |
| Utah | 84,899 | 11.7 | 0.14 | 725 | 8,540 |
| Colorado | 104,091 | 45.1 | 0.43 | 4,116 | 39,542 |
| Nevada | 110,561 | 4.8 | 0.04 | 288 | 2,605 |
| Arizona | 114,000 | 7.0 | 0.06 | 1,515 | 13,289 |
| New Mexico | 121,593 | 15.1 | 0.12 | 1,259 | 10,354 |
| Total | 863,563 | 190.2 | 0.22 | 13,421 | $ 15,540 |
| **Northern Plains** | | | | | |
| North Dakota | 70,702 | 60.3 | 0.85 | 2,746 | $ 38,839 |
| South Dakota | 77,116 | 76,2 | 0.99 | 3,244 | 42,066 |
| Nebraska | 77,355 | 117.7 | 1.52 | 8,210 | 106,134 |
| Kansas | 82,277 | 108.1 | 1.31 | 8,316 | 101,073 |
| Total | 307,450 | 362.3 | 1.18 | 22,516 | $ 73,235 |
| **Southern Plains** | | | | | |
| Oklahoma | 69,956 | 68.7 | 0.98 | 3,653 | $ 50,932 |
| Texas | 266,807 | 192.4 | 0.72 | 12,004 | 44,991 |
| Total | 336,763 | 261.1 | 0.78 | 15,567 | $ 46,226 |
| **Lake States** | | | | | |
| Minnesota | 84,402 | 208.0 | 2.46 | 6,477 | $ 76,740 |
| Wisconsin | 56,153 | 195.6 | 3.48 | 5,260 | 93,673 |
| Michigan | 58,527 | 120.5 | 2.06 | 3,029 | 51,754 |
| Total | 199,082 | 524.1 | 2.63 | 14,766 | $ 74,171 |
| **Corn Belt** | | | | | |
| Iowa | 56,275 | 256.6 | 4.56 | 10,100 | $179,492 |
| Missouri | 69,697 | 180.1 | 2.58 | 4,303 | 61,739 |
| Illinois | 56,345 | 207.0 | 3.67 | 7,337 | 130,216 |

*(continued)*

Table 7.2 (continued)

| Region and State | Total Square Miles | 1990 Farm Population (1,000) | Farm Persons per Square Mile | 1992 Gross Farm Sales ($ million) | Farm Sales per Square Mile |
|---|---|---|---|---|---|
| **Corn Belt** (continued) | | | | | |
| Indiana | 36,185 | 188.1 | 5.20 | 4,633 | 128,036 |
| Ohio | 41,330 | 198.9 | 4.81 | 3,914 | 94,701 |
| Total | 259,832 | 1,030.7 | 3.97 | 30,287 | $116,565 |
| **Delta States** | | | | | |
| Arkansas | 53,187 | 63.6 | 1.20 | 4,160 | $ 78,215 |
| Louisiana | 47,752 | 40.1 | 0.84 | 1,608 | 33,674 |
| Mississippi | 47,689 | 56.2 | 1.18 | 2,337 | 49,005 |
| Total | 148,628 | 159.9 | 1.08 | 8,105 | $ 54,532 |
| **Southeast** | | | | | |
| Alabama | 51,705 | 59.3 | 1.15 | 2,369 | $ 45,818 |
| Georgia | 58,910 | 80.1 | 1.36 | 3,521 | 59,769 |
| South Carolina | 31,113 | 48.6 | 1.56 | 1,066 | 34,262 |
| Florida | 58,664 | 47.4 | 0.81 | 5,266 | 89,765 |
| Total | 200,392 | 235.4 | 1.17 | 12,222 | $ 60,991 |
| **Appalachia** | | | | | |
| Kentucky | 40,410 | 174.2 | 4.31 | 2,664 | $ 65,924 |
| Tennessee | 42,144 | 111.7 | 2.65 | 1,934 | 45,890 |
| West Virginia | 24,232 | 23.8 | 0.98 | 364 | 15,021 |
| Virginia | 40,767 | 80.6 | 1.98 | 2,056 | 50,433 |
| North Carolina | 52,669 | 116.8 | 2.22 | 4,834 | 91,781 |
| Total | 200,222 | 507.1 | 2.53 | 11,852 | $ 59,195 |
| **Northeast** | | | | | |
| Maryland | 10,460 | 32.6 | 3.12 | 1,169 | $111,759 |
| Delaware | 2,045 | 6.5 | 3.18 | 560 | 273,839 |
| New Jersey | 7,787 | 17.3 | 2.22 | 533 | 68,447 |
| Pennsyvania | 45,308 | 117.1 | 2.58 | 3,570 | 78,794 |
| New York | 49,108 | 82.3 | 1.68 | 2,622 | 53,393 |
| Connecticut | 5,018 | 5.3 | 1.06 | 337 | 67,158 |
| Rhode Island | 1,212 | 1.1 | 0.91 | 40 | 33,003 |
| Massachusetts | 8,282 | 9.3 | 1.12 | 351 | 42,371 |
| Vermont | 9,614 | 11.8 | 1.23 | 415 | 43,166 |
| New Hampshire | 9,279 | 5.6 | 0.60 | 114 | 12,286 |
| Maine | 33,265 | 11.0 | 0.33 | 430 | 12,926 |
| Total | 181,380 | 299.9 | 1.65 | 10,141 | $ 55,910 |

Table 7.3
Regions of the Country and Rank for Percent of Land That Is Suitable for Crop
Production, Farm Population per Square Mile, and Gross Farm Sales per Square
Mile

| Region | Percent of Nonfederal Land Suitable for Crop Production | (Rank) | Farm Population per Square Mile | (Rank) | Gross Farm Sales per Square Mile | (Rank) |
|---|---|---|---|---|---|---|
| Corn Belt | 76 | (1) | 3.97 | (1) | 116,565 | (1) |
| Lake States | 59 | (2) | 2.63 | (2) | 74,171 | (2) |
| Northern Plains | 59 | (3) | 1.18 | (5) | 73,235 | (3) |
| Delta States | 55 | (4) | 1.08 | (7) | 54,532 | (8) |
| Southeast | 45 | (5) | 1.17 | (6) | 60,991 | (5) |
| Southern Plains | 44 | (6) | 0.78 | (9) | 46,226 | (9) |
| Appalachia | 43 | (7) | 2.53 | (3) | 59,195 | (6) |
| Northeast | 37 | (8) | 1.65 | (4) | 55,910 | (7) |
| Pacific | 25 | (9) | 0.87 | (8) | 71,518 | (4) |
| Mountain | 18 | (10) | 0.22 | (10) | 15,540 | (10) |

cluding federally owned land), total farm population, gross farm sales, farm
population per square mile, and farm sales per square mile by state and
region for the contiguous 48 states. Table 7.3 shows summary data by
region on the proportion of the total land area that is suitable for crop
production, the farm population per square mile, and gross farm sales per
square mile. The purpose of these tables is to show the effect that soil
quality has on agricultural productivity, as measured by the number of farm
people per square mile and gross farm sales per square mile. An examination of Table 7.2 shows that farm populations tend to be most dense in
areas with better soils. The states with the largest farm population per
square mile include the Corn Belt states of Indiana (5.20 farm persons per
square mile), Ohio (4.81), and Iowa (4.56). At the other extreme, all eight
Mountain states have a farm population density of less than 1 person per
square mile, and all but Idaho have a density of less than .5 farm persons
per square mile. These findings show that the farm population of a state
parallels closely the proportion of the land area in the state that is suitable
for crop production.

Gross farm sales per square mile are also closely related to the availability
of quality soil resources. States producing more than $100,000 worth of
agricultural products per square mile tended to be located in areas of more

extensive soil resources in 1992, while production per square mile was much lower in the mountain states where soil suitable for crop production is limited. Iowa was the state where gross farm sales per square mile were highest, at $179,492.

Table 7.3 provides summary data and ranks the regions on the variables previously discussed. This table shows that the Corn Belt had the highest proportion of its land area with soil suitable for crop production (76 percent); and this area also had the largest farm population (3.97 farm persons per square mile) and greatest gross farm sales per square mile ($116,565). In contrast, the Mountain states had the lowest percentage of land capable of agricultural production; and they also had the lowest farm population per square mile (0.22) and the lowest gross farm sales per square mile ($15,540). The rankings for the other regions on farm population and gross farm sales per square mile generally followed the pattern expected, given the percent of the land that each has with the soil capable of producing crops.

In sum, both historical evidence and data from modern-day U.S. agriculture show that soil resources play an important role in shaping agriculture. A closer look also shows that soil resources likewise play a role in the organizational structure of farming. For example, the proportion of farm operators with off-farm employment is less in areas where soil resources are more substantial (Albrecht and Murdock, 1984).

## Water

Water is another environmental resource that is absolutely essential for successful agricultural production. Approximately three-fourths of the earth's surface is covered with water, yet water remains one of the most severe resource constraints for many agricultural producers. The problem is not that the total amount of water available is insufficient—this amount is relatively constant—it is the distribution of this water, both geographically and temporally. Some areas consistently have too much water, while other areas have constant water shortages. The temporal distribution of the water supply is also problematic. Too much rainfall or extended periods of drought can both severely limit agricultural production.

The distribution of water resources had an enormous influence on the initial settlement of the United States. Areas where water resources were severely limited were simply not settled until ways of obtaining an adequate water source were provided. Some areas in the West have never been settled because they lack a sufficient water supply. In the arid West, farm production is limited to those areas where irrigation can be provided, and consequently, agricultural production is greatly reduced.

Within the contiguous United States, the average annual precipitation ranges from over 100 inches on the Washington coast to less than 5 inches in southern Nevada and southwestern Arizona. Throughout the eastern part of the country and in the Pacific Northwest, rainfall is generally sufficient for agricultural production. Thus, other than for an occasional drought or flood, water is not a major constraint for agriculture in these areas. However, the situation is vastly different in the western United States. Moving westward across the Great Plains, the amount of rainfall received diminishes sharply. Between about the 98th meridian and the West Coast, natural rainfall will not support the levels of crop production that are possible given the soil and climatic conditions of the region. Consequently, the need for irrigation arises (Whittlesey, 1986).

In 1992, nearly 50 million acres were irrigated in the 17 western states. The states with the greatest number of acres irrigated included California (7.6 million), Nebraska (6.3 million), and Texas (4.9 million). There is very little irrigation in the rest of the country. Table 7.4 shows the distribution of this irrigated acreage in the four western USDA farm production regions. As shown, about 60 percent of the irrigated acreage, and about 80 percent of the water utilized in the western United States, is in the Mountain and Pacific states. These Mountain and Pacific states are generally more arid, and thus the amount of water utilized per acre is greater. Table 7.4 also shows that most of the water utilized in the Plains states is from groundwater sources, while the majority of water used in the Mountain and Pacific states is from surface sources.

In much of the West, crop production would be virtually impossible without irrigation. For example, in 1992 over 99 percent of the harvested cropland in the states of Arizona and Nevada was irrigated. In other parts of the West and in much of the Plains, irrigation results in greatly increased production, allows crops to be grown that could not otherwise be produced, and removes the risks of total crop failure that could occur if there was a lack of rainfall. Table 7.5 shows the enormous difference in productivity that results from irrigation. Corn and cotton yields are more than doubled in the West, while irrigated western crops show yields substantially higher than the same crop grown under nonirrigated conditions in the East. Consequently, in 1980 irrigated agriculture produced 27 percent of the value of the farm crops harvested in the United States on only 12 percent of the harvested acres (Sampson, 1981).

Water availability is strongly related to the structure of farming that emerges in different areas. Generally, farms in dryer areas are substantially larger than those in areas with greater amounts of rainfall. This is because per-acre production is lower, and consequently, more acres are needed to make a living (Albrecht and Murdock, 1990).

Table 7.4
Acres Irrigated and Acre Feet of Water Applied in the 17 Western and Plains States by Region

| Region | Total Irrigated Acres (Million) | (Percent) | Millions of Acre Feet | | | | | | Percent of Water Used That Is Ground-water |
|---|---|---|---|---|---|---|---|---|---|
| | | | Total Water Applied | (Percent) | Surface Water Applied | (Percent) | Ground-water Applied | (Percent) | |
| Northern Plains | 10.8 | (21.5) | 14.3 | (9.9) | 3.1 | (3.5) | 11.2 | (20.0) | 78.3 |
| Southern Plains | 9.0 | (17.9) | 13.9 | (9.6) | 2.8 | (3.2) | 11.1 | (19.8) | 79.9 |
| Mountain | 17.1 | (34.1) | 65.3 | (45.3) | 50.9 | (57.6) | 14.5 | (25.8) | 22.2 |
| Pacific | 13.3 | (26.5) | 50.9 | (35.2) | 31.6 | (35.7) | 19.3 | (34.4) | 37.9 |
| Total | 50.2 | (100.0) | 144.4 | (100.0) | 88.4 | (100.0) | 56.1 | (100.0) | 38.9 |

*Source:* Frederick and Hanson (1982).

Table 7.5
Irrigated and Dryland Yields of Selected Crops

| Crop | Location | Yield |
|------|----------|-------|
|      |          | (Bushels per Acre) |
| Corn | Irrigated West | 115.2 |
|      | Dryland West | 48.3 |
|      | East | 88.6 |
| Sorghum | Irrigated West | 77.4 |
|      | Dryland West | 45.5 |
|      | East | 61.4 |
| Wheat | Irrigated West | 39.4 |
|      | Dryland West | 27.1 |
|      | East | 38.1 |
|      |          | (Bales Per Acre) |
| Cotton | Irrigated West | 1.41 |
|      | Dryland West | 0.60 |
|      | East | 1.03 |

*Source*: Sampson (1981:157).

## CONSEQUENCES OF CHANGES IN RESOURCE AVAILABILITY

The resource base of agriculture is in constant transition and the effects of these transitions can be extensive. It is theoretically possible for the quality and quantity of environmental resources to either increase or decrease. Increases in the quantity of resources can result from either the discovery of new and previously unused resources or from a technological development. The latter can increase resource availability by either improving the efficiency with which humans use resources, or by making resources that were previously unusable available for human use. A decrease in the availability of a resource for agricultural purposes can result from either its depletion or from pollution which makes the resource unusable or at least less productive (Buttel, 1982). Several examples of how these changes in resource availability occur, and their consequences, are discussed below.

### Irrigation as Resource Development

One example of a practice which increases resource availability is irrigation. A resource may exist in an environment, but be of little use to that society because it has not yet been discovered, or the technology to extract the resource economically from the environment is not available. Irrigation in the Great Plains provides a prime example of a technological development which made a critical resource available to agriculture. Using longitudinal data from the Census of Agriculture and the Census of Population from 1940 to 1980, Albrecht and Murdock (1985, 1986a, 1986b) have explored the demographic and farm structure consequences of technological developments making water available for irrigated agriculture in the Great Plains. A brief summary of this research follows.

In many respects, the Great Plains is an area ideally suited for agricultural production. Much of the Great Plains is flat, and has rich soils and a sufficiently long growing season to produce numerous crops. The major deterrent to successful agricultural production has been a lack of water (Kraenzel, 1955; Webb, 1936). Annual rainfall in the Great Plains is well below the levels received in the East, and generally is insufficient for dependable crop production. Also, with the exception of a few streams, the region is nearly devoid of surface water (Lawson and Baker, 1981).

From early in the settlement period, it was well-known that much of the Great Plains was underlain by the extensive groundwater resources of the Ogallala Aquifer (Gould, 1907); but since the technology to efficiently pump this water to the surface was not available, the lack of water remained a major constraint to successful agricultural production. Most settlers had windmills, but they generally provided only enough water for household use, to water livestock, and to possibly irrigate a few rows of garden vegetables.

During the 1930s, newly developed pumps made it possible to efficiently lift large amounts of groundwater to the surface for irrigation purposes (Hughes and Magee, 1960; Hughes and Motheral, 1950). Eventually, thousands of water wells were drilled, millions of acres were placed under irrigation, and the Ogallala Aquifer became one of the most intensely developed groundwater resources in the country (Albrecht and Murdock, 1985).

Later technological improvements in irrigation systems further improved their utility. Irrigation in the early days meant hours of intensive human labor. After the groundwater was pumped to the surface, it was immediately set flowing in ditches to the rows of the crop. It was necessary to carefully watch to make sure that the proper amount of water was flowing down each row, and to maintain the system against erosion, weeds, and rodent damage. In addition, the water was not utilized very efficiently with these open-ditch, furrow irrigation systems. It is estimated that as much as 30 percent of the water was lost to seepage and evaporation (Green, 1973). In addition, these furrow irrigation systems could not be used in areas characterized by sandy soils or rolling terrain.

Later, some of the open ditches were replaced by gated pipes with an outlet to each furrow. This helped reduce seepage and evaporation losses. However, the major improvement came with the development of the center-pivot sprinkler system in 1952. Center-pivot sprinklers greatly reduced the labor requirements in irrigated agriculture, improved the efficiency by which water could be used, and increased the number of acres that could potentially be irrigated. In the Great Plains today, millions of acres of sandy or rolling terrain are being irrigated using center-pivot sprinkler systems that could not be irrigated with furrow irrigation systems (Bittinger and Green, 1980).

Having the technology to make water resources available for irrigation provided the impetus for extensive changes in agriculture, and consequently, in the economic and social structure of the Great Plains. The pumpage of groundwater effectively removed (at least temporarily) a critical ecological constraint and allowed the Great Plains to become one of the most productive farming regions in the nation. This increased agricultural productivity resulted in subsequent population and organizational adaptation. When comparing the development of Great Plains counties between 1940 and 1980, Albrecht and Murdock (1985, 1986b) found that counties without the water resources to permit extensive levels of irrigation became substantially different over time from counties with the resources for irrigation. Irrigation has created a system of agriculture that is more labor-intensive and one that has retained profitability on smaller-sized production units. Perhaps most important, the development of irrigation has created a system of agriculture that has been more resistant to farm consolidation, and as a result, more persons have been able to remain in agriculture. As shown in Table 7.6, over the 40-year study period, counties with extensive levels of irrigation development have experienced population increases, while counties with little or no irrigation development have generally experienced population declines. In addition, this more productive agricultural base has resulted in growth of related agricultural industries and in secondary growth to support a more viable rural economy. Irrigated agriculture has thus resulted in both more productive and profitable agriculture and more viable rural communities.

### Resource Depletion

However, just as more and better quality environmental resources enhance farm productivity, the depletion of resources critical to agriculture can constrain production. As noted above, resources are threatened in two primary ways—by depletion and by pollution such that the resources become unusable (Buttel, 1982; Poincelot, 1986). Writers have noted that modern industrial agriculture increases the potential of both depletion and pollution (Bird et al., 1995). Unfortunately, there is a dearth of empirically based sociological research on the consequences of resource depletion for agriculture. However, three examples of the potential consequences of re-source depletion in agriculture are discussed below. The three issues to be discussed are soil erosion, water depletion, and energy depletion.

### Soil Erosion

The erosion of our topsoil resources is a double-edged sword that reduces the productivity of cropland while polluting the water (ReVelle and Re-Velle, 1988). Both of these effects of soil erosion constitute serious threats to our well-being as a nation. Soil is an absolutely essential natural re-source, but one that is both limited and fragile.

The potential for producing food and fiber with limited soil erosion is possible, but seldom achieved, given today's technology. Soil erosion can-not be totally eliminated under any feasible management plan, but it can be reduced to levels that allow the soil to retain productivity. This "toler-able" soil loss might be defined as the maximum rate of annual soil erosion that will permit a high level of crop productivity to be sustained econom-ically and indefinitely. This amount will vary from place to place, depend-ing on how fast new topsoil can be formed to replace the soil lost to erosion. Soil formation is a slow, continuous process, with new soil being formed as minerals break down due to chemical and biological processes. When the soil is being eroded faster than it is being formed, it is essentially being "mined" (Sampson, 1981). Modern farming practices often result in soil being lost at a rate 10 times faster than it can be replenished. Soil losses in the United States from cropland alone amount to about 2 billion tons annually. In the Corn Belt, the production of one bushel of corn consumes about two bushels of topsoil (Pimentel et al., 1976). There are places in America where the entire layer of topsoil has been lost in only 50–100 years of cultivation (Sampson, 1981).

History makes the consequences of excessive soil erosion apparent (Va-sey, 1992). Lowdermilk (1953), for example, found evidence of over 100 dead villages in Syria. These villages now stand on bare rock with the soils completely washed or blown away. Lowdermilk (1953:10) concluded that "If the soils had remained, even though the cities were destroyed and the population dispersed, the area might have been repeopled and the cities rebuilt. But now that the soils are gone, all is gone." Similarly, in Meso-potamia (now Iraq), the rich soils of the Tigris and Euphrates valleys sup-ported some of the world's greatest civilizations. However, through the centuries, the soil has been severely eroded and today the land supports less than one-sixth of the population that lived there during its historic peaks. Iraq is now dependent on oil exports, not agriculture, for its wealth (Sampson, 1981). Dale and Carter state:

Let's not put the blame for the barrenness of these areas on the conquering hordes that repeatedly overran them. True, those conquerors often sacked and razed the

Table 7.6
Level of Irrigation Development by County Characteristics, 1940–1980 (N = 294)

| Variable | Year | | | | | Percent Change | | | | |
|---|---|---|---|---|---|---|---|---|---|---|
| | 1940 | 1950 | 1959 | 1969 | 1980 | 1940–50 | 1950–60 | 1960–70 | 1970–80 | 1940–80 |
| Gross Farm Sales ($1,000) | 1,983 | 10,638 | 11,126 | 20,054 | 54,018 | 436.4 | 4.5 | 80.2 | 169.3 | 2,624.0 |
| High* | 2,505 | 14,251 | 19,241 | 41,809 | 129,496 | 468.9 | 35.0 | 117.2 | 209.7 | 5,069.5 |
| Medium | 1,866 | 10,836 | 11,166 | 19,765 | 53,058 | 480.1 | 3.0 | 77.0 | 168.4 | 2,734.3 |
| Low | 1,875 | 9,152 | 8,083 | 12,184 | 26,683 | 388.1 | -11.6 | 50.7 | 119.0 | 1,323.0 |
| Number of Farms | 1,152 | 981 | 796 | 692 | 589 | -14.8 | -18.8 | -13.0 | -14.8 | -48.8 |
| High | 1,232 | 1,105 | 949 | 834 | 721 | -10.3 | -14.1 | -12.1 | -13.5 | -41.4 |
| Medium | 1,078 | 943 | 782 | 672 | 587 | -12.5 | -17.0 | -14.0 | -12.6 | -45.5 |
| Low | 1,176 | 963 | 750 | 653 | 542 | -18.1 | -22.1 | -12.9 | -16.9 | -53.9 |
| Energy Expenditures ($1,000) | 150 | 481 | 640 | 806 | 2,943 | 220.6 | 33.0 | 25.9 | 265.1 | 1,862.0 |
| High | 200 | 730 | 1,139 | 1,457 | 6,531 | 265.0 | 56.0 | 27.9 | 348.2 | 3,165.5 |
| Medium | 152 | 484 | 625 | 790 | 2,914 | 218.4 | 29.1 | 26.4 | 268.8 | 1,817.1 |
| Low | 130 | 386 | 466 | 576 | 1,631 | 196.9 | 20.7 | 23.6 | 183.1 | 1,154.6 |
| Hired Farm Labor Expenditures ($1,000) | 145 | 730 | 567 | 728 | 1,575 | 403.4 | -22.3 | 28.3 | 116.3 | 986.2 |
| High | 206 | 1,060 | 1,124 | 1,545 | 3,522 | 414.5 | 6.0 | 37.4 | 127.9 | 1,609.7 |
| Medium | 138 | 704 | 529 | 694 | 1,559 | 410.1 | -24.8 | 31.1 | 124.6 | 1,029.7 |
| Low | 127 | 625 | 387 | 450 | 864 | 392.1 | -38.0 | 16.2 | 92.0 | 580.3 |

| | | | | | | | | | | |
|---|---|---|---|---|---|---|---|---|---|---|
| **Proportion of Part-Time Farmers** | 10.6 | 12.8 | 18.6 | 26.0 | 27.5 | 20.7 | 45.3 | 39.7 | 5.7 | 159.4 |
| High | 10.4 | 11.1 | 13.1 | 21.6 | 21.7 | 6.7 | 18.0 | 64.8 | 0.4 | 108.6 |
| Medium | 10.0 | 11.1 | 16.5 | 24.4 | 25.4 | 11.0 | 48.6 | 47.8 | 4.0 | 154.0 |
| Low | 11.0 | 14.7 | 22.2 | 28.7 | 31.2 | 33.6 | 51.0 | 29.2 | 8.7 | 183.6 |
| **Total Population** | 10,813 | 10,902 | 11,086 | 10,469 | 11,045 | 0.8 | 1.6 | -5.5 | 5.5 | 2.1 |
| High | 11,523 | 12,861 | 13,902 | 14,360 | 15,273 | 11.6 | 8.0 | 3.2 | 6.3 | 32.5 |
| Medium | 10,100 | 10,533 | 11,075 | 10,083 | 10,577 | 4.2 | 5.1 | -8.9 | 4.9 | 4.7 |
| Low | 11,071 | 10,439 | 10,047 | 9,307 | 9,805 | -5.7 | -3.7 | -7.3 | 5.3 | -11.7 |
| **Rural Farm Population** | 4,934 | 3,665 | 2,717 | 2,011 | 1,407 | -25.7 | -25.8 | -25.4 | -30.0 | -71.4 |
| High | 5,280 | 4,322 | 3,652 | 2,761 | 1,818 | -18.1 | -15.5 | -24.3 | -34.1 | -65.5 |
| Medium | 4,560 | 3,531 | 2,700 | 2,064 | 1,400 | -22.5 | -23.5 | -23.5 | -32.1 | -69.2 |
| Low | 5,078 | 3,518 | 2,374 | 1,692 | 1,173 | -30.7 | -32.5 | -28.7 | -30.6 | -76.9 |

*High irrigation counties are those with over 100,000 acres irrigated; medium irrigation counties have between 22,000 and 100,000 acres irrigated; while low irrigation counties have less than 22,000 acres irrigated.

cities, burned the villages, and slaughtered or drove off the people who populated them. But while the soil and other resources . . . remained, the cities were usually rebuilt. It was only after the land was depleted or exhausted that the fields became barren and the cities remained dead. (1955:15)

In the United States, little concern was expressed about soil erosion until the 1930s when the "Dust Bowl" phenomenon made the problem apparent. Beginning in 1931 and lasting until about 1940, the Great Plains of the United States was devastated by a severe drought. The combination of the breakup of the native prairie sod, severe drought that killed the soil-holding vegetation, incessant wind, and soils that were subject to wind erosion resulted in some of the most severe dust storms in U.S. history (Hurt, 1981; Lockeretz, 1981). During the 1930s, clouds of dust thousands of feet thick rolled across the plains, causing total darkness in the middle of the afternoon, stranding motorists on the highways, and making breathing difficult. During the most severe storms, schools and businesses were forced to close (Hurt, 1981).

The obvious severity of the Dust Bowl resulted in the creation of the Soil Conservation Service (SCS) and the passage of the Soil Conservation Act of 1935, which was intended to control and prevent soil erosion. However, although over a half century has elapsed since the passage of the Soil Conservation Act and the creation of the SCS, sophisticated technologies and data systems have been developed to address the problem, and $15 billion in federal funds have been spent to prevent it, soil erosion is still a serious problem in the United States. In fact, the United States is losing topsoil at a faster rate than at any time in history, including the Dust Bowl era (Sampson, 1981).

There are many reasons for the lack of success in dealing with the soil erosion problem. Soil conservation measures are expensive to implement, and typically the return on the investment is not realized for many years. Thus, some studies conclude that landowners and farm operators are more interested in increasing their net incomes over a short-term planning horizon. In particular, tenants with short-term leases may have short-term planning horizons that motivate them to emphasize immediate income. This problem is further aggravated by the very small profit margin in farming. Small-sized farms frequently force farmers to exploit the land in order to make a living, regardless of the soil erosion consequences. Finally, some farmers are not fully convinced that reducing soil erosion is essential for long-term soil productivity (Heffernan and Green, 1986; Nowak and Korsching, 1982; Timmons, 1979).

Major gaps remain in the sociological research on soil erosion and many questions are left unanswered. A critical question relates to how the population adapts to changes in the quality and quantity of critical resources such as soil. It seems likely that reduced soil quality will result in more severe limits and constraints being placed on agriculture. Declining farm production caused by extensive soil erosion is likely to mean that the size of the farm population that can be supported in an ecosystem will be reduced and that, unless other sustenance activities emerge, total population and economic resources will decline.

As of yet, however, research has not been completed that explores such questions in a modern setting. Research has shown that topsoil loss reduces crop yields (except legumes) unless liberal amounts of fertilizers are added to replace the nutrients lost from the soil. Soil losses may also reduce the water-holding capacity of the soil and restrict root penetration. Soil erosion thus always increases the costs of production, and in severe cases makes it unprofitable to farm (Sampson, 1981). While economists have explored the consequences of these increased costs of production for the farm firm (Timmons, 1979), the macro-level organizational and demographic consequences have not been examined. Conducting research on these consequences will be difficult and will require interdisciplinary approaches, because they involve biological as well as social and economic dimensions. Obtaining quantitative estimates of the amount of soil lost and the effects of these losses on productivity will be difficult. However, determining how farm populations adapt to changes in soil productivity, and the macro-level consequences of this adaptation, is critical to policy and program formation.

### Water Scarcity and Depletion

Water is generally referred to as a "flow" resource. This means that it appears on a time-installment basis as it moves through the hydrologic cycle. We can use today's water today, or we can store some of it until tomorrow, but we cannot use tomorrow's water until it comes. As such, the water supply cannot be depleted in the sense that soil resources can. However, water supplies can be polluted to the point that they are unusable or even toxic. Also, much of the groundwater used in agriculture is a "fund" resource like petroleum. If groundwater resources are depleted faster than they can be naturally replenished, then the resource will eventually be gone.

Again, history presents graphic evidence of the importance of water resources for agriculture. In ancient Mesopotamia, the waters of the Tigris and Euphrates Rivers were developed for irrigation with an elaborate system of canals. This region is so arid that dependable crop production is not possible without irrigation. The resulting increase in agricultural productivity from irrigation freed many people from primary production and allowed those societies to flourish. However, the river waters were filled with silt resulting from the erosion of the overgrazed highlands, and as the water entered the slow-moving canals, the silt settled out and clogged the canals. Keeping the irrigation ditches open was long a primary concern of the people of the region, and the problem was often solved by slave labor. However, if wars or other events prevented such maintenance activities from being performed, the irrigation system quickly regressed and the food source was threatened. Time and time again, the region experienced periods of mass starvation when the irrigation system failed (Dale and Carter, 1955).

As noted earlier, irrigation plays a vital role in American agriculture today, and both surface and groundwater sources for water are critical. Surface water used for irrigation is a flow resource with a limited seasonal supply. In most of the West, there is no surplus or unused water. Thus, adding more water to presently irrigated land, or bringing other lands into irrigation is generally impossible without decreasing other uses of the water. However, the competitive users of this water, such as industry, municipal uses, power generation, recreation, and fisheries are frequently in a position to place a higher economic value on the water than agriculture, and thus bid water away from agriculture (Whittlesey, 1986).

In contrast to surface water, groundwater is basically a fund resource with limited supply available. While most aquifers experience some re-charge, the amount varies significantly from formation to formation (Lace-well and Collins, 1986). However, throughout the West, the mining of groundwater (extracting more than is naturally recharged) exceeds 22 million acre feet per year (Sloggett, 1979). Groundwater irrigation is also heavily dependent on energy resources to pump the underground water to the surface. As the water tables decline, the energy costs of lifting the water to the surface increase. Thus, groundwater mining, energy costs, alternative uses, and the impairment of groundwater quality all pose serious threats to the long-term outlook for irrigation from groundwater in the West (National Water Commission, 1973).

Some exploratory research has investigated the consequences of ground-water depletion for agriculture. As discussed earlier, technological devel-opments initially made it possible to effectively utilize groundwater for irrigation purposes. In some cases, however, extensive withdrawal has re-sulted in problems of groundwater depletion. Perhaps nowhere is this prob-lem more severe than in the Great Plains.

Years of heavy withdrawal of water from the Ogallala Aquifer resulted in considerable declines in the amount of water available. Of the more than 22 million acre feet of water that is mined from groundwater sources per year in this country, about 14 million of this occurs in Texas and Oklahoma High Plains areas alone. This is equivalent to the average annual flow of the Colorado River (Frederick and Hanson, 1982). In parts of the Texas High Plains, the water table has already declined by more than 100 feet. These declines in the water table have resulted in reduced irrigation in some areas. For example, in Hockley County, Texas, about 201,000 acres of cropland were irrigated in 1969. By 1978, the number of acres irrigated had decreased to 165,000, and the decline has continued. In 1992, only about 101,000 acres of land were irrigated in Hockley County. Other nearby counties have experienced similar declines.

Projections show that reduced irrigation and the reimposition of water constraints may have serious implications for the Great Plains (Albrecht and Murdock, 1985). In some preliminary research in the Great Plains, Albrecht (1988) found that groundwater depletion led to declines in the amount of acreage being irrigated and consequently to reduced agricultural productivity. This reduced productivity, in turn, led to population decline and reduced economic activity.

## Energy Depletion

In recent decades, increases in the productivity of American agriculture have been remarkable. Whether measured in terms of production per man-hour of human labor or per-acre production, the increases have been impressive. To a large extent, however, these enormous increases in productivity have been achieved by channeling extensive amounts of energy (primarily fossil fuels) into agricultural production. In comparison to most of human history, when agricultural production depended upon human and animal power, the capacity for agricultural productivity is increased immensely by the use of fossil fuels (Vasey, 1992). The increased use of fossil fuel energy has directly resulted in a sharp decline in the number of farm operators because a small number of farmers using fossil fuel energy are now able to produce so much. This increased farm productivity from fossil fuel energy has also contributed to our high standard of living and to the relatively plentiful, cheap, and nutritious diet that we enjoy.

Since the early 1970s, however, it has become increasingly apparent that our extreme dependence upon fossil fuel energy in agriculture is not without its drawbacks. The OPEC oil embargo of 1973 resulted in temporary oil supply shortages and in drastically higher energy prices. The higher energy prices resulted in farmers having much higher input costs, which threatened the economic stability of many operations. At the same time, the interruption in the supply of energy products caused many people to realize how dependent we had become upon a nonrenewable resource. Not only will the depletion of world fossil fuel supplies have drastic consequences for agriculture, but the United States has the added quandary of being dependent on the importation of foreign oil from sources that have proven to be unreliable (Dovring, 1988; Tuve, 1976).

The energy crisis has resulted in a great deal of research on the use of alternative sources of energy for agriculture, and the development of renewable energy sources such as methanol, solar energy, and wind energy. Unfortunately, the amount of sociological research on energy depletion and agriculture is limited. A great deal of additional research is needed on farmers' use of, and views toward, energy conserving techniques and alternative

energy sources. Additional research is also necessary on the social consequences of the energy crisis and the depletion of energy supplies. In one of
the few sociological studies exploring energy and agriculture, Buttel and
Larson (1979) examined the relationship between the scale of agriculture
and energy intensity (defined as the ratio of energy input to product yield).
They found that as the scale of agriculture in a state increased, the energy
intensity of agriculture in that state also increased. Substantial additional
sociological work on energy and agriculture must be performed.

## THE ENVIRONMENT AND THE ADOPTION OF AGRICULTURAL TECHNOLOGY

Another area of research concern relative to the interface of agriculture
and the environment is the adoption of agricultural technology. For decades
rural sociologists have explored factors related to farmers' decisions about
the adoption of agricultural innovations (Rogers, 1983). Literally hundreds
of studies have examined the relationship between the adoption of agricultural technology and factors such as the characteristics of the innovation, the structure of the farm (e.g., farm size and nature of ownership),
and the psychological and demographic characteristics of the farmer. Only
recently have researchers included environmental factors in their explanatory models. To a large extent, the use of environmental factors in adoption
research can be traced to an academic debate which occurred in the early
1980s (Dunlap and Martin, 1983). This debate began when Gartrell and
Gartrell (1979) reported on a study of the trial of various agricultural technologies by farmers in India. They found that social status and related
factors explained over 60 percent of the variance in whether or not Indian
farmers tried the various technologies. Despite these impressive findings,
their study came under criticism from Ashby and Coward (1980), who
claimed that the Gartrells had failed to consider the suitability of the technologies for diverse agricultural environments. (See also Gartrell and Gartrell, 1980.) Subsequently, Ashby (1982) found that the adoption behavior
of peasant farmers in Nepal was related to the ecological suitability of the
technology for different types of farms.

In a similar manner, other researchers have found environmental factors
to be important in the explanation of adoption behavior by farmers. After
examining the adoption of "green revolution" technologies in six low-
income countries, Perrin and Winkelmann (1976:893) came to the following conclusion:

The most pervasive explanation of why some farmers do not adopt new varieties
and fertilizers while others do is that the expected increase in yield for some farmers

is small or nil, while for others it is significant, due to differences (sometimes subtle) in soils, climate, water availability, or other biological factors.


Environmental factors have also been found to be important in the adoption of technology in a highly industrialized agricultural setting such as the United States. Albrecht and Ladewig (1985) found that the adoption of irrigation technology in the High Plains of Texas was strongly dependent on the extent to which groundwater resources were available. They found that farmers with limited water resources were generally unwilling to make the substantial financial investment necessary to purchase more efficient irrigation technology. In contrast, farmers living in areas with more extensive groundwater resources were often willing to purchase irrigation technology because they could financially justify the expense. Additional research is needed to determine under what conditions technology will be applied and the extent to which natural resource availability influences adoption behavior.

In addition to expanding the adoption model to include environmental factors, researchers in adoption and diffusion have also recently conducted studies exploring the adoption of technologies developed to conserve natural resources and those which have less severe negative impacts on the environment (Lasley et al., 1990; Thomas et al., 1990). A spirited debate has emerged regarding the applicability of the mainstream adoption literature which emphasizes the importance of both the structure of farms and characteristics of farmers in the adoption of soil conservation technologies (Heffernan and Green, 1986; Nowak, 1987). Some researchers argue that hypotheses from the adoption model can be used to predict the adoption of soil conservation measures (Taylor and Miller, 1978). These researchers argue that what is needed to increase adoption are not better research models, but educational efforts that make farmers aware of the need for the technology and provide them with valid information for implementing and utilizing the technology (Nowak, 1987).

Others, however, note the inconsistencies in the findings of past research and maintain that adoption theory is of little utility in understanding the adoption of conservation technology (Buttel and Swanson, 1986; Lovejoy and Parent, 1982; Pampel and van Es, 1977). In other words, they claim that findings related to who adopts nonconservation technology are of little utility in predicting who adopts conservation technology. They maintain that the costs of most conservation technologies exceed the benefits on a short-term and possibly long-term basis, and that farmers are asked to adopt these technologies for noneconomic reasons. As a result, they claim that the factors important in understanding the adoption of these technologies is different than for commercial or profitable technologies. Because of the inconsistencies of this research in the past, a great deal of additional work is needed on this topic in the future.

## THE ENVIRONMENTAL CONSEQUENCES OF MODERN AGRICULTURE

Not only is agriculture greatly influenced by the environment in which it operates, but in recent decades it has become increasingly apparent that some modern farming practices may harm the environment (Beus and Dunlap, 1990, 1994; Bird et al., 1995; Buttel et al., 1981). In fact, many of the nation's most severe environmental problems are a direct result of modern farming practices (Buttel et al., 1990). There is growing consensus that the massive soil erosion resulting from modern agricultural practices is one of the major sources of the water pollution problem that plagues our society (Carter, 1977; Pimentel et al., 1976). Water pollution is intensified by the run-off of fertilizers, pesticides, and other farm chemicals (Commoner, 1976; Manners, 1978; ReVelle and ReVelle, 1988). In addition, agriculture is the most intensive user of groundwater and other water supplies, and as agricultural users deplete these supplies, competition among alternative uses of the water is intensified (Bittinger and Green, 1980). These are only a few of the many environmental problems stemming from modern agriculture that affect the nonfarm public. In this section, a brief discussion will be provided of nonpoint-source pollution in agriculture as an example of how modern agriculture directly effects the environment for the nonfarm public.

The first European settlers in the Piedmont area of the American Southeast used terms such as "transparent," glittering," and "crystal clear" to describe the streams flowing through the area. Within a century of settlement, however, such terms were no longer appropriate as the formerly clear streams were filled with mud and debris which had washed in from nearby hillsides. Numerous streams and lakes all over the country met a similar fate. The primary factors leading to this problem of muddy streams and lakes included overgrazing and poor farming practices (Clark et al., 1985).

Of course, there were other sources of water pollution besides agricultural soil erosion, and as the nation became increasingly urbanized and industrialized, "point" sources of pollution such as municipal sewage and industrial effluents were seen as the major problems. However, due in large part to the potential sanctions resulting from pollution control laws, industries and municipalities have made progress in cleaning up their wastewater discharges. With some success in controlling water pollution from these sources, "nonpoint" sources—especially from agriculture—have become the major source of water pollution in much of the United States.

Nonpoint-source pollution from agriculture results in part from the massive erosion of topsoil discussed earlier. A 1977 study by the U.S. Department of Agriculture estimated that the annual erosion rate in the United States was equal to 6.42 billion tons. This is equivalent to about 30 tons of erosion per year for every person in the country, or an average of more than 200 tons of erosion per second (Clark et al., 1985). The water pollution problems from agriculture are exacerbated because agricultural herbicides, pesticides, nitrates, and phosphates mix with water run-off and flow into streams, rivers and lakes. According to some estimates (Clark et al., 1985), non-point sources are responsible for as much as 73 percent of the total biochemical-oxygen-demand loading, 99 percent of the suspended solids, 83 percent of the dissolved solids, 82 percent of the nitrogen, 84 percent of the phosphorous, and 98 percent of the bacteria loads in U.S. waterways. Such agricultural pollutants adversely affect fish life, water-based recreation, water-storage facilities, and water-based navigation.

The pollution problems from agriculture are made more severe by the fact that the chemicals used in agriculture enter the food chain. Classic cases of this problem resulted from the chemicals DDT and 2,3,4-T, which killed many unwanted plants. However, instead of dissipating into the environment after they had accomplished their purpose, these chemicals concentrated in animal and human tissue, leading to mutagenic and carcinogenic conditions. The eagle population in the United States declined because DDT accumulated in the fish which were the main food source of eagles. These pollutants led to thin-shelled eagle eggs that broke prematurely. DDT was banned in the United States in 1971, but the compound is still found in fish caught in Lake Michigan (Rogers et al., 1988).

Another severe water pollution problem resulting from agricultural practices involves the leaking of agricultural chemicals into underground water sources. This is a problem of major concern because such groundwater sources supply about 50 percent of the U.S. water supply. There have been situations in recent years where the health of numerous people has been adversely affected by the consumption of contaminated groundwater (Tiner, 1982).

It is obvious that the water pollution problems resulting from modern U.S. agriculture are severe. Modern agricultural practices have also resulted in a number of other major environmental problems. Without question, these problems demand the attention of policy makers and researchers. One additional consequence of the environmental problems of modern agriculture is that calls have been made for a more environmentally pristine form of agricultural production. It is to a discussion of such agriculture that we now turn.

## Sustainable Agriculture

A growing awareness of the environmental problems resulting from modern agriculture has resulted in a call for a form of agriculture that lacks such severe effects for the environment (Bird et al., 1995). To proponents, this form of agriculture has become known as "sustainable" or "alternative" agriculture (Beus and Dunlap, 1990, 1994; Youngberg, 1984). The goals of sustainable agriculture are to avoid or at least reduce the use of synthetically compounded fertilizers, pesticides, growth regulators, and livestock feed additives (Lockeretz, 1986). Instead, sustainable agriculture stresses reliance on crop rotation, crop residues, animal manures, legumes, green manures, mechanical cultivation, and biological pest control (Altieri, 1987). Proponents of sustainable agriculture maintain that a transition to a more sustainable form of agriculture is essential if our society is to avoid being overwhelmed by the magnitude of the environmental problems that result from the current industrialized agriculture. Proponents of conventional industrialized agriculture, on the other hand, argue that while some aspects of sustainable agriculture have merit, large-scale adoption of such programs would have serious repercussions for our society. For example, the reduced production from sustainable agriculture would make it difficult to feed our own population, and reduced exports abroad would help expand an already overwhelming budget deficit. These proponents of conventional industrialized agriculture contend that many of the environmental problems of modern agriculture can be dealt with through technological developments and scientific breakthroughs.

Most research to date has attempted to describe the ecological or economic effects of a widespread adoption of reduced input farming techniques (e.g., Lockeretz and Wernick, 1980; Olsen et al., 1982). Some recent studies have explored the values and attitudes of farmers who have adopted sustainable agricultural techniques and compared them with conventional farmers (Beus and Dunlap, 1990, 1994; Buttel et al., 1986).

As was the case with each of the research areas previously discussed, the need for additional research is evident. Research is needed on the long-term macro-level social and economic consequences of a partial or complete transition to sustainable agriculture. This should include an analysis of the consequences for the farm family, the rural community, and consumers. Also, more research is needed on the views of various populations of producers toward this alternative form of agriculture. It does appear likely that before most farmers utilize reduced input farming methods, it will have to be shown that such methods are economically profitable. Past research has shown that in the aggregate, farmers are among the most anti-environmental of major social groupings in the United States (Buttel et al., 1981).

## SUMMARY AND CONCLUSION

In this chapter, it has been shown that environmental resources have played a vital role in the past development and the current structure of agriculture in the United States. Research has shown that the quality and quantity of resources in an area has had a major effect on initial settlement patterns, agricultural productivity, and farm structure. In addition, either increases or decreases in the availability of a critical environmental resource for agriculture can have a major effect on agriculture and the rest of society.

Throughout the discussion in this chapter, it has been apparent that the level of sociological knowledge on resource issues in the sociology of agriculture is insufficient to answer some of the most critical questions that arise. With breakthroughs in biotechnology, chemicals, fertilizers, and other areas that may have critical implications for resource issues and agriculture in the future, the answers to such questions will be of increasing importance. Such questions must be answered if sociologists are to have an influence on the policy agenda. To answer these questions, improvements are needed in both our theoretical models and our empirical databases.

## REFERENCES

Albrecht, Don E. 1988. "Resource Depletion and Agriculture: The Case of Ground-worker in the Great Plains." *Society and Natural Resources* 1(2):145–157.

Albrecht, Don E., and Howard Ladewig. 1985. "The Adoption of Irrigation Technology: The Effects of Personal, Structural, and Environmental Variables." *Southern Rural Sociology* 3:26–41.

Albrecht, Don E., and Steve H. Murdock. 1984. "Toward a Human Ecological Perspective on Part-time Farming." *Rural Sociology* 49(3):389–411.

Albrecht, Don E., and Steve H. Murdock. 1985. *The Consequences of Irrigation Development in the Great Plains.* Department of Rural Sociology Technical Report 85–1. College Station: Texas Agricultural Experiment Station.

Albrecht, Don E., and Steve H. Murdock. 1986a. "Understanding Farm Structure and Demographic Change: An Ecological Analysis of the Impacts of Irrigation." *Sociological Perspectives* 29(4):484–505.

Albrecht, Don E., and Steve H. Murdock. 1986b. "Natural Resource Availability and Social Change." *Sociological Inquiry* 56(3):381–400.

Albrecht, Don E., and Steve H. Murdock. 1990. *The Sociology of U.S. Agriculture: A Human Ecological Perspective.* Ames: Iowa State University Press.

Altieri, Miguel A. 1987. *Agroecology: The Scientific Basis of Alternative Agriculture.* Boulder, CO: Westview Press.

Ashby, Jacqueline A. 1982. "Technology and Ecology: Implications for Innovation Research in Peasant Agriculture." *Rural Sociology* 47(2):234–250.

Ashby, Jacqueline A., and E. Walter Coward, Jr. 1980. "Putting Agriculture Back into the Study of Farm Practice Innovation: Comment on Status, Knowledge and Innovation." *Rural Sociology* 45(3):520–523.

Beus, Curtis E., and Riley E. Dunlap. 1990. "Conventional versus Alternative Agriculture: The Paradigmatic Roots of the Debate." *Rural Sociology* 55:590–616.

Beus, Curtis E., and Riley E. Dunlap. 1994. "Agricultural Paradigms and the Practice of Agriculture." *Rural Sociology* 59:620–635.

Bird, Elizather Ann R., Gordon L. Bultena, and John C. Gardner (eds.). 1995. *Planting the Future: Developing an Agriculture that Sustains Land and Community*. Ames: Iowa State University Press.

Bittinger, Morton W., and Elizabeth B. Green. 1980. *You Never Miss the Water Till . . . (The Ogallala Story)*. Littleton, CO: Water Resources Publication.

Brown, Lester R. 1981. *Building a Sustainable Society*. New York: Norton.

Buttel, Frederick H. 1982. "Rural Resource Use and the Environment." Pp. 359–372 in *Rural Society in the U.S.: Issues for the 1980s*, edited by D. A. Dillman and D. J. Hobbs. Boulder, CO: Westview Press.

Buttel, Frederick H., Gilbert W. Gillespie, Jr., Rhonda Janke, Brian Caldwell, and Marianna Sarrantonio. 1986. "Reduced-Input Agricultural Systems: A Critique." *The Rural Sociologist* 6(5):350–370.

Buttel, Frederick H., Gilbert W. Gillespie, Jr., Oscar W. Larson III, and Craig K. Harris. 1981. "The Social Bases of Agrarian Environmentalism: A Comparative Analysis of New York and Michigan Farm Operators." *Rural Sociology* 46(3):391–410.

Buttel, Frederick H., Olaf F. Larson, and Gilbert W. Gillespie, Jr. 1990. *The Sociology of Agriculture*. Westport, CT: Greenwood Press.

Buttel, Frederick H., and Oscar W. Larson III. 1979. "Farm Size, Structure, and Energy Intensity: An Ecological Analysis of U.S. Agriculture." *Rural Sociology* 44(3):471–488.

Buttel, Frederick H., and Louis E. Swanson. 1986. "Soil and Water Conservation: A Farm Structural and Public Policy Context." Pp. 26–39 in *Conserving Soil: Insights from Socioeconomic Research*, edited by S. Lovejoy and T. Napien. Ankeny, IA: Soil Conservation Society of America.

Carter, Luther J. 1977. "Soil Erosion: The Problem Persists Despite the Billions Spent on It." *Science* 196(22 April):409–411.

Clark, Edwin H. II, Jennifer A. Haver Kamp, and William Chapman. 1985. *Eroding Soils: The Off-Farm Impacts*. Washington, DC: The Conservation Foundation.

Commoner, Barry. 1976. *The Closing Circle*. New York: Alfred A. Knopf.

Dale, Tom, and Vernon Gill Carter. 1955. *Topsoil and Civilization*. Norman: University of Oklahoma Press.

Dovring, Folke. 1988. *Farming for Fuel*. New York: Praeger.

Dunlap, Riley E., and Kenneth E. Martin. 1983. "Bringing Environment into the Study of Agriculture: Observations and Suggestions Regarding the Sociology of Agriculture." *Rural Sociology* 48(2):201–218.

Franck, Karen A. 1984. "Exorcising the Ghost of Physical Determinism." *Environment and Behavior* 16(4):411–435.

Frederick, Kenneth D., and James C. Hanson. 1982. *Water for Western Agriculture*. Washington, DC: Resources for the Future.

Gartrell, John W., and C. David Gartrell. 1979. "Status, Knowledge, and Innovation." *Rural Sociology* 44(1):73–94.

Gartrell, John W., and C. David Gartrell. 1980. "Beyond Earth, Water, Weather and Wind." *Rural Sociology* 45(3):524–530.

Gould, C. N. 1907. *The Geological and Water Resources of the Western Portion of the Panhandle of Texas*. Washington, DC: U.S. Geological Survey Water Supply Paper 191.

Green, Donald E. 1973. *Land of the Underground Rain*. Austin: University of Texas Press.

Heffernan, William D., and Gary P. Green. 1986. "Farm Size and Soil Loss: Prospects for a Sustainable Agriculture." *Rural Sociology* 51(1):31–42.

Hughes, William F., and A. C. Magee. 1960. *Some Economic Effects of Adjusting to a Changing Water Supply*. Bulletin 966. College Station: Texas Agricultural Experiment Station.

Hughes, William F., and Joe R. Motheral. 1950. *Irrigated Agriculture in Texas*. Miscellaneous Publication 59. College Station: Texas Agricultural Experiment Station.

Hurt, R. Douglas. 1981. *The Dust Bowl: An Agricultural and Social History*. Chicago: Nelson-Hall.

Kraenzel, Carl Frederick. 1955. *The Great Plains in Transition*. Norman: University of Oklahoma Press.

Lacewell, Ronald D., and Glenn S. Collins. 1986. "Energy Inputs on Western Groundwater Irrigated Areas." Pp. 155–176 in *Energy and Water Management in Western Irrigated Agriculture*, edited by N. K. Whittlesey. Boulder, CO: Westview Press.

Lasley, Paul, Michael Duffy, Devin Kettner, and Craig Chase. 1990. "Factors Affecting Farmers' Use of Practices to Reduce Commercial Fertilizers and Pesticides." *Journal of Soil and Water Conservation* 45:132–136.

Lawson, Merlin P., and Maurice E. Baker. 1981. *The Great Plains: Perspectives and Prospects*. Lincoln: University of Nebraska Press.

Lockeretz, William. 1981. "The Dust Bowl: Its Relevance to Contemporary Environmental Problems." Pp. 11–31 in *The Great Plains: Perspectives and Prospects*, edited by M. P. Lawson and M. E. Baker. Lincoln: University of Nebraska Press.

———. 1986. "Alternative Agriculture." Pp. 291–311 in *New Directions for Agriculture and Agricultural Research*, edited by K. A. Dahlberg. Totowa, NJ: Rowman & Allenheld.

Lockeretz, William, and S. Wernick. 1980. "Commercial Organic Farming in the Corn Belt in Comparison to Conventional Practices." *Rural Sociology* 45: 708–722.

Lovejoy, S., and D. Parent. 1982. "Conservation Behavior: A Look at the Exploratory Power of the Traditional Adoption-Diffusion Model." Paper presented at the Annual Meetings of the Rural Sociological Society, San Francisco.

Lowdermilk, Walter C. 1953. *Conquest of the Land Through 7,000 Years*. USDA-SCS Information Bulletin 99. Washington, DC: U.S. Department of Agriculture.

Manners, Ian R. 1978. "Agricultural Activities and Environmental Stress." Pp. 263–294 in *Sourcebook on the Environment*, edited by D. A. Hammond, G. Macinko, and W. B. Fairchild. Chicago: University of Chicago Press.

National Water Commission. 1973. *New Directions in U.S. Water Policy: Summary, Conclusions and Recommendations*. Final Report of National Water Commission, Superintendent of Documents. Washington, DC: U.S. Government Printing Office.

Nowak, Peter J. 1987. "The Adoption of Agricultural Conservation Technologies: Economic and Diffusion Explanations." *Rural Sociology* 52(2):208–220.

Nowak, Peter J., and Peter F. Korsching. 1982. "Social and Institutional Factors Affecting the Adoption and Maintenance of Agricultural BMPs." Pp. 349–73 in *Agricultural Management and Water Quality*, edited by F. Schaller and G. Bailey. Ames: Iowa State University Press.

Olsen, K. D., J. Langley, and E. O. Heady. 1982. "Widespread Adoption of Organic Farming Practices: Estimated Impacts on U.S. Agriculture." *Journal of Soil and Water Conservation* 37:41–45.

Pampel, Fred, Jr., and J. C. van Es. 1977. "Environmental Quality and Issues of Adoption Research." *Rural Sociology* 42(1):57–71.

Perrin, Richard, and Donald Winkelmann. 1976. "Impediments to Technological Progress on Small versus Large Farms." *American Journal of Agricultural Economics* 58:888–894.

Pimentel, D., E. C. Terhune, R. Dyson-Hudson, S. Rochereau, R. Samis, E. Smith, D. Denman, D. Reifschneider, and M. Shepard. 1976. "Land Degradation: Effects on Food and Energy Resources." *Science* 194:149–155.

Poincelot, Raymond P. 1986. *Toward a More Sustainable Agriculture*. Westport, CT: AVI Publishing.

ReVelle, Penelope, and Charles ReVelle. 1988. *The Environment: Issues and Choices for Society*, 3rd ed. Boston: Jones and Bartlett Publishers.

Rogers, Everett. 1983. *Diffusion of Innovations*. New York: Free Press.

Rogers, Everett M., Rabel J. Burdge, Peter F. Korsching, and Joseph F. Donnermeyer. 1988. *Social Change in Rural Societies: An Introduction to Rural Sociology*, 3rd ed. Englewood Cliffs, NJ: Prentice-Hall.

Sampson, R. Neil. 1981. *Farmland or Wasteland: A Time to Choose*. Emmaus, PA: Rodale Press.

Sloggett, Gordon. 1979. *Energy and U.S. Agriculture: Irrigation Pumping, 1974–77*. Economics, Statistics, and Cooperatives Service, Agricultural Economic Report No. 436. Washington, DC: U.S. Department of Agriculture.

Soil Conservation Service. 1961. *Land-Capability Classification*. Agricultural Handbook No. 210. Washington, DC: U.S. Department of Agriculture.

———. 1982. *Basic Statistics 1977 National Resources Inventory*. Statistical Bulletin No. 686. Washington, DC: U.S. Department of Agriculture.

Taylor, David L., and William L. Miller. 1978. "The Adoption Process and Environmental Innovations: A Case Study of a Government Project." *Rural Sociology* 43(4):634–648.

Thomas, John K., Howard Ladewig, and William Alex McIntosh. 1990. "The Adoption of Integrated Past Management Practices among Texas Cotton Growers." *Rural Sociology* 55(3):395–410.

Timmons, John F. 1979. "Agriculture's Natural Resource Base: Demand and Supply Interactions, Problems, and Remedies." Pp. 53–74 in *Soil Conservation Society of America, Soil Conservation Policies: An Assessment*. Ankeny, IA: Soil Conservation Society of America.

Tiner, Tom. 1982. "Public Health Aspects of the Edwards Aquifer." Pp. 60–67 in *Proceedings of the Symposium: Perspectives on the Edwards Aquifer*, edited by B. Luckens and G. Langley. San Marcos, TX: Edwards Aquifer Research and Data Center, Southwest Texas State University.

Tuve, George L. 1976. *Energy, Environment, Populations, and Food*. New York: John Wiley & Sons.

Vasey, David E. 1992. *An Ecological History of Agriculture*. Ames: Iowa State University Press.

Webb, Walter Prescott. 1936. *The Great Plains*. Boston: Houghton Mifflin.

Whittlesey, Norman K. (ed.). 1986. *Energy and Water Management in Western Irrigated Agriculture*. Boulder, CO: Westview Press.

Youngberg, Garth. 1984. "Alternative Agriculture in the United States: Ideology, Politics, and Prospects." Pp 107–1335 in *Alterations in Food Productions*, edited by D. Knorr and T. Waltkins. New York: Van Nostrand Reinhold.

*Chapter 8*

# Energy, Society, and Environment

*Loren Lutzenhiser, Craig K. Harris,*
*and Marvin E. Olsen*

Energy—defined broadly in physics as the ability to perform work—is an indispensable element of all human activities. Because everything we do, individually and collectively, utilizes energy in some way, it would appear to be a fundamental sociological variable that links the social sciences with the physical and biological sciences. But with the exception of Fred Cottrell's (1955) seminal work, energy was largely ignored by sociology until the 1970s, when energy supply crises prompted sociologists to begin to explore the role of energy in social life. Since that time, social science interest in energy has tended to fluctuate with societal concerns about energy-related problems. The energy shortages of the 1970s spurred a variety of scientific and policy initiatives that faded as energy prices fell during the 1980s. A renewed interest in energy occurred in the early 1990s, as some regional energy systems pursued energy efficiency rather than new sources of energy supply, and as international concern grew about global environmental changes resulting from energy use. At the beginning of the twenty-first century, energy systems face additional changes as deregulated energy markets stimulate a revival of power plant building and a vacillating interest in conservation activities.

This chapter explores these developments and their relationship to the growth of sociological knowledge about the role of energy in the environment–society dynamic. It is divided into six major sections. The first considers the treatment of energy by various social theorists, focusing on the parts played by energy and energy conversion technologies in the development of industrial societies. The second section uses the United States as a case study in the application of these perspectives, exploring historical changes in energy sources, levels of consumption, and the social uses of energy. It also presents alternative explanations for energy development trajectories, and inventories some key energy system impacts on society and the environment. The third section briefly chronicles the socio-political contexts of energy analysis from the 1970s to the present, and discusses the shifting grounds of energy policy debates about the social consequences of divergent energy development paths. The next two sections review social research on energy use and conservation. The first of these focuses on social behavior at the levels of the individual, the household, and the community—considering research on energy attitudes, knowledge, decision-making, and social behavior. The second focuses on the macro-social structuring of energy use across demographic categories, within life-style segments, and at the levels of organizational networks and producer/consumer systems. The final section considers the contemporary context of energy research, including emerging trends, challenges for the social sciences, and significant knowledge gaps.

While we cannot undertake a comprehensive discussion of the problem of energy in society in a single chapter, we identify what we believe to be some of the most important developments in the field, and we offer a conceptual orientation to further work on the topic.[1] There is, nevertheless, an overall thesis to this chapter. All social scientists—especially environmental sociologists—must take energy seriously, since it is both fundamental to social organization and a central factor in society–environment interactions. Conversely, analysts in other disciplines more closely connected to energy system operations must appreciate the social nature of energy use before adequate theories and effective energy policies can be formulated.

## THEORIES OF ENERGY AND SOCIETY

Although Herbert Spencer wrote, in 1882, that "Whatever takes place in a society results either from the undirected physical energies around, from these energies as directed by men, or from the energies of men themselves" (quoted in Rosa and Machlis, 1983), the crucial role of energy in human societies has been largely ignored by all schools of sociological theory (Lutzenhiser, 1994b). Even ecological theory, which would seem to be especially receptive to the idea of energy as a critical variable linking the environment, technology, and population, has failed to give it more than passing notice; and although energy studies have become a major component of environmental sociology, none of that work has thus far produced any kind of systematic energetic theory of society (Rosa and Machlis, 1983; Rosa et al., 1988).

Over the past hundred years, several writers who were not sociologists—Patrick Geddes (1884/1979), Wilhelm Ostwald (1909), Frederick Soddy (1912), T. N. Carver (1924), and Lewis Mumford (1934)—have emphasized the importance of energy for human civilization, but their work was never incorporated into sociological theorizing. The writings of anthropologist Leslie White have been known to many sociologists, but not widely used by them. In an attempt to formulate a general theory of societal evolution, White argued that the amount of energy per capita available to a society and the technological efficiency of its use directly influence the level of development attained by that society (White, 1949). He saw social activity as serving to organize matter and energy to achieve a localized reversal of the natural tendency toward entropy.

It was Fred Cottrell's *Energy and Society* (1955), however, that finally brought energy—as a crucial factor in social organization and societal development—to the attention of sociologists. His principal thesis was that "the energy available to man limits what he *can* do and influences what he *will* do" (Cottrell, 1955:2; emphasis in original). His analysis—introduced in early work on the social impacts of railroads (Cottrell, 1940; also see 1970) and elaborated in his later theorizing about the ecological basis of human society (Cottrell, 1972)—treated the technological *conversion* of energy (whether via the use of spears to secure energy from animals, hoes to convert solar energy stored in plants, steam engines to convert fossil energy from coal to motion, or nuclear fission to generate electricity) as a central, and essential, aspect of social life. Cottrell observed that transformative energy shifts—from low-energy to high-energy forms of society— coincided with the shifts toward industrialization, capital accumulation, urbanization, and rationalization involved in the modern transformation that has been sociology's principle focus. Although he did not attempt to formulate an energy-based general theory of society, Cottrell did demonstrate the countless ways in which the shift from low-energy to high-energy forms of society—and from one type of energy to another—has resulted in massive social, economic, and political changes. Such changes, Cottrell argued, depend upon societies' geophysical resources and conditions, their development of conversion technologies and social organization, their values governing expenditure and reinvestment of energy, and their very capacities to appreciate the energetic nature of their interactions with their environments. Cottrell's work was not extended by sociologists in subsequent decades, although its value has periodically been noted (e.g., by Duncan, 1964; Lutzenhiser, 1994b; Rosa et al., 1988).

Three contemporary nonsociologists who have written extensively about the role of energy in social life are economist Nicholas Georgescu-Roegen, biologist Howard Odum, and anthropologist Richard Adams. Georgescu-Roegen (1971, 1976) has dealt primarily with the consequences of finite energy resources in modern economic systems. Attacking orthodox assumptions of the inevitability of continued economic growth, he has argued that economic production, and hence also consumption, ultimately depends on energy availability; and since modern economies rely almost entirely on drawing down finite stocks of fossil fuels, existing forms of economic production cannot continue indefinitely.

Odum, a biologist, bases his work on the assumption that "any and every process and activity on earth is an energy manifestation measurable in energy units" (Odum, 1971:34). He then uses an ecological systems model to demonstrate the ways in which the activities of all living organisms, including humans, depend upon energy flows from the natural environment. Within human societies, he equates physical energy with social power, stating that "The true powers of individuals, groups, and political bodies lie in the useful potential energies that flow under their control" (Odum, 1971: 206). He goes on to demonstrate how energy flows influence economics, politics, and even religion within human societies (Odum, 1995).

Adams—the scholar who has written most extensively about the place of energy in social theory—takes energy as *the* fundamental factor in human life. "Everything in the environment of man is composed of energy forms and processes and can be measured in terms of the energy that is potentially available for conversion or is being converted" (Adams, 1975: 12). In this environment, control over stocks and flows of energy provides persons and organizations with the ability to exercise social power—the actual amounts and uses of power within social life being determined by cultural meanings and values. Adams' concept of energy-based social power is distinguished from Odum's in that energy forms and flows must be relevant to some system of value and meaning—that is, be culturally recognized (Adams, 1975:13). He also breaks with previous writers such as Duncan (1964:43), who had treated energy, matter, and information flows as distinct kinds of phenomena—Adams arguing that energy flows always convey information, and that information transfers always depend upon some sort of energy trigger.

Adams also rejects Leslie White's characterization of human systems as islands of negative entropy—that is, systems that in effect reverse the Second Law of Thermodynamics by concentrating and organizing energy. Drawing on the work of Alfred Lotka, Adams points out that the more extensively humans employ physical energy to perform work and create the social power necessary to construct and operate social systems, the greater the transformation of ordered energy within natural systems into useless heat. From the perspective of ecosystems, then, social organization and evolution *increase* rather than decrease entropy. "As culture advanced, man increasingly has had recourse to extrahuman [energy] triggers. . . . Man, in his immense anthropocentrism, has tended to congratulate himself and see this only as a per capita decrease in the human energy input; until recently, he tended to overlook the cosmic significance of the massive amounts of nonhuman energy required for this advance" (Adams, 1975: 121).

To Adams, all forms of social organization are dissipative systems because they continually disperse energy into the environment, requiring a continuous inflow of energy to maintain their existence. A mature, homeostatic socio-energetic system could be described, then, as a "steady state," since environmental inputs are balanced by outputs to the surrounding environment, although such a state is not necessarily sustainable indefinitely, of course. The basis of social power lies, then, not merely in control of the means of production, as argued by Marx, but in the control of "the *total set of conversion processes*, including consumption and destruction" (Adams, 1975:141; emphasis in original).

As humanity's ability to control ecological processes has increased, so has its capacity to exercise social power at a distance, with resulting persistent growth in the scale and complexity of social organization. Adams concludes, however, that the conversion of energy into power and social evolution cannot continue to increase indefinitely. "Since many of the particular forms of energy that we need are in terminal supply, we cannot indefinitely have an increase in the rate of conversion" (Adams, 1975:304). And rates of energy conversion and social expansion are not limited simply by energy supplies and technologies. Adams (1988) also argues that as energy dissipates it emits perturbations that disrupt both ongoing social life and the natural environment. To cope with these disruptions, humans create organizational structures in response to the consequences of energy use. The resulting social system changes further concentrate and utilize energy, but also transform increasing amounts of material resources into waste heat, and thus further increase the rate of entropy in the world.

## THE SOCIAL SHAPING OF ENERGY SYSTEMS

As all classic and contemporary theorists have pointed out, dramatic changes in the amounts, sources, and forms of energy used in human societies have taken place over the past two centuries. Data on energy consumption in the United States since the beginning of the industrial revolution (circa 1850) can be used to illustrate both the historic linkage between energy and economic development observed in all nations as they have industrialized, and the uncoupling of this relationship in recent decades.

### Changing Energy Sources and Levels of Consumption

In 1850, the United States consumed the equivalent of roughly 44 horsepowerhours (hph) of energy per person. By 1900 that figure had grown to 103 hph, and in 1950 it was 445 hph (Duncan, 1964:63). During those 100 years of industrial growth, the social capacity to expend energy to perform work increased more than *tenfold*. Using the more conventional energy measure of quadrillion Btus (or "quads"), we find that in 1950 the

United States consumed 34 quads of energy, or 229 million Btus per capita. By 1970, consumption had increased to 67 quads, or 334 million Btus per capita. Total energy consumption in the United States then climbed to 81 quads in 1979, but declined for the first time over the next four years as a result of conservation efforts and slowed economic activity. Consumption growth began again in 1984, however, and reached nearly 96 quads in 1999 (the most recent year for which data are available). *Per capita* consumption peaked at nearly the same time in the late 1970s (352 million Btus per person in 1978), but declined by 13 percent to 314 million Btus in 1983. Per capita consumption has grown continuously since 1981, and at 354 million Btus per person in 1999, it is nearly as high as at its peak (U.S. Department of Energy, 2001).

Because growth in economic productivity can outstrip growth in population and energy consumption, another useful measure is the amount of energy consumed per monetary unit (dollars, yen, etc.) of Gross Domestic Product (GDP). For the United States, that figure was 20 thousand Btus per dollar in 1950 and declined slightly to 19 thousand Btus in 1970.[2] Since then, however, the amount of energy consumption associated with each dollar of GNP declined steadily to 11 thousand Btus in 1999 (U.S. Department of Energy, 2001). In short, although energy consumption was closely linked with economic development in the United States until at least 1950, since that time this linkage has weakened as the United States and other industrialized societies have reduced their energy consumption per capita and per unit of GNP (Mazur and Rosa, 1974).

Although the specific sources and forms of the energy used in any particular country depend on its available fuel supplies and the structure of its economy, changes in the United States illustrate the general nature of these trends in most industrialized nations. The tenfold increase in U.S. energy use since 1850 was possible because of a fundamental shift in energy sources. In 1850, waterpower, draft animals, fuelwood, human labor, and wind power provided almost all of the energy then available. That situation changed over the succeeding century as fossil hydrocarbons—first coal, and later petroleum and natural gas—became the dominant energy sources. Significant regional hydroelectric development took place during the first half of the twentieth century, and nuclear fission has become an important—although not major—energy source since the end of World War II.

The amounts of energy obtained from these sources in 1999 are shown in Figure 8.1. This energy flow graphic indicates that 84 percent of the 96.6 quads of energy used in the United States in 1999 was in the form of fossil fuels—petroleum (39%), natural gas (23%), and coal (23%). The remainder was obtained from nuclear power, hydropower, and wood and other biofuels (U.S. Department of Energy, 2001).

The technological means by which energy is utilized in the United States have also changed considerably since 1850. At that time, most waterpower

Figure 8.1
Total U.S. Energy Flow, 1999 (Quadrillion Btu)

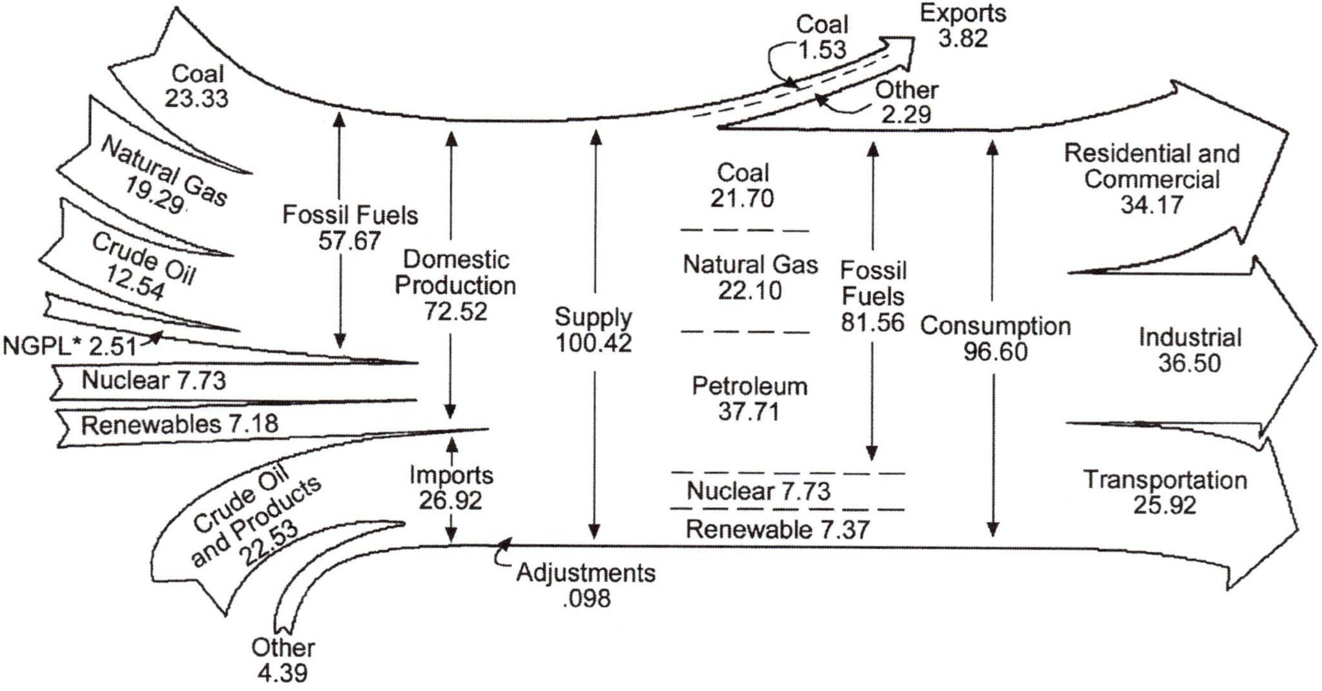

NGPL = Natural Gas Plant Liquids.
Source: U.S. Energy Information Administration, Annual Energy Review, 1999.

and wind power were converted directly into mechanical energy for operating textile factories, milling grains, pumping water, and sailing ships.
Today, all nuclear power, virtually all hydropower, most of the energy
obtained from coal, and portions of the energy obtained from natural gas
and oil are converted into electrical energy. Overall, about 35 percent of
input energy is used for electricity production (although about 66 *percent*
of the energy used for electricity generation is lost in conversion and transmission). As a result, although total U.S. consumption was about 96 quads
in 1999, the net energy actually used *to produce work* was only about 71
quads. Despite the huge energy losses entailed in producing, transmitting,
and using electricity, ever-increasing amounts of energy resources are being
converted into electricity because of the wide variety of uses to which it
can be put and the ease of using it (Starr et al., 1992).

## The Social Uses of Energy

Drawing again upon data from the United States, we can illustrate how
these energy inputs are actually used in industrialized nations by identifying
consumption patterns in the manufacturing, transportation, commercial,
residential, and agricultural sectors. Manufacturing uses directly about 38
percent of the net energy consumed in this country. Since manufacturing
in the United States is generally large in scale, bulkier fuels such as coal
can be used, although natural gas is now the dominant fuel in this sector.
Both of these fuels are used primarily to generate electricity and for process
heat. The transportation sector uses about 27 percent of the net energy
consumption in the United States—fairly evenly divided between freight
and human transportation and relying almost entirely on highly concentrated fuels such as petroleum derivatives. The commercial sector consists
largely of buildings used for business activities, but also includes government and other public buildings and related uses. This sector accounts for
about 12 percent of the net energy used in the United States—roughly half
in the form of natural gas and the other half mainly as electricity. The
residential sector uses about 15 percent of the net energy consumed. Of
this, two-thirds is used for heating and cooling living space, and the balance
for cooking, hot water, lighting, and appliances. Natural gas is now the
main source for space heat and hot water, while electricity dominates other
uses. Finally, agriculture (including fishing and forestry) uses directly only
about 5 percent of the net energy consumed in the country. Liquid fuels
for traction remain important in farming, while irrigation primarily uses
electricity. In addition to direct consumption, this sector indirectly uses a
considerable amount of the energy attributed to manufacturing for the production of all kinds of equipment, fertilizer, and other inputs, as well as in
the processing and distribution of agricultural outputs.

A sectoral view of energy consumption allows us to see that as the composition of activities in a society changes, the amounts, forms, and distribution of energy uses will also change. Many analysts have suggested that as the United States moves toward a postindustrial society with an emphasis on services and information processing, the amount of energy consumed per dollar of GNP will continue to decline as sectoral shifts occur in amounts and types of fuels used. The relationship is hardly straightforward, however. Daly (1973) and Pollock (1987) suggest that higher rates of recycling may require somewhat more energy consumption. Also, greater emphasis on leisure activities may reduce some forms of demand and increase others (Schipper et al., 1989), while shifts in production across a globalized economy will certainly continue to shift the locus of energy use.

## Accounting for Changes in Energy Systems

U.S. patterns are not ubiquitous, however. Other societies exhibit quite different levels of consumption and different sectoral concentrations of energy use—Europe and Japan, for example, use about half the amount of energy per capita. Several explanations have been advanced to account for these differences. One emphasizes *environmental pragmatism*—suggesting that societies rely upon those energy resources that are most readily at hand and can be obtained with the least effort. However, societies may neglect an immediately available energy source, as occurred with coal in England and oil in Mexico—or they may expend considerable effort to obtain an energy resource that is not readily available, as in Japan's worldwide hunt for whale oil or Taiwan's heavy reliance on imported uranium.

An alternative *technological determinism* argument holds that the technologies available for energy production, conversion, and/or consumption determine the amounts, sources, and forms of energy used by a society. Thus, the development of powerful water pumps made possible the deep-shaft mining of coal and the development of offshore oil technology that has extended the production curve of petroleum (Hubbert, 1962). However, the long delay that occurred in utilizing natural gas in the United States indicates that the simple availability of production and conversion technology is not a sufficient condition (Butti and Perlin, 1980). A demand-side version of the argument points to developments such as the expansion of coal mining attributable to the need for coke in manufacturing steel, or the vast growth in petroleum production attributed to the automobile; but counterarguments, such as the languishing of the internal combustion farm tractor in the late 1800s and early 1900s, suggest that technological demand is neither a necessary nor sufficient condition for such change. Relevant technology must certainly exist before an energy source can be utilized, but with deployment of expertise and resources, such technologies can often be developed to exploit new energy sources in a fairly short time.

The third approach sees energy users as trying to optimize the *opera-*

*tional efficiency* of technical systems (e.g., to obtain productive gains). A difficulty with this technical explanation lies in agreeing upon measures of optimal efficiency. Most socio-technical processes require multiple resources or inputs, so that any shift between energy sources generally involves a trade-off of some efficiencies for other inefficiencies. Controversies over the relative efficiencies of truck, rail, and ship transportation of freight illustrate this indeterminacy (Stern and Aronson, 1984). Also, differences between First and Second Law efficiencies sometime support different technical optima, and competing analytic paradigms and contending organizational interests often support competing definitions of efficiency.

A fourth approach suggests that energy sources and forms will be chosen to maximize the amount of *socio-economic power* available within a society. Part of the initial attractiveness of nuclear energy was that it was expected to provide a tremendous increase in available energy at very low cost, which would greatly expand economic productivity, wealth, and power. Significant increases in available energy have often been associated with economic expansion, which in turn generates wealth and power in a society. However, the argument that societies deliberately seek new sources and forms of energy in order to create more socio-economic power does not seem to be a universal principle in social evolution—for example, Tokugawa society eschewed technologies that would have greatly increased its power, and the Chinese emperors, while developing such technology, refrained from its use in world conquest.

A somewhat more sophisticated *political economy* perspective directs attention to the interests served or harmed by different energy systems. The development of wind conversion devices greatly benefitted mercantilists in European societies, for example, but only slightly benefitted landowners (Cottrell, 1955). In the present period, nuclear energy has been seen as beneficial to manufacturing capital but detrimental to the interests of finance capital. What's more, the debate over nuclear energy has taken very different forms in societies with different constellations of political and economic interests (Jasper, 1992). Reece (1979) and others have argued that the development of solar energy would impair the profitability of fossil hydrocarbon firms, leading powerful conglomerates both to slow the development of photovoltaics and take leading positions in the development of large-scale solar-electric facilities. More broadly, Ridgeway (1973) contends that a few large corporations have established effective control over most energy resources in order to minimize competition between the sources and maximize the profits obtained from each.

A political-economic approach need not be inconsistent with others—for example, one might examine the supply and demand technologies of a society with the aim of discovering the interests that have supported the creation of those technologies and the inertial conditions that they impose. A complementary approach that focuses on *socio-technical infrastructure* does just that in examining the structuring of energy systems via elaborate hardware and organizational infrastructures in contemporary societies. For example, the U.S. national investment in highway transportation facilities almost mandates that any future energy source used in transportation must have the same characteristics as petroleum. Similarly, heavy investments in facilities for large-scale production and distribution of electricity suggest that when small-scale photovoltaic technology becomes economically feasible, it is likely to be first adopted in remote rural areas and in societies that lack this infrastructure (Flavin and Lenssen, 1994). Hughes' (1983) cross-national studies of electric power systems and Cowan's (1984, 1989) studies of refrigeration and home heating technologies show how the institutional and cultural dimensions of infrastructure—which are embodied in regulations, customs, obligations, and meanings—also shape and restrain change in complex socio-technical systems. (See Hughes [1989] for a theoretical model of stability and change in such systems.)

We conclude that none of these six approaches (environmental pragmatism, technological determinism, operational efficiency, socio-economic power, political economy, or socio-technical infrastructure) alone provides a satisfactory account of how energy is used in a society. Efforts to explain variations in energy use across all societies, as well as the differences in energy sources and forms used by societies with similar technological endowments, could certainly combine these approaches. All should be taken into account in any analysis of energy system change.

### Energy System Impacts on Society and Environment

To this point, we have considered some of the ways in which various aspects of energy production and consumption result from social conditions; but the *consequences* of energy use also represent an important subject matter for environmental sociology. Emerging concerns about global-scale environmental change currently draw attention to some of these impacts, but a wide range of others is also salient.

Entropy considerations suggest that the production, distribution, and consumption of energy are always significant causes of various kinds of pollution. The mining of coal causes extensive land and water pollution (National Research Council, 1981), as does the mining of lower-grade petroleum resources (e.g., oil shales and tar sands). The extraction of oil and gas is relatively nonpolluting, although accidents involving offshore wells, pipelines, and tankers can cause serious environmental problems (Freudenburg and Gramling, 1994). The refining of oil and the burning of coal and natural gas in electric power plants are persistent sources of air pollution, as are emissions from a rapidly growing number of automobiles, trucks, and buses. The burning of fossil fuels releases carbon dioxide rapidly in large amounts, which contributes to the greenhouse effect, as well as to air pollution and acid precipitation.

Hydroelectric energy is relatively clean—but requires the destruction of wilderness, farmland, and aesthetic amenities by the large-scale damming of rivers, along with the forced relocation of residents and the inundation of habitat. The production of nuclear energy generates large amounts of radioactive waste, both in the mining and concentrating of uranium, as well as in the by-products of nuclear reactors. Although the operations of nuclear plants have not in general seriously polluted the environment, Chernobyl serves as an example of the inherent riskiness of this technology. The thermal generation of electricity (whether using coal, gas, oil, or nuclear fuels) results in the thermal pollution of water and air, and the transmission of electricity through high-voltage lines produces magnetic fields and visual impacts that often result in social conflict.

Renewable energy sources are somewhat more benign in their impacts, although the harvesting of wood can cause land and water pollution, and wood burning is a persistent source of sometimes serious air pollution that contributes to local health problems, atmospheric greenhouse gases, and acid rain. Solar energy (both direct heating and photovoltaics) and wind energy are relatively clean, although solar collectors can cause visual pollution and wind energy can cause noise pollution.

For environmental sociologists, a key aspect of these effects is how they are distributed across segments of society, especially in relation to the distribution of the benefits derived from energy. One dimension of this distribution is geographic location; another is socio-economic status. For example, coal-fired electric generating plants are often sited in rural areas, while urban dwellers receive most of the benefits of electricity availability (Aldrich, 1980); and, while low-income households use less energy than others, their energy costs are a much larger proportion of their total household expenses (Higgins and Lutzenhiser, 1995). Most of the energy consumed by lower-income households is used for basic necessities, whereas a considerable portion of higher-income household energy use is for discretionary purposes (Lutzenhiser, 1997; Morrison, 1978). For these reasons, rising energy prices often have severe negative economic impacts on low-income households (Lutzenhiser and Hackett, 1993)—effects that are generally not mitigated by energy equity policies (Higgins and Lutzenhiser, 1995).

Among the most sociologically interesting impacts of energy systems are their effects on socio-political and economic structure. Since these have been outlined and discussed most extensively in the context of alternative energy systems (Lovins, 1977; Morrison and Lodwick, 1981), we will consider them below.

## CRISIS AND RESPONSE: THE POLICY CONTEXT OF ENERGY RESEARCH

Social science research on energy is best understood in the context of the energy situations and policy debates within which it has developed. The roots of contemporary energy analysis are in the energy crises of the 1970s, but developments since the last oil embargo in 1979 have provided for a continuous elaboration of energy policy and research. At the time of the 1973 oil crisis, the United States had no comprehensive, long-range national energy policy.[3] The first steps toward formulating such a policy were a series of studies conducted by the Ford Foundation. The report of that project—*A Time to Choose* (Energy Policy Project, 1974)—presented a scenario in which zero energy growth could be achieved in the United States by 1990, although the authors viewed this as utopian. In reality, that goal was achieved in 1980.

By the mid-1970s, a number of analysts had begun to realize that the potential for reducing energy consumption in this country was much greater than had previously been imagined. Particularly influential was research by Schipper and Lichtenberg (1976) showing that Sweden then consumed only 54 percent as much energy per capita as the United States, despite its colder climate and higher gross national product per capita. Later research (Darmstadter et al., 1977) demonstrated that all other industrial nations (except Canada) used less than one-half as much energy per capita as the United States. These and subsequent studies suggested to many—including a growing number of economists—that continual energy growth might not be necessary for economic or social well-being in modern nations.

The year 1979 was not only the peak in U.S. energy consumption, but also the high point of energy policy studies. In that year, five major studies of the world's and the nation's energy situation were published, all of which came to essentially the same two basic conclusions.[4] First, the world's known reserves of fossil fuels are rapidly being depleted, and will become prohibitively expensive or essentially exhausted during the twenty-first century (except for coal reserves, which could last into the twenty-second century). Consequently, unless industrial societies are able to reduce drastically their consumption of fossil fuels in the near future, it will probably be impossible to sustain current levels of industrial production for more than 50 to 75 years. Second, if industrial societies are to achieve energy sustainability in the future, they must adopt vigorous national energy conservation programs and shift away from an almost total dependence on fossil fuels toward primary reliance on solar and other renewable energy sources. Most subsequent energy policy studies have continued to support those conclusions.

### Shifting Grounds of Policy Debate

An array of short-term initiatives begun during the 1973 energy crisis were institutionalized in the late 1970s, but despite considerable discussion about the need for a national energy policy during the Carter administration, none was actually formulated. In contrast, the Reagan administration issued a National Energy Policy Plan early in the 1980s—although it was never supported by Congress. The essence of the plan was to place federal emphasis and financial support almost entirely on increasing energy production, primarily nuclear generating plants. While energy conservation was endorsed as a desirable goal, it was to be achieved almost entirely through the marketplace by allowing energy prices to rise according to market forces with conservation to follow from consumer response (see Kraft, 1991).

Two broad, and somewhat contradictory, sets of policy interests tended to dominate national energy debates during those years: energy self-reliance (also described in more militaristic terms as energy security) and energy sustainability. Energy self-reliance/security emphasized sufficiency of energy supply, and led to actions such as the creation of a strategic petroleum reserve and the guarantee of international transit of energy supplies. This approach saw energy largely as a commodity, and sought ways to ensure the availability of energy commodities in the market. Other products of this approach included the synthetic fuels development efforts, oil shale recovery, and the construction of liquefied natural gas facilities. The self-reliance/security viewpoint accepted the operation of oligopolistic energy markets in capitalist societies, and sought to insulate those markets from the intrusion of what are perceived to be illegitimate outside political forces, such as the Organization of Petroleum Exporting Countries (OPEC).

In contrast, the socio-environmental sustainability approach viewed energy both as a societal necessity and an ecological resource, and sought to move the society toward an energy system in which the depletion of non-renewable energy resources and pollution of natural environments would be minimized (Flavin, 1988). Energy, in this view, ought to be provided in ways that minimize the risks involved in both production and consumption. The system should maximize efficiencies, as well as net energy or energy gain, and minimize geographical, political, and economic dependence, while ensuring equity both within the United States and across societies.

Sometimes a third theme—concern for energy and socio-economic equity—did, in fact, enter the policy debate, especially among intellectuals and social activists. Should low-income households be assured of an adequate supply of energy (e.g., by keeping the price for a minimal amount of energy consumption per household below the market level, or by some kind of energy tax rebate to those households)? Or should market prices for energy be unregulated, with the result that low-income households spend a disproportional share of their income for energy, while higher-income households purchase as much energy as they wish?

Falling energy prices in the 1980s, coupled with increased security of international energy supplies and a more efficient energy system, largely rendered these debates moot; but while crises faded from memory, advances in computing power and analytic techniques contributed to improvements in the capacity to model and forecast energy demands, supply alternatives, policy options, and environmental impacts. At the same time, regulatory initiatives during the 1980s produced increased efficiency across a wide range of technologies (from automobiles and lighting systems, to industrial motors and residential buildings), although the pace of change stalled late in the decade, with the leveling of energy efficiency discussed above. Government- and utility-sponsored incentive programs also stimulated the implementation of more efficient technologies, although at much lower than optimum levels (for a detailed review of energy efficiency program evaluation results, see Vine [1994]). In the 1990s, movement toward system deregulation, the opening of energy markets to competition between vendors and fuels, and the expansion of energy production began to shift emphasis further away from efficiency and the environment.

Throughout the 1980s and 1990s, there was, interestingly, little concern for the environmental consequences of energy use in policy discussions. Even those involving environmental advocacy groups centered on technical efficiencies and cost advantages of energy conservation—advantages that are receding with the growing attractiveness of low-cost natural gas. A number of indicators do suggest a generally improving environmental situation, in part as a result of a cleaner energy system (Easterbrook, 1995). But at the same time, there is growing concern about a range of environmental problems, many of which (e.g., acid rain, smog, the accumulation of greenhouse gases) are rooted in energy system operations (Stern et al., 1992). Driven by these concerns and questions about the eventual depletion of fossil energy reserves (and the availability and suitability of alternatives), policy debates about energy security, sustainability, and equity will undoubtedly re-emerge in the future. At that time, unanswered questions are likely to be raised regarding the amount of energy required for social well-being (and how the latter will be defined); which new sources of energy ought to be exploited (nuclear, biomass, solar, conserved energy); rates of population and economic growth (required and desirable); public versus private responsibility (and the relative virtues of markets versus regulation in securing an optimally efficient energy system); emphasis on supply expansion versus demand reduction; and the virtues of centralized versus decentralized systems.

### The Role of Energy in Alternative Developmental Trajectories

All of these dimensions of energy policy debate were brought together two decades ago in Amory Lovins' (1977) concepts of "hard" and "soft" energy paths, which he envisioned as two broad, mutually exclusive policy directions that industrial nations might choose to follow (for a detailed sociological critique, see Morrison and Lodwick, 1981). The "hard energy path"—which has been the policy of the United States and other industrial nations for the past hundred years—is characterized by: (1) maximization of energy use, which is assumed to be necessary for economic and social well-being; (2) primary reliance on "hard" energy resources and high technologies, including petroleum (as long as it lasts anywhere in the world), coal, nuclear fission, and eventually nuclear fusion and/or solar power satellites; (3) promotion of continual economic growth, dominance over the natural environment, and rising material standards of living; (4) assignment of primary responsibility for meeting energy needs to the marketplace, supported by governmental funding and price regulation when necessary to keep the market functioning smoothly; (5) strong emphasis on developing new technologies to provide more energy, and reliance on rising energy prices to persuade consumers to practice conservation; and (6) a highly centralized energy production system dominated by huge energy corporations, in which consumers have no control over energy supply (Lovins, 1977:26). Lovins made clear his conviction that if industrial nations were to continue along this path, it would rather quickly lead to their ecological, economic, and social ruin.

In place of those prevailing policy choices, Lovins outlined a "soft energy path" with the following characteristics: (1) reduction in total energy use to much lower levels, which need not impair national economic or social well-being; (2) development of intermediate and appropriate energy technologies for both supply and conservation that would utilize renewable resources and be diverse, flexible, and matched in quality to end-use needs; (3) creation of a permanently sustainable economy that would function in harmony with the natural environment and provide people with a comfortable but not lavish standard of living; (4) vigorous leadership by all levels of government in promoting and facilitating a shift from the hard to a soft energy path, but with management of the energy system remaining within each local community; and (5) extensive decentralization of the entire energy system, so that its geographical scale was matched to end-use needs and could be controlled by all citizens (Lovins, 1977:38–39). In Lovins' view, only by adopting this path as quickly as possible could industrial societies be assured of an enduring future.

Public opinion surveys have shown consistent support for "soft path" alternatives, and particularly of solar and other renewable energy sources compared to nuclear power (Farhar, 1994). Since Lovins' first writings, a drift away from the hard path trajectory—due, at least in small part, to Lovins' own ability to persuade firms and regulatory bodies to consider the benefits of alternatives—has led in the direction of a sort of "mostly hard" hybrid system. Demands for scarce capital and risks to the environment, public health, and personal well-being would seem to be salient criteria for differentiating the two "paths"—and for deciding upon their ultimate mutual exclusivity. For environmental sociologists, then, an interesting question is: How compatible are "hard" and "soft" path elements, particularly when their social consequences are taken into account?

Although Lovins' primary emphasis has been on energy technologies and systems, he also argued that "Perhaps the most profound difference between the soft and hard paths—the difference that ultimately distinguishes them—is their domestic sociopolitical impact" (Lovins, 1977:54). In Lovins' view, most of the impacts of a soft energy path would be beneficial for society, while most of the impacts of a hard path would be detrimental. Morrison and Lodwick (1981:359–364) enumerated the benefits that, according to Lovins' rather utopian vision, would follow from change to a soft energy path. These include: increased viability of the social system, economic self-sufficiency (including improved viability of enterprises, higher employment, better quality of work life, increased quantity and quality of goods and services, and better satisfaction of basic human needs); increased consumer understanding and participation in the energy system; the growth of humane values, as well as reduced social conflicts and inequalities; less economic concentration; fewer operational problems and negative consequences of failure of technologies; and decreased health, safety, and environmental risks. These claims would seem to call for systematic empirical examination and policy consideration—something that they have yet to receive.

## RESEARCH ON ENERGY AND SOCIAL BEHAVIOR

We turn now to areas in which empirical social science research on energy and behavior has been undertaken over the past two decades. Sociologists, anthropologists, and psychologists have, in fact, conducted a large number of studies of the "human dimensions" of energy systems. A good deal of that work has been focused at the micro or behavioral level (e.g., analyzing energy use by individuals and households). That work is discussed in this section, while research on energy use in larger social groups is considered in the next.

Social science energy research has been motivated, at least in part, by a desire to fundamentally improve understandings of how social choices are made about energy and how energy system impacts are socially perceived and managed. A good deal of social research on energy has also been quite applied in orientation, for example, investigating rates of participation in energy conservation programs and the impacts of such programs. But both sorts of research are part of a societal effort, beginning in the 1970s, to enhance the efficiency of energy use through science-based research and development (R&D). The status of energy as a social problem has shaped sociological interest in energy during this period, as has the scientific R&D environment in which social studies have been undertaken. In the United States and elsewhere, the period from the mid-1970s to the mid-1990s was one of accelerating energy R&D and experimentation with energy policy initiatives—although these activities were certainly much more intense in some regions, and were everywhere affected by the ebb and flow of resources. R&D work included technical innovations in energy production, conversion, distribution, and end use—most in the direction of securing greater technical efficiency for energy systems, and much of it sponsored by the federal government and undertaken through the U.S. national laboratory system (Lutzenhiser and Shove, 1996). Policy interventions included the creation of federal and state tax incentives, grants and loans for the development of alternative energy sources (e.g., solar and geothermal heating, wind-powered electricity generation), and energy efficiency improvements (from home insulation and more efficient lighting, to industrial motor upgrades and the replacement of outdated systems in government buildings). Energy efficiency labels were mandated for home appliances, building codes were rewritten to take energy conservation into account, and regional programs in the Pacific Northwest, New England, California, and parts of the American Midwest were initiated to manage a host of interventions at the regional and local levels. Related innovations in utility rate-setting, environmental impact assessment, low-income equity adjustment, and other areas of energy system operation and energy use were also established in this period; and, in a shift away from the previous logic of continuous expansion of energy supply, the rationalization and politicization of planning for energy system growth (so that the potentials of conservation and renewable energy sources could be taken into account) became widespread in the United States.

## Human Action and Analytic Paradigms

It is important to note that this growth in both energy R&D and energy planning sophistication drew upon knowledge in energy-related scientific disciplines, particularly engineering and economics. To a surprising degree, these perspectives have excluded consideration of the social aspects of energy systems—favoring a narrow focus on the technical efficiency of machines and the assumed directives of economic rationality. This focus has sometimes been undermined by consumer and producer nonresponse to engineering/economic efficiency initiatives, and by user adaptation of new technologies in ways that subvert their effectiveness. It has only been recently, however, that some efficiency advocates have concluded that "those of us who call ourselves energy analysts have made a mistake . . . we have analyzed energy. We should have analyzed human behavior" (Lee Schipper, quoted by Cherfas, 1991:154). But despite such realizations, an engineering/economic model of energy use continues to dominate energy planning, forecasting, and policy analysis. The behaviors of human occupants of buildings, for example, are seen as secondary to building thermodynamics and technology efficiencies, with "typical" patterns of hardware ownership and use being the usual assumption. Growth or decline in energy demand is seen to result primarily from changes made to buildings and equipment—changes that are believed to depend upon "the cost of energy relative to consumer income, as weighted by the priorities of the consumer for services, convenience, comfort and time" (Starr et al., 1992:986).

By assuming human behavior to be a relatively insignificant aspect of consumption, such approaches overlook the central role of human action in shaping energy use. A large body of social science research suggests, however, that engineering/economic analyses exaggerate the importance of energy prices and technological solutions, while underestimating the effects of human behavior (particularly noneconomic social action) in shaping energy flows (e.g., Baumgartner and Midtunn, 1987; Lutzenhiser, 1993; Stern, 1984). Energy use is highly variable across households, for example, even when taking into account the effects of buildings, equipment, and prices. In fact, studies of nearly identical units occupied by demographically similar families have reported 200–300 percent variations in energy use (Hackett and Lutzenhiser, 1991; Socolow and Sonderegger, 1976). Variability is also notable at the end-use level, where vastly different amounts of energy are used via appliances, for household heating and cooling, hot water, and so on (Lecar and Hanford, 1992; Stokes and Miller, 1986). Stern and Aronson (1984:182) observe that "Tremendous variation . . . exists in the needs and practices of energy users, so that analyses based on an average situation are likely to be wrong in many or most particular cases." The "average" consumer has, unfortunately, been a shibboleth in energy analysis.

Behavior also plays a significant role in *changes* in consumption that may result both from investment in more efficient hardware and from changes in the ways that persons occupy space and use equipment. A U.S. Department of Energy study of changes in household energy consumption between 1979 and 1987 estimates that if historic growth trends had not been reversed by efficiency gains, household consumption would actually have increased by about 20 percent in that period (U.S. Department of Energy, 1992). The analysis suggests that behavioral factors account for the bulk of the estimated 4 quads of energy conserved, with 1 quad of those savings attributable to changes in heating and cooling behavior, another 1 quad to the purchase of more efficient appliances and changes in the use of appliances, and about 0.3 quad each to smaller family sizes, migration to the Sun Belt, and the greater use of wood. Less than 1 quad savings could be attributed solely to improved efficiency of housing. Behavior also accounted for increases in some forms of energy use during the study period. Significant new demands were produced, for example, by growth in the use of residential air conditioning, the acquisition of a wider range and larger number of appliances, and increased use of hot water. In short, the energy consumed by households seems to fluctuate significantly from year to year, to vary significantly between households, and to respond to influences producing temporal trends—with human behavior playing a central role in the initiation, maintenance, and alteration of energy flows.

### A Role for Social Actors in the Energy System

Despite this fact, sociologists and other social scientists have been marginal players in the world of energy analysis. One of the earliest pieces of research on energy consumption, the Ford Foundation's study *The American Energy Consumer* (Newman and Day, 1975), did in fact explore social patterns of energy use and social impacts of energy shortage. However, since that time, most social science contributions have maintained a distance from the physical and technical details of consumption, focusing instead on public opinions about energy, attitudes toward conservation, and issues related to consumer information, incentives, and program evaluation (all discussed below). Much of this work has been coupled to policy interventions, with individualistic engineering/economic paradigms often accepted as appropriate for social analysis, that is, one in which "individuals" are seen to select appliances, take conservation actions, and process information about energy programs.

A useful corrective to such thinking is found in public opinion polling, an enterprise that samples individuals in populations and finds among them surprisingly common views. A large number of public opinion polls have been conducted since the early 1970s in which questions have been asked about persons' energy use and conservation beliefs and practices (for reviews, see Farhar et al., 1980; Farhar, 1993). Throughout the past two decades, persons have seen energy firms and government agencies to be primarily responsible for energy crises, and despite record low energy prices in recent years, a significant proportion (84% in 1991) continues to believe that energy is a serious problem. A majority (66%) also believes that energy crises will occur sometime in the future. As a result, public support for renewable energy sources and energy efficiency has been widespread and consistent over the past two decades.

The American public seems to view persistent inefficiency as a real problem, but one rooted in "business and industry priorities" and "decisions by governments," which are seen as "the greatest obstacles to the country using energy more efficiently" (Farhar, 1993:xvii). The amount of conservation behavior reported in households increased throughout the 1980s, with 82 percent reporting in 1990 that they had "cut back significantly" or "somewhat" in heating or air conditioning "to conserve energy." While "the urgency to engage in conservation has decreased markedly" (Farhar, 1993:xvii), these self-reports are corroborated by empirical data that show real declines in consumption (U.S. Department of Energy, 1992). Long-standing public support also continues for automobile fuel efficiency standards, more stringent regulation of energy companies, and recycling efforts and policies. Some survey results also suggest that the persistent environmentalism observed in public opinion polls (Dunlap and Scarce, 1991) may be associated with attitudes toward energy, and that a public which is "beginning to connect energy use and environmental concern" is also willing to pay increased fees and taxes for environmental protection and cleanup—if convinced that the money will actually be used for those purposes (Farhar, 1993:xxxiii). Data from in-depth interviews also suggest, however, that public understandings of the complex connections between environment, energy, conservation, and policy are limited at best (Kempton et al., 1995; Kempton and Montgomery, 1982).

Although opinion polls usually devote few questions to energy or the environment, a number of studies—particularly in the 1970s—have explored energy attitudes in greater detail (e.g., see Farhar-Pilgrim and Unseld, 1982). Common findings have included public support for conservation in principle, uncertainty that it is necessary, poor understanding of the national energy situation, willingness to make equitable sacrifices, and low trust in public institutions. Reviewing this research, Ritchie and McDougall (1985) concluded that the public would strongly support mandated standards, as long as they were viewed as equitable, with public opposition likely to increase with the severity of restrictions.

## Attitudes and Action

Public opinion was not unanimous regarding the severity and importance of the 1970s energy crises, however, nor were all consumers willing to conserve. Some observers even suggested that conservation appeals might have perverse effects (Stern and Kirkpatrick, 1977). As a result, differential willingness to conserve became the object of a number of studies of the linkages between consumer *attitudes* and *conservation action/inaction* (for reviews, see Costanzo et al., 1986; Olsen, 1981). A variety of social attitudes seem to be associated with conservation behavior, including "feelings of obligation," "belief in the importance of conservation," "belief in science," the "role of individuals" in society, as well as with unwillingness to conserve (e.g., "comfort and health concerns") (Heberlein and Warriner, 1982; Seligman et al., 1979). Some researchers have suggested that desires for comfort may compete with pro-conservation values, and have shown that conservers and nonconservers differ along these two dimensions (Seligman et al., 1983).

A series of studies has attempted to model energy conservation decision making, specifying the underlying linkages between conservation attitudes and subsequent behavior. Many have used the Fishbein and Ajzen (1975) model, which views both intentions to act and behaviors themselves as outcomes of a dynamic balance between the individual decision maker's attitudes and the influences of his or her social environment—with "situational" factors (e.g., price, energy supply limits, weather, knowledge or information, and income) that complicate the analysis treated as exogenous to the model. While some of these studies have reported significant relationships between attitudes and subsequent conservation action (Becker et al., 1981; Seligman et al., 1979), others found that situational factors predominate (Stutzman and Green, 1982; Wilhelm and Iams, 1984). Ester's rigorous test of the Fishbein-Ajzen model, when applied to energy behavior, found it, overall, to be a weak predictor, with "energy illiteracy" (lack of information regarding the severity and scale of energy problems, relative energy prices, and consumption alternatives) the most notable influence on persons' willingness and ability to conserve (Ester, 1985). Alternative models that explicitly consider the joint effects of contextual constraints and energy attitudes perform somewhat better, showing that the relative strength of attitude and contexts of choice may depend upon the complexity, difficulty, and cost of the behavior in question (Black et al., 1985). Also, different elements of basic models may differ in their influence on different consumer groups; for example, attitudes may play a larger part in the case of conservation adopters, while social disapproval may be more influential for nonconservers (Macey and Brown, 1983).

Although these studies have offered energy planners some insights (e.g., see Coltrane et al., 1986), social-psychological energy research has steadily diminished in volume since the early 1980s (Lutzenhiser, 1992). Part of the problem lies in the inherent limits of models focused solely on individual decision making. Recognizing these limitations, Stern and Oskamp (1987) have proposed a more complex, multidimensional view of resource psychology—one that treats attitude-behavior processes as embedded in larger systems of beliefs, events, institutions, and influential "background factors" such as income, education, family size, and weather.

## Energy Use in Social Context

Several studies have explicitly considered the effects of factors exogenous to attitude models, and several experiments have examined the ways in which key contextual factors (e.g., information, financial incentives, and prices) influence voluntary conservation. If "energy illiteracy" limits consumers' capacities to compare costs and formulate action plans, then the delivery of higher-quality information might be expected to obtain a greater conservation response. The impacts of efforts to improve consumer energy knowledge and motivate conservation through general information (e.g., via appliance energy labels, utility advertisements, and governmental appeals) are unclear, however (Dyer and Maronick, 1988). Studies of the effectiveness of direct information delivery to consumers (e.g., information about consumption and conservation opportunities via energy bills) find that "prompts" provided to consumers prior to the act are considerably less effective than "feedback" about recent consumption, and that more "humanized" information provided by video images, community role models, personal contacts with consumers, and the distribution of information through local networks is the most effective (see Farhar and Fitzpatrick, 1989 for a detailed review of feedback research).

Other studies have considered the effectiveness of financial incentives (e.g., loans, grants, tax credits) in influencing conservation action. A detailed review of incentive program evaluations (Stern et al., 1986) found that frequent failures of incentives can often be traced to poor economic/ energy information—but also, as economic sociologists would predict, to the fact that "individual" consumers often pursue "social" (and often enough, noneconomic) ends when making energy-related decisions. By this, we mean that factors such as status display, ethical consumption, and pollution reduction also play a part in the assessment of incentives. Also, different subgroups of consumers seem to be differentially attracted to various inducements, leading the reviewers to note the irony that "the stronger the financial incentives are, the more important the nonfinancial factors—especially marketing—become to a program's success" (Stern et al., 1986: 162).

The relationship of energy prices to consumption and conservation has also received empirical attention (although this is fairly unusual, given the common economic assumption that price is obviously significant). Two lines of research have explored the extremes of energy pricing and they present a picture of economic decision making that is profoundly social and at odds with the simple cost-benefit calculations assumed by actors in the engineering/economic approach. These are "master metering" (paying an "average" share of the energy use of some larger group) and "time-of-day" rates (the charging of higher prices for energy used during peak times when its use is most important). Both demonstrate that, as with financial incentives, consumer response to price is both highly variable and dependent upon the social structuring of economic choices.

Rather than receiving a monthly bill for their energy use, some apartment dwellers pay collectively, as a part of their rent. These "master-metered" customers lack information about their own consumption and its contribution to collective energy costs, resulting in about 35 percent more energy consumption on average than for individually metered customers (Craig and McCann, 1980). A number of interventions have attempted to address this "commons dilemma" by calling residents' attention to the collective effects of excessive individual consumption, and by creating "group contingencies" that pit subgroups of master-metered households and living groups against one another in contests with rewards—a strategy that evokes group solidarity and stimulates collective surveillance and social control. Projects have also offered cash rewards for specific conservation behaviors, such as closing windows and monitoring thermostat settings. All suggest that collective welfare can be substituted for self-interest, even when the financial incentive structure might tend to reward the latter (e.g., see McClelland and Cook, 1980).

However, do all residents unaffected by such incentives "naturally" pursue a commons-taxing strategy of optimal energy use in master-metered settings? In principle, this question is unanswerable, since only aggregate consumption information is available for master-metered sites. Hackett and Lutzenhiser (1991), however, were able to observe individual energy use in two master-metered complexes whose 500 apartments were, unknown to their occupants, equipped with individual meters. Rather than finding universal high levels of consumption, differences as large as 300 percent were observed between nearly identical households—differences that were attributable to variations in family size, length of residence in the complex, income, ethnic culture, and minor variations in the physical design and orientation of the units. There were also significant consumption differences between the two complexes, despite the fact that they were nearly identical socially and architecturally—a community or neighborhood effect that seems to reflect locally evolving standards of behavior. These findings suggest that, even where lack of concern for energy use is endemic, cultural practice and collective restraint can produce both highly variegated and lower than expected consumption levels—among households who might, by economic reasoning, be considered likely to exploit common property resources.

At the opposite end of the price continuum, Heberlein and Warriner (1982) considered the effects of a two-year experiment that randomly assigned electricity customers to various "time-of-day" energy price regimes. Participants had limited knowledge of the details of peak hours and peak/off-peak price ratios, but they tended to significantly shift their consumption to off-peak times, and their satisfaction with the new rates was generally high—even among those who were assigned very high (e.g., 8:1) peak-to-off-peak ratios, with peak periods as long as 12 hours. Surprisingly, about 90 percent of the participants thought that the rates were fair and equitable, despite the fact that higher rates took effect at precisely those times of day when energy use was at its highest in households. Subsequent research (Linz and Heberlein, 1984) found that, once persons had accumulated experience with the rates, they developed a sense of social obligation to shift their consumption away from the peaks. The authors argue that, rather than conservation attitudes necessarily preceding behavior, behavioral changes can also result in new energy attitudes—that is, attitudes, actions, and rates are co-determined elements of institutionalized energy-use arrangements.

### Energy and Social Knowledge

The literature on information, price, and incentives suggests that all of these are more social than individualistic models suggest, and more complex than imagined in conventional policy discourse. Several other lines of inquiry have concluded from observation and intensive interviewing that consumer knowledge and calculation are socially structured and inherently limited—to such a degree that conventional engineering/economic assumptions about consumer rationality and economic calculation are untenable. "Price consciousness" seems to be a variable rather than constant condition, and it is only one of a number of modes of normal, energy-related behavior (Heslop et al., 1981). Consumers may not recognize the incentive structure in a given situation, and even if significant opportunities to save energy (and money) are present, only persons with certain rationalistic styles (e.g., technological hobbyists or those interested in accountancy) may be able to appreciate that fact (Kempton, 1984). Ethnographic researchers have reported samples in which a good deal of energy conservation took place, with little evidence of economic calculation—persons instead responding to vague cultural values such as "reducing waste," "being independent," or "making the house tight" (Wilk and Wilhite, 1984). In these cases, energy use and conservation were incorporated by households into their larger "home improvement" plans, and conservation measures were chosen on the basis of visibility to neighbors and visitors (although the investments selected were often among the least effective).

Even when consumers claim to be well-informed about energy and believe themselves to be acting in an economically rational fashion, they may be mistaken. Archer et al. (1984:F.10) find, for example, that there is little evidence of consumer awareness of energy and conservation costs and benefits—in many cases, the "minimal necessary information indispensable to even gross cost calculation" being absent. This view is supported by Kempton and Layne's (1988) studies of consumers' energy accounting behavior, in which they found that while many kept their old bills, and some computed their annual energy costs or claimed to have read their meters in the last year, it was actually impossible for them to have collected the necessary information on weather, heat loss, equipment efficiency, and behavioral effects necessary to perform anything even approximating accurate economic calculations. In several cases of highly rationalistic and cost-conscious behavior (e.g., cases in which persons kept detailed records and attempted to assess the interactions of weather, buildings, and costs), Kempton and Layne found flaws in knowledge and logic that seriously distorted the calculations.

Limited respondent knowledge of the characteristics of buildings, systems, appliances, and fuels is probably widespread. A significant proportion of consumers, in fact, have been found to misrepresent the sizes of their dwellings, the amounts of insulation present, and the fuels used (Singh et al., 1989). Predictable misreporting is found in the cases of renters and low-income respondents, but higher-income, well-educated homeowners also misreport hardware and even fuels in significant proportions. When reported energy-use behaviors are compared with observations, consumer diaries, and/or activity logs, it has been found that, while behavior does tend to be highly patterned and repetitive, persons frequently cannot recall events, nor can they accurately estimate the durations or volumes of consumption (e.g., of hot water use) (Weihl and Gladhart, 1990). Other studies have found that persons often misrepresent thermostat settings, even when they know that the settings are being recorded (Kempton and Krabacher, 1984). Evidence also points to actors' overrepresentation of their own technical competencies, and systematic misreporting of energy-relevant household division of labor by gender (e.g., cooking, cleaning, washing) (Wilhite and Wilk, 1987).

Honest accounting for behavior (even honest accounting to oneself) may, in fact, be fundamentally problematic because of the limits of human cognition. Kempton and Montgomery (1982) note that since energy use is invisible and intrinsically difficult to quantify and analyze (even for experts), persons are forced to develop ad hoc accounting techniques that, quite reasonably, tend to overestimate the cost of conservation investments. Unconscious habit also plays an important role in everyday energy use. Many routine, energy-related actions simply go unnoticed—although it can hardly be otherwise if actors are to competently attend to longer-term goals, task sequences, and higher cognitive functions (Lutzenhiser, 1988). Studies asking consumers to keep diary records of their routines (e.g., cleaning, washing, door opening, refrigerator use) report that persons are surprised by the frequency of these actions and that the self-monitoring causes them to "catch themselves" in the act (e.g., peering into the refrigerator or running hot water) (Hackett and Lutzenhiser, 1985; Wilhite and Wilk, 1987).

A number of researchers have concluded that even the most routine forms of energy consumption involve poorly understood behavioral, cognitive, and social processes—while the two most common theories of energy and behavior ("attitude change" and "economic rationality") underestimate the complexity of energetic action and the importance of social influences (Archer et al., 1984). Some believe that entirely new approaches (e.g., theories of social networks and technology diffusion processes) are required (e.g., Costanzo et al., 1986), while others point to the need for better understandings of the ways in which economic, psychological, and social processes interact, so that models are better able to represent the complexity of real-world consumption (Stern, 1986). Stern and Aronson, in an important mid-1980s review and synthesis of the behavioral literature, point to the confusion caused by conflicting perspectives, and illustrate their point by identifying four quite distinct views of energy commonly used in policy and research (Stern and Aronson, 1984). Despite these differences, there seems to be a consensus, however, that adequate models of energy and behavior must be more directly concerned with the social contexts of individual action—at least a partial recognition that human behavior is inherently social and collective.

### Households and Communities as Units of Analysis

If energy use is social, then it might be argued that its fundamental organizing principles cannot be discovered through studies focused on individuals (even individuals seen to be acting under social influence). Instead, energy-related decisions and behavior must be seen as the properties of social units such as households, firms, organizations, and communities. We will focus on households and communities in this section, and return to a discussion of firms and organizations below.

In the household context, research has pointed toward the energy-relevance of collective processes such as the household division of labor, socially determined work roles, and the differential distribution of knowledge in the family regarding energy and technology (Kempton and Krabacher, 1984; Wilhite and Wilk, 1987). Energy-related gender differences have been reported, with women viewing conservation more seriously and men being less willing to accept regulations in domains of traditional male competence (Claxton et al., 1983). Distinct male and female spheres of energy-related activity have also been identified, even within families claiming an egalitarian division of labor (Wilhite and Wilk, 1987).

Klausner (1979) has argued that the energy consumption of female-headed households increases with larger numbers of ties to kinship networks and other social groups. He also associated the expressiveness of the head (i.e., level of aspiration and aggressiveness) with higher levels of consumption, and the presence of an adult male in the household with reduced consumption—pointing to the role of authority in household energy use. In a partial test of Klausner's hypothesis that "less ordered" matrifocal households are more consumptive, DeFronzo and Warkov (1979) did not detect higher consumption levels in those families, although their sample was biased toward higher incomes and homeowners, and therefore differed significantly from Klausner's sample of lower-class and welfare families.

Some work on parent–child transmission of energy attitudes and values has also been reported, with Wilhelm and Iams (1984) finding, for example, stronger mother–child associations in the cases of ecological and social responsibility attitudes, and "flexibility of energy-use behavior" more highly correlated with fathers' views. They also point to the possible importance of extrafamilial influences (e.g., peers) on childrens' attitudes and behavior.

Two studies have suggested that different types of families respond differently to rapid increases in energy prices. Research by Dillman, Rosa, and Dillman (1983) showed that, when faced with energy price increases, lower-income households made life-style cutbacks across nearly all end uses, while higher-income households maintained their consumption and/or took advantage of tax credits and incentive programs to invest in building conservation and equipment improvements. Marganus and Badenhop (1984), whose research also measured changes in well-being associated with price-induced energy conservation cutbacks and investments, found declines in perceived well-being across household life-cycle (family age) groups. Surprisingly, the oldest age group reported slightly higher well-being than other groups, despite the fact that price increases had doubled their budget share for energy costs.

Other research has pointed to the household as a symbolic realm of energy use (Monnier, 1983), in which items of hardware have collective meanings apart from their utilitarian significance, appliances must conform to status expectations (Hackett and Lutzenhiser, 1990), and relative energy efficiency is only one of many issues salient to social actors (Gordon and Dethman, 1990). This means that buildings, energy improvements, and alternative energy sources such as solar collectors are items that must be seen as meaningful in the symbolic realm of the community (Lutzenhiser and Hackett, 1993; Wilk and Wilhite, 1984).

The linkages between families as energy consumers and larger forms of social organization have also received some attention: for example, in considering the roles of social networks and technology diffusion processes in energy-use behavior and conservation, and the collective consumption and social dynamics of energy use in settings such as the apartment building, the housing complex, the neighborhood, and the small town (see Lutzenhiser, 1993:263–264).

It is clear that the networked social worlds of kin, associates, neighbors, and vendors, conditioned by the dynamics of collective life in buildings, neighborhoods, and communities, provide social organization for energy-relevant behavior; but while social processes structure consumption, so too do physical phenomena such as weather patterns, buildings, mechanical systems, and appliances. A number of researchers have considered the energy-related micro-behavior of persons and groups in physical settings, such as in temperature and device manipulation; customary and ritualized conduct; the patterning of activities across days, weeks, and seasons; and persons' understandings of these (see Lutzenhiser, 1993:264–269). Unfortunately, sociologists have had little contact with this work, in part because of the division of labor between the social sciences, engineering, and energy analysis. An overarching model that can capture elements as disparate as group dynamics, building management, body use, cognitive processes, and human-machine interactions would be needed to handle socio-physical processes at the group level. To date, progress toward such a model has been limited by the theoretical interests of the disciplines involved. Engineering comfort models, for example, assume many human-building interactions to involve straightforward physical relations between temperature, humidity, metabolic activity, clothing, and air movement (e.g., Fanger, 1972)—a view that has only recently been uncovered and questioned by those working in other disciplines (Prins, 1992). Models more along the lines proposed by Latour (1988), in which neither the social nor the physical is seen as privileged, at least at the outset of analysis, might be more useful (e.g., see Fujii and Lutzenhiser's [1992] study of Japanese air conditioners as mechanical and cultural systems).

In summary, research at the levels of the individual, household, and local group, demonstrates that significant variations in consumption can be traced to patterned behavior (conscious and habitual, routine and extraordinary) and to the interactions of actors, buildings, and equipment. It also suggests the value of richer conceptions of how social and material systems function in everyday life. The existing literature provides only a provisional and fragmentary understanding of real-world energy use at the micro or behavioral level, however.

## RESEARCH ON THE MACRO-SOCIAL STRUCTURING OF ENERGY USE

Social research has also focused on energy use across demographic categories and life-style groups, as well as within organizations and economic subsystems. For example, since Newman and Day's (1975) national study of energy, life styles, and equity, several researchers have undertaken more geographically limited studies of energy consumption and conservation across socio-demographic categories and household life-cycle stages (see Lutzenhiser, 1993:270). Age-related differences (primarily those involving older persons) have also been reported in relation to knowledge of energy-using equipment and building functioning (Diamond, 1984), as well as in behavioral response to energy price and billing changes (Hackett, 1984).

Not surprisingly, studies of household energy use have often reported strong income effects. Persons with higher incomes are better able to afford to purchase more energy, but they also have a greater ability and willingness to invest in conservation equipment and in newer, more efficient housing (Dillman et al., 1983), which could reduce their consumption. The effects of wealth on energy use are complex, since income serves as a resource, as well as an indicator of social status. In terms of the latter, social expectations and constraints work to shape many forms of consumption through the use of buildings and equipment in status-marking and via the residential segregation of persons by social class. The macro-patterning of energy use seems to be strongly influenced by the deployment of wealth and material culture (for a discussion of energy and social status, see Lutzenhiser and Hackett, 1993). The literature also shows that household income is strongly associated with the consumption of "indirect energy" embodied in goods and services (Herendeen, 1974), housing characteristics (Lutzenhiser and Hackett, 1993), electricity use and rate structure preferences (Blocker and Koski, 1984), and attitudes toward and access to conservation services (Dillman et al., 1983). In a large study of California households facing rising energy prices in the 1980s, Schwartz and True (1990) looked for price effects on reported conservation actions in various income and life-cycle groups. They found quite different price elasticities for different groups, and for different end uses across groups. The equity implications of differential income effects have also received some attention, for example, in terms of energy pricing schemes, supply technologies, conservation alternatives, and environmental pollution policies (Cramer et al., 1985; Dillman et al., 1983; Lutzenhiser and Hackett, 1993; Morrison, 1978; Schnaiberg, 1975). And, it is useful to note that, while not all low energy users are efficient, nor are all high energy users inefficient (Baxter et al., 1986), persons who actively pursue low energy life styles often use surprisingly little energy, and at the same time report high quality of life (Hackett and Schwartz, 1980).

Quantitative studies of ethnic energy-use patterns, as well as in-depth ethnographic studies of household life and energy use within different cultures, show that energy consumption differences result from cultural practice (Erickson, 1997; Lutzenhiser, 1997), with differential price and policy impacts on low-income minority households identified, particularly among African Americans (Brazzel and Hunter, 1979). Other groups have received less attention. Differences between ethnic groups in family size, housing characteristics, and appliance holdings certainly influence consumption differences (Skumatz, 1988), but little work has been done to assign the appropriate weights to structural, as opposed to cultural, components of consumption. Throgmorton and Bernard (1986) offer a fairly comprehensive review of the literature on minorities and energy through the mid-1980s, in which they conclude that while there are clear and changing energy-use differences between minorities and the Anglo population (e.g., blacks consumed less than other groups prior to the first energy crisis and consumed relatively more by the mid-1980s), a lack of adequate data, due to the small numbers of minorities found in survey samples, has limited efforts to analyze these changes.

## Perspectives on Life Style and Energy Use

Since the early 1970s, the term "life style" has been widely used by energy researchers to refer to patterned differences in behavior and consumption within socio-demographic groups of the sort identified above, but also among other segments that are not captured by conventional demographic categories. The term has been applied to the comparative energy consumption patterns of whole societies (Mazur and Rosa, 1974), and more narrowly to group differences in energy use within a given society (Nader and Beckerman, 1978). The most rigorous definition of "life style" would probably be one that relates to the anthropological concept of *culture*, that is, the totality of practices, meanings, beliefs, and artifacts of a social group (Lutzenhiser, 1992). In the energy literature, however, the concept has no coherence, no single, agreed-upon working definition; but the notion that energy consumption differences are likely to follow from style-of-life differences that are apparent in most communities has appeal, since it points to regularities in behavior and hardware that are both energy-relevant and blurred by conventional demographic, economic, and psychological models of consumption (Lutzenhiser and Gossard, 2000).

Both marketing researchers and social scientists have contributed to life-style research.[5] The two disciplines seem to agree that useful distinctions between subgroups of consumers can be made, but they take opposite analytic approaches to the problem. Social researchers see consumption differences across demographic categories (age, income, ethnicity) as products of underlying class and subcultural differences and constraints, and note the role of consumption styles in defining actors' locations in the status complex (Bourdieu, 1984). Sociologists would agree that other life-style differences (e.g., forms of cultural expression, emergent styles, fads, small-group behavior, local and regional differences in ways of organizing everyday life) certainly warrant investigation, but these would tend to be seen as derivative of social-structural conditions.

Marketing researchers, who have long recognized stylistic differences in consumption, have developed analytic tools that enable clusters of consumer traits to be associated with differences in purchase behavior—but with relatively little regard to social structure. The resulting topologies classify consumers in life style–based "market segments." A number of residential energy market segmentation studies have been performed for energy firms (e.g., electric utilities), because subgroups of consumers seem to have quite different orientations to energy efficiency investments. Several classifications of customer types have, as a result, been proposed for use in targeting energy efficiency programs. A problem with the life-style segmentation approach lies in the fact that, while its categories are often intuitively appealing, it treats consumer preferences as rooted in personalities which are disconnected from social structure. For example, marketing classification schemes have been proposed that segment energy consumers according to their concern for "appearance," "safety," "hassle avoidance," "resistance to electric company control," or "high-tech orientation" (Feldman et al., 1986). Others have identified clusters of "pleasure seekers," "appearance conscious," "life-style simplifiers," "conservers," "hassle avoiders," and "value seekers" (Electric Power Research Institute, 1990). Although a social-class dimension sometimes is implicit in life-style typologies (e.g., in the categories of "survivor," "achiever," or "life-style simplifier"), membership in any given life-style group is treated, by default, as essentially voluntary. More rigorous efforts to link social and environmental values to life style, consumption, and social structure are easily imagined, but they have yet to be undertaken.

### The Life Style–Consumption Linkage at the Societal Level

At the societal level, however, shifts in collective ways of life and resulting energy-use levels have gradually taken place over the past three decades—contradicting one of the most persistent themes in social science writing about energy. This is the notion that societal development is inherently dependent upon the use of increasing amounts of energy. The fact that national measures of energy use and GNP per capita correlate at above .95 in the contemporary world would appear to strongly support this generalization, and the historical record is fairly clear. As societies have moved from horticultural to agrarian to industrial economies, they have become increasingly dependent on inanimate energy sources to perform work previously done by human and animal labor. In the process, total societal energy consumption has risen dramatically. At the present time, the 35 highly industrialized nations that contain 24 percent of the world's population account for 77 percent of total world energy consumption, at a per capita rate 10 times that of all other countries. A key finding, however, is that within this group of industrial nations, *the linkage* between GNP and energy use has been steadily weakening (Olsen, 1992). In fact, several studies have suggested an "uncoupling" of energy-use levels from societal development in the highly industrialized societies. For example, when the relationships are examined between energy consumption and quality-of-life measures other than GNP (e.g., health, education, access to art and media), they are found to be extremely weak or nonexistent across those societies (Buttel, 1979; Mazur and Rosa, 1974; Rosa, 1997). This would seem to imply either a permanent severing of socio-economic development from continuously increasing energy use (e.g., along a soft path), or a plateau of development beyond which some future technological and economic advances may require further expansion in energy consumption. Either outcome will obviously be shaped by the kinds of economies and forms of social organization that emerge in coming decades.

By more closely examining changing life styles, social structures, and patterns of energy use *within* these societies, Lee Schipper and his colleagues at the University of California's Lawrence Berkeley National Laboratory (LBNL) have offered some insights into their different socio-demographic structures and intermediate determinates of consumption. The LBNL research reveals large differences between industrial societies—and significant changes over time—in their use of various fuels, in housing (quality, efficiency, size, style, design), energy-using equipment (types, numbers, efficiencies), and consumer behavior (heating, water use, cooking, travel) (e.g., Schipper et al., 1996). These analyses also show that changing factors such as patterns of employment, household composition, travel, and public versus private consumption of goods and services, as well as changing consumer habits, lie behind changing society-level differences in energy use. Focusing on the United States, Schipper et al. (1989) direct attention to the energy implications of changes in age structure, female employment patterns, longer commutes, housing stock changes, and so on. They also argue that macro-social changes in the use of time and travel by various social groups may have significant energy consequences in the future. Schipper (1991) also points to other trends that may have significant future lifestyle and consumption consequences as well, including societal shifts from "production to pleasure" and shrinking household size.

Clearly, a number of macro-social influences are at work in shaping consumption in modern industrial/consumer societies. Some of these function to homogenize life styles on a global scale, while others (e.g., the constant efforts of higher status groups to stylistically differentiate themselves, supported by manufacturers' continuous offering of new stylistic opportunities) promote differences between groups. In the face of these pressures, we also find a persistence of traditional cultural patterns, with subcultures following strikingly different logics in actors' decision making. We can infer from the ethnographic literature cited above that subcultures differ in their understandings of energy-using appliances, standards of heating and cooling, ways of controlling technologies, and norms regarding bill payment. They also exhibit varying notions of the rights, prerogatives, and responsibilities of different family members, and even how and when animals and plants can become family members requiring heating, cooling, or bathing.

Energy flows through these subcultural worlds, energy bills are delivered there, and cultural actors are faced with opportunities to choose to either maintain or alter their energy-use patterns—choices that are both constrained and shaped by cultural logics. To date, our understandings of these worlds, their movement toward convergence, and the energy implications of their differentiation, are limited.

## Energy and Organizational Systems

Finally, we consider energy and organizations, although it should be noted that the spheres of activity of organizations, households, and communities are not distinct. Energy is used by societies that function as more or less integrated wholes on multiple levels of organization. Household members work in organizations, and organizations manufacture, distribute, and regulate goods and services destined for household use; communities provide the context for organizational systems which, in turn, shape community life. An adequate understanding of energy use in society should take account of these linkages and how they may change in the future. For example, some forms of consumption may occur either in the home or in a public setting, and through time the locus of that activity may shift. Longer work hours and longer commutes may result in eating out more often or eating while in transit. Child care offered by employers may shift some energy use from the home to a collective child care site. Telecommuting (working at home with electronic connections to the workplace) can shift consumption in the opposite direction.

Consumers also acquire goods, services, appliances, information, housing, automobiles, and so on through networks of actors and organizations whose choices may adversely affect consumer utility, energy demand, and the environment (Beldock, 1988). Architects, builders, subcontractors, code officials, automobile dealers, utility company representatives, appliance salesmen, and so on operate through elaborate networks of commercial and regulatory relations that mediate and structure the relationships between consumers and manufacturers (Lutzenhiser, 1994a). Stern and Aronson (1984) note that these intermediaries' incentives to pursue energy efficiency are few, while their disincentives are many. Corporations and their officers seek the short-term accumulation of profits, tend to avoid unfamiliar problems and risks, and are influenced by the competitive, contractual, and regulatory environments in which they must operate. Government agencies frequently adopt regulations and promote development projects that are politically rather than technically motivated—or are technically motivated by nonenergy objectives—and are therefore largely indifferent to energy impacts.

While Stern and Aronson note that research and interventions aimed at key intermediaries could pay large dividends, little effort along those lines has been expended. A few studies merit mention, however. These have focused on institutional barriers to energy efficiency, technology adoption by builders, appliance selection by contractors and architects, the framing of efficiency issues in appliance sales, loan officers' wariness of innovative housing proposals, conservation motivations of apartment owners, institutional barriers to super-efficient factory housing, and builder-installer network barriers to residential cooling innovations (see Lutzenhiser, 1993: 276–277).

Our knowledge of the social dynamics of energy use *within organizations* of various sorts is also limited. The received view assumes that organizational energy use must, of necessity, be carefully managed and rationally allocated—in line with physical and technical realities and energy costs (e.g., Shippee, 1980). But when the National Academy of Sciences panel on the Human Dimensions of Energy Use considered this issue, they concluded that organizations frequently fail to optimize their energy efficiency—among other reasons, because of lack of precise information and conflicting internal interests (Stern and Aronson, 1984). The panel pointed to a variety of circumstances that encourage risk aversion by firms and agencies, imitation of other organizations, and the delegation of energy-related decisions to outside actors (e.g., architects and designers).

Most commercial consumption is, in fact, mediated rather than direct; for example, the majority of commercial energy use is for air conditioning and lighting, often in rented space. Also, all commercial energy efficiency decision making, like other economic action, is socially "embedded" (Granovetter, 1985) and processed through organizational networks, in which mutual obligation, professional prerogatives, and customary practices routinely limit technology transfer (Lovins, 1992; Lutzenhiser, 1994a). Choices in the industrial sector about energy are also often assumed to be determined largely by relative prices and functional efficiencies (e.g., in historical fuel shifts from coal to oil and electricity). However, Ross (1986) and Cebon (1992) show that the process is much more complex and socially embedded, with Cebon offering a detailed review of the literature and an institutional model of industrial energy decision making. The political economy of energy in the industrial sector has significant social ramifications—industries are large, and therefore powerful, energy consumers who are often able to dictate system-wide energy pricing and technology choices.

While energy consumption in agriculture has received considerable attention, very little of that work has been sociological. Although the food system accounts for 20 percent of national energy consumption, less than 5 percent is consumed on the farm. The rest of the food system is divided among the industrial, transportation, commercial, and residential sectors. Since most farm operators are small entrepreneurs, one might expect their energy behavior to be similar to that of energy users in the commercial sector. However, the motivations of most farm operators are composed of a mix of profit maximization, life style, enjoyment, and occupational satisfaction. Thus, their energy behavior is also more complex than would be predicted by simple economic models (Swanson and Maurer, 1983). Although many writers suggest that agricultural development involves the substitution of inanimate energy for labor, some farm subsectors use relatively large amounts of both and some subsectors use relatively little of either (Harris and Macheski, 1988).

In studies of energy use in the transportation sector, the local journey to work via automobile has received the most attention. While there is a rich social-historical literature on suburbanization, cars, and travel (e.g., Jackson, 1985), with a few exceptions (e.g., Lutzenhiser and Hackett, 1993) the sociological aspects of transportation energy use and the environment have scarcely been considered. Even less attention has been paid to freight transportation, or to alternatives to contemporary long-haul freighting systems.

In the end, producers and consumers share in the continuous expansion of consumption via intricate networks of social relations. This expansion—and its range of negative environmental impacts—is rooted in the growth of new uses for energy, population expansion, and expanding economic activity. Study of the complex interactions that take place in these networks requires a sorting out of the processes by which consumers and producers influence one another, such as, through demands for energy-rich goods and services, through the control of goods offered in markets, through the use of advertising, through pricing, and the continuous reinvention of style to induce purchase. To date, our understanding of these processes has been limited—and in fact, muddied by the widely held notion that producers simply strive to satisfy consumer demands over which they have little control. This is a partial view at best (Schnaiberg, 1991). It should be pointed out, however, that the social science energy literature reviewed here can contribute a good deal to the more general analysis of producer/consumer systems—through its critique of models centered on individual choice and action, its warnings against overreliance on rationalistic explanations, and its insights into the social and cultural organization of technical systems and energy flows.

## THE CONTEMPORARY CONTEXT OF ENERGY RESEARCH

Just as there are strengths in the social science energy literature, weaknesses are also apparent. The previous two sections of this chapter have pointed to numerous gaps in our knowledge, some of which have been systematically inventoried by two National Academy of Sciences panels (Stern and Aronson, 1984; Stern et al., 1992), as well as by the prior critical reviews of environmental sociologists (e.g., Farhar, 1991; Lutzenhiser, 1993; Rosa et al., 1988). In this inherently interdisciplinary area, there has been little effort to theoretically link social action with the physical performances of buildings, technologies, and the natural environment—although a few specifications of socio-physical models have been proposed (Cramer et al., 1985; Lutzenhiser, 1997; Lutzenhiser and Hackett, 1993).

In fact, neither disciplinary nor interdisciplinary energy studies have been high on recent social science research agendas (Lutzenhiser, 1992). This is unfortunate, since two decades of research on the human dimensions of energy systems offers significant insights to social theory, applied research, and energy policy analysis.

The global environmental impacts of energy use in the industrialized world are now becoming more widely recognized, however, as is the disproportionate use of energy and other resources (and high pollution rates) of countries such as the United States. There is also a growing recognition that human behavior is central to energy use, that rapid socio-technical change and consumption reductions have occurred in the past, and that the entire system of energy flows and conversion technologies is socially structured. All of these observations suggest an elasticity in consumption requirements that offers openings for increased energy efficiency in such societies.

Because European scholars (as well as European citizens, firms, and policy makers) take energy-related environmental change, equity imbalance, and global competition for energy resources to be potentially serious problems, there is growing interest in energy-related social science in Europe. Perhaps because European analyses of technology and consumption are nearer the social science mainstream (e.g., see Bijker and Law, 1992; Miller, 1987; Otnes, 1988), European research agendas related to the human dimensions of global environmental change are turning social science attention to a wide array of energy, technology, and consumption-related topics. Some of these initiatives are moving in the direction of more detailed, societal-level understandings of how energy-using technologies are structured and how the interaction between social and technical factors shape energy demand.[6] Efforts have been begun in Switzerland and the United Kingdom, for example, to evaluate traditional techno/economic energy modelling systems with the aim of incorporating information on the institutional shaping of technologies and the cultural organization of consumer behavior into such models (e.g., Giovanni and Baranzini, 1997). European studies also have recently been undertaken on the energy impacts of industry practices (e.g., Guy, 1994; Shove, 1995); emerging energy equity issues (Boardman, 1991); the relationships between social and technical determinates of energy use (Hinnells and Lane, 1995); and the cultural meanings of energy information (Strang, 1996), billing arrangements (Wilhite and Ling, 1995), and efficiency incentive schemes (Boardman, 1993; Wilhite, 1994). European panels of social scientists and energy analysts have also been convened to consider larger agendas for social research in areas such as sustainable energy consumption (Norwegian Research Council, 1996) and personal transport (OECD, 1997). A recurrent theme in all of these developments has been movement away from individualistic, economistic, and purely technical perspectives, and toward the sociological study of energy use by, through, and within socio-technical systems (Shove, 1997). Cross-national collaborations and comparative studies demonstrate the relevance of this approach to global efforts to stem environmental decline (Shove et al., 1998).

In the United States, on the other hand, energy-related social science research remains limited—particularly in comparison to work in engineering and economics (disciplines that continue to be strongly supported by the national laboratory system, industry associations, and specialized journals). Unlike the European case, virtually no U.S. science funding has been made available for social analysis of energy systems, and no government energy or environmental agencies have recently supported energy-related social science research (e.g., see Lutzenhiser and Shove [1996] for a discussion of the institutional contexts of energy social science development in the United States and the United Kingdom). The National Science Foundation's program in the Human Dimensions of Global Change—the analog to various expanding human dimensions research efforts in Europe—has been disbanded and dispersed across the agency. Few of the new research and training initiatives recommended by a recent National Academy of Sciences' Human Dimensions of Global Change review panel (see Stern et al., 1992) to stimulate social research on energy consumption and production have been pursued by the federal government in a political climate that has sometimes been openly hostile to social and environmental research.

It seems likely, then, that in the absence of independent academic interest in energy-related environmental issues by social scientists, the social sciences will continue as underlaborers to the technical analysis of energy systems (i.e., invited occasionally to provide "marketing advice" or "evaluation services" in support of techno-economic paradigms). An expansion of independent social science interest is warranted, however, both by the importance of energy to human societies, and because the social study of energy systems offers insights into production and consumption processes that are implicated in other environmental problem areas of interest to sociologists, such as global equity, sustainability, and intrasocietal environmental justice.

There is a substantial body of work upon which such an expansion of interest can build. The sociologies of technology, risk, consumption, and household demographics can contribute useful theoretical perspectives and empirical findings to studies of energy and environment. Since demands for energy are culturally conditioned, work in media and culture studies is also clearly relevant, and because production decisions and energy system dynamics involve both choice in organizations and the mediating effects of organizational networks, work in the sociology of organizations is clearly relevant as well. So too are anthropological approaches to these questions, as well as work by human ecologists, geographers, environmental psychologists, political scientists, and researchers in marketing, management, and home economics. Where appropriate, insights from engineering and economics are crucial elements of an interdisciplinary approach to energy and socio-environmental systems. In short, sociological progress in this area should not be impeded by a lack of intellectual resources.

Environmental sociologists interested in energy have at least four significant tasks at hand, then. The first involves advancing sociological understandings of energy-related phenomena. Key theoretical questions about the relationships between energy producers and consumers remain to be answered by a political economy of energy; basic research on human use of machines and devices is in its infancy; and the sociological analysis of energy policy processes has scarcely begun. The second task involves taking a closer look at the mechanics of scientific paradigm construction in energy analysis and intervention in order to provide a critical appraisal of the complementarities and conflicts (including some fundamental disagreements) between the various disciplinary approaches available (e.g., sociology, engineering, economics, psychology, applied policy analysis). The third involves participating in applied interdisciplinary studies within the context of the energy system, enriching the quality of analysis and the effectiveness of interventions. The final task involves addressing emergent questions about energy and human social evolution. Two decades ago, concerns about energy development and the future of the global environment, for example, would have been secondary to questions about present and local (and mostly human) impacts. However, a larger view and longer time horizon have allowed us to imagine a future when fossil energy supplies are nearing depletion in a much more populous world—perhaps the middle of the twenty-first century, perhaps near its end, perhaps early in the following century. As a result, we are led to wonder about the resilience of the environment as we know it, and to imagine alternative developmental trajectories (and the alternative social arrangements, power structures, and distributional realities associated with various regimes of scarcity and technological possibility). We might ask about our possible ethical obligations to future generations (including persons born late in the twentieth century who will live well into the twenty-first). We might even ask about ethical obligations to ecosystems—both as natural biotic systems in their own right and as sites for future human habitation. If social scientists choose to participate in the emerging discussion of these issues as they relate to the roles of energy and energy-conversion technologies in the world's future, we will be able to contribute unique and useful insights. The theoretical orientations and empirical findings outlined in this chapter offer a starting point.

## NOTES

Professor Olsen passed away before this chapter could be completed. The final version draws upon material in a preliminary draft by Olsen and Harris, and from Lutzenhiser (1993), although it more fully develops and integrates the arguments contained in each. Professor Harris would like to thank the Michigan Agricultural Experiment Station for support which contributed to work on this chapter. Professor Lutzenhiser similarly acknowledges the support of the Washington State University Agricultural Research Center.

1. For other reviews of the energy literature that take somewhat different approaches, see Humphrey and Buttel (1982), Lutzenhiser (1993) and Rosa, Machlis, and Keating (1988).

2. All comparisons are in constant (1996) dollars.

3. Earlier efforts of the Truman administration to formulate and implement national energy policy were not continued during the succeeding years (Goodwin, 1981).

4. These reports included *Energy Future*, by the Energy Project at the Harvard Business School (Stobaugh and Yergin, 1979); *Energy: The Next Twenty Years*, the Ford Foundation (Landsberg, 1979); *Energy in Transition 1986–2010*, a report by the Committee on Nuclear and Alternative Energy Systems of the National Academy of Sciences (1980); *Energy in America's Future* by Resources for the Future (Schurr, 1979); and *The Good News About Energy* by the Council on Environmental Quality (1979).

5. For a detailed discussion of research in these traditions and their relevance to energy, see Lutzenhiser (1993:272–275).

6. For U.S. work in a similar vein, see Stern et al. (1997).

## REFERENCES

Adams, Richard N. 1975. *Energy and Structure: A Theory of Social Power.* Austin: University of Texas Press.
Adams, Richard N. 1988. *The Eighth Day: Social Evolution as the Self-Organization of Energy.* Austin: University of Texas Press.
Aldrich, Brian C. 1980. *Communities of Opposition: Energy Facility Siting in Minnesota.* Winona, MN: Winona State University.
Archer, Dane, Mark Costanzo, Bonita Iritani, Thomas F. Pettigrew, Iain Walker, and Lawrence White. 1984. "Energy Conservation and Public Policy: The Mediation of Individual Behavior." Pp. 69–92 in *Energy Efficiency: Perspectives on Individual Behavior*, edited by W. Kempton and M. Neiman. Washington, DC: ACEEE Press.
Baumgartner, Thomas, and Atle Midtunn (eds). 1987. *The Politics of Energy Forecasting: A Comparative Study of Energy Forecasting in Western Europe and North America.* Oxford: Clarendon Press.
Baxter, Lester, Shel Feldman, Arie P. Schinnar, and Robert M. Wirtshafter. 1986. "An Efficiency Analysis of Household Energy Use." *Energy Economics* 8: 62–73.
Becker, Lawrence J., Clive Seligman, Russell H. Fazio, and James M. Darley. 1981. "Relating Attitudes to Residential Energy Use." *Environment and Behavior* 13:590–609.
Beldock, John A. 1988. "Energy Efficiency Innovations in the Residential Appliance Industries." Doctoral Dissertation, Ecology Graduate Group, University of California, Davis.

Bijker, Weibe, and John Law (eds.). 1992. *Shaping Technology/Building Society: Studies in Sociotechnical Change.* Cambridge, MA: MIT Press.

Black, Stanley J., Paul C. Stern, and Julie T. Elworth. 1985. "Personal and Contextual Influences on Household Energy Adaptations." *Journal of Applied Psychology* 70:3–21.

Blocker, Jean T., and Patricia R. Koski. 1984. "Household Income, Electricity Use, and Rate-Structure Preferences." *Environment and Behavior* 16:551–572.

Boardman, Brenda. 1991. *Fuel Poverty: From Cold Homes to Affordable Warmth.* New York: Belhaven Press.

Boardman, Brenda. 1993. "Energy Efficiency Incentives and UK Households." *Energy and Environment* 4:316–334.

Bourdieu, Pierre. 1984. *Distinction: A Social Critique of the Judgement of Taste.* Cambridge, MA: Harvard University Press.

Brazzel, John M., and Leon J. Hunter. 1979. "Trends in Energy Expenditures by Black Households." *Review of Black Political Economy* 9:276–299.

Brown, George L. 1977. "Invisible Again: Blacks and the Energy Crisis." *Social Policy* 7:39–42.

Buttel, Frederick. 1979. "Social Welfare and Energy Intensity: A Comparative Analysis of Developed Market Economies." Pp. 297–327 in *Sociopolitical Effects of Energy Use and Policy*, edited by C. T. Unseld et al. Washington, DC: National Academy of Sciences.

Butti, Ken, and John Perlin. 1980. *A Golden Thread: Twenty-five Hundred Years of Solar Architecture and Technology.* New York: Van Nostrand Reinhold.

Carver, T. N. 1924. *The Economy of Human Energy.* New York: Macmillan.

Cebon, Peter. 1992. "Twixst Cup and Lip: Organizational Behavior, Technical Prediction and Conservation Practice." *Energy Policy* 20:802–814.

Cherfas, Jeremy. 1991. "Skeptics and Visionaries Examine Energy Savings." *Science* 251:154–156.

Claxton, John, Brent Ritchie, and Gordon McDougall. 1983. "Evaluating Acceptability and Effectiveness of Consumer Energy Conservation Programs." *Journal of Economic Psychology* 4:71–83.

Coltrane, Scott, Dane Archer, and Elliot Aronson. 1986. "The Social-Psychological Foundations of Successful Energy Conservation Programmes." *Energy Policy* 14:133–148.

Costanzo, Mark, Dane Archer, Elliot Aronson, and Thomas Pettigrew. 1986. "Energy Conservation Behavior: The Difficult Path from Information to Action." *American Psychologist* 41:521–528.

Cottrell, Fred. 1940. *The Railroader.* Palo Alto, CA: Stanford University Press.

———. 1955. *Energy and Society: The Relation between Energy, Social Change and Economic Development.* New York: McGraw-Hill.

———. 1970. *Technological Change and Labor in the Railroad Industry: A Comparative Study.* Lexington, MA: Heath Lexington Books.

———. 1972. "Technological Progress and Evolutionary Theory." Pp. 3–34 in *Technology, Man and Progress*, edited by E. Lemert. Columbus, OH: Charles E. Merrill.

Council on Environmental Quality. 1979. *The Good News About Energy.* Washington, DC: U.S. Government Printing Office.

Cowan, Ruth S. 1984. *More Work For Mother: The Ironies of Household Technology from the Open Hearth to the Microwave.* New York: Basic Books.

————. 1989. "The Consumption Junction: A Proposal for Research Strategies in the Sociology of Technology." Pp. 261–280 in *The Social Construction of Technological Systems*, edited by W. Bijker, T. P. Hughes, and T. Pinch. Cambridge, MA: MIT Press.

Craig, Samuel, and John McCann. 1980. "Consumers without Direct Economic Incentive to Conserve Energy." *Journal of Environmental Systems* 10:157–164.

Cramer, James C., Nancy Miller, Paul Craig, Bruce Hackett, Thomas M. Dietz, Mark Levine, and Dan Kowalczyk. 1985. "Social and Engineering Determinants and Their Equity Implications in Residential Electricity Use." *Energy* 10:1283–1291.

Daly, Herman E. 1973. "The Steady-State Economy: Toward a Political Economy of Biophysical Equilibrium and Moral Growth." Pp. 149–171 in *Toward a Steady-State Economy*, edited by H. E. Daly. San Francisco: Freeman.

Darmstadter, Joel, Joy Dunkerly, and Jack Alterman. 1977. *How Industrial Societies Use Energy*. Baltimore, MD: Johns Hopkins University Press.

DeFronzo, James, and Seymour Warkov. 1979. "Are Female-Headed Households Energy Efficient: A Test of Klausner's Hypothesis Among Anglo, Spanish-speaking, and Black Texas Households." *Human Ecology* 7:191–197.

Diamond, Richard C. 1984. "Energy Use among the Low-Income Elderly: A Closer Look." Pp. F52–F67 in *Proceedings of the American Council for an Energy Efficient Economy Summer Study*. Washington, DC: ACEEE Press.

Dillman, Don A., Eugene Rosa, and Joye J. Dillman. 1983. "Lifestyle and Home Energy Conservation in the U.S." *Journal of Economic Psychology* 3:299–315.

Duncan, Otis Dudley. 1964. "Social Organization and the Ecosystem." Pp. 36–82 in *Handbook of Modern Sociology*, edited by R. Faris. Chicago: Rand-McNally.

Dunlap, Riley, and Rik Scarce. 1991. "The Polls—Poll Trends: Environmental Problems and Protection." *Public Opinion Quarterly* 55:651–672.

Dyer, Robert F., and Thomas J. Maronick. 1988. "An Evaluation of Consumer Awareness and Use of Energy Labels in the Purchase of Major Appliances—A Longitudinal Analysis." *Journal of Public Policy and Marketing* 7:83–97.

Easterbrook, Gregg. 1995. *A Moment on the Earth: The Coming Age of Environmental Optimism*. New York: Viking Press.

Electric Power Research Institute. 1990. *Residential Customer Preference and Behavior: Market Segmentation Using CLASSIFY*. Report EM-5908, Electric Power Research Institute, Palo Alto, CA.

Energy Policy Project. 1974. *A Time to Choose: America's Energy Future*. Cambridge, MA: Ballinger.

Erickson, Rita J. 1997. *Paper or Plastic? Energy, Environment and Consumerism and Sweden and America*. London/Westport, CT: Praeger.

Ester, Peter, 1985. *Consumer Behavior and Energy Conservation*. Dordrecht: Martinus Nijhoff.

Fanger, P. O. 1972. *Thermal Comfort: Analysis and Applications in Environmental Engineering*. New York: McGraw-Hill.

Farhar, Barbara. 1991. "Toward a Sociology of Energy." *Sociological Practice Review* 2:81–86.

Farhar, Barbara. 1993. *Trends in Public Perceptions and Preferences on Energy and Environmental Policy.* Report no. NREL/TP-461–4857, National Renewable Energy Laboratory, Washington, DC.

Farhar, Barbara, and Colleen Fitzpatrick. 1989. *Effects of Feedback on Residential Electricity Consumption: A Literature Review.* Report no. SERI/TR-254–3386, Solar Energy Research Institute, Golden, CO.

Farhar, Barbara, Charles T. Unseld, Rebecca Vories, and Robin Crews. 1980. "Public Opinion about Energy." *Annual Review of Energy* 5:141–172.

Farhar, Barbara C. 1994. "Trends: Public Opinion About Energy." *Public Opinion Quarterly* 58:603–632.

Farhar-Pilgrim, Barbara, and Charles T. Unseld. 1982. *America's Solar Potential: A National Consumer Study.* New York: Praeger.

Feldman, Shel, Carl Finkbeiner, and John Berrigan. 1986. "Residential Segmentation for Marketing Utility Programs: General or Specific?" Pp. 5.63–5.74 in *Proceedings of the American Council for an Energy Efficient Economy Summer Study.* Washington, DC: ACEEE Press.

Fishbein, Martin, and Icek Ajzen. 1975. *Belief, Attitude, Intention and Behavior: An Introduction to Theory and Research.* Reading, MA: Addison-Wesley.

Flavin, Christopher. 1988. "Creating a Sustainable Energy Future." Pp. 22–40 in *State of the World,* edited by Lester R. Brown et al. New York: Norton.

Flavin, Christopher, and Nicholas Lenssen. 1994. *Power Surge: A Guide to the Coming Energy Revolution.* New York: Norton.

Freudenburg, William R., and Robert Gramling. 1994. *Oil in Troubled Waters: Perception, Politics, and the Battle over Offshore Drilling.* Albany: State University of New York Press.

Fujii, Haruyuki, and Loren Lutzenhiser. 1992. "Japanese Residential Air Conditioning Technology: Natural Cooling and Intelligent Systems." *Energy and Buildings* 18:221–234.

Geddes, Patrick. [1884] 1979. *Civics as Applied Sociology.* Leicester, UK: Leicester University Press.

Georgescu-Roegen, Nicholas. 1971. *The Entropy Law and Economic Process.* Cambridge, MA: Harvard University Press.

———. 1976. *Energy and Economy Myths.* New York: Pergamon Press.

Giovannini, Bernard, and Andrea Baranzini. 1997. *Energy Modelling beyond Economics and Technology.* Geneva: Center for the Study of Energy Problems, University of Geneva.

Goodwin, Cranfred D. (ed.). 1981. *Energy Policy in Perspective: Today's Problems. Yesterday's Solutions.* Washington, DC: The Brookings Institution.

Gordon, Lois M., and Linda Dethman. 1990. "Efficient Refrigerators and Water Heaters: The Role of Third Party Buyers." Pp. 2.53–2.60 in *Proceedings of the American Council for an Energy Efficient Economy Summer Study.* Washington, DC: ACEEE Press.

Granovetter, Mark. 1985. "Economic Action and Social Structure: The Problem of Embeddedness." *American Journal of Sociology* 91:481–510.

Guy, Simon. 1994. *Developing Alternatives: Energy, Offices and the Environment.* University of Newcastle: Center for Urban Technology.

Hackett, Bruce. 1984. "Energy Consumption and Energy Billing in Apartments." Pp. F106–F118 in *Proceedings of the American Council for an Energy Efficient Economy Summer Study.* Washington, DC: ACEEE Press.

Hackett, Bruce, and Loren Lutzenhiser. 1985. "The Unity of Self and Object." *Western Folklore* 4:317–324.

Hackett, Bruce, and Loren Lutzenhiser. 1990. "Social Stratification and Appliance Saturation." Pp. 2:61–2:68 in *Proceedings of the American Council for an Energy Efficient Economy Summer Study*. Washington, DC: ACEEE Press.

Hackett, Bruce, and Loren Lutzenhiser. 1991. "Social Structures and Economic Conduct: Interpreting Variations in Household Energy Consumption." *Sociological Forum* 6:449–470.

Hackett, Bruce, and Seymore Schwartz. 1980. "Energy Conservation and Rural Alternative Lifestyles." *Social Problems* 28:165–178.

Harris, Craig K., and Ginger E. Macheski. 1988. "The Social Dimensions of Energy Use in Agriculture." Pp. 311–332 in *Energy in Production Agriculture*, edited by R. C. Fluck. Amsterdam: Elsevier.

Heberlein, Thomas A., and Keith Warriner. 1982. "The Influence of Price and Attitude on Shifting Residential Electricity Consumption from On to Off-Peak Periods." *Journal of Economic Psychology* 4:107–130.

Herendeen, Robert A. 1974. "Affluence and Energy Demand." *Mechanical Engineering* 96:18–22.

Heslop, Louise A., Lori Moran, and Amy Cousineau. 1981. " 'Consciousness' in Energy Conservation Behavior: An Exploratory Study." *Journal of Consumer Research* 8:299–305.

Higgins, Lorie, and Loren Lutzenhiser. 1995. "Ceremonial Equity: Low Income Energy Assistance and the Failure of Socio-Environmental Policy." *Social Problems* 42:468–492.

Hinnells, Mark, and Kevin Lane. 1995. "The Relative Importance of Technical and Behavioural Trends in Electricity Consumption of Domestic Appliances." Paper No. 117, *Proceedings of the European Council for an Energy-Efficient Economy Summer Study*, edited by A. Persson. Stockholm, Sweden.

Hubbert, M. King. 1962. *Energy Resources*. Washington, DC: National Academy of Sciences—National Research Council, Publication 1000-D.

Hughes, Thomas P. 1983. *Networks of Power: Electrification in Western Society, 1880–1930*. Baltimore MD: Johns Hopkins University Press.

———. 1989. "The Evolution of Large Technological Systems." Pp. 51–82 in *The Social Construction of Technological Systems*, edited by W. Bijker, T. P. Hughes, and T. Pinch. Cambridge, MA: MIT Press.

Humphrey, Craig R., and Frederick H. Buttel. 1982. *Environment, Energy and Society*. Belmont, CA: Wadsworth.

Jackson, Kenneth T. 1985. *Crabgrass Frontier: The Suburbanization of the United States*. New York: Oxford University Press.

Jasper, James M. 1992. "Three Nuclear Energy Controversies." Pp. 97–111 in *Controversy: Politics of Technical Decisions*, edited by D. Nelkin. Newbury Park, CA: Sage Publications.

Kempton, Willett. 1984. "Residential Hot Water: A Behaviorally Driven System." Pp. 229–244 in *Energy Efficiency: Perspectives on Individual Behavior*, edited by Willett Kempton and Max Neiman. Washington, DC: ACEEE Press.

Kempton, Willett, James Boster, and Jennifer Hartley. 1995. *Environmental Values in American Culture*. Cambridge, MA: MIT Press.

Kempton, Willett, and Shirlee Krabacher. 1984. "Thermostat Management: Intensive Interviewing Used to Interpret Instrumentation Data." Pp. 245–262 in *Energy Efficiency: Perspectives on Individual Behavior*, edited by Willett Kempton and Max Neiman. Washington, DC: ACEEE Press.

Kempton, Willett, and Linda Layne. 1988. "The Consumer's Energy Information Environment," Pp. 11.50–11.66 in *Proceedings of the American Council for an Energy Efficient Economy Summer Study*. Washington, DC: ACEEE Press.

Kempton, Willett, and Laura Montgomery. 1982. "Folk Quantification of Energy." *Energy* 7:817–827.

Klausner, Samuel. 1979. "Social Order and Energy Consumption in Matrifocal Households." *Human Ecology* 7:21–39.

Kraft, Michael E. 1991. "Environmental and Energy Policy in the Reagan Presidency: Implications for the 1990s." Pp. 19–36 in *Energy, the Environment, and Public Policy*, edited by David L. McKee. New York: Praeger.

Landsberg, Hans H. (ed.). 1979. *Energy: The Next Twenty Years*. Cambridge, MA: Ballinger.

Latour, Bruno. 1988. "Mixing Humans and Nonhumans Together: The Sociology of a Door-closer." *Social Problems* 35:298–310.

Lecar, Matt, and James Hanford. 1992. *A Database of Residential End-Use Unit Energy Consumption Estimates*. Report no. LBL-32721/UC-350, Lawrence Berkeley Laboratory, Berkeley, CA.

Linz, Daniel, and Thomas Heberlein. 1984. "Development of a Personal Obligation to Shift Electricity Use: Initial Determinants and Maintenance over Time." *Energy* 9:255–263.

Lovins, Amory B. 1977. *Soft-Energy Paths: Toward a Durable Peace*. Cambridge, MA: Ballinger.

———. 1992. *Energy Efficient Buildings: Barriers and Opportunities*. Boulder, CO: E-SOURCE.

Lutzenhiser, Loren. 1988. "Embodied Energy: A Pragmatic Theory of Energy Use and Culture." Doctoral dissertation, Department of Sociology, University of California, Davis.

———. 1992. "A Cultural Model of Household Energy Consumption." *Energy— The International Journal* 17:47–60.

———. 1993. "Social and Behavioral Aspects of Energy Use." *Annual Review of Energy and the Environment* 18:247–289.

———. 1994a. "Innovation and Organizational Networks: Barriers to Energy Efficiency in the U.S. Housing Industry." *Energy Policy* 22:867–876.

———. 1994b. "Sociology, Energy and Interdisciplinary Environmental Science." *The American Sociologist* (Spring):58–79.

———. 1997. "Social Structure, Culture and Technology: Modelling the Driving Forces of Household Energy Consumption." Pp. 77–91 in *Consumption and the Environment: The Human Causes*, edited by P. C. Stern, T. Dietz, V. W. Ruttan, R. H. Socolow, and J. Sweeney. Washington, DC: National Academy Press.

Lutzenhiser, Loren, and Marcia Hill Gossard. 2000. "Lifestyle, Status and Energy Consumption." Pp. 8.207–8.222 in *Proceedings of the American Council for an Energy Efficient Economy Summer Study*. Washington, DC: ACEEE Press.

Lutzenhiser, Loren, and Bruce Hackett. 1993. "Social Stratification and Environmental Degradation: Understanding Household $CO_2$ Production." *Social Problems* 40:50–73.

Lutzenhiser, Loren, and Elizabeth Shove. 1996. "Coordinated Contractors and Contracting Knowledge: The Organizational Structure of Energy Efficiency Research in the U.S. and UK." Pp. 8:113–8:122 in *Proceedings of the American Council for an Energy Efficient Economy Summer Study*. Washington, DC: ACEEE Press.

Macey, Susan M., and Marilyn A. Brown. 1983. "Residential Energy Conservation: The Role of Past Experience in Repetitive Household Behavior." *Environment and Behavior* 15:123–141.

Marganus, Martin, and Suzanne Badenhop. 1984. "Energy Expenditures and Family Well Being by Stage in the Family Lifecycle." Pp. 391–404 in *Families and Energy: Coping with Uncertainty*, edited by B. M. Morrison and W. Kempton. East Lansing: Michigan State University.

Mazur, Allan, and Eugene A. Rosa. 1974. "Energy and Lifestyle: Cross-National Comparison of Energy Consumption and Quality of Life Indicators." *Science* 186:607–610.

McClelland, Lou, and Stuart W. Cook. 1980. "Promoting Energy Conservation in Master-Metered Apartments through Group Finance Incentives." *Journal of Applied Social Psychology* 10:20–31.

Miller, Daniel. 1987. *Material Culture and Mass Consumption*. Oxford: Basil Blackwell.

Monnier, Eric. 1983. "Energy Inputs and Household Behavior in France." *Journal of Economic Psychology* 4:197–207.

Morrison, Denton E. 1978. "Equity Impacts of Some Major Energy Alternatives" Pp. 164–193 in *Energy Policy in the United States: Social and Behavioral Dimensions*, edited by S. Warkov. New York: Praeger.

Morrison, Denton E., and Dora Lodwick. 1981. "The Social Impacts of Soft and Hard Energy Systems: The Lovins' Claims as a Social Science Challenge." *Annual Review of Energy* 6:357–378.

Mumford, Lewis. 1934. *Technics and Civilization*. New York: Harcourt, Brace and World.

Nader, Laura, and Stephen Beckerman. 1978. "Energy as It Relates to the Quality and Style of Life." *Annual Review of Energy* 3:1–28.

National Academy of Sciences. 1980. *Energy in Transition, 1985–2010: Final Report of the Committee on Nuclear and Alternative Energy Systems. National Research Council National Academy of Sciences*. San Francisco: W. H. Freeman.

National Research Council. 1981. *Surface Mining: Soil, Coal and Society*. Washington, DC: National Academy Press.

Newman, Dawn, and Dorothy Day. 1975. *The American Energy Consumer*. Cambridge, MA: Ballinger.

Norwegian Research Council. 1996. *Report of the Workshop on Sustainable Consumption Research*. Oslo: Norges Forskningsrad.

O'Brien, Robert M., and Sheldon Kamieniecki. 1980. "An Exploratory Study of Social Class and Energy Issues." *Political Behavior* 2:371–384.

Odum, Howard T. 1971. *Environment, Power and Society*. New York: John Wiley & Sons.

————. 1995. *Maximum Power: The Ideas and Applications of H. T. Odum.* Niwot: University Press of Colorado.

OECD. 1997. *Report of the OECD Policy Meeting on Sustainable Consumption and Individual Travel Behavior.* Paris: Organization for Economic Cooperation and Development OCDE/GD(97)144.

Olsen, Marvin E. 1981. "Consumers' Attitudes toward Energy-Conservation." *Journal of Social Issues* 37:108–131.

————. 1992. "The Energy Consumption Turnaround and Socioeconomic Well-Being in Industrial Societies in the 1980s." Pp. 197–234 in *Advances in Human Ecology,* Vol. 1, edited by Lee Freese. Greenwich, CT: JAI Press.

Ostwald, Wilhelm. 1909. *Energetische Grundlagen der Kulturwissenshaften.* Leipzig, Germany: W. Klinkhardt.

Otnes, Per (ed.). 1988. *The Sociology of Consumption: An Anthology.* Atlantic Highlands NJ: Humanities Press.

Pollock, Cynthia. 1987. *Mining Urban Wastes: The Potential for Recycling.* Washington, DC: Worldwatch Institute.

Prins, Gwynn. 1992. "Condis and Coolth." *Energy and Buildings* 18:251–258.

Reece, Ray. 1979. *The Sun Betrayed.* Boston: South End Press.

Ridgeway, James. 1973. *The Last Play.* New York: Dutton.

Ritchie, Brent, and Gordon McDougall. 1985. "Designing and Marketing Consumer Energy Conservation Policies and Programs: Implications from a Decade of Research." *Journal of Public Policy and Marketing* 4:14–32.

Rosa, Eugene A. 1997. "Cross-national Trends in Aggregate Consumption, Societal Well-being and Carbon Releases." Pp. 100–109 in *Environmentally Significant Consumption: Research Directions,* edited by Paul C. Stern, Thomas Dietz, Vernon W. Ruttan, Robert H. Socolow, and James Sweeney. Washington, DC: National Academy Press.

Rosa, Eugene A., and Gary E. Machlis. 1983. "Energetic Theories of Society: An Evaluative Review." *Sociological Inquiry* 53:152–178.

Rosa, Eugene A., Gary E. Machlis, and Kenneth M. Keating. 1988. "Energy." *Annual Review of Sociology* 14:149–172.

Rosa, Eugene, A., Alien E. Radzik, and Kenneth M. Keating. 1980. "Energy, Economic Growth, and Societal Well-Being: A Cross-National Trend Analysis." Paper presented at the annual meeting of the American Sociological Association.

Ross, Marc. 1986. "Capital Budgeting Practices of Twelve Large Manufacturers." *Financial Management* 15:15–22.

Schipper, Lee. 1991. "Lifestyles and Energy: A New Perspective." Lawrence Berkeley Laboratory, Berkeley, CA.

Schipper, Lee, Susan Bartlett, Dianne Hawk, and Edward Vine. 1989. "Linking Lifestyles to Energy Use: A Matter of Time?" *Annual Review of Energy* 14: 273–318.

Schipper, Lee, and Allan J. Lichtenberg. 1976. "Efficient Energy Use and Well-Being: The Swedish Example." *Science* 194:101–113.

Schipper, Lee, Michael Ting, Marta Khrushch, Patti Monahan, and William Golove. 1996. *The Evolution of Carbon-Dioxide Emissions from Energy Use in Industrialized Countries: An End-Use Analysis.* Berkeley, CA: Lawrence Berkeley National Laboratory.

Schnaiberg, Allan. 1975. "Social Syntheses of the Societal-Environmental Dialect: The Role of Distributional Impacts." *Social Science Quarterly* 56:5–20.

———. 1991. "The Political Economy of Consumption: Ecological Policy Limits." Presented at the Annual Meeting of the American Association for the Advancement of Science, Washington, DC.

Schurr, Sam. H. 1979. *Energy in America's Future: The Choices Before Us*. Baltimore, MD: Johns Hopkins University Press.

Schwartz, Donald, and Bruce True. 1990. "What Households Do When Electricity Prices Go Up: An Econometric Analysis with Policy Implications." Pp. 2.121–2.130 in *Proceedings of the American Council for an Energy Efficient Economy Summer Study*. Washington, DC: ACEEE Press.

Seligman, Clive, Don Hall, and Joan Finegan. 1983. "Predicting Home Energy Consumption: An Application of the Fishbein-Ajzen Model." Pp. 647–651 in *Advances in Consumer Research*, edited by R. Bagozzi and A. Tybout. Urbana, IL: Association for Consumer Research.

Seligman, Clive, M. Kriss, J. Darley, R. H. Fazio, L. J. Becker, and J. B. Pryor. 1979. "Predicting Summer Energy Consumption from Homeowners' Attitudes." *Journal of Applied Social Psychology* 9:70–90.

Shippee, Glenn. 1980. "Energy Consumption and Conservation Psychology." *Environmental Management* 4:297–314.

Shove, Elizabeth. 1995. "Threats and Defenses in the Built Environment." Pp. 45–61 in *Perspectives on the Environment* 2, edited by S. Elworthy, I. Coates, M. Stroh, K. Anderson, and P. Stephens. London: Avebury.

———. 1997. "Revealing the Invisible: Sociology, Energy and the Environment." Pp. 261–273 in *The International Handbook of Environmental Sociology*, edited by Michael Redclift and G. Woodgate. Cheltenham: Edward Elgar.

Shove, Elizabeth, Loren Lutzenhiser, Bruce Hackett, Simon Guy, and Harold Wilhite. 1998. "Energy and Social Systems." Pp. 201–234 in *Human Choice and Climate Change*, edited by Steve Rayner and Elizabeth Malon. Columbus, OH: Battelle Press.

Singh, Nirvikar, Paul Ong, and Susanne Holt. 1989. *Evaluating Biases in Conditional Demand Models*. Report to the Universitywide Energy Research Group and the California Energy Commission, University of California, Santa Cruz.

Skumatz, Lisa. 1988. "Energy-Related Differences in Residential Target-Group Customers: Analysis of Energy Usage, Appliance Holdings, Housing, and Demographic Characteristics of Residential Customers." Pp. 11.13–11.43 in *Proceedings of the American Council for an Energy Efficient Economy Summer Study*. Washington, DC: ACEEE Press.

Socolow, Robert H., and Robert C. Sonderegger. 1976. *The Twin Rivers Program on Energy Conservation in Housing: Four Year Summary Report*. Report no. 32, Princeton University, Center for Energy and Environmental Studies, Princeton, NJ.

Soddy, Frederick. 1912. *Matter and Energy*. London: Oxford University Press.

Starr, Chancy, Milton F. Searl, and Sy Alpert. 1992. "Energy Sources: A Realistic Outlook." *Science* 256:981–987.

Stern, Paul, Thomas Dietz, Vernon Ruttan, Robert Socolow, and James Sweeney (eds.). 1997. *Consumption and the Environment: The Human Causes.* Washington, DC: National Academy Press.

Stern, Paul C. 1984. *Improving Energy Demand Analysis.* Washington. DC: National Academy Press.

———. 1986. "Blind Spots in Policy Analysis: What Economics Doesn't Say about Energy Use." *Journal of Policy Analysis and Management* 5:200–227.

Stern, Paul C., Elliot Aronson (eds.). 1984. *Energy Use: The Human Dimension.* Washington, DC: National Academy Press.

Stern, Paul C., Elliot Aronson, James Darley, Daniel H. Hill, Eric Hirst, Willett Kempton, and Thomas J. Wilbanks. 1986. "The Effectiveness of Incentives for Residential Energy-Conservation." *Evaluation Review* 10:147–176.

Stern, Paul C., and Eileen Kirkpatrick. 1977. "Energy Behavior." *Environment* (December):10–15.

Stern, Paul C., and Stuart Oskamp. 1987. "Managing Scarce Environmental Resources." Pp. 1043–1088 in *Handbook of Environmental Psychology*, edited by D. Stokols and I. Altman. New York: John Wiley & Sons.

Stern, Paul C., Oran Young, and Daniel Druckman (eds.). 1992. *Global Environmental Change: Understanding the Human Dimensions.* Washington, DC: National Academy Press.

Stobaugh, Robert, and Daniel Yergin (eds.). 1979. *Energy Future: Report of the Energy Project at the Harvard Business School.* New York: Random House.

Stokes, Gerald, and Nancy Miller. 1986. "Exploratory Analysis of Residential End-Use Consumption." Pp. 7.230–7.245 in *Proceedings of the American Council for an Energy Efficient Economy Summer Study.* Washington, DC: ACEEE Press.

Strang, Veronica. 1996. *Environmental Values and the Energy Label: Report to the Department of the Environment.* Oxford: Environmental Change Unit.

Stutzman, Thomas, and Samuel Green. 1982. "Factors Affecting Energy Consumption: Two Field Tests of the Fishbein-Ajzen Model." *The Journal of Social Psychology* 117:183–201.

Swanson Louis E., and Richard C. Maurer. 1983. "Farmers' Attitudes toward the Energy Situation." *Rural Sociology* 48:647–660.

Throgmorton, James A., and Martin J. Bernard III. 1986. "Minorities and Energy: A Review of Recent Findings and a Guide to Future Research." Pp. 7.259–7.280 in *Proceedings of the American Council for an Energy Efficient Economy Summer Study.* Washington, DC: ACEEE Press.

U.S. Department of Energy. 1992. *Energy Conservation Trends: Understanding the Factors that Affect Conservation Gains in the U.S. Economy.* Report no. DOE/PE-0092, Office of Conservation and Renewable Energy, Washington, DC.

U.S. Department of Energy. 2001. *Annual Energy Review.* Information Administration, Washington, DC. DOE/EIA 0384 (99). htpp://www.eia.doe.gov/emeu/aer/.

Vine, Edward. 1994. "The Human Dimension of Program Evaluation." *Energy—The International Journal* 19:165–178.

Weihl, Jeffrey, and Peter Gladhart. 1990. "Occupant Behavior and Successful Energy Conservation: Findings and Implications of Behavioral Monitoring."

Pp. 2.171–2.80 in *Proceedings of the American Council for an Energy Efficient Economy Summer Study*. Washington, DC: ACEEE Press.

White, Leslie. 1949. *The Science of Culture*. New York: Farrar, Straus and Giroux.

Wilhelm, Mari, and Donna Iams. 1984. "Attitudes and Energy Conservation Behaviors of Desert and Non-Desert Residents of Arizona." Pp. 405–414 in *Families and Energy: Coping with Uncertainty*, edited by B. M. Morrison and W. Kempton. East Lansing: Michigan State University Press.

Wilhite, Harold. 1994. "Market Signals Fall Short as Policy Instruments to Encourage Energy Savings in the Home." Pp. 1:193–1:200 in *Proceedings of the American Council for an Energy Efficient Economy Summer Study*. Washington, DC: ACEEE Press.

Wilhite, Harold, and Richard Ling. 1995. "Measured Energy Savings from a More Informative Energy Bill." *Energy and Buildings* 22:145–155.

Wilhite, Harold, and Richard Wilk. 1987. "A Method for Self-Recording Household Energy-Use Behavior." *Energy and Buildings* 9:73–79.

Wilk, Richard, and Harold Wilhite. 1984. "Household Energy Decision Making in Santa Cruz County, California." Pp. 449–458 in *Families and Energy: Coping with Uncertainty*, edited by B. M. Morrison and W. Kempton. East Lansing: Michigan State University Press.

*Chapter 9*

# Natural Hazards and Disasters

*Joanne M. Nigg and Dennis Mileti*

The consequences of the impacts of natural disaster events on societies are dramatic. For example, over the last 20 years earthquakes, tidal waves, floods, hurricanes, tornadoes, landslides, and wildfires have claimed over 2.8 million lives worldwide. Over a dozen of these events have killed more than 10,000 people each. The accompanying economic losses to the built environment—commercial and municipal buildings, homes, bridges and dams, water and power systems, and communication networks—are staggering. During the past two decades, natural disaster events have resulted in an estimated loss of $25–$100 billion in property damage, and this figure does not include losses due to economic disruption of commercial and governmental activities (National Research Council, 1987). The United Nations declared the 1990s as the International Decade for Natural Disaster Reduction when it was realized that these losses were not only continuing but escalating worldwide.

Although the above description focuses on the magnitude of the *consequences* of natural disaster events, it is not always true that disaster consequences are in proportion to the magnitude (or the physical properties) of the *disaster agent* itself. In other words, the relationship between the "physical" damage and the "social" damage in a natural disaster is often quite tenuous (Dynes, 1970); natural disaster events that have similar physical characteristics may not have similar social consequences. Take, for example, two recent earthquakes—the 1988 earthquake in Armenia and the 1989 Loma Prieta earthquake in California. The earthquake in Armenia, which was 6.9 magnitude on the Richter scale, killed approximately 25,000, injured more than 31,000, and left 514,000 homeless. By contrast, the slightly larger (7.1 magnitude) Loma Prieta earthquake in the San Francisco Bay area killed only 62 people, injured 3,800, and left approximately 12,000 homeless. Because of this inconsistency, research on natural disasters has focused on characteristics of individuals and social systems that make them more or less vulnerable to the impacts of disaster agents.

The existence of a natural hazard—a river capable of flooding, an earthquake fault, or a weather system capable of generating a tornado or hurricane—is necessary for a natural disaster to occur, but it is not sufficient. Natural hazards may be present in the physical environment for extremely long periods of time without a disaster occurring. Even if a river floods, a hurricane develops, or an earthquake fault moves, a disaster—in its *social* sense—may still not result. In order for a natural disaster to occur, human beings, their social systems, and their built environments (their homes, buildings, dams, utility systems, etc.) must be dramatically affected, causing widespread damage, social disruption, and economic interruption.

Because of this linkage between the natural and social worlds, there are obvious linkages between natural disaster research and environmental sociology. Current research efforts in the field of natural hazards and disasters bridge the two prevailing emphases in environmental sociology. One approach emphasizes the *built environment*, while the other focuses on the *natural environment*. Traditionally, "natural hazards" concerns have been included within the natural environment area of environmental sociology, along with other issues such as social impact assessment, outdoor recreation, resource management, and energy (Dunlap and Catton, 1983:114). While natural disaster agents *do* derive from the physical forces of nature (particularly geophysical and atmospheric conditions), their societal consequences are directly related to the extent to which social systems and the built environment are disrupted. The vulnerability of any community to the impact of a disaster event is directly related to the complexity and condition of the built environment and to the extent that affected social systems are able to prepare for, cope with, and respond to the agent itself. The study of natural hazards and disasters, therefore, tends to bridge the gaps between the built and natural environments.

This chapter provides a brief overview of the history of natural hazards and disaster research in the United States, the formulation of a sociological definition of disaster, and major historical and current themes in disaster research.

## THE DEVELOPMENT OF DISASTER RESEARCH

Early sociological work focused primarily on the social consequences of disasters, a topic that has been rigorously studied by social scientists since the late 1940s (e.g., Barton, 1969; Fritz and Marks, 1954; Kreps, 1981; Quarantelli, 1987a). Almost all of the early research (1950–1962) was conducted by sociologists affiliated with one of three research programs—the

National Opinion Research Center (NORC) of the University of Chicago; the University of Oklahoma; and the National Academy of Sciences' National Research Council—that focused on behavioral responses to disaster events. In the course of their work, these groups studied a variety of natural and industrial disaster events in order to better understand human behavior in response to extreme, and often unexpected, situations; that is, situations that created a great amount of disturbance for communities and social systems. Some of the incidents studied by these groups included response to such diverse events as: the 1952 Bakersfield, California earthquake; three airplane crashes in Elizabeth, New Jersey; tornadoes in Arkansas and Texas; hurricanes along the Gulf Coast; a coal mine disaster; and a ship explosion in Texas City.

The early research topics addressed by these three groups were strongly influenced by their principal funding agencies, all of which were part of the U.S. military. During this post–World War II period, the military was quite concerned about the extent to which unexpected nuclear attacks on U.S. cities would disrupt military as well as civilian populations. The military wanted to be able to train soldiers to function according to plans following a nuclear strike as well as to be able to anticipate what problems might result from civilian behavioral responses to such attacks. Large-scale, rapid-onset peacetime disasters and industrial accidents, such as those mentioned above, were seen as providing comparable situations within which such issues could be studied.

There was an implicit assumption made by the funding agencies that underlay this early work—the basic problems in disasters (and, by extrapolation, in wartime situations) are found in the reactions of individuals to danger, loss, and deprivation. For this reason, much of the early research effort focused on victims and their responses to disaster events during the early emergency (or immediate post-impact) period. For example, the emphasis in the early NORC studies was on problems associated with individual behavior, as well as on the attitudes and opinions of those involved in the disaster.

However, because most of these research efforts were administered or conducted by sociologists, the emphasis was *not* psychological but sociological in orientation. For example, implications of the consequences for victims from different and identifiable social groups—the elderly, children, people living in poorer areas—within the context of the overall community affected by the disaster became important concerns.

Since many of these early sociological researchers were also trained in the substantive area of collective behavior (especially from a symbolic interactionist perspective), these studies also focused on the emergence of group phenomena following the onset of the disaster (e.g., the emergence of volunteer search-and-rescue groups before "official" emergency organizations could respond) and on the functions that rumoring served during the warning and early response periods. (For a more complete discussion of the theoretical and substantive approaches that shaped these early disaster research efforts, see Nigg, 1994 and Quarantelli, 1992.)

The significance of this early work was the rejection of the popularly accepted notions that societies affected by a disaster experience some disintegration, and that individuals in such situations engage in irrational and anti-social behavior. Instead of discovering support for this "disorganization" model of societal reaction to disaster events, these early sociological researchers argued that disaster-stricken communities resolve disaster problems through collective approaches, and these approaches allow them to rebound with some degree of resilience (Nigg and Perry, 1988). Although these notions were refuted over 40 years ago, we still see examples of this type of expectation, especially in the formal plans of some emergency management organizations. One only needs to remember the use of thousands of National Guard and federal troops to protect private property from looters during Hurricane Andrew, rather than to provide direct relief assistance to victims. The magnitude of looting (even its very existence) in the wake of many natural disasters has been grossly exaggerated, often resulting in a misuse of resources during the disaster response and early recovery periods.

The effect of the initial emphases in these early studies had two major consequences for the development of disaster research (Quarantelli, 1987a). First, the prototypic disaster was a rapid-onset event with little warning, where the impact was experienced over a wide geographic area. In fact, the problems and impacts generated by a large-magnitude earthquake were believed to be good approximations for those likely to accompany a nuclear attack. This perspective led to the development of a definition of disaster that guided much of disaster research during the next couple of decades:

an event, *concentrated in time and space*, in which a society, or a relatively self-sufficient subdivision of a society, undergoes severe danger and incurs such losses to its members and physical appurtenances that the social structure is disrupted and the fulfillment of all or some of the essential functions of the society is prevented. (Fritz, 1961:655) (emphasis added)

One result of this early emphasis on rapid-onset disasters was a lack of attention to other types of disaster events that were not necessarily concentrated in space or time. Slowly developing disasters such as long-lasting droughts (like the Sahael drought in Africa) or geographically widespread climate changes (like those produced by the El Niño and La Niña phenomena) have not typically been studied by sociologists as "disasters," despite the devastating impacts they have on human populations.

Attempts were made to account for the different levels of systemic disruption (that is, the *social impacts* of such events) suggested by Fritz's definition for different types of disaster events; however, the primary emphasis remained on immediate-onset events. Researchers identified several aspects of disasters that need to be taken into account to explain this variation: the predictability of an event's occurrence; the controllability of the event or its agent; the probability that the event could occur; the agent itself (e.g., whether it is natural or technological in origin); the speed of onset; the scope of impact; the destructive potential of the event; the frequency of the event's occurrence in a particular location; the length of possible forewarning; and the duration of impact (e.g., Dynes, 1970; Fritz, 1961).

Given this approach, the features of the disaster agent were depicted as variable, but their significance was exclusively social in nature. In other words, these features are not viewed as deterministic in and of themselves; rather, their impact on any specific community was directly related to the disruption of the social systems and the built environment in that community. As emphasized in the introductory section of this chapter, disaster events with similar characteristics—despite the type of agent that creates the disaster—may have different impacts in different communities. Given this attention to the variability across the features of disaster events, more recent work in the field of natural disasters has begun to apply this approach to other than rapid-onset disasters (e.g., Nigg, 1993; Quarantelli, 1996).

A second emphasis in the early work that had long-lasting consequences for the field was a focus on the "impact" and immediate "post-impact" periods, especially investigations of emergency response efforts (Nigg and Tierney, 1993). Disaster response studies have focused on the extent to which organizations and communities are systemically disrupted and the factors which are associated with differential levels of disruption. While these studies have primarily been concerned with the response of victims and their communities to the disaster, they have also investigated the extent to which communities were prepared to respond to disaster events (e.g., Gillespie et al., 1993; Kartez and Lindell, 1987). Ostensibly, those communities that were better prepared would be less seriously disrupted or, at least, better able to manage the consequences following the disaster impact. While these studies have looked at impacts on communities of all sizes, greater attention is currently being given to the impact of disasters in major metropolitan areas, since increasing urbanization and increasing population density are worldwide phenomena. For example, extensive research since the mid-1970s has been conducted by sociologists and other social scientists on the ability of both the Los Angeles and San Francisco metropolitan areas' preparedness for and ability to respond to a catastrophic earthquake (e.g., Mileti et al., 1981; Turner et al., 1986).

Again, because of the potential application to military situations, early disaster research focused on reaction, not prevention. This initial constraint resulted in the majority of research efforts investigating disaster planning and response activities rather than mitigation strategies or recovery efforts (Drabek, 1986). Dynes (1993, 1994) also points out, however, how this early usage of emergencies as extensions of "enemy attack" scenarios focused attention on command-and-control capabilities—ostensibly needed because of the chaos that would follow such an event—which developed a set of false assumptions that have been used as the basis of emergency planning for community disasters.

More recently, Quarantelli (1987b), among others in the field of disaster research, has called for a reformulation of the term "disaster" in order to overcome the limitations of earlier conceptualizations. His suggestions to guide this reformulation include:

1. An emphasis on "disaster" as a *sensitizing concept*, in Blumer's use of the term, rather than as an empirical determinant. This would allow the concept to be applied to a wider range of situations that have similar consequences for human communities.
2. A definition that is exclusively *social*. References to the physical characteristics would be important only insofar as they influenced the social dimensions of an agent's impact on a community.
3. Their characterization as *occasions*, in Goffman's terms, rather than events. In this way, disasters could be seen as social occasions that provide multiple possibilities for development, rather than as a singular type of outcome that results along a linear path.
4. Their characterization as *crisis occasions* in order to differentiate between agent- and response-generated demands. By focusing on response-generated demands, crisis occasions would need to be contextualized within the social parameters of the affected community, and would become part of the cycle of social stability and social change that typifies the dynamic properties of all social organization.

## ADJUSTMENTS TO NATURAL HAZARDS

The relationship between human populations and the natural environment has been a subject of investigation by social scientists for a long time. Early efforts (Park, 1936) viewed human collectives as adaptive units that respond to the natural world. Others, like Hawley (1950), have emphasized the study of the mechanisms through which adjustment occurs, and specification of the physical–social relationships that define human-environment interaction (Duncan, 1964). The general field is known as human ecology, and investigations seek the causes of human behavior in the natural environment and the processes that facilitate human adjustment to the physical world through social organization (Duncan and Schnore, 1959).

Extremes in routine natural processes, when they impact a human collective, can cause disaster. Extremes in physical systems become disasters when the social systems they impact have only partially taken such extremes into account when adjusting to the physical world; that is, when human beings don't anticipate how natural hazards might affect their communities. Human collectives typically emphasize adjustment to physical systems on the basis of the probable routine of nature rather than its equally predictable, although less frequent, extremes.

The environmentally routine in a hydrological (water) system, for example, is the presence of a river or lake, average annual rainfall, and other factors to which the human aggregate adjusts and on which it often depends. When extremes in this same physical system occur, for example, as a flood or a drought, they can result in a disaster. Environmental extremes are commonplace. Although they are of lesser probability in the short term than are the environmentally routine, they are certain to occur over the long term. For example, a river is likely to continue to flow within its "normal" banks over a period of years; but, at some time, it will overflow its banks and flood nearby areas. If the river runs through a community, this could result in a disaster.

The balance of this chapter will focus on human *adjustment* to living with natural hazards—the environmental extremes of nature. Historically, this approach derived from human or social ecology (Faupel, 1985), which places a major emphasis on the "human-environment" system; that is, the character and magnitude of a hazard is affected by human action. In other words, disaster impacts are a consequence of both physical and social systems that have been constructed by human effort. This trend in natural hazards and disaster research has shifted attention from studies of disaster response to investigations of how humans have created situations that endanger their communities, and how human action can lessen the potentially disruptive effects of natural hazard agents through various means.

From the perspective of environmental sociology, natural hazards research attempts to explain the choice of collective adjustment to some possible future disaster event. Given this objective, our focus in the remainder of this chapter is to review what is known about adjustment decision making; that is, about the selection of types of adjustment during the nonemergency period before a disaster occurs.

There are two general types of adjustments to environmental hazards—cognitive and behavioral. *Cognitive adjustments* refer to ways of thinking about the hazard. Such cognitions would include: ideas; understandings; feelings; expectations of the frequency, causation, and intensity of the occurrence of the event; and perceptions of the potential impacts of a disaster agent. Such cognitive processes routinely involve some *assessment of risk* to which individuals and their social systems are exposed. Risk, for purposes of this discussion, is defined as the expectation of certain harms or damages to social, political, or economic systems as well as to the built environment.

Developing understandings of peoples' cognitive adjustments to a hazard provides insight into why people are willing either to live with a threat or to do something to reduce the risk to which they believe they are exposed; that is, why some people undertake *behavioral adjustment*—individually or collectively—to reduce risk while others do not. According to Mileti and his colleagues (1981), risk reduction is the consequence of adjustment policies which intensify efforts to lower the potential for loss from future environmentally extreme events.

Sociological researchers conducting studies on natural disaster reduction policy and planning investigate collective attempts (formal and informal, public and private) to reduce vulnerability and risk, especially those that are associated with the threat of natural hazards to urban environments. These efforts have involved both structural (in terms of improving the physical integrity of the built environment as well as the structural relationships among social systems) and nonstructural solutions (for example, land-use planning and zoning policies) to disaster-related problems. Disaster reduction efforts are undertaken to reduce the consequences of the disaster impact both before impact (through the use of mitigation measures) and after impact (through disaster preparedness and response planning efforts). Especially important in these studies is the identification of the social, political, and economic factors that both facilitate and impede the adoption of disaster reduction efforts by organizations, professional associations, and governments.

Concerns about adjustment to natural hazards raise two basic questions. First, what factors account for the emergence of, interest in, awareness of, and concern about an environmental hazard? In other words, when do natural hazards begin to receive a sufficient level of attention, during non-emergency periods, to motivate people to consider or reconsider the level of risk which they are willing to tolerate, and to whom do these assessments become important and why? Second, what solutions (i.e., types of adjustments) are considered to be acceptable, and to whom are they acceptable?

Both of these questions focus on the understanding of natural hazards and their meanings, implications, and consequences for those who may be affected by them or for those who are responsible for the safety and welfare of those who are potentially threatened. By focusing on the social processes through which these understandings are formulated and shared, the importance of the communication process in the formulation of risk perceptions and policy solutions is highlighted. Also central to both of these questions is the concern about differential decision making with regard to adjustment to natural hazards, both within and across communities. When there are competing definitions of the acceptability of risk, what political and policy processes result in the selection of a collective adjustment strategy or mix of strategies?

The following sections review the natural hazards and disaster literature under three headings that shed some light on the above questions: hazard perceptions (i.e., perceptions of risk that facilitate adjustment); emergency preparedness and response planning (i.e., adjustments which increase the capacity of a social system to respond to disaster); and mitigation (i.e., adjustments to reduce risk).

## Hazard Perception

Although used in a variety of ways, *hazard perception* can be defined as beliefs about the existence and characteristics of a natural hazard. Hazard perception studies have been undertaken to investigate how people come to understand the risks from natural hazards to which they are exposed, and how those understandings are related to their behavioral responses. While most of these efforts have been traditionally directed to public perceptions of natural hazards and the risks they entail, more recent research has focused on the development of risk perceptions by professionals and governmental actors who have key roles in the development of disaster reduction initiatives. Particularly important in these studies has been the identification of contextual, cultural, and historical factors that have influenced the ways in which individuals and communities adjust to the risks from a natural hazard agent.

In general, research on natural hazard perception concludes that perception is a necessary but not sufficient cause of human adjustment to natural disaster, and that perception thresholds must be reached or exceeded for action to occur.

Studies of hazard perception have focused on how individuals and collectivities come to understand the character and relevance of the hazard for themselves and their communities. Hazard perceptions are often influenced by the characteristics that are associated with the expected future disaster. Such characteristics include the notions of speed of onset, scope, intensity, duration, frequency, temporal spacing, casual mechanisms, and predictability (Dynes, 1970). Another key component of hazard perception is the development of a *risk perception* (that is, a belief in the seriousness of the threat) that directly influences attitudes and dispositions about the need to consider further adjustments through the enhancement of preparedness and/or mitigation efforts (Mileti, 1980).

Individual, collective, and cultural perceptions of extreme events, as well as hazard-reduction adjustments, are vital to reducing the vulnerability of the built environment to the impact of a natural disaster agent. Perception plays a vital role in the hazard adjustment process, expanding our understanding of the frequent mismatch between selected adjustment options and the objectively determined level of risk (Parker and Harding, 1979).

Although some empirical evidence has been found to support a causal linkage between hazard perception and behavioral adjustment (e.g., Mileti et al., 1975), these linkages have been weak (e.g., Saarinen, 1982). Since the individual is the unit of analysis in studies of perception of natural hazards, behavioral adjustment has been defined variously as actions which can be taken by individuals: the purchase of insurance (Kunreuther, 1978); improvements in household preparedness (Turner et al., 1986); and mobility decisions (Kiecolt and Nigg, 1982). While awareness may be necessary for the eventual decision to engage in behavioral adjustment, it is not sufficient in and of itself.

However, when the hazard perception specifically includes an assessment of risk, slightly stronger relationships are found. Mileti (1980), for example, concluded that the greater the perceived damage or harm that could result from the disaster agent, the more likely hazard adjustments would be undertaken. Several researchers have posited the existence of a "hazard perception threshold" to explain this adjustment process (e.g., Kates, 1962, 1970; Preston et al., 1983; Slovic et al., 1979). Only when expected losses exceed some critical value or threshold will individuals and collectivities begin to consider new adjustment options.

A larger body of literature suggests that past experience with a specific hazard agent may have consequences for behavioral adjustment; however, findings on the influence of past experience are somewhat difficult to reconcile. Simple past experience alone does not account for peoples' current behavioral adjustment (e.g., Hanson et al., 1979). However, Preston and her colleagues (1983) found that awareness of a natural hazard was influenced by the ease with which people recall or imagine the intensity and impact of an event's occurrence, providing an explanation of why rare events (those which occur infrequently) generally do not provide sufficient motivation for adjustments to take place under "normal" (i.e., nonemergency) conditions. When the frequency of disaster events is low, people have little opportunity to become familiar with the likely consequences of experiencing disruption in their environments and how various adjustment options could reduce the extent of that disruption.

Alternatively, however, researchers have also concluded that when disaster events occur more frequently in an area and people have more experience with that hazard agent, they begin to underestimate the threat, thereby not engaging in further behavioral adjustments. Two different lines of reasoning have been used to explain why these underestimates occur— one focuses on cognitive adjustments; the other on the development of disaster subcultures.

### Cognitive Adjustments

All cognitive adjustments involve changes in peoples' awareness of environmental hazards. These changes allow for the reduction of cognitive dissonance (i.e., the psychological discomfort) people feel when they hold two conflicting beliefs simultaneously. In hazardous environments, cognitive dissonance may arise when a person believes that a threat exists but still expects to continue living in that environment (Shippee et al., 1980).

Researchers have identified several solutions to such dissonant situations. Taylor and Hall (1976) suggest that people grow accustomed to the existence of the environmental hazard over time and their concern about the threat is diminished. Weinstein (1983) states that people are unrealistically optimistic about the future, believing that they are less likely to be negatively affected by any possible future event. The most extreme form of cognitive adjustment results in the denial of the existence of the threat from a particular hazard (Slovic et al., 1979).

Slovic and his colleagues (1974) have identified a process whereby cognitive adjustments are made. They suggest that people have "anchors"—starting points for judgments about the hazard—which are adjusted over time to accommodate new information. The worst past experience, therefore, becomes the standard against which future impacts are judged. This explanation of the hazard perception development process accounts for the differential development of adjustment patterns both within and across communities. Those who have directly experienced the impact of a past disaster have greater familiarity with the consequences of disaster impacts and are more willing to undertake and support preparedness and mitigation adjustments than are those who did not have these direct experiences. Those who did not share in these experiences, even though they lived in the same community, may not feel that further behavioral adjustments are warranted. Cognitively, the latters' anchors may be adjusted to reflect this new event; however, the need to reconsider additional behavioral adjustments may not exist since they were relatively unharmed by this worst-case experience.

### Disaster Subcultures

The concept of a disaster subculture was first developed by Moore (1964) to refer to the cultural defenses which groups develop to cope with recurrent dangers. This includes adjustments—cognitive and behavioral, individual and collective—that are used by residents to prepare for, cope with, and respond to a disaster agent that has struck or that tradition indicates will strike in the future.

Wenger and Weller (1973) suggested three factors that facilitate the emergence of a disaster subculture. First, the community must have experienced repetitive disaster impacts and perceive that there is a recurrent, chronic threat from that hazard agent again in the future. Second, the development of a subculture is facilitated if the disaster agent allows for a period of forewarning, providing an opportunity to implement hazard reduction activities to lessen the impact. Third, the belief that damage will be widespread and could affect any part of the community facilitates the emergence of a disaster subculture.

Research in the area of disaster subculture has been sparse (e.g., Turner et al., 1980); however, there are indications that individuals tend to become complacent about making behavioral adjustments to a continuing threat from a natural hazard if the organizational component of the subculture is strengthened. For example, Hannigan and Kueneman (1978) discovered that as government accepts greater responsibility for flood mitigation, individual interest in flood-related matters is weakened. This finding suggests that individuals may be lulled into a false sense of security and become less prepared to cope with or respond to a disaster event because organizational adaptations to the threat appear to be sufficient. Underestimation of the threat, in this case, appears to be related to a sense that the government is responsible for reducing natural hazard threats and risks.

## Emergency Preparedness and Response

Emergency preparedness refers to how and to what extent people, organizations, and communities have adjusted to natural hazards and the disasters they cause by readying themselves to respond to future environmental disasters. Typically, response to natural disasters such as those caused by hurricanes, earthquakes, tornadoes, and other environmental extremes is more effective and more efficient if emergency plans exist before a disaster occurs. The focus of research on emergency preparedness has been on how organizations such as fire and police departments prepare for disasters. Additionally, research has sought to explore how organizations interact and network with one another to mount a coordinated community-level response to disaster. Research findings on this topic fall into two general categories. These are organizational factors (elements within each disaster response organization) and community organizational factors (those pertaining to all responding organizations in the community struck by disaster). This section of the chapter reviews these research findings.

### *Organizational Factors That Affect Disaster Response*

A large number of research studies have focused on the effectiveness of preparedness for, and organized response to, disaster. These studies, when brought together, point out key elements of good emergency preparedness and effective response to disaster. The first of these is normativeness. It has been found (Adams, 1970; Anderson, 1969; Drabek and Quarantelli, 1967) that the less an organization has to change from its routine nondisaster work (that is, its everyday work tasks and roles) to perform in a disaster, the more effective is its actual disaster response. In essence, organizations like fire and police departments, whose daily operations can be switched to handle the emergency at hand, do better than organizations that must adopt new operations that are unique to the emergency.

Second is the ability of an organization to be flexible. Organizations that are better able to vary from standard operating procedures during the disaster are typically more effective than those that cannot be flexible (Drabek et al., 1981; Kreps, 1978; Stallings, 1978). For example, an organization that has very bureaucratic work rules has a difficult time dealing with and adjusting to the uncertainty of disaster situations (Dynes, 1969). The result of inflexibility is that response to the disaster suffers. Flexibility is useful in many ways, including flexibility in doing disaster work, in decision making (Drabek et al., 1981), in mobilizing the organization for disaster response, in taking on new disaster-related tasks and work, and in giving up autonomy in order to become part of the general community response to the disaster (Dynes, 1969:191).

A third major factor that affects the ability of an organization to be effective in responding to disaster is being prepared (Kreps, 1978; Quarantelli, 1970). Disaster preparedness enables members to see how their organization's responsibilities fit into the general community's disaster response plan (Haas and Drabek, 1973). By engaging in preparedness planning, members of an organization become aware of the internal authority structure of that organization during the disaster response process (Dynes, 1969:20); a need that is particularly acute, since authority in organizations during emergencies typically changes from what it is during routine nonemergency operations. Preparedness also defines what functions organizations are expected to perform in a disaster situation (Dynes et al., 1972: 54). A clear definition of anticipated activities, tasks, and priorities is important in emergency situations because internal as well as community demands are so numerous. Organizations that must discover their disaster-related tasks and activities during a disaster are rarely as effective as they could have been if this planning were done before the onset of the disaster agent.

Several other aspects of emergency preparedness affect the effectiveness of organizations in responding to disasters. First, resources (staff and equipment), if adequate, enhance disaster response (Kreps, 1978), as does access to important information (Quarantelli, 1970). Preparedness planning typically pre-identifies resources that can then be allocated as the need arises. Second, preparedness also helps organizations respond more effectively to disasters by legitimating the roles and responsibilities of individual organizations, thus reducing interorganizational conflict during disaster response (Stallings, 1978). Third, preparedness helps an organization respond to disaster by creating cohesion among the members of the organizations included in the planning. Worker commitment (Dynes, 1970), group cohesion (Form and Nosow, 1958), and an absence of role conflict (Dynes, 1969) indicate that organizational workers can be more effective in their postdisaster efforts.

### Community Factors That Affect Disaster Response

Individual organizations certainly do not function independently during disasters. A rich research history has explored the nature and character of preparedness with respect to how different community disaster response organizations relate to one another in emergencies and how such relations determine disaster response effectiveness (Wenger et al., 1986). An over-riding conclusion of this research is that interorganizational coordination enhances the effectiveness of community-level response to any disaster (Quarantelli, 1988, 1992).

Several factors have been identified that enhance overall effectiveness of a community's response to a disaster event. First, at the community level, there must be some agreement or consensus about what organizations are expected to perform what tasks in a disaster situation (Dynes, 1978; Kreps, 1978; Quarantelli and Dynes, 1977). This type of specific planning facilitates organizational interaction by legitimizing the emergency roles of all organizations involved in the process (Dynes, 1978, 1969; Stallings, 1978). Second, it establishes lines of authority among these organizations (Drabek et al., 1981), which helps to avoid conflict and to expedite decision making across the organizations. The result is a better integrated community response to the disaster. Third, the number of organizations included in community-level plans for disaster response should not be large (Dynes, 1969; Warheit, 1968). If too many organizations are included in community-level response plans, integration becomes difficult and effectiveness can actually decrease.

Fourth, integration of the organizations in a community plan is easier to achieve if the organizations normally interact with one another during non-disaster times (Drabek et al., 1981; Dynes, 1978). Organizations that are used to interacting with each other are more readily able to coordinate in an emergency, often because of the personal contacts that have been established by the members of the organizations, and made over a longer period of time. Also, when organizational members understand the internal operations and structure of other organizations, it is easier to coordinate with them during a disaster (Dynes, 1978). When such integration and coordination is absent, the gap can be filled by interorganizational competition, resulting in a decrease of the effectiveness of community disaster response. Fifth, communication between organizations is another essential ingredient for an organized, community-wide emergency response (Dacy and Kunreuther, 1969; Drabek et al., 1981). Communication is essential for the quick dissemination of news about the changing context of the emergency. Sixth, participation in an effective community-wide response requires that organizations relinquish some of their individual autonomy (Dynes, 1970; Mileti et al., 1975). Although individual organizations typically struggle against giving up their autonomy, preparedness planning makes obvious the need to surrender some autonomy to those who are responsible for coordinating the overall disaster response.

### Mitigation

Mitigation refers to those actions undertaken to reduce a community's vulnerability to the possible future impacts of a hazard agent, whether natural or technological. Although individuals can also undertake mitigation measures, most of the emphasis in mitigation efforts as well as in mitigation research is on professional and governmental attempts to reduce vulnerability. Mitigation activities are generally thought of as collective solutions to a threat which could have widely felt effects in a community, region, state, or country.

There are generally five ways of reducing the physical impacts of a natural hazard agent (Petak and Atkisson, 1982). The first two efforts concern ways of preventing or modifying the occurrence of a hazard. First, structural protection for a geographic area can be enhanced—for example, through the construction of dams, levees, channels, and seawalls—to lessen the likelihood of flooding due to severe storms. Second, specific buildings or developments can be protected through site preparation. For example, the installation of hillside drains and debris basins can lessen the impacts of severe storms by reducing the likelihood of erosion and mud floods.

Third, attempts can be made to avoid the hazard by changing where people build. Land-use planning and regulation are the techniques generally used to discourage building in areas where natural hazards have the greatest impacts. Flood plain management, for example, has been used to limit the types and amount of new development in areas that are prone to riverine and coastal flooding. Fourth, the control of building practices through the adoption of building codes is one of the primary methods used to enhance the structural integrity of the built environment. Through the adoption of building codes—particularly those incorporating wind and seismic design—governments make attempts to change how people build, to provide a minimum life-safety standard where the existence of a natural hazard agent is known. Finally, strategies can be developed to remove buildings that are determined to be hazardous from the existing stock of buildings in use.

Numerous factors influence the adoption of these various techniques. Why do some communities adopt certain mitigation measures when other communities that have a similar objective risk do not, opting either for a different mix of techniques or none at all? What characteristics of communities and their histories of experience with a natural hazard agent are related to the preference for some hazard reduction measures over others? How does the political and economic climate of a community affect the adoption of different mitigation strategies? These questions highlight the importance of the need to understand the decision-making process of key actors as they consider different mitigation actions.

Mitigation is one of the newest areas of research emphasis in the natural hazards and disaster field, only attaining significant attention from sociologists within the past 15 years or so. Social geographers led this field with enquiries about the success of flood mitigation efforts (e.g., White, 1964, 1975). More recently, questions have been raised by planners and political scientists about the success of the National Flood Insurance Program—the federal government's primary policy tool to reduce flood risks (e.g., Burby et al., 1985).

Similar questions have also been raised about local, state, and federal attempts to reduce community vulnerability to earthquakes (Panel on Seismic Policy Adoption and Implementation, 1996). Sociologists began investigating how the public assessed earthquake threat in the mid-1970s, when geoscientists in California felt they were on the verge of being able to predict earthquakes and governmental officials were concerned about how the public would react to such announcements (e.g., Mileti et al., 1980; Turner et al., 1986). Contrary to the belief that people would become overly fearful and be likely to engage in mass evacuation if such announcements were issued, these research efforts concluded that the public wanted to be kept informed, even of very low probability events, and was positively disposed toward continued efforts to educate them about how to respond if such announcements were made.

Subsequent assessments of how people did in fact respond to such announcements confirmed the sociological contention (e.g., Nigg, 1982) that people would not panic, but would instead continue to function normally while seeking additional information about the prediction and hazard-reduction measures (Goltz, 1984). Building on this earlier interest in how people understand scientific assessments of earthquake risk and its relationship to behavioral adjustment activities, more recent research is being undertaken to assess public response to the state of California's attempt to inform potentially affected residents about the most recent large-magnitude earthquake prediction (Mileti and Fitzpatrick, 1993).

Although substantial research attention has been focused on California because of its considerable earthquake vulnerability, other areas of the country are also known to be at risk from earthquake threat—for example, the Puget Sound area of Washington; the New Madrid area of the Central states along the Mississippi River; Charleston, South Carolina; Alaska; and Hawaii. Researchers are now turning their attention toward understanding the adoption of earthquake mitigation adjustments in these areas of objectively high seismic risk, high seismic vulnerability (because the built environment has not been constructed with seismic concerns in mind), but a low probability of the occurrence of a damaging earthquake event (e.g., Berke and Beatley, 1992; Mushkatel and Nigg, 1987a, 1987b).

Research has confirmed that the adoption of adjustments is strongly associated with the high frequency of occurrence of a specific natural disaster agent. When such events are infrequent—such as a damaging earthquake—but their occurrence could result in significant life loss and economic and social disruption to a community or region, what conditions are likely to lead to the adoption of mitigation adjustments?

Mileti (1980) has identified two factors which he believes are related to the adoption of community risk mitigation adjustments across natural hazard agents—the capacity to implement various policies, and the perceived costs of the implemented policy. Capacity refers to the resources governmental or administrative entities have to undertake additional adjustment-related tasks in relation to their ongoing responsibilities. The capacity to implement any new mitigation effort is high if it does not require much change in resource allocation and utilization from the status quo. Higher levels of adoption are also related to the availability of both economic resources and expertise, which are necessary to implement new programs.

Even if decision makers believe that their community is exposed to a significant threat, they may believe that the cost involved in attempting to mitigate that hazard is unacceptably high. Costs are not limited to economic concerns solely, but also include calculations of social and political costs as well. Elected officials, especially those at the local governmental level, must weigh the social costs of not taking action (possible life loss and economic disruption) against political costs of supporting litigation actions (unfavorable reactions by interest groups who would be required to bear economic costs for changing their current practices or who would not get support for nonhazard-related programs, such as social welfare programs).

This research emphasis on mitigation adjustments to high risk–low probability natural disaster events has a great deal in common with similar concerns raised about some technological hazards, especially those associated with fixed-site facilities. Why do some communities "accept" the risk associated with a nuclear power plant or a catastrophic earthquake or volcanic eruption, while other communities become actively involved in attempting to reduce the risks associated with these hazards? While some research assessments have been conducted on the differences in the hazard perception related to natural versus technological hazard agents (e.g., Baum et al., 1983; Slovic et al., 1979; Chapter 10 in this volume), the question of willingness to accept risk on a collective basis—and the manner in which individuals and organizations adjust to those decisions—constitutes an important area for future study.

## CROSS-CUTTING CONCLUSIONS

We have tried in this chapter to provide an overview of research directions and findings regarding the perception, mitigation of, and preparedness for natural hazards and disasters. Research and theorizing on natural hazards and disasters has also suggested several insights that cut across these specific areas. In this concluding section of the chapter, we present these general cross-cutting ideas about societal adjustment to natural hazards and the disasters they can create.

Natural disasters are not acts of God, occurring randomly and having societal impacts which must be borne. Natural disasters are simply consequences of extremes in natural inevitable processes; as such, they are low-probability events. These natural extremes become disasters only when they impact the human collective and the constructed or built environment which society has erected. The consequences of natural environmental extremes are disaster events, therefore, only as a consequence of human actions such as building in a floodplain, on a landslide shoot, near an earthquake fault, or along a coastline; or using construction practices that result in buildings not capable of withstanding natural forces like moderate ground shaking in earthquakes or high velocity winds in hurricanes.

Society and communities adjust to the risk of natural disasters through a variety of mechanisms. Some of these mechanisms have been reviewed in this chapter; they include, for example, emergency preparedness, mitigations like building codes, warning systems, and insurance. Societal adjustment to the risk of disaster imposed by natural hazards is not, however, altogether rational and in proportion to the risks faced. In fact, risk is often ignored or, in many cases, unknown until extensive development has already taken place. Adjustment to the risk of low-probability natural events (for example, a damaging hurricane every 60 years or a great earthquake every 140 years) is costly, and the benefits of that increased protection may not be realized for decades. Consequently, it is easy to understand why society has not fully adjusted to risks posed by natural hazards and why natural disasters continue to occur. In fact, if one could predict the future, it might be a safe bet to expect natural disasters to escalate in the magnitude of their impacts. Societal trends, like the growth and increasing concentration of populations in hazard-prone areas, foretell ever-increasing numbers of people and structures at risk despite purposeful attempts at risk mitigation.

Additionally, the adjustment process is hardly proactive. In fact, adjustment to the risk of natural disaster is typically reactive. Society typically readies for and adjusts to the risk of disasters already experienced rather than those which it faces in the future. For example, the state of California has long enforced building codes that increase seismic resistance of structures. Those adjustments to risk largely came after earthquakes occurred, illustrating earthquake damage: in the 1933 Long Beach Earthquake, public school buildings collapsed and this led to legislation to enhance the design of schools; in 1971 the San Fernando Earthquake collapsed a hospital and subsequent legislation was passed to enhance the design of hospitals; in

1989 the Loma Prieta Earthquake caused the collapse of the I-880 freeway in Oakland, resulting in retrofit regulations for all elevated highways and bridges in California. Meanwhile, although the risk of a great earthquake in other parts of the United States is high (for example, in Memphis and Charleston), it has been difficult to alter building codes in those areas and adjust to seismic risks, since a damaging earthquake has not occurred in either area for decades.

The reactive character of the adjustment process has resulted in an uneven and varied distribution of societal adjustments to natural disaster agents across the United States. The historical occurrence of disasters has facilitated adjustment where disasters have recently occurred; yet they are often ignored elsewhere despite the risk that exists. The risk of future disasters may be just as probable and in fact even more likely in some regions of the nation where they have not yet happened or where they infrequently occur. For example, the risk of a future great earthquake is lower in areas where one has recently happened and can be increasing daily in seismically prone areas where one has not occurred for decades.

Despite the innate tendency of the adjustment process for natural hazards to be reactive rather than proactive, and disproportionate to risk rather than proportional to it, advances have been recently made to enhance the adjustment process and increase its rationality. The adjustment process, which largely occurs through the adoption and implementation of mitigation and preparedness actions, continues to become more and more institutionalized into the society of the United States. There are increasingly larger and larger numbers of people who pursue careers devoted to reducing the risk of natural disasters; and there are ever-increasing numbers of national, regional, and state programs devoted to escalating adjustment accomplishments. It is difficult, however, to now estimate what the actual outcome will be of the efforts of this ever-increasing number of adjustment-bearers. It is tempting to hypothesize that some of them must inevitably be successful, resulting in increased societal adjustment to natural disasters. On the other hand, it is also possible that increased adjustment accomplishments and attention to natural disasters may only be a societal reaction to increased risk flowing from trends in processes like increased urbanization. The result of increased adjustment may simply be to keep risk constant or, worse, to only slow its rate of growth.

The inevitable occurrence of extreme natural events in the physical environment ensures that the study of natural hazards and disasters will remain a vital area of inquiry and a crucial arena for the study of societal–environmental interactions.

## REFERENCES

Adams, David. 1970. "The Red Cross: Organizational Sources of Operational Problems." *American Behavioral Scientist* 13(3):392–403.

Anderson, William A. 1969. "Social Structure and the Role of the Military in Natural Disaster." *Sociology and Social Research* 53:242–253.

Barton, Allen. 1969. *Communities in Disaster*. New York: Doubleday.

Baum, Andrew, Raymond Fleming, and Laura M. Davidson. 1983. "Natural Disaster and Technological Catastrophe." *Environment and Behavior* 15:333–353.

Berke, Phillip R., and Timothy Beatley. 1992. *Planning for Earthquakes: Risk, Politics, and Policy*. Baltimore, MD: Johns Hopkins University Press.

Burby, Raymond J., Steven P. French, Beverly A. Cigler, Edward Kaiser, David H. Moreau, and Bruce Stiftel. 1985. *Flood Plain Land Use Management: A National Assessment*. Boulder, CO: Westview Press.

Dacy, Douglas C., and Howard Kunreuther. 1969. *The Economics of Natural Disasters*. New York: Free Press.

Drabek, Thomas E. 1986. *Human System Responses to Disaster: An Inventory of Sociological Findings*. New York: Springer-Verlag.

Drabek, Thomas E., and Enrico L. Quarantelli. 1967. "Scapegoats, Villains, and Disasters." *Transaction* 4:12–17.

Drabek, Thomas E., Harriet L. Taminga, Thomas S. Kilijanek, and Christopher R. Adams. 1981. *Managing Multiorganizational Emergency Responses: Emergent Search and Rescue Networks in Natural Disaster and Remote Area Settings*. Boulder: Institute of Behavioral Science, University of Colorado.

Duncan, Otis D. 1964. "Social Organization and Ecosystems." Pp. 37–82 in *Handbook of Modern Sociology*, edited by Robert E. L. Faris. Chicago: Rand-NcNally.

Duncan, Otis D., and Leo F. Schnore. 1959. "Cultural, Behavioral, and Ecological Perspectives for the Study of Social Organization." *American Journal of Sociology* 58:132–146.

Dunlap, Riley E., and William R. Catton, Jr. 1983. "What Environmental Sociologists Have in Common." *Sociological Inquiry* 53:113–135.

Dynes, Russell R. 1969. *Organized Behavior in Disasters: Analysis and Conceptualization*. Columbus: Disaster Research Center, Ohio State University.

———. 1970. *Organized Behavior in Disaster*. Lexington, MA: Heath.

———. 1978. "Interorganizational Relations in Communities Under Stress." Pp. 49–64 in *Disasters: Theory and Research*, edited by E. L. Quarantelli. Beverly Hills, CA: Sage Publications.

———. 1993. "Disaster Reduction: The Importance of Adequate Assumptions about Social Organization." *Sociological Spectrum* 13:175–192.

———. 1994. "Community Emergency Planning: False Assumptions and Inappropriate Analogies." *International Journal of Mass Emergencies and Disasters* 12:141–158.

———, E. L. Quarantelli, and Gary A. Kreps. 1972. *A Perspective on Disaster Planning*. Columbus: Disaster Research Center, Ohio State University.

Faupel, Charles. 1985. *The Ecology of Disaster: An Application of a Conceptual Model*. New York: Irvington.

Form, William H., and Sigmund Nosow. 1958. *Community in Disaster*. New York: Harper.

Fritz, Charles E. 1961. "Disaster." Pp. 651–694 in *Contemporary Social Problems*, edited by Robert K. Merton and Robert A. Nisbet. New York: Harcourt, Brace, and World.

————, and Eli Marks. 1954. "The NORC Studies of Human Behavior in Disaster." *Journal of Social Issues* 10:26–41.

Gillespie, D. F., R. A. Colignon, M. M. Banerjee, S. A. Murty, and M. Rogge. 1993. *Partnerships for Community Preparedness*. Monograph #53. Boulder: Institute of Behavioral Science, University of Colorado.

Goltz, James. 1984. "Are the News Media Responsible for the Disaster Myths? A Content Analysis of Emergency Response Imagery." *International Journal of Mass Emergencies and Disasters* 2:345–368.

Haas, J. Eugene, and Thomas E. Drabek. 1973. *Complex Organizations: A Sociological Perspective*. New York: Macmillan.

Hannigan, John A., and Rodney M. Kueneman. 1978. "Anticipating Flood Emergencies: A Case Study of a Canadian Disaster Subculture." Pp. 129–146 in *Disasters: Theory and Research*, edited by E. L. Quarantelli. Beverly Hills, CA: Sage Publications.

Hanson, Susan, John D. Vitek, and Perry O. Hanson. 1979. "Natural Disaster: Long-Range Impact on Human Response to Future Disaster Threats." *Environment and Behavior* 11:268–284.

Hawley, Amos H. 1950. *Human Ecology: A Theory of Community Structure*. New York: The Ronald Press.

Kartez, Jack D., and Michael K. Lindell. 1987. "Planning for Uncertainty: The Case of Local Disaster Planning." *American Planning Association Journal* 53: 487–498.

Kates, Robert W. 1962. *Hazard and Choice Perception in Flood Plain Management*. Chicago: University of Chicago, Department of Geography Research Paper #78.

————. 1970. *Natural Hazard in Human Ecological Perspective: Hypotheses and Models*. Toronto: University of Toronto, Department of Geography, Natural Hazard Research Working Paper #14.

Kiecolt, K. Jill, and Joanne M. Nigg. 1982. "Mobility Decisions Based on Perceptions of a Hazardous Environment." *Environment and Behavior* 14:131–154.

Kreps, Gary A. 1978. "The Organization of Disaster Response: Some Fundamental Theoretical Issues." Pp. 65–86 in *Disasters: Theory and Research*, edited by E. L. Quarantelli. Beverly Hills, CA: Sage Publications.

————. 1981. "The Worth of the NAS-NRC (1952–63) and DRC (1963–present) Studies of Individual and Social Responses to Disasters." Pp. 91–121 in *Social Science and Natural Hazards*, edited by J. D. Wright and P. H. Rossi. Cambridge, MA: ABT Books.

Kunreuther, Howard. 1978. *Disaster Insurance Protection: Public Policy Lessons*. New York: Wiley.

Mileti, Dennis S. 1980. "Human Adjustment to the Risk of Environmental Extremes." *Sociology and Social Research* 64:327–347.

————, Thomas E. Drabek, and J. Eugene Haas. 1975. *Human Systems in Extreme Environments: A Sociological Perspective*. Boulder: Institute of Behavioral Science, University of Colorado.

————, and Colleen Fitzpatrick. 1993. *The Great Earthquake Experiment*. Boulder, CO: Westview Press.

————, Janice Hutton, and John Sorenson. 1981. *Earthquake Prediction Response and Options for Public Policy*. Boulder: Institute of Behavioral Science, University of Colorado.

Moore, Harry E. 1964. *And the Winds Blew*. Austin: The Hogg Foundation for Mental Health, University of Texas.

Mushkatel, Alvin H., and Joanne M. Nigg. 1987a. "Opinion Congruence and the Formulation of Seismic Safety Policies." *Policy Studies Review* 6:645–656.

———. 1987b. "The Effect of Objective Risk on Key Actor Support for Seismic Mitigation Policy." *Environmental Management* 11:77–86.

National Research Council. 1987. *Confronting Natural Disasters*. Washington, DC: National Academy Press.

Nigg, Joanne M. 1982. "Communication under Conditions of Uncertainty: Understanding Earthquake Forewarnings." *Journal of Communication* 32:27–36.

———. 1993. "Societal Response to Global Climate Change: Prospects for Natural Hazard Reduction." Pp. 289–294 in *Proceedings of the Symposium on the World at Risk: Natural Hazards and Global Climate Change*, edited by Rafael Bras. New York: American Institute of Physics.

———. 1994. "Influences of Symbolic Interaction on Disaster Research." Pp. 33–50 in *Self, Collective Action and Society: Essays Honoring the Contributions of Ralph H. Turner*, edited by Gerald Platt and Chad Gorden. Greenwich, CT: JAI Press.

———, and Ronald W. Perry. 1988. "Influential First Sources: Brief Statements with Long-Term Effects." *International Journal of Mass Emergencies and Disasters* 6:311–344.

———, and Kathleen J. Tierney. 1993. "Disasters and Social Change: Consequences for Community Construct and Affect." Newark: Disaster Research Center, University of Delaware. Preliminary Paper #195.

Panel on Seismic Policy Adoption and Implementation. 1996. *Working Paper on Seismic Policy Adoption by Local Governments*. Washington, DC: Board on Natural Disasters, National Academy of Sciences/National Research Council.

Park, Robert E. 1936. "Human Ecology." *American Journal of Sociology* 42:1–15.

Parker, D. J., and D. M. Harding. 1979. "Natural Hazard Evaluation, Perception and Adjustment." *Geography* 64:307–316.

Petak, William J., and Arthur A. Atkisson. 1982. *Natural Hazard Risk Assessment and Public Policy: Anticipating the Unexpected*. New York: Springer-Verlag.

Preston, Valerie, S. Martin Taylor, and David C. Hodge. 1983. "Adjustment to Natural and Technological Hazards: A Study of an Urban Residential Community." *Environment and Behavior* 15:143–164.

Quarantelli, E. L. 1970. "The Community General Hospital: Its Immediate Problems in Disaster." *American Behavioral Scientist* 13:380–391.

———. 1987a. "Disaster Studies: An Analysis of the Social Historical Factors Affecting the Development of Research in the Area." *International Journal of Mass Emergencies and Disasters* 5:285–310.

———. 1987b. "What Should We Study? Questions and Suggestions for Researchers about the Concept of Disasters." *International Journal of Mass Emergencies and Disasters* 5:7–32.

———. 1988. "Assessing Disaster Preparedness Planning." *Regional Development Dialogue* 9:48–69.

———. 1992. "Disaster Studies: An Analysis of the Consequences of the Historical Use of a Sociological Approach in the Development of Research in the Area." Unpublished manuscript.

———. 1996. "The Future Is Not the Past: Projecting Disasters in the 21st Century from Present Trends." *Journal of Contingencies and Crisis Management* 4: 228–240.

———, and Russell R. Dynes. 1977. "Response to Social Crisis and Disaster." *Annual Review of Sociology* 3:23–49.

Saarinen, Thomas F. 1982. *Perspectives on Increasing Hazard Awareness*. Boulder: University of Colorado Press.

Shippee, G., J. Burroughs, and S. Wakefield. 1980. "Dissonance Theory Revisited: Perception of Environmental Hazards in Residential Areas." *Environment and Behavior* 12:33–52.

Slovic, Paul, Baruch Fischoff, and Sarah Lichtenstein. 1979. "Rating the Risks." *Environment* 21:14–39.

———, Howard Kunreuther, and Gilbert White. 1974. "Decision Processes, Rationality, and Adjustment to Natural Hazards." Pp. 187–205 in *Natural Hazards: Local, National, Global*, edited by Gilbert White. New York: Oxford University Press.

Stallings, Robert A. 1978. "The Structural Patterns of Four Types of Organizations in Disaster." Pp. 87–104 in *Disasters: Theory and Research*, edited by E. L. Quarantelli. Beverly Hills, CA: Sage Publications.

Taylor, S. M., and F. L. Hall. 1976. "Residential Planning Implications of Subjective Response to Noise: Some Empirical Findings." Pp. 172–179 in *Behavioral Basis of Design*, edited by P. Suedfeld and J. Russell. Stroudsburg, PA: Dowden, Hutchinson, and Ross.

Turner, Ralph H., Joanne M. Nigg, and Denise H. Paz. 1986. *Waiting for Disaster*. Berkeley: University of California Press.

———, Joanne M. Nigg, Denise Heller Paz, and Barbara Shaw Young. 1980. *Community Response to Earthquake Threat in Southern California. Part VII: Vulnerability Zones and Earthquake Subculture*. Los Angeles, CA: Institute for Social Science Research, UCLA.

Warheit, George J. 1968. "The Impact of Four Major Emergencies on the Functional Integration of Four American Communities." Dissertation. Columbus: Ohio State University.

Weinstein, Neil D. 1983. "Unrealistic Optimism about Future Life Events." Unpublished manuscript. Department of Human Ecology and Social Sciences, Rutgers University, New Brunswick, NJ.

Wenger, Dennis, Russell R. Dynes, and E. L. Quarantelli. 1986. *Disaster Analysis: Emergency Management Offices and Arrangements*. Final Report #34. Newark: Disaster Research Center, University of Delaware.

Wenger, Dennis E., and Jack M. Weller. 1973. "Disaster Subcultures: The Cultural Residues of Community Disasters." Columbus: Disaster Research Center, Ohio State University.

White, Gilbert F. 1964. *Choice of Adjustment to Floods*. Chicago: Department of Geography, University of Chicago.

———. 1975. *Flood Hazard in the United States*. Boulder: Institute of Behavioral Science, University of Colorado.

*Chapter 10*

# Technological Hazards and Disasters

*Steve Kroll-Smith, Stephen R. Couch,*
*and Adeline G. Levine*

## INTRODUCTION

In contrast to the relatively constant number of natural calamities, technological disasters are increasing both in number and in the amount of
financial, social, and human devastation they cause (Kates, 1977:250;
Kroll-Smith and Couch, 1990a). The increased capacity of societies to understand natural disasters contrasts sharply with their initial bewilderment
over a variety of complex issues posed by technological disasters, and by
technological hazards as well. However, just as societies have developed
some capacity to mitigate the consequences of natural disasters, so we are
in the midst of developing such capacities in relation to technological disasters and hazards. The emergence of a body of literature on the latter
topic is part of the total effort to understand crises stemming from the often
volatile interplay of technology and environment. What we are observing
and are part of is a process of social change.

Before the 1970s, few scholars who dealt with hazards and disasters
viewed those produced by technology as substantively different in social
process or social effect from those produced by natural forces (see Quarantelli and Dynes, 1977). More recently, a number of scholars have asserted
that technological disaster and hazard agents produce effects quite different
from those of natural origin (e.g., Baum et al., 1983; Bolin, 1985; Erikson,
1991, 1994). On the other hand, Quarantelli (1987) concludes, from his
extensive studies of disasters, that the distinction between natural and technological agents may unfruitfully divert attention from a detailed examination of the variables which affect processes and outcomes in any disaster.

Whatever importance one attributes to the distinction between the types of disaster agents, sociologically a disaster can be viewed as a severe breakdown in the relatively stable relations between human systems and the environment. In the literature we will refer to in this chapter, the authors assume or assert that the attributed cause of that breakdown will clearly influence the environmental dimensions affected and the social and cultural attempts to adapt to the new human/environmental relationship. Serious technological hazards are included in studies of technological disasters because they have the potential to become disasters, and like them, harshly disrupt the taken-for-granted assumptions people make about their relationships with the environment.

For purposes of illustration, let us consider two extreme conditions. Natural disasters disrupt, perhaps destroy, a portion of a community's built and modified environment. A hurricane rolling over a shoreline city is a massive reality unequivocally understood and responded to as a disaster. With little collective doubt about what occurred and how it should be interpreted, governmental and private agencies can implement their emergency response and rehabilitation programs. At the local level, a therapeutic community is likely to emerge temporarily, wherein citizens and their organizations expand their ordinary roles within the community to meet the immediate needs of the injured, the homeless, and the grief-stricken (Fritz, 1961). Eventually, houses and stores are rebuilt and order is restored. In most cases, the physical and social community continues (Wright and Rossi, 1979).

Technological disasters, however, may well not destroy buildings or streets; the built and modified environments often remain as they were before the disaster. What is destroyed when chemicals leach through underground swales and dioxin dust settles on roadways and gardens is the fundamental relationship of communities to primary environmental resources. The water is no longer safe to drink; the air is poisoned; the ground is contaminated. Often, relief from technological disasters may be won only by permanently relocating the residents. The houses and stores may remain, but the community ceases to exist or becomes an empty shell; even if people do remain in their physical community and homes, their feelings about both may undergo profound changes.

Technological disasters and hazards are far more complex than this example suggests, however. Because materials and their impacts may be invisible to the senses, detected and measured only by sophisticated technical apparatuses, it may be difficult to identify all the victims of technological disasters. In addition, the variable experiences and knowledge of the victims can be expected to result in quite different subjective assessments of damage or of potential for harm. Due to these factors, a unique pattern of psychological, social, and cultural disruption can be expected to accompany a technological disaster or hazard that interrupts the relationship of people to environments. Shrivastava, who terms the Bhopal disaster an industrial crisis, states: "Social agents, institutions, and relationships (rather than nature) are responsible for the triggering event in industrial crises and social processes are the vehicles by which crises proliferate. Dealing with the consequences invariably involves social and political conflicts. Thus, industrial crises are fundamentally shaped by existing social order and class relations" (Shrivastava, 1987:19).

This review emphasizes human responses to technological hazards and disasters, focusing on materials produced during the 1980s and 1990s, and summaries of earlier literature. Our interest is in literature that examines the effects of these human-generated crises on individuals, groups, and communities, and on the national and international activities that both produce and interact with those effects.

We begin with a brief look at the confusing plethora of classificatory schemes developed to bring some order to the study of technological hazards and disasters. Then we review the literature on how victims of technological hazards and disasters cope with the considerable stress that such situations generally produce. Next, we examine how individuals and groups appraise the risks of human-caused hazards and disasters and how these appraisals frequently lead to community conflict.

Following this, we shift attention to national and international processes that both create and respond to technological dangers, highlighting work on macro-level social, economic, and cultural structures and processes that affect the nature, distribution, and impacts of technological hazards and disasters. Also considered are works that examine the difficulties of developing and implementing governmental policies to help communities cope with the impacts of hazardous technologies. We discuss several studies that address the complicated roles played by social scientists who investigate contaminated communities; and finally, we draw some brief conclusions about directions for future social scientific studies on the important and timely subject of technological hazards and disasters.

## Typologies

The importance of typologies in the study of hazards and disasters is reflected in the bewildering number of classificatory schemes found in the literature. A well-known typology among natural disaster researchers classifies disasters as social-crisis occasions, and purposely eschews any reference to the characteristics or event-specific qualities of the disaster or hazard agent (see Quarantelli, 1985, 1987; Tierney, 1981). Quarantelli (1987) argues that it is not the characteristics of the agents per se, but their social consequences that are important. Disasters of whatever type should be viewed as a subset of the field of crises studies (1985:50; 1987:240). "The definition of disaster," he writes, "should be exclusively in social terms," and "references to physical phenomena ought to be absent" from any sociology of disaster (1987:22). In discussing the effects of disasters on mental health, for example, he points out that what is important for understanding effects is not the characteristics of the disaster agent itself, but such social variables as the proportion of the population involved; their social centrality; the length, rapidity, depth, predictability, and recurrence of their involvement; and the unfamiliarity of the crisis (1985:58–63).

Several other typologies depart significantly from Quarantelli's approach by focusing explicitly on the differences between the physical characteristics of the disaster or hazard agent itself, particularly the differences between natural and technological agents. Baum, Fleming, and Singer (1983), for example, argue that technological hazards differ from natural hazards along several dimensions, including suddenness, power, destructiveness, and predictability, while Berren, Beigel, and Ghertner (1980) also add potential for occurrence and control over future impact. Shrivastava (1987: 9) describes "industrial crises" caused by four different "triggering events": industrial accidents, environmental pollution, product injuries, and product sabotage. Gill (1986:86–88) suggests that social responses to technological disasters differ, depending upon the speed of onset and whether they are transportation or fixed-site events. Thus, he finds four categories in his analysis of the literature on human-caused disasters: accidents that get out of control at industrial plant sites, the breakdown of fixed structures such as dams, transportation route accidents, and toxic substance disposal site accidents. Couch and Kroll-Smith (1985) cross-tabulate time with level of human involvement to construct a fourfold typology: immediate impact natural or technological disasters, and chronic natural or technological disasters. Erikson (1991:28) also develops a fourfold typology based on whether or not the disaster is of technological origin, but having as the second dimension whether or not toxic contamination is involved.

While there are many ambiguities in these event-quality classifications, what unifies typologies based on the physical characteristics of hazards and disasters is the "crucial possibility that one can at least conceive of systems encompassing both human and physical elements" (Duncan, 1961: 141). Linking each of these classification schemes is the idea that the human social system is influenced by more than social action or the physical environment transformed into a social fact. Physical, or nonsocial factors are treated as necessary for understanding human action in response to natural and technological crises. "Sometimes," as Dunlap and Catton observe, "the physical environment has direct, unmediated impacts upon humans" (1983: 126).

A smaller number of typologies are based on technological and organizational structures likely to create or exacerbate disasters and hazards. Perrow (1982, 1984) coined the term *normal accident* to account for the disaster at Three Mile Island, and argued that the greater the degree of complexity in our industrial and transportation technologies, the greater the chance for "unanticipated multiple failures in the equipment, design, or operator actions" (1982:174). Technological accidents, he concludes, are a normal consequence of profit-driven, high-risk systems. Focusing more on managerial culpability in accounting for technological accidents, Gephart argues that environmental disasters are frequently caused by the "organizational exploitation of ecosystemic resources" and are usefully typed as "organizationally based environmental disasters" (1984:206).

While exemplifying a burst of creative energy and the generation of many thought-provoking ideas, this plethora of typologies also carries with it a lack of standardization, with no one of them having gained common acceptance. There are also differences in usage within common dimensions of different typologies. For example, Perrow (1984) considers an airplane crash to be one type of technological accident, while Berren et al. (1980: 107) see it as a natural disaster because it was "not purposely perpetuated by man." In terms of duration the latter article describes a 27-hour kidnapping as a relatively long-term hazard event, while for other researchers a long-term technological disaster is one which may last for decades.

The variety of classificatory schemes and the differences in the meaning of concepts may be due partly to the fact that researchers have had neither the time nor sufficient empirical studies to sort through the utility of these typologies. In addition, typologies have been developed by scholars from sociology, psychology, political science, geography, administrative science, social work, and other fields. This multidisciplinary effort makes the job of standardizing terminology and developing commonly accepted typological dimensions all the more difficult. It is obvious that there is a need for multidimensional classification of a more complex nature than has been developed so far (see also Drabek, 1986:17 ff.).

Finally, a recently emerging perspective suggests that typologies that ignore the symbolic capacity of human agents are likely to apply classificatory schemes that are inconsistent with people's experiences of crises. In a study of citizen response to a flood, Blocker and Sherkat (1992) found that a majority of respondents interpreted the disaster as preventable and attributed their losses to human agency. To classify a flood as a natural disaster in this case would be inconsistent with most victims' understanding of the event. Kroll-Smith and Couch (1991, 1993; Couch and Kroll-Smith, 1994) suggest the need for an "ecological-symbolic perspective" on hazards and disasters. They would shift attention away from the physical qualities of aversive agents to the type(s) of environment that is damaged (built, modified, or biophysical) and to the subjective interpretations of damage by survivors.

## Coping with Stress

Exposure to calamitous events, whether for short or long periods of time, results in a marked increase in stress and dysphoric feelings. A review of 41 studies of survivors of natural and technological disasters concludes that while long-term health consequences were not reported in all the studies, "[t]he preponderance of the evidence seems to indicate" that mental health problems appear in the period of recovery from a disaster (Melick, 1985: 193).

Because technological disasters and hazards do not necessarily wreak abrupt physical disruption in the way that natural disasters do, it is important not to underestimate the anguish felt by those experiencing the former events. Bolin points out that "[m]an-made disasters often produce prolonged periods of threat and result in prolonged mental stresses" (1985: 16). Lebovits, Baum, and Singer (1986) report that studies of nonoccupational exposure to hazardous substances show "elevated levels of psychological distress, both global and specific, among individuals subsequent to toxic exposure. Specific reactions found include higher than expected levels of demoralization, depression and anxiety. The primary concern . . . is physical health . . . [e]xposed individuals also report feelings of loss of control, helplessness, and powerlessness" (Lebovits et al., 1986: xii). Other behavioral scientists have found difficulty in problem solving and increased levels of measurable psychopathology among victims of technological disasters (e.g., Davidson and Baum, 1991; Edelstein, 1982; Fleming and Baum, 1985; Gibbs, 1982).

Seventeen months after the accident at Three Mile Island, Baum, Fleming, and Singer (1983) assessed the residents' stress by means of self-reports, and behavioral and biochemical measures. They found that the levels of stress were higher than those of a control group of people living near an undamaged nuclear power plant. Gill (1986) studied a community that suffered the consequences of a derailed train carrying hazardous chemicals. The derailment caused fires, leakage of toxic materials, a 14-day evacuation of the population of 1,800 people, and a full year of cleanup activities. Using standardized psychological measurements, he concluded that people in the affected community experienced levels of stress elevated beyond those found in the normal population. In addition, by use of a comparison community with similar demographic characteristics and also located near a railroad, Gill ascertained that residents of the affected community expressed a greater desire to move away from it, perceived that living near a railroad was more dangerous, were less satisfied with the quality of life in their community, and perceived a greater chance of being involved in various technological accidents in the future.

Some authors suggest that technological disasters may create more stress than natural disasters do. Schorr, Goldsteen, and Cortes (1982) found that Three Mile Island residents who had also experienced major floods in 1972 and 1973 reported more long-term social and psychological impacts from the nuclear accident than from the floods. Similarly, Smith, Robins, Przybeck, Goldring, and Solomon (1986) compared the mental status of people who had experienced both floods and dioxin contamination of property at

Times Beach with those exposed only to dioxin and those exposed only to floods in other areas. They found more symptoms reported by people involved in dioxin contamination than in the floods only. "[O]ne year after the disasters only a third of the victims reported that they had fully recovered from the disaster experience. Flood-only victims were twice as likely to report full recovery than were those exposed to dioxin with or without accompanying flooding" (Smith et al., 1986:60).

In contrast to an earlier review of the literature, which found that victims exhibit little or no prolonged adverse psychological effects from experiencing a natural disaster (Mileti et al., 1975:103), other researchers note that the psychological effects of technological disasters may last for months and years (Baum, 1987; Davidson and Baum, 1991; Dyer et al., 1992; Erikson, 1976, 1994; Gleser et al., 1981). While the numbers are small, people affected by this type of calamity report fears and anxieties, sleep disturbances, and a general inability to carry on their normal activities. Some of the reactions resemble post-traumatic stress disorders by virtue of their intrusiveness and persistence (Vyner, 1988).

Persistent stress reactions become part of the individual's psychological context, thus prolonging the sense of disaster. When people perceive that the hazard has not been removed, they may well feel that they are still at risk. Some reactions may be related to the process of remediation, which may contribute to a perception of continuing risk. Some reactions may be related to responses by government, relief agencies, physicians, and other authorities, which may not decrease, but rather add to the sense of confusion and feelings of distress (Kroll-Smith and Couch, 1990a; Prince-Embury and Rooney, 1989, 1995; Vyner, 1988).

Several variables influence the severity of psychological effects reported by individuals and families experiencing technological hazards and disasters. These include the disaster or hazard exposure and experience, as measured by distance from the impact site, separation from family members, relocation experiences, injury, death, and property loss (Bolin, 1985; Fowlkes and Miller, 1982; Gill, 1986; Gill and Picou, 1991; Gleser et al., 1981; Markowitz and Gutterman, 1986; Smith et al., 1986; Walsh, 1981); presence of young children in the household (Dohrenwend et al., 1981; Gill, 1986; Markowitz and Gutterman, 1986); age of household head (Fowlkes and Miller, 1982; Gill, 1986; Levine and Stone, 1986); length of residence in the area of the disaster (Fowlkes and Miller, 1982; Stone and Levine, 1985); gender (Brown and Ferguson, 1995; Hamilton, 1985a; Markowitz and Gutterman, 1986; Weisaeth, 1991); social support (Lindy and Grace, 1985:154); and socio-economic status (Levine and Stone, 1986).

Moving beyond the individual level, in their discussion of toxic exposure, Edelstein and Wandersman (1987:71) find "toxic exposure . . . responsible for influencing community dynamics and structure such as social networks, community solidarity, and community conflict, that are influenced by and, in turn, affect individual responses" (see also, Edelstein, 1988). One noticeable effect on community structure is the emergence of citizen action, or "grassroots" pressure groups (Brown and Ferguson, 1995; Cable and Benson, 1992; Cable and Cable, 1995; Cable and Walsh, 1991; Szasz, 1994). This phenomenon has been reported in recent literature and may occur more often in response to technological than to natural disasters. For example, in one community with two natural and three technological hazards, researchers found that residents were more likely to be aware of technological than of natural hazards, and also "took more . . . actions to modify the impact of . . . [the technological] . . . problems" (Preston et al., 1983:162).

Initially, the organizations form as a communal response to adversaries in industry and sometimes in government, who deny responsibility or adequate relief to people afraid that their homes, their health, and their children's health are threatened (Levine, 1982:ch. 7). Active involvement in such groups affects participants in both positive and negative ways. The formation of support groups serves as a social support, provider of information, and a source of power (Edelstein and Wandersman, 1987:89). Activists at Love Canal more often reported that they had lost friends from the time the crisis began than was reported by nonactivists, but the activists also gained new friends more often. Similarly, activists reported changes in relationships with children and other family members, but most of them were in a positive direction. While activists and nonactivists alike felt changed by the crisis, more of the nonactivists reported negative effects than did the activists. The great majority of activists felt their work influenced decisions made about Love Canal, in contrast to the great majority of nonactivists (Stone and Levine, 1985:171–175). Leaders of such groups undergo a variety of stresses related to their new and demanding roles. They find themselves pressed for time, forced to learn to speak in public, to confront powerful authorities, and to handle intra- as well as intergroup conflicts (Levine, 1987; see also Reich, 1991).

Generally, researchers do not use models incorporating factors that might reduce or increase stressful conditions. Drabek (1986:266), citing Perry and Lindell (1978:108–114), calls for more theoretical work to integrate three classes of variables—characteristics of the disaster, social system, and individuals—in order to understand better the effects of disasters on people. Such work is underway. Warheit's paradigm (1985:204 ff.) for predicting mental health outcomes of disaster incorporates 20 propositions relevant to these variables. Hartsough's "transactional model" (1985:32) outlines a step-by-step process from the occurrence of an environmental event to the outcomes of illness, and psychological and social impairment. The model indicates variables to be measured, including the event characteristics, the physical impacts, characteristics of individuals such as appraisal of losses and coping behavior, and society's relief and support responses. The model emphasizes two forms of stress which may lead to adverse outcomes: "Stress-e" which is produced by the event, and "Stress-r" which is produced by the social responses.

Not surprisingly, several sociological studies of technological disasters focus explicitly on "Stress-r" costs. Erikson's (1976) study of the dam break at Buffalo Creek found recovery efforts often increased the stress of survivors. In their study of a community response to an underground mine fire, Kroll-Smith and Couch (1990a) report residents identifying local conflicts in response to the fire as more stressful than the threat of the fire itself. Not surprisingly, residents of an Alaskan fishing village affected by the Exxon Valdez oil spill report amplified levels of stress due to the effects of mismanaged and uncoordinated efforts to clean up the spill on the community's infrastructure (Picou et al., 1992).

Another response which might lead to "Stress-r" is stigmatization. In contrast to victims of natural disasters, whose plight, at least initially, elicits sympathetic responses from the public (Mileti et al., 1975:105), victims of technological disasters may be stigmatized as a result of the fears of the surrounding community (Edelstein, 1991; Reich, 1991). Stigmatization may occur because of the fear and resentment of the nonexposed part of the community when "there are scientific uncertainties about the nature of the hazard . . . potential adverse impacts on the economy of the area, prolonged debate, political activity among victims and intense media attention" (Kasperson and Pijawka, 1985:16). Some of the stigmatization may be encouraged by community leaders who refer to the victims as chronic complainers, or simply troublemakers (Reich, 1983). Finally, stigmatization also results from what Vyner (1988) has called the "medical invisibility" of most environmental contaminants (see also Edelstein, 1991). That is, all too frequently, physicians are unable to locate the etiology of physical symptoms. Without the legitimation of the medical establishment, many victims of human-caused contamination are labeled hypochondriacs or worse.

Another response which increases stress is blaming. Rather than accepting the technological hazard or disaster as an "act of God" whose impacts can at best be mitigated, affected people may suffer from deep feelings of anger because they perceive the events as avoidable, as someone's responsibility (Baum, 1987:38–41; Baum et al., 1993; Couch and Kroll-Smith, 1994; Davidson and Baum, 1991; Douglas, 1992; Gill, 1986). In what could have been a study of the recent Exxon Valdez oil spill of 1989, but was actually written over 30 years ago, Bucher (1957) found that victims of technological accidents were likely to engage in blame attribution if they perceived that the mishaps occurred because big businesses acted in a morally reprehensible way and were not taking sufficient steps to ameliorate the crises they created. Blame may be directed toward those whose acts led directly to the technological disaster, or those viewed as having allowed those acts to happen, such as public officials who failed to pass or enforce regulatory laws (e.g., Baum, 1987:38; Levine, 1982:176; Picou et al., 1992; Stone and Levine, 1986:170). They may even blame themselves in the attempt to gain some feeling of control over the situation (Baum, 1987:41; Davidson and Baum, 1991). In short, they try to attribute blame, and "seek retribution rather than . . . [integrating] . . . the event into their life experience" (Murphy, 1985:7).

It is not their feelings alone, however, that delay or hamper their recovery. The processes involved in assessing damage to people and environment, fixing the burden for damage repair or cleanup, and implementing remedies may take years. In part the delays occur because as a society we are trying to come to grips with technological disasters, trying to compress into decades what it took hundreds of years to learn about events like floods and hurricanes. More than 15 years after the conditions at the Love Canal disposal site came to the attention of government agencies, and despite vast expenditures of time and money, the full extent of migration of the chemical leachates remains unknown, as does the full extent of the damage to health and environment; decisions about how best to clean up the area are the subjects of current discussions and debates. In part, the delays occur because powerful vested interests, corporations, and government agencies, seem resistant to learning about the full extent of the consequences; they try to minimize them and avoid the high costs of repairing or alleviating the damage (Levine, 1982; Reich, 1991; Shrivastava, 1991). Not surprisingly, a few studies have found that the institutional denial of threat may exacerbate the stress of victims, creating additional obstacles to their ability to cope with the crisis and its aftermath (Gephart, 1984, 1992; Vyner, 1988).

A third source of stress derives from legal actions. On the societal level, a good deal of legislative effort has gone into devising laws and regulations to force companies to prevent, mitigate, or take responsibility for the recovery from technological disasters. Some state as well as national government departments of justice are involved in legal actions alleging violations of existing environmental statutes. Because of factors of responsibility and blame, technological disasters lend themselves to litigation; "toxic torts" is now one of the growing fields in the law, and there are law firms whose entire practice focuses on such cases, some with class action suits involving millions of dollars. On the individual level, involvement in any litigation is a traumatic event for the average person, and involvement in prolonged litigation means that people cannot put the event behind them and go on with their lives.

The stressful conflicts and controversies which accompany technological disasters are in part related to appraisals of their risks. We turn now to the literature of risk perception.

## Risk, Threat, and Community Conflict

Formal risk analysis is derived from a mathematical projection of expected rates of mortality and morbidity, based on known or estimated relationships between such undesirable consequences and the degree of exposure to hazardous substances. However, the analytic assessment of how much risk is officially tolerated is a value question whose answer varies greatly with social factors. Those who profit from the processes creating the risks may assess incremental increases in risk quite differently from those exposed to the hazards (Cuoto, 1986:55). In fact, Perrow (1984:306) argues that formal risk analysis is an exercise of political power, "the power to impose risks on the many for the benefit of the few." Finally, the formal analysis of risk itself is a social act and subject to normative biases and institutional confusion typical of any human enterprise, however rational it may claim to be (Freudenburg, 1988). (A more complete discussion of formal risk analysis is found in Chapter 11).

In addition to analyses made by risk professionals, ordinary people facing technological hazards make their own evaluations of risks and threats. These individual and community evaluations are known as risk perceptions. Not surprisingly, considering the uncertain and frequently invisible nature of human-caused hazards and disasters, theoretical efforts to interpret the field rely on some variant of the social constructionist approach. "The people whose perception is being studied," Douglas writes, "are living in a world constructed from their own concepts. These include the concept of what is hazardous" (1985:26). In technological crises, "perceptions of the event . . . may be more important in interpreting chronic stress . . . than is the actual danger posed" (Baum, 1987:45).

Douglas and Wildavsky (1982) offered a controversial interpretation of risk perception in a theoretical framework of culture and power. While their book has been criticized for what are seen as conservative political biases, it makes the important point that competing definitions of what is risky—environmental contamination or communist threats to democratic freedoms, for example—are ultimately moral judgments about the proper way to organize society. The form of social order based on the threat of a communist invasion will differ from that of a social order based on the threat of the loss of environmental quality. Reality-creating groups, organizations, and social movements, they argue, collide, knock, and push one another about to secure public ratification of their particular idea of risk (Kroll-Smith and Couch, 1992, 1993; Johnson and Covello, 1987).

In his ASA presidential address, "The Social Fabric At Risk: Toward the Social Transformation of Risk Analysis" (1984), James Short relies extensively on a draft of Douglas' 1985 essay to argue for a social construction model of threat and against a positivist view that reduces risk to event-trees and cost-benefit equations. He emphasizes that risk analysis should focus on more than "human life and health, and . . . economic values" (Short, 1984:711). "Few sociologists," he reminds us, "have studied risks to the social fabric in the context of risk analysis" (Short, 1984:716).

In "Explaining Choices Among Technological Risks," Clarke, (1988) outlines a theory of risk appraisal that shifts attention from social construction by individuals to organizations (see also Clarke, 1989). According to Clarke, it is public and private sector bureaucracies "that set the definition of acceptable risk and the terms of a cost-benefit payoff" (Clarke, 1988: 31). Moreover, he argues, the institutional assessment of risk is not the outcome of a rigorous application of the experimental method to potential hazards. It is rather a type of claims-making activity, a ceremonial act of legitimation used by corporations and government agencies "to construct a reality such that actions an organization has already taken will make sense and seem reasonable" (Clarke, 1988:30). This social constructionist work is important for emphasizing that risk and threat are in part derived from the structure of human relations; that conflicting perceptions of risk are in part derived from the social locations of perceivers; and that certain aversive agents can threaten not only the person, but also the social and cultural milieu itself.

Several case studies have examined specific social and spatial variables that influence the perception of risk. Not surprisingly, the closer people live to a hazardous condition, the more danger they believe they are facing (Flynn, 1982:55; George and Southwell, 1986; Kroll-Smith and Couch, 1990a). In a study of a small town's response to a chemical fire caused by a train derailment, the single most important predictor of resident perception of threat was distance of the household from the derailment (Gill, 1986:277). At Love Canal, age and length of residence were important in understanding the variance in people's perceptions of the threat of chemical contamination. Twenty-year residents were less likely to believe they were threatened by toxic chemicals than more recent residents (Fowlkes and Miller, 1982:31–32; Levine and Stone, 1986). Hamilton (1985a:177) found that "newer residents from higher income households and particularly women with young children" were the most disturbed by their community's contaminated water. After a second, comparative study of two towns with contaminated wells, Hamilton concluded that "sex and parenthood effects on toxic waste concern . . . are consistent across three different communities" (Hamilton, 1985b:476; see also, Flynn, 1982:55; Weisaeth, 1991).

Hazard detection technology is also related to appraisals of risk. While hurricane or tornado detection technology is a routinized part of the emergency preparedness of most communities prone to high wind damage, most communities lack the technical ability to assess the risks of human-caused hazards. Looking at specific characteristics of technological hazards and their role in shaping perceptions of risks, Kasperson and Pijawka (1985: 13) conclude that simply detecting the aversive agent "may require a specialized analytical ability lacking in most communities." Chemical or radiological contamination, for example, is "not within the realm of the human sensory capacities to see, smell, taste, touch or hear" (Cuthbertson and Nigg, 1987:469–471; Vyner, 1988:13). But even assuming the presence of appropriate measurement instruments and skills, the ambiguity of the hazard agent and its effects is likely to create conflicting data regarding the scope and severity of the dangers (Couch and Kroll-Smith, 1985:569; Cuoto, 1986:60).

Not surprisingly, the more an aversive agent resists accurate detection the more uncertainty people will experience and the more they are likely to depend on one another, the media, and other social sources to define the dangers besetting them (Covello, 1983). Several families living in Centralia, Pennsylvania, for example, defined the degree of danger they were exposed to by identifying with families who had been relocated because of the poisonous gases. The worst-case families served as reference groups even after they had been relocated, and even though no gas levels of comparable magnitude were recorded in any of the other homes in Centralia (Kroll-Smith and Couch, 1990). At Love Canal, invisible chemicals moved through underground swales, affecting one family but not another; the lack of uniform objective criteria hampered the achievement of consensus about the consequences of exposure. "Each family found itself in the unusual . . . position of having to arrive at its own decision concerning the significance of the presence of the chemicals" (Fowlkes and Miller, 1982:45).

One study reported that the public's perceptions of the risks of nuclear energy were inherently subjective, and concluded that "risks from nuclear power seem to be prime candidates for exaggeration because of extensive media coverage . . . and their association with the vivid, imaginable dangers of nuclear war" (Slovic et al., 1982:45). In another study, residents erroneously assumed that a hazardous waste site was located adjacent to their neighborhood. Their risk perceptions were influenced by media coverage and the behavior of organizations in response to a "threat" which never materialized (Schwartz et al., 1985:68).

These studies illustrate the idea that because of a high degree of subjectivity in assessing the risks of technological versus natural hazards, the social fabric plays a more pronounced role in shaping the interpretation of threat. One way in which society clearly influences assessments of danger is through the formation of shared versus individual appraisals of loss. A few studies have suggested the need to expand the study of the more psychologically oriented risk *perceptions* to include the study of risk *beliefs*. "In . . . situations involving exposure to invisible contaminants . . . one finds that invisible health threats are met by the development of nonempirical belief systems about the nature of the threats" (Kroll-Smith and Couch, 1987; Vyner, 1988:21).

The concept of belief systems applied to the study of risk suggests the importance of collective ideas that acquire permanence, require personal commitment, and serve as the basis for emergent group organization (Kroll-Smith and Couch, 1993). The first and most important grassroots group to emerge at Love Canal was organized on the basis of a shared belief system regarding the amount and kind of dangers it was facing, and what its members were entitled to as taxpaying citizens (Levine, 1982:176–177). Similarly, Love Canal residents talked about chemical migration and risk using "the conditional language of belief" (Fowlkes and Miller, 1982:47). Residents of Centralia responded to the risks of an underground mine fire with a "shared set of linked ideas concerning the amount and kinds of dangers facing their families" (Kroll-Smith and Couch, 1987:264; Kroll-Smith and Couch, 1990a). It is ironic that the steady state of hypervigilance required by a risk belief system may create enough chronic apprehension to amplify the anxiety already caused by the aversive agent itself (Kroll-Smith and Couch, 1987, 1993; Vyner, 1988:128–129).

Shared assumptions about danger are frequently the bases for group emergence. Such groups may, by their very presence and activities, restructure a neighborhood or community. An account of neighborhood responses to water contamination describes "the creation of a 'spatial network,' a community group corresponding to the boundaries of contamination" (Edelstein and Wandersman, 1987:72). Three distinct grassroots groups formed at Love Canal, each organized around a different perception of the amount and kind of danger it was facing (Levine, 1982). Similarly, seven local protest groups emerged in the wake of the accident at Three Mile Island (Walsh, 1981, 1988). The Centralia mine fire resulted in the formation of six citizens' groups in a town of fewer than a thousand people (Kroll-Smith and Couch, 1990a, 1990b). The emergence of several citizens' groups in a town or neighborhood is likely to create new roles, emergent leadership, and public occasions, and thus create the conditions for social conflict.

In contrast to the generally cooperative nature of the informal citizens' groups that emerge in the immediate aftermath of natural calamities (see Quarantelli and Dynes, 1976), groups emerging in response to technological stressors frequently disagree over the correct interpretation of the problem and the proper course of action to resolve it. A team of community psychologists wrote: "Our frustrating and saddening experience in consulting with United Way agencies at Love Canal was that the murkiness and pessimism of the situation resulted in divisions among victims . . . effective community organization was nearly impossible in an atmosphere of hopelessness and misplaced conflict" (Kliman et al., 1982:267). In cases of asbestos and pesticide contamination, competing "victim clusters" emerged, which "attempted to demonstrate the correctness of their own interpretations of the . . . risk level of the disaster agent. . . . (The) emotional climate that emerged was one of anger, frustration (and) bitterness" (Cuthbertson and Nigg, 1987: 480).

In their study of asbestos, Kasperson and Pijawka found "that the non-victimized community (developed) sharp resentment against the disaster victims" (1985:16). Fowlkes and Miller discovered that Love Canal families who believed the chemical migration was not a health threat discredited "any and all claims that migration was widespread" by "categorically discrediting the people who (made) them" (1982:98).

Conflict can, of course, facilitate the stable growth of a community (Coser, 1956). In the recovery and rehabilitation stages of a natural disaster, conflict facilitates the restructuring of neighborhoods and communities by helping to realign group interests and re-establish the competitive milieu necessary for an exchange-based social order (Turner, 1976). The type of conflict that typically emerges in response to technological hazards, however, may place the basic consensus of a community in question. One group interprets the warning and threat cues as remote risks, a potential problem but certainly nothing to warrant the relocation of the settlement. One group charges another with pursuing goals inimical to human health and welfare. In turn, the accused group blames its accuser of seeking to destroy the community's traditional way of life by working for relocation. Understanding this process of reciprocal blame attribution is critical in anticipating the escalating conflict that may, as in the case of Centralia, Pennsylvania, become more debilitating than the hazard agent itself (Kroll-Smith and Couch, 1990a). Freudenburg and Jones (1991) argue convincingly for the corrosive effects of these events on communities. They refer to these transformed human settlements using the provocative phrase "corrosive communities."

Work by Aronoff and Gunter (1992), however, suggests that in cases where communities obtain considerable political and financial resources to address the crisis, community conflict is less likely to emerge. The following discussion expands the study of hazard and disaster response by examining the social distribution of risks and corporate liability.

### Political Economy

The risks of technological development are distributed unequally among individuals, groups, communities, regions, and societies. Overall, the costs of living with technological risks are borne by those least equipped to manage them—the poor. There is a substantial literature on environmental equity which examines the process by which the creation and unequal distribution of technological hazards take place (Bullard, 1990; Napton and Day, 1992). In 1983, the U.S. General Accounting Office reported on four hazardous waste sites threatening communities in one southern state: "at least 26% of the population in all four communities have income below the poverty level" (U.S. General Accounting Office, 1983:1). Similarly, the city of Houston pursued a policy of locating solid waste disposal sites in low-income, "predominantly black neighborhoods" (Bullard, 1983:285, 1990; see also Bullard and Wright, 1986). The convergence of data on the seeming disproportionate amount of toxins polluting the neighborhoods and bodies of racial minorities encouraged the use of the term *environmental racism*, to mount both a research and a protest focus on people and hazardous waste (Bryant and Mohal, 1992; Bullard and Wright, 1992).

The distribution of impacts of hazardous technologies appears to be related to political and economic systems. An interactionist model of resource management and political conflict by Freudenburg and Gramling (1992) is arguably the most comprehensive approach to the problem currently found in the literature. A number of other approaches, however, are also worth pursuing.

In a seminal article dealing with the Santa Barbara oil spill, Molotch (1970) discusses the processes by which "big oil" was able to triumph, even against the residents of an affluent community. In a more general article, Gephart (1984) focuses on "organizationally based environmental disasters" (or "OBEDS"). These are disasters which are caused by an organization and have negative environmental consequences. Gephart views OBEDs as inherently political, involving conflict over whether or not the organization's version of reality concerning the disaster (e.g., that it is not serious, or cannot be blamed on them) will become dominant. For Gephart, the dominance of capital extends to the shaping of reality, in this case the way we think about technological hazards; and for Szasz (1994), technological threats and calamities are also likely to shape perceptions regarding the willingness or capacity of industry to protect the public.

In a somewhat similar vein, Etzkowitz (1984) is interested in disasters caused by corporations having foreknowledge of the environmentally disastrous consequences of their actions. Here, the critical factor is the control of knowledge by the corporation so that it will not be blamed for the catastrophe (see Kliman et al., 1982:265). Shrivastava (1991) also deals with corporate control of knowledge through the development and dissemination of myths concerning industrial crises. In these examples, the reason for the production of corporate-induced disasters is seen to lie in the nature of capitalist organizations. As for culpability, in studying 25 toxic waste incidents, Finsterbusch (1987) found that most illegal waste activities by corporations were not carried out in ignorance, but with full knowledge of the illegal nature of their activities. While primarily interested in technological accidents caused by the normal operation of complex, modern technological systems, Perrow (1984) agrees that the capitalist profit motive is a major factor in technological catastrophes (see also Reich, 1991).

Castleman adds an international dimension to the discussion of capitalism: "as manufacturers in industrial nations are forced to absorb the economic burdens of preventing and compensating occupational and environmental diseases caused by their operations, pressures favoring hazard export will increase. . . . Poverty and ignorance make communities in many parts of the world quite vulnerable to the exploitation implicit in hazard export" (Castleman, 1979:570). Perrolle points to recent efforts to relate ecological theory to Marxism and world systems theory as a positive development in explaining such tragedies as Bhopal (Perrolle, 1985; see Shrivastava, 1987:ch. 2). Operating at the macro-sociological level of analysis, Schnaiberg analyzes the "treadmill of production" inherent to capitalist systems. He argues that growth produced by the treadmill, while environmentally destructive, is supported by institutional structures which gain from it (including not only business, but also labor and government). Technological disasters can be seen as a logical outcome of this system (Schnaiberg, 1980; Schnaiberg and Gould, 1994).

A number of scholars have discussed the effects on individuals and social organizations of technological disasters caused by corporations. For example, in his classic study of the Buffalo Creek flood, Erikson (1976) relates the social and psychological devastation of the survivors to the long history of corporate dominance as well as to the immediate corporate responsibility for the flood itself. A paper on the Love Canal problem discusses the complex psychological problems which result from believing that one's life has been risked for the sake of profit (Kliman et al., 1982).

In addition to the focus on corporations, a number of works analyze the involvement of other institutions, especially the government. Molotch (1970) argues that the federal Department of the Interior was on the side of the corporation in the Santa Barbara oil spill case, helping in the job of reality management. Walsh (1988) describes a collaborative relationship between the Nuclear Regulatory Agency and Metropolitan Edison, the owners of the Three Mile Island facility. Finsterbusch (1987) states that while the situation is improving, the government traditionally has responded inadequately in toxic contamination situations. Along a different line, Castleman (1979) implies that in passing legislation to regulate corporate activity involving technological hazards in their own countries, governments of industrialized nations unintentionally aid in the unequal spread of these hazards worldwide. Szasz (1986) argues that toxic waste disposal regulations, created through political compromise between the government and corporations, unintentionally allow organized crime to become a major player in this institutional structure.

While intracountry government/economic relationships are the subject of a fair number of articles, cross-national comparison of such relationships is the subject of very few. In one exception, the author asserts that environmental regulation in Japan is due more to noneconomic factors than is environmental regulation in the United States (Ikeda, 1986). Another author observes that the success of the nuclear power industry in France, as compared with the United States, is based on the program of direct subsidies to that industry by the French government (Campbell, 1986).

These articles are necessary reminders that international variations in institutional arrangements must be taken into account more than they have been in the past. A crucial question still to be addressed is raised by attributing the creation and distribution of hazardous technologies to monopoly capitalist phenomena: Why then have technological hazards and disasters also been prevalent in noncapitalist societies?

Recently, environmental interest group politics has become a major topic for research concerning technological hazards (e.g., Clarke, 1991; Wolensky, 1991). In one interesting example, Cuoto (1986) identified three interest groups whose competition shaped the outcome of a case involving toxic waste disposal. In another, Brown (1991; see also Brown and Mikkelsen, 1990) analyzes alliances between community residents and health professionals in the Woburn toxic contamination case. In contrast to both psychological and macro-sociological approaches, Clarke (1988) uses bureaucratic theory, interorganizational analysis, and bounded rationality to analyze how the interests and dynamics of various groups influence the outcomes in technological hazard situations (Clarke, 1988, 1989).

In addition to the studies which examine structural conflicts of interest, there are some that look at the shaping of culture and culture conflict in technological hazard situations. Omohundro (1991) discusses how the Saint Lawrence River oil spill sparked the composition of a musical about that spill, and how the musical has influenced the region's disaster subculture. Mazur (1991) examines the way technological hazards become defined as public issues. Molotch (1970), Gephart (1984), and Shrivastava (1991) are concerned with the power of corporations to shape the cultural reality of technological hazards.

Ridington (1982) describes cultural conflict between Native Americans and both corporate and governmental authorities about a toxic gas release from an oil well. The Native Americans value personal autonomy, individual competence, and responsibility, while industrial society values expert knowledge and deference to authority. The Native Americans wanted to move from the site, but the government argued that there was no continuing danger. Different cultural perspectives prohibited the two sides from understanding each other. A related article examines a semi-rural community in Puerto Rico which perceived health problems due to its proximity to a Union Carbide chemical plant. Unlike the case Ridington reported, respondents had apparently abandoned their traditional or folk beliefs regarding the environment and health and had internalized Western categories of risk and health. In this case, socialization to "modern" culture aided residents in forming a collective protest (Susser, 1985).

Finally, there is a line of inquiry which argues that differences in economic, social, and cultural organization are perhaps less important than the characteristics of modern technology itself, and that these characteristics make modern technologies especially hazardous. For example, Perrow (1984) is primarily interested in technological accidents caused by the normal operation of modern technological systems. The Three Mile Island nuclear plant accident, in Perrow's terms, is a "normal accident," one due to a series of interactive technical failures in a complex, tightly coupled technological system. Given the nature of modern technology, normal accidents are seen as inevitable. Pursuing this theme, another author argues that modern technological systems are especially dangerous because of their large size, sensitivity to human error, and catastrophic potential (Westrum, 1986). Working at a macro-sociological level, Giddens (1990, 1991) writes of manufactured risk (i.e., manufactured by humans and their technology) becoming dominant in the modern world, with consequences ranging from the global to the personal levels. Beck (1992, 1995a, 1995b) argues that the catastrophic potential of modern technological risks goes beyond the ability of our current social organizational forms to handle the threat, and that this will lead to very significant social change.

Overall, the studies in this area clearly show that the nature of modern technology, and the way it is organized at the institutional, national, and international levels, affects what the negative consequences of the technology will be, and on whom those negative consequences will fall. We turn now to an examination of studies dealing with another important aspect of the political-economic process: social policy.

### Social Policy

The literature on policy issues recognizes that policies designed for natural hazards and disasters are not adequate for technological crises. Worthley and Torkelson (1981) make policy recommendations specifically developed for toxic waste management. A few investigators have begun to consider the problems associated with technology transfer. Castleman (1979:570) states that "[n]ational efforts to implement environmental controls for hazardous industries may have to be complemented by measures that prevent the mere displacement of killer industries to 'export platforms' in nonregulating countries." He proposes the establishment of an international organization to monitor and disseminate information about the worldwide spread of hazardous technologies. Policy experts also implore decision makers to base their choices on long-term environmental factors rather than short-term economic benefits. They point out that societies differ in their abilities to use toxic materials properly, and suggest monitoring and informational programs that would help societies to develop safer hazardous materials policies (Weiss and Clarkson, 1986).

Several works discuss information programs and problems. The picture they provide of the way information is gathered and disseminated in technological crises is not encouraging. Hewitt and Burton (1971:76–77) pointed out some time ago that the data are inadequate to predict the frequency of human-caused disasters; and they appear to remain inadequate today (Perrow, 1994). Also, the inherent ambiguity of technological hazards makes it difficult to develop policy programs that help people to make decisions concerning technological risks (see Bord, 1985).

A number of studies have considered the difficulties of disseminating information in ways which will quiet public fears about various hazards. For example, while recognizing the public concern over health, safety, and toxic wastes, one study discusses some of these informational difficulties and offers policy suggestions for remedying them (Harris, 1983). Kasperson, Hohenemser, and Kates (1982) are less optimistic. After considering the failure of several attempts to gain consensus on nuclear power, they state: "It is not even clear that the profusion of information helped to eliminate confusion, reduce concerns about risks, or clarify the major issues of debate. . . . In the short term we foresee no events that will quiet vocal opposition and eradicate the deep public distrust of nuclear power" (Kasperson et al., 1982:43–44). This conclusion is supported by an empirical study of residents living near the Diablo Canyon nuclear plant, which found a positive correlation between information about the plant and opposition to licensing (George and Southwell, 1986).

At the same time, these conclusions cannot be taken to indicate that the public is extremely concerned about all hazards. A study of the effectiveness of a state radon information program, designed to alert homeowners of radon dangers, found that "[d]espite the involvement of generally well-motivated homeowners and well-intentioned researchers and government officials . . . the risk information approach . . . failed to induce appropriate, cost-effective voluntary protection. . . . There is a pronounced tendency for respondents to understate their actual risks" (Johnson and Luken, 1987: 78). It seems, then, that information programs, whether designed to increase or decrease the perceptions of risk, have not accomplished their intended effects. Before effective policies in this area can be developed, we may need to know much more than we do about the perception of risks of technological hazards, and about the role of information in increasing or reducing those perceived risks.

Another aspect of the issue is the use of behavioral science information by policy makers. Here, too, the results are disappointing. Studies of evacuation behavior following the Three Mile Island accident (Cutter, 1984), and those of behavior anticipated if a radiological emergency were to occur on Long Island, New York (Johnson and Zeigler, 1983), indicate that people's behavior would depart radically from that predicted by governmental emergency evacuation plans. The authors of these studies argue that evacuation policy makers should take behavioral science findings into account.

Finally, there are a few studies of the administration of policies relevant to technological hazards. For example, Zimmerman (1985) points out that policy concerning technological disasters is usually set by laws and implemented by agencies dealing primarily with environmental issues, rather than emergency management legislation and agencies. While environmental laws and agencies have become powerful tools for controlling and responding to technological disasters, "environmental management programs do not fit easily into the emergency management mode" (Zimmerman, 1985: 37). Shrivastava (1994) examines social structural contradictions likely to precipitate industrial accidents. Other researchers focused on two environmental health agencies to examine the risk assessment process, arguing that "risk assessment is at the heart of the regulatory process in the environmental health area." The federal agencies in this area (such as EPA and FDA) have "important political advantages" since they are granted "broad discretionary authority regarding risk management" (Regens et al., 1983: 142); but movement toward uniformity and coordination may well lessen such discretionary powers.

These articles provide good starting points for a much-needed examination of the development and implementation of laws which, in fact if not always in intention, govern the ways people and communities attempt to prevent and respond to technological disasters. Two recent efforts at such an examination are the first book-length treatment of the passage and effects of Superfund legislation (Hird, 1994), and Szasz's discussion of that legislation as one factor which shaped the nature of social movement response to toxic contamination (1994:11–37).

## The Role of Social Researchers

Several social scientists have commented on the complicated role they found themselves playing in researching communities responding to protracted technological crises. In this section we will consider only a few aspects of the influence of the context on the collection and use of data, and on the influence of the researcher and the research process on the groups, organizations, and communities being studied.

The social researcher's purpose is to collect information about the community and its predicament. Information, however, is a key resource for communities organizing to respond to the uncertainty of technological hazards and disasters. At Love Canal, Levine (1986:80) found her research team greeted with suspicion by government personnel at the Canal but welcomed by residents, because both groups viewed the sociologists as "interpreters and disseminators of information, and possibly as moral judges." Kroll-Smith and Couch (1990b:122) discuss a "fusion of horizons" between the social scientist and the community; "[a]s we interpret the community, its residents are interpreting us and our data." In such situations the traditional distinction between social science and advocacy may seem particularly forced and artificial. Cuoto (1986:69) reached a similar conclusion on the social scientist's role in investigating towns threatened by toxic waste: "participatory research seems to be grounds on which to combine an emphasis on community with the need to acquire knowledge."

There are other information-related problems which the researcher must consider. Omohundro (1982:25) suggests that sociologists and anthropologists can act as "cultural translators" in technological crises, increasing the understanding of people's reactions to threat, the responsibility of government agencies, and the limits of the law. In the ideal case, the social scientist would be acceptable as a "translator" to all involved parties. The role outlined by Omohundro would seem to require exactly the carefully neutral stance prescribed by our disciplines; the scientist's credibility with other scientists is dependent upon adherence to norms of scientific objectivity.

In the field situation, however, issues of advocacy may well arise, making it difficult to maintain a neutral stance. The credibility and the acceptability of the social scientist's contributions may be related to the perceptions of the residents that the social scientist is sympathetic to one side or the other in a controversial situation; credibility and acceptability may be influenced as well by the affected people's knowledge about sources of funding for research. Many of these dynamics are shaped by the methods used by the researchers, the length of time they spend in the community, and the sorts of personal relationships they develop in the course of research.

In the high-stakes legal controversies which develop in technological disasters, social scientists may find themselves trying to protect the confidentiality of research data in the face of requests from litigants preparing legal claims and defenses (Cecil and Boruch, 1988). Fulfilling an ethical obligation to obtain informed consent may require the researcher to tell prospective interviewees that a court order may preclude the maintenance of confidentiality. The researcher may decide not to keep identifying information in the records, preserving confidentiality but preventing the possibility of longitudinal studies.

Finally, the information vacuum created by the uncertainty and ambiguity of the events may place unusual demands on investigators who are asked to provide community groups with data, with leadership, or with insights into their predicament. Social scientists engaged in long-term research may find themselves dealing with the dilemma of how much advice and assistance to provide to such groups, while still maintaining the neutrality which will make their work acceptable to the scientific community (see Edelstein, 1988; Kroll-Smith and Couch, 1990b; Walsh, 1988).

CONCLUSIONS

The literature on technological hazards and disasters is being produced in societies slowly coming to grips with relatively new problems that show their complexity and effects at every level of social organization, from individual to international relations. As societies confront these issues, their responses lead to social changes. Since the early 1970s, there has been a proliferation of new laws and regulations, as well as new applications of existing laws and regulations to matters concerning hazardous technologies. New methods for controlling, storing, and disposing of hazardous waste are in various stages of development.

The mass media, which both reflect and help establish public awareness, report daily on technological hazards and disasters. Organized social responses include familiar ones with new foci, such as the thousands of small groups springing up all over the country to control toxic waste disposal. The spontaneously formed citizens' groups often include in their ideology the prevention or mitigation of future technological crises.

In addition, the "Superfund" legislation which followed the Love Canal disaster mandates citizen participation in decisions about the cleanup of abandoned hazardous waste disposal sites. These citizens' groups may well influence a variety of details in the cleanup processes, and help to set precedents or promote expectations for citizen participation in other situations. In response to the Bhopal disaster, the 99th Congress passed the Superfund Amendment and Reauthorization Act (SARA), which entitled communities to know what hazardous chemicals are being used within their corporate boundaries. A republican-led Congress now refuses to fund the SARA and its future is uncertain.

The organized responses also include new forms and variants of old ones. One example is the Technical Review Committee (TRC), established at Love Canal in 1983, composed of representatives of two federal and two state agencies working in concert to study the question of habitability of the area where remedial construction work to correct the leaking disposal site had taken place. When the TRC empaneled a group of scientists from a number of disciplines, they mandated that the scientific deliberations were to be carried out in a public forum, from the earliest considerations of research design to the final peer review process. New York State now employs "citizen participation specialists" who work with both citizens' groups and government agencies around a variety of water- and toxic-related issues. There are international groups and commissions studying problems of technological hazards and disasters and attempting to develop cooperative solutions.

All the people involved, whether as victims, responders, law makers, industry officials, consultants, and others, are players in the process of social change created by technological crises. The context within which social research is conducted is changing as well. We are dealing with social and environmental phenomena whose parameters are constantly emerging and changing. The changes in context and phenomena should be taken into account when we try to compare the findings and conclusion from studies done at different times.

Most critiques of the literature on individual and collective responses to technological hazards and disasters emphasize that the majority of studies are descriptively strong; some are conceptually weak; generalizations are limited because many lack methodological rigor; most research designs do not include control groups, standardized measures, carefully selected population samples, or baseline data (see e.g., Smith et al., 1988).

These criticisms are true of much of the work on psychological and social-psychological responses to human-induced hazards and disasters; their origin, however, is not in poorly conceived research designs but in the limitations posed by the research context itself. The law and our respect for one another as human beings, for example, prevent us from pre-testing a group, polluting their environment, and then post-testing for elevated levels of stress, coping problems, and so on. The true pre-levels are never unequivocally known and thus a valuable piece of the puzzle is missing. Moreover, it is impossible to randomly assign residents to victim and nonvictim groups. Thus, the control and experimental groups will be nonequivalent. It is not impossible in such cases for the experimental and control groups to be statistically equivalent, but there are no assurances of this and so we must be very cautious in generalizing from these types of data.

While these methodological problems are inherent in research on human responses to technological hazards and disasters, there is an equally important problem that is not intrinsic to this substantive area. In our opinion, there is a mismatch between the academic norm of increasing specialization and the systemic, interdisciplinary, problems of technological calamities. We believe more sophisticated conceptual work is possible now if researchers shift their unit of analysis away from structures and processes that fall short of representing larger affected units, particularly at the community level. While individual and small-group data are necessary for many purposes, "theories about disasters," Torry reminds us, "are inherently theories about communities, that is, community continuity and change" (1979: 43). Often the research already done has focused on one dimension of the disaster, such as emergent groups, risk perception, or policy implementation. These can be analyzed to some extent in isolation from a community's social, political, and cultural patterns. However, isolating the process of groups emerging in response to technological hazards and considering them as representative of social movement organizations, for example, tells us more about social movement organizations than how or why communities respond to chronic states of contingent loss.

Achieving only such narrowly defined research goals diminishes our ability to develop middle- or macro-range theories of technological hazards and disasters. We argue that these human-caused crises are intricately woven into the fabric of modern society. When a board room decision of a multinational corporation eventually results in the contamination of a person's basement, the substantive problem is a systemic one. Our theories and our methods should reflect this reality.

## NOTE

The authors want to thank Murray Levine, Frada Naroll, Lee Clarke, and Duane Gill for their careful reading of previous drafts of this manuscript. Particular thanks go to Dallas McGlinn, a graduate student at the University of New Orleans, for her timely work in preparation of this chapter.

## REFERENCES

Aronoff, Marilyn, and Valerie Gunter. 1992. "It's Hard To Keep a Good Town Down: Local Recovery Efforts in the Aftermath of Toxic Contamination." *Industrial Crisis Quarterly* 6:83–97.

Baum, Andrew. 1987. "Toxins, Technology and Natural Disasters." Pp. 5–54 in *Cataclysms, Crises and Catastrophes*, edited by Gary van den Bos and Brenda Bryant. Washington, DC: American Psychological Association.

Baum, Andrew, Raymond Fleming, and Laura M. Davidson. 1983. "Natural Disaster and Technological Catastrophe." *Environment and Behavior* 15:333–354.

Baum, Andrew, Raymond Fleming, and Jerome E. Singer. 1993. "Coping with Victimization by Technological Disaster." *Journal of Social Issues* 39:117–138.

Beck, Ulrich. 1992. *Risk Society: Towards a New Modernity*. Trans. Mark Ritter. London: Sage.

———. 1995a. *Ecological Enlightenment: Essays on the Politics of the Risk Society*. Trans. Mark A. Ritter. Atlantic Highlands, NJ: Humanities Press.

———. 1995b. *Ecological Politics in an Age of Risk*. Trans. Amos Weisz. Cambridge: Polity Press.

Berren, Michael R., Allan Beigel, and Stuart Ghertner. 1980. "A Typology for the Classification of Disasters." *Mental Health Journal* 16:103–110.

Blocker, Jean T., and Darren E. Sherkat. 1992. "In the Eyes of the Beholder: Technological and Naturalistic Interpretations of a Disaster." *Industrial Crisis Quarterly* 6:153–166.

Bolin, Robert. 1985. "Disaster Characteristics and Psychosocial Impacts." Pp. 3–28 in *Disasters and Mental Health*, edited by Barbara J. Sowder. Washington, DC: U.S. Department of Health and Human Services, National Institute of Mental Health.

Bord, Richard J. 1985. "Problems of Social Control in Organizations with Democratic Norms: The Case of Citizen Participation Programs Involving Risky Technologies." Unpublished paper, Pennsylvania State University.

Brown, Phil. 1991. "The Popular Epidemiology Approach to Toxic Waste Contamination." Pp. 133–155 in *Communities at Risk: Collective Responses to Technological Hazards*, edited by Stephen R. Couch and J. Stephen Kroll-Smith. New York: Peter Lang.

Brown, Phil, and Faith I. T. Ferguson. 1995. "Making a Big Stink: Women's Work,

Women's Relationships, and Toxic Waste Activism." *Gender & Society* 9: 145–172.

Brown, Phil, and Edwin J. Mikkelsen. 1990. *No Safe Place: Toxic Waste, Leukemia, and Community Action.* Berkeley: University of California Press.

Bryant, Bunyan, and P. Mohal. 1992. *Race and the Incidence of Environmental Hazards: A Time for Discourse.* Boulder, CO: Westview Press.

Bucher, Rue. 1957. "Blame and Hostility in Disaster." *American Journal of Sociology* 62:467–475.

Bullard, Robert D. 1983. "Solid Waste Sites and the Black Houston Community." *Sociological Inquiry* 53:273–288.

Bullard, Robert D. 1990. *Dumping in Dixie: Race, Class and Environmental Quality.* Boulder, CO: Westview Press.

Bullard, Robert D., and Beverly H. Wright. 1992. "The Quest for Environmental Equity: Mobilizing the African-American Community for Social Change." Pp. 39–50 in *American Environmentalism: The U.S. Environmental Movement, 1970–1990,* edited by Riley E. Dunlap and Angela G. Mertig. Philadelphia: Taylor and Francis.

Bullard, Robert D., and Beverly Hendrix Wright. 1986. "The Politics of Pollution: Implications for the Black Community." *Phylon* XLVII:71–78.

Cable, Sherry, and Michael Benson. 1992. "Environmental Injustice: The Failure of the Regulatory Process and the Emergence of Grassroots Environmental Organizations." Unpublished paper, University of Tennessee.

Cable, Sherry, and Charles Cable. 1995. *Environmental Problems, Grassroots Solutions.* New York: St. Martin's Press.

Cable, Sherry, and Edward Walsh. 1991. "The Emergence of Organized Protest in Chronic Technical Emergencies." Pp. 113–132 in *Communities at Risk: Collective Responses to Technological Hazards,* edited by Stephen R. Couch and J. Stephen Kroll-Smith. New York: Peter Lang.

Campbell, John L. 1986. "The State, Capital Formation, and Industrial Planning: Financing Nuclear Energy in the United States and France." *Social Science Quarterly* 67:707–721.

Castleman, Barry I. 1979. "The Export of Hazardous Factories to Developing Nations." *International Journal of Health Services* 9:569–606.

Cecil, Joe Shelby, and Robert Boruch. 1988. "Compelled Disclosure of Research Data: An Early Warning and Suggestions for Psychologists." *Law and Human Behavior* 12:181–190.

Clarke, Lee. 1988. "Explaining Choices Among Technological Risks." *Social Problems* 35:22–35.

———. 1989. *Acceptable Risk? Making Decisions in a Toxic Environment.* Berkeley: University of California Press.

———. 1991. "Failure and Success in Social Protest." Pp. 83–111 in *Communities at Risk: Collective Responses to Technological Hazards,* edited by Stephen R. Couch and J. Stephen Kroll-Smith. New York: Peter Lang.

Coser, Lewis. 1956. *The Functions of Social Conflict.* New York: Free Press.

Couch, Stephen R., and J. Stephen Kroll-Smith. 1985. "The Chronic Technical Disaster: Toward a Social Scientific Perspective." *Social Science Quarterly* 66:564–575.

Couch, Stephen R., and J. Stephen Kroll-Smith. 1990. "Patterns of Victimization and the Chronic Technological Disaster." Pp. 159–176 in *The Victimology Handbook*, edited by Emilio Viano. New York: Garland Publishing.

Couch, Stephen R., and Steve Kroll-Smith. 1994. "Environmental Controversies, Interactional Resources and Rural Communities: Siting Versus Exposure Disputes." *Rural Sociology* 59:25–44.

Covello, Vincent T. 1983. "The Perception of Technological Risks: A Literature Review." *Technological Forecasting and Social Change* 23:285–297.

Cuoto, Richard A. 1986. "Failing Health and New Prescriptions: Community-Based Approaches to Environmental Risks." Pp. 53–70 in *Current Health Policy Issues and Alternatives: An Applied Social Science Perspective*, edited by Carole E. Hill. Athens: University of Georgia Press.

Cuthbertson, Beverly H., and Joanne M. Nigg. 1987. "Technological Disaster and the Nontherapeutic Community: A Question of True Victimization." *Environment and Behavior* 19:462–483.

Cutter, Susan L. 1984. "Emergency Preparedness and Planning for Nuclear Power Plant Accidents." *Applied Geography* 4:235–245.

Davidson, Laura, and Andrew Baum. 1991. "Victimization and Self-Blame Following a Technological Disaster." Pp. 33–52 in *Communities at Risk: Collective Responses to Technological Hazards*, edited by Stephen R. Couch and J. Stephen Kroll-Smith. New York: Peter Lang.

Dohrenwend, B. P., B. S. Dohrenwend, G. J. Warheit, G. S. Bartlett, R. L. Goldsteen, K. Goldsteen, and J. L. Martin. 1981. "Stress in the Community: A Report to the President's Commission on the Accident at Three Mile Island." *Annals of the New York Academy of Sciences* 365:159–174.

Douglas, Mary. 1985. *Risk Acceptability According to the Social Sciences*. New York: Russell Sage Foundation.

———. 1992. *Risk and Blame*. London: Routledge.

Douglas, Mary, and Aaron Wildavsky. 1982. *Risk and Culture*. Berkeley: University of California Press.

Drabek, Thomas E. 1986. *Human System Responses to Disaster*. New York: Springer-Verlag.

Duncan, Otis Dudley. 1961. "From Social System to Ecosystem." *Sociological Inquiry* 31:140–149.

Dunlap, Riley E., and William R. Catton, Jr. 1983. "What Environmental Sociologists Have in Common (Whether Concerned With 'Built' or 'Natural' Environments)." *Sociological Inquiry* 53:113–135.

Dyer, Christopher L., Duane A. Gill, and J. Steven Picou. 1992. "Social Disruption and the *Exxon Valdez* Oil Spill." *Sociological Spectrum* 12:105–126.

Edelstein, Michael R. 1982. "The Social and Psychological Impacts of Groundwater Contamination in the Legler Section of Jackson, New Jersey." Report prepared for the law firm Kriendler and Kriendler.

Edelstein, Michael R. 1988. *Contaminated Communities: The Social and Psychological Impacts of Residential Toxic Exposure*. Boulder, CO: Westview Press.

———. 1991. "Community Image in Cases of Radon Gas Exposure." Pp. 205–225 in *Communities at Risk: Collective Responses to Technological Hazards*, edited by Stephen R. Couch and J. Stephen Kroll-Smith. New York: Peter Lang.

Edelstein, Michael R., and Abraham Wandersman. 1987. "Community Dynamics in Coping with Toxic Contaminants." Pp. 69–112 in *Neighborhood and Community Environments*, edited by I. Altman and A. Wandersman. New York: Plenum Press.

Erikson, Kai. 1994. *A New Species of Trouble*. New York: Simon and Schuster.

Erikson, Kai T. 1976. *Everything in Its Path: Destruction of Community in the Buffalo Creek Flood*. New York: Simon and Schuster.

Erikson, Kai T. 1991. "A New Species of Trouble." Pp. 11–29 in *Communities at Risk: Collective Responses to Technological Hazards*, edited by Stephen R. Couch and J. Stephen Kroll-Smith. New York: Peter Lang.

Etzkowitz, Henry. 1984. "Corporate Induced Disaster: Three Mile Island and the Delegitimation of Nuclear Power." *Humanity and Society* 8:228–252.

Finsterbusch, Kurt. 1987. "Typical Scenarios in Twenty-Four Toxic Waste Contamination Episodes." Paper presented at the annual meeting of the International Association of Impact Assessment, Barbados.

Fleming, India, and Andrew Baum. 1985. "The Role of Prevention in Technological Catastrophe." Pp. 139–152 in *Beyond the Individual: Environmental Approaches and Prevention*, edited by Abraham Wandersman and Robert Hess. New York: Haworth Press.

Flynn, Cynthia. 1982. "Reactions of Local Residents to the Accident at Three Mile Island." Pp. 49–63 in *Accident at Three Mile Island*, edited by D. L. Sills, C. P. Wolf, and B. Shelanski. Boulder, CO: Westview Press.

Fowlkes, Martha R., and Patricia Y. Miller. 1982. *Love Canal: The Social Construction of Disaster*. Washington, DC: Federal Emergency Management Agency.

Freudenburg, William R. 1988. "Perceived Risk, Real Risk: Social Science and the Art of Probabilistic Risk Assessment." *Science* 242:44–49.

Freudenburg, William, and Robert Gramling. 1992. "Community Impacts of Technological Change: Toward a Longitudinal Perspective." *Social Forces* 70: 937–955.

Freudenburg, William, and Timothy R. Jones. 1991. "Attitudes and Stress in the Presence of a Technological Risk: A Test of the Supreme Court Hypothesis." *Social Forces* 69:1143–1168.

Fritz, Charles E. 1961. "Disaster." Pp. 651–694 in *Contemporary Social Problems*, edited by Robert K. Merton and Robert A. Nisbet. New York: Harcourt and Brace.

George, David L., and Priscilla L. Southwell. 1986. "Opinion on the Diablo Canyon Nuclear Power Plant: The Effects of Situation and Socialization." *Social Science Quarterly* 67:722–735.

Gephart, Robert P. 1984. "Making Sense of Organizationally Based Environmental Disasters." *Journal of Management* 19:205–225.

Gephart, Robert P., Jr. 1992. "Sensemaking. Communicative Distortion and the Logic of Public Inquiry Legitimation." *Industrial Crisis Quarterly* 6:115–135.

Gibbs, Margaret. 1982. "Psychological Dysfunction in the Legler Litigation Group." Report prepared for the law firm Kriendler and Kriendler.

Giddens, Anthony. 1990. *The Consequences of Modernity*. Stanford, CA: Stanford University Press.

———. 1991. *Modernity and Self-Identity: Self and Society in the Late Modern Age.* Stanford, CA: Stanford University Press.

Gill, Duane A. 1986. *A Disaster Impact Assessment Model: An Empirical Study of a Technological Disaster.* Doctoral Dissertation, Texas A&M University, Department of Sociology.

Gill, Duane A., and J. Steven Picou. 1991. "The Social Psychological Impacts of a Technological Accident: Collective Stress and Perceived Health Risks." *Journal of Hazardous Materials* 27:77–89.

Gleser, Goldine C., Bonnie L. Green, and Carolyn N. Winget. 1981. *Prolonged Effects of Disasters: A Study of Buffalo Creek.* New York: Academic Press.

Hamilton, Lawrence C. 1985a. "Who Cares about Water Pollution? Opinions in a Small-Town Crisis." *Sociological Inquiry* 55:170–181.

———. 1985b. "Concern about Toxic Waste: Three Demographic Predictors." *Sociological Perspectives* 28:463–486.

Harris, Jeffrey S. 1983. "Toxic Waste Uproar: A Community History." *Journal of Public Health Policy* 4:181–201.

Hartsough, Don M. 1985. "Measurement of the Psychological Effects of Disaster." Pp. 22–61 in *Perspective on Disaster Recovery*, edited by Jerry Laube and Shirley A. Murphy. Norwalk, CT: Appleton-Century-Crofts.

Hewitt, Kenneth, and Ian Burton. 1971. *The Hazardousness of Place: A Regional Ecology of Damaging Events.* Toronto: University of Toronto Press.

Hird, John A. 1994. *Superfund: The Political Economy of Environmental Risk.* Baltimore, MD: Johns Hopkins University Press.

Ikeda, Saburo. 1986. "Managing Technological and Environmental Risks in Japan." *Risk Analysis* 6:389–402.

Johnson, Brandon, and Vincent T. Covello (eds.). 1987. *The Social and Cultural Construction of Risk: Essays on Risk Selection and Perception.* Boston: D. Reidel Publishing.

Johnson, F. Reed, and Ralph A. Luken. 1987. "Radon Risk Information and Voluntary Protection: Evidence from a Natural Experiment." *Risk Analysis* 7:97–107.

Johnson, James, Jr., and Donald J. Zeigler. 1983. "Distinguishing Human Responses to Radiological Emergencies." *Economic Geography* 59:386–402.

Kasperson, Roger E., Christoph C. Hohenemser, and Robert W. Kates. 1982. "Institutional Responses to Different Perceptions of Risk." Pp. 39–46 in *Accident at Three Mile Island*, edited by D. L. Sills, C. P. Wolf, and B. Shelanski. Boulder, CO: Westview Press.

Kasperson, Roger E., and K. David Pijawka. 1985. "Societal Response to Hazards and Major Hazard Events: Comparing Natural and Technological Hazards." *Public Administration Review* 45:7–18.

Kates, R. W. (ed.). 1977. *Managing Technological Hazards: Research Needs and Opportunities.* Boulder: University of Colorado, Institute of Behavioral Science.

Kliman, Jodie, Rochelle Kern, and Ann Kliman. 1982. "Natural and Human-made Disasters: Some Therapeutic and Epidemiological Implications for Crisis Intervention." Pp. 253–280 in *Therapeutic Intervention: Healing Strategies for Human Systems*, edited by U. Rueveni, Ross V. Speck, and Joan L. Speck. New York: Human Sciences Press.

Kroll-Smith, J. Stephen, and Stephen R. Couch. 1987. "The Chronic Technical Disaster, Small Town Conflict, and the Social Construction of Threat Beliefs." Pp. 262–269 in *The Small City and Regional Community*, edited by Robert P. Wolensky and Edward J. Miller. Stevens Point, WI: Foundation Press.

Kroll-Smith, J. Stephen, and Stephen R. Couch. 1990a. *The Real Disaster Is Above Ground: A Mine Fire and Social Conflict.* Lexington: University Press of Kentucky.

Kroll-Smith, J. Stephen, and Stephen R. Couch. 1990b. "Sociological Knowledge and the Public at Risk: A 'Self Study' of Sociology, Technological Hazards and Moral Dilemmas." *Sociological Practice Review* 2:120–127.

Kroll-Smith, Steve, and Stephen R. Couch. 1991. "What Is a Disaster? An Ecological-Symbolic Approach to Resolving the Definitional Debate." *International Journal of Mass Emergencies and Disasters* 9:355–366.

Kroll-Smith, Steve, and Stephen R. Couch. 1992. "Editorial: The Sociology of Technological Hazards." *Industrial Crisis Quarterly* 6:79–81.

Kroll-Smith, Steve, and Stephen R. Couch. 1993. "Technological Hazards: Social Responses as Traumatic Stressors." Pp. 62–85 in *The International Handbook of Traumatic Stress Syndromes*, edited by John P. Wilson and Beverly Raphael. New York: Plenum Press.

Lang, Kurt, and Gladys Engel Lang. 1964. "Collective Responses to the Threat of Disaster." Pp. 58–75 in *The Threat of Impending Disaster*, edited by George H. Grosser, Henry Wechsler, and Milton Greenblatt. Cambridge, MA: MIT Press.

Lebovits, Allen H., Andrew Baum, and Jerome E. Singer (eds.). 1986. *Advances in Environmental Psychology: Exposure to Hazardous Substances, Psychological Parameters.* Hillsdale, NJ: Lawrence Erlbaum Associates.

Levine, Adeline G. 1986. "Love Canal: Ethical and Methodological Problems in Field Work." *International Journal of Mass Emergencies and Disasters* 4:79–84.

Levine, Adeline G. 1987. "The Stress of Grassroots Leadership." Paper presented at CCHW conference on Stress for Grass Roots leaders, Arlington, VA.

Levine, Adeline G., and Russell A. Stone. 1986. "Threats to People and What They Value." Pp. 109–130 in *Advances in Environmental Psychology*, Vol. 6, edited by A. H. Lebovits, A. Baum, and J. E. Singer. Hillsdale, NJ: Lawrence Erlbaum Associates.

Levine, Adeline Gordon. 1982. *Love Canal: Science, Politics, and People.* Lexington, MA: Lexington Books.

Lindy, Jacob D., and Mary Grace. 1985. "The Recovery Environment: Continuing Stressor Versus a Healing Psychological Space." Pp. 137–149 in *Disasters and Mental Health: Selected Contemporary Perspectives*, edited by Barbara Sowder. Washington, DC: U.S. Department of Health and Human Services, National Institute of Mental Health.

Markowitz, Jeffrey S., and Elane M. Gutterman. 1986. "Predictors of Psychological Distress in the Community Following Two Toxic Chemical Incidents." Pp. 89–107 in *Advances in Environmental Psychology*, Vol. 6, edited by A. H. Lebovits, A. Baum, and J. E. Singer. Hillsdale, NJ: Lawrence Erlbaum Associates.

Mazur, Alan. 1991. "Putting Radon and Love Canal on the Public Agenda." Pp. 183–204 in *Communities at Risk: Collective Responses to Technological Hazards*, edited by Stephen R. Couch and J. Stephen Kroll-Smith. New York: Peter Lang.

Melick, Mary Evans. 1985. "The Health of Postdisaster Populations: A Review of Literature and Case Study." Pp. 179–209 in *Perspectives on Disaster Recovery*, edited by Jerry Laube and Shirley A. Murphy. Norwalk, CT: Appleton-Century-Crofts.

Mileti, Dennis S., Thomas E. Drabek, and J. Eugene Haas. 1975. *Human Systems in Extreme Environments: A Sociological Perspective*. Boulder: Institute of Behavioral Science, University of Colorado.

Molotch, Harvey. 1970. "Oil in Santa Barbara and Power in America." *Sociological Inquiry* 40:131–144.

Murphy, Shirley A. 1985. "The Conceptual Bases for Disaster Research and Intervention." Pp. 3–21 in *Perspectives on Disaster Recovery*, edited by Jerry Laube and Shirley A. Murphy. Norwalk, CT: Appleton-Century-Crofts.

Napton, Mary Luanne, and Frederick A. Day. 1992. "Polluted Neighborhoods in Texas: Who Lives There." *Environment and Behavior* 24:508–526.

Omohundro, John T. 1982. "The Impacts of an Oil Spill." *Human Organization* 41:17–25.

———. 1991. "From Oil Spill to Greasepaint: Theater's Role in Community Response to Technical Disaster." Pp. 159–181 in *Communities at Risk: Collective Responses to Technological Hazards*, edited by Stephen R. Couch and J. Stephen Kroll-Smith. New York: Peter Lang.

Perrolle, Judith A. 1985. "Beyond Bhopal: Communities Confront the Political Economy of Capitalism." Paper presented at the Annual Meetings of the Society for the Study of Social Problems, Washington, DC, August.

Perrow, Charles. 1982. "The President's Commission and the Normal Accident." Pp. 173–183 in *Accident at Three Mile Island: The Human Dimension*, edited by D. L. Sills, C. P. Wolf, and U. B. Shelanski. Boulder, CO: Westview Press.

———. 1984. *Normal Accidents: Living with High Risk Technologies*. New York: Basic Books.

———. 1994. "Accidents in High-Risk Systems." *Technology Studies* 1:1–20.

Perry, Ronald W., and Michael K. Lindell. 1978. "The Psychological Consequences of Natural Disaster: A Review of American Communities." *Mass Emergencies* 3:105–115.

Picou, J. Steven, Duane A. Gill, Christopher L. Dyer, and Evans W. Curry. 1992. "Disruption and Stress in an Alaskan Fishing Community: Initial and Continuing Impacts of the *Exxon Valdez* Oil Spill." *Industrial Crisis Quarterly* 6:235–257.

Preston, Valerie, S. Martin Taylor, and David C. Hodge. 1983. "Adjustment to Natural and Technological Hazards." *Environment and Behavior* 15:143–164.

Prince-Embury, Sandra, and James F. Rooney. 1989. "A Comparison of Residents Who Moved versus Those Who Remained Prior to Restart of Three Mile Island." *Journal of Applied Social Psychology* 19:959–975.

Prince-Embury, Sandra, and James F. Rooney. 1995. "Psychological Adaptation among Residents Following Restart of Three Mile Island." *Journal of Traumatic Stress* 8:47–59.

Quarantelli, E. L. 1985. "What Is Disaster: The Need for Clarification in Definition and Conceptualization in Research." Pp. 41–73 in *Disasters and Mental Health*, edited by Barbara J. Sowder. Washington, DC: U.S. Department of Health and Human Services, National Institute of Mental Health.

———. 1987. "What Should We Study? Questions and Suggestions for Researchers about the Concept of Disasters." *International Journal of Mass Emergencies and Disasters* 5:7–32.

Quarantelli, E. L., and Russell R. Dynes. 1976. "Community Conflict: Its Absence and Its Presence in Natural Disasters." *Mass Emergencies* 1:139–152.

Quarantelli, E. L., and Russell R. Dynes. 1977. "Response to Social Crisis and Disaster." *Annual Review of Sociology* 3:23–49.

Regens, James L., Thomas M. Dietz, and Robert W. Rycroft. 1983. "Risk Assessment in the Policy-Making Process: Environmental Health and Safety Protection." *Publication Administration Review* 44:137–145.

Reich, Michael. 1983. "Environmental Politics and Science: The Case of PBB Contamination in Michigan." *American Journal of Public Health* 73:302–313.

Reich, Michael R. 1991. *Toxic Politics*. Ithaca, NY: Cornell University Press.

Ridington, Robin. 1982. "When Poison Gas Comes Down Like a Fog: A Native Community's Response to Cultural Disaster." *Human Organization* 41:36–42.

Schnaiberg, Allan. 1980. *The Environment: From Surplus to Scarcity*. New York: Oxford University Press.

Schnaiberg, Allan, and Kenneth Alan Gould. 1994. *Environment and Society: The Enduring Conflict*. New York: St. Martin's Press.

Schorr, John K., Raymond Goldsteen, and Cynthia H. Cortes. 1982. "The Long-Term Impact of a Man-Made Disaster: A Sociological Examination of a Small Town in the Aftermath of the Three Mile Island Nuclear Reactor Accident." Paper presented at the Tenth World Congress of Sociology, Mexico City, Mexico.

Schwartz, Steven P., Paul E. White, and Robert G. Hughes. 1985. "Environmental Threats, Communities, and Hysteria." *Public Health Policy* 6:58–77.

Short, James F. 1984. "The Social Fabric at Risk: Toward the Social Transformation of Risk Analysis." *American Sociological Review* 49:711–725.

Shrivastava, Paul. 1987. *Bhopal: Anatomy of a Crisis*. Cambridge, MA: Ballinger.

———. 1991. "Organizational Myths in Industrial Crises: Obfuscating Revelations." Pp. 263–290 in *Communities at Risk: Collective Responses to Technological Hazards*, edited by Stephen R. Couch and J. Stephen Kroll-Smith. New York: Peter Lang.

———. 1994. "Societal Contradictions and Industrial Crises." Pp. 42–61 in *Learning From Disaster: Risk Management after Bhopal*, edited by Sheila Jasanoff. Philadelphia: University of Pennsylvania Press.

Slovic, Paul, Baruch Fischhof, and Sarah Lichtenstein. 1982. "Psychological Aspects of Risk Perspection." Pp. 11–19 in *Accident at Three Mile Island*, edited by D. L. Sills, C. P. Wolf, and B. Shelanski. Boulder, CO: Westview Press.

Smith, Elizabeth, Carol S. North, and Paul C. Price. 1988. "Response to Technological Accidents." Pp. 52–95 in *Mental Health Response to Mass Emergencies*, edited by Mary Lystad. New York: Brunner/Mazel.

Smith, Elizabeth M., Lee N. Robins, Thomas R. Przybeck, Evelyn Goldring, and Susan D. Solomon. 1986. "Psychosocial Consequences of a Disaster." Pp. 50–76 in *Disaster Stress Studies: New Methods and Findings*, edited by James H. Shore. Washington, DC: American Psychiatric Press.

Stone, Russell A., and Adeline G. Levine. 1985. "Reactions to Collective Stress: Correlates of Active Citizen Participation at Love Canal." *Prevention in Human Services* 4:153–177.

Susser, Ida. 1985. "Union Carbide and the Community Surrounding It: The Case of a Community in Puerto Rico." *International Journal of Health Services* 15:561–583.

Szasz, Andrew. 1986. "Corporations, Organized Crime, and the Disposal of Hazardous Waste: An Examination of the Making of a Criminogenic Regulatory Structure." *Criminology* 24:1–27.

———. 1994. *EcoPopulism: Toxic Waste and the Movement for Environmental Justice*. Minneapolis: University of Minnesota Press.

Tierney, Kathleen J. 1981. "Community and Organizational Awareness of and Preparedness for Acute Chemical Emergencies." *Journal of Hazardous Materials* 4:331–342.

Torry, William I. 1979. "Anthropology and Disaster Research." *Disasters* 3:43–52.

Turner, Barry A. 1976. "The Organizational and Interorganizational Development of Disasters." *Administrative Science Quarterly* 21:378–397.

U.S. General Accounting Office. 1983. "Siting of Hazardous Waste Landfills and Their Correlation with Racial and Economic Status of Surrounding Communities." Washington, DC: General Accounting Office, Resources, Community and Economic Development Division.

Vyner, Henry M. 1988. *Invisible Trauma*. Lexington, MA: Lexington Books.

Walsh, Edward. 1981. "Resource Mobilization and Citizen Protest in Communities around Three Mile Island." *Social Problems* 29:1–21.

———. 1988. *Democracy in the Shadows: Citizen Mobilization in the Wake of the Accident at Three Mile Island*. Westport, CT: Greenwood Press.

Warheit, George J. 1985. "A Propositional Paradigm for Estimating the Impact of Disasters on Mental Health." Pp. 196–214 in *Disasters and Mental Health*, edited by Barbara J. Sowder. Washington, DC: U.S. Department of Health and Human Services, National Institute of Mental Health.

Weisaeth, Lars. 1991. "Reactions in Norway to Nuclear Fall-Out from the Chernobyl Disaster." Pp. 53–80 in *Communities at Risk: Collective Responses to Technological Hazards*, edited by Stephen R. Couch and J. Stephen Kroll-Smith. New York: Peter Lang.

Weiss, Bernard, and Thomas W. Clarkson. 1986. "Toxic Chemical Disasters and the Implications of Bhopal for Technology Transfer." *Millbank Quarterly* 69:216–240.

Westrum, Ron. 1986. "Vulnerable Technologies: Accident, Crime and Terrorism." *Interdisciplinary Science Reviews* 11:386–391.

Wolensky, Robert. 1991. "Political Power, Collective Action and the Giardiasis Crisis in Northeastern Pennsylvania." Pp. 229–261 in *Communities at Risk:*

*Collective Responses to Technological Hazards*, edited by Stephen R. Couch and J. Stephen Kroll-Smith. New York: Peter Lang.

Worthley, John A., and Richard Torkelson. 1981. "Managing the Toxic Waste Problem: Lessons from the Love Canal." *Administration and Society* 13: 145–160.

Wright, James D., and Peter H. Rossi. 1979. *After the Cleanup: Long Range Effects of Natural Disasters*. Contemporary Evaluation Research Series #2. Beverly Hills, CA: Sage Publications.

Zimmerman, Rae. 1985. "The Relationship of Emergency Management to Governmental Policies on Man-Made Technological Disasters." *Public Administration Review* 45:29–39.

*Chapter 11*

# Risk, Technology, and Society

*Thomas Dietz, R. Scott Frey,*
*and Eugene A. Rosa*

## INTRODUCTION

Increased public concern with technological risk has promoted critical scrutiny of new technologies and re-evaluation of older ones. It is both a paradox and a challenge for modern societies that technologies, despite their countless benefits, are increasingly challenged by professionals and laypersons alike. The paradox resides in the generally uncritical acceptance of the benefits of technology but a simultaneous demand for a reduction in the risks of technology. The challenge resides in the difficult issue of how to assess, choose, and manage technology through democratic processes. This problem, in turn, challenges the social sciences to inform debates about technological risk, since the outcomes of these debates will broadly shape the direction of technological and social changes.

Technological risk consists of two separate but interrelated concepts: risk and hazard. Risk is a compound measure of the probability and magnitude of some event or adverse effect. Hazard refers to dangers or threats that can produce adverse effects. Technological risk, therefore, refers to the probability and magnitude of adverse effects of technological hazards on human health and safety and the environment. The adverse effects to human health and safety include death, disease, and injury, whereas the adverse effects to the environment include threats to nonhuman species, ecosystems, biogeochemical cycles, climate, and the biosphere as a whole. Principal technological hazards include dangers that threaten the entire biosphere, such as nuclear holocaust and global warming; the failure of large-scale technological systems, such as nuclear power plants; the use or misuse of mechanical devices, such as power lathes in factories; the misuse or release of hazardous substances, such as toxic chemical spills; and population exposure to low-level, delayed-effect dangers, such as asbestos.[1]

Technological risks have been a problem throughout human history (Covello and Mumpower, 1985), but they have assumed greater importance in recent times because of growing public concern. Whether increased concern reflects an actual increase in the number and severity of technological risks is a matter of debate (e.g., Bailey, 1995; Commoner, 1990; Douglas and Wildavsky, 1982; Lancet, 1992; Proctor, 1995). However, it is clear that technological risks abound in modern industrial societies. Precise estimates are difficult to obtain, but the best available data suggest that at least 20–30 percent of all male deaths and 10–20 percent of all female deaths in the United States each year can be attributed to technological hazards (Harriss et al., 1985:130–143). The economic costs are also great, for Tuller (1985) estimates that in 1979 alone the monetary cost of technological hazards in the United States (including lost productivity, property damage, and public and private sector efforts to control technological hazards) was $179–283 billion or 8–12 percent of the U.S. Gross National Product. Furthermore, technological hazards have hidden effects—especially on the environment—that are not captured by the market. Harriss et al. (1985:144–148), for instance, estimate that one-third of the extinction and endangerment rate of bird and mammal species since 1800 can be attributed to technology, as can 75 percent of the land biomass decline in recent history.

Recent opinion polls indicate that a majority of Americans believe that life is getting riskier and that additional regulations are needed to effectively control health, safety, and environmental risks (Dunlap, 1992). There is growing evidence that such concerns are global (Dunlap et al., 1993). Confidence in institutions responsible for risk regulation and management has been eroding steadily over the past several decades (Lipset and Schneider, 1987; Rosa and Clark, 1999). One consequence of the convergence of these trends is the rise in political controversy over technologies (Jasper, 1988, 1990; Mazur, 1981; Nelkin, 1992). Other consequences include increased government efforts to assess and manage technological hazards (Breyer, 1993; Fiorino, 1995; Regens et al., 1983), and the development of a new profession termed "risk analysis" (Crouch and Wilson, 1982; Lave, 1982; Lowrance, 1976; Rodericks, 1992).

In this chapter, we describe the social and political issues associated with technological risk and outline the emerging social science perspectives for examining them. We organize our discussion around five major themes: (1) formal models of risk assessment, risk evaluation, and risk management; (2) the background and current structure of the risk policy system in the United States and other nations; (3) the major social science perspectives that have emerged to understand risk; (4) the dynamics of the political controversies over risk; and (5) recommended directions for future socio-logical research.

## RISK ASSESSMENT, RISK EVALUATION, AND RISK MANAGEMENT

A proper understanding of technological risk requires some familiarity with the vocabulary, procedures, and range of methods currently used in risk assessment, risk evaluation, and risk management (e.g., Environ, 1988; Rodericks, 1992; U.S. National Research Council, 1983; U.S. Office of Technology Assessment, 1981). Risk assessment is the process of identify-ing technological hazards and estimating and assessing the likelihood of adverse consequences (e.g., death) associated with such hazards. Risk eval-uation is the process of determining the acceptability of identified risks in order to guide policy decision making. Risk management entails efforts to avoid, reduce, control, or mitigate those risks deemed unacceptable.

Proponents of risk assessment and evaluation maintain that these tech-niques are rational scientific tools, essential to the accurate assessment and effective management of technological risks (e.g., Breyer, 1993; Crouch and Wilson, 1982; Lave, 1982; Rodericks, 1992; Russel and Gruber, 1987). But critics argue that formal risk assessment and evaluation have numerous limitations that produce deeply biased and flawed risk management prac-tices (e.g., Clarke, 1988; Perrow, 1984; Proctor, 1995; Shrader-Frechette, 1985, 1991). We will not enter this debate here, but instead describe the dominant techniques and key concepts underpinning formal risk assess-ment, evaluation, and management.

### Risk Assessment

The U.S. National Research Council (1983:17–20) divides risk assess-ment into four distinct but complementary steps: hazard identification, dose-response assessment, exposure assessment, and risk characterization.

Hazard identification is the identification of technologies or features of technologies that are hazardous. Identification is based on a variety of sources: epidemiological and clinical studies, animal experiments, in-vitro tests, and examination of the relationship between molecular structure and the probable molecular activity of a suspect compound (Environ, 1988; Lave, 1982; Rodericks, 1992; U.S. Office of Technology Assessment, 1981). Clinical and epidemiological studies, because they measure effects on hu-mans directly, are probably the best sources of data for identifying tech-nologies hazardous to humans.[2] But because of the difficulty of obtaining reliable data on human exposure levels, the lack of experimental controls, and the fact that some technologies are too new to be evaluated with such data, the results of clinical or epidemiological studies cannot provide complete information on all potential sources of risk. As a result, data from animal experiments or other types of laboratory studies are often used as a substitute for, or supplement to, field and clinical evidence. Despite the utility of these indirect methods and data sources, they are subject to serious shortcomings, most notably the problem of external validity. For example, small doses of some substance may prove hazardous to laboratory rats but may be harmless to humans (or even mice) because of metabolic differences between species (Environ, 1988; Graham et al., 1988).

Dose-response assessment is the determination of the relation between the magnitude of exposure and the probability of adverse consequences. Extrapolation techniques are used to determine such a relation. For instance, in estimating human health effects of hazardous substances, a dose-response curve is calculated from epidemiological data for population groups experiencing different levels of exposure. This curve is used to determine the link between exposure to the compound and its effects. In the absence of human epidemiological data, animal data often must be used for calculating the human dose-response curve. Where human or animal data are meager or nonexistent, hypothetical models are sometimes used to fill gaps in real-world data.

Such techniques are sensitive to the assumptions that underpin them and engender large uncertainties, even in the best of circumstances. The problem of measurement validity at different levels of exposure is particularly vexing. On the one hand, available techniques may be insufficient to detect small exposure levels. On the other hand, aggregate dose-response data may not permit a determination of whether low exposure levels are harmless, or the precise threshold between harmful and harmless levels (Environ, 1988).

Exposure assessment is the determination of the nature and degree of human exposure to a hazard. It consists of determining the source, route, dose, frequency, duration, and timing of hazard exposure, as well as the identification of the types of populations exposed to the hazard. A variety of methods, including mathematical models, are used to specify population and environmental exposure. The physical, biological, and social data and models available to predict exposure are limited, so here, as elsewhere in the risk assessment process, there are serious questions about the validity of results (Lave, 1982).

Risk characterization is the overall summary of what is known about the likelihood and magnitude of adverse consequences. It represents a summary of the other three steps. It often contains a quantitative estimate of the nature and degree of risk associated with exposure to a hazard, and a statement of the uncertainty associated with the risk estimate.

Because of the uncertainties built into each step in the process, not only are risks not known with certainty, but the degree of uncertainty is itself highly uncertain. We refer to this problem as one of meta-uncertainty—

uncertainty about the degree of uncertainty. Such meta-uncertainty pervades all work on risk. With direct threats to human health and safety such as those posed by toxic substances, the sources of uncertainty and meta-uncertainty are easy to identify. The uncertainty embedded in the new class of risks posed by the effects of toxic substances on ecosystems and by global environmental change is much more difficult to identify. It is particularly acute around the problem of climate change. While there is general agreement among climatologists that the earth will experience anthropogenic climate change over the next century, it is difficult to translate this prediction for the planetary climate into forms that can be used to assess human response (Intergovernmental Panel on Climate Change, 1996). Localized effects can be known with much less certainty than the overall global trend, and yet are far more consequential for ecosystems and for humans. The consequences of climate change for the biosphere and for humanity may be immense, but predictions about global temperature are uncertain, and predictions about the effects that have greatest impact on the biosphere and humans are fraught with meta-uncertainty.

**Risk Evaluation**

Various approaches have been proposed for judging whether or not the risks associated with a technological hazard are acceptable. We discuss five major approaches: risk-benefit-cost analysis, multi-objective methods, revealed preferences, expressed preferences, and *de minimis* (Fischhoff et al., 1981; Shrader-Frechette, 1985, 1991).

Risk-benefit-cost analysis is based on the logic of the rational action as described by economic theory (Jaeger et al., 2001); that is, maximizing benefits while minimizing costs (Bentkover et al., 1986). Technological risks are acceptable if the economic benefits of the technology outweigh the economic costs. Subject to a broad range of criticisms, this method is most vulnerable in its emphasis on assigning monetary values to all costs and benefits. Assignment of monetary values not only to benefits such as productivity but also to costs such as human death, disease, and injury as well as environmental degradation rests on assumptions that many critics find problematic (Baram, 1980; Dietz, 1988, 1994). Further, the method frequently ignores the problem of evaluating the distribution of costs and benefits across populations and time.

The multi-objective approach, typically some version of multi-attribute utility theory, acknowledges that the reduction of risks to a single dimension such as money is flawed (Keeney and Raiffa, 1976). As a corrective, this approach uses a set of procedures for identifying the key attributes of a decision (i.e., the desirable and undesirable consequences), for assigning value to those attributes (usually through a ranking or rating system or a combination thereof), and for aggregating the evaluations of the separate attributes into an overall assessment. This approach has two major weaknesses. First, the procedure is complex, and results can be sensitive to methodological assumptions whose implications are hard to determine or analyze. Second, the list of attributes evaluated must be finite, and its selection over alternative lists is always arbitrary.

The method of revealed preferences is based on the assumption that risks tolerated currently or in the past provide a standard for assessing the acceptability of new risks. Proponents of this approach (e.g., Starr, 1969) maintain that the risks of a new technology are acceptable if they are no greater than the risks of existing technologies that have similar benefits. The method is problematic for several reasons (Shrader-Frechette, 1985). It assumes that the political, economic, and social relations underlying extant patterns of risk are legitimate. It is also mute to the possibility that some risks tolerated in the past should be reduced because they are no longer tolerable.

The method of expressed preferences consists of asking people what risks they find acceptable (Fischhoff et al., 1981). An obvious advantage of this approach is that it is more democratic than other methods because it is based on public preferences. Proponents of the approach use opinion surveys and public hearings to elicit preferences. Major criticisms of this method are that people change their views over time; may not be well-informed about complex issues surrounding technological risk; and are seldom forced in surveys to make trade-offs among risks, costs, and benefits associated with technologies.

The method of *de minimis* risk is based on the idea that certain risks are simply too trivial to merit attention (Breyer, 1993; Whipple, 1987). The goal of this method is to establish thresholds to distinguish between risks that are trivial and therefore acceptable, and risks that are nontrivial and therefore unacceptable. One of the most obvious problems with this approach is the difficulty of establishing threshold levels for distinguishing between trivial and nontrivial risks (Menkes and Frey, 1987). In practice, the method of natural standards is typically used to establish cutoff levels. For example, natural background levels of radiation have been used as a basis for establishing standards for human exposure to radiation. The use of such standards leads to the well-known naturalistic fallacy: the flawed logic of presupposing that what is natural is "normal" and what is normal is "moral" (Shrader-Frechette, 1985).

All methods of risk assessment and risk evaluation are based on key assumptions that may be unsound or tenuous. Because of these uncertainties, risk assessments and risk evaluations—despite the fact that they are frequently portrayed as "scientific"—do not lead to unequivocal regulatory or management guidance (Proctor, 1995); nor can they, whatever their scientific validity, provide an unqualified recommendation of what risks are acceptable. Risk policy controversies, therefore, often involve conflict over the normative and methodological bases for deciding which risks are to be regulated and by what means.

## Risk Management

In addition to controversies about risk assessment and evaluation, controversies exist over the appropriate methods for managing risks (Breyer, 1993; Fiorino, 1995; Jasanoff, 1986). Three general strategies are currently used to manage risks: direct regulation, indirect regulation, and alternatives to regulation (Breyer, 1993; Hadden, 1986; Kasperson et al., 1985).

Direct regulation takes two forms: the reduction of risks to zero through the elimination of a hazard, or the reduction of risks to an acceptable level through the establishment of regulatory controls on a hazard. Banning the production, sale, or use of a hazard is a strategy for reducing risks to zero. This strategy is seldom used in risk management. Instead, the reduction of risks to an acceptable level by the use of performance or process criteria is the most common form of direct regulation. Performance criteria are standards setting limits on allowable levels of risks associated with the production or use of a hazard, whereas process criteria mandate the actual methods for the production or use of a hazard (Kasperson et al., 1985). These strategies have been criticized for reducing the liberties of producers and users of hazards and for being ineffective (Commoner, 1990).

Indirect regulation consists of informing parties at risk. The parties are provided with appropriate information so that they can make their own judgments about the acceptability of risks associated with a hazard. Standard techniques include warning labels and recommended practices for safe use, storage, transport, and disposal of a hazard. This approach is often used when the benefits for producers and/or consumers of the hazard are considered to outweigh the risks, and risk acceptance is to some degree voluntary. This strategy has been criticized because it makes questionable assumptions about human behavior, seldom leads to the dissemination of adequate risk information, and is a regressive policy (Hadden, 1986).

Alternatives to direct and indirect regulations take several different forms (Baram and Miyares, 1986). Voluntary compliance with recommended practices for the safe production and use of a hazard is one such form. The provision of incentives for hazard substitution and the safe production and use of a hazard is another. A third form is the use of penalties such as the indemnification of those at risk through the market, courts, or taxes. The final form is the provision of insurance for those at risk. Each of these alternatives to regulation has been criticized for failing to provide effective and fair compensation to those bearing the risks of a hazard.[3]

## RISK AND RISK POLICY

Technological risks generate conflict between various social constituencies and industry over state policy toward risk. Risk policy and the current structure of the U.S. policy system that promotes, critiques, and implements risk policy evolved in response to the interactions between a variety of stakeholders, each with different interests and resources. We first examine the development and current structure of the U.S. risk policy system. We then examine the responses to risk by other developed nations, developing nations, and international organizations.

### Emergence of the U.S. Risk Policy System

Public attempts to deal with risk are, as noted earlier, at least 5,000 years old (Covello and Mumpower, 1985). Before the Progressive era of the late nineteenth and early twentieth century in the United States, problems of environmental risk were generally defined as economic matters and were handled by the courts under tort law. By the late nineteenth century, social critics and their allies challenged the laissez-faire approach to state risk policy (Hofstadter, 1955). Their challenges provided the impetus for increased state intervention in the market through regulation. This "old social regulation" (Weidenbaum, 1977)—including the U.S. Biologies Act of 1902, the Federal Pure Food and Drug Act of 1906, and the Federal Meat Inspection Act of 1906—targeted those industries that had been the subject of reformers' concerns. These regulations were based on the idea that monopoly or market concentration prevented the efficient functioning of markets on the one hand and promoted labor abuses and other social ills on the other. State intervention was required to ensure efficiency and to mitigate the worst costs of capitalism.

The mechanisms that emerged to control risk in this period had several common characteristics. First, they were developed in response to muckraking accounts and the actions of the political left. Second, their scope was usually industry-specific, which facilitated the evolution of strong ties between regulators and the regulated—the "iron triangle" of regulated industries, executive branch agencies, and legislative oversight committees. Third, they spawned industry organizations for both self-regulation and lobbying to influence government regulation.

During this period, in addition to regulation of industry, public bodies expanded substantially to address a variety of public health and welfare concerns. Government began to bear a substantial part of the social costs of industrial production and attendant urbanization. It was during this period that the first environmental science professionals emerged in the fields of forestry, agriculture, and public health, with most of these professionals employed in government agencies or universities (Brulle, 2000; Hays, 1959).

The character of the U.S. risk policy system has changed dramatically in the last 40 years for several reasons (Hays, 1987). First, the growth of the petrochemical and related industries has introduced a large number of anthropogenic (human-generated) compounds into the environment. As a result, the impacts of toxic substances are more pervasive and dangerous than in the past. In addition, catastrophic failure of some new technologies, such as nuclear power and large chemical plants, could harm more people than the worst anthropogenic disasters of the past. Second, the growth of scientific knowledge, particularly in the areas Schnaiberg (1980) characterizes as the "impact sciences," provided credible information on the varied, subtle, and often negative consequences of contemporary technologies. Third, some scientists, the college-educated, and in some cases unionized workers sought increased protection from the new technological risks. Starting with the struggle against nuclear testing in the 1950s and 1960s, the environmental, consumer, and labor movements have been effective at placing risk issues on the political agenda. The interplay between these movements, industrial interests that have usually opposed further risk regulation, and government has generated the current risk policy system.

## Current Structure of the U.S. Risk Policy System

Statutes, enacted in response to the environmental and allied movements of the 1960s have produced regulations written in broad language that address generic environmental issues. One consequence has been a drastic expansion in the scope of regulation, cutting across nearly all industries (Breyer, 1993; Fiorino, 1995; Regens et al., 1983). For example, the Clean Air Act (1970) and the Clean Water Act (1977) empower the Environmental Protection Agency (EPA) to intervene in the operations of nearly every industry and government agency in the United States, to curb offending activities. A second consequence, related to the broad language in the enabling statutes—such as "unreasonable risk or injury to health" or "substantial present or potential hazard"—has been the establishment of agencies with considerable discretionary authority. Agencies such as the EPA, the Nuclear Regulatory Commission, the Occupational Safety and Health Administration, and the Food and Drug Administration have great latitude in determining how regulatory decisions are to be made and enforced. This means that the details of policy implementation are crucial to all stakeholders, so they must actively participate in the policy system to ensure that their interests are reflected in risk policy.

The U.S. risk policy system presently consists of eight major types of organizational actors (Fiorino, 1995; Dietz and Rycroft, 1987). Executive branch agencies responsible for implementing risk regulation employ about

25 percent of all professionals active in the system (Dietz and Rycroft, 1987). Congress and its supporting agencies employ about 10 percent of the active professionals. Law and consulting firms account for about 14 percent of those employed, whereas environmental organizations employ about 12 percent. Corporations and the industry associations that represent them account for about 18 percent of active professionals. Universities and think tanks account for about 9 percent, and all remaining organizations, principally those representing state government, local government, or labor, employ about 12 percent.

Heavy emphasis on formal methods of risk analysis and risk evaluation distinguish the risk policy system from many other policy systems. About half of the core professionals have training in the natural sciences or engineering. Over 95 percent of those working in the system have bachelor's degrees and nearly half hold doctorates (Dietz and Rycroft, 1987). Since expertise is expensive to acquire, it is found mostly in the service of government and industry. Only 8 percent of environmental organization employees have natural science degrees, compared to around 20 percent of industry employees.

This imbalance in expertise is probably a key reason that environmental organizations are suspicious of policy decisions based on formal risk analyses. Their relative lack of expertise limits their ability to critique formal risk assessments and present counteranalyses based upon equally formal procedures. They prefer instead to emphasize the less "scientific" features of risk policy, such as due process and a variety of qualitative considerations, which are largely ignored in formal assessments.

In contrast, industry favors formal risk analysis as the principal basis of risk policy, partly because it can employ or contract for the appropriate expertise to promote its position in technical debates. The imbalance in expertise and difference in strategies that results brings into sharp focus a central if latent theme of risk policy debates: whether policy formation and regulatory guidance should be based primarily on scientific and technical evidence or whether such evidence should be balanced against other considerations, such as fairness and equity. This issue continues to structure policy debates.

### Situation Outside of the United States

Like the United States, other developed nations have a full range of administrative and legal mechanisms for assessing and managing technological risks. The risk policy systems of these nations differ in many ways from the U.S. policy system. For instance, Great Britain, France, Sweden, Japan, and Germany place a heavier emphasis on scientific expertise, give a smaller role to environmental organizations in public policy discussions, and are more likely to have critical decisions made "behind closed doors" than the United States (Brickman, et al., 1985; Jasanoff, 1986).

Developing nations, on the other hand, have a limited ability to assess and manage technological risks (Covello and Frey, 1990; Montgomery, 1990; Smil, 1993). The legislative basis for risk protection is often weak or nonexistent. In turn, existing legislation and regulations are not adequately enforced. The problem is exacerbated by the fact that developing nations do not have enough trained operators and managers with skills necessary for managing risky technologies effectively.

Since the risks of many technological hazards transcend national boundaries, a number of international organizations and international treaties have emerged to manage these risks (see Caldwell, 1990; Covello and Frey, 1990; Dietz and Kalof, 1991; Hackett, 1990; Lipschutz and Conca, 1993; Mathews, 1991; Porter and Brown, 1991; Rummel-Bulksa, 1991; World Commission on Environment and Development, 1987; Young, 1989). Key examples of the agencies involved include the U.N. Environment Programme, the Man and Biosphere Program of UNESCO, the World Health Organization, the International Atomic Energy Agency, and the Food and Agriculture Organization (Caldwell, 1990). Examples of key treaties include the Basel Convention on Hazardous Wastes, the Rome Convention, the Rio Accords and the Vienna and Montreal Ozone Protocols. Multilateral aid agencies, such as the World Bank and the Inter-American Development Bank, are also beginning to pay attention to risk issues in project planning (Holden, 1988). Other nongovernment organizations concerned with technological risk include the International Council of Scientific Unions, the International Trade Union Movement, and the International Union for Conservation of Nature and Natural Resources (McElrath, 1988). These organizations have pursued a variety of activities, including research, dissemination of risk information, training programs, and development of international standards and restrictions on the practices of transnational corporations (Robinson, 1989; World Commission on Environment and Development, 1987). In addition, the international scope of many hazards has led environmental groups, such as Friends of the Earth, Conservation International, Earth Island Institute, Greenpeace, and the World Wildlife Federation, to expand their activities across national boundaries in the form of debt-for-nature swaps and the like (Cartwright, 1989; Princen and Finger, 1994; Taylor, 1995).

## THE SOCIAL CONTEXT OF RISK

Social scientists have increasingly turned their attention to the study of technological risk. Four distinct social science approaches have emerged in the past few years: the psychological, sociological, anthropological, and geographic. Recent (Krimsky and Golding, 1992; Jaeger et al., 2001) volumes provide more detailed coverage of these approaches. Here we critically but briefly review each.

### The Psychological Perspective

Until recently, the field of risk perception was dominated by a psychometric approach that focused on cognitive processes underlying risk perceptions. An impressive body of research indicates that most individuals systematically under- or overestimate risks. Indeed, these biases may reflect fundamental processes in the cognitive organization of risk perception. A number of commonsense strategies, or cognitive "rules of thumb," apparently produce these biases. The *availability* heuristic is one of the most important of these rules (Tversky and Kahneman, 1982); it was discovered, along with other heuristics, in research examining people's assessments of probabilities (numerical representations of risk) in both small sample studies and laboratory experiments.

In a typical study, researchers provide subjects with pairs of causes of death and ask them to judge which of the pair is most likely to occur (Lichtenstein et al., 1978). For example, subjects might be asked the following question: Which cause of death is most likely to occur out of each pair? (1) Lung cancer or stomach cancer?; (2) Murder or suicide? and (3) Diabetes or motor vehicle accident? People tend to answer that lung cancer is responsible for more deaths than stomach cancer, murder for more deaths than suicide, and motor vehicle accidents for more deaths than diabetes. In fact, aggregate data indicate that the second alternative for each pair (i.e., stomach cancer, suicide, and motor vehicle accidents) is more likely to occur than the first. People typically err in making two out of three probability choices.

One conclusion consistent with these findings is that laypersons are not very good at assessing the risks they face. Why are layperson's judgments sometimes correct, but more often incorrect? What cognitive processes could produce such contrary results? The availability heuristic was proposed as an answer to this question (Fischhoff et al., 1981; Tversky and Kahneman, 1982). The extent to which an event is cognitively available, that is, vivid and easy to recall, strongly influences the perceived probability of the event. The familiar is seen as more probable than the unfamiliar and recent events more probable than past events, other things being equal. This suggests that people will typically overestimate causes of death that are highly publicized, such as lung cancer and homicide, relative to less publicized but more frequent causes of death, such as stomach cancer and suicide. The availability heuristic produces a biased perception.

Reliance on the availability and other heuristics, however, does produce valid assessments under some circumstances. Where the vividness of events coincides with their relative frequency, a person's perceptions will be valid—as was the case where subjects judged deaths by motor vehicle accidents to be more frequent than deaths by diabetes. To the individual, the value of cognitive heuristics, and perhaps the reason for their continued use, is that they are efficient and may often be correct. These heuristics may be useful information-processing tools, the product of adaptation through cultural and biological evolution.[4]

The discovery that people use heuristics for assessing risks stimulated an effort to determine whether or not people use them in their perceptions of technological risk. Paul Slovic, Baruch Fischhoff, Sarah Lichtenstein, and their colleagues have produced an impressive body of findings on this topic. The Slovic/Fischhoff/Lichtenstein group (Fischhoff et al., 1981; Lichtenstein et al., 1978; Slovic, 1987) have asked people to rate the risks and benefits associated with a wide variety of hazardous technologies, activities, and substances, such as nuclear power, motor vehicles, handguns, smoking, swimming, commercial aviation, and pesticides. Their work indicates that people tend to overestimate low probability, high consequence events (unlikely events like a nuclear accident that can kill thousands) and to underestimate high probability, low consequence events (like the risks associated with X rays). Furthermore, lay judgments of risk, although sometimes consistent with those of experts, often diverge from them in systematic ways.

Several factors appear to underlie the bias in lay perceptions. Key among these factors is the availability heuristic: People tend to overestimate the frequency of unlikely events that are dramatic in their consequences because the drama of such events makes them cognitively available and thus easier to recall. This may be due to media coverage of the news that emphasizes dramatic rather than routine events, often sensationalizing unlikely but dreadful events (Combs and Slovic, 1979; Sandman et al., 1987). Discrepancies between public and expert perceptions of risk are seen to reside in the sources of information about risk and in the tendency of laypersons to stress qualitative features of risk ignored by experts. For example, risks highly dreaded by the public are those perceived to involve a lack of control, catastrophic potential, fatal consequences, or inequitable distributions of risks and benefits. Such risks are far less acceptable to the public than to experts, who give little or no consideration to these qualitative factors in their formal analyses (Slovic, 1987). In effect, discrepancies in lay and expert judgments of risk are based on different definitions of risk.

If the public does view risk differently than experts, of what importance is public opinion to risk evaluation, and what is the proper role of the public in risk management? One position, often left implicit, is that the public should be excluded or otherwise disenfranchised from risk assessment and decision making (e.g., Breyer, 1993; Cohen, 1987; Starr, 1969). A second, less extreme position, proposes that laypersons' perceptions of risk should be brought into line with those of the experts. Advocates of this view call for efforts by policy makers to improve communication between agencies and the public, to educate citizens so that they are better prepared to evaluate uncertainties, and to develop better risk management strategies that include means for providing the public with accurate, understandable information upon which to make reasonable decisions about risky technologies (Covello et al., 1988). A third position begins with the recognition that nearly all risk assessments and risk management strategies are laden with uncertainty and meta-uncertainty, that experts as well as the public are subject to cognitive biases, and that an emphasis solely on technical information has political implications for the relative power of environmental groups versus corporate interests. For these reasons, laypersons should play a more central role in the process of assessing, evaluating, and managing technological risks (Fischhoff, 1990; Freudenburg, 1988; Perrow, 1984; Stern, 1991; U.S. National Research Council, 1989).

### The Sociological Perspective

Although only two decades old, sociological interest in risk has evolved to produce an incipient specialty with a variety of perspectives. Together, they seek to understand the social influences on risk perception and behavior, the importance of organizational contexts and institutional responses to risk, and the role of risk in large-scale social change. They comprise four distinct research directions, though in some instances there is considerable overlap in orientation or approach. The four directions, discussed below, represent increasing levels of theoretical aggregation, from micro to meso to macro.

A first direction, stemming from the lead of psychometric research, was to re-examine and reconceptualize the psychometric finding with a sociological lens. Several sociologists and psychologists have raised questions about the saliency of risk questions to laypersons and about the external validity of the psychometric findings, citing reliance on laboratory settings and small samples of unrepresentative groups as serious limitations on the generalizability of findings (Gould et al., 1988). The interpretative work of Heimer (1988) suggests that cognitive heuristics operate in natural settings. An extensive sample survey by Gould et al. (1988) and follow-up studies in France (Bastide et al., 1989), Hong Kong (Keown, 1989), Hungary (Englander et al., 1986), Japan (Kleinhesselink and Rosa, 1991, 1993), Norway (Teigen et al., 1988), and Poland (Goszczynska et al., 1991) generally corroborate the findings of the psychometric research. Several recent studies also are consistent with the basic ideas of the psychometric paradigm, but show sharp gender and ethnic differences in risk perception (Davidson and Freudenburg, 1996; Slovic, 1999). However, a number of conceptual and methodological problems remain. These include whether heuristics differ in their impact for trivial versus nontrivial decisions, how perceptions differ across populations facing different life chances, and whether the framing of choices stems primarily from power differences among social actors (Heimer, 1988). The most serious problem is the virtual absence of research on whether risk perceptions predict actual behavior.

The second direction of sociological research offers a fundamental re-conceptualization of the psychometric model. It proposes a model that examines the problem of risk perception by taking into account the social context in which human perceptions are formed (Rosa et al., 1987; Short, 1984). The model proceeds from the assumption, fundamental to all social psychology, that humans do not perceive the world with pristine eyes, but through perceptual lenses filtered by social and cultural meanings transmitted via primary influences such as the family, friends, superordinates, and fellow workers. Secondary influences, such as public figures and especially the mass media, are also presumed to affect risk perceptions (Mazur, 1984).

In addition to these contextual effects, the sociological model notes that people often take actions or form attitudes about hazardous technologies and events prior to developing meaningful perceptions about them. Formal organizations such as government agencies and corporations apparently are also guilty of offering ex post facto explanations that have little to do with the actual reasons a decision about technological risk was made (Clarke, 1989). Such "after the fact" beliefs are often used as a justification for the attitude already formed or the action already taken. This common occurrence is ignored by the unidirectional emphasis of the psychometric model, but it is a central feature of the sociological model.

The third sociological direction has been the organizational and institutional approach that emphasizes the system characteristics and context of complex technologies and the policies that develop for their use. Perrow's (1984, 1994) analysis of "normal accidents," the exemplar of this approach, demonstrates that industrial societies have produced a variety of high-risk technologies in which a main source of risk is part of the very systems designed to ensure their safety. For many of these technological systems, the interaction of system components (including humans) makes accidents—"system accidents"—all but inevitable. Formal risk assessments of complex technologies typically involve computing the probability of failure for each of the system's components and then aggregating these into an overall estimate of accident probability. From an organizational approach, such quantitative assessments are misleadingly precise, because they cannot take into account the vast number of component interactions that could result in conjoint failures. Accidents are therefore bound to happen. This disturbing conclusion of "normal accident" theory is studded with sociological and policy implications. It means that technological risk cannot be understood completely through formal risk assessments. Rather, risks can be understood only by analyzing the way that parts of risky systems fit together (Freudenburg, 1988) and the evolution of socio-technical systems in which technologies are embedded (Burns and Dietz, 1992a). Such an understanding requires a sociological focus on the organizational and institutional contexts of decision making by corporate actors and institutional elites. Just such a focus is beginning to emerge in this line of sociological research (Jaeger et al., 2001; Short and Clarke, 1992).

As stark counterpoint to "normal accident" theory is "high reliability organization" (HRO) theory, most of whose practitioners are associated with the University of California, Berkeley (LaPorte, 1988; LaPorte and Consolini, 1991; Roberts, 1993; Rochlin et al., 1987; Wildavsky, 1988). The Berkeley group has identified organizations that perform with remarkable safety even though their operations are technologically complex and inherently risky. This remarkable performance in the face of complexity and risk leads to the label High Reliability Organization (HROs). In several studies, the Berkeley group has produced a sustained body of empirical work demonstrating the existence of HROs. Extensive fieldwork has been conducted in three HROs: the Federal Aviation Administration's air-traffic control system, the Pacific Gas and Electric Company's power grid (PG&E is one of the largest utilities in the United States and includes the Diablo Canyon nuclear power plant in its grid), and the peacetime flight operations of two U.S. Navy nuclear aircraft carriers.

How are these organizations able to operate so safely? The Berkeley group holds that the development of a "high reliability culture" where safety and reliability are made a priority of the organization's top leadership is essential. Further, organizations can overcome the potential failure of hardware and humans by designing systems with redundancies: the duplication of parts and the incorporation of backup systems. Thus, HRO theory argues that accidents are preventable while normal accident theory says they are not. These antithetical positions will doubtless generate further empirical research on this important issue. Indeed, a notable first effort is this direction is the work of Sagan (1993) on the management of nuclear weapons.

The fourth sociological direction is, if not grand theory, at least macrosociological theory on a grand scale. Grounded in the European sociological tradition, the theme of this line of thinking is worldwide social change: the transformation from modernity to its successor, some form of postmodernity. Risk is the central driving force of this transformation. Key examples of such theorizing are British sociologist Anthony Giddens' *The Consequences of Modernity* (1990) and German sociologist Ulrich Beck's *Risk Society: Toward a New Modernity* (1992). The nets of each theory are too broadly cast, the logic too carefully crafted, and the insights too finely nuanced for us to do them justice in our short compass here. Furthermore, owing to their origins in the European tradition, they have left the operational explication to others. Thus, much work remains to assess their contribution to the sociology of risk. Nevertheless, they are too important to ignore.

Key to Giddens is the observation that modernity—modes of social life and organization emerging in Europe in the seventeenth century and eventually becoming worldwide—resulted in globalization. "Globalization" refers to the "intensification of worldwide social relations which link distant localities in such a way that local happenings are shaped by events occurring many miles away and vice versa" (1990:64). With modernity, locale no longer held a leash on the range of interpersonal interactions available to the individual. People's social relations became "disembedded," in Giddens' terms. As a consequence, people everywhere interact with "absent" and distant others, others who are often never seen or known. With the approach of postmodernity this disembeddedness has second-order consequences: a worldwide division of labor accompanied by a worldwide spread of risks associated with production processes; and a worldwide diffusion of consumption practices and their accompanying risks. Overlaid on this pattern of shared risks has been the appearance of globalized risks—radiation releases from nuclear accidents, global warming, destruction of the ozone layer, the broad diffusion of toxics associated with industrial activities and others—that, because they are not contained by national borders, "do not respect division between rich and poor or between regions of the world" (1990:125). In short, postmodernity introduces new forms of global interdependence, and interdependence grounded in globalized risks. That interdependence, in turn, magnifies the importance of trust.

Beck's theoretical argument, though resembling Giddens' position, was developed independently. It consists of two interrelated theses: risk and what Beck calls "reflexive modernization." To develop his first thesis Beck identifies a fundamental distinction between industrial society and contemporary society: The former is concerned with the distribution of goods, while the latter is concerned with the distribution of "bads" (danger) and is, therefore, aptly titled "the risk society." This shift produced a fundamental restructuring of social organization, from one of class to one of risk positions. It also produced a new culture of shared meaning where "in class positions being determines consciousness, while in risk positions, conversely *consciousness (knowledge) determines being*" (emphasis in the original) (1992:53). This fundamental change results in a decline in the importance of structures, like class, and the individualization of social agents (actors) who, forced to make risk decisions, reflect on the social institutions responsible for those decisions. Like Giddens, Beck delineates the globalization of risks and underscores the role of trust in dealing with them, while adding consideration of future generations.

Beck's second thesis is based on the central role of science in issues of risk, a problem emphasized by other scholars as well (Burns and Dietz, 1992a; Dietz et al., 1989; Dunlap et al., 1993). Science is, on the one hand, partly responsible for the growth of risks and hazards while, on the other hand, it is the principal social institution entrusted with knowledge claims about risk. Therein lies the rub for Beck. Because risks are ambiguous and difficult to define, subject to competing interpretations and conflicting claims, "in definitions of risks *the sciences' monopoly on rationality is broken*" (emphasis in the original) (1992:29). When science is no longer privileged, how are risk societies to make knowledge claims about the increased risks that define those societies? For Beck the answer is "reflexive modernity." By this he means, in essence, a negotiation of knowledge claims between science, political interests, and laypersons—in effect, negotiation between different epistemologies.

These macro-theoretical arguments are not yet well integrated with existing and emerging work on the sociology of risk. The emphasis on the special character of science in the modern world is common in the risk literature, as noted above. The globalization of risk processes is a central theme in discussions of global environmental change (Dietz, 1992; Stern et al., 1992). The integration of scientific with other forms of knowledge has also been emphasized in some streams of the literature on technology, risk, and impact assessment (Burns and Uberhorst, 1988; Dietz, 1987, 1988; Freeman and Frey, 1990–1991; Stern, 1991); but the argument that risk is universal contradicts emerging work on risk distribution (see discussion below). As we will note in the closing section of the chapter, there is a large research agenda around these and related issues.

### The Anthropological Perspective

An anthropological approach to risk analysis has also contributed to the risk literature. In the initial formulation of this approach, Douglas and Wildavsky (1982) argue that the selection of risks for societal attention is purely a social process with little or no linkage to objective risk or physical reality. Instead, individuals affiliate with organizations that resonate with their values. Presumably, these core values are based on personality traits, institutional socialization, or other factors not fully elaborated in the model. Douglas and Wildavsky emphasize the differences between "entrepreneurs" who are comfortable with risks, and "egalitarians" or environmentalists, who are averse to risks. Entrepreneurs receive high praise because they produce affluence and freedom, whereas environmentalists are compared to cultists and witches. Douglas and Wildavsky assert that the need for organizational self-maintenance provides the basis for environmental groups' concerns with technological risks. By invoking a sense of "cosmic doom," the environmentalists ensure member loyalty. This perspective has been subjected to a number of strong critiques (see, e.g., Abel, 1985). Central to these critiques is the idea that Douglas and Wildavsky's scholarly vision is guided by an underlying fear of social change. In addition to the ongoing theoretical debate, there have also been attempts to use this framework to guide ethnographic studies and surveys on risk (Dake, 1991; Dake and Wildavsky, 1991; Douglas, 1992; Rayner and Cantor, 1987; Thompson et al., 1990).

### The Geographic Perspective

Geography has a distinguished tradition of research on human responses to natural disasters and human activities that modify the landscape (e.g., White, 1974). Recently, this tradition has been broadened to include technological risks, producing a growing body of literature, developing a broad theoretical framework for organizing the cumulative social science literature on risk, and pointing the way for future inquiry (Cutter, 1993; Kasperson et al., 1988; Renn, 1992). The framework, borrowed from communication theory and titled "Social Amplification," holds promise for deepening our understanding of the link between risk perception and behavior and for understanding risks thus far ignored in the literature (Machlis and Rosa, 1990).

Classic communications theory emphasizes a source-receiver model in which signals are sent from the source to some receiver. Clusters of signals (the message) sent from source to receiver must typically first flow through intermediate transmitters. Each of the intermediate transmitters "amplifies" the message by intensifying or attenuating certain incoming signals. Thus, the cluster of signals leaving the source will be altered during transmissions to the ultimate receiver.

The social amplification of risk, according to this framework, follows similar processes. Risk events are signals. The message contained in those signals is amplified before reaching the ultimate receiver—the public. The amplification may either be toward heightening or attenuating the risk. Principal amplifiers include information processes, institutions, social milieus, and the variety of individual experiences. Because part of the amplification of risk signals is due to cognitive heuristics, the framework attempts to integrate the psychometric findings on risk perception with the institutional context of risk communication in order to better predict responses to risk.

## RISK, POLITICS, AND SOCIETY

In the United States, many of the sociologically relevant issues stem from continued conflict between key stakeholders in debates over growth and management of technology, especially between industry and social movement organizations. Several key sociological themes emerge from those conflicts.

## Public Goods, Science, and Social Movements.

A critical feature of technological risk is that the benefits derived from risk reduction are public goods. All social actors potentially exposed to the risks, therefore, will benefit from reduced risks, whether they participate in the actions to reduce the risk or not. Thus, actors can "free ride" on the efforts of others. Environmental, consumer, and other social movement organizations must contend with the "free rider" problem in obtaining resources and securing public support (Olson, 1965). As a result, such organizations will always be comparatively short of staff, technical expertise, and funds to hire consultants or support research. In contrast, the benefits associated with many technologies are private goods, so industries that profit from the technologies typically have abundant material resources to deploy in the protection and advancement of their private interests. There are occasions when industry is subject to free rider problems (as in instances where industry trade associations rely on voluntary contributions), but these are relatively rare and generally inconsequential to their lobbying strategies (Dietz and Rycroft, 1987).

Social movement organizations have difficulty acquiring and mobilizing resources in their pursuit of collective goods (Frey et al., 1992; Gamson, 1990; Walsh, 1981). As a result, the amount of public goods supplied, such as the reduction of risk to ideal levels, will be less than optimal; but those seeking collective goods also have a key advantage. The pursuit of private benefits, frequently thought to be a reflection of unbridled self-interest, is easily labeled as selfish, whereas moral virtue may be attributed to groups promoting public goods. Thus, despite attempts by opponents to label environmental, consumer, and other social movements as "special interests," the public and professionals within the risk policy system are generally supportive of these movements and skeptical of industry motives (Dietz and Rycroft, 1987). Furthermore, technological risk and other environmental issues seem to contain a moral component that taps strong norms in most individuals (Stern et al., 1985–1986).

Differential access and command of resources between the proponents and opponents of technology account for the imbalance, noted earlier, of expertise among the key actors in technological controversy. Expertise is a highly prized resource in risk assessment and evaluation, because policy formulation and implementation are heavily dependent on scientific and technical evidence. Recognizing the advantage they hold by controlling expertise, industry and other promoters of technologies seek to define risk policy conflicts as scientific or technical conflicts that can be resolved with formal methods removed from the political process. Opposition groups, recognizing not only their limited control of expertise but also the importance of issues left unaddressed in formal modes of analysis (e.g., consideration of equity or public acceptability of risks), seek to define conflicts over risk as political issues (Dietz et al., 1989). In this context, Warwick (1999) has identified the critical role that external allies can play for local groups seeking to address perceived environmental injustices.

The preponderance of resources in the hands of industry also means that the risk policy system will underestimate risks, because industry can use expertise to generate its own risk estimates and to offer critiques of the risk estimates of others. Opponents of technology usually lack sufficient expertise to balance the technical analyses offered by industry. Thus, public risk assessments will typically be subject to extensive formal critique by those who are concerned that risks may be overestimated, but subject to less scrutiny from those concerned that risks will be underestimated.[5]

Just as environmental and other stakeholder groups are likely to be skeptical of risk policy emphasizing formal analyses, industry will likewise be skeptical of an emphasis on accountability and public preferences. Because the public is often in favor of stricter risk regulation, industry questions the importance of public views. This discrepancy between expert and lay preferences is attributed to lay ignorance, and if the public is ignorant, its views should carry little weight in the formulation and implementation of risk policy. From a sociological perspective, this position is no more or less rational and no more or less self-serving than opponent groups' skepticism of formal analysis. The point of sociological concern is that these conflicting views, stemming from a differential command of resources, set the stage for determining acceptable processes of risk policy formulation and implementation (Dietz et al., 1989).

### The Media

The media play a direct role in shaping public attitudes toward risk and, thereby, indirectly affect the support for social movement organizations critical of technologies. Conservative critics complain of a liberal bias in media coverage, including coverage of risky technologies (Rothman and Lichter, 1987). Available evidence suggests that if media bias exists, it is procedural rather than political (Combs and Slovic, 1979; Sandman et al., 1987). The media are inclined to cover a dramatic events and those elements of news stories that are easy to convey to a mass audience. Coverage of technological risks is often in response to either a disaster, such as Love Canal or Times Beach, or in response to new and dramatic evidence about a technological risk, such as the greenhouse effect. The undramatic is not newsworthy; there is not much to report either when a technology works smoothly or when a product or substance presumed safe has been found safe by yet another study.

In addition to a preoccupation with dramatic events, the media have few specialists covering technology or environmental beats, so reports on risk lack the benefits of "insider" knowledge that come with the coverage of sports, business, or politics. This combination of circumstances means that the media are better equipped to cover the politics of risk and risk controversy than the technical details of formal risk assessments.

The links between media coverage, public opinion, and political action are not well understood, but some work has evolved to fill this gap (e.g., Gamson, 1990; Gamson and Modigliani, 1989; and Stallings, 1990). Although general attitudes toward technologies have been shown to fluctuate with the amount of media coverage devoted to them (Mazur, 1981, 1984), it is not known how these attitudes are translated into public action. For example, it is not clear that media coverage of risky technologies or attendant controversies is the basis for growth in support for or membership in social movement organizations opposed to such technologies, nor is media coverage clearly linked to skepticism of industry practices. Indeed, Perrow (1994) has argued that public concern with technological hazards has increased because industry tends to deny the risks of serious mishaps, only to recant after a serious accident has occurred. Given a long history of this practice, it is not surprising that the public often rejects industry claims of safety and shows a growing mistrust of risk management institutions (Freudenburg, 1993). Thus, sustained sociological inquiry into the impacts of media and other institutions on public opinion about risk is clearly needed.

### Distributional Impacts

All technologies generate impacts—costs and benefits borne by people and the environment. Often large numbers of individuals experiencing little or no benefit from a technology, such as neighbors of a toxic waste site, must bear the risks associated with it (Bryant, 1995; Bullard, 1990; Erickson, 1994; Szasz, 1994). At the same time, smaller groups, such as investors in chemical company stocks, experience great benefit and little risk (Frey, 1995). Conversely, when risks are eliminated or reduced through regulation or other means, broad populations usually receive small benefits, while smaller groups—owners, managers, and workers, for example—bear costs. Because formal risk assessments are typically based on aggregate data, distributional impacts are ignored. Thus, it is quite possible that a credible risk evaluation will show a net benefit to society generally, but neglect to identify the net costs to certain individuals, neighborhoods, or communities. To those experiencing costs, especially where such costs are not compensated, the fairness of the results is clearly in question—and prevalent norms of justice and equity motivate people to participate in the now familiar NIMBY (not in my backyard) movements (Freudenberg, 1984).

The issue of distributional equity reaches a second order of concern once the unfair impacts of policy proposals are identified. It is the most advantaged members of society who have financial and organizational resources to support NIMBY movements or to take other effective opposition actions. The usual effect of this process is to saddle the poorest and least powerful members of society with the brunt of risks (Bryant and Mohai, 1992; Bullard, 1990); see also the discussion of life chances below). Society faces a variety of technological hazards, such as the disposal of high-level nuclear waste, that cannot be avoided and that have serious consequences for those bearing the risks. Siting controversies are unlikely to be settled without serious consideration of equity issues. Risk management procedures ensuring a fair distribution of benefits, costs, and risks are most likely to be successful in bringing closure to controversies. Indeed, such procedures may be the most effective means for turning NIMBYS into PIMBYS (put it in my backyard) (Rosa, 1988). This problem plays itself out at the global level in conflicts between North and South on hazardous technologies and on global environmental change (Covello and Frey, 1990; Frey, 1994). There the less affluent nations call for financial and technological assistance from the more affluent nations in return for action to reduce risks to the global or regional environment.

### Science, Communication, and Public Involvement

The duration and intensity of risk controversies can also be traced to the tension between the roles of science and public participation in risk policy. On the one hand, there is no sound basis for ignoring scientific evidence, however flawed, in decisions about risk; but on the other hand, the fact that the public is often unfamiliar with this evidence does not justify dismissing public concerns. Progress toward conflict resolution requires an approach that provides a legitimate role for each and proper channels for communication. To achieve this end, discussions of risk communication should discard a unidirectional model in which the goal is "informing the public," that is, changing public perceptions and preferences to match those of experts (Covello et al., 1988). Instead, risk communication must be viewed as a two-way process in which public views are seen as legitimate, expert views are valued but also acknowledged as fallible, and the goal of risk communication is "informing the debate" (Stern, 1991; Stern and Fineberg, 1996; U.S. National Research Council, 1989). The scientific evidence, indispensable as it is, needs to be complemented with defensible normative criteria for making value-laden decisions. Sociology already provides guidelines for accomplishing this practice. In particular, work in social impact assessment has outlined methods for integrating scientific analyses with normative considerations (Burns and Uberhorst, 1988; Dietz, 1987, 1988, 1994; Freeman and Frey, 1986, 1990–1991).

The experience from social impact assessment suggests a crucial need to revise the typical process of public involvement. If the process permits public involvement only after a major policy decision has already been reached, the role left to the public is that of "veto group," and the image of the public as ignorant "nay-sayers" is reinforced. The likelihood of conflict resolution is improved considerably if all stakeholders are allowed to participate in the design of risk assessments and in devising proper management strategies. This procedure ensures that factors relevant to those impacted are included in the analysis and that compensation favored by those impacted are included in management strategies (Rosa et al., 1987). Such involvement not only engenders confidence in the analyses but, just as importantly, builds trust among key actors.

## A RESEARCH AGENDA FOR SOCIOLOGY

The sociology of risk appears to be a mixture of orienting perspectives; incipient research programs; and sociologically motivated questions about the social context, politics, and equity of risk. Although not entirely incorrect, such a description would be somewhat misleading. The fundamental concerns of environmental sociology can be defined as questions about risk: risk to humans from exposure to technological hazards; risk to all species from vast alterations in their ecological landscapes; and risk to the long-term sustainability of life from shortsighted consumption and production practices. A variety of well-researched sociological topics, not heretofore subsumed under the rubric of risk, are clearly derivative of and illuminating to issues of technological risk. For example, many social impact studies discuss the uncertain impacts (i.e., the risks) to local areas from siting of large-scale projects (Freudenburg, 1986). Public debates over national energy policy can also be viewed as debates over the acceptability of risks associated with competing energy sources (Rosa et al., 1988). In addition, social movements against technologies can be traced to citizen rejection of the risks of technologies (Mazur, 1981).

Despite the obvious salience of technological risk to existing concerns in sociology and the value of a sociological perspective in understanding risk, the cumulative body of research is small. Although several sociologists have made a compelling case for increased sociological attention to technological risk (see especially Christenson, 1988; Freudenburg, 1988; Short, 1984), key topics of sociological concern remain underresearched. Given this situation, we conclude our examination of the topic by sketching an agenda for future research. Our task is eased considerably by the outlines provided by Perrow (1984), Short, (1984), Heimer (1988), Christenson (1988), and Jaeger et al. (2001). Taken together, their outlines form a starting point for our own analysis. It is convenient to begin by summarizing their working agendas.

Perrow (1984) discusses three forms of rationality underlying current views on the evaluation of risk: absolute rationality, bounded rationality, and social rationality. Absolute or economic rationality, invoked by risk-benefit-cost analysis, has dominated the field of risk evaluation, despite the fact that the quantitative and seemingly precise analyses it generates are often criticized or rejected by the public. Herbert Simon's concept of bounded rationality recognizes limits on human rationality and, in effect, points to the unreasonableness of the fundamental assumptions underlying absolute rationality (Simon, 1982). Although a growing perspective among risk assessors, the bounded rationality approach falls short of capturing key features of human reasoning and action in the face of complex problems of judgment and risk choices. What is needed, Perrow asserts, is the study of social and cultural rationality. In particular, he calls for approaches to risk evaluation that take seriously two defining features of social life: the variation in talents and perspectives among social actors, and the social bonding that coordinates interdependencies and provides a socially "rational" use of this diversity of talents and perspectives.

Short (1984), in his presidential address to the American Sociological Association in 1984, reiterates Perrow's position on the importance to sociology of systematic inquiry into the nature of "social rationality." Short further elaborates the research agenda by pointing to an affinity, previously hidden, between the considerable body of research on the fear of crime and victimization and the small but growing literature on technological risk within the "social fabric."

Heimer (1988), in her review of the psychology of risk, identifies four key weaknesses of the psychological perspective that call for sociological inquiry. These are the inability of the perspective to deal with: voluntarily assumed risks (i.e., those assumed for pleasure); the impact of social position on risk perception; the role of organizational dynamics in selecting risks for attention and "framing" them once selected; and the active role played by people in avoiding risks that are unacceptable but avoidable, reworking existing choices about risk, or seeking more attractive choices.

Christenson's (1988) presidential address to the Rural Sociological Society is a plea for rural sociologists to direct their research to risks "imposed" on rural people. He emphasizes the importance of identifying and estimating the negative consequences of hazards on the life chances of rural people, and determining how such risks can be prevented or reduced. He outlines a research program consisting of several components: the identification of populations at risk, the assessment of such situations in noneconomic terms, and the formulation and assessment of preventive strategies.

Jaeger et al. (2001) develop a sociological approach to risk by first returning to the foundations of risk analysis: the rational actor paradigm of economics and engineering. Mainstream analysis of risk is underpinned by this paradigm which assumes individuals are purposive actors who, given the appropriate information, will act toward risk in "rational" ways. Jaeger et al. neither accept nor reject this orientation a priori, but instead critically evaluate it in the light of empirical evidence, theoretical criteria, and policy demands. The end result is a sociologically enriched, interdisciplinary framework that delineates domains of risk investigation and aligns these domains with appropriate metatheoretical orientations—whether individualistic, as with the rational actor and psychometric traditions; or sociological, as with the cultural, the interactional, and the organizational traditions. Its goal is to match intellectual tools with the appropriate theoretical or policy management needs.

All of these research suggestions represent important directions for future research, but there are many equally important topics worthy of investigation. Without pretending to exhaust all possibilities, we suggest that the following four topics be added to the research agenda of sociology.

## Knowledge, Science, and Politics

Because it plays such a central role in risk assessment, evaluation, and management, science itself is worthy of sociological scrutiny. Some topics derived from the current sociology of science and knowledge are certainly appropriate. For example, what are the historical and social conditions that produced a methodological specialization for the study of the ancient, ubiquitous social problem of technological risk? How does science, the dominant knowledge system in the West, evaluate evidence (or the lack thereof) at the very boundaries of its capabilities? Indeed, how are these boundaries identified, when research is driven in part by the ends of the policy system for "correct" answers in the face of uncertainty and controversy? Do these difficulties point to the need for new scientific practices (Funtowicz and Ravetz, 1992)?

Many sociologists of science have labeled scientific knowledge as socially constructed and therefore ultimately subjective (e.g., Pinch and Bijker, 1984); and some sociologists (Buttel and Taylor, 1994; Hilgartner, 1992; Johnson and Covello, 1987; Stallings, 1990) have adopted social constructionist approaches to the study of risk. Although we recognize the fallibility of all knowledge claims, scientific or otherwise, we judge this view to be too extreme. We take a critical realist view, which, though recognizing the fallibility of all knowledge claims, holds that not all knowledge is equally fallible. It follows that many facts of science, including facts about technological risks, have a basis in reality that is more than a simple social construction (Rosa, 1998). For example, the health effects of lead exposure may have many subjective features (such as why they were dismissed from consideration until the 1950s in the United States [Graebner, 1987]), and may not be precisely quantifiable, but it is known that sufficient doses are toxic in all societies, whatever the shared beliefs of members of the society. Selection processes and cultural transmission processes in turn shape these shared beliefs (Burns and Dietz, 1992a, 1992b).

Nonetheless, it is just as clear that science, in the service of policy, is deeply intertwined in politics, which creates tensions between the pursuit of knowledge and the operation of democracy (Burns and Uberhorst, 1988; Dickson, 1984; Dietz, 1987, 1988). Thus, in the policy arena, scientific beliefs, evidence, and arguments are hardly immune from social and political influences (Proctor, 1995). Unfortunately, we know relatively little about how those influences manifest themselves, especially when we move from theoretical science to the scientific or formal methods used in risk research. The relative importance of professional education and work experience in shaping attitudes toward technological risk has yet to be explored in detail (but see Dietz and Rycroft, 1987). Not much is known about how experts obtain and evaluate information or about how their values and attitudes influence their interpretation of research results. Furthermore, scientist activists have played important roles in risk debates at various times, but we have little understanding of why some scientists choose to become engaged in public debate, or why some scientists choose one side over another. At the structural level, more systematic inquiry is needed to understand the institutional arrangements of policy-relevant science, and especially to understand how funding priorities shape the growth of scientific knowledge and how in turn scientific networks (the so-called "epistemic communities") shape policy.[6]

### Risk Distribution and Life Chances

The notion of "life chances," introduced into the sociological lexicon by Max Weber (1958[1921]) refers to one's quality of life as determined by class position. Placed in the context of technological risks, the term *life chances* becomes more directly reflective of modern social life. Despite the arguments offered by Giddens (1990) and Beck (1992), the costs and benefits of technologies are not equitably distributed in society. The chances of a healthy and long life vary considerably among major social groupings. Despite the widespread recognition of this fact, research on the distribution of risks has evolved slowly (see Bryant and Mohai, 1992; Bullard, 1990, 1992; Freeman, 1989; Frey, 1995, 1996; Taylor, 1992). Still, we have little understanding of how risks are distributed across class, occupational, gender, ethnic and race, regional, and national boundaries and other meaningful social categories, such as generations and species. Further investigation, for example, might show that typical dimensions of social position are reinforced and perpetuated by an unexplored dimension of stratification: stratification by exposure to technological hazards at both the local and global levels (see Frey, 1998, 2001b; Robinson, 1989).

### Risk Perceptions, Worldview, and Political Action

The public does not always perceive risks in the same way as experts, but the evidence on risk perceptions is mixed and its political salience contested. As noted above, most work on risk perception has been based on limited samples, with little attention given to the background and social situation of respondents. Further research, therefore, is needed along these lines.

Although the work of Gould et al. (1988) on the relationship between risk salience and risk perceptions is an excellent beginning, more research is needed. The cost to an individual of obtaining risk information is probably high, and the public probably obtains accurate information only on risks salient to them. Many questions about relative risk are framed at aggregate levels, having little salience to most respondents. For instance, the overall U.S. fatality rate from homicides may not accurately reflect the true risk of homicide to either a young black male in Chicago or an elderly white female in Kansas, so the aggregate risk statistics may bear little relation to their life experience. University undergraduates may be more inclined toward miscalculating risks than commercial fishers or wheat farmers, whose lives depend critically on proper risk assessments. In addition, respondents to surveys about technological risk probably make the reasonable assumption that all items on the survey, including those about "objective facts" such as relative risks, are also asking for an opinion about the desirability of the source of risk. Thus, their responses may blur the researcher's intended distinctions between the objective and subjective.

More attention should be given to sources of risk information and the ways in which risk perceptions change. Although some research exists on media coverage of technological risk (Gamson and Modigliani, 1989; Mazur, 1994; Stallings, 1990), the intricacies of media impacts on public perception have not been fully explored. The impact of media coverage on risk perception should be compared to other sources of information, such as formal education, work experiences, and communication with family and friends. Of particular importance are studies of the impact of dramatic events, such as Chernobyl, Bhopal, and Three Mile Island on public perceptions.

We have already noted that risk issues seem to have a moral dimension, suggesting that moral norms play an important role in support for the environmental movement (Stern et al., 1985–1986). Further research on moral norms and their relationship to activism, worldview, values, attitudes, perceptions of risk, and an individual's position in the social structure seems appropriate. Whitfield (1998) has taken some first steps in this direction, relating perceptions of nuclear risks and other risks to values and general environmental beliefs.

## The Political Economy of International Technological Hazards

Transnational corporations (TNCs) based in developed countries export banned, obsolete, and regulated technologies and products to less developed countries (LDCs). Examples include powdered milk contaminated by radiation from the Chernobyl nuclear power plant accident; pesticides; tobacco; hazardous wastes; and hazardous production processes such as asbestos processing, arsenic production, and copper smelting (Covello and Frey, 1990; Frey, 1995, 1997, 1998, 2001b; Hilz, 1992). Because LDCs have limited resources for the analysis and management of risks, the export practices of TNCs contribute to the overall level of health, safety, and environmental risks of LDCs (Barkin, 1991; Bogard, 1989; Covello and Frey, 1990; Hilz, 1992; O'Connor, 1989). Case studies as well as comparative studies of the export practices of TNCs and the actual practices of TNCs operating in LDCs are needed (Bunker, 1985). Detailed analyses of the full range of health, safety, and environmental risks facing LDCs that can be attributed to the practices of TNCs are needed. Research is also needed on national and international efforts to deal with hazardous export practices. Systematic efforts should also be undertaken to identify the full range of policy options available for managing the problem.

## CONCLUSION

Technological risk is a topic of growing concern in contemporary societies. We have reviewed the formal procedures used to examine such risks, the development of the policy systems that address risk, current social science perspectives on risk, and the dynamics of political controversies over risk. We also have identified a number of areas for further sociological research. Clearly, the topic of risk contains a rich variety of challenging sociological questions. Theoretical and empirical investigations are beginning to address them. As this work progresses, we emphasize the need for integration. Current efforts range in scope from examinations of individual risk perception, through analyses of organizations, institutions, and policy systems to consideration of the transformation of societies and global environmental change. Understanding risk will require theories that can span this range from the micro to the macro, and that are attentive to empirical detail. This in turn will require grounding theoretical and empirical work in specific contexts. In doing so, the sociology of risk must take up questions at the core of social science theory: rationality, agency, collective action, valuation, globalization, social order, reality construction, and socio-cultural transformation. The study of risk will, in turn, make contributions to that theory, recasting it in ways that are more attentive to physical and biological environment and to the technologies humans use to interact with that environment.

## NOTES

Order of authorship is alphabetical. We wish to thank Chip Clarke, Riley Dunlap, Bill Freudenburg, Jim Jasper, Ed Liebow, Jim Miley, Marvin Olsen, Ortwin

Renn, and Jim Short for their comments on earlier versions of this chapter. An earlier version of some of this material appeared in Frey (2001a).

1. Although this definition is widely used, it remains the subject of continued debate (see, e.g., Fischhoff et al., 1984; Renn, 1992; Rosa, 1998; U.S. National Research Council, 1989). We do not discuss risks associated with natural hazards (White, 1974), individual avoidance of health and safety risks (Weinstein, 1987), crime risk (Short, 1984), individual risk-seeking behavior (Machlis and Rosa, 1990), risks of medical procedures (Kolker and Burke, 1994), or the actuarial profession and industries (Heimer, 1985). These are all important topics, and existing work on them is important for the study of technological risk, but space limitations preclude discussing them here. Note also that the use of the term *risk* in policy debates may be value-laden and imply that such risks should be politically acceptable (U.S. National Research Council, 1989). Finally, while the effects we discuss seem to range from the global to the local, it is useful to remember that global risks such as climate change and ozone depletion manifest themselves in local effects, while many technologies whose use is localized, such as nitrogen-based fertilizers or products containing heavy metals, have cumulative effects on the biosphere (Stern et al., 1992). Thus, the global and local distinctions to some degree are arbitrary.

2. To date, most risk analyses have been about direct threats to human health and safety. Our discussion here reflects that focus; but evidence is mounting that there are subtle environmental effects of many technologies on the biosphere, ranging from climate change and ozone depletion to a broad spread of toxics throughout the biosphere. By altering major ecosystems and the biosphere itself, these technologies may in turn pose grave indirect risks to humans. These issues are discussed in more detail in Silver and DeFries (1992) and Stern, Young, and Druckman (1992). The field of ecological risk assessment, which focuses on threats to species other than humans, is developing rapidly (see Norton et al., 1992).

3. Recently, advocates of an "industrial ecology" approach to environmental protection have argued for examining the entire resource extraction-manufacturing-marketing-consumption-disposal cycle to identify leverage points for minimizing environmental impact (Socolow et al., 1994). To date, the industrial ecology literature emphasizes a systems analysis of material and energy flows, and has only begun to address policies that would reduce risk (but see Andrews, 1994; Griefahn, 1994). In parallel, Furger (1997) suggests examining the full institutional context of firms, regulatory agencies, and industry associations in attempting to understand risk. Both these broader approaches suggest innovative approaches to risk regulation that may ultimately prove more effective than the proposals outlined above.

4. There is some evidence that the poor performance of lay persons on such tasks may be a result of questions that are asked in a format that differs from everyday reasoning. For example, Cosmides and Tooby (1996) find that respondents perform well on probability questions posed in a frequentist form and poorly on a Bayesian formulation, while Gigerenzer et al. (1989) provide a theory of mental models that shows the consistency of seemingly incongruous results in probability experiments. As we will note below, this psychological approach could be greatly enhanced by consideration of the social contexts in which human reasoning evolves and develops; the environments that are the selective regimes for human decision making. Most human decision making is about social interaction rather

than about technology, and the calculus of decisions required for interaction may differ from that typically used in normative decision theory.

5. The disproportionate power of the corporate sector relative to that of social movement groups is also brought to bear in "Strategic Law Suits Against Public Participation" (SLAPPs). SLAPPs are used to silence opposition by confronting them with the threat of substantial legal fees that may be required to defend against even a frivolous suit. SLAPPs are carefully documented by Pring and Canan (1996).

6. International relations theorists have recently emphasized the role of international networks of scientists ("epistemic communities") in the development of international regulation (Haas, 1992). This work could be linked fruitfully to both the sociology of science and the substantial body of sociological work on development and dependency.

## REFERENCES

Abel, Richard L. 1985. "Blaming Victims." *American Bar Foundation Research Journal* 2:401–417.

Andrews, Clinton. 1994. "Policies to Encourage Clean Technology." Pp. 405–422 in *Industrial Ecology and Global Change*, edited by R. Socolow, C. Andrews, F. Berkhout, and V. Thomas. Cambridge: Cambridge University Press.

Bailey, Ronald (ed.). 1995. *The True State of the Planet*. New York: Harper-Perennial.

Baram, Michael S. 1980. "Cost-Benefit Analysis: An Inadequate Basis for Health, Safety and Environmental Regulatory Decision-making." *Ecology Law Quarterly* 8:473–531.

Baram, Michael S., and J. Raymond Miyares. 1986. "Alternatives to Government Regulation for the Management of Technological Risks." Pp. 337–357 in *Risk Evaluation and Management*, edited by V. T. Covello, J. Menkes, and J. Mumpower. New York: Plenum Press.

Barkin, David. 1991. "State Control of the Environment: Politics and Degradation in Mexico." *Capitalism, Nature and Socialism* 2:86–108.

Bastide, Sophie, Jean-Paul Moatti, Jean-Paul Pages, and Francis Fagnani. 1989. "Risk Perception and Social Acceptability of Technologies: The French Case." *Risk Analysis* 9:215–223.

Beck, Ulrich. 1992. [1986]. *Risk Society: Toward a New Modernity*. Trans. Mark Ritter. London: Sage Publications.

Bentkover, Judith D., Vincent T. Covello, and Jeryl Mumpower (eds.). 1986. *Benefits Assessment: The State of the Art*. Boston: Reidel.

Bogard, William. 1989. *The Bhopal Tragedy: Language, Logic, and Politics in the Production of a Hazard*. Boulder, CO: Westview Press.

Breyer, Stephen. 1993. *Breaking the Vicious Circle: Toward Effective Risk Regulation*. Cambridge, MA: Harvard University Press.

Brickman, Ronald S., Sheila Jasanoff, and T. Ilgen. 1985. *Controlling Chemicals: The Politics of Regulation in Europe and the United States*. Ithaca, NY: Cornell University Press.

Brulle, Robert. 2000. *Agency, Democracy and the Environment*. Cambridge, MA: MIT Press.

Bryant, Bunyan. 1995. *Environmental Justice: Issues, Policies, and Solutions.* Washington, DC: Island Press.

Bryant, Bunyan, and Paul Mohai (eds.). 1992. *Race and the Incidence of Environmental Hazards.* Boulder, CO: Westview Press.

Bullard, Robert D. 1990. *Dumping in Dixie: Race, Class and Environmental Quality.* Boulder, CO: Westview Press.

Bullard, Robert D. (ed.). 1992. *Confronting Environmental Racism: Voices from the Grassroots.* Boston: South End Press.

Bunker, Stephen G. 1985. *Underdeveloping the Amazon: Extraction, Unequal Exchange and the Failure of the Modern State.* Urbana: University of Illinois Press.

Burns, Tom R., and Thomas Dietz. 1992a. "Technology, Sociotechnical Systems, Technological Development: An Evolutionary Perspective." Pp. 206–238 in *New Technology at the Outset: Social Forces in the Shaping of Technological Innovation,* edited by M. Dierkes and U. Hoffman. Frankfurt am Main: Campus Verlag.

Burns, Tom R., and Thomas Dietz. 1992b. "Cultural Evolution: Social Rule Systems, Selection and Human Agency." *International Sociology* 7:259–284.

Burns, Tom R., and Reinhard Uberhorst. 1988. *Creative Democracy: Systematic Conflict Resolution and Policymaking in a World of High Science and Technology.* New York: Praeger.

Buttel, Frederick H., and Peter J. Taylor. 1994. "Environmental Sociology and Global Change: A Critical Assessment." Pp. 228–255 in *Social Theory and the Global Environment,* edited by Michael Redclift and Ted Benton. London: Routledge.

Caldwell, Lynton Keith. 1990. *International Environmental Policy: Emergence and Dimensions,* 2nd ed. Durham, NC: Duke University Press.

Cartwright, John. 1989. "Conserving Nature, Decreasing Debt." *Third World Quarterly* 11:114–127.

Christenson, James A. 1988. "Social Risk and Rural Sociology." *Rural Sociology* 53:1–24.

Clarke, Lee. 1988. "Politics and Bias in Risk Assessment." *The Social Science Journal* 25:155–165.

———1989. *Acceptable Risk? Making Decisions in a Toxic Environment.* Berkeley: University of California Press.

Cohen, Bernard L. 1987. "Reducing the Hazards of Nuclear Power: Insanity in Action." *Physics and Society* 16:2–4.

Combs, B., and Paul Slovic. 1979. "Newspaper Coverage of Causes of Death." *Journalism Quarterly* 56:837–843, 849.

Commoner, Barry. 1990. *Making Peace with the Planet.* New York: Pantheon.

Cosmides, Leda, and John Tooby. 1996. "Are Humans Good Intuitive Statisticians After All? Rethinking Some Conclusions from the Literature on Judgment under Uncertainty." *Cognition* 58:1–73.

Covello, Vincent T., and R. Scott Frey. 1990. "Technology-Based Environmental Health Risks in Developing Nations." *Technological Forecasting and Social Change* 37:159–179.

Covello, Vincent T., D. McCallum, and M. Pavlova (eds.). 1988. *Effective Risk Communication: The Role and Responsibility of Government.* New York: Plenum Press.

Covello, Vincent T., and Jeryl Mumpower. 1985. "Risk Analysis and Risk Management: An Historical Perspective." *Risk Analysis* 5:103–120.

Crouch, Edmund A. C., and Richard Wilson. 1982. *Risk/Benefit Analysis*. Cambridge, MA: Ballinger.

Cutter, Susan L. 1993. *Living with Risk: The Geography of Technological Hazards*. London: Edward Arnold.

Dake, Karl. 1991. "Orienting Dispositions in the Perception of Risk: An Analysis of Contemporary Worldviews and Cultural Biases." *Journal of Cross-Cultural Psychology* 22:61–82.

Dake, Karl, and Aaron Wildavsky. 1991. "Individual Differences in Risk Perception and Risk-Taking Preferences." Pp. 15–24 in *The Analysis, Communication and Perception of Risk*, edited by B. J. Garrick and W. C. Gekler. New York: Plenum Press.

Davidson, Debra J., and William R. Freudenburg. 1996. "Gender and Environmental Risk Concerns: A Review and Analysis of Available Research." *Environment and Behavior* 28:302–339.

Dickson, David. 1984. *The New Politics of Science*. New York: Pantheon.

Dietz, Thomas. 1987. "Theory and Method in Social Impact Assessment." *Sociological Inquiry* 57:54–69.

———1988. "Social Impact Assessment as Applied Human Ecology: Integrating Theory and Method." Pp. 220–227 in *Human Ecology: Research and Applications*, edited by R. Borden, J. Jacobs, and G. Young. College Park, MD: Society for Human Ecology.

———1992. "The Challenges of Global Environmental Change for Human Ecology." Pp. 30–45 in *Human Responsibility and Global Change*, edited by L. O. Hansson and B. Junger. Göteborg, Sweden: University of Göteborg.

———1994. "What Should We Do? Human Ecology and Collective Decision Making." *Human Ecology Review* 1:277–300.

Dietz, Thomas, and Linda Kalof. 1992. "Environmentalism among Nation-States." *Social Indicators Research* 26:353–366.

Dietz, Thomas, and Robert W. Rycroft. 1987. *The Risk Professionals*. New York: Russell Sage Foundation.

Dietz, Thomas, Paul C. Stern, and Robert W. Rycroft. 1989. "Definitions of Conflict and the Legitimation of Resources: The Case of Environmental Risk." *Sociological Forum* 4:47–70.

Douglas, Mary. 1992. *Risk and Blame*. New York: Routledge.

Douglas, Mary, and Aaron Wildavsky. 1982. *Risk and Culture: The Selection of Technological and Environmental Dangers*. Berkeley: University of California Press.

Dunlap, Riley E. 1992. "Trends in Public Opinion toward Environmental Issues." Pp. 89–116 in *American Environmentalism: The U.S. Environmental Movement, 1970–1990*, edited by Riley E. Dunlap and Angela Mertig. Philadelphia: Taylor and Francis.

Dunlap, Riley E., George H. Gallup, and Alex M. Gallup. 1993. "Global Environmental Concern: Results from an International Opinion Survey." *Environment* 35 (November):6–15, 33–39.

Dunlap, Riley E., Michael E. Kraft, and Eugene A. Rosa (eds.). 1993. *Public Reactions to Nuclear Waste: Citizen's Views of Repository Siting*. Durham, NC: Duke University Press.

Englander, Tibor, Klara Farago, Paul Slovic, and Baruch Fischhoff. 1986. "A Comparative Analysis of Risk Perception in Hungary and the United States." *Social Behaviour* 1:55–66.

Environ. 1988. *Elements of Toxicology and Chemical Risk Assessment.* Washington, DC: Environ.

Erickson, Kai. 1994. *A New Species of Trouble: Explorations in Trauma and Community.* New York: Norton.

Fiorino, Daniel J. 1995. *Making Environmental Policy.* Berkeley: University of California Press.

Fischhoff, Baruch. 1990. "Psychology and Public Policy: Tool or Toolmaker?" *American Psychologist* 45:647–653.

Fischhoff, Baruch, Sarah Lichtenstein, Paul Slovic, Steven L. Derby, and Ralph L. Keeney. 1981. *Acceptable Risk.* New York: Cambridge University Press.

Fischhoff, Baruch, Stephen R. Watson, and Chris Hope. 1984. "Defining Risk." *Policy Sciences* 17:123–129.

Freeman, David M., and R. Scott Frey. 1986. "A Method for Assessing the Social Impacts of Natural Resource Policies." *Journal of Environmental Management* 23:229–245.

Freeman, David M., and R. Scott Frey. 1990–1991. "A Modest Proposal for Assessing Social Impacts of Natural Resource Policies." *Journal of Environmental Systems* 20:375–404.

Freeman, Harold P. 1989. "Cancer in the Economically Disadvantaged." *Cancer* 64 (Supplement):324–334.

Freudenberg, Nicholas. 1984. *Not in Our Backyards! Community Action for Health and the Environment.* New York: Monthly Review Press.

Freudenburg, William R. 1986. "Social Impact Assessment." *Annual Review of Sociology* 12:451–478.

———. 1988. "Perceived Risk, Real Risk: Social Science and the Art of Probabilistic Risk Assessment." *Science* 242:44–49.

———. 1993. "Risk and Recreancy: Weber, the Division of Labor and the Rationality of Risk Perceptions." *Social Forces* 71:909–932.

Frey, R. Scott. 1995. "The International Traffic in Pesticides." *Technological Forecasting and Social Change* 50:151–169.

———. 1996. "Cancer Mortality in Kansas Farmers." *Transactions of the Kansas Academy of Sciences* 99(1–2):51–55.

———. 1997. "The International Traffic in Tobacco." *Third World Quarterly* 18: 303–319.

———. 1998. "The Hazardous Waste Stream in the World System." Pp. 84–103 in *Space and Transport in the World System,* edited by Paul S. Ciccantell and Stephen G. Bunker. Westport, CT: Greenwood Press.

——— (ed.). 2001a. *The Environment and Society Reader.* Boston: Allyn and Bacon.

———. 2001b. "The Migration of Hazardous Industries to the *Maquiladora* Centers of Northern Mexico." Paper in review.

Frey, R. Scott, Thomas Dietz, and Linda Kalof. 1992. "Another Look at Gamson's *Strategy of Social Protest.*" *American Journal of Sociology* 98:368–387.

Funtowicz, Silvio, and Jerome R. Ravetz. 1992. "Three Types of Risk Assessment and Emergence of Post-Normal Science." Pp. 251–297 in *Social Theories of*

*Risk*, edited by Sheldon Krimsky and Dominic Golding. Westport, CT: Praeger.

Furger, Franco. 1997. "Accountability and Systems of Self-Governance: The Case of the Maritime Industry." *Law and Policy* 19:445–476.

Gamson, William. 1990. *The Strategy of Social Protest*, 2nd ed. Belmont, CA: Wadsworth.

Gamson, William A., and Andre Modigliani. 1989. "Media Discourse and Public Opinion on Nuclear Power: A Constructionist Approach." *American Journal of Sociology* 95:1–37.

Giddens, Anthony. 1990. *The Consequences of Modernity*. Stanford, CA: Stanford University Press.

Gigerenzer, Gerd, Zeno Swijtink, Theodore Porter, Lorraine Daston, John Beatty, and Lorenz Kruger. 1989. *The Empire of Chance*. Cambridge: Cambridge University Press.

Goszczynska, Maryla, Tadease Tyszka, and Paul Slovic. 1991. "Risk Perception in Poland: A Comparison with Three Other Countries." *Journal of Behavioral Decision Making* 43:179–193.

Gould, Leroy C., Gerald T. Gardner, Donald R. DeLuca, Adrian Tiemann, Leonard W. Doob, and Jan A. J. Stolwijk. 1988. *Perceptions of Technological Risks and Benefits*. New York: Russell Sage Foundation.

Graebner, William. 1987. "Hegemony through Science: Information, Engineering and Lead Toxicology, 1925–1965." Pp. 140–159 in *Dying for Work: Workers' Safety and Health in Twentieth Century America*, edited by David Rosner and Gerald Makowitz. Bloomington: Indiana University Press.

Graham, John D., Laura C. Green, and Marc J. Roberts. 1988. *In Search of Safety: Chemicals and Cancer Risk*. Cambridge, MA: Harvard University Press.

Griefahn, Monika. 1994. "Initiatives in Lower Saxony to Link Ecology to Economy." Pp. 423–428 in *Industrial Ecology and Global Change*, edited by R. Socolow, C. Andrews, F. Berkhout, and V. Thomas. Cambridge: Cambridge University Press.

Haas, Peter M. 1992. "Epistemic Communities and International Policy Coordination." *International Organization* 46:1–35.

Hackett, David P. 1990. "An Assessment of the Basel Convention on the Control of Transboundary Movements of Hazardous Wastes and Their Disposal." *American University Journal of International Law and Policy* 5:291–323.

Hadden, Susan G. 1986. *Read the Label: Reducing Risk by Providing Information*. Boulder, CO: Westview Press.

Harriss, Robert C., Christoph Hohenemser, and Robert W. Kates. 1985. "Human and Nonhuman Mortality." Pp. 129–155 in *Perilous Progress: Managing the Hazards of Technology*, edited by Robert W. Kates, Christoph Hohenemser, and Jeanne X. Kasperson. Boulder, CO: Westview Press.

Hays, Samuel P. 1959. *Conservation and the Gospel of Efficiency: The Progressive Conservation Movement, 1890–1920*. Cambridge, MA: Harvard University Press.

———. 1987. *Beauty, Health, and Permanence: Environmental Politics in the United States, 1955–1985*. New York: Cambridge University Press.

Heimer, Carol. 1985. *Reactive Risk and Rational Action: Managing Moral Hazard in Insurance Contracts*. Berkeley: University of California Press.

————. 1988. "Social Structure, Psychology, and the Estimation of Risk." *Annual Review of Sociology* 14:491–519.

Hilgartner, Stephen. 1992. "The Social Construction of Risk Objects: Or How to Pry Open Networks of Risk." Pp. 39–56 in *Organizations, Uncertainty and Risk*, edited by James F. Short, Jr. and Lee Clarke. Boulder, CO: Westview Press.

Hilz, Christoph. 1992. *The International Toxic Waste Trade*. New York: Van Nostrand Reinhold.

Hofstadter, Richard. 1955. *The Age of Reform*. New York: Alfred A. Knopf.

Holden, Constance. 1988. "The Greening of the World Bank." *Science* 240:1610.

Intergovernmental Panel on Climate Change. 1996. *Climate Change: The Second Assessment Report*. Cambridge: Cambridge University Press.

Jaeger, Carlo, Ortwin Renn, Eugene A. Rosa, and Thomas Webler. 2001. *Risk, Uncertainty and Rational Action*. London: Earthscan.

Jasanoff, Sheila. 1986. *Risk Management and Political Culture: A Comparative Study of Science in the Policy Context*. New York: Russell Sage Foundation.

Jasper, James M. 1988. "The Political Life Cycle of Technological Controversies." *Social Forces* 67:355–377.

————. 1990. *Nuclear Politics: Energy and the State in the United States, Sweden and France*. Princeton, NJ: Princeton University Press.

Johnson, Branden B, and Vincent T. Covello (eds.). 1987. *The Social and Cultural Construction of Risk: Essays on Risk Selection and Perception*. Dordrecht, Holland: D. Reidel.

Kasperson, Roger E., Robert W. Kates, and Christoph Hohenemser. 1985. "Hazard Management." Pp. 43–66 in *Perilous Progress: Managing the Hazards of Technology*, edited by Robert W. Kates, Christoph Hohenemser, and Jeanne X. Kasperson. Boulder, CO: Westview Press.

Kasperson, Roger E., Ortwin Renn, Paul Slovic, Halina S. Brown, Jacque Emel, Robert Goble, Jeanne X. Kasperson, and Samuel Ratick. 1988. "The Social Amplification of Risk: A Conceptual Framework." *Risk Analysis* 8:177–187.

Keeney, Ralph, and Howard Raiffa. 1976. *Decisions with Multiple Objectives, Preferences and Value Tradeoffs*. New York: John Wiley & Sons.

Keown, Charles F. 1989. "Risk Perceptions of Hong Kongese vs. Americans." *Risk Analysis* 9:401–405.

Kleinhesselink, Randall R., and Eugene A. Rosa. 1991. "Cognitive Representation of Risk Perceptions: A Comparison of Japan and the United States." *Journal of Cross-cultural Psychology* 22:11–28.

Kleinhesselink, Randall R., and Eugene A. Rosa. 1993. "Nuclear Trees in a Forest of Hazards: A Comparison of Risk Perceptions between American and Japanese University Students." Pp. 101–119 in *Nuclear Power at the Crossroads*, edited by G. Hineman, S. Kondo, P. Lowinger, and K. Matsui. Boulder, CO: International Center for Energy and Economic Development, University of Colorado.

Kolker, Aliza, and B. Meredith Burke. 1994. *Prenatal Testing: A Sociological Perspective*. Westport, CT: Bergin and Garvey.

Krimsky, Sheldon, and Dominic Golding (eds.). 1992. *Social Theories of Risk*. Westport, CT: Praeger.

Lancet. 1992. "The Cancer Epidemic: Fact or Misinterpretation?" *The Lancet* 340(August 15):399–400.

La Porte, Todd R. 1988. "The United States Air Traffic System: Increasing Reliability in the Midst of Rapid Growth." Pp. 215–244 in *The Development of Large Technological Systems*, edited by Renate Mayntz and Thomas P. Hughes. Boulder, CO: Westview Press.

La Porte, Todd R., and P. M. Consolini. 1991. "Working in Practice but Not in Theory: Theoretical Challenges of High Reliability Organizations." *Journal of Public Administration Research and Theory* 1:19–47.

Lave, Lester B. (ed.). 1982. *Quantitative Risk Assessment in Regulation*. Washington, DC: The Brookings Institution.

Lichtenstein, Sarah, Paul Slovic, Baruch Fischhoff, Mark Layman, and Barbara Combs. 1978. "Judged Frequency of Lethal Events." *Journal of Experimental Psychology: Human Learning and Memory* 4:551–578.

Lipschutz, Ronnie D., and Ken Conca (eds.). 1993. *The State and Social Power in Global Environmental Politics*. New York: Columbia University Press.

Lipset, Seymour Martin, and William Schneider. 1987. *The Confidence Gap: Business, Labor and Government in the Public Mind*, rev. ed. Baltimore, MD: John Hopkins University Press.

Lowrance, William W. 1976. *Of Acceptable Risk: Science and the Determination of Safety*. Los Altos, CA: William Kaufman.

Machlis, Gary E., and Eugene A. Rosa. 1990. "Desired Risk: Broadening the Social Amplification of Risk Framework." *Risk Analysis* 10:161–168.

Mathews, Jessica Tuchman (ed.). 1991. *Preserving the Global Environment: The Challenge of Shared Leadership*. New York: Norton.

Mazur, Allan. 1981. *The Dynamics of Technical Controversy*. Washington, DC: Communications Press.

———. 1984. "Media Influences on Public Attitudes toward Nuclear Power." Pp. 97–114 in *Public Reactions to Nuclear Power: Are There Critical Masses?*, edited by William R. Freudenburg and Eugene A. Rosa. Boulder, CO: Westview Press.

Mazur, Allan (ed.). 1994. "Symposium on Technological Risk in the Mass Media." *Risk: Health, Safety and Environment* 5:187–282.

McElrath, Roger. 1988. "Environmental Issues and the Strategies of the International Trade Union Movement." *Columbia Journal of World Business* 23:63–68.

Menkes, Joshua, and R. Scott Frey. 1987. "*De Minimis* Risk as a Regulatory Tool." Pp. 9–13 in *De Minimis Risk*, edited by Chris Whipple. New York: Plenum Press.

Montgomery, John D. 1990. "Environmental Management as a Third-World Problem." *Policy Sciences* 23:163–176.

Nelkin, Dorothy (ed.). 1992. *Controversy: Politics of Technical Decisions*. Beverly Hills, CA: Sage Publications.

Norton, Susan B., Donald Rodier, John H. Gentile, William H. Van Der Schalie, William W. Wood, and Michael W. Slimak. 1992. "A Framework for Ecological Risk Assessment at the E.P.A." *Environmental Toxicology and Chemistry* 11:1663–1672.

O'Connor, James. 1989. "Uneven and Combined Development and the Ecological Crisis: A Theoretical Introduction." *Race and Class* 30:1–11.

Olson, Mancur. 1965. *The Logic of Collective Action: Public Goods and the Theory of Groups.* Cambridge, MA: Harvard University Press.

Perrow, Charles. 1984. *Normal Accidents: Living with High Risk Technologies.* New York: Basic Books.

———. 1994. "The Limits of Safety: The Enhancement of a Theory of Accidents." *Journal of Contingencies and Crisis Management* 2:212–220.

Pinch, Trevor J., and Wiebe E. Bijker. 1984. "The Social Construction of Facts and Artifacts: Or How the Sociology of Science and the Sociology of Technology Might Benefit Each Other." *Social Studies of Science* 14:399–441.

Porter, Garth, and Janet Welsch Brown. 1991. *Global Environmental Politics.* Boulder, CO: Westview Press.

Princen, Thomas, and Matthias Finger (eds.). 1994. *Environmental NGOs in World Politics.* London: Routledge.

Pring, George W., and Penelope Canan. 1996. *SLAPPs: Getting Sued for Speaking Out.* Philadelphia: Temple University Press.

Proctor, Richard. 1995. *Cancer Wars: How Politics Shapes What We Know about Cancer.* New York: Basic Books.

Rayner, Steve, and Robin Cantor. 1987. "How Fair Is Safe Enough? The Cultural Approach to Societal Technology Choice." *Risk Analysis* 7:3–13.

Regens, James L., Thomas M. Dietz, and Robert W. Rycroft. 1983. "Risk Assessment in the Policy-Making Process: Environmental Health and Safety Protection." *Public Administration Review* 43:137–145.

Renn, Ortwin. 1992. "Concepts of Risk: A Classification." Pp. 53–79 in *Social Theories of Risk*, edited by Sheldon Krimsky and Dominic Golding. Westport, CT: Praeger.

Roberts, K. H. (ed.). 1993. *New Challenges to Organizations: High Reliability Organizations.* New York: Macmillan.

Robinson, James C. 1989. "Exposure to Occupational Hazards among Hispanics, Blacks, and Non-Hispanic Whites in California." *American Journal of Public Health* 79:629–630.

Rochlin, Gene I., Todd R. La Porte, and Karlene H. Roberts. 1987. "The Self-Designing High-Reliability Organization: Aircraft Carrier Flight Operations at Sea." *Naval War College Review* 40:76–90.

Rodericks, Joseph V. 1992. *Calculated Risks.* Cambridge: Cambridge University Press.

Rosa, Eugene A. 1988. "NAMBY PAMBY and NIMBY PIMBY: Public Issues in the Siting of Hazardous Waste Facilities." *FORUM for Applied Research and Public Policy* 3:114.

———. 1998. "Metatheoretical Foundations for Post-Normal Risk." *Journal of Risk Research* 1:15–44.

Rosa, Eugene A., and Donald L. Clark, Jr. 1999. "Historical Routes to Technological Gridlock: Nuclear Technology as Prototypical Vehicle." *Research in Social Problems and Public Policy* 7:21–57.

Rosa, Eugene, Gary E. Machlis, and Kenneth M. Keating. 1988. "Energy and Society." *Annual Review of Sociology* 14:149–172.

Rosa, Eugene, Allan Mazur, and Thomas Dietz. 1987. "Sociological Analysis of

Risk Impacts Associated with the Sting of a High Level Nuclear Waste Repository: The Case of Hanford." *Proceedings of the Workshop on Assessing Social and Economic Effects of Perceived Risk.* Seattle: Battelle Human Affairs Research Centers.

Rothman, S., and S. Robert Lichter. 1987. "Elite Ideology and Perception in Nuclear Energy Policy." *American Political Science Review* 81:383–404.

Ruckelshaus, William D. 1983. "Science, Risk, and Public Policy." *Science* 221: 1026–1028.

Rummel-Bulska, Iwona. 1991. *Environmental Law in UNEP.* Nairobi, Kenya: United Nations Environment Program.

Russel, Milton, and Michael Gruber. 1987. "Risk Assessment in Environmental Policy-Making." *Science* 236:286–290.

Sagan, Scott D. 1993. *The Limits of Safety: Organizations, Accidents and Nuclear Weapons.* Princeton, NJ: Princeton University Press.

Sandman, Peter M., David B. Sachsman, Michael P. Greenberg, and M. Gotchfeld. 1987. *Environmental Risk and the Press.* New Brunswick, NJ: Transaction Books.

Schnaiburg, Alan. 1980. *The Environment: From Surplus to Scarcity.* New York: Oxford University Press.

Short, James F. 1984. "The Social Fabric at Risk: Toward the Social Transformation of Risk Analysis." *American Sociological Review* 49:711–725.

Short, James F., and Lee Clarke (eds.). 1992. *Organizations, Uncertainties and Risk.* Boulder, CO: Westview Press.

Shrader-Frechette, K. S. 1985. *Risk Analysis and Scientific Method: Methodological and Ethical Problems with Evaluating Societal Hazards.* Dodrecht, Holland: D. Reidel.

———. 1991. *Risk and Rationality: Philosophical Foundations for Populist Reforms.* Berkeley: University of California Press.

Silver, Cheryl Simon, and Ruth S. DeFries. 1992. *One Earth, One Future, Our Changing Global Environment.* Washington, DC: National Academy Press.

Simon, Herbert A. 1982. *Models of Bounded Rationality.* Cambridge, MA: MIT Press.

Slovic, Paul. 1987. "Perception of Risk." *Science* 236:280–285.

———. 1999. "Trust, Emotion, Sex, Politics and Science: Surveying the Risk-Assessment Battlefield." *Risk Analysis* 19:689–701.

Smil, Vaclav. 1993. *China's Environmental Crisis: An Inquiry into the Limits of National Development.* New York: M. E. Sharpe.

Socolow, Robert, C. Andrews, F. Berkhout, and V. Thomas (eds.). 1994. *Industrial Ecology and Global Change.* Cambridge: Cambridge University Press.

Stallings, Robert A. 1990. "Media Discourse and the Social Construction of Risk." *Social Problems* 37:80–95.

———. 1995. *Promoting Risk: Constructing the Earthquake Hazard.* New York: Aldine De Gruyter.

Starr, Chauncey. 1969. "Social Benefit versus Technological Risk." *Science* 165: 1232–1238.

Stern, Paul C. 1991. "Learning through Conflict: A Realistic Strategy for Risk Communication." *Policy Sciences* 24:99–119.

Stern, Paul C., Thomas Dietz, and J. Stanley Black. 1985–86. "Support for Environmental Protection: The Role of Moral Norms." *Population and Environment* 8:204–222.

Stern, Paul C., and Harvey Fineberg. 1996. *Understanding Risk: Informing Decisions in a Democratic Society.* Washington, DC: National Academy Press

Stern, Paul C., Oran R. Young, and Daniel Druckman (eds.). 1992. *Global Environmental Change: Understanding the Human Dimensions.* Washington, DC: National Academy Press.

Szasz, Andrew. 1994. *EcoPopulism: Toxic Waste and the Movement for Environmental Reform.* Minneapolis: University of Minnesota Press.

Taylor, Bron Raymond. 1995. *Ecological Resistance Movements: The Global Emergence of Radical and Popular Environmentalism.* Albany: State University of New York Press.

Taylor, Dorceta. 1992. "The Environmental Justice Movement: No Shortage of Minority Volunteers." *EPA Journal* (March/April):23–25.

Teigen, Karl Halvor, Wibecke Brun, and Paul Slovic. 1988. "Societal Risks as Seen by a Norwegian Public." *Journal of Behavioral Decision Making* 1:111–130.

Thompson, Michael, Richard Ellis, and Aaron Wildavsky. 1990. *Cultural Theory.* Boulder, CO: Westview Press.

Tuller, James. 1985. "Economic Costs and Losses." Pp. 157–174 in *Perilous Progress: Managing the Hazards of Technology*, edited by Robert W. Kates, Christoph Hohenemser, and Jeanne X. Kasperson. Boulder, CO: Westview Press.

Tversky, Amos, and Daniel Kahneman. 1982. "Availability: A Heuristic for Judging Frequency and Probability." Pp. 163–178 in *Judgment under Uncertainty: Heuristics and Biases*, edited by Daniel Kahneman, Paul Slovic, and Amos Tversky. Cambridge: Cambridge University Press.

U.S. National Research Council. 1983. *Risk Assessment in the Federal Government: Managing the Process.* Washington, DC: National Academy Press.

U.S. National Research Council. 1989. *Improving Risk Communication.* Washington, DC: National Academy Press.

U.S. Office of Technology Assessment. 1981. *Assessment of Technologies for Determining Cancer Risks from the Environment.* Washington, DC: U.S. Government Printing Office.

Walsh, Edward J. 1981. "Resource Mobilization and Citizen Protest in Communities around Three Mile Island." *Social Problems* 29:1–21.

Warrick, Cynthia. 1999. "A Theory of Environmental Justice Success: When Impacted Communities Are Likely to Prevail." Doctoral dissertation, George Mason University.

Weber, Max. 1958 [1921]. "Class, Status, Party." Pp. 180–195 in *From Max Weber: Essays in Sociology*, edited by H. H. Gerth and C. Wright Mills. New York: Oxford University Press.

Weidenbaum, Murray. 1977. *Business, Government and the Public.* Englewood Cliffs, NJ: Prentice-Hall.

Weinstein, Neal (ed.). 1987. *Taking Care: Understanding and Encouraging Self-protective Behavior.* New York: Cambridge University Press.

Whipple, Chris (ed.). 1987. *De Minimis Risk.* New York: Plenum Press.

White, Gilbert. 1974. *Natural Hazards: Local, National, Global.* New York: Oxford University Press.

Whitfield, Stephen E. 1998. "Environmental Values, Risk Perception, and Support for Nuclear Technology." Doctoral dissertation, George Mason University.

Wildavsky, Aaron. 1988. *Searching for Safety.* New Brunswick, NJ: Transaction Books.

World Commission on Environment and Development. 1987. *Our Common Future.* Oxford: Oxford University Press.

Young, Oran R. 1989. *International Cooperation: Building Regimes for Natural Resources and the Environment.* Ithaca, NY: Cornell University Press.

*Chapter 12*

# Human Dimensions of Global Environmental Change

*Thomas Dietz and Eugene A. Rosa*

## INTRODUCTION: DEFINING GLOBAL ENVIRONMENTAL CHANGE

*Global environmental change* (GEC), the term used to encompass a variety of ongoing environmental transformations, is the most recent—and perhaps the most threatening—challenge to the biosphere.[1] GEC is usually defined as three interrelated transformations of the biosphere: climate change, loss of biodiversity, and depletion of stratospheric ozone (Stern et al., 1992:18–30). All three of these changes are believed to be generated, or vastly accelerated by, human action. Thus, the GEC literature describes the human component of environmental change as "anthropogenic." These transformations may have substantial impacts on socio-cultural systems as well, though those impacts are even more difficult to anticipate than the biophysical effects.

Because the topic of GEC is of such recent vintage, we cannot review it in the conventional manner, as sociological literature on the topic is just emerging. Our effort, instead, will be to translate the emergent scientific consensus on GEC into a sociological context. This translation highlights a core orientation of environmental sociology: the interpenetration of environmental and social systems, their mutual dependencies, and their reciprocal impacts. We can identify emerging issues and approaches to them, and direct the reader to the literature. We can provide orientation and offer cautions, but not specific directions.[2]

We will examine the key features of each of the three components of GEC in turn, and note the importance of each for humans. We will then outline the systematic features that make an environmental transformation not just local in scope, but global. This outline permits us to identify some emerging candidates for the label "global environmental change," and to sketch its sociological implications.

## Climate Change

Climate has a profound impact on humans. The capacity to support life on earth—including, of course, all human societies—depends on the moderating influences of gases that envelop the planet, warm its surface, and protect it from radiation harmful to life.[3] For perhaps 3.5 billion years of the earth's 4-billion-year history, the earth's envelope of greenhouse gases has been in a proper mix to maintain temperatures in a range in which life flourishes (Benton, 1993). Now, there is growing consensus that human activities are seriously influencing this balance. Humans may be altering the atmosphere in ways that will bring on a very rapid and substantial change in global climate (Bruce et al., 1996; Houghton et al., 1995; Watson et al., 1996).

The most abundant greenhouse gas is carbon dioxide ($CO_2$). As early as 1896, the Swedish physical chemist Svante Arrhenius, winner of the 1903 Nobel Prize in Chemistry, tried to show how human industrial activity since the industrial revolution, by pouring $CO_2$ into the atmosphere, must gradually raise the earth's temperature (Weart, 1992). While no one since has doubted that industrial societies are pumping massive amounts of $CO_2$ into the atmosphere, there has, until recently, been little concern that this would produce noticeable changes in climate. Now, however, there is the more general realization that "The earth has entered a period of hydrological, climatological and biological change that differs from previous episodes of global change in the extent to which it is human in origin" (Stern et al., 1992:17). Among the environmental changes attracting scientific scrutiny, global climate change is one of the principles with which GEC is concerned.[4]

The current scientific consensus is that human activity, especially the release of greenhouse gases, is altering the climate system. To quote the Intergovernmental Panel on Climate Change (IPCC) (1996:22): "the balance of evidence suggests a discernible human influence on global climate." The most credible forecasts suggest an increase in average global temperature of 1.5–3.5°C by the end of the twenty-first century. This change will be distributed unevenly between the equator and the poles (with considerably greater change at the poles), and accompanied by a change in precipitation and soil moisture regimes, sea-level rise, and an increase in weather variability, possibly with extreme events more frequent than they have been in the recent past. The effects of these changes are harder to anticipate, but there is concern that many ecological and socio-cultural systems will face significant stresses. Understanding how human systems might and should respond to these changes is a major research challenge.

Social theorists have, over the course of the past two centuries, pointed to a connection between climate and the social world. Montesquieu wrote: "The laws of Mohammed, which prohibits the drinking of wine, is . . . fitted to the climate of Arabia" (1997:10). Rousseau, writing in the Enlightenment spirit on the unity and natural equality of all humankind, argued that differences among people were "artificial," merely conventional or accidental due to differences in climate (Manicas, 1987:54). The German historian Johann Gottfried Herder saw climate as crucial in the shaping of peoples and civilizations: "The constitution of their body, their way of life, the nature of work and play . . . indeed their whole mentality are climatic" (1969:285).

The idea is even found in the mainstream of sociological thought in the work of Pareto. In his attempt to develop a social system approach to society based upon general equilibrium theory, Pareto explicated the elements determining society's form; among these was climate (1963, Vol. IV). Of course, theories of geographic determinism invoking regional climate to explain cultural features were roundly rejected during the late nineteenth and early twentieth centuries (Harris, 1968). The difference between these climate determinists and more recent work is that the former assumed a direct link between socio-cultural systems or human behavior and average local climate while more recent work emphasizes change in climatic regime. Human ingenuity seems capable of elaborating, in time, a variety of cultural forms within most biophysical systems, so the correlation between average climate and cultural form is attenuated. However, changes in biophysical systems often result in striking transformations of socio-cultural systems. In evolutionary terms, changing climate means that many human actions will have different outcomes than was the case in the past—a change in selection pressures (Burns and Dietz, 1992).

While centuries of social thought have been punctuated with adumbrations to the climate–society connection, it was macro-social historians (scholars seeking to understand the grand sweeps of social history) who explicated links between climate change and society. Climate, for them, played a key role in shaping the modern world. For example, Wallerstein (1974) identifies climate change as one of three physical factors (the other two being the Black Plague[5] and soil conditions) that led to a crisis in Western feudalism.

Similarly, Braudel (1979) documents key climatological events that, on the one hand, brought about the demise of the feudal system while, on the other hand, laid the foundation for the modern social system. Europe experienced a general cooling from around the thirteenth century onward, what has come to be known as the "little ice age," reaching its peak in the reign of Louis XIV (1643–1715).[6] Indeed, the decade of the 1690s was the coldest for seven hundred years, leading Braudel (1979:49) to claim that the little ice age "was more of a tyrant than the Sun King." With their centuries-long lenses of hindsight, macro-social historians have been able to tease out, from proximate social and historical forces, effects of climate change in shaping the modern world. They have fueled a growing scholarly consensus that climate change has had profound historical effects. The sociological imagination points to equally profound effects if current projections of very rapid global climate change are realized.

### Biodiversity Loss

Biodiversity refers to the full range of variability in life, including the genetic variability within a species and the number of species and higher taxa extant in a region and globally. The transformation in forms of human sustenance from food foraging to horticulture depended on favoring genotypes that produced plants and animals with characteristics desirable for domestication. At least since the rise of capitalism, the search for economically productive biodiversity has been an important activity of both the state and private firms (Fowler, 1994). While recent developments in biotechnology may seem to distance human welfare from the genetic diversity of natural systems, humans remain deeply dependent on ecosystem services, such as pollination and nutrient cycling, that are not easily engineered (Daily, 1997). Costanza et al. (1997) have estimated that the flow of ecosystem services for the planet as a whole is worth $16–54 trillion annually. These services take a variety of forms. A number of undomesticated species pollinate both "wild" crops and domesticants, so agricultural activity could be profoundly influenced by a loss of pollinator species. Biogeochemical cycles of critical nutrients, such as nitrogen, are driven in large part by populations of plant and animal species not managed by humans. So too are the hydrologic regimes of most parts of the world. Thus, changes in species composition—one type of change in biodiversity—may have a profound effect on systems critical to humans.

Biodiversity loss is proceeding at a pace unprecedented in human history, and on a scale matching the great geological extinctions that reshaped the taxonomy of life on Earth (Wilson, 1992:24–32; 243–280). Public and policy concerns with biodiversity loss focus on species extinction, but genetic diversity may be lost when a local population dies out, even if the species persists elsewhere, and ecosystem functioning may change as species composition shifts. Thus, all forms of biodiversity loss may be consequential in both practical and ethical terms. There are several proximate driving forces of biodiversity loss, including the destruction of habitat, the introduction of exotic species, and exposure to both persistent and acute toxics.

## Ozone Depletion

Ozone (O$_3$) depletion and the attendant increase in exposure to ultraviolet Type B radiation (UVB) at the earth's surface is the third element in the GEC trinity. Concern with a depletion of stratospheric ozone was first articulated in debates about the development of the commercial supersonic transport in the 1970s (Mazur, 1980). Ozone in the stratosphere provides a "shield" against UVB by absorbing it. A depletion in ozone—the so-called "ozone hole"—leads to a sharp increase in ground-level exposure to UVB. Sustained analytical work by the chemists Rowland, Molina, and Crutzen documented the connection between chlorofluorocarbons (CFCs) and ozone depletion. This research led to the award of the Nobel Prize in Chemistry in 1995, the first given for research on an environmental topic. These researchers and others discovered that some persistent anthropogenic gases change the rates of important chemical reactions in the stratosphere, and thus lead to a reduction in stratospheric O$_3$, which would otherwise absorb ultraviolet Type B (UVB) radiation before it reached the troposphere.

Most important of these ozone-depleting chemicals are a number of chlorofluorocarbon compounds that have found widespread industrial and consumer use since the 1930s (Stern et al., 1992). These compounds were very useful, cheap to produce, and nontoxic. Until they were implicated in stratospheric ozone depletion, they seemed the ideal industrial chemicals.

The increasing loss of ozone and the attendant increase in UVB radiation at the earth's surface have attracted considerable attention. There is concern that increased exposure to UVB will lead to a dramatic rise in skin cancer among human populations with limited skin melanin, and to an increased incidence of cataracts. The effects on other species and ecosystem processes are not well understood, though there are indications that some sensitive species, such as many amphibians, may be severely affected (Blaustein et al., 1995, 1997).

## What Is Global about Global Environmental Change?

What makes a change part of "global environmental change?" Two criteria have been proposed to define an environmental change as global (Stern et al., 1992:25–33; Turner et al., 1991b). First are changes that are globally systemic—they are processes that by their very nature operate at a global level. Second are changes that are local in character but that cumulate into global patterns. Climate changes and ozone depletion are changes of the first type. Biodiversity loss, the destruction of moist forests, and the widespread dispersion of persistent toxics are examples of the second type.

Several other problems are candidates for the label "global environmental change." The global dispersal of persistent toxics, such as heavy metals and compounds that interfere in hormone metabolism, is one. Another is substantial human alteration in global biogeochemical cycles, such as the nitrogen cycle.[7] A third is the change in the global epidemiological regime brought about by several rapid changes, including human population growth, urbanization and urban poverty, high speed global transport, and disruption of tropical ecosystems that have high biodiversity in disease organisms.

While GEC phenomena are global according to at least one of the two defining criteria, they also have local impacts and are generated, at least in part, in the local outcomes of larger social processes; but the context of local actions and impacts are, in the contemporary world, often determined by social, economic, political, and cultural forces that are themselves global. For example, local economic decisions everywhere in the world are conditioned on the structure of the global market. As Frey (1994, 1995, 1998) has documented, the trade in toxic substances, and thus the local use of toxics and exposure to toxics, can only be understood in global terms.

Understanding the human dimensions of global change requires work at both the local and global, or micro and macro levels, and especially work at the meso level that seeks to link phenomena at the micro and macro levels. This is one of the challenges that GEC presents to the social sciences and to environmental sociology in particular.

## Sociology and GEC

There are venerable traditions, such as the macro historians cited above, from which research on the human dimensions of GEC can draw; but for the most part, work on the human dimensions of GEC is in very early stages. Thus, we will structure our review in a way that is admittedly ad hoc, because the field has not yet evolved to the point where a more inductive taxonomy is appropriate. The number of sociological questions raised by contemplating GEC is vast, even daunting. We limit ourselves by discussing only those topics, of the many possibilities, that have begun to yield solid scholarship on GEC per se.

We begin by raising a key metatheoretical issue: What is the nature of the relationship between biophysical phenomena and the perceptions of those phenomena by humans? The debate between social constructivists and realists is a decades-long one. Because understanding of GEC phenomena is rooted in large, broad, complex and uncertain science, GEC has sparked a debate within environmental sociology about these classical issues. Next, we examine this theoretical concern, and also note briefly the problems of spatial and temporal scale and macro-micro linkages involved in understanding the human dimensions of global change (HDGC). We also allude to problems of normative theory.

We then consider the debate over driving forces: the human actions, individual and systemic, that lead to GEC. We emphasize the problem of contextualizing action, which is critical to disentangling arguments about the relative importance of various driving forces. Following this, we consider the role that theory, developed in the tradition of political economy and world systems theory, might play in structuring analysis of driving forces. The new evolutionary theory offers an interesting prospect for integrating these approaches with a more constructivist view.

Perhaps the most venerable tradition in environmental sociology is that of examining public perceptions and concerns. Recent work in this area is becoming more comparative and integrative than has been the case in the past, and it is the subject of the next discussion in this chapter. We then turn to human responses to those perceptions, including individual decision making, social movements, and organizational and state responses; and finally, we consider potential sociological contributions to policy analysis and conclude by reprising key conceptual issues.

## CONSTRUCTING CONSTRUCTIONS AND OTHER THEORETICAL PROBLEMS

### Constructionism and GEC

Social constructivism (see, for example, Buttel and Taylor, 1992; Buttel et al., 1990; Taylor and Buttel, 1992; Wilenius, 1996; Wynne, 1994) can raise serious issues about the ontological realism that underlies the scientific and political claims for GEC. From a strong constructivist perspective, GEC is merely a constructed consensus, not an actual transformation of the state of the world. This reasoning is a form of reductionism—a sociological reductionism: all phenomena, including physical phenomena, can be reduced to socially generated knowledge.

Strong social constructivism has several consequences. First, if widely accepted it would shift the focus of inquiry away from an understanding of GEC per se and toward sociology of knowledge. The key questions would include: Why did a scientific consensus over GEC emerge? What are the social and policy forces shaping this consensus? Whose interests stand to benefit or lose from dominant conceptions or formulations of GEC? These are interesting problems, but the danger here is that focusing on them exclusively would involve a shift in intellectual talent away from addressing the myriad of other GEC problems, and in particular would leave the study of the driving forces of GEC to other disciplines, rendering sociology mute on those issues (Dunlap, 1994). Second, the scientific community will proceed, whatever sociology has to say about the matter, to conduct inquiry on the presupposition that GEC is an ontological state of the world. Should sociology choose to treat GEC only as a sociology of knowledge topic, rather than as a substantive focus of sociological investigation, the discipline will miss an unprecedented opportunity to contribute knowledge to the most comprehensive environmental conceptualization to date. The traditional sciences, having identified the importance of anthropogenic factors in driving global change, now look—more than ever—to the social sciences to provide an understanding of those factors.

Our own position, briefly stated in Chapter 11 of this volume and elaborated in Rosa (1998), is one of ontological realism coupled with an epistemological hierarchy. We agree with the scientific consensus that GEC is a real phenomenon, serious and worthy of attention. However, we also agree with the contructivists that our knowledge of the transformations constituting GEC is inevitably socially constructed, as is all human knowledge. Furthermore, we argue, following Rosa (1998), that this knowledge varies in credibility, if not validity, and therefore forms a hierarchy. Nature imposes constraints, a set of limitations imposed by a world beyond ourselves. It also sends signals about those constraints. Some constraints are easy to discern (such as gravity), while others are very difficult, if not impossible to discern (such as risks of nuclear waste). If, on the one hand, nature's signals are highly ostensible (we can point to instances) and are repeatable, then the constraint will be highly discernable. If, on the other hand, the signals are too weak or too filled with noise to be ostensible and repeatable, then the constraint becomes illusive. The result is a hierarchy of knowledge about nature's constraints. The hierarchy can be illustrated in the context of GEC by pointing to our considerable knowledge of deforestation practices compared to our uncertain knowledge about whether global climate change is occurring.

### Evolutionary and Normative Theory

Rosa's position is consistent with another new contender in the arena of social theory: the new evolutionary theory. The new evolutionary theory focuses on the dynamics of cultural change and on the resulting diversity of culture (Burns and Dietz, 1992; Dietz and Burns, 1992; Eder, 1996; Epstein and Axtell, 1995; Jaeger, 1994; Jaeger et al., 2001; McLaughlin, 1998, 2001). It has several features of interest to environmental sociologists concerned with GEC and other phenomena that work themselves out over large spatial and temporal scales. One is the notion of selection processes, due to feedback from the biophysical environment, that shape culture. This provides a mechanism for linking the social realm with the biophysical that is lacking in strong constructivist theories. But selection can also result from the intentional exercise of power and from biases embedded in culture and existing social arrangements, so the insights of a constructivist position are not lost. The new evolutionary theory is a micro-theory in that it is centrally concerned with how individuals come to take certain actions and not others. This approach is consistent with the methodological approaches we will describe in the next section. Finally, because of its emphasis on culture and language, the new evolutionary theory has implications for normative theory.

Normative theory underlies, and thus is very important in, policy debates on global change. At present, the logic of classical welfare economics dominates discussion of GEC policy. Individuals are assumed to act rationally to maximize individual benefit. In that case, and under some equilibrium assumptions about the functioning of markets, prices reflect social value. When a good or service is not priced in a market, the policy challenge becomes one of identifying what the price should be, so that trade-offs can be made. A number of sociologists have criticized the neoclassical welfare economics approach to social value, but emphasized that the valuation problem is central to policy analysis (Dietz, 1987, 1994; Dietz and Stern, 1998; Freeman, 1992; Freeman and Frey, 1990–1991). Unfortunately, most sociological theory does not offer a systematic theory of value that can be used to develop a mode of policy analysis. Thus, sociologists lack a strong voice in debates about proper methods for coming to collective decisions. The neo-evolutionary approach draws on Habermas in offering a normative theory that emphasizes open discourse for coming to appropriate value positions on policy issues (Dietz, 1994). While not all sociologists will embrace the evolutionary position, we feel it is critical that environmental sociologists work toward a systematic normative theory rather than ceding that territory to welfare economics.

## DRIVING FORCES

It is useful to distinguish human actions that drive global change ("human proximate causes") from the effects of GEC on what people value and attendant responses by people to those effects. This distinction is admittedly arbitrary but provides a useful way to structure an examination of the emerging literature. So we will proceed accordingly, always keeping in mind that driving forces and responses are part of a single dynamic system.

### Understanding Context

A key first principle of sociology is that context matters. We believe, therefore, that a pivotal sociological contribution to GEC research is the recognition of the importance of context and the disciplined incorporation of context into GEC research—matching contexts appropriately to the level of analysis, whether macro, micro, or meso. The incorporation of context into sociological investigation of GEC can proceed in either of two general directions. Progressive contexualization analysis begins with elementary units of analysis, such as individuals and their actions, and incrementally layers social context onto the explanation of what is being investigated. Progressive decomposition analysis begins with macroscopic phenomena and units of analysis, such as the $CO_2$ emissions of a nation-state, and incrementally peels off layers of context until arriving at more elementary units. Using both approaches as complements to one another is more likely to yield robust findings than use of either alone.

The proximate driving forces of GEC are often described as industrial metabolism[8] and land-use change, but to the social scientist, these simple covering terms hide a world of complexity. The problem of identifying driving forces borders on the philosophical because there are so many layers and entry points to the system. Consider an American suburbanite driving an auto to work. The car emits $CO_2$ and thus contributes to global warming. This is an example of industrial metabolism. Consider a Peruvian small landholder cutting tropical forest to clear land for a homestead and attendant fields. The deforestation contributes to biodiversity loss (and with the decomposition of the vegetation, increases the atmospheric $CO_2$ load as well). This is land-use change; but what causes these actions that are presumed to drive GEC?

When the car key turns and the ax swings, where do we attribute causation? The decision to drive can be thought of in social-psychological terms and related to awareness of and concern with global warming and other environmental problems, as well as preferences about various transportation modes and the costs associated with them. However, the ease and cost of taking public transportation, and even attitudes about private cars versus buses or subways, are structurally conditioned. Government agencies and corporations have, for decades, followed policies that make the choice of the private auto easier and cheaper, and public transit harder and more expensive than might otherwise have been the case. So, too, for the Peruvian smallholder—the local political economy shapes opportunities, making some things easy, others difficult, and still others impossible; and the local political economy is embedded in a history of a global political economy and political ecology.

This is a critical issue for anyone thinking about the driving forces of global change. One useful way of conceptualizing the problem is to begin with individual action and successively examine ever-broader contexts in which the action is embedded (Vayda, 1988). The idea is to model in centrifugal fashion analogous to the dropping of a pebble into a pond that produces concentric circles of waves.

## Individuals Act

The context of the individuals' actions, the basis for their decisions, includes personal history and their environmental, community, organizational, and institutional circumstances, as they perceive and interpret them. Thus, while individual action (and its biophysical consequences) is the starting point for analysis, more explanatory power may come from variables that describe the context than from those that describe the individual. Circumstances in which all individuals in one context exhibit the same behavior, which is quite distinct from the behavior of seemingly similar individuals in a different context, suggests that the variables describing contextual variation are more important than those explaining individual variation. On the other hand, there will be circumstances in which substantial variation persists across individuals, even when they face the same context.

While this approach provides a logic for assessing the explanatory power of alternative levels of explanation and types of theory, it is difficult to implement. The strategy applied to real problems involving many individual characteristics and many overlapping levels of contextualization (class, community, culture, local political economy, position in the world system, etc.) requires challenging analytical frames and very substantial amounts of data. Furthermore, the data must have a structure that allows differentiation among key variables and concepts so that their effects can be distinguished and compared. Analysis of particular problems, such as energy consumption in the United States or deforestation in Latin America, usually cannot be disciplined with adequate data, and so debates about the proper level of explanation continue.

### Some Cautions

As Palloni (1994) emphasizes in his excellent meta-analysis of the relationship between population and deforestation, phenomona such as deforestation are multidimensional. A single term like *deforestation* may or may not adequately describe biophysical effects, because it aggregates a series of social phenomona that have very different causes. Deforestation may occur because of clearing by landless peasants or smallholders seeking living and crop space. It may occur in the search for fuelwood; or it may occur because of clearing for cattle or large-scale farming, logging, or clearing as an ancillary to road building, mining, or other activities. The same trees may be cut in the same area and the biophysical effects of deforestation carried out for each of these reasons may be the same, but the human actions are motivated by very different factors, and thus the driving forces for each type of deforestation will be different.

There also is a practical problem for those considering research on GEC. It is important that scarce social science resources be directed to understanding the most consequential drivers of global change. We endorse the attention to priorities suggested by Stern et al. (1992:44–53). When choosing a particular phenomenon for study, researchers should work backwards from the environmental impact to determine how consequential the phenomenon really is. We note, for example, a substantial body of research on household recycling. This research may be useful if results can be generalized to other behaviors that are more environmentally significant, but recycling per se, while a convenient object for study, is certainly not the most environmentally significant behavior undertaken in the affluent nations. Even in the domain of waste reduction, studies of demand for recycled products seem more important than studies of household recycling.

Stern et al. (1992:44–52) apply this strategy to greenhouse gas emissions. They note that fossil fuel use contributes about 46 percent of human contributions to greenhouse warming, CFCs (which are potent greenhouse gases as well as ozone depletors) about 25 percent, biomass burning about 15 percent, agriculture about 8 percent, and landfills and other sources about 6 percent. Of the 46 percent of greenhouse warming that can be attributed to fossil fuel use, transportation is responsible for 12 percent of greenhouse warming (or about a quarter of fossil fuel use), buildings about 14 percent (30% of fossil fuel use), and industrial uses about 20 percent (43% of fossil fuel use). This suggests that industrial energy use should be a high priority for research.

### Energy Consumption as an Example

The tradition of energy consumption research begun in the 1970s is being invigorated as various aspects of individual, household, and organizational consumption are examined (Cramer et al., 1985; Lutzenhiser, 1993; Lutzenhiser and Hackett, 1993; Rosa et al., 1988:160–163; Stern et al., 1997). In the past, this research has tended to focus on either social-psychological or social-structural factors. As is the case for the closely related literature on environmental attitudes reviewed below, the next step would seem to be theory that integrates social-structural and social-psychological factors as causes of individual behavior. That is, social-psychological understanding of energy consumption must be embedded in a social-structural understanding of what constrains choices and what shapes attitudes, perceptions, and life styles.

The energy research literature can also act as a model for broader research on consumption. Inter- and intranational variation in consumption is immense, and is not entirely a result of differences in income and prices, as economic theory would emphasize. Differing consumption patterns lead to substantial differences in environmental impact. More research is needed on consumption as a driving force of global change (Stern et al., 1997).

Little work has been done on resource consumption and decision making at higher levels of aggregation. Lough (1996) offers provocative evidence regarding the energy efficiency of organizational form in the U.S. economy. The emerging literature on industrial ecology notes the importance of corporate decisions about production and marketing and government decisions regarding regulation and purchasing, but this area has not been much explored by social scientists (but see Dietz and Hawley, 1983). Below we will review the limited literature on corporate and governmental response to GEC.

### Macro-modeling

While we advocate the use of progressive contextualization, it is sometimes useful to follow a strategy of progressive decomposition that moves in the opposite direction, starting with aggregate, or macro, phenomena and examining the processes from which they are built. The popular but simple IPAT model provides a useful starting point for examining macro-modeling (Dietz and Rosa, 1994, 1997a, 1997b). The IPAT model holds that:

$$\text{Impact} = \text{Population} \times \text{Affluence} \times \text{Technology}.$$

We have recast this into a stochastic framework:

$$I = aP^b A^c T^d e$$

and suggest that I, P, A, T, and e must be thought of as sets of variables rather than single variables. We call this approach STIRPAT, for "Stochastic Impacts by Regression of Population, Affluence and Technology." The challenge is to develop a reasonable theoretical specification of these variables as drivers of environmental impact. While any aggregate unit of analysis, from the household to the biosphere as a whole, might be used in estimating such a model, most work has focused on the nation-state, in part because data are readily available at that level and in part because the nation-state figures prominently in macro-comparative theory that can be brought to bear on the problem. In a provocative paper, Richerson and Boyd (1997/1998) provide a model that integrates social and biophysical factors. They suggest how social structure (including differential power and exploitation) can be included in an environmental model. The model suggests key relationships to be investigated in the STIRPAT framework.

Dietz and Rosa (1997a) have estimated a model of national $CO_2$ emissions using population size for P and gross domestic product per capita as A. The residual term e then captures all other factors. They find a nonproportional effect of population, with diseconomies of scale at the largest population sizes. Affluence has the effect that has been labeled the "Kuznets" curve (Kuznets, 1955). The effect of affluence, in terms of gross domestic product per capita, reaches a peak at about $10,000 and declines thereafter. (See also Cropper and Griffiths, 1994; Grossman and Krueger, 1995; Holtz-Eakin and Selden, 1995; Knapp and Mookerjee, 1996; Selden and Song, 1994; Shafik, 1994; Tucker, 1995.) These models are being elaborated in several recent papers by sociologists (Crenshaw and Jenkins, 1996; Roberts and Grimes, 1997). This literature demonstrates the potential for macro-level modeling of global change that integrates realistic understanding of biophysical processes with insights of the sociological theory of the state and world system.

Another macro approach is quantitative historical analysis that looks at the other side of the climate change question: namely, what are the societal concomitants of the industrialization that drives the need for fossil fuel— the principle source of $CO_2$ load? (Rosa, 1997). Are high $CO_2$-producing nations better off than lower-producing nations? Does societal well-being, broadened beyond purely economic measures, track trends in $CO_2$ loads? An answer to these questions will improve our understanding of the relationship between the anthropogenic causes of climate change and overall social change. It also would provide a basis for international strategies and policies for averting or mitigating climate change.

A number of works have focused on national or regional determinants of deforestation or biodiversity loss (Allen and Barnes, 1985; Brown and Pearce, 1994; Burns et al., 1994; Cropper and Griffiths, 1994; Deacon, 1994; Dietz et al., 1991; Kick et al., 1996; Rudel, 1989; Rudel and Horowitz, 1993). The model specifications and data sets used vary so much across studies that it is hard to draw any general conclusions. A variety of divergent theoretical arguments suggest a diversity of candidate causal factors. Population growth, rural poverty, and inequality in land ownership, export-dominated economies, failure of property rights and explicit government policies to promote deforestation have all been indicted in the literature. Palloni's (1994) meta-analysis of many of these studies suggests that population pressure may influence deforestation, but he notes (1994: 137) the complexity involved in understanding population effects:

First, population growth operates *through* [emphasis in original] land inequality and both factors are part of a rather lengthy causal chain: the more remote the connection (the higher the number of intermediate stages) the less relevant population growth will be and the higher the likelihood that its effects will be twisted, bent and even dissipated by a sequel of contingencies punctuating the chain. This does not mean that population growth does not have any effects; it only implies that its effects are felt insofar as they are efficiently transmitted by mediating factors. Second, the effects of population growth can be attenuated and delayed within social and political contexts that favor the reallocation of wealth and cushion the fall in per capita yields. These social and political conditions are thus contingencies that alter the responses to changes in population growth.

These remarks could also be applied to the effects of any other driving force. The causal linkages are complex, context-specific, and contingent on other variables. Indeed, this is why, with even as simple a model as IPAT, we insist that the variables explicitly included in the equation are actually a subset of the relevant variables. Thus, estimated effects must be seen as conditional on model specification, and improved understanding will come from exploring alternative models.

Rudel (1995) has examined reforestation associated with the Tennessee Valley Authority's efforts in the U.S. Southwest. His analysis provides insights into both structural effects and the effectiveness of government action in restoring biodiversity. A more common approach is examining the driving forces of biodiversity loss (Balmford and Long, 1995; Ceballos and Brown, 1994; Forester and Machlis, 1996; Kerr and Currie, 1995; McNeely et al., 1996; Neumann and Machlis, 1989). As with the work noted above on deforestation, the models and data sets used are diverse and the literature too new to allow a discernment of generalizable patterns. Nevertheless, it is indicative of moves toward developing macro-comparative social models of a broader diversity of biophysical phenomena.[9]

### Local and Regional Case Studies

In addition to these quantitative analyses at the aggregate level, there are a substantial number of local or regional case studies of deforestation, including those by Babu and Hassan (1995), Faber (1992), Jones (1990), Moran (1993), Rudel and Horowitz (1993), and Stonich (1993). The varied conclusions of these case studies indicate the difficulty in unraveling the casual links among the drivers of global environmental change. Palloni (1994) uses Ragin's (1987) method for applying Boolean logic to case studies to examine the effects of population on deforestation in 55 such studies. As with his examination of cross-national studies, he concludes that the effects of population pressure on deforestation are contingent on other factors, and vary depending on the reason deforestation is taking place. Population pressure by itself can generate clearing by smallholders or clearing for fuel. Any other effects of population are contingent on land distribution, access to credit, markets and technologies, land tenure, and government policies. While this result is complex, it demonstrates how human action generates global change and how various political, economic, cultural, and other factors shape the contexts in which actions are taken.

As some case studies and many policy discussions note, social stratification must be considered in understanding GEC. Policy debates often center around the appropriate actions to be taken by the affluent industrial nations that generated much of the current atmospheric load of greenhouse gases and ozone-depleting compounds, and the less affluent nations who hope to increase their degree of affluence and standard of living. If the less affluent nations follow a development trajectory that has even a fraction of the environmental impacts of those generated over the last century by the currently industrialized nations, massive reductions in emissions by the rich nations will be required to stabilize or reduce overall environmental impact. Looking at the "environmental Kuznets curve" referred to above, increases in affluence and population over the next quarter century will move all but a very few nations toward increasing impacts—there are very few nations at a level of affluence that leads to declining impacts.

In addition, impacts differ by social class. Within nearly every nation there are the affluent and the poor. The activities of the affluent drive industrial emissions and also have some responsibility for biodiversity loss. The activities of the poor are more likely to generate local pollution, especially water pollution, and may have some link to biodiversity loss when land is cleared for farming or firewood.

## THEORIES OF THE DRIVING FORCES

Current research on the driving forces of GEC accepts the reality of the biophysical phenomena involved in global change, such as $CO_2$ emissions and changes in ecosystem function and structure. Thus, theories that can structure work on driving forces must adhere to a neorealist perspective, in contrast to the social constructionist approaches to GEC described above. By neorealist we mean approaches that view the socially constructed claims or the culturally discoursed aspects of human life as a transcendent structure that rests upon a foundation that presupposes a material world independent of percipient human actors (Rosa and Dietz, 1998). The fruitful tradition of research on the political economy of environmental problems, the world systems tradition, and the emerging evolutionary approach all provide neorealist scaffoldings on which to build a theory of driving forces.

### Development Theory

Economists argue that environmental quality is a luxury good that is not of much interest until societies reach a high level of affluence. This argument is directly parallel to classical development theory in sociology and also to Inglehart's (1995) postmaterialist thesis. The curvilinear relationship of the so-called Kuznet's curve between impact and affluence obtains because a threshold is reached where willingness to pay for environmental protection becomes greater than the costs associated with achieving it, or because competing risks to health, safety, and well-being have been sufficiently reduced that environmental quality becomes the next societal priority. In this formulation, Inglehart's hypothesis specifies the social-psychological mechanism underpinning the societal shift. It is also possible that shifting consumption patterns that accompany greater affluence will lead to reduced impact and dematerialization (Stern et al., 1997). As the ratio of information to material in goods consumed increases, and as information per se becomes an ever more important consumption good, environmental impact will decrease.

A less optimistic explanation is that the new international division of labor has shifted the most environmentally disruptive activities to the least affluent nations, leaving relatively clean service industries in the most affluent nations. Reduced environmental impact from industries in the affluent nations is thus an artifact of changes taking place for other reasons. The impacts still occur, but in different locations.

### Political Economy of Environmental Problems

The neorealist political economy of the environment has origins that stretch back at least to Malthus and the debate about resource limitations on human welfare, but contemporary work can be traced to Charles Anderson's (1976) *The Sociology of Survival*. Anderson, drawing on the work of Baran and Sweezy (Baran, 1957; Baran and Sweezy, 1966; Sweezy, 1968/1942; Sweezy and Magdoff, 1972), argued that capitalism requires growth, and that growth will ultimately lead to dire environmental consequences.[10] Schnaiberg (1980) expands on this idea that growth and the need to externalize costs of production leads to environmental degradation, in his very influential work *The Environment: From Surplus to Scarcity*.[11] Schnaiberg adds a critical political and social dimension to the problem of growth. The key concept for Schnaiberg is the "treadmill of production"— the momentum for environmental degradation caused by the need to produce profits to fulfill the capitalist imperative of growth. Coalitions emerge from diverse segments of society who are committed to the treadmill of production. It is this treadmill that produces the growth necessary for capitalist profits, increasing benefits to labor and state tax revenues so it is difficult for any of these sectors to "step off the treadmill."[12]

The political economy tradition takes the reality of environmental impacts and their potential adverse effects as relatively unproblematic,[13] but analysis of local environmental struggles and conflicts with growth machines opens an interesting space for social construction within the political economy tradition. While neorealists see health effects of toxics, for example, as real and not primarily social constructions, emerging work acknowledges that it is hard for people to detect these effects and to go from detection to an understanding of the contamination that produces them and the political and economic situation that allows or even encourages such problems (Brown and Mikkelsen, 1990). The reconstruction of community understanding takes place through agentic action by those dealing with local problems but opposed by structural forces. The large-scale political economy of a society and many of its impacts on the biophysical environment are repeated and ostensible in modern society, and thus are adequately theorized with a neorealist perspective; but local manifestations are far more subtle and idiosyncratic. Specific manifestations are hard to pin down and are much more subject to definitional struggles of the sort emphasized by the interpretive approach. Indeed, it has been suggested that definitions play a major role in struggles over environmental policy (Dietz et al., 1989).[14] The tensions between the macro and the micro are the focus of recent work by Schnaiberg and his collaborators (Gould et al., 1996).

## World Systems Theory

While Anderson emphasized problems of development and the Third World, Schnaiberg and his collaborators have focused on developed countries, especially the United States. In the early twenty-first century, as environmental sociology struggles to understand climate change and other global phenomena, an approach that goes beyond individual nations is needed. As noted above, pioneers in world systems theory, including Braudel and Wallerstein, considered climate change a phenomenon of great historical importance in generating social transformation. So we might expect that world systems theory would have carefully examined the causes and consequences of environmental problems over the last quarter century and provided a useful perspective on the relationship of development to environment. However, as Roberts and Grimes (2001) have noted, world systems theory has largely ignored environmental change as either a cause or consequence of human action.

World systems theory is thoroughly materialist and neorealist, but its emphasis on structural determinants of national actions and conditions seems to have left some of the insights of its founders at the periphery of its vision. In contrast to the political economy tradition, the environment is undertheorized in world systems theory.[15] The initial attempts to examine environmental degradation treat it as one more social phenomenon that can be explained with the same variables used to model economic growth, income inequality within a nation, or quality of life. The more peripheral or dependent a nation, the more its environment will be degraded, just as peripheral and dependent nations will have slower growth, more inequality, and lower quality of life.

There are some important exceptions to this current limitation of world systems theory. Bunker (1984, 1985, 1996) has noted that the extraction of "rents" by exploitation of land and other natural resources can be an important source of profit for capitalists, and can lead to severe environmental degradation in the Third World. Roberts (1996) has suggested some of the domestic political factors that may influence a nation's participation in international environmental treaties. In a series of papers, Frey (1994, 1995, 1998) has examined the internal factors that make peripheral nations especially susceptible to technological hazards. These efforts provide important starting points for embedding the theoretical insights of the political economy approach in the broader historical and comparative perspective offered by world systems theory. This integration should lead to neorealist accounts of environmental issues at the global level that draw on the strengths of both world systems theory and national-level analyses of political economy.

In an interesting extension of world systems theory Roberts and Grimes (1997) argue that there is no overall Kuznets curve of the sort adopted by economists and described above. Rather, since the oil crisis of the 1970s, affluent nations in the core have become more carbon efficient, that is, they produce more GDP per unit carbon dioxide emissions. In contrast, the carbon efficiency of middle-income nations has gone down slightly and the carbon efficiency of the least affluent nations has dropped substantially. They explain this pattern using world systems theory. The poorest nations are locked into a pattern of high and even increasing environmental impact per unit affluence, while affluent nations may indeed follow the patterns proposed by development theory. If this is true, then any conclusions drawn from a developmental logic are seriously flawed, since only core nations follow the developmental pattern postulated.[16]

Political, economic, and world systems approaches present clear arguments for why the environment will be degraded in capitalist societies, and in the dependent nations in the world system. Capitalism generates growth that is supported by local and national elites. The unequal division of wealth and power across and within nations exacerbates the problem, but arguments as to why the driving forces of GEC might be altered are not as well developed. A theory of environmental protection is particularly important when dealing with climate change and other global environmental problems. For local or regional environmental problems there are ostensible and repeated adverse effects from environmental degradation. Groups opposing the treadmill of production emerge because the members of these oppostional groups come to see the harm to them caused by environmental degradation. But climate change and other global environmental problems are planetary collective goods. Emissions of carbon dioxide, methane, and chlorofluorocarbons, the principle greenhouse gases, produce no circumscribed local environmental problems. The adverse effects of such environmental disruption only come on time scales of decades to centuries and at global spatial scales.

The logic for opposing emissions of substances toxic to humans and the degradation of local ecosystems does not generalize to greenhouse gas emissions; and, as noted above, climate change impacts can be understood only through the application of rather sophisticated modeling and analysis. The impacts are neither ostensible nor repeated. The growing concern with climate change must be explained, at least in part, by the rise of environmentalist worldviews and values that emphasize concern with the welfare of other people distant in time and space from the local community and environmental protection, even in the face of scientific uncertainty.[17] To understand responses to climate change threats, we must have a theory that involves both the structural constraints emphasized by neorealist theory and the consciousness formation and agency emphasized by the interpretive tradition.

### Toward an Integrative Theory

McLaughlin (1998, 2001) has suggested that sociology's problems in integrating agency and structure are deep rooted, resting on the nominalist/essentialist distinction that first developed in Greek philosophy. The nominalist (or sometimes "idealist") position corresponds to the interpretive approach in modern social theory, while the essentialist approach matches the modern neorealists'. McLaughlin concludes that the only way past this problem is to adopt an evolutionary approach grounded in population and selection dynamics.[18] There are several emerging strains of evolutionary thinking, including work by Boyd and Richerson (1985), Burns and Dietz (1992), Eder (1996), Epstein and Axtell (1995), Jaeger (1994; Jaeger et al., 2001), and McLaughlin and Khawaja (2000). The evolutionary approach intends to link biophysical phenomena to the social construction of cultural views, and to incorporate both power and agency in accounts of social dynamics. While still in the early stages of development, it appears that this approach holds great promise.

## PERCEIVING GEC

For 25 years, researchers have examined public perceptions of environmental problems (Chapter 15, this volume). Recently, this community of environmental attitude researchers has begun important new initiatives related to both the theoretical and substantive problems of GEC. The substantive changes are themselves interesting—researchers have moved attention from either general environmental concern or local and regional problems such as air and water pollution to public understanding of and concern with global problems such as ozone depletion, climate change, and loss of biodiversity (Berk and Schulman, 1995; Jaeger et al., 1993; Lave and Dowlatabadi, 1993; Löfstedt, 1991, 1992; Rebetez, 1996). Some of this work has been qualitative, exploring the character of public beliefs and concerns through in-depth interviews rather than the usual survey instruments (Kempton et al., 1995); but perhaps more important, there has been a move toward more integrative theory.

Until recently, there were two rather distinct lines of research on environmental concern. One was social-psychological. It emphasized such theories as Schwartz's model of norm activation and altruism (Heberlein, 1977; Stern et al., 1986); or work following Rokeach that emphasizes values (Dunlap et al., 1983; Stern and Dietz, 1994; Stern et al., 1995, 1999); or Dake's, (1991) derivations of "orienting dispositions" from Douglas and Wildavsky's (1982) so-called "cultural theory" of risk; or Inglehart's (1995) use of his theory of postmaterialism as an explanation for environmental concern. The other tradition emphasized socio-demographic variation in environmental concern. However, with the exception of correlations with age/cohort, ethnicity, and gender, it was undertheorized (Jones and Dunlap, 1992; Van Liere and Dunlap, 1980).

Interest in global environmental phenomena has facilitated cooperation, funding, and attempts at integrative theorizing. Stern et al. (1995, 1999) have attempted to develop models that link the social-psychological with the social-structural and ask how individuals come to form opinion about emergent problems such as ozone depletion or climate change that were not on the public agenda even a few years ago. Dunlap and his collaborators have begun analysis of the broadly comparative "Health of the Planet" survey (Dunlap et al., 1993; Dunlap and Mertig, 1995, 1997). This survey, which includes data on environmental perceptions and concerns from 24 nations, is beginning to answer broad, comparative questions about the relationship between environmental concern and national development, individual characteristics, and other important theoretical constructs.

## Movements and Organizations

Public concern and individual and household behavior are hardly the endpoint of understanding human response to GEC. A new and more comparative interest in social movements is emerging. This was prompted to some degree with theorizing about the environmental movement as a "new social movement" and the engagement of environmental sociology with the work of Habermas and Foucault (Brulle, 1995). At the broadest level, the new work on the environmental movement suggests that social movements should be considered as the nexus in which new perceptions, analyses, and strategies emerge in response to new social problems (Brulle, 1993). Empirical work has emphasized the historical developments of the various strains of the U.S. environmental movement, its links to other institutions, and the comparative and global analysis of environmental movements (Brulle, 1995; Dunlap and Mertig, 1995; Lipschutz and Conca, 1993; McLaughlin and Khawaja, 2000; Princen and Finger, 1994; Taylor, 1995).

Private organizations are also responding to the public arguments regarding GEC.[19] Some of these changes have produced resistance by major corporations and nations that believe they will be adversely influenced by policies developed to mitigate global change.[20] One manifestation of this resistance has been the rise to prominence of a series of global change nay-sayers who impugn the consensus science. Because of a media dynamic that suggests all sides to an argument should have equal time, the press gives substantial coverage to critics who have little or no record of scientific work in the areas under debate. Property rights and "wise-use" movements in the United States have been vociferous opponents of the endangered species act and various measures to manage ecosystems for sustainability. In some cases in the United States and elsewhere, environmentalists have been subject to terrorism, murder, and in the case of Nigerian environmental activist Ken Saro-Wiwa and his colleagues, even execution at the hands of the state.

These examples of resistance and denial represent an extreme, albeit common form of corporate or state response. More reasoned and reasonable strategies also occur. At the individual and small-firm level, some have suggested that GEC is sufficiently small in magnitude and sufficiently slow in its pace that rational strategists such as small farmers will easily adapt by shifting production strategies (Nordhaus, 1994). One may anticipate some division between industrial sectors and within an industrial sector. DuPont, the major manufacturer of the chlorofluorocarbon compounds implicated in ozone depletion may have been relatively quick to endorse a ban on such compounds because the company felt it could shift to alternatives more quickly and profitably than its competitors (Benedick, 1991). In other cases, some industries, such as insurance, may see unmitigated climate change as a major threat to their future viability, and may urge public policy at odds with that supported by other industries (Tucker, 1996). Furger (1998) has offered the provocative argument that insurance mechanisms and the institutions that enforce insurance rules create a strong concern with factors such as climate change that increase overall risk. These institutions, and others private bodies like them that establish, and in some cases enforce, environmental standards within an industry may provide an interesting and efficient mechanism for environmental regulation in situations that fall beyond national sovereignty.

Political scientists have suggested that global environmental problems have led to new international regulatory regimes and they have tried to understand why some nations participate and others do not (Lipschutz and Conca, 1993; Young et al., 1996).[21] They have also highlighted the role of the scientific community in helping to shape regulatory treaties and the organizational mechanisms to monitor and enforce them, suggesting that "epistemic" international communities of scientists have emerged (Haas, 1993, 1997; Haas and Haas, 1995). Presumably, it is these networks that are engaged in the social construction of problems that have interested some sociologists. Sociologists to date have paid little heed to this work, though Dietz and Kalof (1992) have developed a measure of "state environmentalism" based on participation in international treaties. The structural determinants of this measure have been examined by Roberts (1996).

Frank (1997) provides a quantitative historical analysis of conceptual and structural factors driving the adoption of international environmental treaties. Canan (1993) monitored in detail the efforts to implement the ozone protocol by government and industry officials, environmentalists, and scientists, but clearly there is a need for a more sociological approach to international environmental policy.

## CONCLUSION

Global Environmental Change (GEC) invokes serious international concerns among scholars and politicians while simultaneously embedding historical irony. The first irony is that GEC is the belated recognition of the global scale of a variety of environmental problems; indeed, it is that scale that not only defines these problems as global but also underpins their reconceptualization. It was over a century ago, as noted above, that the Swedish chemist and physicist Svante Arrhenius, who had a knack for finding meaningful patterns in seemingly random data, argued that carbon dioxide in the atmosphere trapped heat like a greenhouse and, therefore, was the basis for the periodic episodes of global warming and cooling. Furthermore, the fossil fuel revolution of industrialization was pumping ever-larger amounts of $CO_2$ into the atmosphere, thereby increasing the chances of trapping more heat. This was not only a germinal hypothesis; it was a fundamental reconceptualization of the relationship between human activities and natural processes—a fundamental reconceptualization of scale to include the entire globe.

Decades later the Russian chemist Vernadsky (1965) coined the term *biosphere*—again advancing a reconceputalization of human ecological processes to a global scale. Human life was intimately and inextricably dependent on the biosphere; man [*sic*] could not "cut the umbilical cord between himself and the biosphere of the earth." (Laptev, 1977[1973]:112). A decade later the chemists F. Sherwood Rowland and Mario Molina warned of the dangers to the protective upper atmospheric ozone due to the use of chlorofluorocarbons (CFCs). After considerable early controversy, their findings were adopted as part of scientific consensus, and two decades later they were, along with Paul Crutzen, awarded the Nobel Prize in Chemistry. These developments, plus many similar scientific advances, fostered the awareness that certain environmental problems could best be understood at the global level.

The reconceptualization in science was followed by political awareness. A series of international agreements were forged to protect the ozone layer by reducing emissions of CFCs and other compounds that deplete stratospheric ozone (Benedick, 1991). At the Earth Summit held in Rio de Janeiro in 1992, treaties to protect global biodiversity and to reduce the emissions of greenhouse gases were also debated, though there was, and is, far less consensus on these problems than on ozone depletion, because the interests of more nations and more corporations seem at risk from strong action on biodiversity or climate change. Yet while these treaties are the most prominent, there is a long history of international cooperation to protect the environment. For example, an Antarctic Treaty was developed in 1959, a nuclear test ban treaty in 1963, and the Ramsar Treaty to protect wetlands in 1971 (World Resources Institute 1992:357–367). As early as 1900, colonial powers agreed to the Convention for the Preservation of Animals, Birds and Fish in Africa (Bonner, 1993); but the GEC tryptich seems to have placed a new emphasis on international cooperation to solve problems that are global and long term.

The second irony is that a scientific consensus is emerging that GEC can, for the most part, be traced to anthropogenic—that is, human—causes. Thus, while the biological and physical sciences have identified the biophysical process leading to GEC ($CO_2$ buildup, deforestation, loss of biodiversity, ozone depletion, etc.), they are not accustomed to understanding either the human driving forces nor the human responses to GEC. The social sciences are, or at least should be, well suited to this task, yet sociology has barely engaged GEC.

In this unorthodox review of the literature, we have attempted to identify the major biospheric transformations constituting GEC. While our understanding of the many nuances of GEC is still meager, the overall contours of GEC are coming into view. Biospheric transformations that are globally systemic, such as climate change, or cumulative on a large geographical scale, such as biodiversity loss, are properly labeled "global." Conceptualizing the environment at this scale provides a vantage point for examining large-scale biospheric change. Conceptualizing at this scale also reveals the daunting magnitude of GEC problems.

We also outlined the importance of sociological work on GEC, especially with respect to contexts, and provided some analytic guidelines of how we might proceed with such work. Then, the incipient sociological literature—consisting primarily of sociology of knowledge questions, macro-modeling, and assessment of perceptions and attitudes—was reviewed. This early work is promising, but much more is needed.

Finally, we pointed to one of the principal insights and key opportunities of GEC, namely, that GEC has been a stimulus to the integration of theory and analysis; not only theoretical integration among the various social sciences, but also theoretical integration between the biological and physical and the social sciences. This is an exciting opportunity and challenge. To the extent that sociology is up to the challenge, it will represent significant progress in the substance and stature of environmental sociology.

## NOTES

This work was supported in part by National Science Foundation grants SES-9109928 and SES-9311593, by the Dean of the College of Liberal Arts at Washington State University, and by funds from the Edward R. Meyer Distinguished Professorship in Environmental and Natural Resource Policy. We thank Henrietta Bullinger for her careful reading of the manuscript.

1. The term *global environmental change* is often abbreviated to global change in the scientific and policy community. Sociologists sometimes try to appropriate the term *global change* for such global phenomena as the spread of democratic forms and capitalist markets. While there is some flexibility about what is covered by the term *global environmental change*, attempting to expand it to cover socio-economic phenomena is imprecise and confusing.

2. We will emphasize work in sociology because that is the focus of this volume. For a review of the literature from a much broader range of disciplines, we recommend Stern et al. (1992). Turner et al. (1991a) provide an overview of anthropogenic environmental change. The psychological literature has been reviewed by Stern (1992).

3. Indeed, it is this "greenhouse" phenomonon that accounts for the prevalence of life on Earth, in contrast to its closest planetary neighbors. In what is sometimes called the "Goldilocks effect," Venus, with a "runaway" greenhouse effect, is too warm to support carbon-based life, while Mars, at least in recent times, has insufficient greenhouse warming to provide life-supporting temperatures. The temperature on Earth is "just right."

4. Global warming was one the pivotal topics at the 1992 Earth Summit in Brazil, where leaders from around the world expressed an urgency to develop international agreements to reduce global $CO_2$ emissions.

5. Climate is even implicated in the spread of plague, for hot summers could have led to the multiplication of the rat and flea populations, the principal carriers of plague.

6. Braudel (1979:49) writes: "There was a general cooling down of the northern hemisphere, for example, in the fourteenth century. The glaciers advanced, ice-floes were more numerous and winters became more severe. The Vikings' route to America was cut short by dangerous icebergs. . . . This climatic drama appears to have interrupted Scandinavian colonization in Greenland; the bodies of the last survivors, found in the frozen earth, are thought to be poignant testimony to this." It also appears that the climate of some areas, such as Scandinavia and China, was unusually warm from the ninth to the fourteenth centuries A.D. (Hughes and Diaz, 1994). Emerging evidence suggests that there are other periodicities in climate with frequencies ranging from years to millennia (Bond et al., 1997; Oppo, 1997; Stern and Easterling, 1999). The effects of these fluctuations on human history have yet to be investigated.

7. Since the "Greenhouse effect" is driven in large part by $CO_2$, it is a result of changes in the global carbon cycle.

8. The term *industrial metabolism*, drawing on a physiological metaphor, was coined by Robert Ayres (1989). It suggests an analytical framework for accounting

for all the processes by which an industrial society, like a living body, takes in substances, uses them, and disposes of them.

9. We suggest two cautions in macro-comparative modeling. First, there is an unfortunate tendency among sociologists to mix linear, log, and quadratic terms in a model, resulting in a functional form that is uninterpretable. Second, there is a tendency to attend to measurement error in social variables while ignoring such error in biophysical variables.

10. In an interesting complement, Jaeger (1994), in offering a general theory of human ecology and social change, suggests that sustainable societies must have an average corporate rate of profit of zero.

11. The influence of Anderson's arguments about growth is evident in Schnaiberg's work. He cites Anderson in seven of his nine chapters.

12. There is a parallel neo-Marxist approach to environment, flowing from O'Connor's work on the crisis tendencies of capitalism (O'Connor, 1994). Like the world systems theorists we discuss below, the American neo-Marxist tradition has only recently begun to theorize about the environment, so in the interests of brevity, we do not examine this approach in any detail.

13. Schnaiberg (1980:277–361) has noted the imbalance in the development of our scientific knowledge of impacts compared to the development of production-oriented science and engineering. This provides an interesting starting place for a political economy of environmental knowledge.

14. The nation-state is usually the nexus for definitional struggles. The neo-Marxist literature on which the political economy tradition draws includes a long and active debate on the relative autonomy of the state, but these discussions have only occasionally emerged in discussions of the environment (Buttel, 1985; Schnaiberg 1994).

15. For example, in Chase-Dunn (1989), environmental problems are mentioned only twice, once in a paragraph summarizing Bunker's work (p. 234) and once in passing while dismissing concerns with rapid population growth (p. 262). In a recent review paper, Chase-Dunn and Grimes (1995) mention environmental issues in only two paragraphs dealing with limits to trends in the world system. However, during the time this chapter was in press, the electronic *Journal of World Systems Research* (http://csf.colorado.edu/wsystems/jwsr.html) published a special issue (V3, #3) on the environment. This engagement of world systems theorists with environmental sociology offers substantial promise.

16. Rosa (1997) finds variation among affluent nations in the trajectory of their carbon intensity, lending further doubt to the developmental logic.

17. Of course, much of the work on environmental concern and on the environmental movement is directly relevant to understanding the basis for such opposition. See, for example, Brulle (1995); Dunlap and Mertig (1995); Stern et al. (1999).

18. It is important to distinguish evolutionary theory from the evolutionist or developmental approaches that sometimes are mislabeled as evolutionary. The latter are theories of stages and obstacles, the former are theories of process and contingency. For a fuller discussion of the distinction, see McLaughlin (1998) and Dietz et al. (1990).

19. See Hoffman (1996) for an examination of trends in corporate attention to

environmental problems, while Cebon (1992) examines corporate decisions regarding the environment.

20. There are also a number of nations and industries that anticipate substantial adverse effects from global change. Among nations, these include island nations and other nations with much of their land area near sea level. The sea-level rise that will accompany climate change will inundate these lands. Among corporations, these include insurance companies who cover coastal areas and areas subject to tropical storms. It is anticipated that climate change will increase the frequency and severity of flooding in many areas and perhaps the frequency and severity of tropical storms.

21. Jones (1991) discussed the response of American states to global climate change and Abel and Stephan (2000) has examined local government efforts. Since states, provinces, cantons, and other subnational units are an important nexus of policy in many nations, and since states or provinces within a nation may be differentially affected by global change, this is an important line of inquiry. There has not been much systematic exploration of government decision making at the level of the agency (but see Andrews, 1994; Cropper et al., 1992; and Metrick and Weitzman, 1996).

## REFERENCES

Abel, Troy D., and Murk Stephan. 2000. "The Limits of Civic Environmentalism." *American Behavioral Scientist* 44:614–628.

Allen, Julia C., and Douglas F. Barnes. 1985. "The Causes of Deforestation in Developing Countries." *Annals of the Association of American Geographers* 75:163–184.

Anderson, Charles H. 1976. *The Sociology of Survival: Social Problems of Growth.* Homewood, IL: Dorsey Press.

Andrews, Clinton. 1994. "Policies to Encourage Clean Technology." Pp. 405–422 in *Industrial Ecology and Global Change,* edited by R. Socolow, C. Andrews, F. Berkhout, and V. Thomas. Cambridge: Cambridge University Press.

Ayers, Robert U. 1989. "Industrial Metabolism." Pp. 23–49 in *Technology and Environment,* edited by J. H. Ausbel and H. E. Sladovich. Washington, DC: National Academy Press.

Babu, Suresh Chandra, and Rashid Hassan. 1995. "International Migration and Environmental Degradation—The Case of Mozambican Refugees and Forest Resources in Malawi." *Journal of Environmental Management* 43:233–247.

Balmford, Andrew, and Adrian Long. 1995. "Across-Country Analyses of Biodiversity Congruence and Current Conservation Effort in the Tropics." *Conservation Biology* 9:1539–1547.

Baran, Paul A. 1957. *The Political Economy of Growth.* New York: Monthly Review Press.

Baran, Paul A., and Paul M. Sweezy. 1966. *Monopoly Capital: An Essay on the American Economic and Social Order.* New York: Monthly Review Press.

Benedick, Richard E. 1991. *Ozone Diplomacy.* Cambridge, MA: Harvard University Press.

Benton, Michael. 1993. "Life and Time." Pp. 22–36 in *The Book of Life*, edited by Stephen Jay Gould. New York: Norton.

Berk, Richard A., and Daniel Schulman. 1995. "Public Perceptions of Global Warming." *Climatic Change* 29:1–33.

Blaustein, Andrew R., Brian Edmond, and D. Grant Hokit. 1995. "Ambient Ultraviolet Radiation Causes Mortality in Salamander Eggs." *Ecological Applications* 5:740–600.

Blaustein, Andrew R., Joseph M. Kiesecker, and Robert G. Anthony. 1997. "Ambient UV-B Radiation Causes Deformities in Amphibian Embryos." *Proceedings of the National Academy of Sciences* 94:13735–13738.

Bond, Gerard, William Showers, Maziet Cheseby, Rusty Lotti, Peter Almasi, Peter deMenocal, Paul Priore, Heidi Cullen, Irka Hajdas, and Georges Bonani. 1997. "A Pervasive Millenial-Scale Cycle in North Atlantic Holocene and Glacial Climates." *Science* 278:1257–1266.

Bonner, Raymond. 1993. *At the Hand of Man: Peril and Hope for Africa's Wildlife.* New York: Alfred A. Knopf.

Boyd, Robert, and Peter J. Richerson. 1985. *Culture and the Evolutionary Process.* Chicago: University of Chicago Press.

Braudel, Fernand. 1979. *The Structures of Everyday Life: The Limits of the Possible.* New York: Harper & Row.

Brown, Katrina, and David W. Pearce (eds.). 1994. *The Causes of Tropical Deforestation: The Economic and Statistical Analysis of Factors Giving Rise to the Loss of the Tropical Forests.* London: University College London Press.

Brown, Phillip, and Edwin J. Mikkelsen. 1990. *No Safe Place: Toxic Waste, Leukemia and Community Action.* Berkeley: University of California Press.

Bruce, J., Hoesung Lee, and E. Haites (eds.). 1996. *Climate Change 1995: Economic and Social Dimensions of Climate Change.* Contribution of Working Group III to the Second Assessment Report of the Intergovernmental Panel on Climate Change. Cambridge: Cambridge University Press.

Brulle, Robert J. 1993. "Environmentalism and Human Emancipation." Pp. 2–12 in *Human Ecology: Crossing Boundaries*, edited by Scott D. Wright, Thomas Dietz, Richard Borden, Gerald Young, and Gregory Guagnano. Ft. Collins, CO: Society for Human Ecology.

———. 1995. "Environmental Discourse and Environmental Movement Organizations: A Historical and Rhetorical Perspective on the Development of U.S. Environmental Organizations." *Sociological Inquiry* 65:58–83.

Bunker, Stephen G. 1984. "Modes of Extraction, Unequal Exchange and the Progressive Underdevelopment of an Extreme Periphery: The Brazilian Amazon, 1600–1980." *American Journal of Sociology* 89:1017–1064.

———. 1985. *Underdeveloping the Amazon: Extraction, Unequal Exchange and the Failure of the Modern State.* Urbana: University of Illinois Press.

———. 1996. "Raw Material and Global Economy: Oversights and Distortions in Industrial Ecology." *Society and Natural Resources* 9:419–429.

Burns, Tom R., and Thomas Dietz. 1992. "Socio-cultural Evolution: Social Rule Systems, Selection and Agency." *International Sociology* 7:259–283.

Burns, Tom R., Edward L. Kick, and Dixie A. Murray. 1994. "Demography, Development and Deforestation from a World-Systems Perspective." *International Journal of Comparative Sociology* 35:221–239.

Buttel, Frederick H. 1985. "Environmental Quality and the State: Some Political-Sociological Observations on Environmental Regulation." Pp. 167–188 in *Research in Political Sociology*, vol. 1, edited by R. G. Braungart and M. M. Braungart. Greenwich, CT: JAI Press.

Buttel, Frederick H., Ann P. Hawkins, and Alison G. Power. 1990. "From Limits to Growth to Global Change: Constraints and Contradictions in the Evolution of Environmental Science and Ideology." *Global Environmental Change* 1:57–66.

Buttel, Frederick H., and Peter J. Taylor. 1992. "Environmental Sociology and Global Environmental Change: A Critical Assessment." *Society and Natural Resources* 5:211–230.

Canan, Penelope. 1993. "Ozone Partnerships, the Construction of Regulatory Communities and the Future of Global Regulation." *Pace Law and Policy Review* 15(10):61.

Canan, Penelope, Stephen J. DeCanio, and Nancy Reichman. 1996. "Implementing the Montreal Protocol through Network Action." Paper presented at the Annual Meeting of the International Conference on Ozone Layer Protection Technologies. Washington, DC.

Canan, Penelope, and Nancy Reichman. 1996. "The Role of Epistemic Community in Creating the Meaning of Global Environmental Regulations." Paper presented at the Meeting of the Law and Society Association and the Research Committee on the Sociology of Law of the International Sociological Association, Glasgow, Scotland.

Ceballos, Gerardo, and James H. Brown. 1994. "Global Patterns of Mammalian Diversity, Endemism and Endangerment." *Conservation Biology* 9:559–568.

Cebon, Peter B. 1992. "Twixt Cup and Lip: Organizational Behavior, Technical Prediction and Conservation Practices." *Energy Policy* 20:802–814.

Chase-Dunn, Christopher. 1989. *Global Formation: Structures of the World-Economy*. Oxford: Blackwell.

Chase-Dunn, Christopher, and Peter Grimes. 1995. "World Systems Analysis." *Annual Review of Sociology* 21:387–417.

Costanza, Robert, Ralph D'Arge, Rudolf de Groot, Stephen Farber, Monica Grasso, Bruce Hannon, Karin Limburg, Shahid Naeem, Robert V. O'Neill, Jose Paruelo, Robert G. Raskin, Paul Sutton, and Marjan van den Belt. 1997. "The Value of the World's Ecosystem Services and Natural Capital." *Nature* 387:253–260.

Cramer, James C., Thomas Dietz, Nancy Miller, Paul Craig, Bruce Hackett, Don Kowalczyk, Mark Levine, and Edward L. Vine. 1985. "Social and Engineering Determinants and Their Equity Implications in Residential Energy Use." *Energy* 10:1283–1291.

Crenshaw, Edward M., and J. Craig Jenkins. 1996. "Social Structure and Global Climate Change: Sociological Propositions Concerning the Greenhouse Effect." *Sociological Focus* 29:341–358.

Cropper, Maureen, and Charles Griffiths. 1994. "The Interaction of Population Growth and Environmental Quality." *American Economic Review* 84:250–254.

Cropper, Maureen L., William N. Evans, Stephan J. Berardi, Maria M. Ducla-Soares, and Paul Portney. 1992. "The Determinants of Pesticide Regulation:

A Statistical Analysis of EPA Decision Making." *Journal of Political Economy* 100:175–197.

Daily, Gretchen C. (ed.). 1997. *Nature's Services: Societal Dependence on Natural Ecosystems*. Washington, DC: Island Press.

Dake, Karl. 1991. "Orienting Dispositions in the Perception of Risk: An Analysis of Contemporary Worldviews and Cultural Biases." *Journal of Cross-Cultural Psychology* 22:61–82.

Deacon, Robert T. 1994. "Deforestation and the Rule of Law in a Cross-Section of Countries." *Land Economics* 70:414–430.

Dietz, Thomas. 1987. "Theory and Method in Social Impact Assessment." *Sociological Inquiry* 57:54–69.

———. 1994. "What Should We Do? Human Ecology and Collective Decision Making." *Human Ecology Review* 1:301–319.

Dietz, Thomas, and Tom R. Burns. 1992. "Human Agency and the Evolutionary Dynamics of Culture." *Acta Sociologica* 35:187–200.

Dietz, Thomas, Tom R. Burns, and Frederick H. Buttel. 1990. "Evolutionary Theory in Sociology: An Examination of Current Thinking." *Sociological Forum* 5:155–171.

Dietz, Thomas, and James P. Hawley. 1983. "The Impact of Market Structure and Economic Concentration on the Diffusion of Alternative Technologies: The Photovoltaics Case." Pp. 17–38 in *The Social Constraints on Energy Policy Implementation*, edited by Max Neiman and Barbara J. Burt. Lexington, MA: Heath.

Dietz, Thomas, and Linda Kalof. 1992. "Environmentalism among Nation States." *Social Indicators Research* 26:353–366.

Dietz, Thomas, Linda Kalof, and R. Scott Frey. 1991. "On the Utility of Robust and Resampling Procedures." *Rural Sociology* 56:461–474.

Dietz, Thomas, and Eugene A. Rosa. 1994. "Rethinking the Environmental Impacts of Population, Affluence and Technology." *Human Ecology Review* 1:277–300.

Dietz, Thomas, and Eugene A. Rosa. 1997a. "Effects of Population and Affluence on $CO_2$ Emissions." *Proceedings of the National Academy of Sciences, USA* 94:175–179.

Dietz, Thomas, and Eugene A Rosa. 1997b. "Environmental Impacts of Population and Consumption." Pp. 92–99 in *Environmentally Significant Consumption: A Research Directions*, edited by P. C. Stern, T. Dietz, V. Ruttan, R. H. Socolow, and J. Sweeney. Washington, DC: National Academy Press.

Dietz, Thomas, and Paul C. Stern. 1998. "Science, Values and Biodiversity." *BioScience* 48:441–444.

Dietz, Thomas, Paul C. Stern, and Robert W. Rycroft. 1989. "Definitions of Conflict and the Legitimation of Resources: The Case of Environmental Risk." *Sociological Forum* 4:47–70.

Douglas, Mary, and Aaron Wildavsky. 1982. *Risk and Culture: An Essay on the Selection of Technological and Environmental Dangers*. Berkeley: University of California Press.

Dunlap, Riley E. 1994. "Struggling with Human Exemptionalism: The Rise, Decline and Revitalization of Environmental Sociology." *The American Sociologist* 25:5–30.

Dunlap, Riley E., G. H. Gallup, Jr., and A. M. Gallup. 1993. "Global Environ-
    mental Concern: Results from an International Public Opinion Survey." *En-
    vironment* 35(9):7–15, 33–39.
Dunlap, Riley E., J. Keith Grieneeks, and Milton Rokeach. 1983. "Human Values
    and Pro-Environmental Behavior." Pp. 145–168 in *Energy and Mineral Re-
    sources: Attitudes, Values and Public Policy*, edited by David W. Conn.
    Washington, DC: American Association for the Advancement of Science.
Dunlap, Riley E., and Angela G. Mertig. 1995. "Global Concern for the Environ-
    ment: Is Affluence a Prerequisite?" *Journal of Social Issues* 51(4):121–137.
Dunlap, Riley E., and Angela G. Mertig. 1997. "Global Environmental Concern:
    An Anomaly for Postmaterialism." *Social Science Quarterly* 78:24–29.
Eder, Klaus. 1996. *The Social Construction of Nature*. London: Sage Publications.
Epstein, Joshua M., and Robert L. Axtell. 1995. *Growing Artificial Societies: Social
    Science from the Bottom Up*. Washington, DC: The Brookings Institution.
Faber, Daniel. 1992. *Environment under Fire: Imperialism and the Ecological Crisis
    in Central America*. New York: Monthly Review Press.
Forester, Deborah J., and Gary E. Machlis. 1996. "Modeling Human Factors that
    Affect the Loss of Biodiversity." *Conservation Biology* 10:1253–1263.
Fowler, Cary. 1994. *Unnatural Selection: Technology, Politics and Plant Evolution*.
    Yverdon, Switzerland: Gordon and Breach.
Frank, David John. 1997. "Science, Nature and the Globalization of the Environ-
    ment, 1870–1990." *Social Forces* 76:409–437.
Freeman, David M. 1992. *Choice against Choice: Constructing a Policy-Assessing
    Sociology for Social Development*. Niwot: University of Colorado Press.
Freeman, David M., and R. Scott Frey. 1990–1991. "A Modest Proposal for As-
    sessing Social Impacts of Natural Resource Policies." *Journal of Environ-
    mental Systems* 20:375–404.
Frey, R. Scott. 1994. "The International Traffic in Hazardous Wastes." *Journal of
    Environmental Systems* 23:165–177.
———. 1995. "The International Traffic in Pesticides." *Technological Forecasting
    and Social Change* 50:151–169.
———. 1998. "The Hazardous Waste Flow in the World-System." Pp. 84–103 in
    *Space and Transport in the World System*, edited by P. Ciccantell and S. G.
    Bunker. Westport, CT: Greenwood Press.
Furger, Franco. 1998. "Accountability and Systems of Self-Governance: The Case
    of the Maritime Industry." *Law & Policy* 19:445–476.
Gould, Kenneth A., Allan Schnaiberg, and Adam S. Weinberg. 1996. *Local Envi-
    ronmental Struggles: Citizen Activism in the Treadmill of Production*. New
    York: Cambridge University Press.
Grainger, Alan. 1993. "Rates of Deforestation in the Humid Tropics: Estimates
    and Measurements." *The Geographical Journal* 159:33–44.
Grossman, G., and A. Krueger. 1995. "Economic Growth and the Environment."
    *Quarterly Journal of Economics* 110:353–377.
Guagnano, Gregory A., Thomas Dietz, and Paul C. Stern. 1994. "Willingness to
    Pay: A Test of the Contribution Model." *Psychological Science* 5:411–415.
Haas, Peter. 1993. "Epistemic Communities and the Dynamics of International
    Environmental Cooperation." Pp. 168–201 in *Regime Theory and Interna-
    tional Relations*, edited by V. Rittberger. Oxford: Oxford University Press.

Haas, Peter M. 1997. *Knowledge, Power and International Policy Coordination.* Columbia: University of South Carolina Press.

Haas, Peter M., and Ernst B. Haas. 1995. "Learning to Learn: Improving Global Governance." *Global Governance* 1:225–284.

Habermas, Jürgen. 1993. *Justification and Application: Remarks on Discourse Ethics.* Cambridge, MA: MIT Press.

Harris, Marvin. 1968. *The Rise of Anthropological Theory.* New York: Thomas Y. Crowell.

Heberlein, Thomas A. 1977. "Norm Activation and Environmental Action." *Journal of Social Issues* 33:79–87.

Herder, Johann Gottfried. 1969. *J. G. Herder on Social and Political Culture.* Cambridge: Cambridge University Press.

Hoffman, Andrew J. 1996. "Trends in Corporate Environmentalism: The Chemical and Petroleum Industries." *Society and Natural Resources* 9:47–64.

Holtz-Eakin, Douglas, and Thomas M. Selden. 1995. "Stoking the Fires? $CO_2$ Emissions and Economic Growth." *Journal of Public Economics* 57:85–101.

Houghton, J. J., L. G. Meiro Filho, B. A. Callander, N. Harris, A. Kattenberg, and K. Maksell (eds.). 1995. *Climate Change 1995: The Science of Climate Change.* Contribution of Working Group I to the Second Assessment Report of the Intergovernmental Panel on Climate Change. Cambridge: Cambridge University Press.

Hughes, Malcolm K., and Henry F. Diaz. 1994. "Was There a 'Medieval Warm Period,' and If So, Where and When?" *Climatic Change* 26:109–142.

Inglehart, Ronald. 1995. "Public Support for Environmental Protection: Objective Problems and Subjective Values in 43 Societies." *PS: Political Science and Politics* 15:57–71.

Intergovernmental Panel on Climate Change (IPCC). 1996. *Intergovernmental Panel on Climate Change, IPCC Second Assessment: Climate Change 1995.* Cambridge: Cambridge University Press.

Jaeger, Carlo. 1994. *Taming the Dragon: Transforming Economic Institutions in the Face of Global Change.* New York: Gordon and Breach.

Jaeger, Carlo, G. Dürrenberger, H. Kastenholz, and B. Trugger. 1993. "Determinants of Environmental Action with Regard to Climatic Change." *Climatic Change* 23:193–211.

Jaeger, Carlo, Ortwin Renn, Eugene A. Rosa, and Thomas Webler. 2001. *Risk, Uncertainty and Rational Action.* London: Earthscan.

Jones, Bradford S. 1991. "State Responses to Global Climate Change." *Policy Studies Journal* 19:73–82.

Jones, Jeffrey R. 1990. *Colonization and the Environment: Land Settlement Projects in Central America.* Tokyo: United Nations University Press.

Jones, Robert E., and Riley E. Dunlap. 1992. "The Social Bases of Environmental Concern: Have They Changed over Time." *Rural Sociology* 57:28–47.

Kempton, Willett, James S. Boster, and Jennifer A. Hartley. 1995. *Environmental Values in American Culture.* Cambridge, MA: MIT Press.

Kerr, Jeremy T., and David J. Currie. 1995. "Effects of Human Activity on Global Extinction Risk." *Conservation Biology* 9:1528–1538.

Kick, Edward L., Thomas J. Burns, Byron Davis, David A. Murray, and Dixie A. Murray. 1996. "Impacts of Domestic Population Dynamics and Foreign

Wood Trade on Deforestation: A World Systems Perspective." *Journal of Developing Societies* 12:68–87.

Knapp, Tom, and Rajen Mookerjee. 1996. "Population Growth and Global $CO_2$ Emissions." *Energy Policy* 24:31–37.

Kuznets, Simon. 1955. "Economic Growth and Income Inequality." *American Economic Review* 45(1):1–28.

Laptev, I. 1977[1973]. *The Planet of Reason: A Sociological Study of Man-Nature Relationships*. Moscow: Progress Publishers.

Lave, Lester B., and Hadi Dowlatabadi. 1993. "Climate Change: The Effects of Personal Beliefs and Scientific Uncertainty." *Environmental Science and Technology* 27:1962–1972.

Lipschutz, Ronnie, and Ken Conca (eds.). 1993. *The State and Social Power in Global Environmental Politics*. New York: Columbia University Press.

Löfstedt, Ragnar E. 1991. "Climate Change and Energy-Use Decisions in Northern Sweden." *Global Environmental Change* 1:321–324.

———. 1992. "Lay Perspectives Concerning Global Climate Change in Sweden." *Energy and Environment* 3:161–175.

Lough, Thomas S. 1996. "Energy Analysis of the Structures of Industrial Organizations." *Energy* 21:131–139.

Lutzenhiser, Loren. 1993. "Social and Behavioral Aspects of Energy Use." *Annual Review of Energy and the Environment* 18:247–289.

Lutzenhiser, Loren, and Bruce Hackett. 1993. "Social Stratification and Environmental Degradation: Understanding Household $CO_2$ Production." *Social Problems* 40:50–73.

Manicas, Peter T. 1987. *A History and Philosophy of the Social Sciences*. Oxford: Blackwell.

Mazur, Allan. 1980. *The Dynamics of Technological Controversy*. Washington, DC: Communications Press.

McLauglin, Paul. 1998. "Rethinking the Agrarian Question: The Limits of Essentials and the Promise of Evolution." *Human Ecology Review* 5:25–39.

———. 2001. "Toward an Ecology of Social Action: Merging the Ecological and Constructivist Traditions." *Human Ecology Review* 8:in press.

McLaughlin, Paul, and Marwan Khawaja. 2000. "The Organization Dynamics of the U.S. Environmental Movement: Legitimation, Resource Mobilization, and Political Opportunity." *Rural Sociology* 65:422–439.

McNeely, J. A., M., Gadgil, C. Leveque, C. Padoch, and K. Redford. 1996. "Human Influences University on Biodiversity." Pp. 712–821 in *Global Biodiversity Assessment*, edited by V. H. Heywood. Cambridge: Cambridge University Press.

Metrick, Andrew, and Martin L. Weitzman. 1996. "Patterns of Behavior in Endangered Species Preservation." *Land Economics* 72:1–16.

Montesquieu, Charles de Secondat. 1977. *The Spirit of Laws*. Berkeley: University of California Press.

Moran Emilio F. 1993. "Deforestation and Land Use in the Brazilian Amazon." *Human Ecology* 21:1–21.

Neumann, Roderick P., and Gary E. Machlis. 1989. "Land-use and Threats to Parks in the Neotropics." *Environmental Conservation* 16:13–18.

Nordhaus, William D. 1994. *Managing the Global Commons*. Cambridge, MA: MIT Press.

O'Connor, Martin. 1994. *Is Capitalism Sustainable? Political Economy and the Politics of Ecology*. New York: Guilford Press.

Oppo, Delia. 1997. "Millenial Climate Oscillations." *Science* 278:1244–1246.

Pareto, Vilfredo. 1963. *The Mind and Society: A Treatise on General Sociology*. New York: Dover Publications.

Palloni, Alberto. 1994. "The Relation Between Population and Deforestation: Methods for Drawing Causal Inferences from Macro and Micro Studies." Pp. 125–165 in *Population and Environment: Rethinking the Debate*, edited by Lourdes Arizpe, M. Priscilla Stone, and David C. Major. Boulder, CO: Westview Press.

Princen, Thomas, and Mathias Finger (eds.). 1994. *Environmental NGOs in World Politics*. London: Routledge.

Ragin, Charles. 1987. *The Comparative Method: Moving Beyond Qualitative and Quantitative Strategies*. Berkeley: University of California Press.

Rebetez, Martine. 1996. "Public Expectation as an Element of Human Perception of Climate Change." *Climatic Change* 32:495–509.

Redclift, Michael, and Ted Benton. 1994. *Social Theory and the Global Environment*. London: Routledge.

Reichman, Nancy, and Penelope Canan. 1996. "Peer Review, Social Capital and the Law: The Politics and Careers of Ozone Layer Protection." Paper presented at the Annual Assembly of the Consortium on Globalization, Law and the Social Science, Glasgow, Scotland.

Richerson, Peter J., and Robert Boyd. 1997/1998. "Homage to Malthus, Ricardo and Boserup: Toward a General Theory of Population, Economic Growth, Environmental Deterioration, Wealth and Poverty." *Human Ecology Review* 4:85–90.

Roberts, J. Timmons. 1996. "Predicting Participation in Environmental Treaties: A World-Systems Analysis." *Sociological Inquiry* 66:38–57.

Roberts, J. Timmons, and Peter Grimes. 1997. "Carbon Intensity and Economic Development: 1962–1991: A Brief Exploration of the Environmental Kuznets Curve." *World Development* 25:181–198.

Roberts, J. Timmons, and Peter Grimes. 2001. "World-Systems and the Environment: Toward a New Synthesis." In *Sociological Theory and the Environment*, edited by Riley E. Dunlap, Frederick H. Buttel, Peter Dickens, and August Gijwijt. Lanham, MD: Rowman and Littlefield.

Rosa, Eugene. 1998. "Metatheoretical Foundations for Post-Normal Risk." *Journal of Risk Research* 1:15–44.

Rosa, Eugene A. 1997. "Cross-National Trends in Fossil Fuel Consumption, Societal Well-Being, and Carbon Releases." Pp. 100–109 in *Environmentally Significant Consumption*, edited by Paul C. Stern, Thomas Dietz, Vernon W. Ruttan, Robert H. Socolow, and James L. Sweeney. Washington, DC: National Academy Press.

Rosa, Eugene A., and Thomas Dietz. 1998. "Climate Change and Society: Speculation, Construction and Scientific Investigation." *International Sociology* 13:419–453.

Rosa, Eugene A., Gary E. Machlis, and Kenneth M. Keating. 1988. "Energy and Society." *Annual Review of Sociology* 14:149–172.

Rudel, Thomas. 1995. "Did TVA Make a Difference? An Organizational Dilemma and Reforestation in the Southern Appalachians." *Natural Resources and Society* 8:493–508.

Rudel, Thomas K. 1989. "Population, Development and Tropical Deforestation: A Cross-national Study." *Rural Sociology* 54:327–338.

Rudel, Thomas K., and Bruce Horowitz. 1993. *Tropical Deforestation: Small Farmers and Land Clearing in the Ecuadorian Amazon.* New York: Columbia University Press.

Sachs, Aaron. 1995. *Eco-Justice: Linking Human Rights and the Environment.* Washington, DC: World Watch Institute.

Schnaiberg, Alan. 1980. *The Environment: From Surplus to Scarcity.* New York: Oxford University Press.

———. 1994. "The Political Economy of Environmental Problems and Policies: Consciousness, Conflict and Control Capacity." *Advances in Human Ecology* 3:23–64.

Selden, Thomas M., and Daqing Song. 1994. "Environmental Quality and Development: Is There a Kuznets Curve for Air Pollution Emissions?" *Journal of Environmental Economics and Management* 27:147–162.

Shafik, Nemat. 1994. "Economic Development and Environmental Quality: An Econometric Analysis." *Oxford Economic Papers* 46:757–773.

Stern, Paul C. 1992. "Psychological Dimensions of Global Environmental Change." *Annual Review of Psychology* 43:269–302.

Stern, Paul C., J. Stanley Black, and Julie T. Elsworth. 1983. "Adaptation to Changing Energy Conditions among Massachusetts Households." *Energy* 12:339–353.

Stern, Paul C., and Thomas Dietz. 1994. "The Value Basis of Environmental Concern." *Journal of Social Issues* 50:65–84.

Stern, Paul C., Thomas Dietz, and J. Stanley Black. 1986. "Support for Environmental Protections: The Role of Moral Norms." *Population and Environment* 8:204–222.

Stern, Paul C., Thomas Dietz, Troy Abel, Gregory A. Guagnamo, and Linda Kalof. 1999. "A Social Psychological Theory of Support for Social Movements: The Case of Environmentalism." *Human Ecology Review* 6:81–97.

Stern, Paul C., Thomas Dietz, Linda Kalof, and Gregory Guagnano. 1995. "Values, Beliefs and Proenvironmental Action: Attitude Formation toward Emergent Attitude Objects." *Journal of Applied Social Psychology* 25:1611–1636.

Stern, Paul C., Thomas Dietz, Vernon W. Ruttan, Robert H. Socolow, and James Sweeney (eds.). 1997. *Consumption and the Environment: The Human Causes.* Washington, DC: National Academy Press.

Stern, Paul C., and William Easterling (eds.). 1999. *Making Climate Forecasts Matter.* Washington, DC: National Academy Press.

Stern, Paul C., Oran R. Young, and Daniel Druckman. 1992. *Global Environmental Change: Understanding the Human Dimensions.* Washington, DC: National Academy Press.

Stonich, Susan C. 1993. *"I Am Destroying the Land!" The Political Ecology of Poverty and Environmental Destruction in Honduras.* Boulder, CO: Westview Press.

Sweezy, Paul M. 1968 (1942). *The Theory of Capitalist Development*. New York: Monthly Review Press.

Sweezy, Paul M., and Harry Magdoff. 1972. *The Dynamics of U.S. Capitalism: Corporate Structure, Inflation, Credit, Gold and the Dollar*. New York: Monthly Review Press.

Taylor, Bron Raymond (ed.). 1995. *Ecological Resistance Movements: The Global Emergence of Radical and Popular Environmentalism*. Albany: State University of New York Press.

Taylor, Peter J., and Frederick H. Buttel. 1992. "How Do We Know We Have Global Environmental Problems? Science and the Globalization of Environmental Discourse." *Geoforum* 23:405–416.

Tucker, Michael. 1995. "Carbon Dioxide Emissions and Global GDP." *Ecological Economics* 15:215–223.

———. 1996. "Climate Change and the Insurance Industry: The Cost of Increased Risk and the Impetus for Action." Fairfield, CT: School of Business, Fairfield University.

Turner, B. L. II, W. C. Clark, R. W. Kates, J. F. Richards, J. T. Mathews, and W. B. Meyer. 1991a. *The Earth as Transformed by Human Action*. New York: Cambridge University Press.

Turner, B. L. II, R. E. Kasperson, W. B. Meyer, K. Dow, D. Golding, J. X. Kasperson, R. C. Mitchell, and S. J. Ratick. 1991b. "Two Types of Global Environmental Change: Definitional and Spatial Scale Issues in Their Human Dimensions." *Global Environmental Change* 1:14–22.

Van Liere, Kent D., and Riley E. Dunlap. 1980. "The Social Bases of Environmental Concern: A Review of Hypotheses, Explanations and Empirical Evidence." *Public Opinion Quarterly* 44:181–199.

Vayda, Andrew P. 1988. "Actions and Consequences as Objects of Explanation in Human Ecology." Pp. 9–18 in *Human Ecology: Research and Applications*, edited by Richard J. Borden, Jamien Jacobs, and Gerald L. Young. College Park, MD: Society for Human Ecology.

Vernadsky, V. I. 1965. *The Chemical Composition of the Biosphere of the Earth and Its Environment*. Moscow: Progress Publishers.

Wallerstein, Immanuel. 1974. *The Modern World System: Capitalist Agriculture and the Origins of the European World Economy in the Sixteenth Century*. New York: Academic Press.

Watson, R. T., M. C. Zinyowera, and R. H. Moss (eds.) (IPCC). 1996. *Climate Change 1995: Impacts, Adaptations and Mitigation of Climate Change: Scientific-Technical Analyses*. Contribution of Working Group II to the Second Assessment Report of the Intergovernmental Panel on Climate Change. Cambridge: Cambridge University Press.

Weart, Spencer. 1992. "From the Nuclear Frying Pan into the Global Fire." *The Bulletin of the Atomic Scientists* 48:18–27

Wilenius, Markku. 1996. "From Science to Politics: The Menace of Global Environmental Change." *Acta Sociologica* 30:5–30.

Wilson, Edward O. 1992. *The Diversity of Life*. Cambridge, MA: Belknap Harvard.

World Resources Institute. 1992. *World Resources 1992–93*. Oxford: Oxford University Press.

Wynne, Brian. 1994. "Scientific Knowledge and the Global Environment." Pp. 169–

189 in *Social Theory and the Global Environment*, edited by Michael Redclift and Ted Benton. London: Routledge.

Young, Oran R., George J. Demko, and Kilapartik Ramakrishna (eds.). 1996. *Global Environmental Change and International Governance*. Hanover, NH: University Press of New England.

*Chapter 13*

# Social Impact Assessment and Technology Assessment

*Kurt Finsterbusch and William R. Freudenburg*

## INTRODUCTION

Both Social Impact Assessment (SIA) and Technology Assessment (TA) involve efforts to assess, in advance, the likely social implications of various technological alterations that we humans make in our physical environment. The dividing line between the two fields is not a sharp one, but assessments of relatively specific facilities or installations are more likely to be called social impact assessments, while assessments of entirely new technologies (such as enhanced telecommunication technologies or power-producing satellites) are more likely to be called technology assessments. Technology assessments are also likely to consider a full range of biological and physical impacts (e.g., species diversity and climate change) as well as social and economic impacts, and they tend to deal with concerns at a broader level of generalization. In this chapter, we will use the phrase "social impact assessment" (often known as "socio-economic impact assessment" or "SIA") to refer to the social science components of both areas.

This chapter will begin by providing a brief discussion of the historical background and some basic terminology. We will move next to a review of several major areas of SIA work and then to a discussion of SIA methods, including impact mitigation techniques. The chapter will conclude with a discussion of key issues that appear to deserve continued attention in the future.

## HISTORICAL AND LEGAL CONTEXT

Sociologists (and others) have been assessing the impacts of technological change since the dawn of the discipline. Prendergast (1989) argues that the true beginning of SIA was Condorcet's canal study in the nineteenth century. Examples of impact assessment in the broader social science literature range from Lynn White's analysis (1962), which traced the emergence of feudalism to the invention of the stirrup, to Weber's broader lament (1958) that industrialization had led to "the disenchantment of the world." The fields of TA and SIA as we know them today, however, can be traced to much more recent origins—particularly to developments of the 1960s and 1970s (the following discussion draws heavily from Freudenburg, 1989).

Social and behavioral scientists have played a variety of roles in environmental management, but involvement was greatly increased by the National Environmental Policy Act (NEPA), passed in 1969 (Finsterbusch, 1995). This was the law that set up the requirement that federal agencies prepare environmental impact statements (EISs) for "major federal actions significantly affecting the quality of the human environment." Along with this call for attention to "the human environment," Section 101 of the NEPA states that the purpose of the Act is not only to maintain environmental quality but also to "fulfill the social, economic and other requirements" of U.S. citizens. Section 102(2)(A) of the Act requires federal agencies to make "integrated use of the natural *and social sciences* . . . in decisionmaking which may have an impact on man's environment" (emphasis added). Section 1508.8 of the official *Regulations for Implementing NEPA* (U.S. Council on Environmental Quality, 1978:40 CFR 1500 *et seq.*) notes that EISs need to consider direct and indirect social and cultural impacts, as well as physical and biological impacts. Section 1508.14 of the *Regulations* notes that while social and economic effects by themselves do not require preparation of an EIS, "When an environmental impact statement *is* prepared" because of physical environmental impacts, and when the social and the bioenvironmental impacts are interrelated, "then the environmental impact statement will discuss *all* of these effects upon the human environment" (U.S. Council on Environmental Quality, 1978:29; emphasis added; see also Freudenburg and Keating, 1985; Interorganizational Committee, 1994; Jordan, 1984; Llewellyn and Freudenburg, 1990; Meidinger and Freudenburg, 1983; Savatsky, 1974).

By the early 1990s, the practice of SIA in connection with the NEPA and other government regulations had matured to the point where representatives from the major social science professional associations were able to compile a set of consensus guidelines and principles for SIA, to assist agencies and private interests in fulfilling their statutory obligations (see Interorganizational Committee, 1994). These guidelines will be discussed in the methods section later in this chapter.

### Definitions

The social and behavioral science components of EISs soon became part of a field generally known as social or socio-economic impact assessment.

A brief definition of the three terms in "socio-economic impact assessment" will be provided here. In essence, the *socio-* half of the term *socio-economic* can be seen as covering social and cultural impacts of development, and as incorporating the traditional subject matter of sociology, anthropology, and psychology, in particular, with input from other fields as well. The *-economic* half of the term is generally seen as including not only economics, but also demography and planning, again with input from other fields, as needed. These are emphases rather than rigid distinctions.

The *impacts* are the indirect as well as direct "effects" or consequences of an action (U.S. Council on Environmental Quality, 1978), where the actions can include building a dam, digging a coal mine, or issuing an air quality permit. In many cases (Merton, 1936), the most important aspects for affected residents involve not the stated intentions but the unintended side effects. In short, impacts include all of the significant changes that take place because of what an agency does and that would not have occurred otherwise. They are the difference between the "future with" a project or decision and the "future without" that same influence (Murdock and Leistritz, 1979; National Academy of Sciences, 1984).

*Assessment*, in the SIA/TA context, tends to have an unusual meaning: In many but not all cases, the "assessment" of impacts is carried out before the impacts actually occur. In other words, an SIA is often anticipatory rather than empirical. It attempts to assist the planning process by identifying the likely effects before they take place. Done well, however, the estimates of likely future impacts are based on the existing empirical knowledge of the impacts of similar actions in the past (Finsterbusch, 1980; Freudenburg and Keating, 1985; Knight et al., 1993; Wolf, 1977; World Bank, 1994).

A fourth term also deserves attention here—the *mitigation* or lessening of negative impacts. The major policy contribution of SIA/TA is to help plan for, manage, and then mitigate any negative impacts (or enhance any positive ones) that may be created by a proposed action (see the fuller discussion provided by Halstead et al., 1984). The legal definition of mitigation (U.S. Council on Environmental Quality, 1978) can be simplified into three primary components. The first and best is impact *avoidance*, preventing negative impacts from occurring in the first place rather than applying corrective measures later, once the problems have been created. Examples include both "brick and mortar" solutions, such as altering proposed developments or access routes to avoid or minimize the impacts on particularly sensitive communities (Berger and Associates, 1982), and "nonstructural" solutions, such as management or scheduling changes to slow down the rapid building up or laying off of project workforces, thus helping to "even out" the boom-bust effects of development that could otherwise result (Freudenburg, 1979; Halstead et al., 1984; Murdock and Leistritz, 1979).

Second, for impacts that cannot be avoided completely, attention is focused on impact *minimization*, or on efforts to lessen or alleviate any deleterious results. Most efforts toward impact alleviation are monetary ones, such as the provision of funds for building or expanding facilities, and services for dealing with negatively affected persons (for discussions, see Davenport and Davenport, 1979; Halstead et al., 1984). Perhaps the most common nonmonetary minimization measures are public involvement programs. These can range from "opportunities to blow off steam" that have little practical effect, to arrangements that give local residents a genuine opportunity to alter the course of development (see discussions in Babiuch and Farhar, 1994; Creighton, 1981; Freudenburg and Olsen, 1983; Gagnon et al., 1993; Howell et al., 1981; see also the discussion of mediation in the semi-final section of this chapter). One published example concerns a proposed nuclear waste facility in Tennessee. Given the facility's potential to lead to increased risks and a reduction in local residents' control over their own futures, a local task force negotiated and reached agreement in principle with the Department of Energy to establish a locally selected committee with considerable control over the facility, including the power to shut it down if the committee felt operations were becoming unsafe (Peelle, 1987). While this arrangement helps to illustrate what is possible, it appears unlikely to become the norm, even though other localities, such as the state of Pennsylvania, have reportedly experienced success with comparable approaches, including one involving an effort to develop a facility for low-level nuclear waste (Dornsife et al., 1989).

Monetary provisions and participation opportunities are important mechanisms for minimizing negative impacts, but usually they should be combined with considerate management. Many negative impacts can be greatly reduced by management decisions. Peak work forces could be reduced and work force levels made less volatile and disruptive through management practices that are sensitive to community problems. Early SIAs gave very little attention to impact monitoring and management, but now these activities are being advocated by residents of affected communities, SIA professionals, and many managers (see Burdge, 1994; Halstead et al., 1984; Interorganizational Committee, 1994; Leistritz and Ekstrom, 1986; Leistritz and Murdock, 1986; Lodwick and Ridge, 1990; and the discussion in a later section).

Third, socio-economic impacts that cannot be avoided in advance and cannot be effectively alleviated raise the controversial question of *compensation* for affected parties. The simplest forms of compensation usually involve money, while the unmitigable impacts often have no clear monetary equivalents. What is the economic "value," for example, of a low juvenile delinquency rate, an unimpeded view of the mountains, or a quiet and friendly community where "everybody knows everybody else?" Even the suggestion that people might be paid for such losses can raise a storm of criticism, both from project proponents who feel that such concerns are impossible to measure and compensate fairly, and from project opponents who object to the idea of "selling out" on things that should not be bought or sold (for discussions, however, see O'Hare, 1977; Smith and Desvouges, 1986). An additional problem is that, as economists are discovering, financial compensation often has less appeal to local residents than policy makers tend to assume (Kunreuther and Easterling, 1990; see also Freudenburg and Gramling, 1994).

Yet it is possible to identify more creative and more appropriate compensation strategies, even where money is involved. One creative approach is to develop "positive impacts" to help offset unavoidable negative ones. One of the proposals to increase the acceptability of offshore oil drilling along the coast of California, for example, sought to counterbalance the visual impact of having platforms "in the middle of the scenery" (as one local opponent put it) by offering offsetting (positive) recreational impacts through the creation or development of state parks or through investments in the financially strapped state trail system (Dornbusch et al., 1987). Similarly, given that the development of a nuclear waste repository may create unknown risks for future generations, perhaps it would be possible for today's beneficiaries of nuclear technologies to set up a trust fund for the benefit of those future generations. The fund might be used to correct problems that were not adequately foreseen when the repository was first developed. One of the challenges for SIA will be to develop compensation strategies for controversial cases that can be sufficiently equitable to achieve a reasonably high level of acceptance by both proponents and opponents. The issue of mitigation will receive further discussion in the concluding section of this chapter.

## MAJOR SIA SUBFIELDS

It is possible to divide SIA work into an almost infinite number of subfields; for purposes of this discussion, however, we will concentrate on six. The first two have to do with the impacts created by specific facilities. First are the major construction projects that have been the most common focus of SIA efforts to date, and second are the risk-inducing projects that have received increasing attention in recent years. The third brings us to the consideration of impacts created by entire technological systems rather than individual facilities. The fourth and fifth examine the impacts induced by new resource-use plans and by changes in broader policies and programs. Sixth and finally, we will discuss the special challenges involved in assessing the impacts of international development efforts.

### Construction Projects

Throughout the 1970s and 1980s, one of the most controversial areas of SIA concerned the social problems created by large construction projects in rural areas—particularly projects that caused rapid community growth. The literature in this area can be seen as having evolved through a series of four stages which are summarized below (this discussion draws on Freudenburg, 1989; see also Freudenburg, 1986c; Freudenburg and Jones, 1992; Seyfrit, 1986; for more detailed reviews, see especially Cortese, 1982; Finsterbusch, 1980; Freudenburg, 1982a).

### Economic Opportunities

With relatively few exceptions (e.g., Smith et al., 1971), the literature before approximately 1975 referred almost entirely to the *positive* implications of economic growth. In the most extensive review of this early work, Summers et al. (1976:1) noted that rural industrialization was generally seen as beneficial, providing "an important tool for solving the twin problems of rural poverty and urban crisis." Similarly, in reviewing federal impact statements produced up to that time, Friesema and Culhane (1976: 343) noted, "The statements generally consider only one social consequence—the economic impact of the project" (see also Freudenburg, 1976; Little, 1977; Schnaiberg, 1980). As a result, the "early" or rural industrialization studies devoted relatively little attention to potential drawbacks.

### Boomtown Disruptions

Beginning in roughly the middle-1970s, particularly after the 1973–1974 oil embargo and the subsequent development of massive projects in sparsely populated regions of the western United States and Canada, researchers began to draw increasing attention to social problems associated with rapid community growth. If earlier studies had drawn on classic economic logic, the literature in this second and shorter-lived tradition tended to draw more directly from classical sociologists such as Durkheim and Tönnies, who emphasized the disruptive consequences of rapid social change. This framework was commonly applied to the energy boomtowns (see the reviews by Cortese, 1982; Freudenburg, 1982a; Wilkinson et al., 1982). In retrospect, some of this work appears to have represented in part an overreaction against the excessively favorable perspective taken by earlier work. In fact, some of the literature (see, e.g., the compilation by Davenport and Davenport, 1979) was produced by human service providers whose primary focus was on helping communities and individuals cope with problems rather than on documenting their occurrence.

### Doubting the Disruptions

The third era began in 1982, as a reaction against the second. While critical voices had been raised earlier (e.g., Freudenburg, 1981), the critique by Wilkinson et al. (1982) marks the eclipse of the second era and the beginning of the third. While this review has been the focus of considerable criticism itself (see, e.g., Albrecht, 1982; Finsterbusch, 1982; Freudenburg, 1982b; Gale, 1982; Gold, 1982; Murdock and Leistritz, 1982), there was clearly merit in the review's contention that much of the literature on the "boomtown disruption hypothesis" showed a too-easy acceptance of assertions about the presumably negative consequences of rapid community growth. On the other hand, just as works of the second era may have overreacted against the problems of the first, some of the work during the post-1982 era could reflect an overreaction against the biases of the second.

### Balanced Assessments

In our judgment the field has moved into a fourth era—a period of empirical research that seeks to provide a balanced and comprehensive assessment of social impacts. Most analysts recognize that rapid economic growth has complex impacts of both positive and negative kinds, and some groups adjust to disruptions far better than others (for early reviews noting this trend, see Finsterbusch, 1985; Murdock et al., 1985). Impact research, therefore, has become more precise and detailed, focusing on the differentiation of impacts for different social groups (see, e.g., Elkind-Savatsky, 1986; Freudenburg, 1986a, 1986b). Impacts are also differentiated for different social *functions* (e.g., Boothroyd et al., 1995; Freudenburg, 1986a; Freudenburg and Jones, 1992). Finally, work in the late 1980s and early 1990s showed that impacts must be differentiated over time.

The rediscovery of a genuinely "pre-boom" data set in the late 1980s (Brown et al., 1989) showed that some of the most significant social impacts may have taken place during the so-called "pre-development" phase—before large numbers of construction workers began moving into the area—and that satisfaction levels failed to return to pre-boom levels later on. Such findings would have been missed if the study had focused strictly on the "boom" phase of development that had been almost the sole focus of attention in earlier research. Freudenburg and Gramling (1992: 941) note:

In the physical or biological sciences, it may in fact be true that no impacts take place until a project leads to concrete alterations of physical or biological conditions. In the case of the human environment, by contrast, observable and measurable impacts can take place as soon as there are changes in *social* conditions— which often means from the time of the earliest announcements or rumors about a project. Speculators buy property, politicians maneuver for position, interest groups form or redirect their energies, stresses mount, and a variety of other social and economic impacts take place, particularly in the case of facilities that are large, controversial, risky, or otherwise out of the range of ordinary experiences for the local community. These changes have sometimes been called "predevelopment" or "anticipatory" impacts, but they are far more real and measurable than such terminology might imply. Even the earliest acts of speculators, for example, can drive up the *real* costs of real estate.

The longer-term examination of impacts also includes the "bust" or completion phase of development projects (see also Gramling and Freudenburg, 1992). Communities seldom return to pre-project conditions after project completion; in fact, one potential problem involves *overadaptation*. In the very process of adapting to a large-scale industry or project, a community can fail to maintain the human as well as the biophysical capital required to participate successfully in traditional industries. The heavy investments that articulate with the new industries may appear rational in the short term but may have little chance of being converted to other uses once the new industry pulls out (see also Freudenburg, 1992a; Gulliford, 1989).

### Risk-Inducing Projects

Although all projects involve risks—the risks of community disruption or economic dependency, for example, in the case of the energy boomtowns just discussed—many facilities are seen by local residents as involving high levels of technological risks, even when technical experts describe them as being perfectly safe (e.g., see Rothman and Lichter, 1987). Since the topic of risk is discussed in Chapter 11 in this volume, our discussion of it will be an abbreviated one, limited to three categories of implications for social impacts (the following discussion draws from Freudenburg, 1988; for additional analyses, see Erikson, 1976, 1990; Finsterbusch, 1988; Freudenburg, 1992b, 1993, 1996; Kasperson et al., 1988; Short, 1984; Short and Clarke, 1992).

The first category involves *impacts created by serious accidents*. The accidents can range from disasters such as Bhopal or Chernobyl, which can ultimately affect the health of thousands of persons, to those that pose less direct risk for human health. For example, the *Exxon Valdez* spill—which disrupted oil prices, jeopardized some of the world's richest fishing grounds, and harmed Exxon's corporate image—had little impact on human health. Accidents can also be "serious" even in cases where neither the human health toll nor the direct ecological damage are extensive. A classic example is the Goiania incident in Brazil (see Petterson, 1988, for further details). Two scavengers had entered an abandoned medical clinic in search of scrap metal; they found a small capsule and later pried it open, releasing a mere 100 grams of cesium-137. The release led eventually to 121 known cases of skin contact with the material and four deaths, with another 3–5 deaths expected within the next five years. As Petterson notes, this death toll could scarcely be considered out of line with "any other industrial accident," but just the labor costs of decontamination exceeded $20 million (U.S.) within a short time, and the broader economic and social costs were far greater. Within just two weeks of the time when the event was first announced in the media, the wholesale value of agricultural products from the entire Brazilian state of Goias fell by 50 percent, and even the demand for manufactured goods (including textiles, clothing, and other finished products) was affected—despite the fact that Petterson was unable to find "even a published suggestion" that the agricultural products or manufactured goods could have been contaminated. Severe impacts were also felt through treatment and research costs, declining property values, canceled conventions, and a broader decline in the tourist trade. More than 100,000 residents lined up at monitoring stations to be checked for radioactive contamination; more than 8,000 residents requested (and received) certificates that they were not contaminated; and even well-trained doctors and dentists refused to treat patients who did not have certificates of non-contamination.

Second, *uncertainty costs* may be created for affected communities even in cases where "nothing goes wrong." Real costs are incurred when communities invest in emergency-preparedness training or the preparation of evacuation plans; when societal strains are created by inequitable distributions of technological risks; or even when individuals "invest" in the psychic costs of worrying about potential disasters, whether such disasters actually occur or not (Baum, 1987; Freudenburg and Pastor, 1992; Short, 1984). As Freudenburg (1988: 44) notes, such uncertainty costs are comparable to insurance that proves in retrospect not to have been "needed": "Insurance companies keep the premiums even if the house does not burn down." The costs are created by the need to deal with the existence of a *possibility* of harm, not just by the experience of harmful outcomes.

The third and perhaps most subtle category of risk-induced effects involves *signal incidents* (Slovic, 1987). These are the cases of otherwise "minor" incidents that send to the public and/or relevant officials a kind of "signal" that the situation may not be fully under control. An example is provided by the accident at Three Mile Island (TMI), which was found by official investigations to have released very little radioactivity, although it did lead to significant mental health consequences for nearby populations (Dohrenwend et al., 1981; Flynn, 1984). Among its other consequences, the TMI accident appears to have sent a signal both to the policy community and to the broader public that nuclear power plants were less safe than the public had formerly been led to believe. The consequences of the accident appear to have included a significant decline in public support for nuclear power (Freudenburg and Baxter, 1984, 1985), and the accident appears to have been little short of disastrous for the nuclear power industry more broadly (Lovins, 1986; see also Rosa and Freudenburg, 1993).

## Technology Assessments

SIAs can also focus on entire technological systems, particularly through the performance of technology assessments (TAs). Because of their scope, TAs tend to be interdisciplinary assessments that require considerable imagination, often in the absence of direct prior experience. TAs are increasingly necessary, however, given that new technologies can have unanticipated negative consequences, some of which could have been averted if properly anticipated. Barbour (1980:194–195) points out that TA is an early warning system:

The crucial decisions in the social management of a new technology should be made at an early point in its deployment, before heavy financial investments and employment patterns have built up pressures for its perpetuation. The benefits of a technology usually are immediate and obvious; the costs and risks often are delayed, remote, and cumulative. Careful study and foresight can identify some of these effects before the new technology has acquired a momentum that is difficult to control.

The principal institutional bases for TAs were the TA program in the National Science Foundation (NSF) and the Office of Technology Assessment (OTA), an agency of Congress. The TA program in NSF began in 1971, funding 43 TAs (and 23 additional studies associated with TAs) through 1977). A reorganization in NSF in 1978 and new emphases of the Reagan administration in 1981 led to the end of NSF's funding for TAs as we have defined them. OTA was established in 1972 to advise Congress of the consequences of technologies. At first it contracted out studies, but it soon developed its own in-house capacity for TAs. Again at OTA, however, a major political shift, in this case involving the Republican landslide in the 1994 congressional elections, led to the decision to abolish the governmental TA capacity; as a congressional rather than an executive branch agency, the OTA became the first agency to be abolished after the new congressional majority took office in 1995.

To illustrate the range of technology assessments, we draw on the Arnstein and Christakis (1975) summary of technology assessments funded by the NSF from 1971 to 1975, when the NSF invested heavily in TAs. In the first one, the Stanford Research Institute examined the impacts of seeding clouds to increase the snowfall in the Rockies. For example, the enhanced flow of the Colorado River could allow farmers to grow more fruit in California, but do the people in colder regions want more snow, particularly if someone is frozen to death in a government-induced snowstorm?

The second TA examined the impact of no-fault automobile insurance, illustrating that TAs not only apply to engineering or biological technologies, such as offshore oil operations or biological pest controls, but also to social technologies. Other examples of TAs for social technologies involved the conversion to the metric system (which did not take hold) and alternative work schedules. Examples of TAs that mix engineering technologies with social technologies are those focusing on the political and scientific aspects of nuclear materials control, the impacts of remote sensing of the environment, and the applications of earthquake prediction techniques, as well as the impacts of cable television, energy conservation strategies, and human rehabilitation techniques.

In most actual TAs, however, the assessment of social impacts has tended to be either minimal or nonexistent. For example, in the mid 1970s the OTA funded a TA of three potential offshore energy facilities—offshore tanker ports, offshore oil and gas drilling, and floating nuclear power plants. The TA analyzed the technical issues and some of the political aspects of using these technologies but no strictly social impacts (OTA, 1976).

In short, while TAs often strive to be interdisciplinary and, at least in theory, to assess impacts on "society," they often tend in practice to reflect little knowledge either of social science or of social impacts, with the possible exception of a concern about public opinion. Governments and businesses are finding, however, that they must deal with public concerns in more than the cursory way that the public hearing process allows. By the late 1980s, a pair of TAs provided examples of the use of extensive public opinion research and exemplified the trend toward assessing at least the attitudes of affected citizens toward technical changes in their environments; Lough and White (1988) reported on a TA of nuclear plant decommissioning, and Stoffle and his colleagues (1988) reported on a TA of a proposed Superconducting Super Collider.

One of the newest yet broadest areas of SIA/TA involves the examination of the impacts of global environmental change (GEC). Geographically dispersed and inadequately understood impacts, both on the environment and on society, can be created by ozone depletion, rainforest destruction, global warming, and other forms of wide-scale climate change. These phenomena are by definition widespread; yet some of the most insightful and useful analyses that have become available to date (see, e.g., Rudel, 1993) have been those that build on the same kinds of careful understanding of specific affected regions that have long been a hallmark of some of the best SIAs. Overall, while efforts to understand the social impacts of these complex, global changes are still at a very early stage (see Dietz and Rosa, 1994; Stern et al., 1993), there is likely to be a need for significantly increased attention to the social science challenges of understanding global-scale changes in the future.

### Resource-Use Plans

Vast areas of land and water are managed by federal agencies. The plans for the multiple uses of these lands require EISs that include the assessment of social impacts. The Forest Service, Bureau of Land Management, National Park Service, Army Corps of Engineers, and Fish and Wildlife Service are some of the federal agencies that have begun to incorporate SIA into their planning processes, and state and local agencies have moved in this direction as well. The Forest Service and the National Marine Fisheries Service were also the agencies that sponsored the printing of the *Guidelines and Principles for Social Impact Assessment* (Interorganizational Committee, 1994). In fact, as Finsterbusch (1995) shows from EPA records, while resource-use plans constituted an insignificant proportion of federal SIAs in the 1970s, the Forest Service filed more than twice as many final EISs with EPA by 1993 than did any other agency (54 compared to 24 for the Federal Highway Administration, 16 for the Army Corp of Engineers, and 15 for the Bureau of Land Management).

Many SIAs for resource-use plans have focused on citizen participation, particularly in the search for alternatives and supplements to public hearings (see Blahna and Yonts-Shepherd, 1989; Burdge, 1984; Creighton, 1981; Daneke et al., 1983; Hanchey, 1975; Hendee, 1977; Vining, 1988). These have ranged from general population surveys to community forum and jury panel techniques. Other than the citizen participation component, however, SIAs in resource-use plans have been generally deficient, being unreliable and inappropriately narrow. Dietz (1984) concludes, from his review of a large number of environmental impact statements of the Bureau of Land Management, that they rely "heavily, and in many cases exclusively, on economic-demographic models to assess social impacts" (p. 1624). He points out that the data for these models are usually out-of-date and often drawn from a different area. Moreover, the model relationships can vary dramatically in a short period of time, so the models' point estimates give a false appearance of precision. He also points out that "The models used by BLM and other agencies only examine impacts that are closely linked to economic changes. Changes in lifestyles, culture, and local institutions, which may be of great concern to those impacted, are ignored or treated in an informal, ad-hoc manner" (Dietz, 1984:1625).

### Policies and Programs

The sociological study of policies and programs, often called evaluation research, differs somewhat from other areas of SIA. In particular, the "typical" evaluation is done *after* a program/policy is implemented and tends to be focused on the intended rather than the unintended impacts. The ideal model for evaluation involves the explicit identification of program goals, the selection of appropriate variables for measuring intended effects, and the quantitative comparison of the target population against a comparable, "control" population (both before and after the program implementation), to determine whether the programs had the intended effects (see Rossi and Freeman, 1993, or Finsterbusch and Motz, 1980, for reviews of the methods and difficulties of evaluation research).

For purposes of this chapter, the application of SIA to program/policy evaluation will be taken to mean that the investigation is not limited to the stated goals of the program, but instead considers all the important social impacts—the unintended as well as the intended ones. In this context, SIA methodology accordingly encounters all the difficulties of a standard evaluation study, and additional ones as well. Partly for this reason, the evaluation community has been slow to adopt SIA as an appropriate evaluation methodology for programs. Increasingly, however, agencies are looking at negative impacts in addition to program achievements. Since 1979, for example, the Office of Evaluation of the Agency for International Development has been producing Program Impact Evaluation Reports that examine the negative impacts of programs and projects, especially on women and the poor.

Although SIAs for programs and policies are not numerous, their range is broad. Examples include assessments of the national 55 mph special limit (Braddock et al., 1974); nonstructural flood control measures (Motz, 1979); tourism as a development strategy (de Kadt, 1979; Noronha, 1979); a national park conservation program (Peters, 1994/1995); and the impacts of national defense (Boulding, 1983). An early landmark study evaluated the income maintenance experiment, which focused on the degree to which the family allowance program was a disincentive to work. It found that the work disincentive "was almost undetectable" for working-age, able-bodied males with family responsibilities, although it was larger for wives, teenagers, and older workers (Kershaw and Fair, 1976:20).

An example that demonstrates the superiority of an evaluation with SIA over an evaluation without SIA is Morash's (1983) study of a Community Arbitration Project (CAP), a new method of screening juveniles whose offenses are not serious enough to require court processing. Three of the differences between CAP and traditional screening procedures are that under CAP police arrest youths by giving them a citation instead of taking them to the police station, the arbitrator is an attorney instead of a social worker, and the juvenile is to redress his anti-social action by doing work for the community. The Morash SIA produced data on a wider range of impacts than a traditional evaluation would have. She found, just as a traditional evaluation would, that the program reduced recidivism rates and increased diversion of youths away from formal courts (two major goals of the program). Because her SIA approach directed her to look for other significant impacts, she also found that the program led to an increased number of youth arrests. When this finding was communicated to the police departments involved, the police responded by returning to normal arrest rates.

### SIA in International Development

With few exceptions (see, e.g., Bailey, 1985; Bunker, 1984; Schurman, 1992), sociologists have been slow to produce analyses that consider the interrelated social and environmental impacts of international development efforts. In recent years, however, the U.S. Agency for International Development (AID) has developed a requirement for conducting "social soundness analysis" on AID projects. These are not full-scale SIAs, but are concerned largely with the socio-cultural fit of a development project or program with the values and institutions of the host country. In reality, most project design documents feature technical, economic, and financial analysis criteria for selecting and justifying the project. Some of these documents include a socio-cultural analysis that describes the culture and interests of the intended beneficiaries and points out what some of the obvious consequences of the project might be. In most cases, however, very little original research is conducted and few social impacts are carefully considered. As a result, the use of SIA for AID projects is generally inadequate, and socio-cultural factors often contribute substantially to poor performance of projects (for a fuller discussion, see Finsterbusch and Van Wicklin, 1989; Morgan, 1985).

AID has conducted about 70 impact assessment studies of completed projects to improve the design, implementation, and maintenance of development projects. These studies demonstrate the importance of competent staff, good management, and coordination with other organizations, as one would expect. They also demonstrate the importance of factors that are external to the project, such as pricing policies, although these are not as important as the internal factors (Finsterbusch, 1988; Finsterbusch et al., 1992). Finally, they demonstrate the value of encouraging the participation of intended beneficiaries in the design (or redesign), implementation, and maintenance of the project (Finsterbusch and Van Wicklin, 1987, 1989; Gran, 1983).

The World Bank and the Inter-American Development Bank use SIA in their project planning even less than AID. Perhaps this is to be expected, because they are banks, and they mainly use banking criteria when they lend money for development projects. Still, the World Bank has a number of sociologists and anthropologists on staff who offer inputs into World Bank policies and project decisions, and it currently is exploring ways to improve the use of SIA in its projects. The Inter-American Development Bank is also trying to be more sensitive to social factors in project planning, but has not yet made a major commitment along these lines.

Development agencies have been widely criticized for the negative impacts of their projects; two criticisms are of special interest because SIAs could help correct them. First, the development agencies are accused of doing the wrong things. Their major wrongs, according to critics, are helping the rich more than the poor (Nelson, 1985) and failing to anticipate the chains of events started by projects that have adverse consequences (see Kottak, 1985; Paddock and Paddock, 1973). Second, development agencies are criticized for doing things the wrong way (see Derman and Whiteford,

1985; Gran, 1983; Paddock and Paddock, 1973). In particular, they are seen as failing to take socio-cultural factors into account (Kottak, 1985) and to sufficiently involve intended beneficiaries in the design, implementation, and maintenance of the projects (Narayan, 1995). Development agencies tend to be top-down bureaucracies that lack the flexibility or inclination to implement participatory projects readily (Gran, 1983; Korten, 1980, 1986, 1990). According to Morgan (1985), by the time most design documents are drafted, AID and the host county leaders are committed to the project and the design document is really an advocacy document.

We agree that SIA needs to be more strongly asserted in development project planning. Some of the problems and failures of development projects could have been prevented or alleviated through better SIAs. Kottak (1985:328) even concludes, from his study of 68 projects, that good SIAs are cost-effective:

Many of the experiences documented here illustrate the tendency to address technical and financial factors and to neglect social issues. Perhaps the most significant finding of the present study is that attention to social issues, which presumably enhances sociocultural fit and results in a better social strategy for economic development, pays off in concrete economic terms: the average economic rates of return for projects that were socioculturally compatible and were based on an adequate understanding and analysis of social conditions were more than twice as high as those for socially incompatible and poorly analyzed projects.

Materials that can help SIAs for development projects include Cochrane (1979); Delp et al. (1977); Derman and Whiteford (1985); Finsterbusch et al. (1990); Jiggins (1995); Narayan (1995); Partridge (1984); and Salmen (1987).

## SIA METHODOLOGY

Perhaps the clearest progress in the field of SIA to date is seen in the area of methodology. In the early and mid-1970s there was a frantic effort to develop an effective and efficient (low-cost) SIA methodology. By the end of the 1970s there was considerable agreement on the general outlines of this methodology. In the 1980s, the outline of the general SIA methodology was filled in and gradually came to be relatively standardized. The final report from the *Guidelines and Principles* project (Interorganizational Committee, 1994) presents this outline in ten steps:

1. Develop a Public Involvement Plan
2. Describe Proposed Action and Alternatives
3. Describe Relevant Human Environment
4. Identify Probable Impacts

5. Investigate Probable Impacts
6. Determine Probable Responses of Affected Publics
7. Estimate Indirect and Cumulative Impacts
8. Recommend Changes in Proposed Action
9. Develop a Mitigation Plan
10. Develop a Monitoring Program

Importantly, this document also spells out the principles that should be used in making the kinds of professional judgments that are required of SIA practitioners—the importance of considering the distribution and equity implications of likely impacts, for example, and not just their overall magnitude—and in planning for and dealing with inevitable gaps in the data. As noted in this final report, it is more important to identify the full range of likely social impacts than to quantify precisely just the subset of impacts that are most likely; it is more important to use professional social scientists in cases where less is available in the way of reliable data; and in cases where the evidence is not definitive, the properly conservative conclusion is that the impact cannot be ruled out with confidence—not that the impact is "not proven."

For analysts seeking help with specific methods, on the other hand, several useful guides are available, particularly for assessing the impacts created by the building of a large facility in a rural area (e.g., Canter et al., 1985; Leistritz and Murdock, 1981; Palinkas et al., 1985). The first two are largely quantitative and have the same framework, practically forming a two-volume set. Together they provide formulas, coefficients, models, and numbers for assessors to use in their SIAs. These volumes can be used in tandem with the work of Palinkas et al. (1985), which illustrates qualitative methods, or of Finsterbusch et al. (1983), which describes both basic and special methods.

Other guides are even broader, particularly the manual by Branch et al. (1984), which is designed to apply not just to large-scale industrial or resource development projects, but also to "infrastructure development, social policy changes, the introduction of new technologies, and the alteration of the economic structure" (Branch et al., 1984:xiii). Even this guide is designed to have a community focus, however, and it may not apply without modification to programs, policies, and new technologies that are not site-specific. Given that it is somewhat weak on public participation programs, it could be supplemented with Creighton's (1981) guide and the lessons of the Daneke, Garcia, and Delli Priscoli reader (1983) on public participation.

Not surprisingly, SIA uses many of the methods of the social sciences, including respondent surveys, informant interviews, field studies, analyses of census-type and secondary data, content analysis, case analysis, historical research, experiments, pilot studies, simulation models, trend extrapolation, and a full array of statistical methods. Many of these are treated in the books just cited and will not be discussed here. Rather, we will touch briefly on six special methods that do or can have an important role in SIAs: mini-surveys, group surveys, rapid rural appraisals, standard information modules, quantitative models of growth, and importance weighting.

The first three of these methods—mini-surveys, group surveys, and rapid rural appraisals—offer low-cost options for field data collection. Each is a method that sacrifices pinpoint accuracy and some degree of reliability in exchange for low costs. The mini-survey includes the randomized selection of survey respondents, but abnormally small sample sizes (20 to 100 respondents). Given that the law of diminishing returns applies to each additional respondent, and that SIAs generally require simple frequencies or zero-order correlations rather than more detailed analyses, mini-surveys provide a useful tool for gauging the dominant attitudes and characteristics of a population. Policy decisions seldom *require* the more precise description or multivariate analyses that large samples permit (for more details, see Finsterbusch, 1976a, 1976b, 1977).

The other two low-cost special methods have been developed for SIAs or evaluation studies in Third World countries, and AID has produced a monograph on each method (Kumar, 1987a, 1987b). In the first of these, group interviews, one or more researchers guide a group discussion using probes but letting group members discuss the topic among themselves. Two types of group interviews have been found useful: focus group interview and community interview. The focus group interview borrows techniques from the focused individual interview (Merton et al., 1956) and essentially has a group of 6 to 10 participants discuss issues set out by the researcher. The researcher usually uses an interview guide but minimally structures the discussion (see Kruger, 1994; Morgan, 1993). The community interview is a public meeting open to all members and is more fruitful when conducted by more than one researcher.

Group interviews have several limitations. First, they do not give quantitative estimates of characteristics of a population such as the frequency of use of a new practice. Second, they are susceptible to interviewer biases, especially the "hypothesis confirmation bias." Third, there are many things that participants will not reveal in group situations. On the other hand, group interviews have several advantages. "Group interviews can . . . provide background information for designing projects and programs, generate ideas and hypotheses for intervention models, provide feedback from beneficiaries, and help in assessing responses to recommended innovations. They are also useful for obtaining data for monitoring and evaluation purposes and for interpreting data that are already available" (Kumar, 1987a: v). Finally, group discussion leads to a fuller examination of topics and often the presence of the group increases the honesty and accuracy of the informants.

The final low-cost method is rapid rural appraisal (RRA) (see Chambers, 1981, 1991; Gow, 1990; Honadle, 1982; Kumar, 1987b; Scrimshaw and Gleason, 1992). RRA is not a single method but an approach and a philosophy. The approach is to gather information rapidly by any practical method, and the philosophy is that the community members should have considerable input into the information used for policy or planning decisions. In part, this approach grows out of dissatisfaction with the inappropriate and wasteful ways in which surveys are so often used in the Third World (Gow, 1990). Rather than using time and budget-consuming surveys of a hundred or more people, Kumar (1987b) suggests using key informant interviews, focus group interviews, community interviews, direct observation, and informal surveys. Gow (1990) adds to this list the use of existing information and aerial inspections.

With the fourth special method, involving standard information modules, the emphasis shifts away from the gathering of new information from potentially affected regions. For projects such as roads, where considerable knowledge on impacts has accumulated over the years, it is possible to create a standard information module (SIM) describing the common pattern of impacts. SIAs for specific projects can use the SIM as the basis for estimating social impacts of the study project. Some fieldwork and interviews with informants and experts is required, however, to test how well the general pattern will hold in the specific case. For a more extensive discussion of SIMs, see Finsterbusch, 1995; Finsterbusch and Hamilton, 1978.

At the other end of the spectrum are methods that are often (although not always) quite expensive, and that are oriented toward the formal and/or quantitative modeling of systems, rather than the gathering of field information about those systems. The most familiar of these techniques are quantitative models of the impacts of growth in rural areas (for guides, see Canter et al., 1985; Leistritz, 1994; Leistritz et al., 1994/1995; Leistritz and Murdock, 1981; Murdock and Leistritz, 1983). These guides tell how to begin with an estimate of the number and kind of new jobs involved in a new economic activity, to decide how many of the new workers are likely to be locals, commuters, and immigrants, and then to estimate the implied changes in demands for services and housing and in the fiscal circumstances for local communities. Each of these estimates feeds into the next, and the authors supply readers with coefficients or standards to simplify the calculations. Canter et al. (1985) even take the brave step of estimating associated quality-of-life impacts, presenting and evaluating nine possible quality-of-life indices, although these tend to differ from indices that a sociologically oriented assessor might use. Finally, the authors discuss methods for weighting the various impacts and making decisions based on these calculations.

The final special method is *importance weighting* (Canter, 1995; Canter and Canty, 1993; Canter et al., 1985; Finsterbusch, 1981); this method has considerable similarity to the multi-attribute utility analyses that are noted in Chapter 11 in this volume. The basic principle is that once all the costs and benefits of a set of alternative courses of action have been estimated, they have to be weighted relative to one another before a choice between alternatives is possible. Normally, the SIA simply presents estimates of impacts without concluding which course of action is the best choice; the subjective weights that are informally employed are those of the decision maker and those who influence him/her. Formal importance-weighting methodologies strive to make the process more explicit and conscious, although they do raise additional issues. For example, does the choice of methodology substantially affect the outcome, that is, the choice? According to Eckenrode's (1965) analysis, six importance-weighting methodologies (ranking, rating, and four paired comparison-weighting schemes) produced essentially the same results in three different decisions settings. The decisions, however, involved 12 or fewer dimensions, so Eckenrode's conclusion might not apply to more complex impact assessments. More important than the selection of the formal importance weighting scheme is the selection of judges. Experts, decision makers, and the general public often have different perceptions and values and would make different judgments. In addition, given that the public is not an undifferentiated mass, we recommend that the stakeholder groups, or types of persons likely to be affected by a decision, be identified and asked to rate the options.

## MITIGATION, MANAGEMENT, AND MONITORING

Most SIAs have been conducted in connection with environmental impact statements and include descriptions of the project area and the estimation of potential impacts. A few of these SIAs have also proposed measures for mitigating the negative social impacts, but on the whole, mitigation, management, and monitoring have received less attention than they deserve. Accordingly, we are encouraged to see the increased attention to these issues among social impact assessors starting in the mid-1980s—including a chapter devoted to mitigation and monitoring in the Branch et al. (1984) guidebook, 100 pages of annotated references in the Leistritz and Ekstrom bibliography (1986), and the publication by Halstead, Chase, Murdock, and Leistritz of *Socioeconomic Impact Management* (1984).

Pragmatism and equity both suggest that, once impacts have been estimated, we should take steps to avoid, minimize, or compensate for the negative ones. Tried-and-true mitigation measures include noise barriers for highways, compensation for taken properties, payments for moving expenses, adjustment of construction schedules and workforce size to reduce peak in-migration, policies to hire local residents first, training programs, and prepayments of taxes, to mention just a few. In any given case, it is worth keeping in mind the hierarchy of mitigation sketched out in the early pages of this chapter—*avoiding* negative impacts where possible, *minimizing* any negative impacts that cannot be avoided, and *compensating* affected persons and communities for any negative impacts that can neither be avoided nor minimized. Often, mitigation also requires nonproject actions, such as passing a special state bill to give affected counties and municipalities the necessary powers for dealing with the impacts. These mitigations, however, require a thorough analysis of the institutional capacity of the local authorities and of state and federal laws and political processes. In addition, the mitigation measures need to be subject to impact assessments themselves, to ensure that they are truly appropriate (Cortese and Jones, 1977).

One type of mitigation activity that has shown a good deal of promise is the practice of mediation (Amy, 1983a, 1983b; Curtis, 1983; Lake, 1980; Mernitz, 1980; Talbot, 1983; Watson and Danielson, 1982). It is employed when a proposed project is contested and the parties agree to use a third-party mediator to compromise and resolve the dispute. Its objectives are to ensure that all parties having an interest have been represented; to achieve a mutually satisfactory settlement relatively quickly and at a low cost; to provide for continued dialogue on future matters; and to ensure that the community at large views the settlement as just and fair (Curtis, 1983:18). Mediation is not a panacea, but it has already achieved many notable successes (see especially, Talbot, 1983; Watson and Danielson, 1982).

Most of the impact management literature deals with fiscal impacts affecting local governments and the actions that local governments can take to manage the problems of rapid growth. Barrows and Charlier (1982:195) identify four sets of growth management techniques for local governments: obtaining state/federal grants; negotiating with companies for assistance such as financial aid or tax prepayment, in-kind services, information, or technical assistance; using local planning and regulation to control and manage growth; and raising local revenues through taxation or borrowing.

Perhaps the major technique is regulation, and the major type of regulation is zoning based on permit powers. Zoning is a form of land-use control that can be used to promote, slow, stop, channel, or encourage growth. Barrows and Charlier (1982) describe some variations of zoning techniques that are promising for boomtown situations. First, "contract zoning . . . is a means by which communities can extract money and other assistance from companies; zoning changes are granted in exchange for special actions by the developer" (p. 203). Second, "interim zoning [places] a moratorium on zoning changes or on existing uses, allowing time to develop a plan or zoning map that protects community residents from the adverse impacts of development" (p. 203). Third, "bonus zoning allows communities to offer developers higher development densities if they provide the community with certain services or dedications." Fourth, phased zoning spells out zoning stages dependent on the extension of municipal services.

Planning and fiscal actions are also important growth-management techniques. In particular, land-use plans and public facility plans set forth the community leaders' vision of how the community should or should not grow. If debated, revised, and widely accepted, they can provide a democratically legitimated guide for zoning decisions and managing growth. Fiscal actions principally include taxes on property, sales and/or income, users' fees, and borrowing as a means to finance the extra services that growth requires.

Less well-developed is the literature dealing with ways in which the management of impact-creating projects themselves could help in avoiding or minimizing negative impacts. There is widespread agreement, however, that developers can reduce the impacts by reducing the number of relocated workers, can offer financial and/or technical assistance to local governments in dealing with impacts, and can establish and/or finance monitoring programs for identifying and managing negative impacts, especially for projects that subject area populations to some risks (Freudenburg, 1979; Halstead et al., 1984; Leistritz and Murdock, 1986; see also Carley, 1986:290–296; Carley and Bustelo, 1984:69–71; for a more critical view, however, see also Gramling and Freudenburg, 1990).

## CURRENT DEVELOPMENTS AND ISSUES

While many of the issues that proved highly contentious during earlier eras of SIA/TA have been resolved, others have not. In this section, accordingly, we turn to what appear to be some of the most contentious and complex of the remaining issues.

### Quantification, Participation, and Politics

Perhaps the issue that has been identified most frequently in past reviews of SIA (Boothroyd, 1982; Bowles, 1982; Carley and Bustelo, 1984; Freudenburg, 1986b; Freudenburg and Olsen, 1983) is the potential for tension between "scientific" and "political" orientations toward the field. To simplify only slightly, proponents of the "scientific" approach tend to call for documenting impacts dispassionately and preferably quantitatively, rather than becoming "politically" involved in efforts to produce change; those proponents tend to be found predominantly in the United States. Proponents of the "political" approach tend to see true objectivity as unobtainable, and they see quantification as working to the advantage of relatively powerful groups in society, and to the disadvantage of the predominantly small and less powerful communities likely to be affected by developments. They tend instead to emphasize a participatory function for SIA, working with affected communities to help them develop their own capacities to deal with development and any attendant disruptions (Dietz, 1987).

Several of the most articulate proponents of the "political" approach to SIA (see, for example, the compilation by Tester and Mykes, 1981) are from Canada, where the roots of SIA emerge not from U.S. environmental law, but from precedent, particularly from the MacKenzie Valley Pipeline Inquiry (Berger, 1977). Justice Thomas R. Berger of the British Columbia Supreme Court was appointed to examine the social, economic, and environmental impacts of the proposed pipeline, which would have brought natural gas from the Canadian Arctic to mid-continent. The pipeline would have crossed a region as large as Western Europe but which was inhabited by only 30,000 people, half of them natives. Berger held hearings in a series of northern communities, complete with native translations, helping to educate his countrymen about their neighbors to the north as well as to identify the implications of the pipeline itself. His final recommendation—to delay pipeline permits for 10 years to allow the settlement of native claims—did not carry the force of law, but it had a major impact on policy outcomes. At least since the time of the Berger inquiry, many SIA practitioners have argued that SIAs in general ought to place greater emphasis on changing outcomes and less on simply studying them.

Partly because both of us have been identified with the "scientific" pole of this debate, we will refer readers to the more detailed treatments of this topic available elsewhere (see, in particular, Carley and Bustelo, 1984; Freudenburg, 1986b), rather than attempting to resolve it here. Instead, we will offer three brief observations that have received relatively little emphasis in work to date.

First, this issue is directly related to the long-standing debate in sociology between "research" and "action" (or "praxis") orientations and to the argument by many in the sociology of science about the impossibility of doing "value-free" research (Fox Keller, 1985; Knorr-Cetina and Mulkay, 1983; Whitehead, 1925). It is also affected by differences in disciplinary backgrounds. In particular, SIA practitioners often come from fields such as community development, planning, and applied sociology, where the professional's role is explicitly envisioned as that of a change agent, rather than as a person who will study a process scientifically without "getting involved" in it.

Second, the issue of client relations is a particularly thorny one for SIA, even for proponents of the "scientific" orientation, given that the SIA may become the focus of contention in court. Under U.S. environmental law, legal vulnerability for a proposal is created not by the creation of negative impacts, but by the failure to disclose those negative impacts in an EIS

(Freudenburg, 1989; Llewellyn and Freudenburg, 1990; Meidinger and Freudenburg, 1983). Organizations that contract for SIAs, however, often are either the project proponents or else agencies that want the project to be described in the most favorable terms possible (see the more detailed reviews in Freudenburg and Keating, 1985, or Chapter 16 in this volume).

Third, some unresolved questions remain about public participation issues. Even we, as proponents of the "scientific" approach, have argued for the importance of encouraging public involvement in social impact assessment—both because local residents are an important source of expertise on their own way of life and because of the importance in a democracy of having significant citizen input into decisions that may affect the broader public. Nevertheless, giving public participation an important role in the evaluation of siting options can be tantamount to advocating that objectionable facilities be placed in the communities that raise the weakest complaints. Given the realities of public participation patterns, these are likely to be the poorest communities—which implies in turn that they could be the localities having the fewest resources for dealing with any problems that may result (Freudenburg and Olsen, 1983).

### Values and the Management of Technology

Many technological decisions require the consideration of both facts and values. Even under optimal conditions, for example, risk disputes are likely to involve at least two types of questions: How safe is the technology? and Is that safe enough? Often the decisions turn on a third question: What are we overlooking? The first or factual question, is at least in principle, answerable in a scientific sense; yet the second simply cannot be answered except with reference to personal values, and the third is one in which the blind spots of scientists often prove to be at least as significant as those of affected publics (Freudenburg, 1996).

The sides involved in many technological controversies, moreover, tend to have unequal access to technical expertise, as well as unequal access to political influence. As Dietz et al. point out in Chapter 11 in this volume, industries and government agencies have the resources necessary to afford the often-expensive scientific expertise that can be decisive in technological disputes, while local communities for the most part do not, needing instead to resort to fund-raising on a scale as "modest . . . as bake sales and car washes" (Freudenburg, 1992b:29). More broadly, local citizens and project proponents often differ in what they perceive to be the proper weightings of values. In the case of a question about how safe is safe enough, for example, local residents might wish for a weighting that would err on the side of increasing costs for industry (see the fuller discussion by Freudenburg and Pastor, 1992). Given that safety-related decisions are often characterized by irreducible ambiguity, there can be a considerable advantage to the regulated industry to demand that government agencies be required to demonstrate that a regulation is *unambiguously* justified before imposing it.

Some value differences, moreover, may be less than obvious. One example is the effects of having risk-related decisions made by scientists. Johnson and Petcovic (1988) found that radiation health professionals tend to have Myers-Briggs personality profiles that favor abstract, empirical, and logical orientations and that emphasize making judgments rather than merely perceiving events. Such a personality type is found in only about 1 percent of the U.S. population. It has important assets, but it can also lead to impatience about considerations that other types of people consider to be important—such as equity of outcomes. One need only reflect on the obvious frustrations of many scientific professionals toward the "illogical, emotional" reactions of affected citizens to realize that such personality variables, while rarely seen as sources of "bias" by the professionals in question, may in fact lead those professionals to make value-based and hence nonscientific decisions that differ dramatically from the decisions that would be preferred by the public at large.

The parties involved are also likely to have differing orientations on what questions ought to be on the agenda and how they ought to be discussed. As noted in some detail by Freudenburg and Gramling (1994), in addition to genuine differences of opinion about what the "real issues" are, differences over the agenda and over the broader "framing" of debates can often be traced to differing tactical interests. As a congressional staffer once put it to one of the authors, "It's something I learned from one of my law school professors: If you let me define what the case is 'about,' then nine times out of ten, I'll be able to win the case."

Project proponents tend to have a greater advantage through "agenda control" than is commonly recognized. As critical authors have pointed out, monetarily powerful interests often have the potential to exert a good deal of influence through "non–decision making"—through the ability to prevent an issue from getting on a policy agenda in the first place (Bachrach and Baratz, 1970; Crenson, 1971; Gaventa, 1980; Stone, 1980). In addition, as Kunreuther and his colleagues have noted (1982), bureaucratic procedures usually give project proponents considerable control over agendas (see also Galanter, 1974). Discussion is likely to focus on relatively narrow questions—on whether the proponent has complied with specific agency regulations, for example—and not on broader questions about whether a different option or technology could lead to socially superior outcomes. Additional advantages are likely to be provided by the nonneutrality of data availability: As Schnaiberg (1980) has pointed out, the "production sciences," which focus on the efficiency and profitability of industrial production, tend to receive far more funding than the "impact sciences," which focus instead on the negative externalities and/or unforeseen implications of production systems. As a result, the data and analyses advanced by project opponents often appear to be (and may well be) "less scientific" than the data and analyses supporting project proponents. Finally, even the terms that are used to discuss the issues on the agenda are likely to work to the advantage of project proponents. Indeed, our usual terminology reflects any number of implicit value judgments. We will tend to weigh factors such as the "national need" for energy, for example, against the "desire" of local communities to maintain a given way of life, rather than discussing the "need" to protect local residents against disruptions that are the result of the "desire" for bigger air conditioners or the "failure" to invest more in energy efficiency.

### Risk and Uncertainty

Perhaps the most troublesome problem for SIAs and TAs is the need to face the irreducible difficulty of predicting the future. In some cases, SIAs/ TAs are asked not only to look into the future, but into futures of almost breathtaking complexity and uncertainty. This is most easily seen in technology assessments, where specialists have been asked to anticipate the wide-ranging implications of everything from home computers to thermonuclear war. Skeptics judge these efforts to be indistinguishable from sheer speculation. Yet the same problem is evident in SIA as well; to cite just the most obvious example, current efforts to assess the likely impacts of a high-level nuclear waste repository are being asked to project impacts 10,000 years into the future (Slovic et al., 1991). For a comparative perspective, 10,000 years is roughly twice the age of the oldest known human civilization, and roughly comparable to the time that has elapsed since humans first started putting seeds into the ground, an act that led eventually to the emergence of horticulture, then agriculture, and then civilization as we know it today.

Even if we focus on less daunting challenges, and on the subfields of SIA that are relatively developed—as in projecting population changes that are likely to be created by the construction of well-understood facilities in isolated rural areas, where no other developments of similar magnitude are taking place—the record to date is not necessarily one to inspire confidence. In a study that examined the accuracy of demographic projections in 225 environmental impact statements prepared during the 1970s, Murdock et al. (1984) found that the average absolute error had been over 50 percent. In another assessment that examined the projections for a single technology in a single region, Moen (1984) found fluctuations so wild as to inspire an article on "Voodoo Forecasting."

Intriguingly, the largest source of error in the Murdock et al. study came not from the social scientists who worked on the projections, but rather from the engineers and physical scientists involved, who routinely underestimated the number of construction workers required to build the industrial facilities in question. Lest we be tempted to assume that social scientists are somehow immune from such errors, however, Henshel (1982) found that demographers' projections of national population counts, while reasonably accurate under "steady-state" conditions, consistently failed to foresee socially significant changes, such as the "baby boom" of the 1940s and 1950s and the "birth dearth" of the 1960s and 1970s. The commonly prescribed antidote of increased sophistication proved not to be a helpful one; Henshel actually found the more complex and sophisticated assessments to do slightly *worse* than those that were more simple and straightforward (see also Moen, 1984).

As might be expected, specialists in the field have long grappled with the problems associated with crystal-ball gazing, and it appears that three principal responses have emerged. First, a number of authors (including both of us) have emphasized the need for relevant, empirical data. Theory is a way of making sense of data; it is not an adequate substitute for data the analyst needs but does not have (Finsterbusch, 1980; Freudenburg and Keating, 1985). Physical scientists often do just as badly as social scientists at foreseeing "surprises" or predicting the future in the absence of relevant data. A widely respected geologist was literally standing on Mount St. Helens, measuring the mountain's behavior, when the top quarter-mile of the mountain blew off in 1980; he appears to have anticipated the eruption only by the length of time required to transmit his last radio message: "Vancouver! Vancouver! This is it!" In part due to the analysis of data obtained from this first eruption, however, it became possible to predict the timing and magnitude of subsequent eruptions with what many observers found to be an impressive level of accuracy. In SIA as well, perhaps the best prediction is that the first "eruption" of any given sort is likely to come as a surprise, while doing the appropriate research on the first such incident can make it possible to do better in anticipating the incidents that follow (Finsterbusch, 1995).

The second response is that monitoring—the process of tracking social and economic changes over time—can be a helpful way of compensating for the things that are not known at the outset. If the number of construction-worker children turns out to be twice as high as originally expected, for example, then payments to the local school districts can be increased proportionately. It needs to be noted explicitly, however, that for this approach to provide a genuinely useful antidote to the problem of placing the burden of uncertainty on "innocent bystanders" (Freudenburg and Gramling, 1992:952), it is first necessary for the potential problem to have been successfully foreseen, for the appropriate institutional safeguards and funding mechanisms to have been set up, for the developer to have stayed in business, and for most or all of the safeguards to work as planned.

The third response is that the SIA practitioner makes "projections," not "predictions." Rather than saying what *will* happen, the SIA practitioner projects what will happen *if* a given set of assumptions is borne out. Unfortunately, clients and affected communities often pay far more attention to the "best estimate" projections than to the caveats. As an SIA practitioner once put it to one of the authors, "The locals really like those nice, solid numbers. What they usually don't realize is that I have about as much say over the *actual* work force planning as [the local priest] has over the selection of the pope."

It helps to remember that the purpose of social impact assessments is to reduce the uncertainties, not to eliminate them. In fact, most SIAs are done for reasonably routine projects and are fairly adequate (Finsterbusch, 1995). Often, however, we have too little information to produce professionally credible assessments, and often, as noted above, even assessments that are based on extensive information and analysis and that appear to be quite credible, at least at the time, will turn out in retrospect to have missed the kinds of "surprises" that can turn the assessments from science to science fiction (Freudenburg, 1992b). Even changes that can easily be foreseen may lead to social impacts that are virtually impossible to predict; what will be the educational implications, for example, of having personal computers in 60 percent of American homes? and what will the implications be for the distribution of wealth and population between rural and urban areas of the United States? How might these trends, in turn, affect the likely viability of a proposed mine or power plant?

At times, in short, the field's three typical responses to the problem of uncertainty are unsatisfactory, even collectively. Providing communities and clients with *caveats* is a useful first step, but it is scarcely sufficient. Local officials must decide to expand services and facilities enough to meet one population size or another, secure only in the knowledge that they will be blamed whether the facilities ultimately prove to be either "too big" or "too small." In addition, evidence from a variety of fields shows that experts routinely suffer from overconfidence, failing to provide sufficiently careful caveats in part because they fail to foresee many of the ways in which their "projections" might go awry (Clarke, 1990; Freudenburg, 1988, 1992b). Finally, a reliance on monitoring will make sense only in a subset of real-world situations—those in which the relevant causal mechanisms are reasonably well understood and in which the likely outcomes are clustered around a single estimate. Monitoring provides far less reassurance when the probability density function is multimodal (a variety of widely differing outcomes are roughly equally likely), binary (as when the outcome will depend heavily on X, where X has roughly a 50/50 chance of occurring/not occurring), or completely unknown. Still other problems are presented by cases involving what might be called "unknown unknowns"—that is, in cases where the analyst is unaware of his or her ignorance. As one practitioner put it, "It's one thing to come across a field of land mines if you know they're out there but just don't know where they're buried. It's another thing entirely when you don't even know the field is mined."

All in all, the situation appears to us to call for new approaches to the problem of dealing with uncertainty. In coping with systems where understanding is relatively high and where remaining uncertainty is not likely to present major problems, it may prove appropriate to continue following the practices that have been common in the past. In coping with systems that are less well understood, however, or those for which it is clear that even a maximum-likelihood estimate has little likelihood of occurring as envisioned, it may be that a completely different approach is needed. The prudent approach may be to invest relatively little effort in predicting the estimated outcome—making it clear that one is offering simply a "rough guess"—and instead devoting the majority of analytic effort to *anticipating how much difference it makes if the estimate is wrong.*

Notably, this would differ from the kinds of sensitivity analyses that have been done in the past. In assessing the likely impacts of a nuclear waste repository on the city of Las Vegas, for example, the "best guess" might well be that a radiological accident involving spent nuclear fuel would probably not occur anywhere within or near the city limits. Still, as most readers—and most residents of affected communities—are all too well aware, "unexpected" incidents have occurred many times in the past; Bhopal, Chernobyl, and the *Exxon Valdez* are just three examples of incidents that were not expected to occur (for further discussion, see Clarke, 1990; Freudenburg, 1992b). If an "unlikely" incident were to occur in or near Las Vegas, moreover, the consequences could be devastating for the city's tourism-based economy, even if few or no radiation-related deaths would occur. When seen realistically and dispassionately, in fact, many of the purportedly "irrational" concerns of the public about serious accidents are not as unwise as risk experts judge them to be (Freudenburg, 1993).

## CONCLUSION

The field of SIA has accomplished a great deal, and yet a great deal remains to be done. It has reached a degree of maturity for assessing impacts from the construction of facilities such as highways, dams, and power plants. A consensus has been reached on the basic methodology for assessing the impacts of these projects, and a considerable database has been developed on their impacts and the management of their negative effects.

Other areas are less developed but are improving. SIAs for resource-use plans have matured in the sense of becoming relatively routinized in the procedures of the agencies involved, although the information needed for fully informed decisions is often still not available. The fastest-developing field today is SIAs for risk-inducing projects, such as hazardous facilities, many of which present troublesome issues that have not been fully resolved.

Technology assessments will always be a difficult field for SIA because they tend to be so unique and extraordinarily complex. SIAs for development projects in the Third World continue on average to lag in analytical sophistication behind the level of analysis prevalent in the United States. Much more progress is needed in this area.

A major conclusion that we draw from our review of the SIA record is that the unexpected may be the rule rather than the exception, and that "surprises" need to be factored into the planning process more realistically and effectively. Impact assessors and local businessmen both anticipated the boom from the Exxon oil shale development in Colorado, for example, but were totally unprepared for Exxon's sudden shutdown in 1982 (Gulliford, 1989). Even projects described as being "destined" to "go ahead as planned" have wound up being abandoned, for reasons that range from poor planning to unanticipated swings in world commodity markets (Gramling and Freudenburg, 1990); and those that do go forward often succumb to the economic pressures well before they complete their anticipated period of operation (Freudenburg, 1992a; Moen, 1984). We are not criticizing the failure to predict all possible fluctuations in the conditions affecting such projects, but we are calling for greater consideration of the possibility of sharp deviations from the planned course of events, and for improved contingency planning.

In sum, the "normal-science contributions" of SIA have tended in the past to be of the sort that simplified the management of relatively predictable processes. The field has documented a number of consistent patterns in certain types of development, has developed a reasonably respectable set of methods, and has produced the kinds of research that are necessary for relatively dramatic improvements in the estimation of the coefficients that those methods require. Increasingly, however, the challenges that remain for the future may have to do not so much with efforts to make sure our projections are "right," but with understanding the steps that are most prudent to take when even the best of projections are virtually guaranteed to be wrong.

## REFERENCES

Albrecht, Stan L. 1982. "Commentary." *Pacific Sociological Review* 25(3)(July): 297–306.

Amy, Douglas James. 1983a. "The Politics of Environmental Mediation." *Ecology Law Quarterly* 11:1–19.

———. 1983b. "Environmental Mediation: An Alternative Approach to Policy Stalemates." *Policy Sciences* 15:343–365.

Arnstein, Sherry R., and Alexander H. Christakis (eds.). 1975. *Perspectives on Technology Assessment.* Jerusalem: Science and Technology Publishers.

Babiuch, William M., and Barbara C. Farhar. 1994. *Stakeholder Analysis Meth-*

*odologies: Resource Book*. National Renewable Energy Laboratory, Golden, CO, March.

Bachrach, Peter, and Morton S. Baratz. 1970. *Power and Poverty*. New York: Oxford University Press.

Bailey, Conner. 1985. "The Blue Revolution: The Impact of Technological Innovation on Third-World Fisheries." *The Rural Sociologist* 5(4)(July):259–266.

Barbour, Ian G. 1980. *Technology, Environment, and Human Values*. New York: Praeger.

Barrows, Richard, and Marj Charlier. 1982. "Local Government Options for Managing Rapid Growth." Pp. 193–221 in *Coping with Rapid Growth in Rural Communities*, edited by Bruce A. Weber and Robert E. Howell. Boulder, CO: Westview Press.

Baum, Andrew. 1987. "Toxins, Technology and Natural Disasters." Pp. 5–53 in *Cataclysms, Crises, and Catastrophes: Psychology in Action*, edited by G. R. VandenBos and B. K. Bryant. Washington, DC: American Psychological Association.

Berger, L. and Associates. 1982. *Forecasting Enclave Development Alternatives and Their Related Impact on Alaskan Coastal Communities as a Result of OCS Development* (Technical Report No. 88). Anchorage, AK: U.S. Minerals Management Service.

Berger, Thomas R. 1977. *Northern Frontier, Northern Homeland: The Report of the MacKenzie Valley Pipeline Inquiry*. Ottawa: Supplies and Services Canada.

Blahna, Dale J., and Susan Yonts-Shepherd. 1989. "Public Involvement in Resource Planning: Toward Bridging the Gap between Policy and Implementation." *Society and Natural Resources* 2(3):209–227.

Boothroyd, Peter. 1982. "Overview of the Issues Raised at the International Conference on Social Impact Assessment." Presented at the International Conference on Social Impact Assessment, Vancouver, B.C., Canada.

Boothroyd, Peter, Nancy Knight, Margaret Eberle, June Kawaguchi, and Christiane Gagnon. 1995. "The Need for Retrospective Impact Assessment: The Megaprojects Example." *Impact Assessment* 13(1)(September):253–271.

Boulding, Kenneth E. 1983. "Impact Assessment of National Defense." *Impact Assessment Bulletin* 2(4)(Fall):13–20.

Bowles, Roy T. 1982. "A Quick and Dirty Profile of the Social Impact Assessment Community." Presented at the International Conference on Social Impact Assessment, Vancouver, B.C., Canada.

Braddock, Dunn and McDonald. 1974. *Impact Considerations of the National 55 m.p.h. Speed Limit*. Washington, DC: National Science Foundation (September 27).

Branch, Kristi, Douglas A. Hooper, James Thompson, and James Creighton. 1984. *Guide to Social Assessment: A Framework for Assessing Social Change*. Boulder, CO: Westview Press.

Brown, Ralph B., H. Reed Geertsen, and Richard S. Krannich. 1989. "Community Satisfaction and Social Integration in a Boomtown: A Longitudinal Analysis." *Rural Sociology* 54(4)(Winter):568–586.

Bunker, Stephen G. 1984. "Modes of Extraction, Unequal Exchange, and the Progressive Underdevelopment of an Extreme Periphery: The Brazilian Amazon 1600–1980." *American Journal of Sociology* 89(5)(March):1017–1064.

Burdge, Rabel J. 1984. "Getting and Staying in Touch: Sociological Techniques for Evaluation of Range Management Decision Alternatives." Pp. 1635–1658 in *Developing Strategies for Rangeland Management*, National Research Council/National Academy of Sciences. Boulder, CO: Westview Press.

———. 1994. *A Conceptual Approach to Social Impact Assessment: Collection of Writings by Rabel J. Burdge and Colleagues*. Middleton, WI: Abt Books.

Canter, Larry W. 1995. *Environmental Impact Assessment*, 2nd ed. New York: McGraw-Hill.

Canter, Larry W., Samuel F. Atkinson, and F. Larry Leistritz. 1985. *Impact of Growth: A Guide for Socio-Economic Impact Assessment and Planning*. Chelsea, MI: Lewis.

Canter, Larry W., and G. A. Canty. 1993. "Impact Significance Determination—Basic Considerations and a Sequenced Approach." *Environmental Impact Assessment Review* 13:275–297.

Carley, Michael J. 1986. "From Assessment to Monitoring: Making Our Activities Relevant to the Policy Process." *Impact Assessment Bulletin* 4(3/4)(Spring):286–303.

Carley, Michael J., and Eduardo S. Bustelo. 1984. *Social Impact Assessment and Monitoring: A Guide to the Literature*. Boulder, CO: Westview Press.

Chambers, Robert. 1981. "Rapid Rural Appraisal: Rationale and Reportoire." *Public Administration and Development* 1(1):95–106.

———. 1991. "Shortcut and Participatory Methods for Gaining Social Information for Projects." In *Putting People First: Sociological Variables in Rural Development*, 2nd ed., edited by Michael M. Cernea. New York: Oxford University Press.

Clarke, Lee. 1990. "Organizational Foresight and the *Exxon Valdez* Oil Spill." Paper prepared for presentation at annual meeting of Society for the Study of Social Problems, Washington, DC, August.

Cochrane, Glynn. 1979. *The Cultural Appraisal of Development Projects*. New York: Praeger.

Cortese, Charles F. 1982. "The Impacts of Rapid Growth on Local Organizations and Community Services." Pp. 115–135 in *Coping with Rapid Growth in Rural Communities*, edited by Bruce A. Weber and Robert E. Howell. Boulder, CO: Westview Press.

Cortese, Charles F., and Bernie Jones. 1977. "The Sociological Analysis of Boom Towns." *Western Sociological Review* 8:76–90.

Creighton, James L. 1981. *Public Involvement Manual*. Cambridge, MA: ABT Books.

Crenson, Matthew A. 1971. *The Un-Politics of Air Pollution: A Study of Non-Decisionmaking in the Cities*. Baltimore, MD: Johns Hopkins University Press.

Curtis, Fred A. 1983. "Integrating Environmental Mediation into EIA." *Impact Assessment Bulletin* 2(3)(Summer):17–25.

Daneke, Gregory A., Margot A. Garcia, and Jerome Delli Priscoli (eds.). 1983. *Public Involvement and Social Impact Assessment*. Boulder, CO: Westview Press.

Davenport, Judith A., and Joseph Davenport, Jr. 1979. *Boom Towns and Human Services*. Laramie: University of Wyoming Press.

de Kadt, Emanuel. 1979. *Tourism: Passport to Development?* New York: Oxford University Press.

Delp, Peter, Arne Thesen, Juzar Motiwalla, and Neelakantan Seshadri. 1977. *Systems Tools for Project Planning*. Washington, DC: Agency for International Development.

Derman, William, and Scott Whiteford (eds.). 1985. *Social Impact Analysis and Development Planning in the Third World*. Boulder, CO: Westview Press.

Dietz, Thomas. 1984. "Social Impact Assessment as a Tool for Rangeland Management." Pp. 1613–1634 in *Developing Strategies for Rangeland Management*, National Research Council/National Academy of Sciences. Boulder, CO: Westview Press.

———. 1987. "Theory and Method in Social Impact Assessment." *Sociological Inquiry* 57(1)(Winter):54–69.

Dietz, Thomas, and Eugene A. Rosa. 1994. "Rethinking the Environmental Impacts of Population, Affluence and Technology." *Human Ecology Review* 1 (Summer/Autumn):277–300.

Dohrenwend, Bruce P., Barbara Snell Dohrenwend, George J. Warheit, Glen S. Bartlett, Raymond L. Goldsteen, Karen Goldsteen, and John L. Martin. 1981. "Stress in the Community: A Report to the President's Commission on the Accident at Three Mile Island." Pp. 159–174 in *The Three Mile Island Nuclear Accident: Lessons and Implications*, edited by Thomas H. Moss and David L. Sills. New York: New York Academy of Sciences.

Dornbusch, David and Company. 1987. *Impacts of Outer Continental Shelf (OCS) Development on Recreation and Tourism*. Los Angeles: U.S. Minerals Management Service.

Dornsife, William, P. Serie, and J. Kauffman. 1989. "Including Local Leaders in Public Participation." Presented to Waste Management '89, Tucson, AZ, March.

Eckenrode, R. T. 1965. "Weighting Multiple Criteria." *Management Science* 12(3)(November):180–192.

Elkind-Savatsky, Pamela D. 1986. *Differential Social Impacts of Rural Resource Development*. Boulder, CO: Westview Press.

Erikson, Kai T. 1976. *Everything in Its Path: The Destruction of Community in the Buffalo Creek Flood*. New York: Simon and Schuster.

———. 1990. "Toxic Reckoning: Business Faces a New Kind of Fear." *Harvard Business Review* (1 January–February):119–126.

Finsterbusch, Kurt. 1976a. "The Mini Survey: An Underemployed Research Tool." *Social Science Research* 5(1)(March):81–93.

———. 1976b. "Demonstrating the Value of Mini Surveys in Social Research." *Sociological Methods and Research* 5(1)(August):117–136.

———. 1977. "The Use of Mini Surveys in Social Impact Assessments." Pp. 291–296 in *Methodology of Social Impact Assessment*, edited by Kurt Finsterbusch and C. P. Wolf. Stroudsburg, PA: Dowden, Hutchinson & Ross.

———. 1980. *Understanding Social Impacts: Assessing the Effects of Public Projects*. Beverly Hills, CA: Sage Publications.

————. 1981. "A Summary of Methods for Evaluating Social Impacts." Pp. 343–360 in *Methodology of Social Impact Assessment*, 2nd ed., edited by Kurt Finsterbusch and C. P. Wolf. Stroudsburg, PA: Hutchinson Ross.

————. 1982. "Boomtown Disruption Thesis: Assessment of Current Status." *Pacific Sociological Review* 25(3)(July):307–322.

————. 1985. "State of the Art in Social Impact Assessment." *Environment and Behavior* 17(2)(March):193–221.

————. 1987. "What Are the Ingredients for Successful Development Projects? Answers from a Systematic Review of 52 Project Evaluations." Presented at annual meeting of American Sociological Association, Chicago, August.

————. 1988. "Citizens' Encounters with Unresponsive Authorities in Obtaining Protection from Hazardous Wastes." Presented at annual meeting of Society for the Study of Social Problems, Atlanta, August.

————. 1995. "In Praise of SIA—A Personal Review of the Field of Social Impact Assessment: Feasibility, Justification, History, Methods, Issues." *Impact Assessment* 13(3)(September):229–252.

Finsterbusch, Kurt, and Mary R. Hamilton. 1978. "The Rationalization of Social Science in Policy Studies." *International Journal of Comparative Sociology* 19(192):88–106.

Finsterbusch, Kurt, Jay Ingersoll, and Lynn Llewellyn (eds.). 1990. *Fitting Projects: Methods of Social Analysis for Projects in Developing Countries*. Boulder, CO: Westview Press.

Finsterbusch, Kurt, Lynn Llewellyn, and C. P. Wolf (eds.). 1983. *Social Impact Assessment Methods*. Beverly Hills, CA: Sage Publications.

Finsterbusch, Kurt, Chris Mausolff, and Warren Van Wicklin III. 1992. *Factors Contributing to the Effectiveness and Sustainability of Development Projects*. College Park, MD: Report for the International Development Management Center of the University of Maryland and the U.S. Agency for International Development (June).

Finsterbusch, Kurt, and Annabelle Bender Motz. 1980. *Social Research for Policy Decisions*. Belmont, CA: Wadsworth.

Finsterbusch, Kurt, and Warren A. Van Wicklin III. 1987. "The Contribution of Beneficiary Participation to Development Project Effectiveness." *Public Administration and Development* 7(1):1–23.

Finsterbusch, Kurt, and Warren A. Van Wicklin III. 1988. "Unanticipated Consequences of A.I.D. Projects: Lessons from Impact Assessment for Project Planning." *Policy Studies Review* 8(1)(Autumn):126–136.

Finsterbusch, Kurt, and Warren A. Van Wicklin III. 1989. "Beneficiary Participation in Development Projects: Empirical Tests of Popular Theories." *Economic Development and Cultural Change* 37(3)(April):573–593.

Flynn, Cynthia B. 1984. "The Local Impacts of the Accident at Three Mile Island." Pp. 205–232 in *Public Reactions to Nuclear Power: Are There Critical Masses?*, edited by William R. Freudenburg and Eugene A. Rosa. Boulder, CO: Westview Press.

Fox Keller, Evelyn. 1985. *Reflections on Science and Gender*. New Haven, CT: Yale University Press.

Freudenburg, William R. 1976. "The Social Impact of Energy Boom Development on Rural Communities: A Review of Literatures and Some Predictions." Presented at the Annual Meeting of American Sociological Association, New York, August.

———. 1979. "An Ounce of Prevention: Another Approach to Mitigating the Human Problems of Boomtowns." Pp. 55–62 in *Energy Resource Development: Implications for Women and Minorities in the Intermountain West*, U.S. Commission on Civil Rights. Washington, DC: U.S. Government Printing Office.

———. 1981. "Women and Men in an Energy Boomtown: Adjustment, Alienation, and Adaptation." *Rural Sociology* 46(2):220–244.

———. 1982a. "The Impacts of Rapid Growth on the Social and Personal Well-being of Local Community Residents." Pp. 137–70 in *Coping with Rapid Growth in Rural Communities*, edited by Bruce A. Weber and Robert E. Howell. Boulder, CO: Westview Press.

———. 1982b. "Balance and Bias in Boomtown Research." *Pacific Sociological Review* 25(3)(July):323–338.

———. 1986a. "The Density of Acquaintanceship: An Overlooked Variable in Community Research?" *American Journal of Sociology* 92(1)(July):27–63.

———. 1986b. "Assessing the Social Impacts of Rural Resource Developments: An Overview." Pp. 89–116 in *Differential Social Impacts of Rural Resource Development*, edited by Pamela D. Elkind-Savatsky. Boulder, CO: Westview Press.

———. 1986c. "Social Impact Assessment." *Annual Review of Sociology* 12:451–478.

———. 1988. "Perceived Risk, Real Risk: Social Science and the Art of Probabilistic Risk Assessment." *Science* 242(7)(October):44–49.

———. 1989. "Social Scientists' Contributions to Environmental Management." *Journal of Social Issues* 45(1):133–152.

———. 1992a. "Addictive Economies: Extractive Industries and Vulnerable Localities in a Changing World Economy." *Rural Sociology* 57(3)(Fall):305–332.

———. 1992b. "Nothing Recedes Like Success? Risk Analysis and the Organizational Amplification of Risks." *Risk: Issues in Health and Safety* 3(1)(Winter):1–35.

———. 1993. "Risk and Recreancy: Weber, the Division of Labor, and the Rationality of Risk Perceptions." *Social Forces* 71(4)(June):909–932.

———. 1996. "Strange Chemistry: Environmental Risk Conflicts in a World of Science, Values, and Blind Spots." Pp. 11–36 in *Handbook of Environmental Risk Decision Making: Values, Perceptions, and Ethics*, edited by C. Richard Cothern. Boca Raton, FL: CRC Press.

Freudenburg, William R., and Rodney K. Baxter. 1984. "Host Community Attitudes toward Nuclear Power Plants: A Reassessment." *Social Science Quarterly* 65(4)(December):1129–1136.

Freudenburg, William R., and Rodney K. Baxter. 1985. "Nuclear Reactions: Public Attitudes and Public Policies Toward Nuclear Power Plants." *Policy Studies Review* 5(August):96–110.

Freudenburg, William R., and Robert Gramling. 1992. "Community Impacts of Technological Change: Toward a Longitudinal Perspective." *Social Forces* 70(4):937–955.

Freudenburg, William R., and Robert Gramling. 1994. *Oil in Troubled Waters:*

*Perceptions, Politics, and the Battle over Offshore Drilling.* Albany: State University of New York Press.

Freudenburg, William R., and Robert E. Jones. 1992. "Criminal Behavior and Rapid Community Growth: Examining the Evidence." *Rural Sociology* 56(4)(January):619–645.

Freudenburg, William R., and Kenneth M. Keating. 1985. "Applying Sociology to Policy: Social Science and the Environmental Impact Statement." *Rural Sociology* 50(4):578–605.

Freudenburg, William R., and Darryll Olsen. 1983. "Public Interest and Political Abuse: Public Participation in Social Impact Assessment." *Journal of the Community Development Society* 14(2):67–82.

Freudenburg, William R., and Susan K. Pastor. 1992. "Public Responses to Technological Risks: Toward a Sociological Perspective." *Sociological Quarterly* 33(3)(August):389–412.

Friesema, H. Paul, and Paul J. Culhane. 1976. "Social Impacts, Politics, and the Environmental Impact Statement Process." *Natural Resources Journal* 16: 339–356.

Gagnon, Christiane, P. Hirsch, and Robert Howitt. 1993. "Can SIA Empower Communities?" *Environmental Impact Assessment Review* 3:229–253.

Galanter, Marc. 1974. "Why the 'Haves' Come Out Ahead: Speculations on the Limits of Legal Change." *Law and Society Review* 9:95–160.

Gale, Richard. 1982. "Commentary." *Pacific Sociological Review* 25(3)(July):339–348.

Gaventa, John. 1980. *Power and Powerlessness: Quiescence and Rebellion in an Appalachian Valley.* Urbana: University of Illinois Press.

Gold, Raymond L. 1982. "Commentary." *Pacific Sociological Review* 25(3)(July): 349–356.

Gow, David D. 1990. "Rapid Rural Appraisal: Social Science as Investigative Journalism." Pp. 143–163 in *Fitting Projects: Methods of Social Analysis for Projects in Developing Countries,* edited by Kurt Finsterbusch, Jay Ingersoll, and Lynn Llewellyn. Boulder, CO: Westview Press.

Gramling, Robert, and William R. Freudenburg. 1990. "A Closer Look at 'Local Control': Communities, Commodities, and the Collapse of the Coast." *Rural Sociology* 55(4):541–558.

Gramling, Robert, and William R. Freudenburg. 1992. "Opportunity-Threat, Development, and Adaptation: Toward a Comprehensive Framework for Social Impact Assessment." *Rural Sociology* 57(2)(Summer):216–234.

Gran, Guy. 1983. *Development by People.* New York: Praeger.

Gulliford, Andrew. 1989. *Boomtown Blues: Colorado Oil Shale, 1885–1985.* Niwot: University of Colorado Press.

Halstead, John M., R. A. Chase, Steve H. Murdock, and F. Larry Leistritz. 1984. *Socio-economic Impact Management: Design and Implementation.* Boulder, CO: Westview Press.

Hanchey, James P. 1975. *Public Involvement in the Corps of Engineers Planning Process.* Fort Belvoir, VA: Institute for Water Resources, IWR Research Report 75–R4.

Hendee, John C. 1977. "Public Involvement in the U.S. Forest Service Roadless-Area Review: Lessons from Case Study." Pp. 89–103 in *Public Participation in Planning*, edited by W. R. Derrick Sewell and J. T. Coppock. London: John Wiley & Sons.

Henshel, Richard L. 1982. "Sociology and Social Forecasting." *Annual Review of Sociology* 8:57–79.

Honadle, George. 1982. "Rapid Reconnaissance for Development Administration: Mapping and Moulding Organizational Landscapes." *World Development* 10(8):633–645.

Howell, Robert E., Darryll Olsen, Marvin E. Olsen, and Riley E. Dunlap. 1981. *Citizen Participation in Nuclear Waste Repository Siting*. Corvallis, OR: Western Rural Development Center.

Interorganizational Committee on Guidelines and Principles for Social Impact Assessment. 1994. *Guidelines and Principles for Social Impact Assessment*. Forest Service, U.S. Department of Agriculture and National Marine Fisheries Service, U.S. Department of Commerce. NOAA Technical Memorandum, NMFS-F/SPO-16 (May). Also published in *Environmental Impact Assessment Review* 15 (1995):11–43.

Jiggins, Janice. 1995. "Development Impact Assessment: Impact Assessment of Aid Projects in Nonwestern Countries." *Impact Assessment* 13(1)(Spring):47–69.

Johnson, Raymond, and W. L. Petcovic. 1988. "What Are Your Chances of Communicating Effectively with Technical or Non-Technical Audiences?" Paper Presented at Annual Meeting, Society for Risk Analysis, Washington, DC, November.

Jordan, William S. III. 1984. "Psychological Harm after PANE: NEPA's Requirements to Consider Psychological Damage." *Harvard Environmental Law Review* 8:55–87.

Kasperson, Roger E., Ortwin Renn, Paul Slovic, and Halina S. Brown. 1988. "The Social Amplification of Risk: A Conceptual Framework." *Risk Analysis* 8 (2):177–187.

Kershaw, David, and Jerilyn Fair. 1976. *The New Jersey Income Maintenance Experiment*, Vol. 1. New York: Academic Press.

Knight, Mancy, Peter Boothroyd, Margaret Eberle, June Kawaguchi, and Christiane Gagnon. 1993. *What We Know about the Socio-economic Impacts of Canadian Megaprojects: An Annotated Bibliography of Post-Project Studies*. Centre for Human Settlements. University of British Columbia, December.

Knorr-Cetina, Karin D., and Michael Mulkay (eds.). 1983. *Science Observed: Perspectives on the Social Study of Science*. London: Sage.

Korten, David C. 1980. "Community Organization and Rural Development: A Learning Process Approach." *Public Administration Review* 40(5):480–510.

———. 1990. *Getting to the 21st Century: Voluntary Action and the Global Agenda*. West Hartford, CT: Kumarian Press.

Korten, David C. (ed.). 1986. *Community Management: Asian Experience and Perspectives*. West Hartford, CT: Kumarian Press.

Kottak, Conrad Phillip. 1985. "When People Don't Come First: Some Sociological Lessons from Completed Projects." Pp. 325–350 in *Putting People First: Sociological Variables in Rural Development*, edited by Michael M. Cernea. New York: Oxford University Press.

Kruger, Richard A. 1994. *Focus Groups: A Practical Guide for Applied Research*, 2nd ed. Thousand Oaks, CA: Sage Publications.

Kumar, Krishna. 1987a. *Conducting Group Interviews in Developing Countries*. Washington, DC: U.S. Agency for International Development, Program Design and Evaluation Methodology Report No. 8.

————. 1987b. *Rapid, Low-Cost Data Collection Methods for A.I.D.* Washington, DC: U.S. Agency for International Development, Program Design and Evaluation Methodology Report No. 10.

Kunreuther, Howard, and Douglas Easterling. 1990. "Are Risk-Benefit Tradeoffs Possible in Siting Hazardous Facilities?" *American Economics Association Papers and Proceedings* 80(2)(May):252–256.

Kunreuther, Howard, John Lathrop, and Joanne Linnerooth. 1982. "A Descriptive Model of Choice for Siting Facilities." *Behavioral Science* 27:282–297.

Lake, Laura M. (ed.). 1980. *Environmental Mediation: The Search for Consensus*. Boulder, CO: Westview Press.

Leistritz, F. Larry. 1994. "Economic and Fiscal Impact Assessment." *Impact Assessment* 12(3)(Fall):305–317.

Leistritz, F. Larry, Randal C. Coon, and Rita R. Hamm. 1994/1995. "A Microcomputer Model for Assessing Socioeconomic Impacts of Development Projects." *Impact Assessment* 12(4)(Winter):373–384.

Leistritz, F. Larry, and Brenda L. Ekstrom. 1986. *Social Impact Assessment and Management: An Annotated Bibliography*. New York: Garland Publishing.

Leistritz, F. Larry, and Steven H. Murdock. 1981. *The Socioeconomic Impact of Resource Development: Methods for Assessment*. Boulder, CO: Westview Press.

Leistritz, F. Larry, and Steven H. Murdock. 1986. "Impact Management Measure to Reduce Immigration Associated with Large-Scale Development Projects." *Impact Assessment Bulletin* 5(2):32–49.

Little, Ronald L. 1977. "Some Social Consequences of Boomtowns." *North Dakota Law Review* 53:401–425.

Llewellyn, Lynn G., and William R. Freudenburg. 1990. "Legal Requirements for Social Impact Assessments: Assessing the Social Science Fallout from Three Mile Island." *Society and Natural Resources* 2(3):193–208.

Lodwick, Dora G., and Linda K. Ridge. 1990. "A Community Sensitive Management Strategy for High Tech Development: The Case of SSC." *Impact Assessment Bulletin* 8(4):67–85.

Lough, W. Timothy, and K. Preston White, Jr. 1988. "A Technology Assessment of Nuclear Power Plant Decommissioning." *Impact Assessment Bulletin* 6(1):71–88.

Lovins, Amory B. 1986. "The Origins of the Nuclear Power Fiasco." Pp. 7–34 in *The Politics of Energy Research and Development: Energy Policy Studies*, Vol. 3, edited by John Byrne and Daniel Rich. New Brunswick, NJ: Transaction Books.

Meidinger, Errol E., and William R. Freudenburg. 1983. "The Legal Status of Social Impact Assessments: Recent Developments." *Environmental Sociology* 34: 30–33.

Mernitz, S. 1980. *Mediation of Environmental Disputes: A Sourcebook*. New York: Praeger.

444  *Handbook of Environmental Sociology*

Merton, Robert K. 1936. "The Unanticipated Consequences of Purposive Social Action." *American Sociological Review* 1:894–904.

Merton, Robert K., M. Fiske, and Patricia A. Kendall. 1956. *The Focused Interview: A Manual of Problems and Procedures*. Glencoe, IL: Free Press.

Moen, Elizabeth W. 1984. "Voodoo Forecasting: Technical, Political and Ethical Issues Regarding the Projection of Local Population Growth." *Population Research and Policy Review* 3:1–24.

Morash, Merry. 1983. "The Application of Social Impact Assessment to the Study of Criminal and Juvenile Justice Programs: A Case Study." *Journal of Criminal Justice* 11:229–240.

Morgan, David L. (ed.). 1993. *Successful Focus Groups*. Newbury Park, CA: Sage Publications.

Morgan, E. Phillip. 1985. "Social Analysis and the Dynamics of Advocacy in Development Assistance. Pp. 21–31 in *Social Impact Analysis and Development Planning in the Third World*, edited by William Derman and Scott Whiteford. Boulder, CO: Westview Press.

Motz, Annabelle Bender. 1979. *Nonstructural Flood Control Measures: A Sociological Study of Innovation*. Ft. Belvoir, VA: Institute of Water Resources, U.S. Army Corps of Engineers.

Murdock, Steve H., and F. Larry Leistritz. 1979. *Energy Developments in the Western United States: Impact on Rural Areas*. New York: Praeger.

Murdock, Steve H., and F. Larry Leistritz. 1982. "Commentary." *Pacific Sociological Review* 25(3)(July):357–366.

Murdock, Steve H., and F. Larry Leistritz. 1983. "Computerized Socioeconomic Assessment Models." Pp. 171–190 in *Social Impact Assessment Methods*, edited by Kurt Finsterbusch, Lynn Llewellyn, and C. P. Wolf. Beverly Hills, CA: Sage Publications.

Murdock, Steve H., F. Larry Leistritz, and Rita Hamm. 1985. "The State of Socioeconomic Analysis: Limitations and Opportunities for Alternative Futures." Presented at the annual meeting of the Southern Association of Agricultural Scientists, Biloxi, MS, February.

Murdock, Steve H., F. Larry Leistritz, Rita R. Hamm, and Sean-Shon Hwang. 1984. "An Assessment of the Accuracy and Utility of Socio-economic Impact Assessments." Pp. 265–296 in *Paradoxes of Western Energy Development*, edited by C. M. McKell, Donald G. Browne, Elinor C. Cruze, W. R. Freudenburg, Richard L. Perrine, and F. Roach. Boulder, CO: Westview Press.

Narayan, Deepa. 1995. *The Contribution of People's Participation: Evidence from 121 Rural Water Supply Projects*. Environmentally Sustainable Development Occasional Paper Series No. 1. Washington, DC: World Bank.

National Academy of Sciences, National Research Council. 1984. *Social and Economic Aspects of Radioactive Waste Disposal: Considerations for Institutional Management*. Washington, DC: National Academy Press.

Nelson, Paul. 1985. "Development Aid: An Agenda for Change." Background Paper No. 86, Bread for the World (November).

Noronha, Raymond. 1979. *Social and Cultural Dimensions of Tourism*. World Bank Staff Working Paper No. 326. Washington, DC.

O'Hare, Michael. 1977. "Not on My Block, You Don't—Facility Siting and the Strategic Importance of Compensation." *Public Policy* 25:407–458.

Office of Technology Assessment (OTA). 1976. *Coastal Effects of Offshore Energy Systems.* Washington, DC: U.S. Office of Technology Assessment.

Paddock, William, and Elizabeth Paddock. 1973. *We Don't Know How—An Independent Audit of What They Call Success in Foreign Assistance.* Ames: Iowa State University Press.

Palinkas, Lawrence A., Bruce M. Harris, and John S. Petterson. 1985. *A Systems Approach to Social Impact Assessment: Two Alaskan Case Studies.* Boulder, CO: Westview Press.

Partridge, William L. (ed.). 1984. *Training Manual in Development Anthropology.* Washington, DC: American Anthropological Association.

Pelle, Elizabeth. 1987. The MRS Task Force: Economic and Noneconomic Incentives for Local Public Acceptance of a Proposed Nuclear Waste Repository. Paper presented at Waste Management '87, Tucson, AZ.

Peters, Dai. 1994/1995. "Social Impact Assessment of the Ranomafana National Park Project of Madagascar." *Impact Assessment* 12(4)(Winter):385–408.

Petterson, John S. 1988. "The Reality of Perception: Demonstrable Effects of Perceived Risk in Goiania, Brazil." *Practicing Anthropology* 10(3–4):8–9, 12.

Prendergast, C. 1989. "Condorcet's Canal Study: The Beginnings of Social Impact Assessment." *Impact Assessment Bulletin* 7(4):25–38.

Rosa, Eugene A., and William R. Freudenburg. 1993. "The Historical Development of Public Reactions to Nuclear Power: Implications for Nuclear Waste Policy." Pp. 32–63 in *Public Reactions to Nuclear Waste: Citizens' Views of Repository Siting,* edited by Riley E. Dunlap, Michael E. Kraft, and Eugene A. Rosa. Durham, NC: Duke University Press.

Rossi, Peter, and Howard E. Freeman. 1993. *Evaluation: A Systematic Approach,* 5th ed. Newbury Park, CA: Sage Publications.

Rothman, Stanley, and S. Robert Lichter. 1987. "Elite Ideology and Risk Perception in Nuclear Energy Policy." *American Political Science Review* 81(2)(June): 383–404.

Rudel, Thomas K. 1993. *Tropical Deforestation: Small Farmers and Land Clearing in the Ecuadorian Amazon.* New York: Columbia University Press.

Salmen, Lawrence. 1987. *Listen to People.* New York: Oxford University Press.

Savatsky, Pamela D. 1974. "A Legal Rationale for the Sociologist's Role in Researching Social Impacts." Pp. 45–47 in *Social Impact Assessment,* edited by C. P. Wolf. Stroudsburg, PA: Dowden, Hutchinson & Ross.

Schnaiberg, Allan. 1980. *The Environment: From Surplus to Scarcity.* New York: Oxford University Press.

Schurman, Rachel. 1992. "Squandered Surpluses and Foregone Rents: The Tale of the Fishing Sector Boom in Southern Chile, 1973–1990." Presented at the Annual Meeting of the Latin American Studies Association, Los Angeles, September 24–27.

Scrimshaw, N. S., and Gary Gleason. 1992. *Rapid Assessment Methodologies for Planning and Evaluation of Health Related Programs.* Boston: INFDC.

Seyfrit, Carole L. 1986. "Migration Intentions of Rural Youth: Testing an Assumed Benefit of Rapid Growth." *Rural Sociology* 51(2)(Summer):199–211.

Short, James F. 1984. "The Social Fabric at Risk: Toward the Social Transformation of Risk Analysis." *American Sociological Review* 49(December):711–725.

Short, James F., and Lee Clarke (eds.). 1992. *Organizations, Uncertainties and Risk*. Boulder, CO: Westview Press.

Slovic, Paul. 1987. "Perception of Risk." *Science* 236(17 April):280–285.

Slovic, Paul, James H. Flynn, and Mark Layman. 1991. "Perceived Risk, Trust, and the Politics of Nuclear Waste." *Science* 254(13 December):1603–1607.

Smith, V. Carey, and William H. Desvouges. 1986. "The Value of Avoiding a LULU: Hazardous Waste Disposal Sites." *The Review of Economics and Statistics* 48(2)(May):293–299.

Smith, Courtland L., Thomas C. Hogg, and Michael J. Reagan. 1971. "Economic Development: Panacea or Perplexity for Rural Areas?" *Rural Sociology* 36(2)(June):173–186.

Stern, Paul C., Oran R. Young, and Daniel Druckman (eds.). 1993. *Global Environmental Change: Understanding the Human Dimensions*. Washington, DC: National Academy Press.

Stoffle, Richard S., Michael W. Traugott, Camilla L. Harshbarger, Florence V. Jensen, Michael J. Evans, and Paula Drury. 1988. "Risk Perception Shadows: The Superconducting Super Collider in Michigan." *Practicing Anthropology* 10(3–4):6–7.

Stoffle, Richard W., Florence V. Jensen, and Robert Copeland. 1987. *Social Assessment of High Technology: The Superconducting Super Collider in Southeast Michigan*. Ann Arbor: Institute for Social Research, University of Michigan.

Stone, Clarence N. 1980. "Systemic Power in Community Decision Making: A Restatement of Stratification Theory." *American Political Science Review* 74: 978–990.

Summers, Gene F., Sharon D. Evans, Frank Clemente, Elwood M. Beck, and Jon Minkoff. 1976. *Industrial Invasion of Nonmetropolitan America: A Quarter Century of Experience*. New York: Praeger.

Talbot, A. R. 1983. *Settling Things: Six Case Studies in Environmental Mediation*. Washington, DC: The Conservation Foundation.

Tester, Frank, and B. Mykes (eds.). 1981. *Social Impact Assessment: Theory, Method and Practice*. Calgary, Alberta: Detselig.

U.S. Council on Environmental Quality. 1978. *Regulations for Implementing the Procedural Provisions of the National Environmental Policy Act* (40 CFR 1500–1508). Washington, DC: U.S. Government Printing Office.

Vining, Joanne. 1988. *Public Involvement in Natural Resource Management*. Guest editor for special issue of *Society and Natural Resources* 1(4).

Watson, J. L., and L. J. Danielson. 1982. "Environmental Mediation." *Natural Resources Lawyer* 15: 687–723.

Weber, Max. 1958. *The Protestant Ethic and the Spirit of Capitalism*. Trans. Talcott Parsons. New York: Charles Scribner's Sons.

White, Lynn, Jr. 1962. *Medieval Technology and Social Change*. London: Oxford University Press.

Whitehead, Alfred North. 1925. *Science and the Modern World*. New York: Free Press.

Wilkinson, Kenneth P., James G. Thompson, Robert R. Reynolds, Jr., and Lawrence M. Ostresh. 1982. "Local Social Disruption and Western Energy

Development: A Critical Review." *Pacific Sociological Review* 25(3)(July): 275–296.

Wolf, C. P. 1977. "Social Impact Assessment: The State of the Art Updated." *Social Impact Assessment* 20:3–22.

World Bank. 1994. *Resettlement and Development: The Bankwide Review of Projects Involving Involuntary Resettlement: 1986–1993*. Washington, DC: The World Bank, Environment Department. April 8.

*Chapter 14*

# The Environmental Movement in the United States

*Angela G. Mertig, Riley E. Dunlap,
and Denton E. Morrison*

The U.S. environmental movement has been one of the most successful and enduring social movements of the twentieth century. The social and environmental changes that have resulted from the movement are many and far-reaching, although the latter is significantly weaker than most environmental advocates would prefer (Dowie, 1995; Sale, 1993; Shabecoff, 1993). Since the first Earth Day in 1970, environmental organizations have grown significantly—despite fluctuations—in number and membership (Brulle, 2000; Mitchell et al., 1992); legislation and lawsuits on behalf of the environment have proliferated (Futrell, 1988); environmental educational programs have been developed around the country (see, e.g., Weilbacher, 1993); and public concern for the environment has generally remained substantial (Dunlap, 1995, 2000; Mertig and Dunlap, 1995). Ecologically responsible behavior among individuals has risen alongside a growing demand for environmental accountability from public officials and business executives (Bowman and Davis, 1989; Dunlap and Scarce, 1991). Recent political events have likewise underscored the importance of environmental issues to the American public. Widespread negative reaction to efforts in the Republican-dominated 104th Congress to undo environmental protection (Kriz, 1996); Democrats' adoption of "Social Security, Medicare, Education, and Environment" as their 1996 campaign slogan, the emphasis placed on environmental issues by democratic presidential candidate Al Gore in 2000; the insistence by a Republican pollster that the party become more environmentally friendly for the 2000 campaign (McFeatters, 2000); and the negative public reaction to the environmental policies of George W. Bush (Fineman, 2001) are all among the most recent indicators in a long-standing trajectory of widespread concern for the fate of the environment.

A social movement can broadly be defined as "a collectivity acting with some continuity to promote or resist a change in the society or group of which it is a part" (Turner and Killian, 1987:223). The myriad of sympathizers, activists, and organizations that constitute the "collectivity" known as the American Environmental Movement strive—with varying tactics and frequently divergent ideologies—to protect their local, regional, national, *and* global environments. This chapter examines key characteristics of the Environmental Movement in the United States and is divided into two sections. In the first section we discuss the emergence and evolution of the Environmental Movement from its roots in the Conservation Movement at the turn of the century up to the present, noting that the movement has become a strong and diversified force that has nonetheless engendered formidable opposition. In the second section of this chapter we examine the structure of the Environmental Movement, focusing on the roles and characteristics of the mainstream organizations, their institutionalized counterparts, and the growing "alternatives": groups devoted to local, grassroots issues and environmental justice as well as groups that espouse direct action techniques.

## THE EMERGENCE AND EVOLUTION OF THE ENVIRONMENTAL MOVEMENT

While recent scholarship has emphasized the existence of organizations and activists concerned with urban environmental issues (e.g., the creation of urban parks and the protection of industrial workers' health and safety) from the mid-1800s to the mid-1900s (Taylor, 1998), it is commonly recognized that the primary ideological and organizational roots of the Environmental Movement stem back to the Conservation Movement that began in the late nineteenth century. Fed largely by concerns over the profligate use of resources, in addition to other progressive concerns of the time, this movement eventually split between utilitarian conservationists concerned about the scientifically managed use of resources and preservationists concerned primarily about preserving nature for its own sake and for its aesthetic and recreational values (Hays, 1959; Nash, 1982).

Early preservationist interests, led by naturalist John Muir, were represented by the Sierra Club (founded in 1892) and the National Audubon Society (1905), both voluntary social movement organizations. Other social movement organizations later joined the preservationist thrust forming the core of the Conservation Movement; for example, the National Parks and Conservation Association (1919), the Wilderness Society (1935), the Defenders of Wildlife (1947), and the Nature Conservancy (1951). The preservationist goals also became institutionalized in the National Park Service (1916), whose purpose was to preserve natural beauty and facilitate recreation in the national parks.

Utilitarian interests, led by Gifford Pinchot, the nation's first professional forester, were based less on organized public support, but were very successful at getting their agenda incorporated into new government agencies—especially due to the close relationship between Pinchot and President Theodore Roosevelt (Hays, 1959). The professional bureaucrats in these agencies—most notably the Forest Service (1905) and the Bureau of Reclamation (1902)—attempted to manage natural resources efficiently through the systematic accumulation and application of scientific information.

While the advent of two world wars dimmed the visibility of conservationism, the movement nonetheless persisted (Nash, 1974; O'Riordan, 1971). New Deal–era conservation programs, such as the Civilian Conservation Corps, simultaneously dealt with the social devastation of the Great Depression and the environmental disasters of massive flooding and the Dust Bowl. Aldo Leopold developed his now-famous "land ethic" in the 1930s and spearheaded the development of the first wilderness area in the Gila National Forest. In the 1950s and 1960s the Sierra Club and the Wilderness Society successfully curbed the building of dams inside the Dinosaur National Monument and the Grand Canyon, gaining significant popularity in the process. Encouraged by success, the Wilderness Society led the fight for passage of the Wilderness Act in 1964. In the decade before the first Earth Day in 1970, the conservationist cause had clearly gained momentum and support.

### From Conservationism to Environmentalism

Despite important continuities with the earlier Conservation Movement, contemporary environmentalism is considered, both popularly and academically, as a distinct movement. However, no specific date or event marks a clean separation of the conservation era and the advent of the modern Environmental Movement. Still, the publication of Rachel Carson's *Silent Spring* in 1962 was an important early articulation of "environmental" as distinct from "conservation" concerns and, perhaps more importantly, the beginnings of an "ecological" conceptual framework for understanding environmental concerns (Mitchell, 1989). The conceptual framework embodied by a social movement, variously called a social movement's "frame" (Snow et al., 1986) or "discourse" (Brulle, 1996), is the ideological glue with which various organizations, groups, and activists are loosely bound together and through which public perceptions of the movement are formed. Rachel Carson played a key role in the development of an environmental frame, as she persuasively articulated to an educated lay audience research concerning the detrimental effects of the new array of chemicals and pesticides unleashed by postwar industry and agriculture.

The new conceptual framework, combined with a growing array of environmental issues, was embodied in the development of several new organizations toward the end of the decade, such as the Environmental Defense Fund (1967; renamed Environmental Defense in 2000) and the Natural Resources Defense Council (1970). The new environmental concerns—often buttressed and verified by subsequent environmental events (such as the Santa Barbara oil spill of 1969)—broadened rapidly and fueled considerable political mobilization in the late 1960s. The decade culminated in the late-1969 passage of the National Environmental Policy Act (NEPA), the establishment of the Environmental Protection Agency (EPA) in 1970, and the massive climax of environmental concern that preceded and followed the original Earth Day in 1970 (Dunlap and Mertig, 1992).

Some scholars have referred to the contemporary Environmental Movement (from the 1960s to the present) as "second generation" environmentalism, in order to mark the qualitative distinctions between the modern movement and the earlier conservation era, referred to as "first generation" environmentalism (Mitchell, 1989). The conservationist discourse was by no means abandoned in second-generation environmentalism; rather, the slate of newer issues—and a newly articulated frame—was affixed to the older agenda, augmenting rather than displacing it (Brulle, 2000). Table 14.1 highlights important differences between the frame of "conservationism" and the "environmentalism" frame that supplanted it, as well as the emerging frame of "ecologism" to be discussed later.

As can be seen in the table, conservationism encompassed concern for the preservation of relatively specific features of the natural environment (e.g., a specific wilderness area or species) and for the professional, scientific, and efficient management of a fairly narrow range of natural resources (e.g., national parks, public rangelands, forests, eroded soils). The causes and consequences of first-generation environmental problems were considered largely specific, direct, and unambiguous, for example, ranchers whose sheep overgrazed public lands or utilities whose dams inundated unique sites. The necessary solutions were therefore fairly straightforward in principle, however difficult it may have been in practice to implement and enforce corrective policies (Dunlap and Mertig, 1994; Mitchell, 1989).

The contemporary discourse of environmentalism has broadened the scope of concern considerably. In addition to concerns about human impacts on the natural environment, environmentalism encompasses concern for urban environments and the impact of environmental problems on human health, the quality of life, and social systems. The issues of environmentalism are more likely than those of conservationism to involve complex technology and scientific research, and are characterized by less obvious, less immediate, and more complex causes, consequences, *and* so-

Table 14.1
Three Stages of Environmental Activism

| | Conservationism | Environmentalism | Ecologism |
|---|---|---|---|
| Approximate Beginnings | Late nineteenth century | Mid-twentieth century | Late twentieth century |
| Primary Goals | Conservation of natural resources | Protection of environmental quality | Maintenance of ecological sustainability |
| Dominant Ideology | Natural resources should be used efficiently for the good of all society | Environmental quality should be protected for a high quality of life | Ecosystems should be protected for the benefit of all species |
| Worldview | Anthropocentric | Anthropocentric | Ecocentric |
| Nature of Issues | Geographically bounded (typically rural), specific, unambiguous | Geographically dispersed (often urban); delayed, subtle, and indirect effects; potentially harmful to human health | Extremely diverse; systemic and synergistic effects; potentially irreversible and harmful to all life on Earth |
| Example | Over-logging of a specific forest area | Urban air and water pollution | Global environmental change |
| Cost of Solution | Relatively small, localized | Often substantial | Potentially infinite |
| Tactics | Lobbying | Lobbying, litigation, citizen participation | Lobbying, litigation, electoral action, direct action, life-style change |
| Opposition/ Culprits | Natural-resource industries; local economic interests (loggers, hunters) | Corporations, economic growth, modern life styles | Status quo; excess human production, consumption, and population |

lutions (Dunlap and Mertig, 1994; Mitchell, 1989). For instance, oil spills from freighters or from offshore drilling platform accidents result in immediate, obvious damage to marine wildlife and to shorelines; but environmentalism includes concern for longer-term, more subtle human disruptions of marine ecosystems plus concern for economic and social disruptions in coastal communities dependent on fishing and tourism. Moreover, underlying the oil spills is a transportation system of petroleum-thirsty private automobiles serving an expanding population of affluent consumers living energy-intensive life styles in sprawling, freeway-connected suburbs. Solving the problem of frequent oil spills thus becomes nothing less than trying to change the life style of the typical American as well as entrenched corporate practices—a formidable task by any standards.

The modern Environmental Movement (and the frame of environmentalism) was born in a time rife with conflict and change, much of it associated with various social movements: the civil rights movement, the student movement, the anti–Vietnam War movement, the farm workers' movement, the welfare rights movement, the counterculture movement, and the women's movement—to name only the most visible contemporaries of emerging environmentalism in the United States (see, e.g., Gottlieb, 1993; Scheffer, 1991). These other movements, coupled with the strong foundation of the conservation-era organizations, were sources of encouragement, strategies, activists, and other resources for the fledgling Environmental Movement (see, e.g., Mitchell, 1989; Mitchell et al., 1992).

In retrospect, the 1960s embodied a "regime crisis" of the kind that presents fertile opportunities for the development of social movements (McAdam et al., 1988). The "environmental crisis" became part of the American consciousness, especially as the decade came to an end. Environmental problems were presented by the movement as real, important, pervasive, and urgently in need of concerted, immediate attention—and initially they appeared readily amenable to rational solutions. Early on, these solutions seemed to pose little threat to the status quo, especially to the existing patterns of power and privilege—unlike many other movements. The Environmental Movement was comparatively modest in its goals and mild in its tactics compared to the often radical goals, shrill claims, and occasionally socially disruptive tactics of the other movements. In fact, leftist critics were wary of widespread acceptance of the Environmental Movement, claiming that it was a deliberate attempt to divert the energies of young people away from the more important social causes of the time (Gale, 1983). However, the nonthreatening appearance of the movement faded rather quickly, as various interests found themselves at the receiving end of environmental condemnation (Morrison, 1973).

By the late 1960s television was in virtually all American households, and an aggressive media industry was eager to meet the public demand for news, especially for news that would vary the standard fare of the latter part of the decade (i.e., the dismal reports on the endless war in Vietnam and the societal conflict it engendered). Pictures of citizens attempting to rescue oil-soaked wildlife on severely damaged Santa Barbara beaches, and of a lonely, fragile spaceship earth were accompanied by accounts of a new type of crisis and a scientific perspective for understanding and addressing it—ecology. Although relatively slow in adopting environmental stories at the onset, television and other media played an increasingly important role in fostering public perceptions of the environment as a social problem (Schoenfeld et al., 1979).

Demographic changes in America also helped fuel the growth of support for environmental causes. Increasing levels of education, affluence, and urbanization, all of which are positively related to environmentalism (as well as other causes) were rising in postwar America (Hays, 1987). The affluence of postwar America allowed people to worry less about just earning a living and more about pursuing a high quality of life, which gradually came to include a healthy environment. A corresponding shift in values from a relatively materialistic vein emphasizing economic growth and security, to what has been labeled "post-materialism," emphasizing goals such as beauty and personal freedom, also helped foster environmental causes (Inglehart, 1990; Milbrath, 1984).

Greater affluence brought increased leisure time which people increasingly spent in the outdoors, where they sometimes came to revere (and then fight for) landscapes that were threatened by development (Gale, 1972). Prior to the environmental era, conservation organizations such as the Sierra Club successfully used recreational field trips to draw members into their ranks (Faich and Gale, 1971). Riding high from hard-won victories protecting natural areas in the 1950s and 1960s, these organizations continued to use field trips as a means of mobilizing people—not only to join their ranks but to fight threats to the natural environment.

These same organizations, plus numerous new organizations devoted to the environmental cause, were further aided by the development of direct mail techniques for soliciting a mass membership and, consequently, a substantial increase in finances (Godwin and Mitchell, 1984). While direct mail techniques began to be used as early as the 1950s, it wasn't until the 1970s that environmental organizations began to use them extensively (Mitchell et al., 1992). Corporations and major foundations (e.g., the Ford Foundation) joined in on the environmental bandwagon by sponsoring the development of new organizations (Robinson, 1993) such as the Environmental Defense Fund (1967) and the Natural Resources Defense Council (1970), both of which began as organizations specializing in the scientific and legal aspects of environmental issues (Mitchell, 1989). Furthermore, changes in the tax laws in the late 1960s allowed greater flexibility in tax exempt status, and gradual changes in the definition of legal standing throughout the 1960s provided environmental organizations greater standing and leverage in the courtroom (Mitchell, 1989). These changes, plus the proliferation of environmental legislation at the time, gave environmentalists a powerful base from which to work.

The larger organizations increasingly became committed to influencing political decisions to bring about environmental reforms. Theirs was basically, although not solely, a "power-orientation" aimed at wielding political power to generate new laws and influence public agencies to implement them. Such a power-orientation, used successfully by the large, national environmental organizations (both old and new), can usefully be contrasted to the "participation-orientation" that was the more publicly visible feature of environmental concern in the early part of the movement (Morrison, 1980; Morrison et al., 1972). This orientation emphasized the important role that individuals and groups could play through their own voluntary behavioral changes (e.g., picking up litter or recycling waste materials). In the heady tenor of media-hyped enthusiasm surrounding Earth Day in 1970, there was an implicit tendency to assume that environmental reforms would come about through the participatory efforts of individuals, families, corporations, and communities. The new awareness of the need to protect the environment was thought sufficient to cause narrow self-interests or bad habits to be put aside in pursuit of the common good.

The development of a power-orientation at the organizational core of the movement, coupled with a participation-orientation among individual activists, the public, and smaller, local and regional organizations, effectively protected environmental concerns from the political winds of change. The former ensured that environmental reform would not depend solely on voluntary behavior, which could fade as quickly as it began. However, by itself a power-orientation was (and is) not sufficient. The arrival of an environmentally hostile political administration in the 1980s—and more recently with the 1994 Congress as well as the early activities of the George W. Bush administration—showed that environmental laws and regulations, as the most visible products of a power-orientation, are vulnerable to political change (Dowie, 1995; Shabecoff, 1993).

The Environmental Movement today flourishes in a substantially more diverse form than when it began. As the movement has evolved, it has incorporated a broader—and more sophisticated—array of issues, organizations, strategies, and tactics. Just as the earlier blending of the frames of conservationism and environmentalism led to greater breadth in the movement, current trends suggest that yet another frame or generation of environmentalism may be evolving, bringing with it a more sophisticated ideology or framework, a more comprehensive list of issues, and a plethora of new organizations, activists, and tactics (Dunlap and Mertig, 1994; Snow, 1992b). In Table 14.1, we refer to this new stage as "ecologism." We use the term *ecologism* to denote the fact that even though an ecological perspective helped stimulate the growth of second-generation environmentalism, this perspective has become even more dominant with this newest wave of activism (Caldwell, 1990; Oates, 1989; Thiele, 1999).

Ecologism broadens environmental concern in various ways, namely, by fighting on a greater number of fronts, from local to global, and by extending concern not only to the entire human race but also to other species and ecosystems (Dunlap and Mertig, 1994; Thiele, 1999). Ecologism embodies a greater emphasis on both macro and micro concerns. At the macro level, ecologism is concerned with issues of international import and ecological sustainability, such as global warming, ozone destruction, and the loss of rainforests. Especially noteworthy is the incorporation of transnational—especially Third World—environmental concerns into the agendas of national environmental organizations (Wapner, 1996); the establishment of various international environmental organizations (e.g., Conservation International [1987]; Rainforest Action Network [1985]) (Caldwell, 1992); and the growth of indigenous protest in the Third World (Guha and Martinez-Alier, 1997; Taylor, 1995), as well as the development of "green" parties in many countries, particularly in Europe (Barbosa, 1993; Dalton, 1994; McCormick, 1989). At the micro level, grassroots groups around the country are mobilizing protests against garbage incinerators and hazardous waste repositories and other presumably hazardous sites (Freudenberg and Steinsapir, 1992). Minorities in particular are mobilizing on behalf of "environmental justice" to oppose the disproportionate location of environmentally noxious facilities in their communities (Bullard and Wright, 1992).

Ideologically, ecologism focuses on the broadest—and most complex—picture possible, the ultimate sustainability of life on earth and a concern for all of creation, including all of humanity (both present and future generations) and all species and ecosystems (Thiele, 1999). A key component of ecologism is the growth of radical, direct action–oriented groups that espouse an ecocentric worldview, in stark contrast to the anthropocentric worldview of both conservationism and environmentalism (Devall, 1992; Manes, 1990; Scarce, 1990). These adherents of ecologism believe that nature has a right to exist in and of itself, apart from human values. While facets of this position existed earlier, only recently has it become a potent voice in the evolving Environmental Movement. Additionally, grassroots/environmental justice groups have not only incorporated issues of class, race, and gender—essentially bringing in groups of humans heretofore largely unacknowledged in the movement—but they have evolved a sophisticated critique of the overall sustainability of technological systems (Freudenberg and Steinsapir, 1992).

Ecologism entails an expanded critique of the status quo, based on a systemic and large-scale view of human impact on the natural environment. The pivotal concerns of ecologism are typically those that involve long-

term, irreversible, synergistic, and often unpredictable consequences of human actions. Global warming and loss of biodiversity, for instance, are not
only long-term and possibly irreversible, but they stem from a complex
interplay of factors. While environmentalism has often addressed these issues, it has looked at them in a piecemeal fashion. Ecologism, on the other
hand, views them in the context of the larger, ecological-evolutionary
global system. Advocates of ecologism talk about the "end of nature," mass
extinction, the halt of evolution, and so forth—unless human practices are
altered, and soon. The purported causes and consequences, as well as the
costs needed to remedy them, are therefore truly colossal.

Just as the issues have broadened, so have the tactics employed by environmental activists. Conservationism and environmentalism relied primarily on relatively polite forms of action, including lobbying, litigation,
research, and citizen participation in letter-writing campaigns and mass
demonstrations. Ecologism incorporates these same tactics but increasingly
employs more aggressive tactics such as consumer boycotts, taking government officials hostage (at Love Canal), and various forms of sabotage or
"direct action," such as tree-spiking and "monkeywrenching" (Foreman
and Haywood, 1987).

Grassroots/environmental justice groups and direct action groups, to a
large extent, developed in response to perceived weaknesses in the mainstream, national environmental organizations. The national organizations
have increasingly been portrayed as ossified, overly professionalized and
centralized, and too willing to compromise on issues that affect the daily
lives of many citizens (Devall, 1992; Dowie, 1995; Snow, 1992a). Indeed,
both the radicals and especially the grassroots/environmental justice groups
have been heralded not only as contributing to a healthy diversification of
the Environmental Movement, but as representing its revitalization (Dowie,
1995; Gottlieb, 1993; Manes, 1990; Szasz, 1994).

### The Decline of the Environmental Movement?

Immediately after the first Earth Day in 1970, the Environmental Movement appeared to be a growing and vital actor in the nation's political
arena. However, this quickly changed, as the years following the active and
participatory fervor of Earth Day witnessed some dampening of support
for environmental issues, due partly to the realization that there were substantial costs—and inequities in bearing them—to environmental cleanup
(Morrison, 1973). This change was exacerbated by the coming of the energy crisis in 1973–1974, and a growing public awareness that environmental reforms would involve crucial trade-offs with energy supplies
(Morrison, 1980).

By 1973, many observers thought the movement was on its way out
(Downs, 1972). In fact, social movement theorists have frequently offered

models of the "natural history of social movements," in which movements are assumed (as ideal types) to evolve from idealistic enthusiasm to a climax of success and to eventual decline (Dunlap and Mertig, 1992). For such theorists, the Environmental Movement appeared in the mid-1970s to have undergone its incipient period of enthusiasm, reached a climax of success, and already begun the slow road to eventual demise, for various reasons ranging from "in-fighting" among activists to co-optation by the status quo, especially when the Carter administration appointed many leading activists to government positions.

However, the Environmental Movement appears to have defied this fate, hanging on not only through the 1970s but experiencing a resurgence of support in the 1980s. A majority of the public, despite some dips in the public opinion polls, continued to support environmental protection throughout the 1970s (Dunlap, 1992), and the numbers of organizations and the members they attracted continued to grow as well (Mitchell et al., 1992). Reagan-era attempts to slash environmental programs provoked a substantial increase in public concern over the environment and a dramatic growth in organizational membership in the 1980s, offering a fertile climate for environmental organizations to launch successful recruitment efforts (Dunlap, 1992; Mitchell et al., 1992). While some national organizations in the late 1980s felt financial and membership losses (Dowie, 1995)— particularly as threats to environmental legislation appeared to be some- what lessened during the Bush administration—the Environmental Move- ment remained relatively healthy, having largely withstood political attempts to weaken the legislative and administrative bases of environmen- tal protection (Sale, 1993; Shabecoff, 1993). The media-laden *Exxon Val- dez* oil spill of 1989 further substantiated movement claims that environmental protection could not be ignored.

Earth Day 1990 marked the twentieth anniversary of the first Earth Day, and it involved millions of people in the United States and around the world. It proved to be an even greater success nationally and internationally than was its 1970 predecessor. By 1990 environmental concern registered an all-time high in public opinion polls, as the percentage of the public supporting environmental protection or identifying themselves as "environ- mentalists" reached strong majority status (Dunlap, 1992). Environmental organizations, both old and new, attracted an even larger membership base and continued to pursue their power-oriented agenda, with several of the national organizations becoming major players in the political arena (Mitchell et al., 1992). The election of an ostensibly environmentally friendly administration in 1992 seemed to solidify the importance of en- vironmental issues in the United States.

However, as the decade proceeded, the Environmental Movement ap- peared to be losing some of its momentum once again, as memberships and finances declined for several national organizations (Brick, 1995; Dowie,

1995), as hope in the new political administration's rhetoric on the environment dwindled, and especially as Republicans took control of Congress in 1994 and the anti-environmental implications of the "Contract with America" gradually became apparent. However, the Environmental Movement has yet again proven its tenacity by mobilizing opposition to the Republicans' anti-environmental agenda. Public opinion polls showing public disapproval of efforts to weaken environmental regulations led Republicans to moderate their rhetoric and opposition to the Clean Air Act (Shabecoff, 1996). In short, as was true in the Reagan era, this recent attempt to weaken environmental protection efforts generated a "backlash," apparent not only in the form of rising public concern, but in expanding membership rolls and coffers for the national environmental organizations (AAFRC Trust for Philanthropy, 1995; Kriz, 1996).

Rather than experiencing the expected demise of social movements, the Environmental Movement has proven tremendously resilient. In fact, the Environmental Movement may be a fairly unique enduring phenomenon, due in no small part to the increasing visibility of "old," worsening environmental problems and the continual discovery of new ones (Dunlap, 1993; see also Downs, 1972), and to the fact that ultimately the environment is where we all live. Even so, the Environmental Movement is increasingly faced with an exceptionally formidable—and, more recently, well-organized—foe whose opposition will undoubtedly continue to challenge the evolving movement and to which we now turn our discussion.

### Opposition to the Environmental Movement: The Wise Use Movement

If a movement is successful it will inevitably engender opposition among groups who see themselves as negatively affected by its suggested reforms. While opposition to conservationist and/or environmentalist actions has always existed to some degree, and certainly played key roles in the earlier years of the Environmental Movement (see, e.g., Albrecht, 1972; Helvarg, 1994; Morrison, 1973), the recent guise of opposition—commonly referred to as the "Wise Use" movement (although Switzer [1997] carefully uses this term to denote only one component of opposition to the environmental movement)—may be the most threatening adversary the Environmental Movement has ever faced (Dowie, 1995). According to Brick (1995:19), "for the first time, the environmental movement faces an opposition that has political and ideological coherence and is capable of organizing on a broad scale."

The Wise Use Movement, supported by conservative/far-right politicians and media spokespersons (e.g., Rush Limbaugh, George Will), sees itself as waging a holy war against environmentalists, who they claim want to destroy free enterprise, private property rights, and jobs through misguided efforts at increasing government regulations, "taking" the value out of private land without just compensation, and forcing entire industries to close their doors to needy workers and their families (Brick, 1995; Helvarg, 1994; see also, Switzer, 1997). The primary constituency of the Wise Use Movement are laborers and middle managers in resource-intensive industries in the West who feel threatened by industry cutbacks, blaming them on excessive environmental regulations (Helvarg, 1994). However, the Wise Use Movement draws support from around the country from various groups who feel shafted by environmental reforms: loggers, miners, ranchers, farmers, hunters, industrialists, motorized recreationists, property owners, and factory workers. Some scholars have also noted direct links between the Wise Use Movement and white supremacist and anti-government or militia groups (Brick, 1995; Helvarg, 1994).

These disparate interests have only recently coalesced to form a viable movement to combat environmentalism. Under the leadership of Ron Arnold—an ex-environmentalist whose self-avowed goal is to destroy the Environmental Movement—a conference of sympathetic interests was convened in Reno, Nevada, in 1988 to start building a coalition of Wise Use organizations and draw up guidelines (*The Wise Use Agenda*) for the movement. According to some estimates, in 1988 there were only 200 organizations actively considered as Wise Use organizations, but by 1995 there were approximately 1,500 such organizations (Brick, 1995). Arnold himself coordinates grassroots Wise Use efforts through his national umbrella group, the Center for the Defense of Free Enterprise out of Bellevue, Washington (Brick, 1995).

The movement's leaders claim to have millions of followers, but dues-paying and active members of Wise Use organizations probably number considerably less than 100,000 (Helvarg, 1994). The Wise Use Movement also claims to be largely a grassroots movement, composed of ordinary individuals and families whose livelihoods and/or property have been significantly hampered by environmentalist activity. Indeed, the movement has been very successful in mounting grassroots efforts such as letter writing or phone campaigns on behalf of resource issues, a useful tactic they borrowed from their opponents in the Environmental Movement (Brick, 1995; Helvarg, 1994). However, some movement organizations are supported substantially, and in some cases almost entirely, by natural-resource and industry groups (Brick, 1995; Deal, 1993; Helvarg, 1994).

Additionally, movement organizations and activists are aided considerably by conservative think tanks (e.g., the Heritage Foundation and the Cato Institute) that provide technical support and political access; by law firms/foundations (e.g., the Mountain States Legal Foundation and the National Legal Center for the Public Interest) that offer legal advice and pro bono counseling; and by public relations firms (e.g., E. Bruce Harrison Co. and Burson-Marstellar) that attempt to sway the public away from environmentalists and/or put a "green" spin on activities that harm the environment but benefit industry and Wise Use interests (Deal, 1993; Helvarg, 1994). Interestingly, many of the Wise Use organizations have also attempted to appear environmentally inclined by giving themselves "green-sounding" names like the Environmental Conservation Organization or the Abundant Wildlife Society of North America (Brick, 1995; Deal, 1993; Helvarg, 1994).

While leaders of the Wise Use Movement gloat that they borrowed some of the devil's tools (i.e., tactics employed by the Environmental Movement) to defeat the devil, some anti-environmental activists and organizations have gone far beyond the legal, political, and financial maneuverings common to modern social movement organizations. There have been numerous reports of environmental activists being intimidated, threatened, and/or violently assaulted by individuals and groups who sympathize with the Wise Use Movement (Dowie, 1995; Helvarg, 1994).

The Wise Use Movement poses a considerable challenge to the contemporary Environmental Movement, one that will likely escalate in the coming years. It is probable, given its resilient history, that the Environmental Movement as a whole will successfully evolve in response to this latest, albeit quite powerful, threat. Part of this response, however, will likely entail a growing sensitivity to local concerns and increased reliance on grassroots organizations—currently the Achilles' heel of large national organizations. The American public continues to expect a level of environmental protection that, despite considerable "greenwashing" by industrial and Wise Use interests, is clearly threatened by unregulated resource-use.

## THE STRUCTURE OF THE ENVIRONMENTAL MOVEMENT

The Environmental Movement has traditionally been considered synonymous with the mainstream national environmental organizations that work on behalf of environmental protection. While these organizations certainly do not represent the movement in its entirety—and not even the bulk of individuals affiliated with the movement—they certainly play a central role. Hence, we begin our overview of the movement's structure by discussing the large national organizations.

### The Mainstream: Large, National Environmental Organizations

The Environmental Movement is comprised of thousands of organizations, over 1,000 of which can be considered relatively large organizations with budgets in excess of $100,000 (Brulle, 2000). Of these there are several national organizations, such as the Sierra Club and the National Audubon Society, that command substantial name recognition and that are considered the major movement players in the environmental policy arena. These voluntary environmental social movement organizations (VESMOs) make up the central core of the movement, mobilizing mass memberships, substantial sums of money, and intensive lobbying efforts on behalf of environmental causes.

The organizations listed in Table 14.2 are the major national VESMOs that engage in lobbying (as well as other activities). While lobbying is a vital activity for any social movement, not all movement organizations choose to do so, as this can lead to a loss of nonprofit status (Mitchell et al., 1992). Of these central VESMOs, seven were established during the conservation era, from the turn of the century up until the beginnings of the modern Environmental Movement in the 1960s. These organizations were all direct or delayed products of the Conservation Movement.

By 1960, most of these organizations remained heavily focused on particular geographic regions (e.g., the Sierra Club originally concentrated on the Sierra Mountains of California) and drew the bulk of their members from those regions (Mitchell, 1989). As individual organizations their memberships were small, totaling only around 124,000 in 1960. The concerns of the organizations were, at that time, fairly narrow, focusing on traditional conservation issues such as wilderness, wildlife and habitat preservation, and outdoor recreation. However, in the 1950s, several years before the publication of *Silent Spring*, the National Audubon Society and the National Wildlife Federation fought to prohibit DDT spraying in certain areas—a distinctively environmental issue (Bosso, 1987). Some of the organizations, especially the Sierra Club and the Wilderness Society, as noted earlier, had also periodically become nationally visible by assuming moderately aggressive postures toward preservationist issues (Mitchell, 1989). In the early 1960s, these conservation-era organizations were moving toward the cutting edge of new, expanded concerns that would transform them into full-blown environmental organizations in the next decade: The frame of conservationism was slowly being converted into that of environmentalism.

One important aspect of this transformation was a sharp growth in memberships, starting toward the end of the 1960s, as public awareness of and concern for environmental issues grew and as the organizations themselves directed their efforts to recruiting a national, mass membership. Membership requirements, where they existed (e.g., sponsorship by existing members), were mostly dropped and/or greatly relaxed and membership basically became open to all interested citizens willing to pay dues. Much of this membership growth occurred prior to and shortly after the first Earth Day in 1970 (Mitchell, 1989).

The concerns of the older organizations became increasingly national as well, broadening beyond the traditionally rather narrow issues of conser-

Table 14.2
National Environmental Lobbying Organizations

| Time Period/Organization | Year Founded | Membership (Thousands) | | | | | | | | |
|---|---|---|---|---|---|---|---|---|---|---|
| | | 1960 | 1969 | 1972 | 1979 | 1983 | 1989 | 1990 | 1995 | 2000 |
| *Conservation Era* | | | | | | | | | | |
| Sierra Club | 1892 | 15 | 83 | 136 | 181 | 346 | 493 | 560 | 550 | 550 |
| National Audubon Society | 1905 | 32 | 120 | 232 | 300 | 498 | 497 | 600 | 600 | 550 |
| National Parks & Conservation Association | 1919 | 15 | 43 | 50 | 31 | 38 | 83 | 100 | 450 | 500 |
| Izaak Walton League | 1922 | 51 | 52 | 56 | 52 | 47 | 47 | 50 | 40 | 50 |
| The Wilderness Society | 1935 | (10) | (44) | (51) | 48 | 100 | 333 | 370 | 310 | 300 |
| National Wildlife Federation | 1936 | — | (465) | (525) | (784) | (758) | (925) | 975 | (975) | 945 |
| Defenders of Wildlife | 1947 | — | (12) | (15) | (48) | 63 | 68 | 80 | 80 | 250 |
| *Environmental Era* | | | | | | | | | | |
| Environmental Defense | 1967 | — | — | 30 | 45 | 50 | (130) | 150 | 300 | 300 |
| Friends of the Earth | 1969 | — | — | 8 | 23 | 29 | (30) | 30 | 35 | 20 |
| Natural Resources Defense Council | 1970 | — | — | 6 | 42 | 45 | 105 | 168 | 170 | 400 |
| Environmental Action | 1970 | — | — | 8 | 22 | 20 | (13) | 20 | 10 | — |
| Environmental Policy Institute | 1972 | Not a membership group. | | | | | | | | |
| Total | | 123 | 819 | 1,117 | 1,576 | 1,994 | 2,724 | 3,103 | 3,520 | 3,865 |

*Note:* Data through 1990 adopted from Mitchell et al., 1992. Data for 1995 come from either Jaszczak, 1996, or the organization's membership person. Data for 2000 come from National Wildlife Federation, 2000, or the organization's membership person. Data in parentheses are estimates.

vationism and adopting the newer issues of environmentalism. Mitchell (1989) points out, for instance, that in the mid-1960s the Sierra Club added urban amenities and population to its action agenda, two concerns heavily associated with the newer frame of environmentalism.

Shortly before and after the first Earth Day, several new, national environmental organizations joined the older organizations (see the five organizations listed under the "Environmental Era" in Table 14.2). One of the organizations, Environmental Action, was specifically involved in the creation of the Earth Day Environmental Teach-In, and in the process successfully generated massive student involvement in environmental issues (Environmental Action, 1970). Since their beginnings in the 1960s and 1970s, the new VESMOs have grown substantially in membership and in influence, and, except for Environmental Action, which disbanded in the mid- to late 1990s, the new VESMOs are a major part of the present core of the movement (Mitchell et al., 1992). These new VESMOs were initiated specifically around second-generation environmental issues; that is, their focus was on national—and sometimes international—problems of pollution and resource depletion, all interpreted via an emerging ecological framework. Some of the new VESMOs were greatly assisted by start-up grants from foundations, such as the Ford Foundation (Robinson, 1993), from the older VESMOs, and from wealthy individual patrons. Foundations also made some grants to the older VESMOs, and foundations remain an important source of support for some of the VESMOs. However, most of the new groups, like the older groups, rely substantially on contributions from individuals.

Members and leaders of large, national environmental organizations, like those for many social causes, typically have "above-average" socioeconomic status, exhibiting higher levels of income, occupational prestige, and—especially—education than the average member of the public (Milbrath, 1984; Morrison and Dunlap, 1986). These environmentalists further tend to be found primarily in nonextractive occupations such as professional, service, and creative art careers (Morrison and Dunlap, 1986). Environmentalists—at least those constituting the bulk of the membership in the large VESMOs—have further been distinguished on the basis of age, race, and sex. In general, organization members have been found to be younger on average than their counterparts in the general public, although this is not consistent across all studies (Manzo and Weinstein, 1987). Organization activists and leaders have also been primarily white and the majority have been male (Dowie, 1995). It is important to emphasize, however, that research has consistently shown that sympathy and support for the goals of the Environmental Movement—if not involvement in it—are widely dispersed throughout most segments of society (Mertig and Dunlap, 2001; Morrison and Dunlap, 1986).

## Resource Mobilization and the Professionalization of VESMOs

The national VESMOs at the core of the Environmental Movement exhibit many of the characteristics of social movement organizations highlighted by the resource mobilization perspective on social movements and social movement organizations (McCarthy and Zald, 1987). This perspective was very popular among scholars in the 1970s and 1980s, the same time that the VESMOs (and other social movement organizations [SMOs]) were becoming quite adept at mobilizing resources (e.g., foundation support and mass memberships via mail campaigns). Prior to the 1960s, social movements were widely considered ephemeral, irrational, and loosely organized around shared "grievances" and charismatic leaders, and some appeared to fit this characterization. However, in the 1960s scholars began to recognize the development of well-organized, professional, bureaucratic, and centralized social movements and social movement organizations that became masters at mobilizing resources, enabling them to grow larger, endure longer, and be more effective than most movements and movement organizations of the past. The large national VESMOs are excellent examples of this phenomenon.

The major national environmental organizations have come to rely on professional staff and professionalized, bureaucratic strategies for generating resources and for influencing specific targets (Mitchell, 1989; Mitchell et al., 1992; Snow, 1992a; see also Ingram and Mann, 1989). These VESMOs have full-time offices where individuals develop managerial and professional careers, frequently transferring between the various VESMOs or moving into other nonprofit organizations or government positions to promote their careers. The VESMOs command the resources of legal and scientific experts to support their cause and they have become adept at marketing diverse ideologies and a wide array of goods—all in the name of mobilizing resources needed in order to fight for environmental protection. They have had impressive results in obtaining resources and in the skillful, effective use of these resources to increase the supply of public environmental goods (e.g., pollution control legislation or court injunctions on logging operations). In addition to the primary tactics of lobbying, litigating, and educating the public, some VESMOs have also developed innovative strategies such as land acquisition or trades for nature preservation (e.g., the Nature Conservancy) and, more recently, debt-for-nature swaps with developing countries. Other VESMOs, like the League of Conservation Voters, have honed their political skills, devoting themselves full-time to monitoring politicians and their campaigns.

In the last three decades the national VESMOs have learned to create, refine, buy, and exchange mailing lists for remarkably productive use in direct-mail fund-raising (Godwin and Mitchell, 1984). The VESMOs have similarly used national telephone soliciting techniques for fund-raising, with great payoffs. These and other techniques, including advertising campaigns in national print media, have resulted in generally growing—albeit irregularly—memberships, public support, and coffers. Members recruited through such efforts often join several organizations, but participate little if at all in the major VESMO policy and action decisions (Mitchell et al., 1992). The primary way the relatively small cadre of VESMO professionals who set policy and manage the organizations interact with their massive constituencies is in the form of regularly published magazines and/or newsletters received by the constituents in exchange for their monetary contributions. Additionally, mailings are occasionally made to constituents regarding the election of VESMO officers and board members, special environmental issues, referenda, and for special fund-raising and letter-writing campaigns on special issues.

The VESMO professionals and their staffs assemble and analyze huge amounts of complex scientific, legal, and economic information. They also develop much insider know-how about federal legislation, agency, and court processes and personnel. Additionally, they are intricately involved in well-oiled, personal influence networks with other VESMO professionals and staffs (most located in Washington, DC), legislators and legislative/committee staffs, and regulatory personnel. Ad hoc coalitions of VESMOs are often formed to collaborate on specific causes. In addition, an informal coalition of 10 of the largest and most influential national environmental organizations, referred to as the "Group of Ten" or "the Green Group," met regularly, occasionally with representatives of other VESMOs as well, throughout the 1980s and 1990s to make decisions regarding the Environmental Movement and its agenda (Dowie, 1995; McCloskey, 1992). The book entitled *An Environmental Agenda for the Future* (Cahn, 1985) was a product of their efforts. In addition, because of the wide array of organizations and their ideological and strategic differences, the organizations tend to voluntarily divide up types of environmental issues amongst themselves based on their expertise and interests (McCloskey, 1992).

The professionalization of the VESMOs has disheartened many observers of the Environmental Movement, who claim that this has led to dampened concern about environmental outcomes, since bureaucrats and professionals care more about organizational stability and career success than about ideological goals (see, e.g., Dowie, 1995; Snow, 1992a). Others, particularly the growing grassroots sector and radical fringe, believe the movement has been co-opted by the status quo and has accommodated economic and industrial interests, embracing those very elements that it originally sought to overcome (Devall, 1992; Freudenberg and Steinsapir, 1992).

Traditional models of social movements (drawing on Weber and Michels) incorporate the notion that enduring movements and movement organizations will inevitably become professionalized, centralized, and bureaucratic, losing ideological fervor and becoming willing to compromise with decision makers and opponents (McCarthy and Zald, 1987). While the major national VESMOs have indeed become professionalized—and even pride themselves on this—and have become concentrated in Washington, it is important to note that these VESMOs exist in a very competitive and sophisticated organizational environment (Mitchell, 1989; Mitchell et al., 1992). They must be able to relate effectively to the media and to public opinion; congressional staff; the judicial system; the scientific community; industrial organizations; and units of federal, state, and local governments in terms of constantly changing, very complex scientific, technological, legal, and economic information. This is not a job that can be done by loosely organized amateurs or volunteers. The national VESMOs have necessarily and successfully adapted to a changing, evolving organizational environment. Whether this has resulted in "too much" compromise or a "sell out" of environmental goals remains to be seen.

## The VESMOs' Institutionalized Counterparts: The IESMOs

It is not conventional in the analysis of social movements to explicitly designate institutionalized organizations (IOs) such as government agencies or public foundations as an integral, important part of the movement under consideration. This is not to say that analyses of movements do not generally recognize their importance, but in most analyses of social movements the voluntary social movement organizations remain as the central, driving element—the social force that, in effect, *is* the movement. Where IOs have been considered they are often discussed as adversaries and impediments of the movement (Gale, 1986), or, at best, as mere auxiliary facilitators of movement goals. IOs, however, frequently develop, at least in part, from the activities of social movements—a point that has been recognized most explicitly in political science (see, e.g., Sabatier and Mazmanian, 1980)— and remain integral to the continued workings of social movements, providing a movement with access to the most direct and powerful instruments of change (Morrison, 1973, 1986; Morrison et al., 1972).

Government agencies, such as the U.S. Environmental Protection Agency and the various state environmental and natural resource departments, are institutionalized organizations created directly or indirectly to advocate and implement environmental regulations and reforms—reforms often pushed by the VESMOs—and can be considered as Institutionalized Environmental Social Movement Organizations (IESMOs) (Morrison, 1973, 1986). The IESMOs carry many of the ideological genes of the VESMOs, albeit in a politically more constrained body. Often the personnel of the IESMOs have had leadership experience in the VESMOs and vice versa (Rudel, 1982). Both the Carter and Clinton administrations, for instance, tapped (some say, drained) the leadership of the Environmental Movement to fill important positions in their administrations (Ingram and Mann, 1989; Kriz,

1996). Typically, VESMOs monitor, lobby, and even litigate IESMOs (and other IOs) to ensure their compliance with environmental reforms.

Many IESMOs were created during the early years of the Environmental Movement and continue to be created, albeit at a substantially slower rate. Similarly, special organizational units to deal with environmental issues have been created in private industries, in business associations, in labor organizations, in various professions, in private foundations, and especially in public and private institutions of higher education (Morrison, 1986). Many pre-existing IOs (such as municipal planning commissions) were transformed into IESMOs as they incorporated a greater emphasis on environmental protection into their agendas (Rudel, 1982). Some of the pre-existing natural resource IOs (stemming from the conservation era) were readily transferred into IESMOs. For instance, the National Park Service was an easy candidate for IESMO status because it was created specifically to protect the environment.

On the other hand, agencies such as the Bureau of Land Management (BLM) and the National Forest Service (NFS), which developed around the "multiple use" of natural resources (a legacy of the utilitarian branch of the early Conservation Movement), developed a largely antagonistic relationship with the Environmental Movement (Gale, 1986) and may even be considered handmaidens to the contemporary Wise Use Movement. Similarly, some of the new organizations created or reconstituted in the wake of rising environmentalism, especially in industry, were negatively *re*-active, specifically created to deal with and to resist the growing number of new and transformed environmental agencies, policies, and regulations emanating from government at all levels (Albrecht, 1972). Such organizations, including the BLM and NFS, constitute what could be considered institutionalized environmental countermovement organizations, often using the same tactics used by VESMOs and IESMOs to defeat efforts at environmental protection (Morrison, 1973).

While a relatively fluid relationship existed between the movement and IESMOs throughout the 1970s, particularly with many of its leaders in agency positions during the Carter administration, this relationship became hostile in the 1980s as the Reagan administration attempted to weaken environmental regulations (Ingram and Mann, 1989). This underscored the extent to which relations between social movements and IOs—even between a movement and the IOs it helped to generate—can vary over time and across political administrations (Gale, 1986). It further highlighted the degree to which a movement could have drastically different relations with IOs affiliated with different branches of government. During the Reagan years, what were originally executive-level IESMOs (e.g., the EPA under Anne Burford), became strong adversaries of the movement, if not institutionalized countermovement organizations. A Democratic Congress—and a vehement, flourishing core of VESMOs—was the only barrier preventing the administration from dramatically transforming the missions of federal agencies such as the EPA, the Department of Energy, and the Department of the Interior (Shabecoff, 1993). Under the Clinton administration the pendulum swung back in the other direction, at least rhetorically restoring the original intent of the various national-level IESMOs, and it was the Republican Congress that exerted pressure to "de-institutionalize" environmentalism within government agencies. The situation changed again with the George W. Bush administration and a Republican Congress (until Senator Jeffords' defection cost the Republicans control of the Senate), and VESMOs are clearly working hard to offset the anti-environmental initiatives of the administration (Fineman, 2001).

## Alternatives to the Mainstream: Grassroots and Direct Action

In recent years the mainstream of the Environmental Movement has been criticized heavily, not only by anti-environmentalist elements, but also by activists and groups who could easily be labeled environmentalist, and many certainly accept this label. The latter feel that the mainstream organizations have become largely ineffective, overly homogeneous, professionalized and centralized, and remarkably indifferent to the concerns faced by many ordinary citizens. Among these critics have occasionally been subnational groups affiliated with the nationals (e.g., local chapters of the Sierra Club), who often feel slighted by the national leadership's decisions on issues that affect them directly (Dowie, 1995). However, the most impassioned criticisms have come from two relatively new players in the Environmental Movement, the grassroots/environmental justice groups and radical/direct action groups. Both of these groups embody to some extent the emerging frame of ecologism discussed earlier and are considered viable and healthful "alternatives" to the mainstream (Gottlieb, 1993).

While there are literally thousands of subnational groups involved in the Environmental Movement—many of which have come and gone—the grassroots groups that have developed in reaction to local environmental hazards and/or oppose the location of hazardous facilities are considered the fastest growing—and most dynamic—segment of the modern Environmental Movement (Bullard, 1993; Szasz, 1994). Community protest against present and potential local environmental hazards has grown dramatically since the late 1970s, when a group of Love Canal citizens successfully organized to protest the toxic contamination of their neighborhood (Levine, 1982). The events surrounding the toxic contamination and resultant activism of the Love Canal residents drew considerable media attention and proved to be a powerful catalyst for a burgeoning grassroots movement (Freudenberg and Steinsapir, 1992; Szasz, 1994). The early 1980s saw a rapid escalation in actions opposed to a broadening array of "locally unwanted land uses" (LULUs) as well as a concentrated effort at networking and coalition building (Gottlieb, 1993; Szasz, 1994). By the early 1990s over 7,000 groups across the country were considered part of this grassroots effort, up from an estimate of 600 in the early 1980s (Szasz, 1994).

By the late 1980s it also became increasingly clear that such grassroots issues were tightly intertwined with issues of class and race (Gottlieb, 1993; Taylor, 1993). Several studies suggest that minority and poorer communities tend to be home to a disproportionate share of environmental hazards such as waste sites (Bryant and Mohai, 1992; Bullard and Wright, 1992; Freudenberg and Steinsapir, 1992). Government agencies and private businesses have subsequently been accused of practicing environmental racism and injustice, locating environmentally noxious facilities in poor and/or minority communities on the belief that such communities would welcome the jobs despite the potential hazards and, in any case, would not have enough resources (e.g., money, knowledge, social leverage) to block such facilities. Thus, the fight over local environmental hazards has been translated into a social equity issue, with minority communities—as well as working-class whites who felt disproportionately targeted—pursuing the goal of "environmental justice" (Capek, 1993). Not surprisingly, many of the groups fighting for environmental justice have borrowed heavily from the tactical repertoire of the civil rights movement (Bullard, 1993).

In recent years, regional coalitions and national-level organizations have developed to coordinate and facilitate the growing number of local protest groups by distributing information, providing technical and legal assistance, and lobbying political leaders on behalf of local concerns (Freudenberg and Steinsapir, 1992). One of these, the Citizen's Clearinghouse for Hazardous Waste (which has recently been renamed the Center for Health, Environment and Justice), was started by Lois Gibbs, a local leader in the Love Canal dispute. Another, the Environmental Research Foundation in Princeton, New Jersey, collects research information on the effects of toxic and hazardous waste in order to provide scientific support to local activists who mistrust government and industrial scientific "experts" (Szasz, 1994). Rather than attempting to control the grassroots movement, these national-level, "grassroots" organizations aim to assist local citizens and communities in educating and empowering themselves (Brown and Masterson-Allen, 1994). Grassroots organizations, especially at the local level, are by nature extremely participatory and empowering, relying almost entirely on a cadre of volunteers (Freudenberg and Steinsapir, 1992). Indeed, grassroots activists are highly distrustful of the mainstream organizations because of their heavy reliance on centralized, professional staff and bureaucratic routines, both of which reinforce the mainstream's observed tendency to compromise on vital issues (Dowie, 1995; see also Salazar, 1996).

Grassroots protests have often been cynically labeled "NIMBY" (not in my backyard) protests to highlight a seemingly parochial and selfish emphasis on protecting local areas and communities. Indeed, a prime motivator of NIMBY protests is concern over the local health hazards that often accompany certain land-uses (e.g., toxic waste dumps, garbage incinerators). Yet, the NIMBY label, while it may have been appropriate in the early stages of the grassroots movement—which was marked by largely solitary actions, no overarching frame or ideology, and activists with little or no experience in other social movements—is no longer considered appropriate. As the grassroots effort has evolved (and as activists themselves change) it has become considerably more sophisticated, embracing more of a "NIABY"—or not in anyone's backyard—attitude that promotes the prevention and reduction of environmental hazards through economic and social reforms (Brown and Masterson-Allen, 1994; Freudenberg and Steinsapir, 1992; Gottlieb, 1993; Szasz, 1994).

Unlike their mainstream counterparts, grassroots organizations attract a surfeit of women members, activists, and leaders (see, e.g., Brown and Ferguson, 1995; Gottlieb, 1993). These women, often housewives, have typically had no experience in political activism but become motivated to act because of fears for their family's health (Brown and Masterson-Allen, 1994; Gottlieb, 1993). Many of these women report becoming completely transformed from complacent housewives with innocent beliefs in the efficacy of government and industry, and no prior experience in political participation, into sophisticated and empowered community (and sometimes regional or national) leaders (Brown and Ferguson, 1995; Brown and Masterson-Allen, 1994; Freudenberg and Steinsapir, 1992).

Because LULUs are disproportionately sited in poor, working/lower class, and especially minority communities, and because the mainstream groups have largely ignored issues of class and race, the grassroots movement also attracts a far larger proportion of members from the lower/working classes and minority groups than do the VESMOs (see, e.g., Brown and Masterson-Allen, 1994; Bullard, 1993; Gottlieb, 1993). Until recently, grassroots organizations were largely separated on the basis of race, sometimes with parallel organizations of working-class whites and working-class minorities fighting the same environmental hazard (Gottlieb, 1993). Grassroots organizations, despite their social justice themes, have certainly not been immune to the tensions between race and class issues. Nonetheless, the goal of environmental justice is increasingly being used in efforts to promote greater cooperation among grassroots groups with varying racial-ethnic composition (Gottlieb, 1993). Many national organizations, in turn, are attempting to respond to these issues by diversifying their leadership and broadening their concerns, but their efforts have been considered shallow and less than adequate by some observers (Bullard, 1993; Taylor, 1993).

Overall, the grassroots segment of the Environmental Movement is dynamic and often successful. Grassroots activists are credited with not only achieving many of their specific goals (e.g., blocking the location of hazardous waste sites), but also with expanding citizen participation, empowering communities, changing public opinion, and even altering the practices and policies of corporations (Freudenberg and Steinsapir, 1992). Consequently, grassroots environmental activism is often seen as having considerable potential for transforming the overall Environmental Movement into a more effective effort (Freudenberg and Steinsapir, 1992; Szasz, 1994). According to Gottlieb (1993:320) the grass roots involve "a redefinition that leads toward an environmentalism that is democratic and inclusive, an environmentalism of equity and social justice, an environmentalism of linked natural and human environments, an environmentalism of transformation." The grassroots effort should prove at least as transformative for contemporary environmentalism as was Rachel Carson's *Silent Spring*.

Another potential wellspring of transformation for the modern Environmental Movement are the "radical" groups devoted to direct action techniques and the anti-industrial ideology of "deep ecology." Indeed, the radical tactics and ideology of these groups are what sets them far apart from any other actors involved in the modern Environmental Movement, especially the national VESMOs (Manes, 1990; Scarce, 1990). Tactically, these groups engage in some of the things that other groups do, but they often add direct action tactics that are considered by the mainstream movement to be too extreme, if not bordering on "terroristic." While Greenpeace is typically considered the pioneer of direct action techniques, such as plugging effluent pipes and steering inflatable Zodiacs between whalers and whales, groups such as Earth First! (which appears to have moderated its stance in recent years, leading to the development of an even more radical splinter group, the Earth Liberation Front) and the Sea Shepherd Conservation Society have gone even further, condoning actual property damage (e.g., contaminating fuel for bulldozers used at logging operations, spiking trees to halt potential timber sales, or ramming drift-net ships on the high seas) (see, e.g., Foreman and Haywood, 1987; see also Manes, 1990; Scarce, 1990).

Many of these tactics, often referred to as "monkeywrenching," are geared to attracting attention, not just from their immediate targets, but from the mass media and an attentive public. Indeed, according to Scarce (1990), radical groups typically do not believe they will actually succeed in influencing their targets (and most of the time they do not), but hope to be sufficiently dramatic to attract public attention and to make the mainstream organizations more effective by appearing more reasonable (see also Manes, 1990). For instance, the founders of Earth First!—many of them ex-staffers of mainstream VESMOs—were conscious of their attempts to create such a "radical flank" effect (Lee, 1995), hoping in turn to re-energize what they perceived as an overly professionalized, centralized, and compromising mainstream movement (Devall, 1992; Manes, 1990; Scarce, 1990).

Radical groups justify their actions through a correspondingly radical ideology often labeled "deep ecology." According to Dowie (1995:226), "of all the new ideologies to surface during the past 25 years, few have challenged the environmental imagination as deeply as deep ecology." In contrast to what radicals label the "shallow" ecology and anthropocentric worldview of reformist, mainstream organizations, deep ecology revolves around a biocentric ethic and a passionate self-identification with nature (Devall, 1992; Manes, 1990; Scarce, 1990). Rather than protecting the environment for the sake of humans, radicals seek to protect the environment for its own sake. In this sense, they take the theme of social equity—a primary theme of the emerging ecologism frame—and expand it beyond the human species to all of nature. Activists' identification with nature— solidified through frequent contact with wilderness and rituals like the "Council of All Beings"—is thought to transform them from activists working to protect nature to that of nature working to protect itself (Devall, 1992).

Organizationally, radical groups attempt to defy the professionalization and bureaucratization that they despise in the mainstream organizations. Earth First!, the most visible of the radical groups, has overcome major fractures and grown substantially from a small group in 1980 to having an estimated following of over 10,000 from all over the nation—and the world—and an annual budget of over $200,000 by the end of its first decade (Lee, 1995). Yet, the activists of Earth First!, despite the pressures to routinize that come with such growth in numbers and finances, are committed to remaining decentralized and informal—to remaining a movement, not an organization (Lee, 1995). Despite being a national movement, with a national journal, local activists and groups affiliated with Earth First! act largely on their own (Scarce, 1990).

The Sea Shepherd Conservation Society, the seafaring arm of the radical movement, is similar to Earth First! in its acceptance of sabotage as an appropriate tactic and deep ecology as a motivating ideology. Paul Watson, the founder of the Society, shares with Earth First! a deep distaste for the mainstream Environmental Movement and its apparent malaise. Indeed, Watson was ousted from Greenpeace, a group he helped to co-found, for being too radical. The Society has also grown substantially from its founding in the late 1970s, as in the late 1980s it had an estimated membership of 15,000 and a budget of over $500,000 (Scarce, 1990). While the Society, as a membership organization that solicits individual contributions, remains "all volunteer and nonbureaucratic" (Scarce, 1990: 107), the actual campaigns are of necessity coordinated by Watson and a few others on the Society's board of directors.

Other groups considered part of the radical segment of the Environmental Movement, and who share many of the characteristics discussed above, include the Rainforest Action Network and the Rainforest Information Center, both of which act as networks to facilitate international grassroots action on rainforest protection (Devall, 1992; Scarce, 1990). Additionally, Scarce (1990) places animal rights and animal liberation groups, like the Animal Liberation Front, in the radical environmental camp as well, although some would question this. Because of their direct challenges to property, many of these groups, including Earth First!, the Sea Shepherd Conservation Society, and the Animal Liberation Front, have been the focus of FBI investigations and various legal disputes nationally and internationally.

While radical activists tend to be highly educated, most of them having college educations, they also tend to be quite poor—by choice (Scarce, 1990). Many are only part-time workers and/or purposefully choose low-paying jobs that accord with their values. Their self-imposed poverty or voluntary simplicity coincides with their desires to engage in life styles that have only a minimal impact on the environment.

While radical groups, especially Earth First! and the Sea Shepherd Conservation Society, have male-dominated origins as well as relatively "macho" images, women have played a greater role in these groups than has been common in the mainstream national organizations. Women in Earth First! have complained about gender limitations in the radical movement, yet this appears to be changing, especially as activists concerned heavily with social justice have become more influential within the overall movement, and as women have come to constitute significant portions of the activists and leaders in local Earth First! groups (Lee, 1995; Scarce, 1990). Hence, like the grassroots/environmental justice movement and *unlike* the mainstream organizations, radical groups are more likely to attract participation by women and people of lower economic status (although the latter is often by choice). Unlike the grassroots/environmental justice movement, however, the radical groups, at least in the United States, do not appear to draw substantial support from minorities—despite attempts by radical activists to incorporate social equity themes in their discourse.

The radical segment of the Environmental Movement, while often deemed less than successful in stopping its specific targets, has certainly had some influence on how environmental issues are handled in this country (Manes, 1990). Mainstream organizations, for instance, have increasingly considered some of the "tamer" proposals ventured by Earth First!ers (Zakin, 1993), and a former Earth First! leader, Dave Foreman, was recently elected to the Sierra Club board of directors. Furthermore, monkey-wrenching has escalated the costs of "doing business" to the tune of $20 to $25 million a year (Manes, 1990), a figure that must give industry at least some pause to think. In sum, radical activists may have few tangible victories to point to, but they certainly represent a serious ideological challenge to the mainstream organizations and to society as a whole. As such, they continue to be prominent agents in the transformation of the modern Environmental Movement—and, hence, in how humans relate to nature.

## CONCLUSION

The Environmental Movement must be counted as one of the last few decades' most important forces for change. It has evolved from a relatively narrowly focused movement, drawing a small amount of support from a limited sector of society, to a broadly focused, powerful, and widely supported social movement. It has grown considerably in strength and numbers, registering strong support from the general public (Dunlap, 2000; Mertig and Dunlap, 2001), garnering substantial followers and finances; and enrolling a proliferating number of groups and organizations with varying ideologies and tactics. It has become a major player in developing and implementing environmental policies, and clearly left its mark on the broader social landscape. Of course, it has had its share of detractors, the most recent—the Wise Use Movement—proving to be perhaps the most challenging. We suspect, however, that the Environmental Movement will continue to evolve and thrive—probably in substantially altered form—as it strives to adapt to this opposition and to its growing diversity.

Nevertheless, despite environmentalism's success as a movement—gauged by its endurance and growth relative to most social movements—we must note that it has been far less successful in achieving its goal of protecting and improving environmental quality. Clearly, there have been notable improvements in areas such as air and water quality, and it seems clear that many conditions would have deteriorated even more without the movement, but one could make a convincing case that overall environmental deterioration has continued and perhaps even accelerated in recent decades (Commoner, 1990). Environmentalism started to emerge almost 30 years ago and problems continue to be discovered. While this trend virtually guarantees the continued existence of the Environmental Movement, ultimately the movement's success will be judged less by its endurance than by its effectiveness. The latter remains problematic.

## NOTES

Denton E. Morrison acknowledges the help of his Graduate Research Assistant, Valerie Gunter, and his faithful newsclipper Ariel Maas. Sherry Cable, Richard Gale, Craig Harris, Kenneth Hornback, Allan Mazur, Robert Cameron Mitchell, and Edward Walsh provided useful feedback on earlier drafts of this chapter.

## REFERENCES

AAFRC Trust for Philanthropy. 1995. *Giving USA 1995*. New York: American Association of Fundraising Council.

Albrecht, Stan L. 1972. "Environmental Movements and Counter-Movements: An Overview and an Illustration." *Journal of Voluntary Action Research* 1:2–11.

Barbosa, Luiz C. 1993. "The 'Greening' of the Ecopolitics of the World-System: Amazonia and Changes in the Ecopolitics of Brazil." *Journal of Political and Military Sociology* 21(Summer):107–134.

Bosso, Christopher J. 1987. *Pesticides and Politics: The Life Cycle of a Public Issue.* Pittsburgh, PA: University of Pittsburgh Press.

Bowman, James S., and Charles Davis. 1989. "Industry and the Environment: Chief Executive Officer Attitudes, 1976 and 1986." *Environmental Management* 13(2):243–249.

Brick, Phil. 1995. "Determined Opposition: The Wise Use Movement Challenges Environmentalism." *Environment* 37(8):17–20, 36–42.

Brown, Phil, and Faith I. T. Ferguson. 1995. " 'Making a Big Stink' Women's Work, Women's Relationships, and Toxic Waste Activism." *Gender and Society* 9(2):145–172.

Brown, Phil, and Susan Masterson-Allen. 1994. "The Toxic Waste Movement: A New Type of Activism." *Society and Natural Resources* 7(3):269–287.

Brulle, Robert J. 1996. "Environmental Discourse and Social Movement Organizations: A Historical and Rhetorical Perspective on the Development of U.S. Environmental Organizations." *Sociological Inquiry* 66(1):58–83.

———. 2000. *Agency, Democracy and the Environment: The U.S. Environmental Movement from the Perspective of Critical Theory.* Cambridge, MA: MIT Press.

Bryant, Bunyan, and Paul Mohai (eds.). 1992. *Race and the Incidence of Environmental Hazards.* Boulder, CO: Westview Press.

Bullard, Robert D. 1993. "Anatomy of Environmental Racism and the Environmental Justice Movement." Pp. 15–39 in *Confronting Environmental Racism: Voices from the Grassroots*, edited by R. D. Bullard. Boston: South End Press.

Bullard, Robert D., and Beverly H. Wright. 1992. "The Quest for Environmental Equity: Mobilizing the African-American Community for Social Change." Pp. 39–49 in *American Environmentalism: The U.S. Environmental Movement, 1970–1990*, edited by R. E. Dunlap and A. G. Mertig. Philadelphia: Taylor and Francis.

Cahn, Robert. 1985. *An Environmental Agenda for the Future.* Washington, DC: Island Press.

Caldwell, Lynton K. 1990. *Between the Worlds: Science, the Environmental Movement and Policy Choice.* New York: Cambridge University Press.

Caldwell, Lynton K. 1992. "Globalizing Environmentalism: Threshold of a New Phase in International Relations." Pp. 63–76 in *American Environmentalism: The U.S. Environmental Movement, 1970–1990*, edited by R. E. Dunlap and A. G. Mertig. Philadelphia: Taylor and Francis.

Capek, Stella M. 1993. "The 'Environmental Justice' Frame: A Conceptual Discussion and an Application." *Social Problems* 40(1):5–24.

Commoner, Barry. 1990. *Making Peace with the Planet.* New York: Pantheon.

Dalton, Russell J. 1994. *The Green Rainbow: Environmental Groups in Western Europe.* New Haven, CT: Yale University Press.

Deal, Carl. 1993. *The Greenpeace Guide to Anti-Environmental Organizations.* Berkeley, CA: Odonian Press.

Devall, Bill. 1992. "Deep Ecology and Radical Environmentalism." Pp. 51–62 in *American Environmentalism: The U.S. Environmental Movement, 1970–1990,* edited by R. E. Dunlap and A. G. Mertig. Philadelphia: Taylor and Francis.

Dowie, Mark. 1995. *Losing Ground: American Environmentalism at the Close of the Twentieth Century.* Cambridge, MA: MIT Press.

Downs, Anthony. 1972. "Up and Down with Ecology—the 'Issue-Attention Cycle'." *The Public Interest,* No. 28(Summer):38–50.

Dunlap, Riley E. 1992. "Trends in Public Opinion Toward Environmental Issues: 1965–1990." Pp. 89–116 in *American Environmentalism: The U.S. Environmental Movement, 1970–1990,* edited by R. E. Dunlap and A. G. Mertig. Philadelphia: Taylor and Francis.

———. 1993. "From Environmental to Ecological Problems." Pp. 707–738 in *Social Problems,* edited by C. Calhoun and G. Ritzer. New York: McGraw-Hill.

———. 1995. "Public Opinion and Environmental Policy." Pp. 63–113 in *Environmental Politics and Policy,* 2nd ed., edited by J. P. Lester. Durham, NC: Duke University Press.

———. 2000. "The Environmental Movement at 30." *The Polling Report* 16 (April 24):1, 6–8.

Dunlap, Riley E., and Angela G. Mertig. 1992. "The Evolution of the U.S. Environmental Movement from 1970 to 1990." Pp. 1–10 in *American Environmentalism: The U.S. Environmental Movement, 1970–1990,* edited by R. E. Dunlap and A. G. Mertig. Philadelphia: Taylor and Francis.

Dunlap, Riley E., and Angela G. Mertig. 1994. "The Environmental Movement." Pp. 211–214 in *Encyclopedia of the Environment,* edited by Ruth A. Eblen and William R. Eblen. Boston: Houghton Mifflin.

Dunlap, Riley E., and Rik Scarce. 1991. "The Polls—Poll Trends: Environmental Problems and Protection." *Public Opinion Quarterly* 55(4):651–672.

Environmental Action, National Staff. 1970. *Earth Day—The Beginning.* New York: Arno Press.

Faich, Ronald G., and Richard P. Gale. 1971. "The Environmental Movement: From Recreation to Politics." *Pacific Sociological Review* 14(3):270–287.

Fineman, Howard. 2001. "W's Green War." *Newsweek* (April 23):26–28.

Foreman, Dave, and Bill Haywood (eds.). 1987. *Ecodefense: A Field Guide to Monkeywrenching,* 2nd ed. Tucson, AZ: Ned Ludd.

Freudenberg, Nicholas, and Carol Steinsapir. 1992. "Not in Our Backyards: The Grassroots Environmental Movement." Pp. 27–37 in *American Environmentalism: The U.S. Environmental Movement, 1970–1990,* edited by R. E. Dunlap and A. G. Mertig. Philadelphia: Taylor and Francis.

Futrell, J. William. 1988. "Environmental Law—Twenty Years Later." Pp. 191–197 in *Crossroads: Environmental Priorities for the Future,* edited by Peter Borrelli. Washington, DC: Island Press.

Gale, Richard P. 1972. "From Sit-In to Hike-In: A Comparison of the Civil Rights and Environmental Movements." Pp. 280–305 in *Social Behavior, Natural*

*Resources and the Environment*, edited by William R. Burch, Neil H. Cheek, and Lee Taylor. New York: Harper & Row.

———. 1983. "The Environmental Movement and the Left: Antagonists or Allies?" *Sociological Inquiry* 53(2/3):179–199.

———. 1986. "Social Movements and the State: The Environmental Movement, Countermovement, and Government Agencies." *Sociological Perspectives* 29(2):202–240.

Godwin, R. Kenneth, and Robert Cameron Mitchell. 1984. "The Implications of Direct Mail for Political Organizations." *Social Science Quarterly* 65(3): 829–839.

Gottlieb, Robert. 1993. *Forcing the Spring: The Transformation of the American Environmental Movement.* Washington, DC: Island Press.

Guha, Ramachandra, and Juan Martinez-Alier. 1997. *Varieties of Environmentalism: Essays North and South.* London: Earthscan.

Hays, Samuel. 1959. *Conservation and the Gospel of Efficiency.* Cambridge, MA: Harvard University Press.

———. 1987. *Beauty, Health, and Permanence: Environmental Politics in the United States, 1955–1985.* New York: Cambridge University Press.

Helvarg, David. 1994. *The War against the Greens: The "Wise Use" Movement, the New Right, and Anti-Environmental Violence.* San Francisco: Sierra Club Books.

Inglehart, Ronald. 1990. *Culture Shift in Advanced Industrial Society.* Princeton, NJ: Princeton University Press.

Ingram, Helen M., and Dean E. Mann. 1989. "Interest Groups and Environmental Policy." Pp. 135–157 in *Environmental Politics and Policy*, edited by James P. Lester. Durham, NC: Duke University Press.

Jaszczak, Sandra (ed.). 1996. *Encyclopedia of Associations.* Detroit: Gale Research.

Kriz, Margaret. 1996. "Not-So-Silent Spring." *National Journal* (March 9):522–526.

Lee, Martha F. 1995. *Earth First! Environmental Apocalypse.* Syracuse, NY: Syracuse University Press.

Levine, Adeline Gordon. 1982. *Love Canal: Science, Politics and People.* Lexington, MA: Lexington Books.

Manes, Christopher. 1990. *Green Rage: Radical Environmentalism and the Unmaking of Civilization.* Boston: Little, Brown.

Manzo, Lynne C., and Neil D. Weinstein. 1987. "Behavioral Commitment to Environmental Protection: A Study of Active and Nonactive Members of the Sierra Club." *Environment and Behavior* 19(6):673–694.

McAdam, Doug, John McCarthy, and Mayer Zald. 1988. "Social Movements." Pp. 695–737 in *Handbook of Sociology*, edited by Neil Smelser. Beverly Hills, CA: Sage Publications.

McCarthy, John D., and Mayer N. Zald. 1987. "The Trend of Social Movements in America: Professionalization and Resource Mobilization." Pp. 337–391 in *Social Movements in an Organizational Society: Collected Essays*, edited by Mayer N. Zald and John D. McCarthy. New Brunswick, NJ: Transaction Books.

McCloskey, Michael. 1992. "Twenty Years of Change in the Environmental Movement: An Insider's View." Pp. 77–88 in *American Environmentalism: The*

*U.S. Environmental Movement, 1970–1990*, edited by R. E. Dunlap and A. G. Mertig. Philadelphia: Taylor and Francis.

McCormick, John. 1989. *Reclaiming Paradise: The Global Environmental Movement*. Bloomington: Indiana University Press.

McFeatters, Ann. 2000. "Voters See the Forest—and the Trees." *The Blade* (July 30). http://www.toledoblade.com:80/editorial/mcfeatters/0g30ann.htm. [Accessed August 4, 2000]

Mertig, Angela G., and Riley E. Dunlap. 1995. "Public Approval of Environmental Protection and Other New Social Movement Goals in Western Europe and the United States." *International Journal of Public Opinion Research* 7(2): 145–156.

Mertig, Angela G., and Riley E. Dunlap. 2001. "Environmentalism, New Social Movements, and the New Class: A Cross-National Investigation." *Rural Sociology* 66(1):113–136.

Milbrath, Lester W. 1984. *Environmentalists: Vanguard for a New Society*. Albany: State University of New York Press.

Mitchell, Robert Cameron. 1989. "From Conservation to Environmental Movement: The Development of the Modern Environmental Lobbies." Pp. 81–113 in *Government and Environmental Politics: Essays on Historical Developments Since World War Two*, edited by Michael J. Lacey. Washington, DC: The Wilson Center Press.

Mitchell, Robert Cameron, Angela G. Mertig, and Riley E. Dunlap. 1992. "Twenty Years of Environmental Mobilization: Trends among National Environmental Organizations." Pp. 11–26 in *American Environmentalism: The U.S. Environmental Movement, 1970–1990*, edited by R. E. Dunlap and A. G. Mertig. Philadelphia: Taylor and Francis.

Morrison, Denton E. 1973. "The Environmental Movement: Conflict Dynamics." *Journal of Voluntary Action Research* 2 (April): 74–85.

———. 1980. "The Soft, Cutting Edge of Environmentalism: Why and How the Appropriate Technology Notion Is Changing the Movement." *Natural Resources Journal* 20(2):275–298.

———. 1986. "How and Why Environmental Consciousness Has Trickled Down." Pp. 187–220 in *Distributional Conflicts in Environmental-Resource Policy*, edited by Allan Schnalberg, Nicholas Watts, and Klaus Zimmerman. Hants, England: Gower.

Morrison, Denton E., and Riley E. Dunlap. 1986. "Environmentalism and Elitism: A Conceptual and Empirical Analysis." *Environmental Management* 10(5): 581–589.

Morrison, Denton E., Kenneth E. Hornback, and W. Keith Warner. 1972. "The Environmental Movement: Some Preliminary Observations and Predictions." Pp. 259–279 in *Social Behavior, Natural Resources and the Environment*, edited by William Burch, Neil Cheek, and Lee Taylor. New York: Harper & Row.

Nash, Roderick. 1974. *The American Conservation Movement*. St. Charles, MO: Forum Press.

———. 1982. *Wilderness and the American Mind*, 3rd ed. New Haven, CT: Yale University Press.

National Wildlife Federation. 2000. *2000 Conservation Directory*. Washington, DC: National Wildlife Federation.

Oates, David. 1989. *Earth Rising: Ecological Belief in an Age of Science*. Corvallis: Oregon State University Press.

O'Riordan, Timothy. 1971. "The Third American Conservation Movement: New Implications for Public Policy." *American Studies* 5(2):155–171.

Robinson, Marshall. 1993. "The Ford Foundation: Sowing the Seeds of a Revolution." *Environment* 35(3):10–41.

Rudel, Thomas K. 1982. "Activists, Agencies, and the Division of Labor in Environmental Protection." *Journal of Environmental Management* 15:205–211.

Sabatier, P., and D. Mazmanian. 1980. "The Implementation of Public Policy: A Framework of Analysis." *Policy Studies Journal* 8:538–560.

Salazar, Debra J. 1996. "The Mainstream-Grassroots Divide in the Environmental Movement: Environmental Groups in Washington State." *Social Science Quarterly* 77(3):626–643.

Sale, Kirkpatrick. 1993. *The Green Revolution: The American Environmental Movement 1962–1992*. New York: Hill and Wang.

Scarce, Rik. 1990. *Eco-Warriors: Understanding the Radical Environmental Movement*. Chicago: Noble Press.

Scheffer, Victor B. 1991. *The Shaping of Environmentalism in America*. Seattle: University of Washington Press.

Schoenfeld, A. Clay, Robert F. Meier, and Robert J. Griffin. 1979. "Constructing a Social Problem: The Press and the Environment." *Social Problems* 27(1): 38–61.

Shabecoff, Philip. 1993. *A Fierce Green Fire: The American Environmental Movement*. New York: Hill and Wang.

———. 1996. "Greens vs. Congress: A Play-by-Play." *Amicus Journal* 18(Fall):24–29.

Snow, Donald. 1992a. *Inside the Environmental Movement: Meeting the Leadership Challenge*. Washington, DC: Island Press.

Snow, Donald (ed.). 1992b. *Voices from the Environmental Movement: Perspectives for a New Era*. Washington, DC: Island Press.

Snow, Donald A., E. Burke Rochford, Jr., Steven K. Worden, and Robert D. Benford. 1986. "Frame Alignment Processes, Micromobilization and Movement Participation." *American Sociological Review* 51:464–481.

Switzer, Jacqueline Vaugn. 1997. *Green Backlash: The History and Politics of Environmental Opposition in the U.S.* Boulder, CO: Lynne Rienner.

Szasz, Andrew. 1994. *Ecopopulism: Toxic Waste and the Movement for Environmental Justice*. Minneapolis: University of Minnesota Press.

Taylor, Bron Raymond (ed.). 1995. *Ecological Resistance Movements: The Global Emergence of Radical and Popular Environmentalism*. Albany: State University of New York Press.

Taylor, Dorceta E. 1993. "Environmentalism and the Politics of Inclusion." Pp. 53–61 in *Confronting Environmental Racism: Voices from the Grassroots*, edited by R. D. Bullard. Boston: South End Press.

———. 1998. "The Urban Environment: The Intersection of White Middle-Class and White Working-Class Environmentalism (1820–1950s)." *Advances in Human Ecology* 7:207–292.

Thiele, Leslie Paul. 1999. *Environmentalism for a New Millennium: The Challenge of Coevolution.* New York: Oxford University Press.

Turner, Ralph H., and Lewis M. Killian. 1987. *Collective Behavior*, 3rd ed. Englewood Cliffs, NJ: Prentice-Hall.

Wapner, Paul. 1996. *Environmental Activism and World Civic Politics.* Albany: State University of New York Press.

Weilbacher, Mike. 1993. "Earth Day: The New Children's Crusade." *E Magazine* 4(2):31–35.

Zakin, Susan. 1993. *Coyotes and Town Dogs: Earth First! and the Environmental Movement.* New York: Viking Press.

*Chapter 15*

# Environmental Concern:
# Conceptual and Measurement Issues

*Riley E. Dunlap and Robert Emmet Jones*

Given social scientists' penchant for survey research, it is not surprising that the emergence of environmental problems on our nation's agenda in the late 1960s was quickly followed by a spate of surveys aimed at understanding how people perceive such problems. Besides trying to document the degree to which the public (and segments thereof) saw environmental problems as serious and supported efforts to solve them, these early studies examined variation in concern for environmental quality among differing sectors of the public as well as trends in environmental concern over time (Buttel, 1975; Murch, 1971). Such studies quickly grew in number, and by the end of the 1970s one could find approximately 300 empirical studies of "environmental concern" by sociologists and other researchers from a wide variety of disciplines (Dunlap and Van Liere, 1978a).

Unfortunately, the divergent disciplinary backgrounds and resulting diversity of approaches of the investigators compounded the problem that most of these studies were ad hoc and atheoretical, seldom building upon one another or attitude theory. This situation led Heberlein (1981:242) to qualify his early overview of work in the area—a highly selective review of efforts to measure environmental attitudes—by noting that "the goal of this paper is *not* to review an almost hopelessly disorganized and fundamentally unintegratable literature (emphasis added)." Given that the empirical literature has expanded enormously in subsequent years, we are faced with the daunting task in this chapter of trying to make sense of the burgeoning body of research on environmental concern produced by sociologists and other scholars. While we cannot begin to provide a comprehensive summary of this huge and diverse body of work, we shall nonetheless attempt to provide readers with a good sense of major issues involved in the conceptualization and measurement of environmental concern.

Specifically, we begin with a discussion of the difficulties inherent in measuring attitudes toward an object as ambiguous as "the environment," paying particular attention to the complex and evolving nature of environment as an "attitude object." Then we turn to efforts to conceptualize environmental attitudes, typically treated as concern for environmental quality or "environmental concern." We discuss the relative strengths and weaknesses of two major types of approaches, those that rely on attitude theory versus those that employ a more policy-relevant approach, and present a conceptual summary that may help to integrate the two and allow for a more consistent and cumulative approach.

Next, we examine concrete examples of efforts to measure the construct of environmental concern, noting that the combination of diverse conceptualizations and varying measurement approaches has yielded an incredibly diverse set of measures or operational definitions of environmental concern. We will try to bring some order to this diversity, by classifying major types of measures, providing a basis for comparing them, and offering suggestions for future efforts. A recurring theme in the measurement literature is whether it is appropriate to conceive of environmental concern as a single construct or whether it is inherently multidimensional, and we will end the measurement section by reviewing recent efforts designed explicitly to answer this question.

## THE CHANGING NATURE OF "ENVIRONMENT" AS ATTITUDE OBJECT

In his review, Heberlein (1981:242) aptly pointed out that "The great difficulty with even thinking about environmental attitudes is the ambiguity of the object itself," and then continued by noting that

The environment as an object is constantly present and has multiple sub-objects which do not, as individual objects, represent the totality. We have attitudes about specific objects in the environment such as pine trees, a particular river, the Rocky Mountains, etc. The environment is an experiential object, but no one experiences "the environment" as a whole, but rather separate distinct aspects of the environment. (p. 243)

Consistent with Heberlein's position, many early environmental attitude surveys in the 1960s and early 1970s focused on specific and readily identifiable attitude objects such as local air and water pollution with which individuals often had firsthand experience (e.g., Crowe, 1968; Dynes and Wenger, 1971). However, throughout the 1970s and 1980s, a wide range of additional environmental issues such as toxic waste, urban sprawl, groundwater contamination, energy and other resource shortages, acid rain, and nuclear power and other hazardous technologies emerged, while in the 1990s deforestation, loss of biodiversity, ozone depletion, and climate change came to the fore—and all have been the subject of surveys.

While there are exceptions, several broad trends are apparent in this evolving set of environmental problems: (1) the problems tend to be less localized and less visible, making awareness of them more dependent on media and other information sources than on firsthand experience; (2) the causes, effects, and solutions of the problems are seen as inherently related to complex social processes; and (3) the continuing emergence of such problems, which are often seen as interrelated, likely gives greater credence to more general notions of environmental deterioration and ecological destruction. The first two trends make the study of environmental attitudes even more challenging than when Heberlein wrote, as the processes of attitude formation toward environmental issues are far more complex and less dependent on personal experience, while the attitudes themselves are more likely to be interrelated with attitudes toward other issues such as the role of government (Eagly and Kulesa, 1997). On the other hand, the continual emergence of new threats to environmental quality has likely made broad concepts such as "environmental problems," "environmental quality," and "ecological deterioration" more meaningful attitude objects for much of the public than was the case two decades ago.

Not only have environmental problems become more complex, but efforts to measure attitudes toward them are compounded by the fact that the meaning of environment is more ambiguous than Heberlein implied. In recent years, social analysts have noted that environment is equated by some people with nature or natural settings like wilderness, and by others with their immediate surroundings (their environs), or with specific settings like countryside (Barry, 1999: ch. 1; Reser and Bentrupperbäumer, 2000). Compounding the problem that environment connotes different things to different people and cultures is that environments can be classified in a multitude of ways: according to their biophysical properties (terrestrial/ land, aquatic/water, and atmospheric/air), their intersubjective or socially shared properties (rural, urban, natural, wilderness, etc.), or by the subjective or personal interpretations applied to them (good, bad, ugly, etc.)[1]

We cannot begin to deal with all of these nuances adequately, but fortunately it is possible to provide an overview of sociological and related work on environmental attitudes without doing so. A beginning point is to follow Ester's (1981:85) recognition that environmental attitudes are largely synonymous with *environmental concern*, the term typically used in the empirical literature. As we will see in the next section, environmental concern is a broad concept that refers to a wide range of phenomena— from awareness of environmental problems to support for environmental protection—that reflect attitudes, related cognitions, and behavioral intentions toward the environment. Our goals are to clarify and specify the meaning of environmental concern, to help make better sense of existing studies of the construct, and to provide suggestions that will prove useful in designing future studies aimed at increasing cumulative knowledge in this area of inquiry.

## CLARIFYING THE MEANING OF ENVIRONMENTAL CONCERN

As noted above, the universe of environmental concern research is complex, continuously evolving and ever expanding, and this makes it particularly difficult to map its boundaries and key features. Our effort along these lines will draw upon facet theory as developed by Louis Guttman. Facet theory provides guidance for mapping the conceptual space and empirical boundaries of research domains, and for systematically decomposing complex concepts such as environmental concern into their key dimensions or facets—thereby facilitating the development of adequate measurement of such concepts (see, e.g., Shye et al., 1994).[2] In this section we attempt to map out the boundaries of environmental concern research by clarifying its key conceptual components, and in the subsequent section we will apply the resulting conceptual distinctions in a review of existing efforts to measure environmental concern. In the process we hope to contribute to the solution of the problem Reser and Bentrupperbäumer (2000:3) recently noted when they wrote that "We clearly need a more useful and precise language for talking about environmental concern."

We begin with a definition of *environmental concern*, something that Reser and Bentrupperbäumer (2000) note that most researchers fail to provide—perhaps because the meaning seems obvious and is at least implicitly conveyed by their operational definitions. The earliest definition we have encountered was provided by the Dutch scholars Scheurs and Nelissen, who argued that environmental concern represented "the totality of ideas on the protection and control of and interference with the natural and artificial environment, as well as the behavioral dispositions connected with them" (quoted in Ester, 1981:86). More succinctly, Ester and van der Meer (1982: 72) define environmental concern "as the degree to which a person recognizes environmental problems and is ready to contribute to their solution." Our preference would be to modify the later definition slightly, so that environmental concern refers to the degree to which people are aware of problems regarding the environment and support efforts to solve them and/or indicate a willingness to contribute personally to their solution.

Regardless of one's explicit or implicit definition of the concept, researchers investigating environmental concern must inevitably choose from a wide range of environmental issues or substantive topics, and from the numerous ways in which concern over these issues/topics can be expressed by respondents. Consequently, environmental concern is a multifaceted construct consisting of two conceptual components: the "environmental" and "concern" components (Ester and van der Meer, 1982; Gray, 1985; Van Liere and Dunlap, 1981). The environmental component represents the substantive content of environmental concern, and is operationalized by the particular issue (e.g., acid rain) or set of issues (e.g., pollution) chosen by the researcher from the "universe of environmental issues," to use the language of facet theory. This universe is composed of major clusters of issues that represent important "substantive topics" or "objects of concern" (e.g., pollution, resource depletion, habitat destruction, etc.). The concern component represents the way in which environmental concern is expressed and is operationalized by the particular manner employed by the researcher to elicit people's expressions of concern about environmental issues, drawn from the "universe of expressions of concern." This universe is composed of forms of expressions representing major theoretical constructs in attitude-behavior theory (attitudes, beliefs, intentions, and behaviors).

Two decades ago, Van Liere and Dunlap (1981) reviewed a variety of early measures of environmental concern in an effort to determine if the way in which the concept was measured made a difference in the results obtained by various studies. They distinguished between what they labeled the "substantive issues" being investigated and the "theoretical conceptualizations" being employed in these studies, and found that variations in both of these components of environmental concern contributed to inconsistent findings.

By variation in substantive issues Van Liere and Dunlap (1981:653) meant that measures of environmental concern varied in terms of the environmental issue(s) or substantive topic(s) they focused on—such as pollution, natural resources, population, wildlife, and so on, and various combinations thereof. Some studies focused on specific topics while others focused on a wide range of topics. By variation in theoretical conceptualization, they meant the various ways in which investigators obtained expressions of people's environmental concern. Some researchers drew upon social-psychological theories about attitudes, beliefs, and behaviors (e.g., Heberlein and Black, 1976; Maloney et al., 1975), while others took a more practical but policy-relevant approach and asked about perceptions of the seriousness of environmental problems, the perceived causes of such problems, respondents' willingness to support and/or engage in efforts to solve the problems, and so forth (see, e.g., Buttel and Flinn, 1976; Dunlap, 1975; Murch, 1974).

After Van Liere and Dunlap's (1981) review of existing studies and their own data showed that variation in both substantive issues and theoretical conceptualizations affected the results obtained in studies of environmental concern, subsequent studies began to pay attention to the implications of measuring environmental concern in differing ways (e.g., Carman, 1998; Gray, 1985; Guber, 1996; Keeter, 1984; Klineberg et al., 1998; Wall, 1985). However, researchers have not systematically examined the conceptual and empirical variation produced jointly by use of different "objects of concern" and different "expressions of concern" (for an exception, see Schahn and Holzer, 1990, n.d.). Yet, as we will subsequently see, the diverse ways in which each of these two components can vary individually, and especially in combination, yield an enormous variety of potential measures of environmental concern. Use of such a wide range of measures of environmental concern by researchers contributes to problems of validity, limits comparability across studies, and thereby inhibits accumulation of knowledge. A first step in contributing to the solution of these problems is to specify carefully the nature of these two fundamental components and thus the potential universe of meanings and measures associated with the multifaceted construct of environmental concern.

## The Environmental Component of Environmental Concern

The term *environment* as it is employed in studies of environmental concern has multiple meanings and is multifaceted, as the universe of environmental issues is vast. Van Liere and Dunlap (1981) illustrated their notion of "substantive issues" by distinguishing among pollution, conservation, and population issues—what Gray (1985:47) calls the "three human processes"—but this is simply one of many ways in which environmental issues can be differentiated.[3] The substantive nature of environmental issues can also be conceptualized in terms of a variety of other facets and their constituent elements that are more exhaustive in coverage and/or logically rigorous in conceptualization.

For example, we can treat the set of clusters of phenomena that constitute the biophysical environment—atmosphere (air), hydrosphere (water), lithosphere (land), flora (plants), and fauna (animals)—as comprising a biophysical facet. We might also distinguish among the differing functions that the biophysical environment serves for human societies—it supplies us with natural resources, absorbs our waste products, and serves as our living space (Dunlap, 1994)—and treat these as elements of a biophysical facet. Or, we can distinguish among different outcomes of human activities on the biophysical environment, such as resource depletion versus conservation, pollution generation versus abatement, and development versus preservation, and treat these as elements of a biophysical facet. Each example represents a way of organizing the enormously complex universe of biophysical properties into a manageable set of elements that comprise a conceptually meaningful facet. In other words, each represents a way of cutting up complex biophysical phenomena into a manageable set of "environmental objects" that enables researchers to construct measures of "environmental concern."[4]

While the foregoing represent ways of conceptualizing the substance of environmental issues, or their biophysical properties, there are a number of other facets that are useful in representing important properties of the environmental component of environmental concern research. Three in particular are suggested by past research: First, environmental issues can be organized along a generality-specificity continuum that reflects the level of specificity with which the issues are conceptualized in various studies. For example, studies may focus on environmental problems or degradation, or on pollution more specifically. Further, studies of concern about pollution may examine attitudes toward pollution in general (Van Liere and Dunlap, 1981), attitudes toward air or water pollution (Crowe, 1968; Dynes and Wenger, 1971), or attitudes toward a specific form of air pollution such as acid rain (Neuman, 1986). Second, past research suggests the utility of a spatial facet, distinguishing between environmental issues at various geographical scales such as the neighborhood, community, regional, national, and global levels (deHaven-Smith, 1991; Dunlap et al., 1993; Furman, 1998; Murch, 1971). Finally, the importance of a temporal facet that distinguishes between past, present, and future (including both short-term and long-term) environmental conditions is also suggested by past research (Dunlap et al., 1993; Hackett, 1995).

The inherent complexity of the environmental component helps account for the huge diversity in existing measures of environmental concern. As we will see when we review measuring instruments in the next section, such instruments vary considerably not only in content, but also in their ability to cover the universe of substantive topics that constitute the environmental component.

In sum, the substantive component of the construct of environmental concern is incredibly complex.[5] What Van Liere and Dunlap and others have referred to as substantive issues (or topics) can potentially vary in diverse ways. Not only are there a variety of ways of distinguishing among properties of the biophysical environment (as suggested above), but they can be studied at various levels of generality, at differing geographical scales, and in differing time frames. Existing studies of environmental concern have often failed to take note of these important features, and some of the measurement problems and inconsistent findings may stem from the many ways biophysical, spatial, temporal, and other facets of the environmental component are haphazardly combined in creating measures of environmental concern. Thus, the nature of environment as attitude object is far more complex than Heberlein implied, and care must be taken when trying to conceptualize and measure it.

## The Concern Component of Environmental Concern

The second major source of variation in environmental concern research stems from the ways in which investigators conceptualize the "concern" component of the construct. What Van Liere and Dunlap (1981) termed "theoretical conceptualizations" can be separated into two broad approaches: On the one hand, a theoretical approach is used in studies that conceptualize the concern component based on the investigator's knowledge—drawn from attitude theory—of the nature of beliefs, attitudes, intentions, and behaviors and their theoretical and empirical relationships. On the other hand, a policy approach is used in studies that conceptualize this component based on the investigator's understanding of environmental problems and their policy implications.

### *The Policy Approach*

The policy approach to conceptualizing and measuring concern employs items that are constructed by researchers in an effort to measure crucial, policy-relevant aspects of environmental concern. Individual items as well as multi-item measures are designed, often rather subjectively, to tap such phenomena as perceptions of the seriousness of environmental problems; opinions about the major causes of such problems and who (industry, government, or individuals) should have primary responsibility for solving them; preferred solutions to such problems; individual support for various solutions, such as increased government regulations on industry to willingness to pay higher taxes and/or prices; and self-reports of pro-environmental behaviors, ranging from consumer behaviors to political actions.

Use of such policy-relevant measures is particularly common in studies of public opinion toward environmental issues (see, e.g., Dunlap and Scarce, 1991), but—as we will see later—in numerous in-depth surveys as well. By relying on researchers' intuitive understanding of environmental problems and policy, rather than attitude theory, these studies are vulnerable to Heberlein's (1981) charge of not contributing to attitude theory. Yet, they have nonetheless yielded important findings that establish useful empirical generalizations about the overall level of environmental concern among the public, variations in such concern among sectors of the public, and changes in both levels and variation over time (see, e.g., Jones and Dunlap, 1992). Furthermore, reflecting their policy relevance, such findings have increasingly found their way into the policy arena, as policy makers and environmental activists often make use of or are influenced by the results of policy-oriented studies of public concern for environmental quality.[6]

## The Theoretical Approach

Although fewer in number, and more likely to be conducted by psychologists than sociologists, several studies of environmental concern are clearly based upon various forms of attitude theory. Such studies typically conceptualize the concern component in terms of the classical tripartite conceptualization of "attitude" as consisting of affective, cognitive, and conative dimensions (Gray, 1985). Ester (1981:85), for instance, argues that the concept of environmental concern is equivalent to "environmental attitude" and consists of cognitions, affects, and behavioral dispositions toward the natural environment. Other theorists include overt actions as conative responses, but classify them separately from behavioral intentions since the classical notion of attitude includes *predispositions* to behavior rather than behavior itself (Fishbein and Ajzen, 1975). We include behavior in our conceptualization of environmental concern because we believe that such concern can often be inferred from a person's overt actions, and also because behavior (both observed and self-reported) has often been treated as an indicator of environmental concern in empirical studies (Maloney and Ward, 1973).

Generally speaking, the cognitive expression of environmental concern is usually treated as the beliefs and knowledge an individual has about the nature of an environmental problem, its assumed causes, and possible solutions (Gray, 1985). The cognitive expression of concern can vary from the minimum of knowledge needed to be aware of a specific problem or issue to broad beliefs about the biosphere and humans' relationship to it. Cognitive expressions of concern can be classified along a continuum ranging from cognitions that have high empirical probability of being accurate (i.e., environmental knowledge) to cognitions that have high intersubjective expectation of being correct or desirable for society (environmental norms). In between these two lie cognitions that have high intrasubjective expectation of being correct for the individual (personal environmental beliefs). For now, the universe of cognitive expressions of concern will be treated as a multidimensional construct (environmental cognition) that can be inferred from peoples' expressed knowledge and beliefs about environmental issues.

The affective expression of concern involves an emotive and evaluative element which is synonymous with a more restricted conceptualization of attitude (Fishbein and Ajzen, 1975). In fact, indicators that tap affective expressions of environmental concern are often referred to simply as environmental attitudes (e.g., Kaiser et al., 1999). These attitudinal indicators tap personal feelings or evaluations (good-bad, like-dislike, etc.) about environmental conditions or issues (acid rain, ozone depletion, recycling, etc.). They can range from attitudes toward very specific problems or issues, such as toxic wastes or recycling, to very broad ones like environmental problems or protection.

The conative expressions of concern reflect a readiness to perform, or a commitment to support, a variety of actions that can potentially impact environmental quality. These may include willingness to perform specific individual actions (e.g., recycling newspapers) or a set of individual actions (e.g., green consumerism), as well as stated support for a specific public policy proposal (e.g., a curbside recycling program) or general public policy proposals (e.g., spending more on environmental protection). The former are indicators of personal commitment to protect environmental quality, while the latter are indicators of public commitment to this goal. This universe of conative expressions of environmental concern will be lumped under the rubric of "environmental intentions and commitments."

Finally, the behavioral expression of concern represents the actual or reported actions taken by individuals (recycling paper, buying eco-friendly products, etc.) and their behavioral expressions of support (or nonsupport) for environmental policies, programs, and organizations (e.g., voting for environmental programs, writing letters to public officials, and being active in an environmental organization). Behavioral expressions of concern for the former are indicators of "personal environmental behavior," while expressions of support for the latter are indicators of "public environmental behavior" or "environmental activism."

Given this conceptualization of the concern component, we can classify studies of environmental concern based on the degree to which they encompass the universe of expressions of concern for the environment. Broad-coverage studies of the concern component are those that examine all or nearly all forms of expression of environmental concern—the cognitive, affective, conative, and behavioral facets. Narrow-coverage studies are those at the opposite end of the continuum, limiting their focus to only one facet—typically the cognitive, conative, *or* behavioral expression of environmental concern.[7]

### Comparing the Two Approaches

By emphasizing either policy-relevant aspects of environmental concern, or the attitudinal components of such concern, the policy and theoretical approaches clearly differ in their emphases; but they can be further distinguished by the implicit and sometimes explicit assumptions they make about the roles played by individuals and social institutions in both environmental degradation and protection. Studies drawing upon attitude theory, such as Maloney and Ward's (1973) important early effort, tend to emphasize the role of individuals and their behaviors in creating and solving environmental problems. They typically focus on such things as individuals' beliefs, attitudes, behavioral intentions, and actual behaviors regarding household wastes, energy use, recycling, consumer purchases, and related phenomena.

In contrast, policy-relevant studies tend to emphasize the role of social institutions (e.g., industry, government, education), environmental policies, and collective action in degrading and protecting the environment. They are more likely to investigate individuals' support for governmental regulations and spending for environmental protection; perceived blame among industry, government, and consumers for environmental degradation; and expressed willingness to engage in various forms of collective action (joining organizations, voting, boycotting, protesting, etc.) aimed at protecting the environment. In short, attitude theory studies generally have a micro or individual-level focus while policy-relevant studies often have a macro or more structural-level focus.[8]

Despite these obvious differences, we want to point out two potential sources of convergence in the two approaches. First, many of the items employed in policy-relevant studies can, upon careful inspection, be classified as indicators of attitudes, beliefs, behavioral intentions, or actual behaviors—key components of attitude theories. Paying attention to such conceptual similarities offers a potential avenue for blending the strengths of both approaches into a more fruitful framework for studies of environmental concern. Furthermore, recent efforts to build theoretical models of the sources of environmental concern combine both the policy and theoretical approaches by explicitly incorporating policy-relevant variables into a social-psychological theoretical framework (see, e.g., Stern et al., 1999).

Thus we see that the concern component as well as the environmental component of the construct of environmental concern is incredibly complex. What Van Liere and Dunlap (1981) and others referred to as theoretical conceptualizations can vary in diverse ways. Not only are there a variety of expressions of concern for the environment, but they can be conceptualized in terms of the practical needs of policy development or with the goal of examining theoretical relationships suggested by attitude-behavior theory.

### Summary

When one considers the diverse ways in which both the environment and concern components of the construct "environmental concern" can be conceptualized, it should come as no surprise that one finds enormous diversity among existing studies of environmental concern. Researchers can focus on a wide range of elements or properties of the environment and do so at a variety of levels of specificity and at varying geographical and temporal scales. Then, regardless of how they conceptualize the environment, they have nearly as many options in obtaining expressions of concern for it—

whether they adopt a policy or theoretical approach to conceptualizing concern.

Using the terminology of attitude theory, but keeping in mind that many policy-relevant measures can often loosely be classified as affective, cognitive, conative, or behavioral expressions of concern, we can summarize this section by presenting a simple typology of efforts to conceptualize and measure environmental concern. At the simplest level, we can dichotomize efforts to conceptualize/measure both the environment and concern components. First, studies can focus on a single environmental issue or substantive topic (the latter being the preferred term for now), or on multiple topics; second, studies can focus on a single expression of concern, or on multiple ones.[9]

Putting these two together yields a fourfold typology of potential measuring instruments consisting of the following categories: (1) Multiple-topic, multiple-expression instruments that examine phenomena such as beliefs, attitudes, intentions, and behaviors concerning various environmental topics; (2) multiple-topic, single-expression instruments that measure beliefs, attitudes, intentions, *or* behaviors across a range of substantive topics; (3) single-topic, multiple-expression instruments that measure beliefs, attitudes, intentions, and behaviors toward specific topics such as population or air or water pollution; and (4) single-topic, single-expression instruments that measure beliefs, attitudes, intentions, *or* behaviors concerning a specific topic like global warming.[10]

For the purpose of comparing studies, rather than specific measuring instruments, it might be helpful to trichotomize both dimensions of the typology to more closely match the diversity found in existing studies: Narrow-range studies examine single topics and a single expression; broad-range studies examine a wide range of environmental topics and expressions (cognitive, affective, conative, and behavioral) of concern; and medium-range studies typically examine two or more topics and/or two or more expressions of concern.[11]

## CLARIFYING THE MEASUREMENT OF ENVIRONMENTAL CONCERN

In this section we examine efforts to operationalize environmental concern by building upon the preceding conceptual distinctions, but we must warn readers that clarifying existing efforts to measure environmental concern is difficult due to the diversity and sheer numbers of such efforts. From our own files we estimate that there are at least 700–800 and perhaps over 1,000 published studies that purport to measure some aspect of environmental concern. Since only a small proportion employ pre-existing measures, it follows that several hundred varying operational definitions have been employed.

We will try to keep the task manageable by ignoring studies employing single-item indicators—even though longitudinal studies using such indicators have proven useful in tracking long-term trends in public opinion on environmental issues (Jones and Dunlap, 1992)—because of their inherent limitations concerning reliability and validity (Heberlein, 1981:253), and focusing on efforts to develop multi-item measures of various aspects of environmental concern. Even this task is extremely challenging, for several reasons: First, there is the inherent difficulty of classifying multi-item measures (especially their individual items) unambiguously in terms of our conceptual typology. Second, some broad-range studies examine a wide range of substantive topics and expressions of concern via several separate measures, while others attempt to combine various topics (and occasionally expressions of concern) into a single, multi-item measure. Finally, some researchers create their measuring instruments subjectively, largely on the basis of face and/or content validity, while others do so methodologically, typically on the basis of factor analysis. The resulting diversity in multi-item measures of environmental concern tends to be overwhelming, but hopefully, by reviewing a number of existing measures in the next section, we can illustrate the conceptual distinctions noted in the prior section and in the process provide readers with a roadmap for understanding existing measurement efforts.

In what follows we will review a wide variety of existing efforts to measure environmental concern, beginning with those that develop measures derived from attitude theory and then moving to those that approach the measurement of environmental concern from a policy-relevant perspective. In the process of reviewing the strengths and weaknesses of both, we will attempt to offer some useful guidelines for future efforts to measure environmental concern. A key issue underlying these discussions will be whether environmental concern is inherently multidimensional or whether it is legitimate to treat it as a unidimensional construct. Our review will therefore end by focusing on recent studies that have explicitly addressed the issue of dimensionality.

### Measures Derived from Attitude Theory

Undoubtedly, the best-known effort to examine environmental concern with measures drawn from attitude theory is the early study by Maloney and Ward (1973). The measures in this study, subsequently shortened in Maloney et al. (1975), have been used by several other researchers and deserve careful attention. What Maloney and Ward termed a "Scale for the Measurement of Ecological Attitudes and Knowledge" is an inventory that consists of four multi-item measures (which they called "subscales" but we will term "scales") of Knowledge (K), Affect (A), Verbal Commitment (VC), and Actual Commitment (AC) regarding ecological issues.[12]

The K Scale is designed to measure a particular type of cognition or belief, namely, "factual knowledge related to ecological issues"; the A Scale to measure the affective, evaluative, and emotional aspect of environmental concern; the VC Scale to measure behavioral intention or commitment; and the AC Scale to measure actual (self-reported) behavior. Thus, these four scales clearly aim to measure the four key facets of concern that are suggested by traditional attitude theory, although knowledge is a specific and narrow type of cognition (as we noted earlier). The individual items included in each scale cover a variety of environmental topics of varying specificity (ranging from ecological problems to pollution to air pollution to smog), indicating that each scale represents a multiple-topic/single-expression measure in our typology.[13]

The original and shortened versions of the A, VC, and AC Scales were found to have adequate internal consistency, but such information was not presented for the K Scale. However, Maloney and colleagues did *not* factor-analyze the entire set of items to determine if, in fact, four dimensions representing the presumably distinct facets of environmental concern would emerge. Instead, they used a subjective rather than methodological approach, apparently selecting items for each facet on the basis of face and/or content validity (with the assistance of other judges). Yet the pattern of intercorrelations obtained with these scales by Maloney et al. (1975) and subsequent researchers (Borden and Francis, 1978; Dispoto, 1977; Smythe and Brook, 1980) suggest that the scales are *not* measuring the same phenomena. Indeed, knowledge typically correlates only weakly with the other facets. In contrast, affect correlates very strongly (about .6) with verbal commitment and moderately (about .4) with actual (self-reported) behavior, while the two behavioral measures correlate strongly (above .5) with one another. That affect and verbal commitment are most strongly related is reasonable, since both are often treated as crucial indicators of overall attitude, whereas knowledge is a very specific form of belief and the link between attitude and actual behavior is often modest at best.

Subsequent users of Maloney et al.'s scales also took them at face value and did not attempt to determine if they were empirically as well as analytically distinct, until Symthe and Brook (1980) factor-analyzed responses obtained from a Canadian sample to all items in the shortened versions of the A, VC, and AC (but not the K) Scales. Smythe and Brook found these 30 items to yield eight factors which were difficult to interpret, and unfortunately they did not describe them.[14] They then factor-analyzed each of the three 10-item scales separately, and found the A Scale to yield two interpretable factors, the VC Scale to yield three, and the AC Scale to yield four—and proceeded to treat these new factors as 10 separate measures.

While many of the items in Maloney et al.'s scales have become somewhat dated, and some are not very applicable outside of urban areas, their study is instructive because it remains the most comprehensive effort to measure the key facets of concern suggested by attitude theory. We think they were largely successful in measuring the affective, cognitive, conative, and behavioral facets of concern, but we note that they focused on knowledge—a very specific form of belief. Had they focused on more general beliefs or cognitions, it is likely that they would have found them to be more highly correlated with their measure of affect and probably with verbal commitment as well.

Although Maloney and Ward did not explicitly use facet theory, their effort to construct multi-item scales for each of the key aspects or facets of "concern" suggested by attitude theory—affect, cognitions, behavioral intentions, and actual behavior—is compatible with a facet approach. In the ideal case a subsequent factor analysis of all of their items would have yielded four dimensions roughly corresponding to these facets. However, if forced to choose between carefully designed measures of theoretically distinct facets that prove to have good internal consistency, or the post hoc creation of measures based on atheoretical factor analyses, we believe the former is preferable. Unfortunately, as we will see later, many environmental measures have been constructed post hoc on the basis of such factor analyses.

We have found three other studies that clearly used the conceptual components of attitudes to construct multiple measures of environmental concern and employed factor analysis to verify the match between theoretical components and empirical dimensions. First, Schahn and Holzer (1990, n.d.) used a unique approach to construct measures of the same four components as Maloney and colleagues: Affect, Verbal Commitment, Self-Reported Actual Commitment, and Knowledge. They chose items in such a fashion that each served as an indicator of one of these components and simultaneously as one of seven distinct "topical" areas as well (water conservation, recycling, energy conservation, etc.). While not labeled as such, their study is thus a superb example of the use of facet design, as each item was designed to tap both a conceptual and topical facet of environmental concern. Schahn and Holzer (n.d.) then employed a special version of factor analysis to determine if their overall set of items yielded dimensions reflecting both the theoretical components and the substantive topics they had designed—except that the Knowledge items were not included. They found two rather than three conceptual dimensions, as the Affect and Verbal Commitment items loaded onto a single dimension, whereas the Self-Reported behaviors loaded onto the second (and similarly found four rather than the hypothesized seven topical dimensions). Their results are thus consistent with the above-noted finding that Maloney et al.'s A and AC Scales are strongly intercorrelated.

Similarly, after distinguishing between cognitions, affect, and behavioral dispositions and employing items to measure each component, Ester (1981) found via factor analysis that the cognitive and affective items loaded onto a single dimension and he therefore used them to create an "Attitude toward the Natural Environment Scale." In contrast, the behavioral disposition items formed two dimensions and led to creation of separate "readiness to sacrifice" and "readiness for action" scales. Ester's findings are consistent with Gray's (1985:23, 38) claim that empirically it is difficult to distinguish clearly between affect and cognitions (at least when the latter are not measuring the special beliefs we call "knowledge").

Finally, in a recent article, Kaiser et al. (1999) report that factor analyses confirmed the presence of three hypothesized dimensions of environmental knowledge, behavioral intentions, and what they term "values" (but which are clearly evaluative and therefore reflective of the affective facet of concern). These dimensions were then employed in a model used to predict reported behavior.

Taken as a whole, the above studies suggest that with careful conceptualization and item selection researchers can create sets of measures of environmental concern that approximate the classical tripartite conceptualization of attitude—affective, cognitive, and conative (including both behavioral intentions and actual behaviors)—that we suggest constitute the major social-psychological expressions of environmental concern. However, although the diverse methods employed preclude drawing firm conclusions, it does appear that while knowledge may be treated as a separate dimension or facet it is probably harder to separate more general beliefs or cognitions from the affective dimension. Finally, what is impossible to judge from these articles and their varying methods is the possibility that factor analyses of both the entire set of items employed as well as of the various sets used to construct the measures of affect, knowledge (or broader beliefs), and behavioral intent might yield further factors reflecting specific topical areas such as pollution and conservation.

We are not aware of any other articles that set out to measure all of the facets of concern suggested by attitude theory, and would especially like to see additional efforts that employ Schahn and Holzer's (1990, n.d.) technique of creating individual items to serve simultaneously as indicators of both differing substantive topics and varying expressions of concern. Many researchers do develop measures of specific components such as environmental knowledge (e.g., Furman, 1998) or environmental behavior (e.g., Tarrant and Cordell, 1997), and typically do so with items tapping various substantive topics, but their efforts are not guided by attitude theory. Others seeking to develop and test more elaborate models of the development of environmental concern (e.g., Stern et al., 1999) construct measures of beliefs such as "awareness of consequences" and behavioral intentions, but are aiming to measure variables in their theoretical models as opposed to operationalizing the facets of concern based on attitude theory per se.

### Policy-Relevant Measures

The variety of policy-relevant measures of environmental concern is vast, as basically every operational definition that does not build on attitude theory falls into this category (although admittedly, some are only marginally related to policy issues, and might be more accurately labeled as "ad hoc" or "atheoretical" operationalizations). Furthermore, while the measures reviewed in the prior section were confined to efforts to measure the four components of attitudes—cognitive, affective, conative, and behavioral expressions of environmental concern—the range of policy-relevant measures is confined only by the ingenuity of those who design them. Consequently, one finds an almost bewildering variety of operational definitions of environmental concern employed by those who have adopted a policy-relevant approach (see Dunlap and Van Liere, 1978a for a list of early ones). In addition, many studies employ as many as half a dozen or more separate measures. Finally, whereas measures based on attitude theory almost always cover multiple topics, policy-relevant measures range from single- to multiple-topic in content.

Perhaps the most fundamental source of divergence among policy-relevant studies stems from the methodological strategy used to construct the measures they employ. On the one hand, there are numerous studies that employ one or more measures developed on the basis of an intuitive approach, in which items are constructed and combined on the basis of their presumed similar content (basically on the basis of face and content validity). On the other hand, there are even more studies that employ a methodological technique such as factor or cluster analysis to create measures reflecting the dimensions revealed by such analyses.[15] We shall use this fundamental dichotomy to organize our overview of policy-relevant measures of environmental concern, first reviewing studies that develop multiple measures constructed on the basis of at least implicit judgments about face and content validity, and then reviewing those that use factor analysis or similar techniques to develop multiple measures. In both cases there are so many potential examples that we can only review a few, selected to illustrate the distinctions in our fourfold conceptual typology.

### *Subjectively Constructed Measures*

We will begin by looking at several *broad-range* studies, from early to more recent, that subjectively constructed several different multi-item, policy-relevant measures. To our knowledge, the first such study was that of Tognacci et al. (1972). They constructed two "general" measures that they termed "Importance of a Pure Environment" and "Attainment of a Pure Environment," both of which included eight items tapping a variety of topics such as clean air and water, wilderness protection, and litter elimination. The former was more of an evaluative measure, asking respondents how important achieving each goal was to them personally, while the second was more of a cognitive measure, asking respondents how well they thought the country was doing in attaining the goals. Thus, we can regard both as examples of multiple-topic/single-component measures. They also constructed five more scales designed to measure "attitudes toward" the following topics: (1) conservation, (2) pollution, (3) power-plant pollution (air pollution from coal-burning power plants), (4) individual population control, and (5) overpopulation. The general description of the latter five suggests that they each included a variety of items tapping beliefs, attitudes, and behavioral commitments, indicating that they are examples of single-topic/multiple-expression scales.

Tognacci et al. (1972) noted that each of their scales possessed adequate internal consistency (alphas of .8 or higher), and reported the intercorrelations among them. The conservation, pollution, and power-plant scales correlated very highly (.7 to .8) with one another, suggesting "that it is difficult to argue empirically for the uniqueness of these measures" (p. 79), but less so with the two population scales. Their two general measures correlated moderately (.40 or higher) with these three conservation/pollution topical scales, while somewhat lower with the population scales.

The Tognacci et al. study is a good example of a subjective, policy-relevant approach to measuring environmental concern. On the one hand, it measured attitudes toward a variety of important substantive issues via the five topical scales, and on the other hand, it developed two more general measures dealing with personal evaluations of, and perceptions of national progress, in achieving a variety of goals. This approach enabled them first to examine the intercorrelations among the various measures (as noted above) to determine the degree to which their sample's views on the differing issues were consistent. The pattern of scale intercorrelations suggests, however, that a factor analysis would likely yield a single dimension consisting of conservation and pollution items. What is unknown is whether such an analysis might also yield dimensions reflecting conceptual variation in items—along the lines of beliefs, attitudes, and behavioral intentions.

The second purpose of Tognacci et al.'s (1972) study was to investigate the ideological and demographic correlates of these various facets of environmental concern, and their results revealed that several measures of political ideology were significantly related to nearly all of the measures of environmental concern, with liberals consistently expressing higher levels of concern. Similarly, they found that younger, well-educated adults were more likely to have higher levels of environmental concern than were their counterparts. In both cases, however, the pattern of correlations tended to be stronger for the specific measures than for the general measures (especially "Importance of a Pure Environment") of environmental concern. Their overall results led Tognacci et al. to question the conventional wisdom of the time that environment was a highly consensual issue that would receive support from all sectors of society.

Whereas Tognacci et al. (1972) constructed individual scales designed to focus on several key environmental topics, or substantive facets of environmental concern, the previously mentioned Van Liere and Dunlap (1981) study explicitly designed measures to tap *both* differing substantive topics and policy-relevant expressions of such concern. As noted earlier, they developed Likert-type pollution, natural resources, and population scales, each consisting of a mix of attitude/belief items that tap both the affective and cognitive facets of concern, and thus represent examples of single-topic/multiple-expression measures. They also constructed three other scales (all dealing with pollution and resource issues, in an effort to hold the substantive content constant) tapping differing policy-relevant expressions of concern: support for environmental regulations, support for environmental spending, and reported behavior. The first two are difficult to equate with components of attitudes, but seem to imply an evaluative dimension, while the latter is clearly a behavioral measure. Thus, the three can be considered as multiple-topic/single-expression measures. All six of the scales were found to have adequate levels of internal consistency.

Van Liere and Dunlap's (1981) results were similar to those of Tognacci et al. in several respects. First, they too found strong intercorrelations among scales dealing with pollution and natural resources, and noted that a factor analysis revealed that most of the Likert-type items dealing with these topics could be combined into a single measure, but that the population scale was even more weakly related to these topics than in the case of Tognacci et al. Van Liere and Dunlap also found that their measure of reported behavior (not examined by Tognacci et al.) correlated poorly with most of the other measures. Finally, Van Liere and Dunlap found that political ideology, age, and education were consistently related in the same direction as reported by Tognacci et al., with the four nonbehavioral measures dealing with pollution and natural resources (and that females and urban residents were also generally more likely to express pro-environmental positions on these measures), but less so with the population and reported behavior scales.

The final study in this genre is a recent one by Klineberg et al. (1998) that argued that four broad types of environmental concern measures were suggested by prior literature: (1) economic/government trade-offs that posed environmental protection against other economic and political goals, (2) perceived seriousness of pollution, (3) reported pro-environmental behaviors, and (4) items dealing with broad issues reflecting an "ecological worldview"—and constructed multiple items for each measure. A careful inspection of the actual items reveals that the trade-off items focus not only on differing topics, but tap both the cognitive and affective facets of concern, producing a multiple-topic/multiple-expression measure. The seriousness-of-pollution items generally suggest a single-topic/single (cognitive)-expression focus; the pro-environmental-behaviors items a multiple-topic/single-expression focus; and the ecological-worldview items presumably a multiple-topic/multiple-expression focus (it is difficult to classify them clearly).

Interestingly, Klineberg et al. (1998) conducted a factor analysis of all of their items "to test the empirical basis for the distinctions," and found limited support: While the behavioral items yielded a dimension, the perceived-seriousness items formed two dimensions representing local and statewide pollution, and the rest of the items dealing with economy/government trade-offs and ecological wordview cross-loaded onto two ambiguous dimensions (Klineberg et al, 1998:footnote 7). Consequently, Klineberg et al. maintained their original measures, except for creating separate local and statewide perceived-pollution measures, but also decided to analyze each item separately as well. Unfortunately, the authors confined their analyses to examining correlations between environmental concern and a range of demographic, political, and religious variables, ignoring relationships among the various measures of environmental concern.

Not surprisingly, Klineberg et al. (1998) observed a good deal of variation, based on logistic regression coefficients, between many of the numerous *individual* items and most of their social and demographic variables, as only education and age were consistently related in the expected directions (positively and negatively, respectively) with every item. However, the pattern of relationships found with their presumably more reliable summary measures (all of which represent "indexes," since they summed responses to individual items in each one but failed to provide any evidence of internal consistency to justify doing so) is consistent across all five indexes, as younger, well-educated, female, and liberal respondents consistently expressed higher levels of environmental concern than did their counterparts.

These three broad-range studies, each employing a variety of policy-relevant measures, reveal both the strengths and weaknesses of this approach to conceptualizing and measuring environmental concern. On the positive side, these studies employ measures that are generally readily comprehensible not only to other scholars, but to lay people and policy makers, which may not be the case, for example, with measures of concepts such as "affect" and "verbal commitment." Their measures are also typically relevant to policy aspects of environmental issues (such as perceived seriousness, support for protection and pro-environmental behaviors). As such, their measures generally appear to tap a wide range of meaningful facets of environmental concern, and it becomes interesting and important to see how responses to these measures relate not only to one another (in order to judge the consistency in public responses to a range of environmental issues), but with various social and demographic variables (in order to determine variation in environmental concern across differing sectors of society). Further, in the case of Klineberg et al. (1998), who not only report responses to individual items but provide longitudinal data covering 1990–1996 from their statewide Texas surveys, it is possible—with caution—to draw conclusions about the overall level of environmental concern existing among the sampled population, and especially changes in these levels over time.[16] Such information is, as noted earlier, useful to those interested in environmental policy making.

On the negative side, it is clear that use of an "intuitive" or "subjective" approach to constructing measures of environmental concern can lead to an incredible variety of measures (as a quick perusal of the many studies we have not covered would reveal). Even though the three studies tend to draw upon existing literature, and are among the more thoughtful efforts we have encountered, they nonetheless generated a variety of measures designed to tap a wide range of facets of environmental concern. One result is that it is impossible to draw conclusions about patterns of relations among these facets along the lines of earlier conclusions we drew concerning emerging patterns of correlations among the various attitudinal components measured with the Maloney et al. (1975) scales.

Similarly, whereas measures drawn from attitude theory are typically "single-expression" measures, aimed at tapping the cognitive, evaluative, conative, or behavioral facets of concern, we have seen that the policy-relevant measures cover the full gamut of all four possibilities in our typology. However, most focus either on a single topic (or a narrow range of topics such as pollution and resources) but employ two or more expressions of concern (e.g., Likert statements covering both the cognitive and evaluative aspects of attitudes), or use a single policy-relevant expression such as perceived seriousness but focus on numerous environmental topics. In some cases, such as Klineberg et al.'s (1998) "trade-off" and "worldview" items, the resulting measures appear to include both multiple topics and multiple expressions of concern.

One consequence of using such a variety of items to construct measures subjectively is that the results, either in the form of high correlations among measures or factor analyses conducted to check if the measures are empirically distinct, often suggest that two or more measures are tapping the same underlying construct rather than distinct facets of environmental concern (as in the case of the pollution and natural resource measures employed by Tognacci et al. [1972] and Van Liere and Dunlap [1981]). Thus, the separation of measures on the basis of face and/or content validity may not hold up empirically. Furthermore, multi-item measures that are found to have a high degree of internal consistency may not prove to be unidimensional, as factor analysis might yield dimensions reflecting distinct topics or components or mixtures of both. And, as Klineberg et al's (1998) results reveal, variation in geographical scale may lead to distinct dimensions necessitating separate measures for differing geographical levels (as noted in our previous discussion of the importance of a geographical facet for measuring environmental concern).

Despite these problems, in the next section we will see that simply substituting the use of factor analyses or similar methodological techniques for the a priori development of policy-relevant measures on the basis of face and content validity leads to problems at least as serious as those we have just discussed plaguing the more intuitive/subjective approach to measuring environmental concern.

### Methodologically Derived Measures

Instead of being designed prior to data collection, as were the measures just described, the policy-relevant measures reviewed in this section were constructed after collection and analysis of the data. The researchers begin with a large set of items and after data collection employ methodological techniques, typically a version of factor analysis, to construct their measures. Thus, we label these methodologically derived measures, although technically it is the empirical results of the analyses that provide the basis for the construction of the measures. While such measures solve problems of unidimensionality, at least for the specific studies involved, they raise numerous problems of their own.

Unfortunately, the methodological approach to constructing measures of environmental concern is seldom prefaced by a careful delineation of crucial facets of this concept and careful construction of items tapping them prior to data collection and analysis; thus, factor analysis and related techniques become substitutes for, rather than complements to, careful conceptualization. This highlights the contrast between facet and factor analysis noted long ago by Foa (1958): Facet analysis is an a priori technique emphasizing careful measurement design prior to data collection, whereas factor analysis is an a posteriori technique that occurs after data collection.[17] Ideally, the two should be used in conjunction with one another, but this has rarely been the case for measures of environmental concern (see Braithwaite and Law, 1977; and Mayton, 1986 for rare exceptions). Rather, various multi-item measures are constructed ex post facto corresponding to the differing factors or dimensions that emerge from the empirical analyses.

The inherent ambiguity and complexity of environmental concern and the popularity of employing methodologically derived strategies for measuring it have resulted in a plethora of measures (see, e.g., Gray, 1985:37–44). This makes it difficult to identify and summarize general patterns in these studies. However, by distinguishing between substantive topics and expressions of concern, we can offer insights into the results of efforts to construct measures of environmental concern via methodological tools such as factor analysis.[18]

Factor-analytic studies that examine a wide range of environmental topics but employ the same expression (such as having respondents rate the seriousness of a variety of environmental problems), and thus take a multiple-topic/single-expression approach, inevitably produce a series of measures that each consists of related sets of topics.[19] For example, a recent study in Botswana (Chanda, 1999) had respondents rate the seriousness of 23 community problems (mostly environmental, but some social as well), and developed four factor-based measures dealing with "litter/indecent behavior (public urination)," "socioeconomic well-being," "aesthetics and recreational space," and "dust, air, and noise pollution." Conversely, studies that limit their attention to a single environmental topic, but employ various expressions (thus taking a single-topic/multiple-expression approach), will yield dimensions reflecting various sets of related expressions. For example, a recent study by Guagnano and Markee (1995) factor-analyzed nine Likert-type items that all dealt with the generally comparable topics of environment, environmental problems, and environmental protection. The nine items were found to form four dimensions dealing with trust, responsibility, complexity, and economic trade-offs aspects of environmental problems and protection. Because such studies are essentially holding one of the two components of environmental concern constant, either the topic or the expression, they inevitably yield factors reflecting dimensions of the other component.

What becomes unpredictable, however, are results from studies that factor-analyze a wide range of items that vary in both topic and expression. Such studies may yield dimensions reflecting differing topical areas (e.g., Berberoglu and Tosunoglu, 1995), differing expressions (e.g., Buttel and Flinn, 1976), or a mixture of both (e.g., Horvat and Voelker, 1976; Keeter, 1984). What makes the situation even more confusing is that dimensions often emerge from these studies that reflect other phenomena, such as differences in geographical scale and methodological artifacts of factor analysis.

It was noted earlier that studies finding that respondents tend to perceive the seriousness of environmental problems or rate the quality of the environment differently at differing geographical levels suggest the importance of a geographical scale facet for the environmental component of environmental concern (deHaven-Smith, 1991; Dunlap et al., 1973; Murch, 1971). It is therefore not surprising that a growing number of factor-analytic studies employing items dealing with various geographical levels have yielded distinct factors corresponding to differing geographical scales. We noted previously that Klineberg et al. (1998) found separate dimensions consisting of local and statewide environmental problems, respectively, in their Texas survey. An earlier five-nation study by Rohrschneider (1988) found local and national problems to form distinct dimensions in all five countries. Finally, an Australian study by McAllister (1994) examined problems at the local, national, and international levels. Although a factor analysis yielded three dimensions, one consisted of a combination of the national and international problems while the other two reflected different types of local problems (essentially pollution versus landscape). Such findings suggest the importance of paying attention to geographical scale when asking respondents about environmental problems; yet, it should be noted that all three studies presented the differing sets of problems to respondents via separate lists, each with their own introductions, as opposed to including them in a single list. This procedure, while certainly appropriate, nonetheless raises the possibility that the distinct factors obtained may reflect, at least partially, methodological artifacts (Green and Citrin, 1994).

Because the results of factor-analytic methods depend upon the intercorrelations among the items being analyzed, anything that affects these correlations can affect the resulting factor structure (see, e.g., Zeller and Carmines, 1980:ch.5). This raises the possibility that the factors obtained reflect a variety of methodological artifacts (Guber, 1996). For example, Keeter (1984:282) notes that the items constituting the four factors emerging in his analysis reflect not only common themes, but share "contiguous placement on the questionnaire." Item contiguity is reinforced by use of varying *sets* of contiguous items that have differing introductions and/or response formats. It is not surprising, therefore, that one finds separate dimensions formed by items included in a list of environmental problems that respondents are asked to rate in terms of their seriousness, and those included in a list that respondents are asked to agree or disagree with (e.g., Buttel and Flinn, 1976; Blocker and Eckberg, 1989).[20] More troubling is the possibility that question direction (pro versus anti-environment) may have a major effect on the factors obtained (see, e.g., Green and Citrin, 1994).

In fact, when one reviews factor-analytic studies reporting two or more dimensions of environmental concern, it is striking as to how many report dimensions that differ in terms of the direction of their constituent items. The previously cited Blocker and Eckberg (1989) study, for example, found that eight "general environmental concern" items formed two dimensions reflecting concern for the environment and concern for the economy, respectively; yet, a careful inspection suggests that the major difference between items in the two dimensions is that all four in the former are worded in a pro-environment direction and all four in the latter in an anti-environment direction. Similarly, a more recent study by Vaske and Donnelly (1999) found nine items designed to measure basic beliefs toward wildland preservation forming two dimensions, presumably reflecting "biocentric" and "anthropocentric" orientations toward preservation; however, all of the former are stated in a pro-preservation direction and all of the latter in an anti-preservation direction. Most notable, however, are three recent studies analyzing data obtained from the International Social Survey

Program's 1993 environmental survey. Employing data from Britain, Witherspoon (1994:110) found 11 items separating into two dimensions that she labeled a "romantic" and a "materialist" orientation toward nature, respectively; but a key difference between the two sets is that the former are all "pro-environment" and the latter all "anti-environment" in direction. Strikingly, two recent analyses of the U.S. ISSP data, employing some but not *all* of the items used by Witherspoon, report similar dimensions that again differ only in terms of direction (Dietz et al., 1998:466–467; Uyeki and Holland, 2000:652).

The possibility that the results of factor-analytically derived efforts to develop measures of environmental concern are heavily contaminated by methodological artifacts reinforces Gray's (1985:40–44) criticisms of this approach to measuring environmental concern. He first notes (p. 40) the "equivocal" nature of the interpretation given to many factors reported in the literature, a point well-illustrated by those (often tortuously) assigned to dimensions differing primarily in directionality. Gray (p. 43) then emphasizes that factors often have limited generalizability to other samples, a problem exacerbated by the use of highly unrepresentative samples such as college students (a common occurrence in factor-analytical studies). Consequently, Gray (1985:43) cautions that "only factors that have some generalizablity should find a place in the future literature" and it is a telling commentary that 15 years later one still searches in vain for well-replicated dimensions of environmental concern identified in factor-analytic studies.

For these reasons, we concur with Gray's conclusion that while exploratory or "blind" factoring may have been appropriate in early efforts to measure environmental concern, it is of limited utility at this point. Specifically, we believe basic factor analysis remains useful for examining the unidimensionality of individual measures of environmental concern (to be discussed next), and appropriate for empirically examining the utility of simple conceptual distinctions such as geographical scale. However, for the purpose of developing valid and reliable measures of environmental concern, confirmatory factor analysis appears to offer more promise (as we shall see shortly).

In sum, although developing measures of environmental concern on the basis of methodological techniques such as factor analysis can avoid the potential problem of employing multidimensional measures that plague the use of subjectively developed measures, and occasionally produces dimensions that are theoretically meaningful (e.g., Buttel and Johnson, 1977), a range of new problems is introduced. Besides those noted above, the often ambiguous nature of the resulting dimensions and their frequently equivocal interpretation lead to measures that sometimes lack face validity and clear interpretability—making it difficult to communicate their meaning to other scholars and policy makers.

## Single Scales for Measuring Environmental Concern

From the beginning of behavioral scientists' interest in public concern for environmental quality, there has been a continuing effort to create multi-item measures of environmental concern that overcome the validity and reliability problems posed by use of single items, but that nonetheless yield a single measure of respondents' levels of environmental concern (see Dunlap and Van Liere, 1978a). These have included efforts to develop measures that focus on environmental concern in the broad sense, such as Dunlap et al.'s (1973) "Concern for Environmental Rights Scale," as well as those that focus on more limited aspects of such concern. The latter include Moffet's (1974) "Conservationism Scale," designed to measure a "conservationist/preservationist versus exploitative attitude," and others that focus on specific topical areas such as Watkins' (1974) previously cited "Water Concern Scale" and McCutcheon's (1974) "Population Opinion Poll," designed to measure attitudes toward population control. What these efforts have in common is the assumption that all of the items employed are measuring the same construct, and can therefore be summed up to yield a single quantitative score for each respondent (Heberlein, 1981:249).

None of the single scales constructed early on (first half of the 1970s) ever attracted the attention and subsequent levels of use achieved by Maloney and Ward's (1973) early effort;[21] however, two subsequent scales gradually received at least comparable use. The first, Weigel and Weigel's (1978) "Environmental Concern Scale" (ECS), was designed as "an attitude measure capable of assessing an individual's relatively enduring beliefs and feelings about ecology such that predispositions to engage in pro- or anti-environment behavior could be anticipated." Beginning with a pool of Likert-type items originally used in the Tognacci et al. (1972) study, the Weigels selected 16 that appeared to form an internally consistent, summated rating scale in that study, and then, over a period of several years, conducted an extensive research program to test the scale's validity and reliability.

Two subsequent surveys by the Weigels in another region of the country again found the 16 items to form an adequate scale; another study found it to have strong test-retest reliability over a six-week period; a comparison of Sierra Club members' scores with the public samples' scores established the scale's known-group validity; and a unique field study documented the scale's ability to predict observed (as opposed to self-reported) pro-environmental behaviors (Weigel and Newman, 1976). This impressive body of work led Gray (1985:29) to note that "The diversity, amount, and quality of psychometric support place [Weigel and Weigel's Environmental Concern Scale] in a class of its own." For this reason, plus the fact that it continues to be used (Tarrant and Cordell, 1997), the ECS deserves closer examination.

Although Weigel and Weigel (1978) did not indicate that they selected items designed explicitly to tap the three major aspects of attitudes, their stated purpose of measuring "beliefs and feelings" that would reveal "predispositions" to engage in behaviors clearly suggests an interest in the affective, cognitive, and conative aspects of environmental concern. Not surprisingly, then, one finds items that appear to tap each of these attitudinal components among the 16 in the ECS; and while many of the items deal with pollution, topics such as resource conservation and wildlife preservation are also included. The ECS thereby achieves relatively broad-range environmental coverage by including items dealing with several environmental topics, as opposed to using items that focus on environmental problems or environmental quality as does the Guagnano and Markee (1995) study noted earlier. Thus, Weigel and Weigel's Environmental Concern Scale represents a multiple-topic/multiple-expression measuring instrument, one that appears to provide a valid and reliable means of measuring environmental concern.

The prior distinction between subjectively and methodologically derived measures (two contrasting ways of developing *multiple* measures of differing aspects of environmental concern) does not directly apply to the construction of single measures such as the ECS. Yet, related methodological issues play a key role in constructing single scales. In the original selection of the 16 items from a larger pool, and subsequent evaluation of the items with new data sets, Weigel and Weigel emphasized internal consistency—as measured by the degree to which each item correlates with the other items (item-total correlations) and the resulting coefficient alpha (the mean of all possible split-half reliabilities).[22] However, internal consistency is generally a necessary but not sufficient condition for unidimensionality (Zeller and Carmines, 1980), and some researchers believe that scales should possess unidimensionality.[23]

Weigel and Weigel did *not* report the results of a factor analysis of the ECS, but on the basis of unpublished studies in which he and colleagues factor-analyzed the 16 ECS items along with other items, Gray (1985:29) questions the unidimensionality of the scale. This is not surprising for a scale of this length, since the goal of factor analysis is to break a set of items into more homogeneous subsets reflecting differing dimensions, and it is rare to see only a single factor emerging from an analysis of 16 items. (While we do not have access to the results, our suspicion is that the ECS would yield multiple factors corresponding to the major topical areas of pollution, wildlife, and conservation and/or attitudinal facets of concern—i.e., items primarily reflecting affect, cognitions, or intentions.) Yet, the strong internal consistency of the ECS, along with the impressive evidence of validity and reliability presented for it, suggests that it is a very good, broad-range measure of environmental concern—one that is particularly useful in predicting environmental behavior (Weigel and Newman, 1976).

Despite the impressive performance of the ECS it seems to have gone out of favor, as by the 1990s very few studies were using it. We suspect this is because it seems somewhat out-of-date. Although the individual items are less dated than some of those in Maloney et al.'s (1975) four scales, they nonetheless fail to deal with many currently pressing environmental problems, ranging from toxic wastes to global warming. This points to the difficulty of creating a general environmental concern scale that will remain relevant for a long period of time (by using sets of individual items dealing with relatively specific problems), and the advantage of using items dealing with broader referents such as environmental problems, quality, and protection, as did Guagnano and Markee (1995), among others.

The advantage of using items with a broader focus is well illustrated by the second scale to be reviewed. Sensing that environmentalism was beginning to pose a challenge to our fundamental views of nature and humans' relationship to it, Dunlap and Van Liere (1978b) set out to measure key aspects of the developing "environmental worldview." They formulated items dealing with beliefs about humanity's ability to upset the balance of nature, the existence of limits to growth, and humanity's right to rule over the rest of nature (anthropocentrism). In a 1976 study in Washington, they found that a set of 12 Likert items measuring these three facets of a new social paradigm or worldview exhibited a good deal of internal consistency, yielding an alpha of .81, and strongly discriminated between samples of known environmentalists and the general public. Dunlap and Van Liere argued that the items could therefore be treated legitimately as a summated rating scale, called the "New Environmental Paradigm Scale" or "NEP Scale."

The amorphous concept of "social paradigm" was particularly ambiguous in the mid-1970s, when it was just beginning to be used, and Dunlap and Van Liere did not attempt to link their measure to traditional social-psychological concepts.[24] However, over time they (Dunlap et al., 2000) and others (Gray, 1985:32; Stern et al., 1995) have come to regard the NEP items as tapping primarily "primitive beliefs" about humans' relationship with nature, although clearly there is a normative or value dimension to some of the items as well. Further, to the degree that all of the items are designed to measure a new paradigm, one can think of the NEP Scale as tapping a single (cognitive) expression of concern. Gray (1985:32) classifies the NEP Scale as a "single-topic" measure, apparently because all of the items deal broadly with human–environment relations, but one could also interpret items on the "balance of nature," the "rights of plants and animals," and the existence of "limits to growth" as reflecting multiple topics. Thus, we think it is most appropriate to label the NEP Scale a multiple-topic/single-expression measure, while admitting that the value aspect of some items might make "multiple-expression" more fitting. By focusing broadly on human relations with the natural environment, the

NEP Scale does achieve broad-range environmental coverage—broader than Weigel and Weigel's (1978) ECS—but with a narrower degree of coverage of the concern component of the construct of environmental concern.

The NEP Scale has had an interesting history, as early on it was not used as widely as Weigel and Weigel's Environmental Concern Scale. It gradually became more popular, however, and by the 1990s was considered "by far the most widely used" measure of environmental concern (Stern et al., 1995:725). There are several reasons for this. First, NEP items such as "Humans must live in harmony with nature in order to survive" have not become dated like some in the Weigel and Weigel ECS or Maloney et al. (1975) scales. Second, by the 1990s, ozone depletion, climate change, and other evidence of global environmental change made the prospect of human alteration of the global ecosystem appear more likely than in the 1970s, and thus NEP items such as "When humans interfere with nature it often produces disastrous consequences" seem to have more plausibility than when they were formulated. Finally, the continuing strength and evolution of environmentalism has made the ecocentric or biocentric worldview (versus the more traditionally dominant anthropocentric worldview) being tapped by the NEP Scale more "mainstream" than in the 1970s.[25]

The NEP Scale has now been used in scores of studies worldwide, and many of them have documented its validity by showing that NEP scores distinguish between the general public and environmental activists (known-group validity), and are related to both self-reported and observed behavior on behalf of the environment (predictive validity). A few have also shown that the NEP Scale performs as expected when incorporated into theoretical models predicting a range of more specific environmental attitudes and behaviors, thus suggesting that it has construct validity (see Dunlap et al., 2000, for a review of these studies). Also, importantly, a recent qualitative study providing an in-depth investigation of the "cultural models" by which Americans attempt to make sense of environmental issues produced a set of beliefs remarkably similar to those tapped by the NEP items, suggesting that the NEP Scale has content validity as well (Kempton et al., 1995:ch.3).

Despite its widespread use, the NEP Scale has come under criticism on both conceptual and methodological grounds. Stern et al. (1995) noted its tenuous links to attitude theory, and Reser and Bentrupperbäumer (2000) have questioned whether the items truly measure environmental concern. To the extent that the NEP items measure environmental beliefs the scale is certainly tapping a major aspect of environmental concern, and is therefore widely regarded as a measure of this construct (e.g., Fransson and Gärling, 1999). Yet, it is clear that the NEP Scale (like many other measures) does not fully tap the richness of the construct and clearly fails to measure the conative and behavioral aspects of environmental concern. For this reason we expect the NEP Scale will continue to be employed as a measure of environmental concern (more specifically, as a measure of an ecocentric worldview) per se, but also as a fundamental component (along with values) in theoretical models designed to predict more specific beliefs, attitudes, and behaviors reflecting environmental concern (e.g., Stern et al., 1995, 1999). Or, in practical terms, we expect to see the NEP Scale used as both a dependent and an intervening variable, depending on the purpose of the study.

Methodological criticisms of the NEP Scale have focused on whether it measures a single construct or is inherently multidimensional. After some early studies produced similar results via factor analysis suggesting that the NEP is composed of three distinct dimensions—balance of nature, limits to growth, and anthropocentrism—some researchers began to routinely measure each dimension separately. However, a review of studies that have factor-analyzed the NEP Scale reveals considerable inconsistency in the number of dimensions obtained (see Dunlap et al., 2000), reinforcing Gray's (1985) assertion that factors are often unstable across different samples. Furthermore, the most consistent finding—that the anthropocentrism items form a distinct dimension—may stem from a methodological artifact, as these were the only items worded in an anti-NEP direction. A revised NEP Scale (reported in Dunlap et al., 2000) has been developed to solve this problem, as well as tap a broader range of features of an ecological worldview, and it will be interesting to see the results of future tests of its dimensionality.

Both of the scales just reviewed, despite their substantial differences in content, reflect efforts to establish single measures of environmental concern that allow researchers to classify respondents in terms of their levels of concern, and illustrate the strengths and weaknesses of this approach. Both have been found to possess adequate internal consistency, yet questions have also been raised (particularly for the NEP Scale) concerning their unidimensionality. The broader question of the dimensionality of environmental concern is the topic of the next section.

## EXAMINING THE DIMENSIONALITY OF ENVIRONMENTAL CONCERN

We have seen that some researchers attempt to achieve broad coverage of the concept of environmental concern by creating several measures—based either on theoretical or policy-relevant grounds—of its crucial aspects, sometimes subjectively and sometimes methodologically; and we have seen others attempt to measure the concept with a single scale. These various approaches tend to make differing assumptions and often come to differing conclusions about a key issue: Is it appropriate to consider environmental concern as a single construct, or is it inherently multidimensional? Unfortunately, none of the previously discussed approaches provide

adequate answers to this question. With a few exceptions, studies that create multiple measures subjectively seldom explicitly address the issue of
whether they all measure the same construct, while those that do so methodologically inevitably (by virtue of factor analysis or related techniques)
create distinct dimensions of environmental concern. Finally, efforts to establish single measures assume they are measuring a single construct, but
the unidimensionality of the scales is often questioned. Thus, none of the
foregoing studies provide evidence that would rebut the claim of deHaven-
Smith (1991:97), who argues that peoples' views of environmental issues
are so dependent upon the specific issue involved and the context in which
it emerges "that researchers should abandon survey designs and statistical
techniques that presuppose the existence of a generalized concern for the
environment."

Fortunately, methodological techniques that allow for a more sophisticated examination of the dimensionality of environmental concern are now
beginning to be used. Confirmatory factor analysis (CFA) appears to offer
an excellent technique for assessing the dimensionality of environmental
concern, and particularly for answering the question of whether it is a
meaningful construct, *if* CFA is coupled with careful conceptualization
along the lines of facet design. Unlike exploratory factor analysis, CFA
requires the analyst to specify in advance the hypothesized measurement
model—making it an ideal complement to facet analysis—and also allows
the analyst to take into account both random and nonrandom sources of
measurement error (directionality of items being an example of the latter).
Furthermore, CFA allows one to hypothesize that two or more factors reflect an underlying construct, thus making it feasible to test for the possibility that empirically distinct dimensions of environmental concern are
nonetheless measuring the same latent construct. CFA would have offered
an ideal technique for examining the degree to which the multiple measures
used in the Tognacci et al. (1972) and Van Liere and Dunlap (1981) studies, as well as those employed by Maloney et al. (1975), are all tapping an
underlying construct of environmental concern.

Two recent studies highlight CFA's potential for helping advance our
understanding of environmental concern. The first, by Guber (1996),
set out explicitly to investigate the dimensionality of environmental concern. After pointing out weaknesses in prior studies (including measurement error) that could be addressed by CFA, Guber used national Gallup
surveys to develop and test a model of environmental concern. Guber
posited three crucial aspects of such concern: perceived seriousness of
environmental problems; (self-reported) pro-environmental behaviors; and
self-identification as an environmentalist. She treated each as a latent dimension, and measured the first with two multi-item scales tapping perceived "general pollution" and perceived "global environmental problems";
the second with three multi-item scales tapping environmental activism,

conservation behavior, and green consumer behavior; and the third with a single self-identification item. The resulting LISREL model not only revealed that each scale clearly measured the hypothesized dimension, *but* that these three dimensions were themselves highly correlated after measurement error was taken into account. This led her to conclude that it is appropriate to treat environmental concern as a reasonably coherent and empirically meaningful construct.

Unfortunately, there are several problems in Guber's study. First, she did not carefully distinguish between environmental topics and expressions of concern, and the three aspects of environmental concern she hypothesized all represent differing policy-relevant expressions: perceived seriousness, pro-environmental behaviors, and self-identification as an environmentalist (the latter being a defensible but idiosyncratic indicator of environmental concern). She largely ignored environmental topics in the creation of the two perceived seriousness measures (both of which are thus examples of multiple-topic/single-expression scales), but used the geographical scale facet to separate items clearly dealing with global problems from those dealing with other (but not specifically local or national) problems. Worse, she gave little justification for how the six items used to construct these two measures were chosen from a list of 11; and why she bothered to construct two measures when an initial factor analysis showed all 11 to be unidimensional is puzzling. The separation of the self-reported behaviors, which Guber too readily accepts as valid behavioral indicators, seems more justifiable, and the resulting scales again represent multiple-topic/single-expression measures. Finally, Guber ignored items dealing with support for pro-environmental policies, a key aspect of most policy-relevant expressions of environmental concern. In short, because the model of environmental concern Guber set out to test ignored key facets of environmental concern, and especially failed to deal effectively with both differing topics and expressions, her analysis—despite showing the promise of CFA—leaves much to be desired.

A second CFA study by Carman (1998), using Michigan's National Election Survey data, took a somewhat narrower focus, as his goal was to measure environmental policy support rather than environmental concern more broadly. For this reason Carman, unwisely in our view, eschewed behavioral indicators, and argued that there are three key dimensions of environmental policy support: an economic dimension reflecting a willingness to give environmental protection priority over economic growth; an environmental regulations dimension reflecting support for such regulations; and an environmental quality assessment dimension reflecting perceived seriousness of environmental problems. Carman constructed multi-item measures of each presumed dimension (with adequate internal consistencies) based on the face validity of respective items. The "regulations" scale is clearly a multiple-topic/single-expression measure that asks respondents if they favor government action on a range of different problems, and the "assessment" scale is similar, even though it focuses only on the perceived seriousness of air and water pollution. The "economic" scale is more difficult to classify clearly, as three of the items involve explicit trade-offs while the other one simply asks if respondents favor more federal spending on environmental programs; similarly, three of the items focus on the environment while one focuses on pollution.

After verifying the existence of the three dimensions empirically via an exploratory factor analysis, Carman (1998:725) first conducted a second-order factor analysis of the three separate measures and found that they all "loaded on a single dimension of support for environmental policy." Then, and most importantly, he conducted a CFA that took into account measurement error to confirm the existence of this model, and found considerable support for it: Each individual item loaded on the appropriate first-order factor, and each of these factors loaded heavily on the second-order factor reflecting overall environmental policy support (although the assessment factor loaded less heavily than the economic and regulation factors). This led Carman (1998:727) to conclude that "both exploratory and confirmatory factor analytic techniques support the hypothesis that support for environmental policy is a hierarchical attitude comprised of three subdimensions, economic concern, regulatory concern, and qualitative assessment." Although these results led Carman, like Guber, to acknowledge the utility of an overarching construct of environmental concern (or, more specifically in his case, environmental policy support), he seems to place more emphasis on the distinctiveness of the three dimensions constituting it.[26]

While Carman's (1998) procedures seem defensible, like Guber's his study has some weaknesses. By ignoring the important distinction between environmental topics and expressions, Carman failed to see the possibility that his measure of perceived seriousness may not correlate as highly as the economic and regulatory dimensions, at least in part, because the substantive topics (air and water pollution) covered in it differ considerably from those in the other two dimensions. Similarly, even though the assessment scale contained two items focusing on the perceived seriousness of "local" pollution and two on "national" pollution, Carman gave little consideration to the utility of taking into account a geographical scale facet that clearly distinguished between the two levels. Perhaps most importantly, Carman's dismissal of the relevance of behavioral indicators is troubling, not only because of the traditional emphasis placed on conative indicators, but because behaviors such as voting and contacting officials are critical indicators of support for environmental policy.

Both the Guber (1996) and Carman (1998) studies have shortcomings, particularly in their conceptualization of environmental concern. Yet, each demonstrates the utility of CFA, with its ability to control for measurement error and to test for the existence of a latent construct underlying a set of empirically meaningful dimensions, for helping to document the structure of environmental concern. Hopefully, future CFA studies will develop models of environmental concern that more fully tap the range of facets involved in both the environmental and concern components, and thereby do a better job of building upon the conceptual distinctions explicated in this chapter.[27] Nonetheless, both Guber (1996) and Carman (1998) provide evidence to show that public attitudes toward environmental issues are organized in a reasonably coherent fashion (also see Pierce et al., 1987), and that, deHaven-Smith's (1991) claims to the contrary, it is therefore appropriate to treat environmental concern as a meaningful construct. Indeed, despite the increased complexity of environmental issues over the past three decades, such evidence suggests that environmental concern may have become a more cognitively consistent, stable, and consequential phenomenon than at the time of the first Earth Day.

## CONCLUSION

By clarifying the conceptual ambiguities inherent in the multifaceted construct of environmental concern, and the methodological difficulties involved in measuring it, we hope this chapter will prove useful to those interested in understanding peoples' concern for environmental quality. We have tried to provide a roadmap that will be helpful both in terms of comprehending existing efforts to study environmental concern and in designing future research on the topic. We believe that many inconsistent findings in the literature stem from comparing results from studies employing noncomparable measures of environmental concern, measures tapping very different facets of the environment and/or concern components of the construct. We hope that our efforts will enable scholars to make more discerning comparisons among studies, as well as to design more adequate measures for their own research. In terms of the latter, it is impossible to offer a short list of hard-and-fast rules, but we trust that the clarifications, examples, and suggestions we have offered throughout this chapter will prove useful. Researchers obviously need to think clearly at the outset about what aspects or facets of environmental concern they want to measure, and then carefully conceptualize them prior to attempting to measure them.

Of course, we are cognizant that many new approaches to studying environmental concern that go well beyond the standard survey/psychometric approaches we have reviewed are beginning to be used. Efforts to employ in-depth, ethnographic interviews and focus groups (e.g., Kempton et al., 1995), the use of narratives (e.g., Shanahan et al., 1999) and content analyses of public comments on environmental controversies (e.g., Vining and Tyler, 1999), among others, offer promising techniques for shedding further light on the nature of public concern for environmental quality. Such alternative approaches offer useful complements to the more traditional survey research strategies reviewed in this chapter, and we look forward to their continued development. While they may be seen by some as competitors to the approaches reviewed here, we see them as offering opportunities to refine and strengthen, as well as to confirm or disconfirm, findings from more traditional approaches. For example, in differing ways both the Kempton et al. (1995) and Shanahan et al. (1999) studies deepen the understanding of the "New Environmental Paradigm" obtained with the NEP Scale.

Finally, it goes without saying that in this chapter we have not come close to doing justice to the immense literature on environmental concern. In particular, we have ignored the large number of efforts to explain the sources of environmental concern, ranging from quasi-theoretical efforts to explain variation in such concern with various social and demographic variables (see, e.g., Jones and Dunlap, 1992; Van Liere and Dunlap, 1980) to more recent efforts to develop theoretical models of its sources (see, e.g., Fransson and Gärling, 1999; Stern et al., 1999).[28] Although Reser and Bentrupperbäumer (2000:22) suggest that the conceptual and measurement confusion in the current literature makes it "pointless to report actual research findings," our primary reason for ignoring "explanatory" work is more pragmatic: Space limitations prohibit us from doing so. Yet, we agree that efforts to develop theoretical models explaining the nature and sources of environmental concern will likely prove more successful if they are built upon improved conceptualization and measurement of environmental concern. Our hope is that this chapter will contribute to achieving this improvement.

## NOTES

1. Environmental psychologists study humans' perceptions and evaluations of such environmental phenomena. See Bechtel (1997:ch. 5) for an introduction to this research.

2. For an example of the use of facet theory in developing and testing a measuring instrument dealing with environmentally relevant issues, see Braithwaite and Law (1977) and Mayton (1986). For a more ambitious but problematic (in the sense of being less convincing and difficult to follow) effort to use facet theory to map the meaning of environmental concern empirically, see Hackett (1995).

3. What Van Liere and Dunlap (1981) called "substantive issue" is equivalent to what Ester (1981:85) calls the "environmental subconcept," Gray (1985: 27–28) calls the "environmental topic," Schahn and Holzer (1990:769) call "topical areas," and Heberlein (1981) and Stern et al. (1995) call "attitude object" (a term we also employ).

4. As these examples suggest, a facet and its constituent elements are analogous to a variable and the attributes that comprise it. The difference is that a facet is a

conceptual device that may, or may not, end up having the empirical utility of a variable (Shye et al., 1994).

5. In reality the complexity is even greater than we have portrayed. We have concentrated on clarifying the universe of *biophysical* issues inherent in the environmental component of environmental concern. However, as our examples of the functions that the environment serves for human societies, or the distinctions between resource depletion/conservation and pollution generation/abatement illustrate, a "social" dimension is always at least implicit—and often explicit—in environmental issues. Technically then, it is the universe of *socio-biophysical* issues that yields the environmental component of environmental concern, as human phenomena such as population and technology and activities such as production, consumption, and disposal are inherently interwoven with the biophysical dimension of environmental issues (see, e.g., Reser and Bentrupperbäumer, 2000). For the sake of manageability and brevity, we will not focus on these social dimensions in this chapter.

6. For example, environmental organizations often cite (and sometimes sponsor) public opinion polls that document public support for environmental protection (see, e.g., Dunlap and Scarce, 1991) to strengthen their credibility, and the League of Conservation Voters conducts polls to help design electoral campaigns.

7. In an effort to avoid confusion, note that we are here discussing broad-range *studies* that employ several measuring instruments to tap different facets of environmental concern, while later we will discuss broad-range *measures* that include items tapping numerous environmental topics (or refer to "ecological" or "environmental" problems) and/or more than one component of attitudes. Thus, broad versus narrow-range is a distinction that can apply both to individual measures and to studies.

8. It should also be noted that theoretical studies are more apt to investigate a wide range of personality and other social-psychological variables, whereas policy-relevant studies tend to investigate the role of demographic and political (party preference and ideology) variables. In addition, policy-relevant studies are more likely to employ representative samples of the public, ranging from the community to national level.

9. For purposes of clarity it should be noted that common usage forces us to employ "component" to refer *both* to the environmental and concern components of environmental concern, as well as to the cognitive, affective, and conative components of attitudes. Hopefully, the context will always make our meaning clear.

10. This typology is similar to, and benefited considerably from, Gray's (1985: 28–37) distinction among "general measures," "specific-topic measures," "multiple-topic measures," and "multicomponent measures." However, we believe that upon careful inspection there is no difference between Gray's categories of general measures and multiple-topic measures, and he also fails to include "single-topic/single-component" measures as a separate category.

11. Complicating matters is that—as noted previously—some studies employ measures that achieve broad-range coverage of the environmental component of environmental concern by focusing on several topics (e.g., population, pollution, and conservation), while others do so by focusing on environmental quality or ecological problems per se.

12. Since neither Maloney and Ward (1973) nor Maloney et al. (1975) combine

all four into a single measure, it is more accurate to label their overall set of items an inventory and the four multi-item measures as "indexes" or "scales." By index we mean a measure based on the sum of responses to multiple individual items, while we call the same measure a scale (specifically, a summated rating scale) once it has been found to possess adequate internal consistency and/or unidimensionality.

13. Had Maloney and colleagues combined responses to all of the items in their inventory (either the original or short versions) into a single measure, then the entire inventory would represent an example of a multiple-topic/multiple-component measure.

14. Gray (1985:38) cites a German study by Amelang and associates that factor-analyzed all of the items in Maloney and Ward's (1973) original inventory, and says that "The resulting factors fit the classical tripartite model quite well." How-ever, Kaiser et al. (1999:15) cite the same study along with Smythe and Brook (1980) as failing to yield dimensions matching Maloney and Ward's four measures. Unable to read German, we are unsure how to treat Amelang et al.'s study.

15. The distinction between these two types of studies is blurred somewhat by the fact that researchers who construct multi-item measures on the basis of face/content validity often subsequently employ statistical techniques to judge the inter-nal consistency (via coefficient alpha) or unidimensionality (via factor analysis) of their measures, and to refine them by deleting items if necessary. However, there is a fundamental difference between using factor analysis to establish the unidimen-sionality of a measure constructed beforehand and using it to create two or more measures based on the dimensions revealed by the results. For an example of the former approach, see Dunlap et al. (2000). The latter approach is illustrated by several examples to be reviewed shortly.

16. Schuman (1986) demonstrates that great caution is called for when gener-alizing from answers to specific questions to actual levels of public support for policies, due to the effects of question wording; but this problem is attenuated somewhat by use of a wide range of questions and is not so problematic when using longitudinal data to draw conclusions about changes over time rather than absolute levels of support (see, e.g., Dunlap and Scarce, 1991).

17. More specifically, Foa (1958:236) notes that the "way of explaining the relationship among variables on the basis of their facet composition is similar to factor analysis. In factor analysis, however, the factors are inferred a posteriori from the empirical observation of the intercorrelations. In facet design the factors are already spelled out in the conceptual composition of the variables. The problem of factor analysis is: Since the variables are intercorrelated, what factors do they have in common? In facet theory the problem is: Since these variables have similar conceptual composition, how does this reflect on their empirical relationship?"

18. Gray (1985:37–44) distinguishes four types of studies that derive measures of environmental concern factor analytically: (1) those that attempt to identify dimensions reflecting the major components of attitudes discussed earlier (with little success, as noted previously); (2) those that examine a broad range of ecological issues; (3) those that examine a narrow range of ecological issues; and (4) those that attempt to validate the unidimensionality of a single measure. The problem with Gray's review of both broad- and narrow-range studies is that he fails to distinguish between topics and components/conceptualizations. This is not so prob-lematic for narrow-range studies, but ignoring the distinction makes it particularly

difficult to clarify findings from broad-range studies. Those reviewed by Gray produced a huge variety of dimensions that reflect both topics and components/conceptualizations, and this is true of others as well. For example, an early factor-analytic study by Horvat and Voelker (1976) yielded dimensions labeled "use/abuse of nature," "overpopulation," "general environmental concern," and "eco-responsible behavior," while a cluster analysis employed by Lounsbury and Tornatzky (1977) yielded separate clusters for "environmental degradation," "environmental action," and "overpopulation."

19. The exception would be if all items load on a single factor and thus the entire set of items is found to be unidimensional.

20. This example reveals that in many instances different forms of "expressions" require differing question and response formats, which inevitably conflates efforts to isolate their effects from those of methodological artifacts.

21. It should be noted that a few items from Dunlap et al's. (1973) scale were used by Van Liere and Dunlap (1981), and the attempt to measure support for "environmental rights" versus traditional American values in that study evolved into an effort to measure support for the "Dominant Social Paradigm" and the "New Environmental Paradigm" in later studies (to be discussed shortly).

22. This is also the approach taken by Tognacci et al. (1972) and Van Liere and Dunlap (1981) in the construction of the various individual scales included in their larger inventories.

23. Keeter (1984) provides an insightful application of these criteria for constructing a measure of environmental concern. Unfortunately, to our knowledge his measure has never been used by other researchers, which is why we do not review it.

24. Drawing upon a spate of literature in the late 1970s and early 1980s that more fully explicated the contrast between the emerging environmental paradigm and the dominant social paradigm (see Dunlap and Van Liere, 1984, on the "DSP"), subsequent researchers provided more comprehensive conceptualizations of the NEP and DSP, and in some cases operationalized both belief and value dimensions in each one (Olsen et al., 1992). However, these elaborate measuring instruments have proven unwieldy, and the original NEP Scale has become far more widely used.

25. The latter is reflected by the fact that in the 1990s a number of other scales designed to measure ecocentric versus anthropocentric orientations were developed (see references in Dunlap et al., 2000).

26. To some degree this is because Carman compared the degree to which the three dimensions, as well as overall environmental policy support, could be predicted by a set of demographic and political variables, and found some differences across the measures. Yet, we think he tends to exaggerate the differences. Two well-established measures, political ideology and age, were significant predictors of all four measures (with liberals and younger adults being more pro-environment). While education was not a significant predictor, this is likely due to the fact that its effect was washed out by the inclusion (unwise in our view) of attention to news and efficacy in the same regression model. Thus, Carman's results are not only consistent with past research (Jones and Dunlap, 1992; Van Liere and Dunlap, 1980), but exhibit less inconsistency across the four measures, at least for the well-established predictors of environmental concern, than he implies.

27. Berberoglu and Tosunoglu (1995) also used CFA to develop a scale that consists of four dimensions reflecting substantive topics, but since it was limited to a study of Turkish college students we will not review it. However, the fact that all of their items had a similar form of expression, being stated in the form of Likert items with the same agree-disagree format, reinforces a point we made earlier about exploratory factor analysis: When items with the same form of expression are factor-analyzed, the dimensions will inevitably reflect differing topical areas.

28. Although we have cited studies conducted in various nations, space limitations have also prevented us from dealing with the recent spate of comparative studies investigating environmental concern cross-nationally (see, e.g., Brechin, 1999; Dunlap et al., 1993), as well as the methodological problems involved in studying environmental concern across nations and cultures.

## REFERENCES

Barry, John. 1999. *Environment and Social Theory*. New York: Routledge.

Bechtel, Robert B. 1997. *Environment and Behavior: An Introduction*. Thousand Oaks, CA: Sage Publications.

Berberoglu, Giray, and Canan Tosunoglu. 1995. "Exploratory and Confirmatory Factor Analyses of an Environmental Attitude Scale (EAS) for Turkish University Students." *The Journal of Environmental Education* 26:40–43.

Blocker, T. Jean, and Douglas L. Eckberg. 1989. "Environmental Issues as Women's Issues: General Concerns and Local Hazards." *Social Science Quarterly* 70:586–593.

Borden, R. J., and J. F. Francis. 1978. "Who Cares about Ecology? Personality and Sex Differences in Environmental Concern." *Journal of Personality* 46:190–203.

Braithwaite, V. A., and H. G. Law. 1977. "The Structure of Attitudes to Doomsday Issues." *Australian Psychologist* 12:167–174.

Brechin, Steven R. 1999. "Objective Problems, Subjective Values, and Global Environmentalism: Evaluating the Postmaterialist Argument and Challenging a New Explanation." *Social Science Quarterly* 80:793–809.

Buttel, Frederick H. 1975. "The Environmental Movement: Consensus, Conflict, and Change." *Journal of Environmental Education* 7:53–63.

Buttel, Frederick H., and William L. Flinn. 1976. "Economic Growth versus the Environment: Survey Evidence." *Social Science Quarterly* 57:410–420.

Buttel, Frederick H., and Donald E. Johnson. 1977. "Dimensions of Environmental Concern: Factor Structure, Correlates, and Implications for Research." *The Journal of Environmental Education* 9:49–64.

Carman, Christopher Jan. 1998. "Dimensions of Environmental Policy Support in the United States." *Social Science Quarterly* 79:717–733.

Chanda, Raban. 1999. "Correlates and Dimensions of Environmental Quality Concern among Residents of an African Subtropical City: Gaborone, Botswana." *The Journal of Environmental Education* 30:31–39.

Crowe, M. Jay. 1968. "Toward a 'Definitional Model' of Public Perceptions of Air Pollution." *Journal of the Air Pollution Association* 18:154–157.

deHaven-Smith, Lance. 1991. *Environmental Concern in Florida and the Nation*. Gainesville: University of Florida Press.

Dietz, Thomas, Paul C. Stern, and Gregory A. Guagnano. 1998. "Social Structural and Social Psychological Bases of Environmental Concern." *Environment and Behavior* 30:450–471.

Dispoto, Raymond G. 1977. "Interrelationships among Measures of Environmental Activity, Emotionality, and Knowledge." *Educational and Psychological Measurement* 37:451–459.

Dunlap, Riley E. 1975. "The Impact of Political Orientation on Environmental Attitudes and Actions." *Environment and Behavior* 7:428–454.

———. 1994. "The Nature and Causes of Environmental Problems: A Socio-Ecological Perspective." Pp. 45–84 in *Environment and Development: A Sociological Understanding for the Better Human Conditions*, edited by Korean Sociological Association. Seoul: Seoul Press.

Dunlap, Riley E., Richard P. Gale, and Brent M. Rutherford. 1973. "Concern for Environmental Rights among College Students." *American Journal of Economics and Sociology* 32:45–60.

Dunlap, Riley E., George H. Gallup, Jr., and Alec M. Gallup. 1993. "Of Global Concern: Results of the Health of the Planet Survey." *Environment* 35(November):7–15, 33–39.

Dunlap, Riley E., and Rik Scarce. 1991. "The Polls—Poll Trends. Environmental Problems and Protection." *Public Opinion Quarterly* 55:651–672.

Dunlap, Riley E., and Kent D. Van Liere. 1978a. "Environmental Concern: A Bibliography of Empirical Studies and Brief Appraisal of the Literature." *Public Administration Series: Bibliography*, P-44. Monticello, IL: Vance Bibliographies.

Dunlap, Riley E., and Kent D. Van Liere. 1978b. "A Proposed Measuring Instrument and Preliminary Results: The 'New Environmental Paradigm'." *Journal of Environmental Education* 9:10–19.

Dunlap, Riley E., and Kent D. Van Liere. 1984. "Commitment to the Dominant Social Paradigm and Concern for Environmental Quality." *Social Science Quarterly* 65:1013–1028.

Dunlap, Riley E., Kent D. Van Liere, Angela G. Mertig, and Robert Emmet Jones. 2000. "Measuring Endorsement of the New Ecological Paradigm: A Revised NEP Scale." *Journal of Social Issues* 56:425–442.

Dynes, Russell R., and Dennis Wenger. 1971. "Factors in the Community Perception of Water Resource Problems." Water Resources Bulletin, *Journal of the American Water Resources Association* 7:644–651.

Eagly, Alice H., and Patrick Kulesa. 1997. "Attitudes, Attitude Structure, and Resistance to Change: Implications for Persuasion on Environmental Issues." Pp. 122–151 in *Environment, Ethics, and Behavior*, edited by M. H. Bazerman, D. M. Messick, A. E. Tenbrunsel, and K. A. Wade-Benzoni. San Francisco: New Lexington.

Ester, Peter. 1981. "Environmental Concern in the Netherlands." Pp. 81–108 in *Progress in Resource Management and Environmental Planning*, Vol. 3, edited by Timothy O'Riordan and R. Kerry Turner. Chichester: John Wiley & Sons.

Ester, Peter, and F. van der Meer. 1982. "Determinants of Individual Environmental Behaviour: An Outline of a Behavioural Model and Some Research Findings." *The Netherlands' Journal of Sociology* 18:57–94.

Fishbein, Martin, and Icek Ajzen. 1975. *Belief, Attitude, Intentions, and Behavior.* Reading, MA: Addison-Wesley.

Foa, Uriel G. 1958. "The Contiguity Principle in the Structure of Interpersonal Relations." *Human Relations* 11:229–238.

Fransson, Niklas, and Tommy Gärling. 1999. "Environmental Concern: Conceptual Definitions, Measurement Methods, and Research Findings." *Journal of Environmental Psychology* 19:369–382.

Furman, Andrzej. 1998. "A Notes on Environmental Concern in a Developing Country: Results from an Istanbul Survey." *Environment and Behavior* 30: 520–534.

Gray, David. 1985. *Ecological Beliefs and Behaviors.* Westport, CT: Greenwood Press.

Green, Donald P., and Jack Citrin. 1994. "Measurement Error and the Structure of Attitudes: Are Positive and Negative Judgements Opposites?" *American Journal of Political Science* 38:256–281.

Guagnano, Gregory A., and Nancy Markee. 1995. "Regional Differences in the Sociodemographic Determinants of Environmental Concern." *Population and Environment: A Journal of Interdisciplinary Studies* 17:135–149.

Guber, Deborah L. 1996. "Environmental Concern and the Dimensionality Problem: A New Approach to an Old Predicament." *Social Science Quarterly* 77: 644–662.

Hackett, Paul. 1995. *Conservation and the Consumer: Understanding Environmental Concern.* London and New York: Routledge.

Heberlein, Thomas A. 1981. "Environmental Attitudes." *Zeitschrift fur Umweltpolitik* 2:241–270.

Heberlein, Thomas A., and J. Stanley Black. 1976. "Attitudinal Specificity and the Prediction of Behavior in a Field Setting." *Journal of Personality and Social Psychology* 33:474–479.

Horvat, Robert E., and Alan M. Voelker. 1976. "Using a Likert Scale to Measure 'Environmental Responsibility'." *Journal of Environmental Education* 8:36–47.

Jones, Robert Emmet, and Riley E. Dunlap. 1992. "The Social Bases of Environmental Concern: Have They Changed over Time?" *Rural Sociology* 57:28–47.

Kaiser, Florian G., Sybille Wölfing, and Urs Fuhrer. 1999. "Environmental Attitude and Ecological Behaviour." *Journal of Environmental Psychology* 19:1–19.

Keeter, Scott. 1984. "Problematical Pollution Polls: Validity in the Measurement of Public Opinion on Environmental Issues." *Political Methodology* 10:267–291.

Kempton, Willett, James S. Boster, and Jennifer A. Hartley. 1995. *Environmental Values in American Culture.* Cambridge, MA: MIT Press.

Klineberg, Stephen L., Matthew McKeever, and Bert Rothenbach. 1998. "Demographic Predictors of Environmental Concern: It Does Make a Difference How It's Measured." *Social Science Quarterly* 79:734–753.

Lounsbury, John W., and Louis G. Tornatzky. 1977. "A Scale for Assessing Attitudes toward Environmental Quality." *The Journal of Social Psychology* 101:299–305.

Maloney, Michael P., and Michael P. Ward. 1973. "Ecology: Let's Hear from the

People: An Objective Scale for the Measurement of Ecological Attitudes and Knowledge." *American Psychologist* 28:583–586.

Maloney, Michael P., Michael P. Ward, and G. Nicholas Braucht. 1975. "Psychology in Action: A Revised Scale for the Measurement of Ecological Attitudes and Knowledge." *American Psychologist* 30:787–790.

Mayton, Daniel M. 1986. "The Structure of Attitudes to Doomsday Issues: A Replication." *Australian Psychologist* 21:395–403.

McAllister, Ian. 1994. "Dimensions of Environmentalism: Public Opinion, Political Activism and Party Support in Australia." *Environmental Politics* 3:22–42.

McCutcheon, Lynn E. 1974. "Development and Validation of a Scale to Measure Attitude toward Population Control." *Psychological Reports* 34:1235–1242.

Moffet, Louis A. 1974. "Conservationism toward the Natural Environment." *Psychological Reports* 34:778.

Murch, Arvin W. 1971. "Public Concern for Environmental Pollution." *Public Opinion Quarterly* 35:100–106.

Murch, Arvin W. (ed.). 1974. "Who Cares about the Environment? The Nature and Origins of Environmental Concern." In *Environmental Concern: Personal Attitudes and Behavior Toward Environmental Problems*. New York: MSS Information Corporation.

Neuman, Keith. 1986. "Trends in Public Opinion on Acid Rain: A Comprehensive Review of Existing Data." *Water, Air, and Soil Pollution* 31:1047–1059.

Olsen, Marvin E., Dora G. Lodwick, and Riley E. Dunlap. 1992. *Viewing the World Ecologically*. Boulder, CO: Westview Press.

Pierce, John C., Nicholas P. Lovrich, Jr., Taketsugu Tsurutani, and Takematsu Abe. 1987. "Environmental Belief Systems among Japanese and American Elites and Publics." *Political Behavior* 9:139–159.

Reser, Joseph P., and Joan M. Bentrupperbäumer. 2000. "Unpackaging the Nature & Management Implications of 'Environmental Concern'." Presented at the Eighth International Symposium on Society and Resource Management, Western Washington University, Bellingham, WA.

Rohrschneider, Robert. 1988. "Citizens' Attitudes toward Environmental Issues: Selfish or Selfless?" *Comparative Political Studies* 21:347–367.

Schahn, Joachim, and Erwin Holzer. 1990. "Studies of Individual Environmental Concern: The Role of Knowledge, Gender, and Background Variables." *Environment and Behavior* 22:767–786.

Schahn, Joachim, and Erwin Holzer. n.d. "Construction, Validation and Application of Scales for Measuring Individual Environmental Concern." Unpublished manuscript, Department of Psychology, University of Heidelberg.

Schuman, Howard. 1986. "Ordinary Questions, Survey Questions, and Policy Questions." *Public Opinion Quarterly* 50:432–442.

Shanahan, James, Lisa Pelstring, and Katherine McComas. 1999. "Using Narratives to Think about Environmental Attitude and Behavior: An Exploratory Study." *Society & Natural Resources* 12:405–419.

Shye, Samuel, and Dov Elizur with Michael Hoffman. 1994. *Introduction to Facet Theory*. Thousand Oaks, CA: Sage Publications.

Smythe, Padric C., and Robert C. Brook. 1980. "Environmental Concerns and Actions: A Social-Psychological Investigation." *Canadian Journal of Behavioral Sciences* 12:175–186.

Stern, Paul C., Thomas Dietz, Troy Abel, Gregory A. Guagnano, and Linda Kalof. 1999. "A Value-Belief-Norm Theory of Support for Social Movements: The Case of Environmentalism." *Human Ecology Review* 6:81–97.

Stern, Paul C., Thomas Dietz, and Gregory A. Guagnano. 1995. "The New Ecological Paradigm in Social-Psychological Context." *Environment and Behavior* 27:723–743.

Tarrant, Michael A., and H. Ken Cordell. 1997. "The Effect of Respondent Characteristics on General Environmental Attitude-Behavior Correspondence." *Environment and Behavior* 29:618–637.

Tognacci, Louis N., Russell H. Weigel, Marvin F. Wideen, and David T. A. Vernon. 1972. "Environmental Quality: How Universal is Public Concern?" *Environment and Behavior* 4:73–86.

Uyeki, Eugene S., and Lani J. Holland. 2000. "Diffusion of Pro-Environment Attitudes?" *American Behavioral Scientist* 43:646–662.

Van Liere, Kent D., and Riley E. Dunlap. 1980. "The Social Bases of Environmental Concern: A Review of Hypotheses, Explanations and Empirical Evidence." *Public Opinion Quarterly* 44:181–197.

Van Liere, Kent D., and Riley E. Dunlap. 1981. "Environmental Concern: Does It Make a Difference How It's Measured?" *Environment and Behavior* 13: 651–676.

Vaske, Jerry J., and Maureen P. Donnelly. 1999. "A Value-Attitude-Behavior Model Predicting Wildland Preservation Voting Intentions." *Society & Natural Resources* 12:523–537.

Vining, Joanne, and Elizabeth Tyler. 1999. "Values, Emotions and Desired Outcomes Reflected in Public Responses to Forest Management Plans." *Human Ecology Review* 6:21–34.

Wall, Glenda. 1995. "General versus Specific Environmental Concern. A Western Canadian Case." *Environment and Behavior* 27:294–316.

Watkins, George Alfred. 1974. "Developing a 'Water Concern' Scale." *The Journal of Environmental Education* 5(Summer).

Weigel, Russell H., and Lee S. Newman. 1976. "Increasing Attitude-Behavior Correspondence by Broadening the Scope of the Behavioral Measure." *Journal of Personality and Social Psychology* 33:793–802.

Weigel, Russell, and Joan Weigel. 1978. "Environmental Concern: The Development of a Measure." *Environment and Behavior* 10:3–15.

Witherspoon, Sharon. 1994. "The Greening of Britain: Romance and Rationality." Pp. 107–139 in *British Social Attitudes, The 11th Report*, edited by Roger Jowell, John Curtice, Lindsay Brook, and Daphne Ahrendt with Alison Park. Aldershot, UK: Dartmouth.

Zeller, Richard A., and Edward G. Carmines. 1980. *Measurement in the Social Sciences*. New York: Cambridge University Press.

# Chapter 16

# Environmental Sociology in Nonacademic Settings

*Barbara A. Payne and Christopher Cluett*

## INTRODUCTION

The preceding chapters have covered a wide range of the theoretical, methodological, and substantive components of environmental sociology. The application of these perspectives and techniques outside of academia is the focus of this chapter. Although the range of topics included earlier was wide, the range of ways in which environmental sociology is practiced is even wider. Every substantive specialty can be applied in numerous ways, and every specialist can be employed in many capacities. Applied environmental sociologists have an opportunity not typically available to those who are in academia full-time to observe firsthand the interaction of humans and their natural and built environments. Environmental sociologists participate in planning and managing environmental projects, identify social impacts of proposals and projects, evaluate policies and proposals from a social science perspective, and work with citizens' groups. The insights gained in these activities provide a rich source of knowledge to the discipline, including new applications of theory, tests of hypotheses, suggestions for research topics, and evaluations of academic research findings.

Some environmental sociologists are concerned that issues surrounding human interaction with the natural environment often are addressed in a political context that discounts or ignores the role of behavioral and institutional factors, and fails to consider the perspectives and suggestions of environmental sociologists or other social scientists (Freudenburg and Keating, 1982; Meidinger and Schnaiberg, 1980; Schnaiberg, 1977). Others are concerned that too much emphasis is placed on atheoretical work that is descriptive and problem-specific and not very helpful for decision making, rather than as input that could lead to better decisions (Freudenburg and Keating, 1985; Gramling and Freudenburg, 1992; Rossi, 1980). To date, few policies have been enacted or substantially altered on the basis of the work of environmental sociologists in nonacademic (or academic) settings. In applications to the built environment, in contrast, sociologists have had somewhat more influence in developing and implementing new approaches to architectural and community design (e.g., Gutman, 1966; Zeisel, 1984). However, we see evidence of greater attention now being given to the human dimensions of environmental policy and expanded opportunities for environmental sociologists to play a substantive role (Burdge et al., 1995). These changes include increased environmental awareness, a globalization of environmental issues, and attention to the human dimensions of global environmental change (Miller, 1992; Stern et al., 1992), as well as increased demands for public involvement in a wide range of public and private management activities and policy decisions (Aggens, 1991).

Nonacademic environmental sociologists are becoming increasingly involved and influential in environmental decision making. Environmental sociologists are now participants in the research, planning, evaluation, and implementation aspects of environmental, architectural, construction, and assessment projects. Environmental sociologists are working for government agencies, large engineering and construction firms specializing in technology development and application, nonacademic research and consulting firms, architectural firms, and local and national environmental groups.

This chapter is divided into three parts. In the first part, the growing application of environmental sociology is discussed. In the second part, we discuss where nonacademic sociologists work, what work settings are like, what practitioners do, and the types of training and experience that contribute to success in these settings. In these sections, we rely heavily on a survey we made, for the Environment and Technology Section (formerly the Environmental Sociology Section) of the American Sociological Association (ASA) in 1983, of environmental sociologists employed in nonacademic settings (Cluett and Payne, 1984),[1] adding recent insights from practitioners. In the third part, we will discuss the ways in which environmental sociology is used, the success of its application, the contribution that the *practice* of environmental sociology is making to the field, and the challenges we see for the future.

## FOUNDATIONS OF ENVIRONMENTAL SOCIOLOGY IN NONACADEMIC SETTINGS

The passage of the National Environmental Policy Act (NEPA) of 1969 (P.L. 91–190, 42 U.S.C. 4321 *et seq.*) was significant for the movement into nonacademic settings of environmental sociologists focusing on the natural environment (Dunning, 1985; Freudenburg and Keating, 1982).

NEPA reflected the increasing public awareness of events and activities that were impinging on the environment and the ecological connections between technological, environmental, and social events and conditions. While social and environmental analysis in applied settings had been around for decades prior to NEPA, the Act gave it new focus and salience for the discipline (Wolf, 1974). The Act required the interdisciplinary assessment of the impacts of "major federal actions significantly affecting the quality of the human environment" and the "integrated use" of the social and environmental sciences (NEPA, Section 102 (2)(c)). The intent of the Act was to protect environmental resources from development activities likely to have significant adverse environmental impacts. As part of the environmental assessment, NEPA called for assessment of the social and economic environment, thereby energizing the field of social impact assessment (SIA). Amendments to the Act, passage of the Council on Environmental Quality regulations, and other legislation at the federal and state levels reinforced general concern and attention to the environment and to the role of SIA.

Initially, social analyses for environmental impact statements (EISs) and assessments were often cursory and conducted by non–social scientists. As the quality and adequacy of these social assessments came under public and legal scrutiny in the project approval and permit processes, new opportunities emerged for social scientists with private developers and in government agencies to provide better quality and more comprehensive SIAs. Public demand for greater attention to the human aspects of environmental change and new regulations have persisted despite fluctuations in the national political and economic climate.

Opportunities for environmental sociologists in nonacademic settings also have come about as a result of three trends: (1) growing awareness on the part of developers and government agencies, such as the Department of Interior (DOI), the Department of Energy (DOE), and the Environmental Protection Agency (EPA), that the societal milieu in which a risky technology operates or the social patterns that a multi-use development serves may have a larger bearing on a successful outcome than engineering or architectural design attributes; (2) greater demand and requirements for public participation in decision making in many large-scale developments, particularly public ones, above and beyond requirements under NEPA; and, (3) increasing public interest group attention to the social, economic, and cultural impacts of technologies perceived as risky (e.g., nuclear power development or hazardous waste management), that have been traditionally ignored in siting and planning these operations.

## Awareness of the Importance of the Social Milieu

Nonacademic environmental sociologists in SIA have long pointed out serious local, social, and economic effects of technologies, particularly those perceived by the public as risky. Such effects can include lower quality of life, demographic changes, or stigmatization of individuals and local products (Mitchell et al., 1988). Agencies, such as the DOE, EPA, DOT, and the National Oceanic and Atmospheric Administration (NOAA), that are involved in technology deployment at a community level or in activities that may pose a health and safety risk, have historically ignored social impacts or considered them less important than other impacts (such as those to the physical environment). However, developers and regulators have found that in proposing these facilities and choosing appropriate sites, they are being challenged by communities to anticipate and to mitigate or compensate for social impacts.

An example of the perils of short-changing the SIA process is provided by the legal suit brought against the U.S. Department of the Interior by the Northern Cheyenne tribe. The tribe contended that an EIS, prepared hastily in 1981, failed to examine potential social, economic, and cultural impacts of a proposed coal lease program on nearby tribal communities. The courts eventually decided in favor of the tribes and voided the leases (Boggs, 1988).[2] Public, interest group, and local government opposition to decisions on siting new facilities (both "noxious" developments, as in the case of municipal, hazardous, or radioactive waste operations; and other developments, such as shopping centers, offices, and condominiums, or senior citizen housing) has drawn attention to the need for careful analysis of social and economic conditions and potential impacts in candidate site areas. The DOE nuclear waste repository program has been stalled and costs have escalated due to failure both to account for the social dimensions of the siting problem and to establish a siting process perceived as fair by those most affected (Dunlap et al., 1993).

In response to this trend, private corporations in real estate development and the management of hazardous wastes, and the government agencies that oversee these activities, are employing environmental sociologists. Many agencies and companies find it less costly to have a social scientist in-house than to hire a consultant each time one is needed. The logic is that an employee will have an identification and familiarity both with the particular needs of the employer and with the kind of analysis needed to conform to the law (Haber, 1983). The environmental sociologist is already seen as the "expert" for analyzing the social and economic consequences of controversial project proposals (e.g., the siting of a wastewater treatment plant). She is seen as a reliable authority on the nature of the public's response to such proposed projects, as well as on the development and negotiation of mitigation and incentive plans to enhance public acceptance, or to reduce or compensate for negative impacts. In the case of proposals dealing with the built environment, the environmental sociologist is helping architects and developers to appreciate the relationship between human behavior and quality of life and the design of housing, buildings, and living areas.

Thirty years ago, one prominent sociologist observed that, due to the influence of practicing sociologists, the public housing movement in the United States "now is concerned principally with the amenities provided in buildings rather than with building form" (Gutman, 1966:51). In 1984, Boothroyd and Rees (1984:11) stated that environmental sociology was becoming "a major component of the development planning process rather than . . . a pure research activity." Today, environmental sociologists are applying their knowledge of and experience with social adaptation to building design and engineering project development, with attention to local and regional effects as well as the worldwide consequences of these human activities for the global environment (Cernea, 1991; Rickson et al., 1990).

### Increased Attention to Public Participation Programs

Years of dealing with strong opposition from local and national citizens' and environmental action groups, hostile meetings, and cancelled or delayed projects and resultant legal challenge and escalating costs have taught managers of controversial projects that they must pay more attention to the people affected by their actions. Managers and staff of large projects, particularly technologies perceived as entailing high risk, have difficulty in communicating with the public, in part because the public tends not to trust them. Over the same years, vocal citizens and organized opposition groups have made government agencies and elected officials aware of their desire to participate in decisions being made about their communities. In response, state and local legislation has been passed that requires formal input from local citizens and other stakeholders in siting, planning, constructing, and operating new facilities. Affected parties and influential environmental lobbying organizations—such as the Natural Resources Defense Council, the Sierra Club, and other state and local interest groups—have demanded a more active, central role in consensus-based decision making that goes well beyond attending hearings and exchanging information. Environmental sociologists have been instrumental in providing research, guidance, and training to agencies that are trying to improve the quality of their interaction with the public. In response to the need to develop creative strategies for involving the public in decision processes, environmental sociologists have joined together with researchers and practitioners from the social, natural, and physical sciences, as well as representatives of industry and government, to form the International Association of Public Participation Practitioners (IAP3).[3]

The environmental sociologist's field work has provided experience in interviewing public officials and affected citizens on sensitive issues, such as those dealing with risk communication and conflict resolution. His experience has led to his being relied on to facilitate, interpret, and often mediate the participation of the public in the planning of controversial projects, sometimes in conjunction with professional arbitrators and mediators. The sociologist has come to be seen as one who can measure and enhance the social acceptability of a project (Dunning, 1985).

In the efforts to site low-level radioactive waste operations over the past decade in several states, environmental sociologists are not only assessing social and economic impacts on the host community and working on compensation and mitigation strategies, but they also are planning and implementing public information, participation, and oversight programs. They are advising state personnel on how to present information, and, as the projects progress, will actually be part of conducting the public participation program.

Another example occurred under a federal program to clean several sites contaminated with radioactive and hazardous wastes during the World War II effort to develop the atomic bomb, DOE's Formerly Utilized Sites Remedial Action Program (FUSRAP). An environmental sociologist (Dr. B. Payne) planned and implemented a series of meetings between local citizens and officials of the DOE and the EPA responsible for the Weldon Spring, MO site, to overcome an impasse in planning the cleanup created by local resistance to the proposed engineering alternatives. Out of these meetings came a new alternative for cleanup and disposal of the wastes, acceptable to both federal officials and local citizens, and eventually chosen as the "preferred alternative." Based on her familiarity with individuals and agencies on both sides of the controversy, gained through her interviews and data gathering in the communities surrounding the contaminated site, Dr. Payne was able to help bring the factions together to make decisions jointly. In a similar way an environmental sociologist (Dr. J. Zeisel), working on the design of housing geared to the social needs of senior citizens, used his survey results to develop information programs to advise seniors on choosing housing.

### Increasing Public Interest Group Attention to the Social, Economic, and Cultural Impacts of Risky Technologies

Public interest groups often actively oppose projects that involve risky technologies or are perceived to be high risk, and have hired environmental sociologists to help them deal with the social dimensions of these problems. More recently, these concerns extend to risks experienced on a global scale, such as climate change impacts of sea-level rise, air pollution, ozone depletion, or acid rain, and to environmental justice (Szasz, 1994).

Schnaiberg (1977:502) points out that environmental assessment and the application of the "impact sciences" have been made especially difficult due to the "domination of the economy by high-technology groups," a structural constraint that has resulted in the allocation of funding priority to "production science" rather than to "impact science." Organized opposition groups, on the other hand, consider social impacts to be central in evaluating a risky technology, and they have used arguments about potential community impacts to rally grassroots support for legal suits to delay projects or deny local permits necessary for project implementation.

Environmental sociologists now are being hired by groups opposed to projects, to advise them or to perform an SIA that is not paid for by the developer or a federal permitting agency. Using money allocated by Congress to protect state interests in the siting of the nation's first high-level nuclear waste repository, the states of Nevada, Texas, and Washington hired environmental sociologists, both academic and nonacademic, to perform SIAs independent of those performed by environmental sociologists funded by the DOE. The states encouraged social and cultural assessments that probed such topics as perceived risk, stigma, tourism, and tribal impacts to a greater degree than the staffs and contractors of federal agencies were allowed. Nevada's governor cited potential impacts identified in the state's SIA as part of a suit to stop further DOE investigations of the Nevada site. Thus, increased public concern about technological risks and pressure for more public participation in decisions are resulting in the potential for more balanced and thorough assessments.

In another case, the elected officials of a small town in Illinois, which was chosen by the state as a candidate site for a low-level radioactive waste disposal facility, were worried that social, psychological, and economic impacts to their community were being underrated in the assessment prepared by the proposed developers of the facility. They hired a nonacademic environmental sociologist (Dr. E. Peelle) to make an independent assessment of the social and economic impacts that might occur should the facility be built in their community. Her findings confirmed many of those found in the developer's assessment, but in addition, she addressed particular local issues and developed mitigation and compensation programs to address local concerns that the developer failed to deal with adequately.

## ATTRIBUTES OF ENVIRONMENTAL SOCIOLOGY IN NONACADEMIC SETTINGS

Our working definition of environmental sociology in nonacademic settings is the application of sociological research, theory, and methodology to: solving problems concerning the relationship of humans to their physical and social environment, developing and implementing policy and programs, and assessing social impacts of environmental changes. Environmental sociologists apply their skills to projects dealing for the most part with the natural environment; only one person responding to the Cluett and Payne (1984) survey reported being able to use them in companies or government agencies dealing with the built environment. In this section we will describe characteristics of the nonacademic settings of environmental sociologists who apply their knowledge and training outside of academics.

### The Product

The work for which environmental sociologists in nonacademic settings are compensated and evaluated usually involves a well-defined project with a specific product requirement, such as a report summarizing research, SIA work, or literature; formulating policy or action programs; or recommending a building design, a decision, or course of action. As project staff members, sociologists may be involved in implementing portions of several short- or long-term projects at the same time, and they also may help in contract negotiations with clients to define the products. Projects are subject to strict budgets and well-defined schedules, often concentrated over a few months. The emphasis is on the highest-quality product that can be produced within those budget and time constraints.

### Working for a Client

In the nonacademic setting, work is done primarily for a client, and the role of the client in shaping the work is particularly salient (Freeman, 1983b; Freudenburg and Keating, 1985; Rossi and Whyte, 1983).[4] The client, who has requested and paid for the product, can be expected to be closely involved in defining the scope of work in terms of his programmatic and policy requirements. The sociologist approaches the problem from a scientific perspective, formulating hypotheses, generating appropriate data, applying sociological methods and analyses, and deriving policy-relevant implications from the work. While the research methods used in the nonacademic and academic settings may be the same, variables of sociological interest or theoretical importance may be of much less interest to the client (Rossi, 1980; Rossi and Whyte, 1983). For example, such variables as trust in decision makers, perceptions of risk to public health and safety, or potential project effects on community cohesion may be viewed as too complex or too politically sensitive by the client to include in the work scope, notwithstanding the sociologist's arguments for the centrality of these issues to long-term program success.

Serving as a reviewer in nonacademic settings, the sociologist looks at the work of others for what is missing in the way of sociological analyses. For example, she may find that an assessment of the impacts of a construction project or the design of an urban development prepared by engineers or architects ignores important social impacts and issues. Analysis of data may consist of merely describing the results of data collection or applying complex statistical analyses to such data. The environmental sociologist may be expected by the client to use methods developed for evaluation, policy analysis, institutional analysis, or impact assessment in addition to traditional sociological methods (Burdge et al., 1995; Cluett and Payne, 1984; Dunning, 1985; Love, 1983).

Potential clients have access to a wide range of roles for environmental sociologists, as reflected in the variety of work respondents to the 1983 survey who said they performed in nonacademic settings. They stated that they are researchers, research managers, program evaluators, policy makers, modelers, demographers, statisticians, planners, consultants, teachers, analysts (policy and otherwise), educators, forecasters, internal consultants, and fund-raisers—all as sociologists (Cluett and Payne, 1984; Love, 1983). They may be called sociologists, socio-economists, researchers, demographers, impact assessors, planners, engineers, or social scientists. Job titles that include sociologist or positions that call for sociological training may mean that the incumbent is actually doing sociological research, or that he is just identified by background and training rather than by the tasks performed.

Despite the variety of work performed by environmental sociologists, they often are in competition for clients with others having similar skills for a few positions, and other disciplines may be seen to offer more to the client. Clients may feel that social issues need not be analyzed by a specialist. Although researchers in other disciplines (e.g., economics) may have similar statistical and data collection skills, they will approach problems from a different perspective and look for solutions in different ways (Freeman, 1983b). The opportunity to provide a sociological perspective may arise only when the client sees social problems as terribly complex and important, when budgets are large, or when a regulation explicitly requires a sociologist on the team. To keep themselves employed or in business in nonacademic settings, environmental sociologists need to be part educator, part activist, and part salesperson in communicating to clients the practical benefits of contributions from a sociological perspective to solving their problems. A record of achievement on projects is important, but at times, applied social scientists need to play "a more aggressive role . . . to assert a broader legitimacy for themselves" and their perspective (Boggs, 1988).

## Employing Organizations and Activities Performed

Traditionally, applied sociologists were employed primarily for their knowledge about large, archival data sets on populations, about methods for quantifying public opinion and behavior, or for their skills in developing and conducting surveys (Costner, 1983). They worked primarily in government agencies and private firms concentrating on these topics (e.g., demography for the U.S. Bureau of the Census, or public opinion research for polling and marketing firms). If a social scientist was needed by other organizations, even large, private corporations, a consultant was hired for the project, rather than adding one to the permanent staff.

In some ways, our 1983 survey of environmental sociologists working full-time in nonacademic settings confirmed that employers, or at least funding sources, are largely in the public sector. The results showed that the great majority (26 of 33) worked in fairly large organizations that manage, regulate, or develop some aspect of the natural (as opposed to the built) environment (Cluett and Payne, 1984). Employing government agencies included: the U.S. Department of Agriculture (Forest Service, Bureau of Land Management, Soil Conservation Service, and a national forest), the Army Corps of Engineers, the National Institutes of Mental Health, the National Aeronautics and Space Administration, the Library of Congress, the Bonneville Power Administration, the Alaska Outer Continental Shelf Office, and Canada's Ministry of the Environment. Of this sample of environmental sociologists, only two were employed by the same agency: the Forest Service. One respondent worked for a state environmental agency (in Illinois) and another as a planner for a California county (based on his master's degree in planning rather than on his Ph.D. in sociology).

In addition to government agencies, respondents gave other employing organizations: large consulting firms (e.g., Battelle: four respondents); national laboratories (specifically Argonne, Oak Ridge, and Pacific Northwest Laboratories, whose funding is primarily from the U.S. Department of Energy: three respondents); social science research organizations (the Social Science Research Council and the Social Impact Research Center: two respondents); a large university hospital administration (one respondent); the Digital Corporation (one respondent); the World Bank (one respondent); and, the Conference Board of Canada (one respondent). Three had their own consulting firms. Two worked for large power companies (one in Florida and one in California), and one for an environmental action organization, the Sierra Club. The distribution of nonacademic employment settings for environmental sociologists is much the same today, with the addition of state environmental agencies.

Large employing organizations are generally bureaucratic and interdisciplinary (Burdge and Opryszek, 1983; Dunning, 1985), have proscribed hours of operation when support staff are available (although professionals often work more or different hours), rarely have more than one sociologist on the staff and even more rarely in a managerial position, and often do not have research as their major purpose. Frequently, a team used on a project is made up of members from several disciplines (the components of which may change from one project to another), so that the sociologist is usually communicating with nonsociologists as well as with nonscientists. One works "for" a superior, and evaluation is based not on sociological publication, but primarily on teamwork, timeliness, verbal and written communication, productivity, and quality of contribution to the project and to the organization as a whole. At the other extreme, small consulting firms may consist of only one or two professionals who, of necessity, perform a wider range of tasks.

A standard promotional ladder in many large, nonacademic organizations, even research laboratories, moves the successful person into positions such as manager, marketer, policy maker, or program administrator. Of those surveyed in 1983, five had reached management positions or developed and managed successful consulting firms (Cluett and Payne, 1984).[5] With advancement in a large organization or expansion of one's own consulting business, the sociological components of one's work are often reduced, and use of other skills, training, and experience increases. However, over the past decade, the sociological perspective has to some degree become "institutionalized," as employers come to value both the substance of the discipline and the insight it provides on organizational and institutional structures and processes (Dunning, 1985; Farhar, 1991). The environmental sociologist is becoming increasingly credible as an employee who can manage projects, guide policy, attract project funding, participate in strategic planning, and work effectively in bureaucratic settings, while remaining a sociologist.

## Pathways into Nonacademic Sociology Positions

Environmental sociologists enter nonacademic work settings directly from graduate school; as academics who only work part-time in a nonacademic setting; and as transfers from academic settings, from other nonacademic work, and sometimes from other fields of sociology.

Academic departments recruiting sociology graduate students immediately after graduate school often request that a candidate have specific substantive and methodological specialties, and hire someone who has training and experience (courses, assistantship duties, research experience) in those specialties. Hiring for nonacademic settings often is based on practical experience with the topics and tasks the organization or client needs performed, such as SIA, along with classroom work and research experience. Because "on-the-job training" is costly in delays and start-up time, it is often the experience gained during a practicum, part-time job, or an internship on a practical project that may not have been the main focus of one's training that makes a student look good to the nonacademic employer or client (Freudenburg, 1981).

Another route for entering the nonacademic setting is from the academic setting. As Freeman and Rossi (1984) have pointed out, many famous sociologists have been able to work both in academia and as consultants for nonacademic employers. Consulting work is popular in environmental sociology, as those who have developed new techniques or become known for their ideas in the field are called on by nonacademic organizations or by sociologists employed in nonacademic settings for assistance. A few choose to leave academia for full-time nonacademic positions. Others do not leave their academic positions, but may keep one foot in each setting over the course of their careers. These "part-time" nonacademics provide a valuable link between the two arenas.

Once in the nonacademic setting, successful performers often work on a wide variety of projects, expanding their knowledge and experience base, and making themselves more desirable for other nonacademic organizations. Because standards for judging success often differ greatly in academic and nonacademic settings, a sociologist seldom moves back into academia from extended full-time work in a nonacademic setting. First, the publication record so valued by academic employers is not valued in many nonacademic settings, and may even be discouraged by employers and clients worried about proprietary data and results. Second, because of the project orientation and the importance of conforming to budgets and schedules, there is little time and money in nonacademic settings to devote to long-term, empirical sociological research, the typical basis for a strong publication record in sociological journals. Some environmental sociologists, however, have reversed this pattern by moving from consulting firms into academic settings renowned for their faculties in environmental disciplines (for example, Michigan State University and Clark University), conducting their teaching and research (as well as part-time consulting) using experiences and insights gained from years of full-time work in nonacademic settings.

### Requirements and Desired Skills

An environmental sociologist in a nonacademic setting must be able to combine theoretical and applied perspectives, communicate to nonsociologists, present ideas effectively in written and oral form, and have a strong curiosity about many areas in sociology as well as other disciplines (e.g., engineering, biology). Basic (and sometimes advanced) research and methodological skills, computer modelling, econometrics, architectural or planning skills, business acumen, and other such interests and knowledge may also help, depending on the setting. Some of these skills are learned in graduate school; others are acquired on the job.

Educational credentials are an important requirement for working in nonacademic settings. The majority of respondents (30 of 33) to the 1983 survey of environmental sociologists in nonacademic settings held Ph.D.s, although some said that their organizations hired social scientists with M.A. degrees (Cluett and Payne, 1984).[6] Additionally, high grades in graduate school and strong letters of reference are often important to potential employers.

Skills acquired in undergraduate and graduate sociology training that respondents found useful in their applied work settings were: survey and field work, SIA techniques, familiarity with data sources, and collection and statistical analysis of data. Experience in evaluation of research and analytical and critical thinking were also mentioned. For some in our survey, their formal training had included, by design or luck, preparation in other social sciences, such as economics or political science, or in the physical or natural sciences. These respondents said that this training was among the most valuable components of their coursework, as it taught them how other disciplines approach problems and search for answers. In fact, most of those polled said that graduate training for nonacademic settings should include forays into coursework of other social sciences, and often other sciences. Contact with other disciplines provided knowledge of the merits and limits of sociology, and allowed them to interact more easily with and draw from nonsociologist colleagues. It also gave them knowledge critical to meeting performance standards. For example, an organization hiring an environmental sociologist to help in the development of health care programs and facilities in rural areas would like a person who has relevant sociological knowledge and skills, but also knows something about health care availability and needs of rural people. A consulting firm hiring a sociologist to help in siting hazardous waste facilities would prefer one who already has some understanding of the nature of hazardous wastes and the regulations controlling their disposal.

Despite the necessity of an advanced degree for employment, respondents did not typically mention training received in graduate school among the top skills needed to perform their jobs. The first skills mentioned were: writing concisely, quickly, and for nonsociologists; timeliness; and working with people, particularly as a manager or in sales or marketing. These were followed by: cross-disciplinary communication, interpersonal and group leadership, efficiency, and ability to compromise in research design without reducing the quality of the results. In their influential article on sociology in nonacademic settings, Freeman and Rossi (1984) concur that the personal skills of tact and diplomacy; a problem-solving orientation; a willingness to compromise; and abilities to work well under pressure, be responsive to deadlines, be organized, and manage others, whether inherent or learned, are important in determining success in the nonacademic setting.

Another point made by many respondents to the survey is that a sociologist in a nonacademic setting must be both a specialist in environmental sociology and a generalist in sociology and other disciplines that are relevant to one's work setting. Familiarity with a range of "social" topics, from demography to collective action, from voting behavior to deviance, from urban to rural sociology locally and internationally, seems desirable to employers and appropriate for interdisciplinary and problem-solving settings.

## Professional Identity and Communication

Socialization in graduate school still encourages the idea that an academic position is the "best" setting to enter with a new degree (Freeman, 1983a). Although she may receive recognition and rewards from her employer and in other arenas, the individual who chooses the nonacademic work setting may receive negative feedback from her graduate academic department and colleagues. Prestige bestowed by the discipline generally goes to those in academic settings who publish in journals aimed only at other sociologists. Further, the feeling is often expressed that the discipline does not recognize the value of the work of those who produce technical reports and solutions to problems.

Part of this disciplinary discomfort with nonacademic career tracks is likely associated with a lack of criteria and experience in evaluating the "professional and intellectual accomplishments of those with careers in the broader markets of public agencies or private firms" (Carter, 1992:4). Local and national sociological professional organizations (and the editors of their publications) do little or nothing to improve this situation, and usually serve only to reinforce it (Freudenburg, 1981). Applied work is often seen by academic sociologists as more client-influenced and thus less objective or thorough than is acceptable for publication (Gans, 1971).

Few sociological journals publish applied environmental sociology research. *Rural Sociology* publishes some social impact work, as does the *Journal of Applied Sociology*. Journals outside of sociology, such as *Impact Assessment Bulletin, Environmental Impact Assessment Review*, or *Risk Assessment*, are publication outlets more compatible with issues of assessment and of applying environmental sociology. Practitioners tend to develop bases other than publication for measuring success, such as growing business revenues, demand for services from clients, or recognition from trade specialists. The reliance by practitioners on nonsociological audiences and colleagues may be contributing to a disproportionate influence of "trends and fashion" or nonsociological paradigms in nonacademic environmental sociology (Kenig, 1987). There is recent evidence that reflects efforts to bring together representatives of the social and natural sciences, academic and nonacademic, to address the compelling issues raised by global environmental change (Miller, 1992; Stern et al., 1992). Interdisciplinary collaborative research in this area, both "basic" and "applied," is being encouraged and funded.

Communication regarding work by environmental sociologists in nonacademic settings usually occurs through technical reports, memos, or verbal presentations, aimed at people whose backgrounds are not in sociology (Burdge and Opryszek, 1983; Dunning, 1985; Freudenburg and Keating, 1985). Because the audience for the work is primarily the client, final reports may omit discussion of theory or complex methodological issues, as well as sociological terminology that may be considered "jargon." Further, data collected in a project not in the public sector are often seen by clients as proprietary, and thus not available for publication.

Direct communication with environmental sociologists and others in academic settings occurs when representatives of both settings work on the same project, for example, when academics serve as consultants or work part-time on a project. It can also occur through professional organizations and their meetings. For example, in panel discussions about risk, nonacademic sociologists have drawn from their experiences to inform academics what research needs to be done on the long-term community consequences of perceived risk in cases where actual health risk is measured below regulatory standards, or what methods are useful for assessing social and organizational patterns that determine how multi-use facilities should be designed. Additionally, to improve access to other practicing environmental sociologists, sociologists in applied settings can join and publish in the journals of interdisciplinary organizations, such as the International Association for Impact Assessment (IAIA), the Society for Risk Assessment, or the Society of Applied Sociology. The Rural Sociological Society, the Society for the Study of Social Problems, the IAIA, and the Environmental Design Research Association have established subgroups on environmental sociology where nonacademic and academic sociologists share their work and research findings.

Many practicing environmental sociologists receive little or no reward from their employers for participation in sociological associations or for publication in sociological or other nontrade journals, further reducing communication between academics and nonacademics in the discipline. Some practitioners feel that participation is a drawback because of the time taken away from projects or from working on nonsociological publications that publicize their successful applications (Cluett and Payne, 1984). They are more likely to receive rewards and attention for presenting their work and ideas at business conferences or for publishing the results of project work in in-house reports or in technical trade publications. While academics may believe that they are subjected to tougher professional review and scrutiny of their work, "critical standards may be more stringent for applied research conducted external to academia" (Carter, 1992:4). In addition to needing to meet academic standards, nonacademic environmental sociologists' "research addressing important policies and programs must be crafted to withstand the scrutiny of attorneys, agency analysts, and legislative staffs," as well as other nonacademic sociologists. "Success" and rewards in nonacademic settings are measured not only by a resumé full of publications, but by a growing client base and reputation for reliable, thorough, timely, and sound applied products.

## ETHICAL ISSUES

Many discussions about working in nonacademic settings point out problems associated with working for clients or sponsors, such as the influence these parties may exert on the approach to and results of the work (e.g., Freudenburg and Keating, 1985; Rossi and Whyte, 1983). As one respondent to the 1983 survey of environmental sociologists states it, "The transition from pure knowledge to the bottom line is not easy. Academics think that our clients pressure us to give them the 'right' answer but that's not true. They do pressure us to give a scientifically sound answer to the question they are paying us to answer" (Cluett and Payne, 1984). Focusing on the question and producing a "scientifically" sound answer can be difficult, given the pressures of deadlines and budget limits. One way to manage problems of potential influence would be to choose carefully both one's client and one's employer, and in all situations guard the quality and integrity of nonacademic work. However, such choices are not always realistic when there are few nonacademic positions or consulting jobs to be found.

Another important ethical problem faced by a nonacademic sociologist arises when his work is used only to endorse decisions already made (Cohen and Lindblom, 1979). In some cases, the decision or policy will appear the same whether sociologists have input or not (before or after), as sociological input is not the major determinant of the outcome. The problem only becomes troublesome if the outcome would have been different had we been able to make our contribution before the fact, and had our input been attended to. The issue can be resolved on the individual level by commitment to standards of objectivity, and on the organizational level by the employment of environmental sociologists as integral parts of staffs assigned to provide the input or to make decisions (i.e., becoming institutionalized in the decision-making structure of an organization).

## OPPORTUNITIES IN A NONACADEMIC SETTING

In the sections that follow we will discuss some of the opportunities and frustrations of work in the nonacademic setting.

### Policy and Organizational Impacts

The strongest attraction offered by nonacademic settings is the potential to use sociological knowledge and training to help solve significant, "real-world" problems and to foster more socially beneficial policies. Ideally, we can help protect, enhance, and guide the future of our natural environment and affect the nature and development of the built environment. In practice, the ability to influence policy and decisions is realized only gradually over a series of projects, programs, and decisions, and a significant gap remains between what we have achieved and would like to achieve.

By working with developers and managers in government, business, and industry, we can expand our clients' perspectives beyond dollars, materials, and engineering concerns and help them (and affected citizens as well) to see the social and psychological implications of their proposals and actions (Farhar, 1991). For example, interviews conducted by a sociologist in the course of an impact assessment revealed the social basis of the conflict between the community and government contractors: A town's long-range plan for commercial development of the site proposed for a large radioactive waste operation. Uncovering this incompatibility through the application of public involvement and conflict resolution techniques resulted in joint planning by town officials and contractors to choose a site more satisfactory to all.

We are positioned to sensitize sponsors to the possibility of public backlash if the program does not consider various affected groups, variables, and scenarios—backlash that could change the definition of interests, political alignments, and distribution of influence (Burdge et al., 1995; Meidinger and Schnaiberg, 1980). The work of environmental sociologists to promote public participation programs has helped foster decision-making processes that are viewed as fair and equitable by all the participants.

On the other hand, decision makers sometimes complain that sociologists are reluctant to make clear and concrete recommendations. Such reluctance may be a function of the nature of the discipline and its training. Sociology claims to take a detached, impersonal view of society for the purpose of making generalizations (usually in probabilistic terms) about social behavior. Problem solving in nonacademic settings calls for concrete problem formulation, deterministic results, and findings explicitly addressed to the problem (Gans, 1971), rather than broad generalizations. Constrained by clients, problem proscription, budgets, data and variable limitations, and deadlines, the nonacademic sociologist knows that his research may be less comprehensive and balanced than desired. He is learning how to overcome these constraints to focus on the most important issues and to make his work concrete, policy-relevant, and responsive to the public interest (Burdge et al., 1995).

## Use of Theory and Contribution to Knowledge

Theory specifically developed in environmental sociology is not seen by some as very useful for direct answers to questions on policy, development plans, or the choice of action for a client. However, we would argue that theory and research findings from sociology in general, and environmental sociology in particular, contribute to quality work in the nonacademic setting (Finsterbusch, 1984; Gale, 1984), though some argue that "very little attention has been focused on the use of traditional theory in applied settings" (Kenig, 1987). SIAs have drawn from theories and research on community change and on collective action on environmental issues to project impacts of proposed developments on community structure, organization, and power relationships (e.g., Argonne National Laboratory, 1984). Results of research on attitudes toward environmental issues are used as a basis for setting up public involvement programs with the appropriate representation of citizens, and to provide information that specific groups will want to use to forecast impacts on quality of life or on markets for goods from communities hosting a waste incinerator (Liebow et al., 1989), and to determine mitigation and compensation strategies (Sorensen et al., 1987). Other program examples include a citizen involvement program in Washington State (Howell et al., 1987), the low-level radioactive waste (LLW) programs implemented in several states, and the World Bank's efforts to "put people first" in rural development programs (Cernea, 1991).

The use of environmental sociology in nonacademic settings provides opportunities for contributing to the development of sociological theory and knowledge. First, practitioners provide new insights acquired from firsthand observations of people adapting to new technologies or responding to actual or planned environmental changes. For example, we have had considerable opportunity to observe the formation and effectiveness of citizen's action groups or task forces and the role that they have played in (1) enhancing public acceptance of controversial technologies, (2) facilitating power sharing between citizens and government, and (3) enhancing collective decision making (Peelle, 1987). In the topical area of risk perception and communication, we in the field have abstracted from our observations and experience to point to policy implications and to identify relevant theory to use in explanations and research (Black, 1989; Bradbury, 1989). We have passed these observations on to colleagues through conversation, presentations at meetings (e.g., Williams and Payne, 1985), and reviews of their work. The lesson taught by practicing environmental sociologists that the social milieu of a proposed project can have as great a bearing on its success as engineering considerations also has been communicated to academic environmental sociologists, and has helped to attract interest in research into such topics as how citizens and politicians respond to waste facility siting (Bord, 1987), and the importance of the social, psychological, and health effects of indoor air pollution from toxics such as radon gas (Edelstein, 1988).

Second, in the course of gathering data to characterize the social environments and impacts of many projects and preparing comprehensive literature reviews for their reports, practitioners can judge the value and adequacy of existing sociological theory and research in contributing to the solution of practical problems, and share their observations with colleagues (Rickson et al., 1990). The most obvious examples of this have been in assessments of communities expecting to experience rapid growth as a result of construction of a large energy-production plant nearby (see Gulliford, 1989). On many projects, nonacademic environmental sociologists (e.g., Cluett et al., 1980) have been able to talk to community members and officials about their concerns about community change, quality-of-life impacts, and other impacts they expected or feared, and what they planned to do if the facility was built and rapid growth occurred. This information was provided as feedback to academic colleagues, and entered into discussions in the discipline over the effects of rapid growth. Practicing environmental sociologists more recently are applying sociological theory to the personal, social, and institutional issues confronting policy makers on energy and global climate change (Farhar, 1991).

Third, even though very innovative work is often discouraged, we can make improvements in the measurement of social phenomena needed to test theory. A good example is provided by the work of several social scientists at the University of Michigan who have developed the concept of risk perception "shadows" to capture the spatial extent of perceived risk in the context of siting a low-level nuclear waste facility. This new measurement technique has been adopted by the Michigan LLW authority as the basis for establishing the affected area boundaries for site social analysis (Stoffle, 1991). Another example involves the use of quality-of-life social indicators in an effort to improve measurement of the social consequences of environmental change, and to better operationalize the general model of social impact processes that has been derived from the theoretical perspective of human ecology (Olsen et al., 1981).

One sociologist who applies his training to the built environment described the contribution to theory and knowledge in environmental sociology as circular. The sociologist applies social design criteria and sociological methods of investigation and evaluation to develop behavioral criteria for architectural design, such as for senior housing or for corporate headquarters (also see Stubbs, 1989; Zeisel, 1984). The method and design are successful and are adopted by other developers and government agencies, and eventually accepted as standard. The sociologist's contribution is incorporated into architectural reviews and texts as an example of what is needed for successful design of such buildings or communities (Langdon, 1987). The consulting firm of the sociologist becomes recognized as expert in this approach to architectural design. Academic environmental sociologists who work on applied topics in the built environment in turn teach these methods to their students, resulting in the completion of the circle and incorporation of new knowledge in both academic and applied realms.

### Research in the Nonacademic Setting

The client's budget and work scope for a single project rarely provide the flexibility and resources needed (e.g., for research assistants and library searches) to pursue research in the applied setting (Freudenberg and Keating, 1982; Rossi, 1980). However, sometimes clients are willing and interested enough to support research on underlying causes into applied tasks in ways that contribute both to the advancement of social science disciplines and to doing a better job of meeting client needs.

The DOE has funded projects to look at individual and community responses to its efforts to clean up sites contaminated with radioactive and chemical wastes. The U.S. Army has supported research into community-level factors contributing to public acceptance of the dismantling and decommissioning of chemical warheads (Bradbury et al., 1995). The U.S. Nuclear Regulatory Commission (NRC) has funded surveys aimed at understanding public attitudes toward nuclear power and radioactive waste (Nealey, 1990). In the course of work on another NRC project to clean up a radioactively contaminated site, environmental sociologists were able to study the effects of proximity to the site on housing values (Payne et al., 1987). After the accident at the Three Mile Island Nuclear Power Plant, the NRC and the state of Pennsylvania paid for surveys on community reponses to the accident, conducted by sociologists (Flynn, 1979; Sorensen et al., 1987). States that are studying options for low-level radioactive waste disposal also have sponsored surveys of citizens and local decision makers (Bord 1987; Dames and Moore, 1995) Environmental sociologists working at Oak Ridge National Laboratory have studied incentive plans aimed at communities being considered as sites for noxious facilities (Carnes et al., 1983).

The Nuclear Waste Policy Act (1982) explicitly called for social research into the potential impacts of siting a national high-level nuclear waste repository (U.S. Department of Energy, 1988). Conducted by academic and nonacademic contractors (including environmental sociologists) working for the implementing agency and for affected states and tribes, these studies funded under the Act have investigated issues not ordinarily examined in large, federal EISs, including: public perceptions of risk; impacts of stress and stigma on individuals, groups, and organizations; trust and attitudes toward decision makers, scientists, technologists, and federal agencies; and, the relationship between these social impact variables unique to nuclear or hazardous projects and more conventional growth-related impacts, such as community infrastructure and population change (Dunlap et al., 1993; Mitchell et al., 1988; Pijawka and Mushkatel, 1991).

## SOME CHALLENGES FOR NONACADEMIC ENVIRONMENTAL SOCIOLOGY

Nonacademic environmental sociologists played a major role in the development of the field of SIA. The methods and approaches to SIA have matured over the last several decades, but important challenges remain in this field. We need to understand better the causal linkages between projects and the impacts they produce. Attention needs to be paid more to indirect as well as direct effects, such as the impact of increased median incomes on a community from higher salaries paid on a construction project (Meidinger and Schnaiberg, 1980). It is important to point out to clients that inappropriate conclusions may be drawn by failing to consider new variables, issues, or approaches to the program or project. We need to gather and analyze data on many similar projects and their observed impacts (in post hoc studies) to test our hypothesized causal relationships and our projections, and to improve our understanding of the role of decision makers in those situations. Understanding cumulative impact processes, as effects from several sources interact over time, has become particularly important. We have an opportunity to help agencies carry out Executive Order 12898 of February 11, 1994, that instructs each federal agency to make achieving environmental justice a part of its mission by identifying and addressing disporportionately high and adverse health or environmental effects of its programs, policies, or activities on minority and low-income populations. We need to convince funding agencies and corporations of the importance of supporting research into these issues, and we need to look internationally both to help developing countries avoid mistakes and to learn from their societal and environmental programs.

Some success already has occurred in these efforts. A study by sociologists, funded by the Electric Power Research Institute, retrospectively analyzed a number of energy-production projects for which SIAs had been performed (as part of a total environmental impact assessment) and compared the impacts that actually occurred with those that had been projected (Denver Research Institute and Browne, Bortz, and Coddington, 1982). Mountain West Research conducted surveys on construction workers in the 1970s to identify impacts from their migration into small communities hosting large facility developments (Gale, 1982; Mountain West Research, 1975, 1979). Edison Electric Institute (1992) has compiled a two-volume collection and analysis of results of surveys of perceived impacts of electrical transmission facilities to help in the environmental analysis of future facilities. The National Renewable Energy Laboratory provides a comprehensive assessment of trends in public opinion on energy-related topics by analyzing a database of approximately 2,000 items from nearly 600 separate surveys conducted between 1979 and 1992 "to help policymakers assess the congruence of energy and environmental policy options with public preferences" (Farhar, 1993:xv). These studies offer examples of the utility of having a strong base of empirical research to support applied environmental sociology.

Although environmental sociologists are working on a widely diverse range of applied problems in such areas as fishery policy, hazardous waste management, transportation technology, recycling, sustainable development, and environmental justice, federal and state agencies and private clients often fund only those studies that are required to meet a law or regulation. Success in acquiring research support, or in influencing decisions, is not guaranteed, no matter how convincing the arguments, data, and interpretation, or how cogent the reports; and one runs the risk of jeopardizing future contracts or client confidence with performance deemed inappropriate.

Another challenging issue that is being faced by nonacademic (and academic) environmental sociologists who are interested in the impacts of engineered systems on social structures relates to quantification of the amount of change that it takes to produce a significant social impact. Thresholds or tolerance levels for negative impacts on the natural environment (e.g., groundwater, air quality, and geology) routinely have been identified by federal agencies. No such thresholds have been established for social and economic impacts; therefore, we have difficulty saying what is *too* rapid a pace of growth or change for a community, or what is the minimum level of service, such as health services, needed to maintain an "acceptable quality of life." The answer depends on the complex interplay between the activity or environmental change and the community being impacted, and that community's capacity to manage or absorb stress and change. Such work would be particularly useful in developing ways for organizations, communities, and nations to adapt to technological and behavioral changes necessary to slow damage to the global environment, such as ozone depletion (Canan, 1992).

## FINAL COMMENTS

The discipline of sociology and the subdiscipline of environmental sociology have been undergoing a transition characterized by decreasing opportunities in the academic setting, and increasing interest in the application of sociology to practical, problem-solving opportunities in nonacademic settings (Manderscheid and Greenwald, 1983). During this period, individual and organizational attention to the environment in both the public and private sectors, locally, nationally, and globally, have fluctuated, as evidenced in part by the worldwide focus on the U.N. Conference on Environment and Development held in Rio de Janeiro in 1992, tempered by continuing tension between forces for economic development and environmental protection. Arguably, because of its well-established participation in the nonacademic world, environmental sociology operates at the cutting edge of these challenging issues. Through their extensive contacts and networks with the other social and physical sciences working in nonacademic settings, these environmental sociologists are taking less-parochial, more interdisciplinary perspectives on the complex, environmental problems, ranging from local to global, of our day. The perspectives and findings emerging from these problem-solving experiences are feeding back into and enriching the parent discipline of sociology, just as sociological insights are informing the creation of sound public policy.

## NOTES

We thank Riley Dunlap, Bill Freudenburg, Dick Gale, Ed Liebow, and Bill Michelson for their comments that have helped us to improve this chapter substantially.

1. The survey was sponsored by the Environment and Technology Section of the American Sociological Association (ASA) and was sent to all section members whose addresses indicated nonacademic employment. The purposes of the survey were: (1) to develop a list of environmental sociologists willing to speak to graduate students about their work, and (2) to find out about work settings, skill and experience requirements, and suggestions for training and communication between sociologists from those working in nontraditional settings. Of the 99 sent surveys, 43 responded (even after repeated efforts to gain response), of whom 33 were actually in nonacademic settings and considered themselves environmental sociologists. The results of the survey may be unrepresentative for several reasons. First, many sociologists in nonacademic settings may not be members of the ASA, as they often complain that membership in the national associations is irrelevant to their work (Freudenburg, 1981). Second, because of the request for volunteers to give time to a speakers' program, some may have chosen not to respond to any part of the survey. The time pressures felt in nonacademic settings and the lack of organizational rewards for professional activities also may have affected the willingness to respond.

2. According to the author, to his knowledge this is the only example of a "major NEPA suit in which a remedy has been granted based on social science grounds" (Boggs, 1988:4).

3. The first annual conference of this organization was held in Portland, Oregon, on September 10–12, 1992. See Cluett and Love, 1992.

4. We note that grant funding, for example, markedly shapes the research that can and does take place in the academic setting too.

5. Others have undoubtedly made this career move, but in doing so may have left the ASA and thus would not be included in the survey sample.

6. This finding may have been a function of the fact that the sample was from a national organization that draws members almost exclusively from academic Ph.D. programs.

## REFERENCES

Aggens, Lorenz W. 1991. "Report on the Bonneville Power Administration's *Programs in Perspective* (PIP) Public Involvement Program." Prepared for the Bonneville Power Administration, U.S. Department of Energy. Portland, OR.

Argonne National Laboratory, Environmental Impact Studies Division. 1984. *Sustina Hydroelectric Project, FERC No. 7114, Alaska. Draft Environmental Impact Statement, Volume I: Main Text,* and *Appendix N: Socioeconomics.*

Prepared for Federal Energy Regulatory Commission, Office of Electric Power Regulation. Washington, DC.

Black, J. Stanley. 1989. "I Have *What* in My Backyard? Some Social and Psychological Implications of the 1986 Superfund Provisions on 'Community Right-To-Know' about Hazardous Chemicals in Local Facilities." Unpublished paper presented at the Annual Meeting of the Rural Sociological Society, Seattle, August 5–8.

Boggs, James P. 1988. "SIA in Legal Theory and in Practice: *The Northern Cheyenne Tribe v. Hodel.*" *Social Impact Assessment* 12(1–2)(January–June):3–11.

Boothroyd, Peter, and William Rees. 1984. "Impact Assessment from Pseudo-Science to Planning Process: An Educational Response." *Impact Assessment Bulletin* 3(2):9–18.

Bord, R. J. 1987. "Judgments of Policies Designed to Elicit Local Cooperation on LLRW Disposal Siting: Comparing the Public and Decision Makers." *Nuclear and Chemical Waste Management* 7:99–105.

Bradbury, J., K. Branch, J. Heerwagen, and E. Liebow. 1995. "Public Involvement in Chemical Demilitarization." Pp. 177–185 in *Environmental Challenges: The Next 20 Years*. Proceedings of the NAEP 20th Annual Conference. Washington, DC: NAEP Publications.

Bradbury, Judith A. 1989. "The Policy Implications of Differing Concepts of Risk." *Science, Technology, & Human Values* 14(4):380–399.

Burdge, R. J., G. Williams, L. Llewellyn, K. Finsterbusch, W. Freudenburg, R. Stoffle, L. Leistritz, C. P. Wolf, J. Thompson, P. Fricke, R. Gramling, J. S. Petterson, A. Holden, and Interorganizational Committee on Guidelines and Principles for Social Impact Assessment. 1995. "Guidelines and Principles for Social Impact Assessment." *Environmental Impact Assessment Review* 15(1):11–43.

Burdge, Rabel J., and Paul Opryszek. 1983. "On Mixing Apples and Oranges: The Sociologist Does Impact Assessment with Biologists and Economists." Pp. 107–117 in *Integrated Impast Assessment*, edited by F. Rossini and A. Porter. Boulder, CO: Westview Press.

Canan, Penelope. 1992. "The Problem of Ozone Depletion: A Call for Sociological Action." *Sociological Practice Review* 3(4):67–73.

Carnes, S., E. Copenhaver, J. Sorensen, E. Soderstrom, J. H. Reed, D. Bjornstad, and E. Peelle. 1983. "Incentives and Nuclear Waste Siting: Prospects and Constraints." *Energy Systems and Policy* 7(4):323–351.

Carter, Lewis F. 1992. "From Academia to the Market Place: Sociologists in Business and Public Administration." *Footnotes* 20(2):4. Washington, DC: The American Sociological Association.

Cernea, Michael M. (ed.). 1991. *Putting People First: Sociological Variables in Rural Development*, 2nd ed. London: Oxford University Press.

Cluett, Christopher, Marjorie R. Greene, and Linda Radford. 1980. "Individual and Community Response to Energy Facility Siting: An Annotated Bibliography." Public Administration Series, P-493. Monticello, IL: Vance Bibliographies.

Cluett, Christopher, and Ruth L. Love. 1992. "International Association of Public Participation Practitioners (IAP3) First Annual Conference." *Environment,*

*Technology, and Society*. Newsletter of the Section on Environment and Technology, American Sociological Association 69:5–7.

Cluett, Christopher, and Barbara A. Payne. 1984. "Training for Non-Academic Employment in Environmental Sociology and Environmental Sociologists in Non-Academic Settings Willing to Speak on Their Work. Results of a Survey by the American Sociological Association Section on Environmental Sociology, 1984." Unpublished manuscript.

Cohen, D. K., and C. E. Lindblom. 1979. "Solving Problems of Bureaucracy, Limits on Social Science." *American Behavioral Scientist* 22(5):547–560.

Costner, Herbert L. 1983. "Introduction" to "Part Two: Sociologists in Diverse Settings." Pp. 65–76 in *Applied Sociology*, edited by H. E. Freeman, R. R. Dynes, P. H. Rossi, and W. F. Whyte. San Francisco: Jossey-Bass.

Dames & Moore, Inc. 1995. "Final Report. Citizen Questionnaire. Connecticut Low-Level Radioactive Waste Facility Siting. July." Prepared for State of Connecticut Hazardous Waste Management Service. Unpublished report.

Denver Research Institute and Browne, Bortz, and Coddington. 1982. "Socioeconomic Impacts of Power Plants. Final Report." EPRI EA-2228, Research Project 1226-4. Prepared for Electric Power Research Institute.

Dunlap, Riley E., Michael E. Kraft, and Eugene A. Rosa (eds.). 1993. *Public Reactions to Nuclear Waste: Citizens' Views of Repository Siting*. Durham, NC: Duke University Press.

Dunning, C. Mark. 1985. "Applying Sociology in Natural Resource Management Agencies: Some Examples from the Corps of Engineers." *Sociological Practice* 5(2):193–207.

Edelstein, Michael R. 1988. *Contaminated Communities: The Social and Psychological Impacts of Residential Toxic Exposure*. Boulder, CO: Westview Press.

Edison Electric Institute. 1992. *Perceived Impacts of Electrical Transmission Facilities: A Review of Survey-Based Studies*. Washington, DC: Edison Electric Institute.

Farhar, Barbara C. 1991. "Toward a Sociology of Energy." *Sociological Practice Review* 2(2):81–86.

———. 1993. *Trends in Public Perceptions and Preferences on Energy and Environmental Policy*. NREL/TP-461-4857 (February).

Finsterbusch, Kurt. 1984. "Social Impact Assessment as a Policy Science Methodology." *Impact Assessment Bulletin* 3(2):37–43.

Flynn, C. 1979. *Three Mile Island Telephone Survey: Preliminary Report on Procedures and Findings*. Report presented to the U.S. Nuclear Regulatory Commission. Seattle, WA: Social Impact Research, Inc.

Freeman, Howard E. 1983a. "Introduction" to "Part One: Current Status of Applied Sociology." Pp. xxi–xxvi in *Applied Sociology*, edited by H. E. Freeman, R. R. Dynes, P. H. Rossi, and W. F. Whyte. San Francisco: Jossey-Bass.

———. 1983b. "Preface." Pp. 1–4 in *Applied Sociology*, edited by H. E. Freeman, R. R. Dynes, P. H. Rossi, and W. F. Whyte. San Francisco: Jossey-Bass.

Freeman, Howard E., and Peter H. Rossi. 1984. "Furthering the Applied Side of Sociology." *American Sociological Review* 49:571–580.

Freeman, Howard E., Russell R. Dynes, Peter H. Rossi, and William Foote Whyte (eds.). 1983. *Applied Sociology*. San Francisco: Jossey-Bass.

Freudenburg, William. 1981. "Environmental Sociology in Non-Academic Settings: Where Do We Go from Here?" *Environmental Sociology: Newsletter of the American Sociological Association's Section on Environmental Sociology*, No. 27:7–14.

Freudenburg, William R., and Kenneth M. Keating. 1982. "Increasing the Impact of Sociology on Social Impact Assessment: Toward Ending the Inattention." *The American Sociologist* 17:71–80.

Freudenburg, William R., and Kenneth M. Keating. 1985. "Applying Sociology to Policy: Social Science and the Environmental Impact Statement." *Rural Sociology* 50(4):578–605.

Gale, M. 1982. *Transmission Line Construction Worker Profile and Community/ Corridor Resident Impact Survey*. Final Report. Prepared by Mountain West Research, Inc., for Bonneville Power Administration. Billings, Montana.

Gale, Richard P. 1984. "The Evolution of Social Impact Assessment: Post-Functionalist View." *Impact Assessment Bulletin* 3(2):27–36.

Glans, Herbert J. 1971. "Social Science for Social Policy." Pp. 13–33 in *The Use and Abuse of Social Science*, edited by I. L. Horowitz. New Brunswick, NJ: Transaction Books.

Gramling, Robert, and William R. Freudenburg. 1992. "Opportunity-Threat, Development, and Adaptation: Toward a Comprehensive Framework for Social Impact Assessment." *Rural Sociology* 57(2):216–234.

Gulliford, A. 1989. *Boomtown Blues: Colorado Oil Shale, 1885–1985*. Niwot: University Press of Colorado.

Gutman, Robert. 1966. "The Questions Architects Ask." Pp. 47–82 in *Transactions of the Bartlett Society* 4: 1965–1966. Bartlett School of Architecture. London: University College.

Haber, Lawrence D. 1983. "Government Policy Research." Pp. 128–137 in *Applied Sociology*, edited by H. E. Freeman, R. R. Dynes, P. H. Rossi, and W. F. Whyte. San Francisco: Jossey-Bass.

Howell, R., M. Olsen, and D. Olsen. 1987. *Designing a Citizen Involvement Program: A Guidebook for Involving Citizens in the Resolution of Environmental Issues*. Corvallis, OR: Western Rural Development Center.

Kenig, Sylvia. 1987. "The Use of Theory in Applied Sociology: The Case of Community Mental Health." *The American Sociologist* 18(3):242–257.

Langdon, P. 1987. *American Houses*. New York: Stewart, Tabori and Chang.

Liebow, Edward, Kristi Branch, and Kathleen Morse. 1989. *Potential Economic and Social Effects of Risk Perceptions Associated with a Proposed Hazardous Waste Facility in Grant County, Washington*. Report prepared for The Environmental Security Corporation, Seattle, Washington. BHARC-800/89/020. Seattle: Battelle Human Affairs Research Centers.

Love, Ruth. 1983. "Some Roles of Sociologists in Organizational Decision Making." *Sociological Practice* 4(2):133–149.

Manderscheid, Ronald W., and Mathew Greenwald. 1983. "Trends in Employment of Sociologists." Pp. 51–63 in *Applied Sociology*, edited by H. E. Freeman, R. R. Dynes, P. H. Rossi, and W. F. Whyte. San Francisco: Jossey-Bass.

Meidinger, Errol, and Allan Schnaiberg. 1980. "Social Impact Assessment as Evaluation Research, Claimants and Claims." *Evaluation Review* 4(4):507–535.

Miller, Roberta B. 1992. "Social Science and the Challenge of Global Environmental Change." *Footnotes* 20(5):9. Washington, DC: The American Sociological Association.

Mitchell, R. C., B. Payne, and R. Dunlap. 1988. "Stigma and Radioactive Waste: Theory, Assessment, and Some Empirical Findings from Hanford, WA." Pp. 95–102 in *Waste Management '88: Proceedings of the Symposium on Waste Management at Tucson, Arizona*, edited by Roy G. Post. Tucson: University of Arizona Press.

Mountain West Research, Inc. 1975. *Construction Worker Profile. Summary Report and Final Report*. Prepared for Old West Regional Commission. Billings, Montana.

———. 1979. *Pipeline Construction Worker and Community Impact Surveys. Final Report*. Prepared on behalf of Environmental Research and Technology, Inc., for Northern Tier Pipeline Company. Billings, Montana.

National Environmental Policy Act (NEPA) of 1969. 1969. P.L. 91-190, 42 U.S.C. 4321 *et seq.*, as amended.

Nealey, Stanley M. 1990. *Nuclear Power Development: Prospects in the 1990s*. Columbus, OH and Richland, WA: Battelle Press.

Nuclear Waste Policy Act of 1982. 1982. 42 U.S.C. 10101–10226, as amended.

Olsen, Marvin E., Barbara D. Melber, and Donna J. Merwin. 1981. "A Methodology for Conducting Social Impact Assessments Using Quality of Social Life Indicators." Pp. 43–78 in *Methodology of Social Impact Assessment*, edited by Kurt Finsterbusch and C. P. Wolf. Stroudsburg, PA: Hutchinson Ross.

Payne, B. A., S. J. Olshansky, and T. S. Segel. 1987. "Effects on Residential Property Values of Proximity to a Site Contaminated with Radioactive Waste." *Natural Resources Journal* 27:579–590.

Peelle, Elizabeth. 1987. "The MRS Task Force: Economic and Non-Economic Incentives for Local Public Acceptance of a Proposed Nuclear Waste Packaging and Storage Facility." *Waste Management '87: Proceedings of the Symposium on Waste Management at Tucson. Arizona* (2):117–121, edited by Roy G. Post. Tucson: University of Arizona Press.

Pijawka, D. K., and A. H. Mushkatel. 1991. "Public Opposition to the Siting of the High Level Nuclear Waste Repository: The Importance of Trust." *Policy Studies Review* 10(4):180.

Rickson, R. E., T. Hundloe, G. T. McDonald, and R. J. Burdge (eds.). 1990. "Social Impact of Development: Putting Theory and Methods into Practice." *Environmental Impact Assessment Review* 10(1/2) (entire issues).

Rossi, Peter H. 1980. "The Presidential Address: The Challenge and Opportunities of Applied Social Research." *American Sociological Review* 45:889–904.

Rossi, Peter H., and William Foote Whyte. 1983. "The Applied Side of Sociology." Pp. 5–31 in *Applied Sociology*, edited by H. E. Freeman, R. R. Dynes, P. H. Rossi, and W. F. Whyte. San Francisco: Jossey-Bass.

Schnaiberg, Allan. 1977. "Obstacles to Environmental Research by Scientists and Technologists: A Social Structural Analysis." *Social Problems* 24(5):500–520.

Sorensen, John, Jon Soderstrom, Emily Copenhaver, Sam Carnes, and Robert Bolin. 1987. *Impacts of Hazardous Technology: The Psycho-Social Effects of Restarting TMI-1*. Albany: State University of New York Press.

Stern, P. C., O. R. Young, and D. Druckman (eds.). 1992. *Global Environmental*

*Change: Understanding the Human Dimensions.* Washington, DC: National Academy Press.

Stoffle, Richard W. 1991. "Risk Perception Mapping: Using Ethnography to Define the Locally Affected Population for a Low-Level Radioactive Waste Facility in Michigan." *American Anthropologist* 93(3):611–635.

Stubbs, M. S. 1989. "80's Retrospective: Attention to Its Users. Successful Programming and Reprogramming of H. A. Brett Headquarters in San Antonio." *Architecture* 78(12):54–57.

Szasz, Andrew. 1994. *Ecopopulism: Toxic Waste and the Movement for Environmental Justice.* Minneapolis: University of Minnesota Press.

U.S. Department of Energy. 1988. *Section 175 Report.* Secretary of Energy Report to the Congress Pursuant to Section 175 of the Nuclear Waste Policy Act, as amended. November.

Williams, R. G., and B. A. Payne. 1985. "Emergence of Collective Action and Environmental Networking in Relation to Radioactive Waste Management." Presented at the Annual Meeting of the Rural Sociological Society, Blacksburg, VA, August 21–25. Unpublished manuscript.

Wolf, C. P. 1974. "Social Impact Assessment: The State of the Art." Pp. 1–44 in *Social Impact Assessment*, edited by C. P. Wolf. Stroudsburg, PA: Dowden, Hutchinson & Ross.

Zeisel, J. 1984. *Inquiry by Design. Tools for Environment-Behavior Research.* Cambridge: Cambridge University Press.

# Index

# About the Contributors

SHERRY AHRENTZEN is Professor of Architecture at the University of Wisconsin–Milwaukee. Her teaching, scholarship, and community work address the means by which architecture can be more responsive to social changes in American culture, particularly those affecting women and marginalized people and groups. She is co-editor of *New Households, New Housing* (with Karen A. Franck, 1989).

DON E. ALBRECHT is Professor of Rural Sociology at Texas A&M University. He has conducted extensive research on the consequences of resource depletion for rural society. He has published two books, *The Sociology of U.S. Agriculture* (1990) and *Human Populations and Environmental Resource Use* (2001), and more than 100 book chapters, refereed journal articles, and other reports.

FREDERICK H. BUTTEL is Professor of Rural Sociology and Environmental Studies at the University of Wisconsin–Madison. He is currently President of the Environment and Society Research Committee (RC 24) of the International Sociological Association. He is co-editor of *Labor and the Environment* (with Charles C. Geisler and Irving W. Wiswall) (Greenwood, 1984) and *Environment and Global Modernity* (with Gert Spaargaren and Arthur P. J. Mol, 2000), and his forthcoming works include *Environment, Energy, and Society* (with Craig R. Humphrey and Tammy L. Lewis, 2002).

CHRISTOPHER CLUETT is a Senior Research Scientist at Battelle Memorial Institute's Seattle Research Center. He has served on the Council of the American Sociological Association's Section on Environment and Technology, and has conducted research primarily in the areas of energy and transportation, with a focus on the human and built environments. From 1995 to 2000 he chaired the Societal Issues Task Force of the Intelligent Transportation Society of America.

STEPHEN R. COUCH is Professor of Sociology and Director of the Center for Environment and Community at Penn State's Capital College. He has written extensively on social and psychological responses to technological hazards and disasters. His current research interests include recovery from environmental contamination, the relationship of lay and scientific knowledge, the collective construction of meaning by victimized groups, and the popular culture of disasters.

THOMAS DIETZ is College of Arts and Sciences Distinguished Professor and Professor of Sociology and Environmental Science and Public Policy at George Mason University and Chair of the U.S. National Research Council Committee on Human Dimensions of Global Change. He conducts research on the anthropogenic driving forces of environmental change, environmental values, and deliberative processes in environmental policy. He recently co-edited *The Drama of the Commons* (with Elinor Ostrom, Nives Dolsak, Paul C. Stern, Susan Stonich, and Elke Weber, 2001) and *New Tools for Environmental Protection* (with Paul C. Stern, 2001).

RILEY E. DUNLAP is Boeing Distinguished Professor of Environmental Sociology at Washington State University and Past President of the International Sociological Association's Research Committee on Environment and Society. He has published extensively on the foundations of environmental sociology as well as on his empirical research on environmental concern and activism. He is co-editor of *American Environmentalism* (with Angela G. Mertig, 1992), *Public Reactions to Nuclear Waste* (with Eugene A. Rosa and Michael E. Kraft, 1993), and *Sociological Theory and the Environment* (with Frederick Buttel, Peter Dickens, and August Gijswijt, 2002).

KURT FINSTERBUSCH is Professor of Sociology at the University of Maryland. He specializes in Social Impact Assessment, the Sociology of Development, and Environmental Sociology. In the first area he wrote *Social Research for Policy Decisions* (with Annabelle Bender Motz, 1980) and *Understanding Social Impacts* (1980) and edited three major works on social impact assessment methodology. In the second area he wrote *Organizational Change as a Development Strategy* (with Jerry Hage, 1987). In the third area he is currently writing a book on society and the environment.

WILLIAM R. FREUDENBURG is Professor of Rural Sociology and Environmental Studies at the University of Wisconsin–Madison. In addition to his work on socioeconomic impact assessment, his research interests include resource-dependent communities, issues of risk and technological controversy, and the dynamics of social change over time. He is co-author of *Oil in Troubled Waters* (with Robert Gramling, 1994) and co-editor of *Public Reactions to Nuclear Power* (with Eugene A. Rosa, 1984).

R. SCOTT FREY is Professor of Sociology and Chair of the Department of Sociology, Anthropology, and Criminal Justice at the University of North Florida. He is the editor of *Environment and Society Reader* (2001), has contributed chapters to several recent books on environmental issues, and has published his work in numerous journals, including the *American Journal of Sociology* and the *American Sociological Review*.

CRAIG K. HARRIS is Associate Professor of Sociology at Michigan State University, where he holds appointments in the Michigan Agricultural Experiment Station, the African Studies Center, and the Asian Studies Center. He is Past President of the International Section of the American Fisheries Society, and former editor of the newsletter of the Section on Environment, Technology and Society of the American Sociological Association. He has published extensively on energy conservation, fisheries management, and sustainable agriculture.

CRAIG R. HUMPHREY is a former chair of the Section on Environment and Technology in the American Sociological Association. He now holds the position of Associate Professor of Sociology Emeritus at the Pennsylvania State University. With Tammy L. Lewis and Frederick H. Buttel, he recently published *Environment, Energy, and Society* (2001). With Professors Lewis and Buttel he will publish a related anthology of readings, *Environment, Energy, and Society: Exemplary Works*, in 2002.

ROBERT EMMET JONES is an Associate Professor in the Environment & Society Program in the Department of Sociology and is affiliated with the Energy, Environment, and Resources Center at the University of Tennessee. He has an interdisciplinary education in the social and natural sciences and his work examines the human dimensions of environmental change and ecosystem management. Dr. Jones has published articles on these topics in a range of journals and serves as an Associate Editor of the journal *Society and Natural Resources*.

LESLIE KILMARTIN is Professor of Regional and Urban Studies at La Trobe University, Australia. He is a Past President of Research Committee 43 (Housing and the Built Environment) of the International Sociological Association. He is the co-author of *Cities Unlimited* (with David C. Thorns, 1978) and *Social Theory and the Australian City* (with David C. Thorns and Terry Burke, 1985). As Foundation Director of La Trobe University's Centre for Sustainable Regional Communities, he is involved in applied research and community outreach programs concerned with regional economic and social development.

STEVE KROLL-SMITH is Professor and Head of the Sociology Department at the University of North Carolina, Greensboro. He is co-author of *Bodies in Protest* (with H. Hugh Floyd, 1997) and co-editor of *Illness and the Environment* (with Phil Brown and Valerie J. Gunter, 2000). Among his current projects is a sociology of sleep and a textbook on environmental sociology.

ADELINE G. LEVINE is Professor Emeritus of Sociology at the State University of New York at Buffalo. In 1978 she began field work at Love Canal, days after the area was declared a health hazard to the residents. Her book, *Love Canal: Science, Politics and People*, was published in 1982, and she produced a videotape, *Love Canal: Issues and Controversies*, in 1983.

LOREN LUTZENHISER is Associate Professor of Sociology and Rural Sociology at Washington State University. His research examines relationships between technology and the environment, with a particular focus on consumer energy use and conservation practices. He has published widely in both social science and policy/applied journals, and is Chair-elect of the American Sociological Association's Section on Environment and Technology.

ANGELA G. MERTIG is Assistant Professor in the Department of Sociology and the Department of Fisheries and Wildlife at Michigan State University. She also works closely with the Michigan Department of Natural Resources Wildlife Division. She is co-editor of *American Environmentalism* (with Riley E. Dunlap, 1992). Her research focuses on the environmental movement, public opinion of environmental/natural resource issues, and landscape and land use change.

WILLIAM MICHELSON is S. D. Clark Professor of Sociology and Associate Dean, Social Sciences, at the University of Toronto. His longstanding research interests focus on the place of social and physical contexts in people's everyday lives. Among his previously published books are *Man and His Urban Environment* (1976) and *Environmental Choice, Human Behavior, and Residential Satisfaction* (1977).

DENNIS MILETI is Professor and Chair of the Department of Sociology at the University of Colorado at Boulder, where he also is Director of the

Natural Hazards Research and Applications Information Center in the Institute of Behavioral Science. Professor Mileti is author of over 100 publications on the topic of natural hazards mitigation and preparedness and he serves on the Boards of Directors or as a member of a variety of groups and organizations related to hazards research and mitigation.

DENTON E. MORRISON, Professor Emeritus of Sociology, Michigan State University, is one of the founders of the field of Environmental Sociology. Since 1970 his work has analyzed the environmental movement, technology and society, and the social dimensions of energy. His contributions have been recognized in awards from the profession. Since retiring he has focused on recycling goods in an antique and collectibles business.

STEVE H. MURDOCK is Regents Professor and Head of the Department of Rural Sociology at Texas A&M University. He is a recipient of Faculty Distinguished Achievement and Distinguished Performance in Research Awards from Texas A&M University. He is the author of 10 books and more than 100 articles and technical monographs on the implications of current and future demographic, socioeconomic, and natural resource change.

JOANNE M. NIGG is Professor of Sociology in the Department of Sociology and Criminal Justice and Co-Director of the Disaster Research Center at the University of Delaware. She has served as a member of the National Academy of Science/National Research Council's Board on Natural Disasters and as the President of the Earthquake Engineering Research Institute. Dr. Nigg is the author or editor of seven books and over 60 articles and papers on individual, organizational, and governmental response to, preparation for, and recovery from natural and technological threats and disasters.

MARVIN E. OLSEN was Professor of Sociology at Michigan State University at the time of his death. Olsen's work in the area of environmental sociology focused primarily on energy issues, particularly energy policy. His authored publications include *Designing a Citizen Involvement Program* (with Robert E. Howell and Darryll Olsen, 1987) and *Viewing the World Ecologically* (with Dora G. Lodwick and Riley E. Dunlap, 1992), and his co-edited publications include the *Handbook of Applied Sociology* (with Michael Micklin, 1981).

BARBARA A. PAYNE has applied sociology in the public and private sectors for 25 years, working for General Motors, Argonne National Laboratory, and as a freelance consultant in environmental sociology. She has conducted social impact assessments and research on energy facilities and radioactive waste projects from Connecticut to Alaska. She currently works out of her home in Arlington, Massachusetts.

DAVID POPENOE is Professor of Sociology at Rutgers University, New Brunswick, New Jersey, where he is also Co-Director of the National Marriage Project and former Dean of Social and Behavioral Sciences. He specializes in the study of family and community life in modern societies and is the author or editor of nine books, including *Life Without Father* (1996, 1999) and *Promises to Keep* (edited with Jean B. Elshtain and David Blankenhorn, 1996).

EUGENE A. ROSA is Professor and Chair of Sociology and the Edward R. Meyer Distinguished Professor of Natural Resource and Environmental Policy at Washington State University. He is a Past Chair of the American Sociological Association's Section on Environment and Technology and current chair of the American Association for the Advancement of Sciences Section on Social, Economic, and Political Sciences. He is co-editor of *Public Reactions to Nuclear Power* (with William R. Freudenburg, 1984), *Public Reactions to Nuclear Waste* (with Riley E. Dunlap and Michael E. Kraft, 1993), and co-author of *Risk, Uncertainty, and Rational Action* (with Carlo Jaeger, Ortwin Renn, and Thomas Webler, 2001).

GLENN STALKER is a Doctoral Candidate in Sociology at the University of Toronto. He is particularly interested in the study of built environments and theory within Environmental Sociology, while maintaining research interests in the areas of Social Ecology and Political Sociology. His dissertation investigates how variations in the social use of time are changing the ecological context of social capital formation.

WILLEM VAN VLIET-- is Professor in the College of Architecture and Planning at the University of Colorado, Boulder. He is the editor of *The Encyclopedia of Housing* (1998), *International Handbook of Housing Policies and Practices* (1990), *Handbook of Housing and the Built Environment in the United States* (with Elizabeth Huttman) (Greenwood, 1988), and *Housing and Neighborhoods* (Greenwood, 1987).